the creative reins. *In Look Homeward, Avenger!* the Black Panther reveals his origin to his fellow teammates.

Hot on the heels, comes *Panther's Rage*, as **Don McGregor** and **Rich Buckler** pit the king of Wakanda against the merciless might of Killmonger! 'Nuff said!

We follow up with **Black Panther #1**, written and illustrated by Jack Kirby! An action-packed almost film-noir tale reminiscent of The Maltese Falcon, that finds the Panther in a race to claim King Solomon's Frog! But why is everyone after such a small artefact? What secrets does it hold that men are willing to kill for it?! The Black Panther is going to find out the hard way!

If there's one thing that comic fans love is a good ol' fashioned team-up! And that's just what **Chris Claremont** and **John Byrne** provide, as Ororo Monroe, AKA Storm of the X-Men, discovers that she and T'Challa are the target of mysterious assassins! But who would be mad enough to try and kill the mutant mistress of lightning and king of Wakanda?!!

Under the watchful eyes of **Christopher Priest**, **Joe Quesada** and **Mark Texeira**, T'Challa returns to New York on the hunt for a child-killer. As the reigning monarch of a foreign nation the US government assign hapless agent Everett K Ross to be his liaison. A job that proves to be a little harder than Ross envisioned.

In Coming to America, **J Torres** and **Ryan Bodenheim** appear to be treading familiar ground as Everett K Ross is once again assigned to escort an African monarch. However, this time it's King Akaje of Dakenia, and to help Everett has called upon his old friend T'Challa. Yet not everything is as it seems!

Once again, we present another tremendous turning point in Marvel history, brought to you by **Reginald Hudlin**, **Kaare Andrews** and **Scot Eaton**, as the king of Wakanda takes a bride. It promises to be the wedding of the decade as esteemed guests from across the globe and super human community gather for the union of T'Challa and his bride-to-be Ororo Munroe!

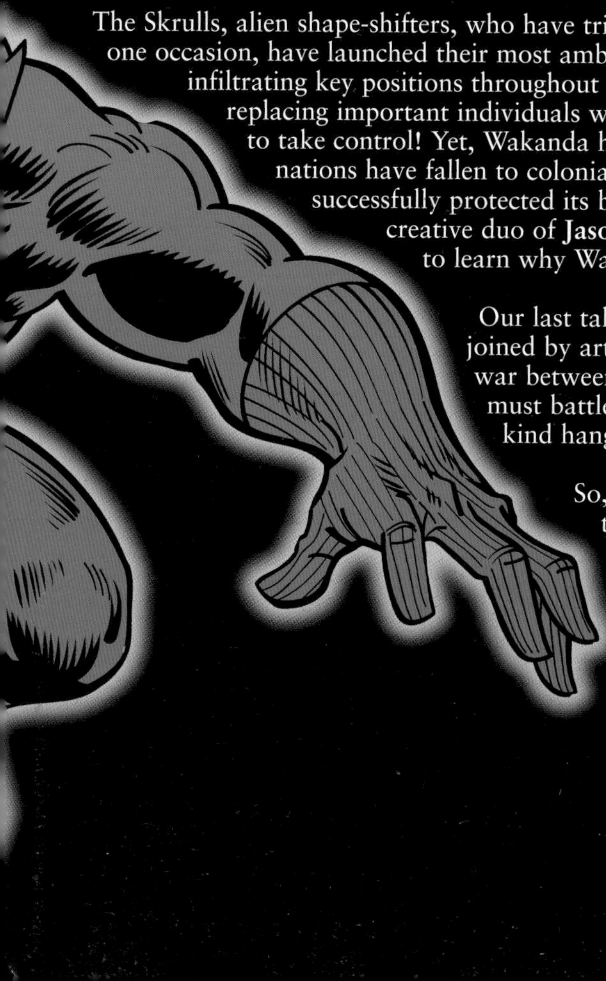

The Skrulls, alien shape-shifters, who have tried to conquer the Earth on more than one occasion, have launched their most ambitious plot ever! Secretly, they have been infiltrating key positions throughout the world and the superhuman community, replacing important individuals with their own operatives – now they are ready to take control! Yet, Wakanda has never been conquered. While other African nations have fallen to colonial interlopers, the hidden nation has always successfully protected its borders from all invaders. Now, thanks to the creative duo of **Jason Aaron** and **Jefté Palo**, the Skrulls are going to learn why Wakanda has never been defeated!

Our last tale is truly heartbreaking, as Jason Aaron is joined by artist **Tom Raney**, as against the back drop of a war between the Avengers and the X-Men, Black Panther must battle Storm as the fate of humanity and mutant-kind hangs in the balance!

So, True Believer, it leaves me just to say, dim the lights, lock the door, switch off your phone and TV. Settle down with a black cat on your lap and prepare to prowl the night in the search of vile villains as we join the hunt with the Black Panther!

Excelsior!

Brady Webb 2017

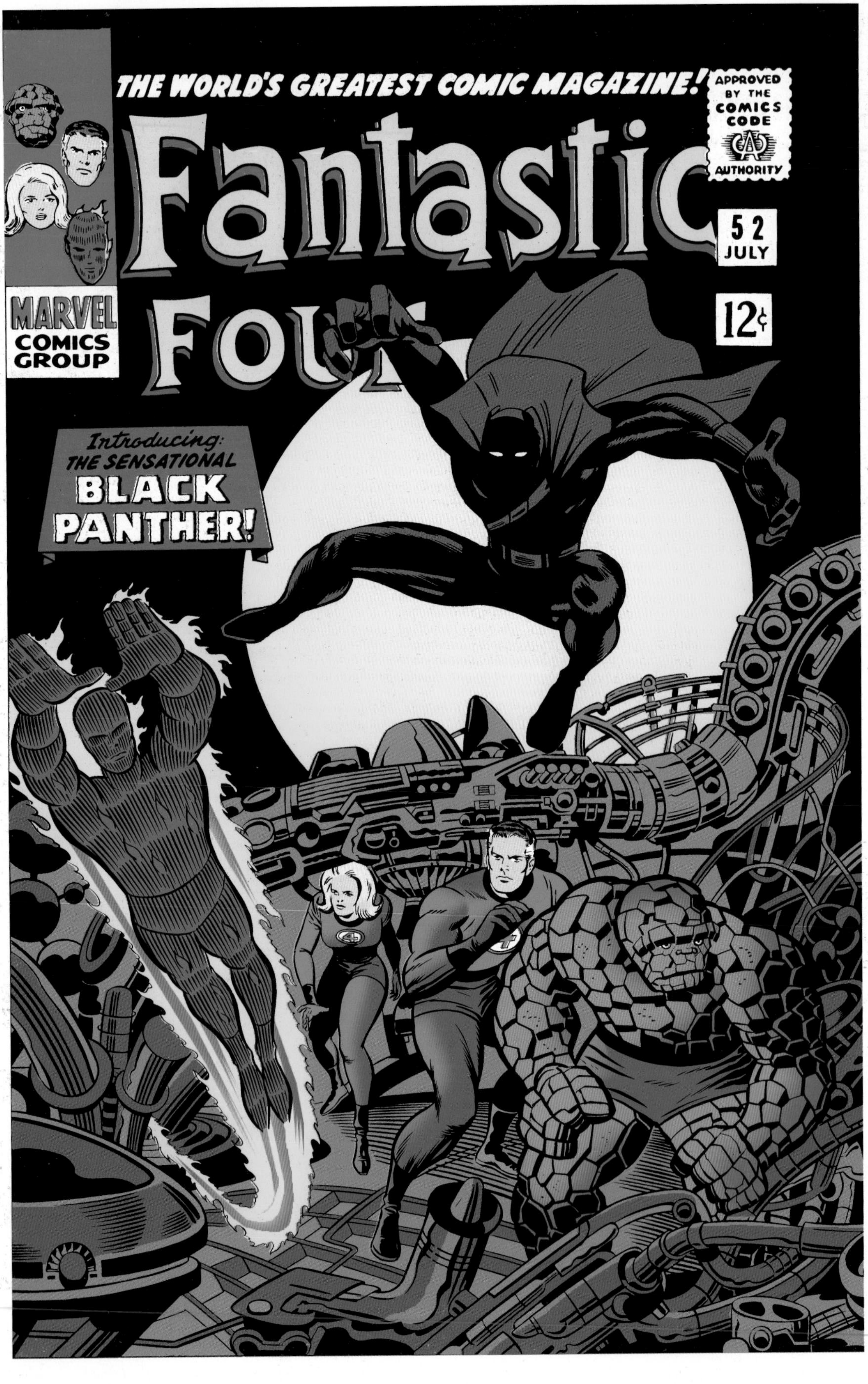
THE WORLD'S GREATEST COMIC MAGAZINE!
APPROVED BY THE COMICS CODE AUTHORITY
Fantastic Four
52 JULY
12¢
MARVEL COMICS GROUP
Introducing: THE SENSATIONAL BLACK PANTHER!

MARVEL PLATINUM
THE DEFINITIVE
BLACK PANTHER

FANTASTIC FOUR #52
JULY 1966
WRITER: STAN LEE
PENCILLER: JACK KIRBY
INKER: JOE SINNOTT
LETTERS: SAM ROSEN

FANTASTIC FOUR #53
AUGUST 1966
WRITER: STAN LEE
PENCILLER: JACK KIRBY
INKER: JOE SINNOTT
LETTERS: ART SIMEK

THE AVENGERS #87
APRIL 1971
WRITER: ROY THOMAS
PENCILLER: FRANK GIACOIA
INKER: SAL BUSCEMA
LETTERS: MIKE STEVENS

JUNGLE ACTION #6
SEPTEMBER 1973
WRITER: DON McGREGOR
PENCILLER: RICH BUCKLER
INKER: KLAUS JANSON
LETTERS: TOM ORZECHOWSKI
COLOURS: GLYNIS WEIN

BLACK PANTHER VOL. 1 #1
JANUARY 1977
WRITER: JACK KIRBY
PENCILLER: JACK KIRBY
INKER: MIKE ROYER
LETTERS: MIKE ROYER
COLOURS: DAVE HUNT

MARVEL TEAM-UP #100
DECEMBER 1980
WRITERS: CHRIS CLAREMONT &
JOHN BYRNE
PENCILLER: JOHN BYRNE
INKER: BOB McLEOD
LETTERS: ANNETTE KAWECKI
COLOURS: ROB CAROSELLA

BLACK PANTHER VOL. 3 #1
NOVEMBER 1998
WRITERS: CHRISTOPHER PRIEST &
JOE QUESADA
PENCILLER: MARK TEXEIRA
INKER: ALITHA MARTINEZ
LETTERS: RICHARD STARKINGS &
COMICRAFT'S SIOBHAN HANNA
COLOURS: BRIAN HABERLIN

BLACK PANTHER VOL. 3 #57
JUNE 2003
WRITER: J TORRES
PENCILLER: RYAN BODENHEIM
INKER: WALDEN WONG
LETTERS: PAUL TUTRONE
COLOURS: JENNIFER SHELLINGER

BLACK PANTHER VOL. 3 #58
JUNE 2003
WRITER: J TORRES
PENCILLER: RYAN BODENHEIM
INKER: WALDEN WONG
LETTERS: PAUL TUTRONE
COLOURS: JENNIFER SHELLINGER

BLACK PANTHER VOL. 4 #18
SEPTEMBER 2006
WRITER: REGINALD HUDLIN
PENCILLERS: KAARE ANDREWS &
SCOT EATON
INKERS: KAARE ANDREWS &
KLAUS JANSON
LETTERS: VC'S RANDY GENTILE
COLOURS: DEAN WHITE

BLACK PANTHER VOL. 4 #39
SEPTEMBER 2008
WRITER: JASON AARON
PENCILLER: JEFTÉ PALO
INKER: JEFTÉ PALO
LETTERS: VC'S CORY PETIT
COLOURS: LEE LOUGHRIDGE

BLACK PANTHER VOL. 4 #40
OCTOBER 2008
WRITER: JASON AARON
PENCILLER: JEFTÉ PALO
INKER: JEFTÉ PALO
LETTERS: VC'S CORY PETIT
COLOURS: LEE LOUGHRIDGE

BLACK PANTHER VOL. 4 #41
NOVEMBER 2008
WRITER: JASON AARON
PENCILLER: JEFTÉ PALO
INKER: JEFTÉ PALO
LETTERS: VC'S CORY PETIT
COLOURS: LEE LOUGHRIDGE

AVX VERSUS #5
OCTOBER 2012
WRITER: JASON AARON
PENCILLER: TOM RANEY
INKER: TOM RANEY
LETTERS: VC'S JOE CARAMAGNA
COLOURS: JIM CHARALAMPIDIS

COVER ART: KABAM
BLACK PANTHER CREATED BY STAN LEE & JACK KIRBY

Do you have any comments or queries about Marvel Platinum: The Definitive Black Panther? Email us at graphicnovels@panini.co.uk.
Join our Facebook group at Panini/Marvel Graphic Novels.

presents: MARVEL PLATINUM: THE DEFINITIVE BLACK PANTHER

by Marvel Characters B.V. through Panini S.p.A., Italy. All Rights Reserved. First printing 2017. Third impression 2018. Published by Panini
g, a division of Panini UK Limited. Mike Riddell, Managing Director. Alan O'Keefe, Managing Editor. Mark Irvine, Production Manager. Marco M.
blishing Director Europe. Brady Webb, Reprint Editor. Angela Gray, Designer. Office of publication: Brockbourne House, 77 Mount Ephraim,
e Wells, Kent TN4 8BS. This publication may not be sold, except by authorised dealers, and is sold subject to the condition that it shall not be
stributed with any part of its cover or markings removed, nor in a mutilated condition. Printed in Italy by Terrazzi. ISBN: 978-1-84653-846-9.

FOREWORD

Greetings, Pantherites!

Welcome to **Marvel Platinum: The Definitive Black Panther!**

You know, a lot has been said about the importance of the Black Panther on pop culture and the fact that T'Challa was the world's FIRST black superhero. Heck, we even have a brilliant and informative essay on the matter in this venerable tome! The True Origin of the Black Panther, by esteemed comic journalist Mike Conroy, discusses, explains and illuminates T'Challa's place in comics history.

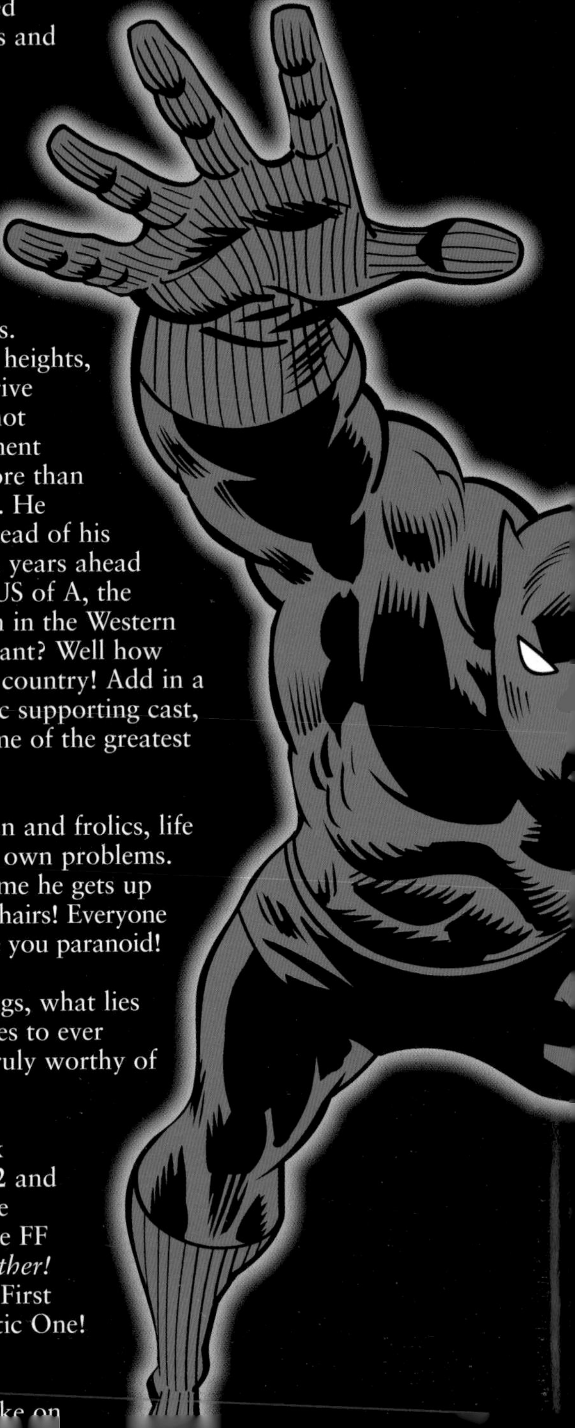

But being a first is not all that makes the Black Panther great. He's awesome because of the depth that his creators, the legends that are **Stan 'The Man' Lee** and **Jack 'The King' Kirby**, gave him. From the moment the Black Panther made his debut in **Fantastic Four #52** (1966), the character leapt off the page, striking a cord with readers from all backgrounds. For our heroes are meant to inspire us to greater heights, to be better than we thought we could be and strive against all odds. And here was a hero who was not only black, at a time when the civil rights movement was fighting its hardest battles, but powerful, more than a match for Marvel's First Family of superheroes. He was also intelligent, always two or three steps ahead of his opponents, and possessing wondrous technology, years ahead of anything his contemporaries had access to in US of A, the supposedly most technologically advanced nation in the Western world. What more could any young comic fan want? Well how about he was also the king of his own enigmatic country! Add in a good mix of tragedy, rights of passage, a fantastic supporting cast, vile villains, and you have one heady mix for some of the greatest stories ever told as only Mighty Marvel can!

Of course, being the Black Panther is not all fun and frolics, life as a monarch and spiritual leader comes with its own problems. T'Challa's kingdom seems to be usurped every time he gets up off the throne, like some bizarre game of musical chairs! Everyone wants to be ruler of Wakanda! It's enough to make you paranoid!

Anyway, enough of my meaningless meanderings, what lies ahead is some of THE greatest Black Panther tales to ever come forth from the House of Ideas! Each one truly worthy of its place within this Marvel Platinum collection.

We kick off with where it all began – the Black Panther's astounding debut in **Fantastic Four #52** and **53**! The legendary creative duo and fathers of the Marvel Universe, Stan Lee and Jack Kirby, pit the FF against T'Challa in a story called *The Black Panther!* But why is the king of Wakanda challenging the First Family? You'll have to read on to find out, Frantic One!

Next, we hit you with another mighty Marvel milestone, as **Roy Thomas** and **Frank Giacoia** take on

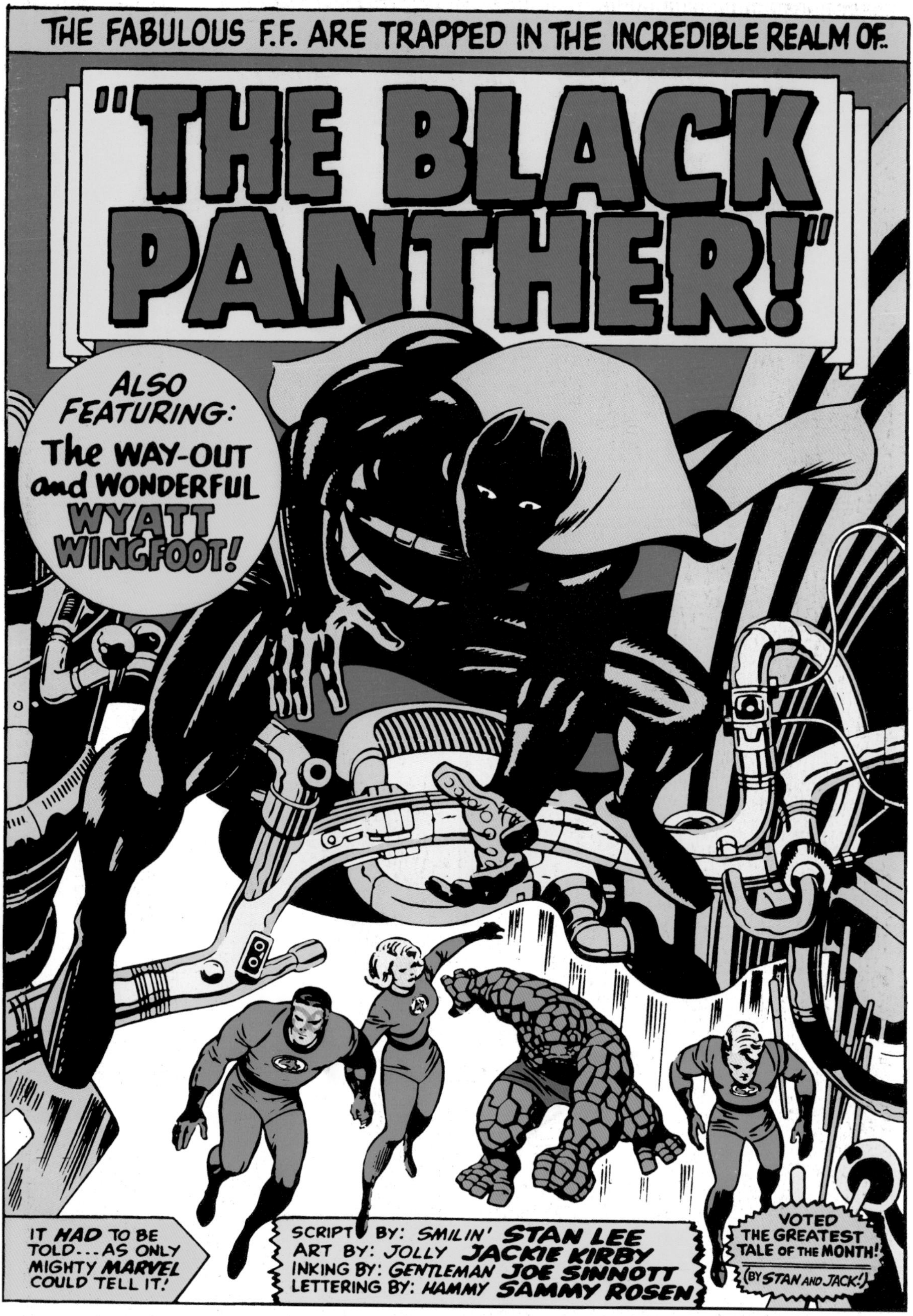
THE FABULOUS F.F. ARE TRAPPED IN THE INCREDIBLE REALM OF..
"THE BLACK PANTHER!"
ALSO FEATURING: The WAY-OUT and WONDERFUL WYATT WINGFOOT!
IT HAD TO BE TOLD... AS ONLY MIGHTY MARVEL COULD TELL IT!
SCRIPT BY: SMILIN' STAN LEE
ART BY: JOLLY JACKIE KIRBY
INKING BY: GENTLEMAN JOE SINNOTT
LETTERING BY: HAMMY SAMMY ROSEN
VOTED THE GREATEST TALE OF THE MONTH! (BY STAN AND JACK!)

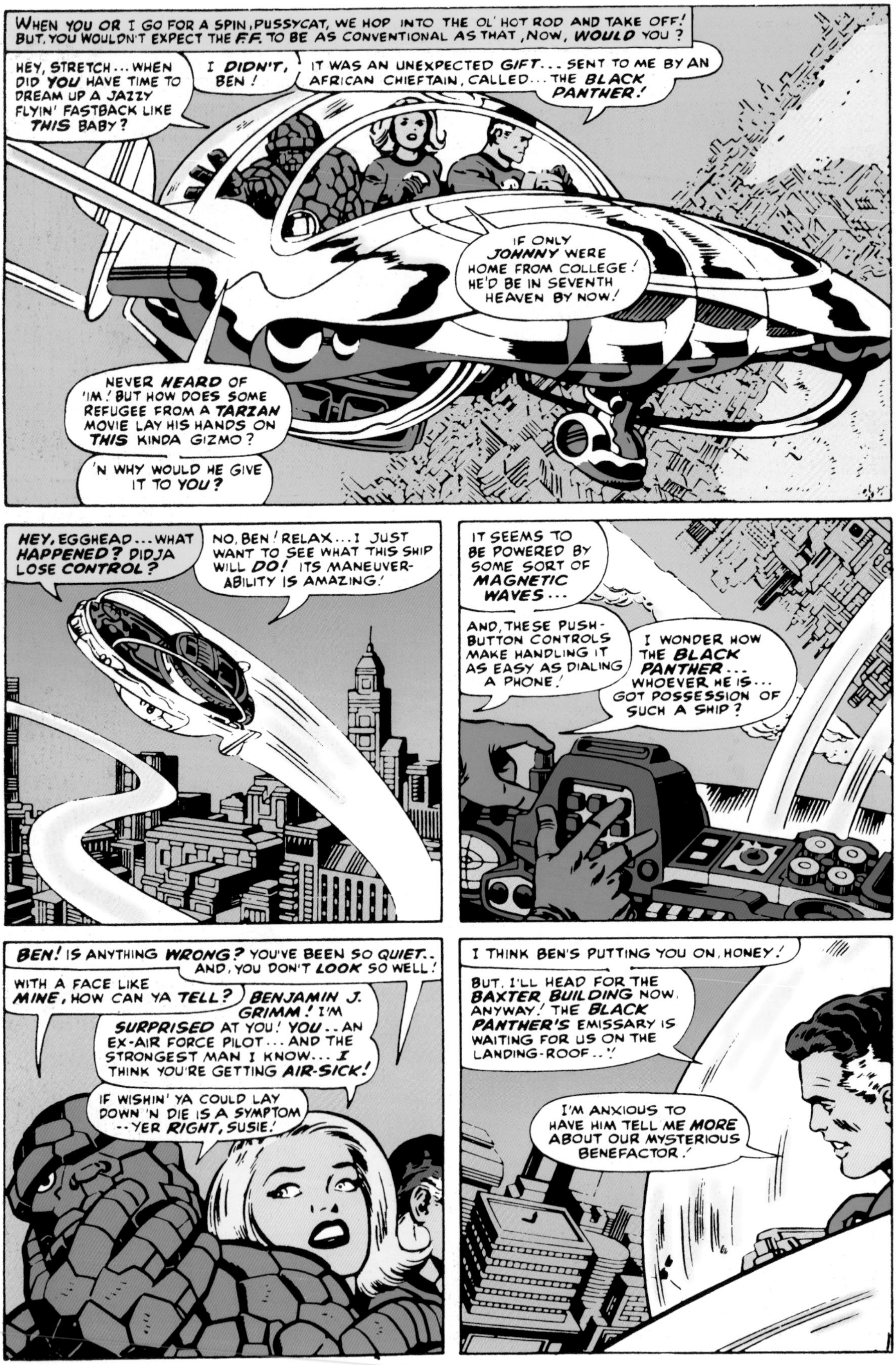
WHEN YOU OR I GO FOR A SPIN, PUSSYCAT, WE HOP INTO THE OL' HOT ROD AND TAKE OFF! BUT, YOU WOULDN'T EXPECT THE F.F. TO BE AS CONVENTIONAL AS THAT, NOW, WOULD YOU?
HEY, STRETCH... WHEN DID YOU HAVE TIME TO DREAM UP A JAZZY FLYIN' FASTBACK LIKE THIS BABY?
I DIDN'T, BEN!
IT WAS AN UNEXPECTED GIFT... SENT TO ME BY AN AFRICAN CHIEFTAIN, CALLED... THE BLACK PANTHER!
IF ONLY JOHNNY WERE HOME FROM COLLEGE! HE'D BE IN SEVENTH HEAVEN BY NOW!
NEVER HEARD OF 'IM! BUT HOW DOES SOME REFUGEE FROM A TARZAN MOVIE LAY HIS HANDS ON THIS KINDA GIZMO?
'N WHY WOULD HE GIVE IT TO YOU?
HEY, EGGHEAD... WHAT HAPPENED? DIDJA LOSE CONTROL?
NO, BEN! RELAX... I JUST WANT TO SEE WHAT THIS SHIP WILL DO! ITS MANEUVER-ABILITY IS AMAZING!
IT SEEMS TO BE POWERED BY SOME SORT OF MAGNETIC WAVES...
AND, THESE PUSH-BUTTON CONTROLS MAKE HANDLING IT AS EASY AS DIALING A PHONE!
I WONDER HOW THE BLACK PANTHER... WHOEVER HE IS... GOT POSSESSION OF SUCH A SHIP?
BEN! IS ANYTHING WRONG? YOU'VE BEEN SO QUIET.. AND, YOU DON'T LOOK SO WELL!
WITH A FACE LIKE MINE, HOW CAN YA TELL?
BENJAMIN J. GRIMM! I'M SURPRISED AT YOU! YOU.. AN EX-AIR FORCE PILOT... AND THE STRONGEST MAN I KNOW... I THINK YOU'RE GETTING AIR-SICK!
IF WISHIN' YA COULD LAY DOWN 'N DIE IS A SYMPTOM --YER RIGHT, SUSIE!
I THINK BEN'S PUTTING YOU ON, HONEY!
BUT, I'LL HEAD FOR THE BAXTER BUILDING NOW, ANYWAY! THE BLACK PANTHER'S EMISSARY IS WAITING FOR US ON THE LANDING-ROOF..!
I'M ANXIOUS TO HAVE HIM TELL ME MORE ABOUT OUR MYSTERIOUS BENEFACTOR!

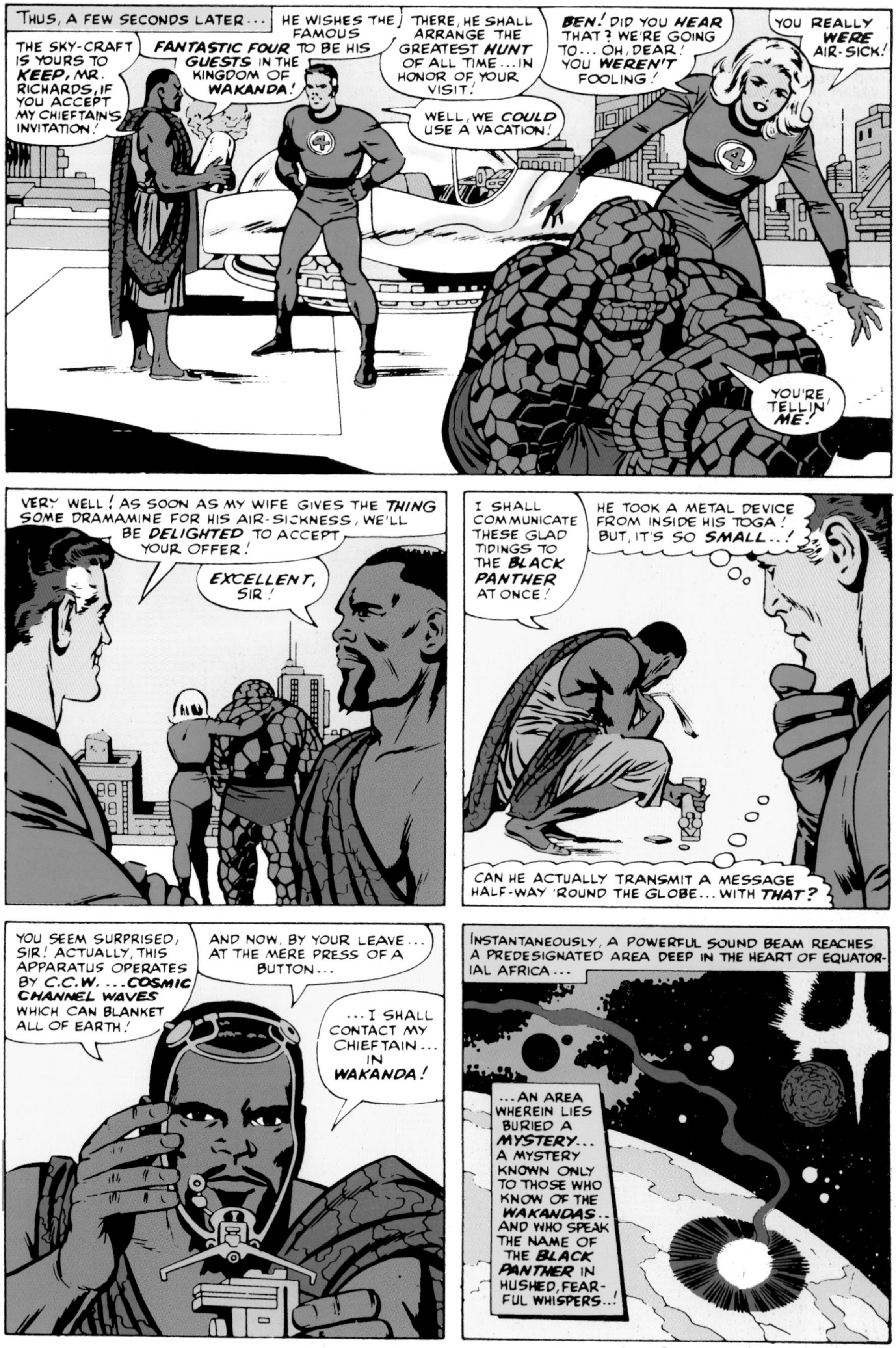
THUS, A FEW SECONDS LATER...
THE SKY-CRAFT IS YOURS TO KEEP, MR. RICHARDS, IF YOU ACCEPT MY CHIEFTAIN'S INVITATION!
HE WISHES THE FAMOUS FANTASTIC FOUR TO BE HIS GUESTS IN THE KINGDOM OF WAKANDA!
THERE, HE SHALL ARRANGE THE GREATEST HUNT OF ALL TIME...IN HONOR OF YOUR VISIT!
WELL, WE COULD USE A VACATION!
BEN! DID YOU HEAR THAT? WE'RE GOING TO... OH, DEAR! YOU WEREN'T FOOLING!
YOU REALLY WERE AIR-SICK!
YOU'RE TELLIN' ME!
VERY WELL! AS SOON AS MY WIFE GIVES THE THING SOME DRAMAMINE FOR HIS AIR-SICKNESS, WE'LL BE DELIGHTED TO ACCEPT YOUR OFFER!
EXCELLENT, SIR!
I SHALL COMMUNICATE THESE GLAD TIDINGS TO THE BLACK PANTHER AT ONCE!
HE TOOK A METAL DEVICE FROM INSIDE HIS TOGA! BUT, IT'S SO SMALL..!
CAN HE ACTUALLY TRANSMIT A MESSAGE HALF-WAY 'ROUND THE GLOBE... WITH THAT?
YOU SEEM SURPRISED, SIR! ACTUALLY, THIS APPARATUS OPERATES BY C.C.W. ...COSMIC CHANNEL WAVES WHICH CAN BLANKET ALL OF EARTH!
AND NOW, BY YOUR LEAVE... AT THE MERE PRESS OF A BUTTON...
...I SHALL CONTACT MY CHIEFTAIN... IN WAKANDA!
INSTANTANEOUSLY, A POWERFUL SOUND BEAM REACHES A PREDESIGNATED AREA DEEP IN THE HEART OF EQUATORIAL AFRICA...
...AN AREA WHEREIN LIES BURIED A MYSTERY... A MYSTERY KNOWN ONLY TO THOSE WHO KNOW OF THE WAKANDAS.. AND WHO SPEAK THE NAME OF THE BLACK PANTHER IN HUSHED, FEARFUL WHISPERS..!

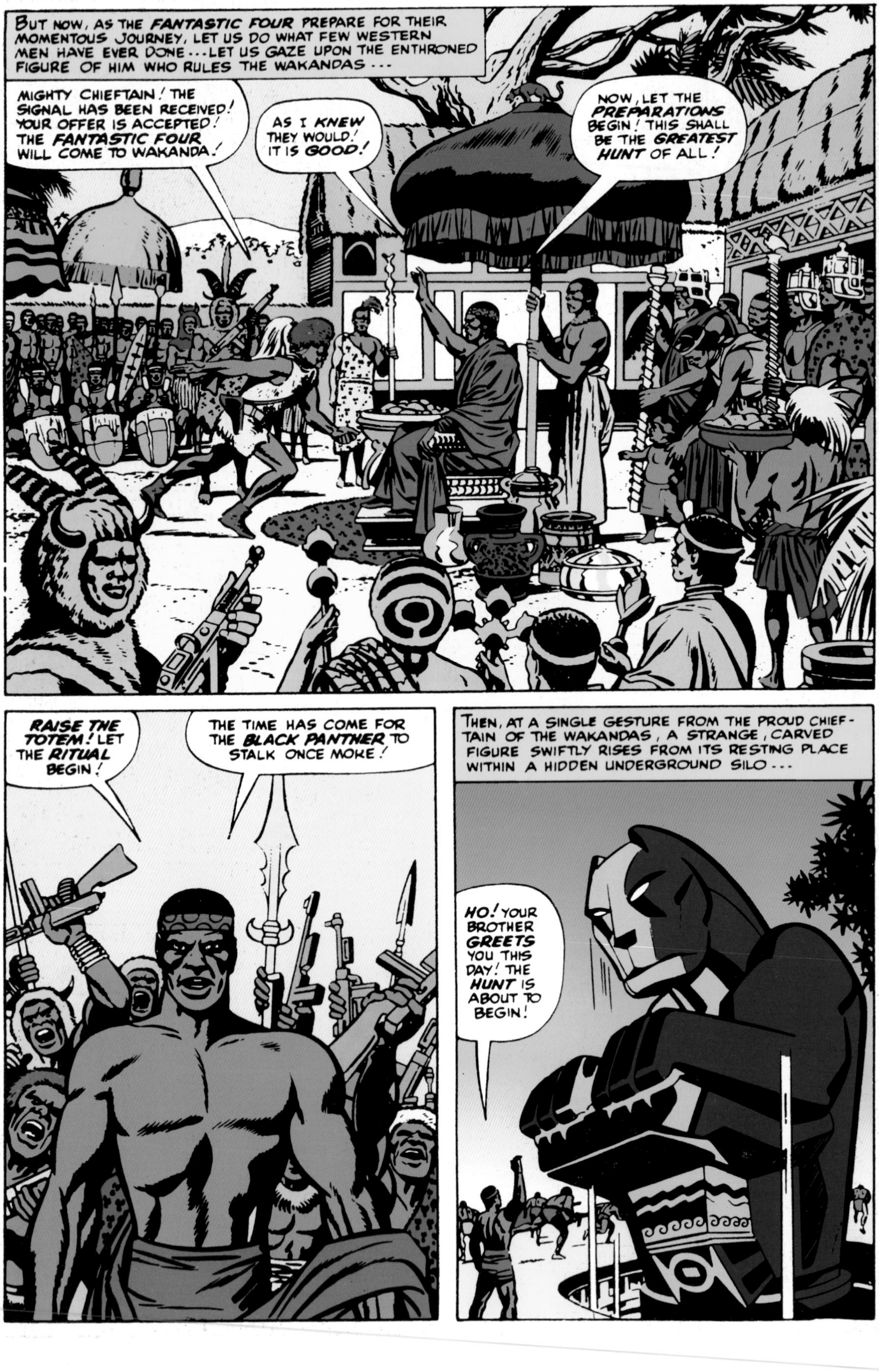

BUT NOW, AS THE FANTASTIC FOUR PREPARE FOR THEIR MOMENTOUS JOURNEY, LET US DO WHAT FEW WESTERN MEN HAVE EVER DONE... LET US GAZE UPON THE ENTHRONED FIGURE OF HIM WHO RULES THE WAKANDAS...
MIGHTY CHIEFTAIN! THE SIGNAL HAS BEEN RECEIVED! YOUR OFFER IS ACCEPTED! THE FANTASTIC FOUR WILL COME TO WAKANDA!
AS I KNEW THEY WOULD! IT IS GOOD!
NOW, LET THE PREPARATIONS BEGIN! THIS SHALL BE THE GREATEST HUNT OF ALL!
RAISE THE TOTEM! LET THE RITUAL BEGIN!
THE TIME HAS COME FOR THE BLACK PANTHER TO STALK ONCE MORE!
THEN, AT A SINGLE GESTURE FROM THE PROUD CHIEFTAIN OF THE WAKANDAS, A STRANGE, CARVED FIGURE SWIFTLY RISES FROM ITS RESTING PLACE WITHIN A HIDDEN UNDERGROUND SILO...
HO! YOUR BROTHER GREETS YOU THIS DAY! THE HUNT IS ABOUT TO BEGIN!

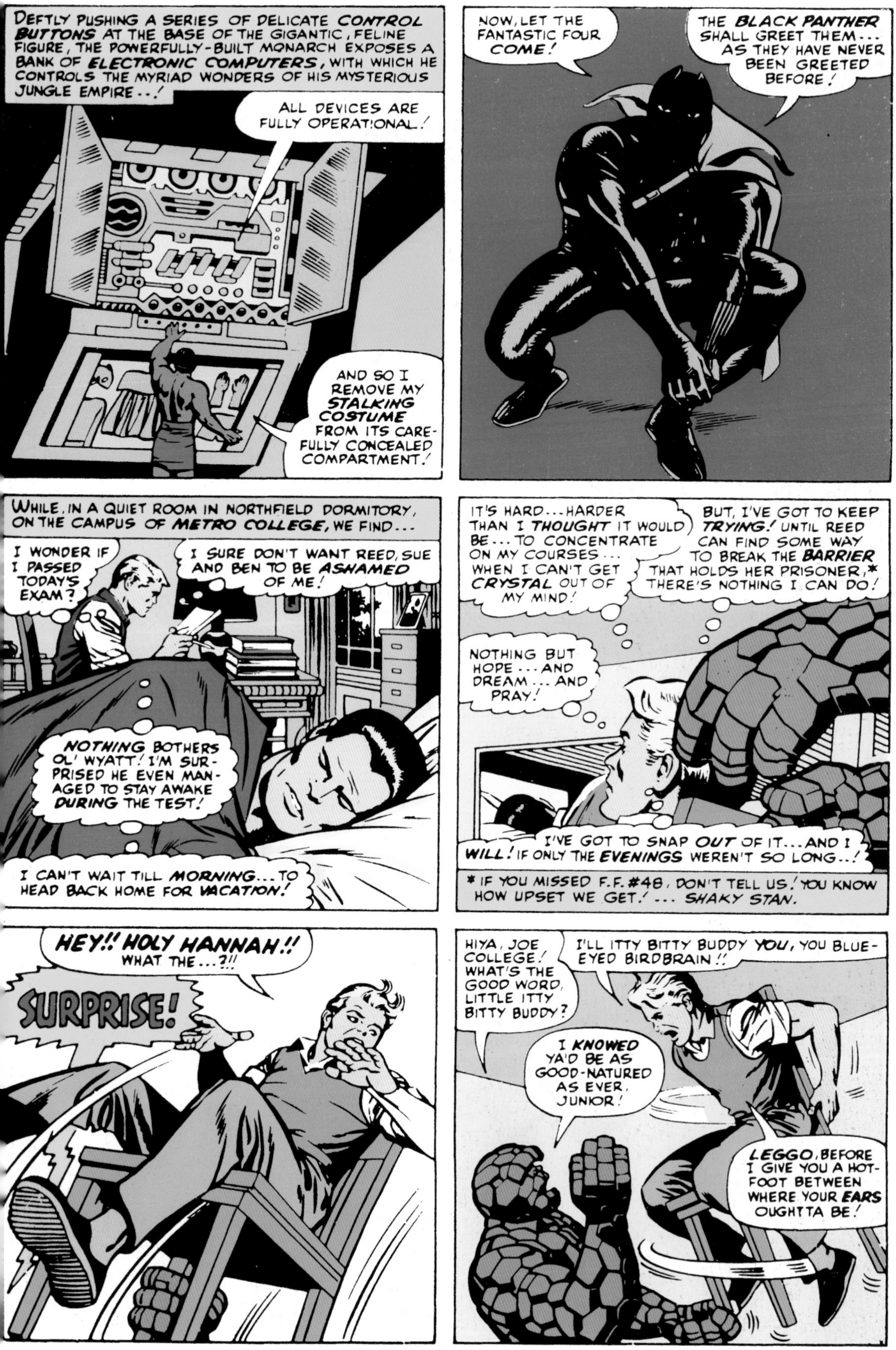

DEFTLY PUSHING A SERIES OF DELICATE CONTROL BUTTONS AT THE BASE OF THE GIGANTIC, FELINE FIGURE, THE POWERFULLY-BUILT MONARCH EXPOSES A BANK OF ELECTRONIC COMPUTERS, WITH WHICH HE CONTROLS THE MYRIAD WONDERS OF HIS MYSTERIOUS JUNGLE EMPIRE..!
ALL DEVICES ARE FULLY OPERATIONAL!
AND SO I REMOVE MY STALKING COSTUME FROM ITS CAREFULLY CONCEALED COMPARTMENT!
NOW, LET THE FANTASTIC FOUR COME!
THE BLACK PANTHER SHALL GREET THEM... AS THEY HAVE NEVER BEEN GREETED BEFORE!
WHILE, IN A QUIET ROOM IN NORTHFIELD DORMITORY, ON THE CAMPUS OF METRO COLLEGE, WE FIND...
I WONDER IF I PASSED TODAY'S EXAM?
I SURE DON'T WANT REED, SUE AND BEN TO BE ASHAMED OF ME!
NOTHING BOTHERS OL' WYATT! I'M SURPRISED HE EVEN MANAGED TO STAY AWAKE DURING THE TEST!
I CAN'T WAIT TILL MORNING... TO HEAD BACK HOME FOR VACATION!
IT'S HARD... HARDER THAN I THOUGHT IT WOULD BE... TO CONCENTRATE ON MY COURSES... WHEN I CAN'T GET CRYSTAL OUT OF MY MIND!
BUT, I'VE GOT TO KEEP TRYING! UNTIL REED CAN FIND SOME WAY TO BREAK THE BARRIER THAT HOLDS HER PRISONER,* THERE'S NOTHING I CAN DO!
NOTHING BUT HOPE... AND DREAM... AND PRAY!
I'VE GOT TO SNAP OUT OF IT... AND I WILL! IF ONLY THE EVENINGS WEREN'T SO LONG..!
* IF YOU MISSED F.F. #48, DON'T TELL US! YOU KNOW HOW UPSET WE GET! ... SHAKY STAN.
HEY!! HOLY HANNAH!! WHAT THE...?!!
SURPRISE!
HIYA, JOE COLLEGE! WHAT'S THE GOOD WORD, LITTLE ITTY BITTY BUDDY?
I'LL ITTY BITTY BUDDY YOU, YOU BLUE-EYED BIRDBRAIN!!
I KNOWED YA'D BE AS GOOD-NATURED AS EVER, JUNIOR!
LEGGO, BEFORE I GIVE YOU A HOT-FOOT BETWEEN WHERE YOUR EARS OUGHTTA BE!

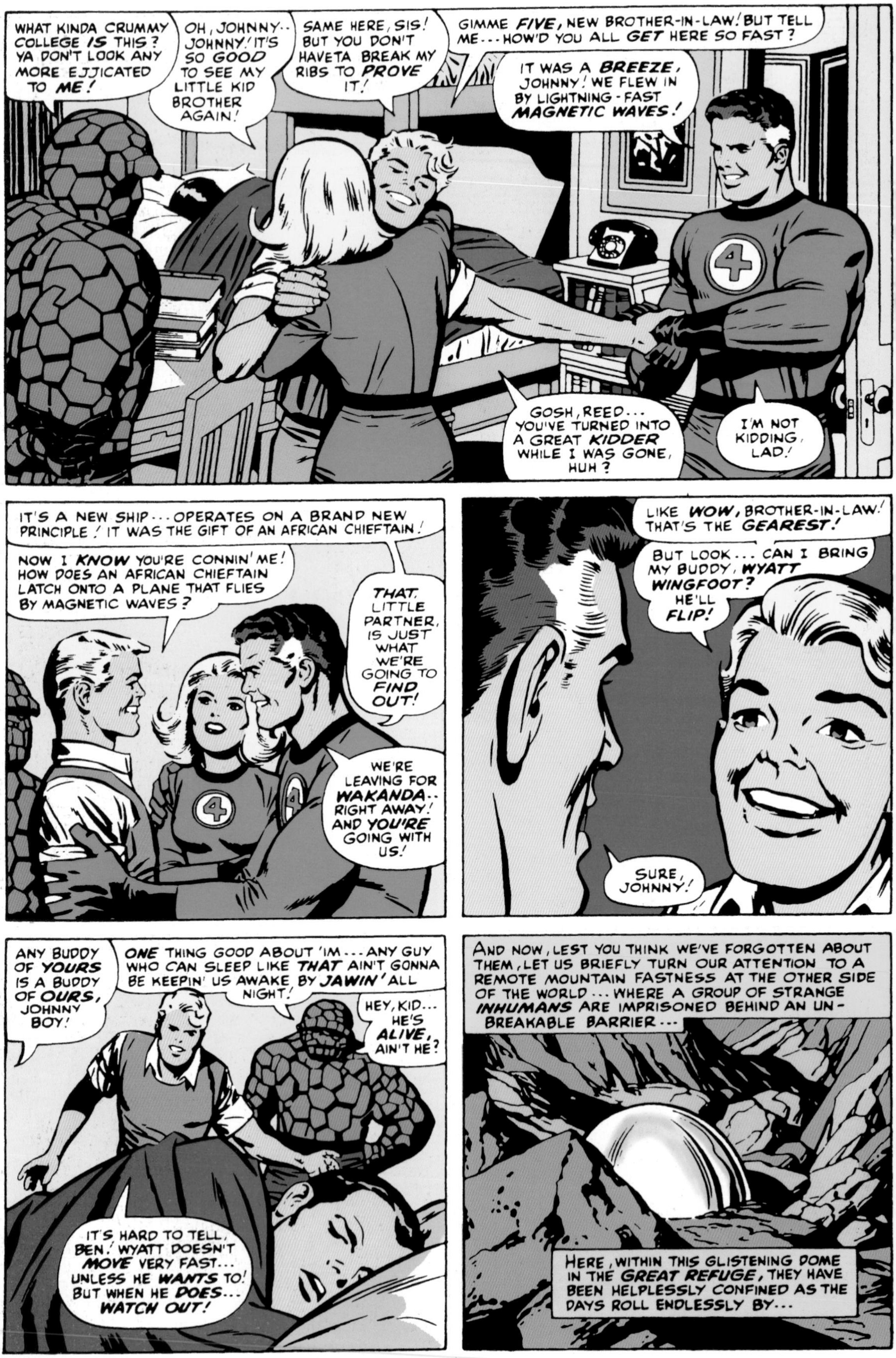
WHAT KINDA CRUMMY COLLEGE IS THIS? YA DON'T LOOK ANY MORE EJJICATED TO ME!
OH, JOHNNY.. JOHNNY! IT'S SO GOOD TO SEE MY LITTLE KID BROTHER AGAIN!
SAME HERE, SIS! BUT YOU DON'T HAVETA BREAK MY RIBS TO PROVE IT!
GIMME FIVE, NEW BROTHER-IN-LAW! BUT TELL ME... HOW'D YOU ALL GET HERE SO FAST?
IT WAS A BREEZE, JOHNNY! WE FLEW IN BY LIGHTNING-FAST MAGNETIC WAVES!
GOSH, REED... YOU'VE TURNED INTO A GREAT KIDDER WHILE I WAS GONE, HUH?
I'M NOT KIDDING, LAD!
IT'S A NEW SHIP... OPERATES ON A BRAND NEW PRINCIPLE! IT WAS THE GIFT OF AN AFRICAN CHIEFTAIN!
NOW I KNOW YOU'RE CONNIN' ME! HOW DOES AN AFRICAN CHIEFTAIN LATCH ONTO A PLANE THAT FLIES BY MAGNETIC WAVES?
THAT, LITTLE PARTNER, IS JUST WHAT WE'RE GOING TO FIND OUT!
WE'RE LEAVING FOR WAKANDA.. RIGHT AWAY! AND YOU'RE GOING WITH US!
LIKE WOW, BROTHER-IN-LAW! THAT'S THE GEAREST!
BUT LOOK... CAN I BRING MY BUDDY, WYATT WINGFOOT? HE'LL FLIP!
SURE, JOHNNY!
ANY BUDDY OF YOURS IS A BUDDY OF OURS, JOHNNY BOY!
ONE THING GOOD ABOUT 'IM... ANY GUY WHO CAN SLEEP LIKE THAT AIN'T GONNA BE KEEPIN' US AWAKE BY JAWIN' ALL NIGHT!
HEY, KID... HE'S ALIVE, AIN'T HE?
IT'S HARD TO TELL, BEN! WYATT DOESN'T MOVE VERY FAST... UNLESS HE WANTS TO! BUT WHEN HE DOES... WATCH OUT!
AND NOW, LEST YOU THINK WE'VE FORGOTTEN ABOUT THEM, LET US BRIEFLY TURN OUR ATTENTION TO A REMOTE MOUNTAIN FASTNESS AT THE OTHER SIDE OF THE WORLD... WHERE A GROUP OF STRANGE INHUMANS ARE IMPRISONED BEHIND AN UN-BREAKABLE BARRIER...
HERE, WITHIN THIS GLISTENING DOME IN THE GREAT REFUGE, THEY HAVE BEEN HELPLESSLY CONFINED AS THE DAYS ROLL ENDLESSLY BY...

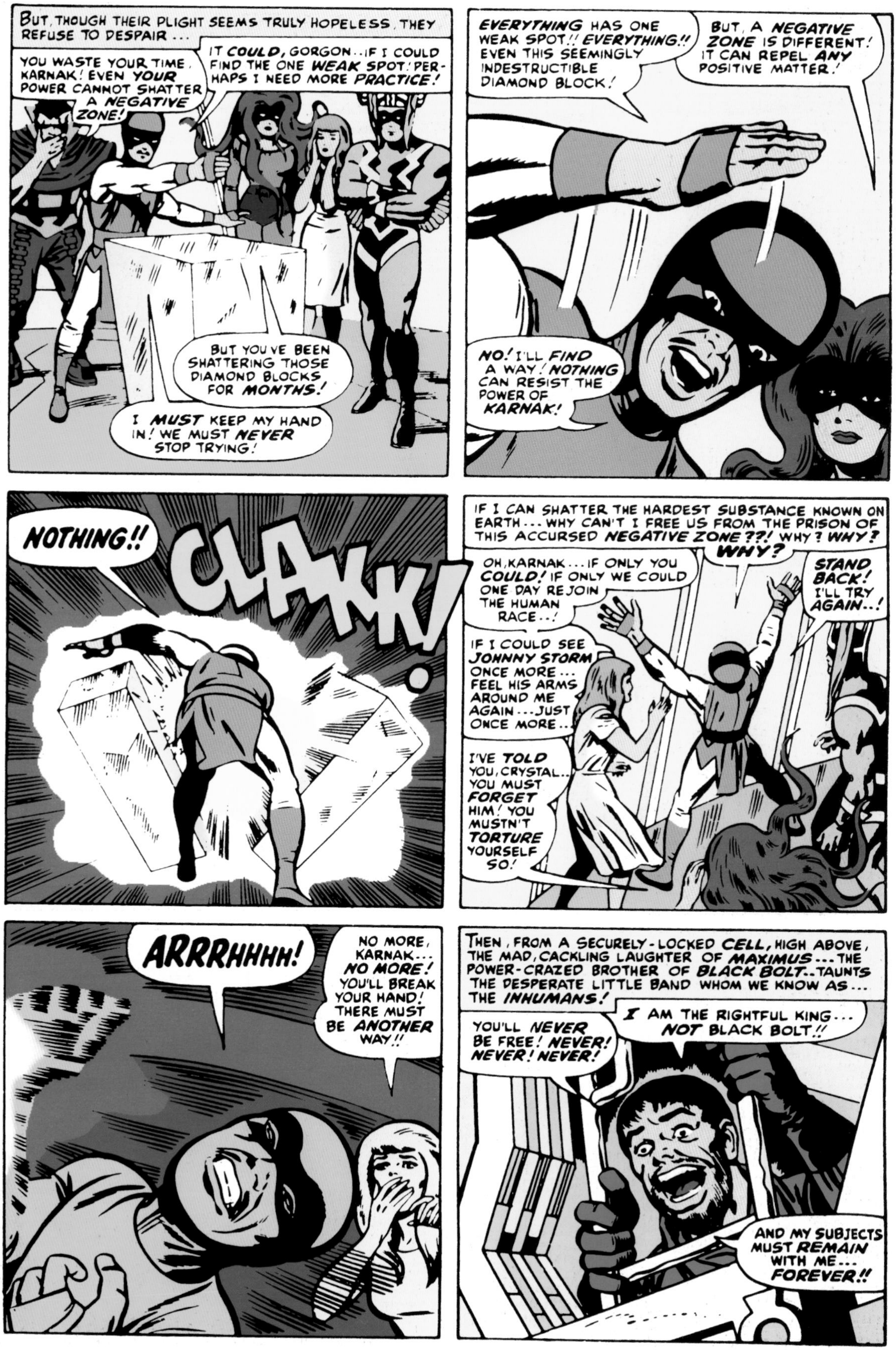
BUT, THOUGH THEIR PLIGHT SEEMS TRULY HOPELESS, THEY REFUSE TO DESPAIR...
YOU WASTE YOUR TIME, KARNAK! EVEN YOUR POWER CANNOT SHATTER A NEGATIVE ZONE!
IT COULD, GORGON...IF I COULD FIND THE ONE WEAK SPOT! PERHAPS I NEED MORE PRACTICE!
BUT YOU'VE BEEN SHATTERING THOSE DIAMOND BLOCKS FOR MONTHS!
I MUST KEEP MY HAND IN! WE MUST NEVER STOP TRYING!
EVERYTHING HAS ONE WEAK SPOT!! EVERYTHING!! EVEN THIS SEEMINGLY INDESTRUCTIBLE DIAMOND BLOCK!
BUT, A NEGATIVE ZONE IS DIFFERENT! IT CAN REPEL ANY POSITIVE MATTER!
NO! I'LL FIND A WAY! NOTHING CAN RESIST THE POWER OF KARNAK!
NOTHING!!
CLAKK!
IF I CAN SHATTER THE HARDEST SUBSTANCE KNOWN ON EARTH... WHY CAN'T I FREE US FROM THE PRISON OF THIS ACCURSED NEGATIVE ZONE??! WHY? WHY? WHY?
OH, KARNAK... IF ONLY YOU COULD! IF ONLY WE COULD ONE DAY REJOIN THE HUMAN RACE...!
STAND BACK! I'LL TRY AGAIN...!
IF I COULD SEE JOHNNY STORM ONCE MORE... FEEL HIS ARMS AROUND ME AGAIN...JUST ONCE MORE...
I'VE TOLD YOU, CRYSTAL... YOU MUST FORGET HIM! YOU MUSTN'T TORTURE YOURSELF SO!
ARRRHHHH!
NO MORE, KARNAK... NO MORE! YOU'LL BREAK YOUR HAND! THERE MUST BE ANOTHER WAY!!
THEN, FROM A SECURELY-LOCKED CELL, HIGH ABOVE, THE MAD, CACKLING LAUGHTER OF MAXIMUS... THE POWER-CRAZED BROTHER OF BLACK BOLT.. TAUNTS THE DESPERATE LITTLE BAND WHOM WE KNOW AS... THE INHUMANS!
YOU'LL NEVER BE FREE! NEVER! NEVER! NEVER!
I AM THE RIGHTFUL KING... NOT BLACK BOLT!!
AND MY SUBJECTS MUST REMAIN WITH ME... FOREVER!!

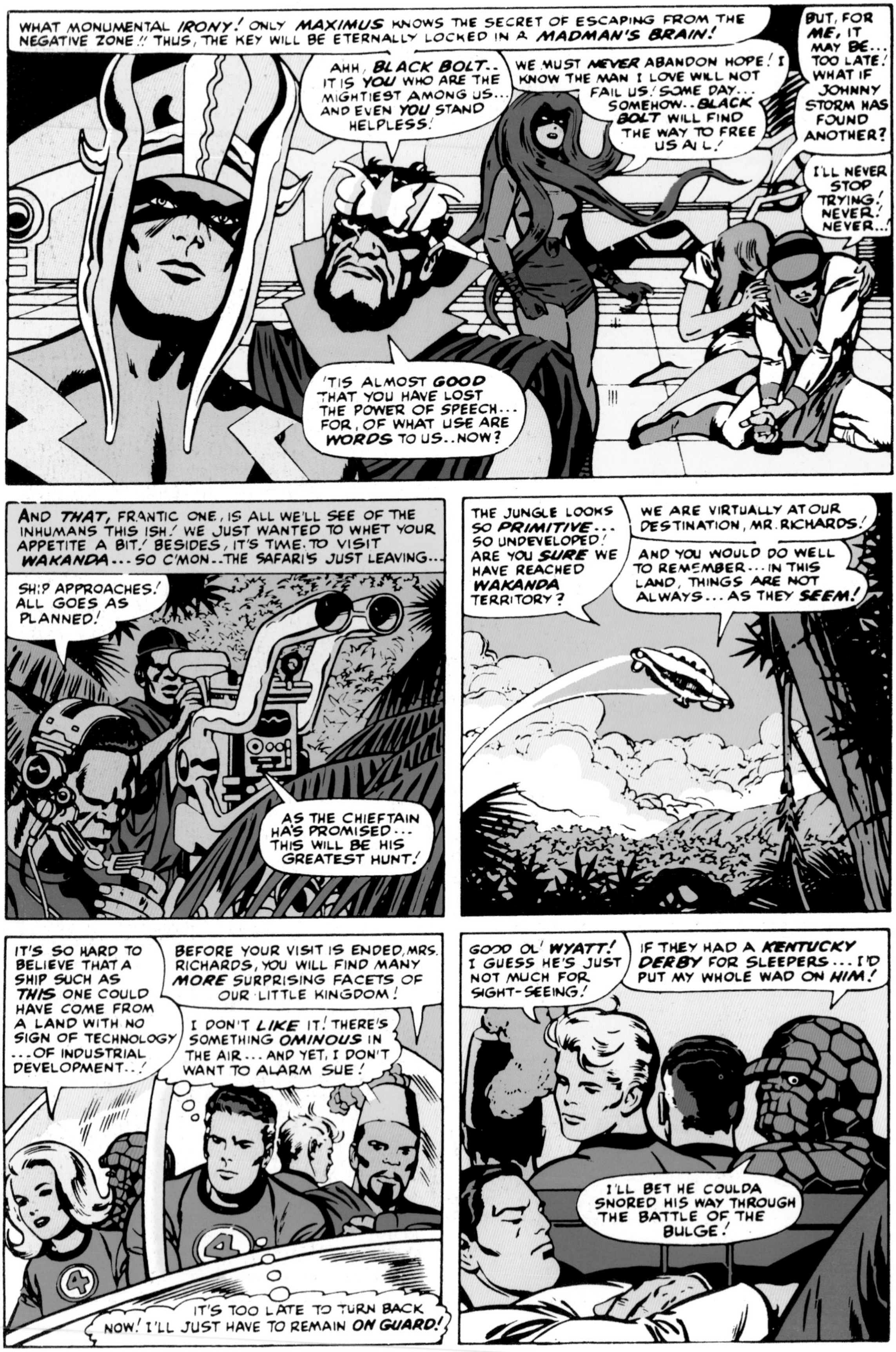
WHAT MONUMENTAL IRONY! ONLY MAXIMUS KNOWS THE SECRET OF ESCAPING FROM THE NEGATIVE ZONE!! THUS, THE KEY WILL BE ETERNALLY LOCKED IN A MADMAN'S BRAIN!
AHH, BLACK BOLT.. IT IS YOU WHO ARE THE MIGHTIEST AMONG US... AND EVEN YOU STAND HELPLESS!
WE MUST NEVER ABANDON HOPE! I KNOW THE MAN I LOVE WILL NOT FAIL US! SOME DAY... SOMEHOW.. BLACK BOLT WILL FIND THE WAY TO FREE US ALL!
BUT, FOR ME, IT MAY BE... TOO LATE! WHAT IF JOHNNY STORM HAS FOUND ANOTHER?
I'LL NEVER STOP TRYING! NEVER! NEVER...!
'TIS ALMOST GOOD THAT YOU HAVE LOST THE POWER OF SPEECH... FOR, OF WHAT USE ARE WORDS TO US.. NOW?
AND THAT, FRANTIC ONE, IS ALL WE'LL SEE OF THE INHUMANS THIS ISH! WE JUST WANTED TO WHET YOUR APPETITE A BIT! BESIDES, IT'S TIME TO VISIT WAKANDA... SO C'MON.. THE SAFARI'S JUST LEAVING...
SHIP APPROACHES! ALL GOES AS PLANNED!
AS THE CHIEFTAIN HAS PROMISED... THIS WILL BE HIS GREATEST HUNT!
THE JUNGLE LOOKS SO PRIMITIVE... SO UNDEVELOPED! ARE YOU SURE WE HAVE REACHED WAKANDA TERRITORY?
WE ARE VIRTUALLY AT OUR DESTINATION, MR. RICHARDS!
AND YOU WOULD DO WELL TO REMEMBER... IN THIS LAND, THINGS ARE NOT ALWAYS... AS THEY SEEM!
IT'S SO HARD TO BELIEVE THAT A SHIP SUCH AS THIS ONE COULD HAVE COME FROM A LAND WITH NO SIGN OF TECHNOLOGY ...OF INDUSTRIAL DEVELOPMENT...!
BEFORE YOUR VISIT IS ENDED, MRS. RICHARDS, YOU WILL FIND MANY MORE SURPRISING FACETS OF OUR LITTLE KINGDOM!
I DON'T LIKE IT! THERE'S SOMETHING OMINOUS IN THE AIR... AND YET, I DON'T WANT TO ALARM SUE!
IT'S TOO LATE TO TURN BACK NOW! I'LL JUST HAVE TO REMAIN ON GUARD!
GOOD OL' WYATT! I GUESS HE'S JUST NOT MUCH FOR SIGHT-SEEING!
IF THEY HAD A KENTUCKY DERBY FOR SLEEPERS... I'D PUT MY WHOLE WAD ON HIM!
I'LL BET HE COULDA SNORED HIS WAY THROUGH THE BATTLE OF THE BULGE!

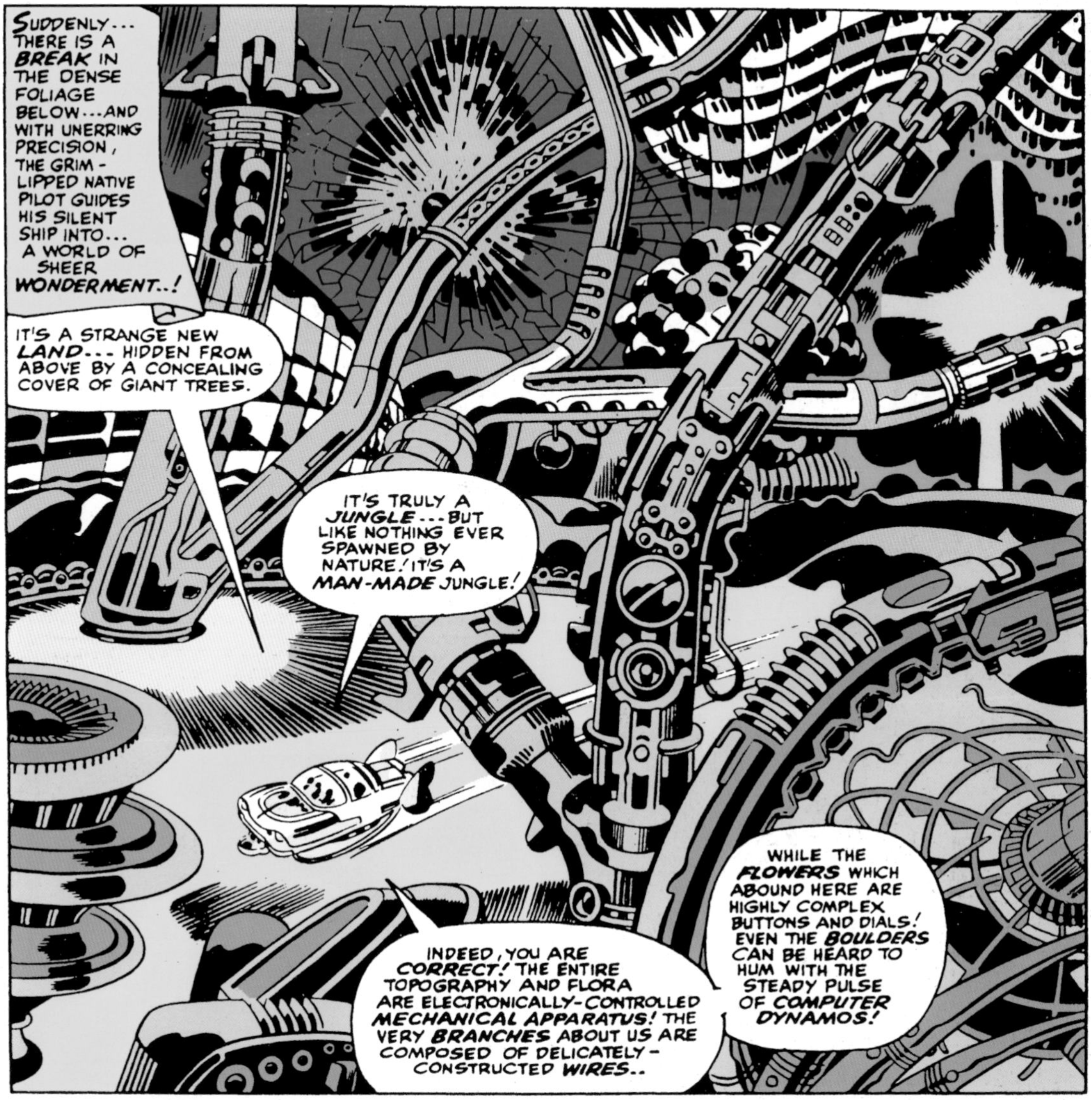
SUDDENLY... THERE IS A BREAK IN THE DENSE FOLIAGE BELOW...AND WITH UNERRING PRECISION, THE GRIM-LIPPED NATIVE PILOT GUIDES HIS SILENT SHIP INTO... A WORLD OF SHEER WONDERMENT..!
IT'S A STRANGE NEW LAND... HIDDEN FROM ABOVE BY A CONCEALING COVER OF GIANT TREES.
IT'S TRULY A JUNGLE... BUT LIKE NOTHING EVER SPAWNED BY NATURE! IT'S A MAN-MADE JUNGLE!
INDEED, YOU ARE CORRECT! THE ENTIRE TOPOGRAPHY AND FLORA ARE ELECTRONICALLY-CONTROLLED MECHANICAL APPARATUS! THE VERY BRANCHES ABOUT US ARE COMPOSED OF DELICATELY-CONSTRUCTED WIRES..
WHILE THE FLOWERS WHICH ABOUND HERE ARE HIGHLY COMPLEX BUTTONS AND DIALS! EVEN THE BOULDERS CAN BE HEARD TO HUM WITH THE STEADY PULSE OF COMPUTER DYNAMOS!

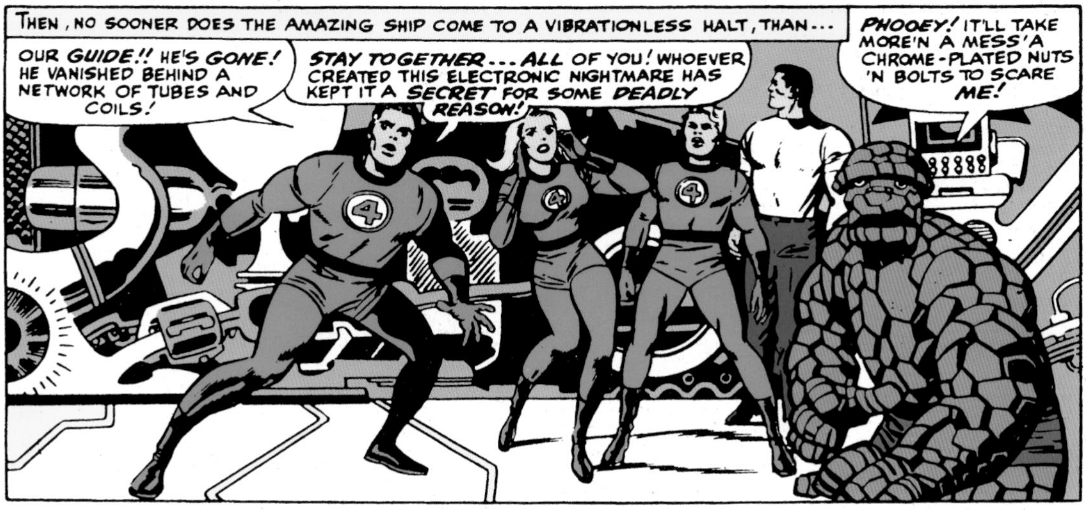
THEN, NO SOONER DOES THE AMAZING SHIP COME TO A VIBRATIONLESS HALT, THAN...
OUR GUIDE!! HE'S GONE! HE VANISHED BEHIND A NETWORK OF TUBES AND COILS!
STAY TOGETHER... ALL OF YOU! WHOEVER CREATED THIS ELECTRONIC NIGHTMARE HAS KEPT IT A SECRET FOR SOME DEADLY REASON!
PHOOEY! IT'LL TAKE MORE'N A MESS'A CHROME-PLATED NUTS 'N BOLTS TO SCARE ME!

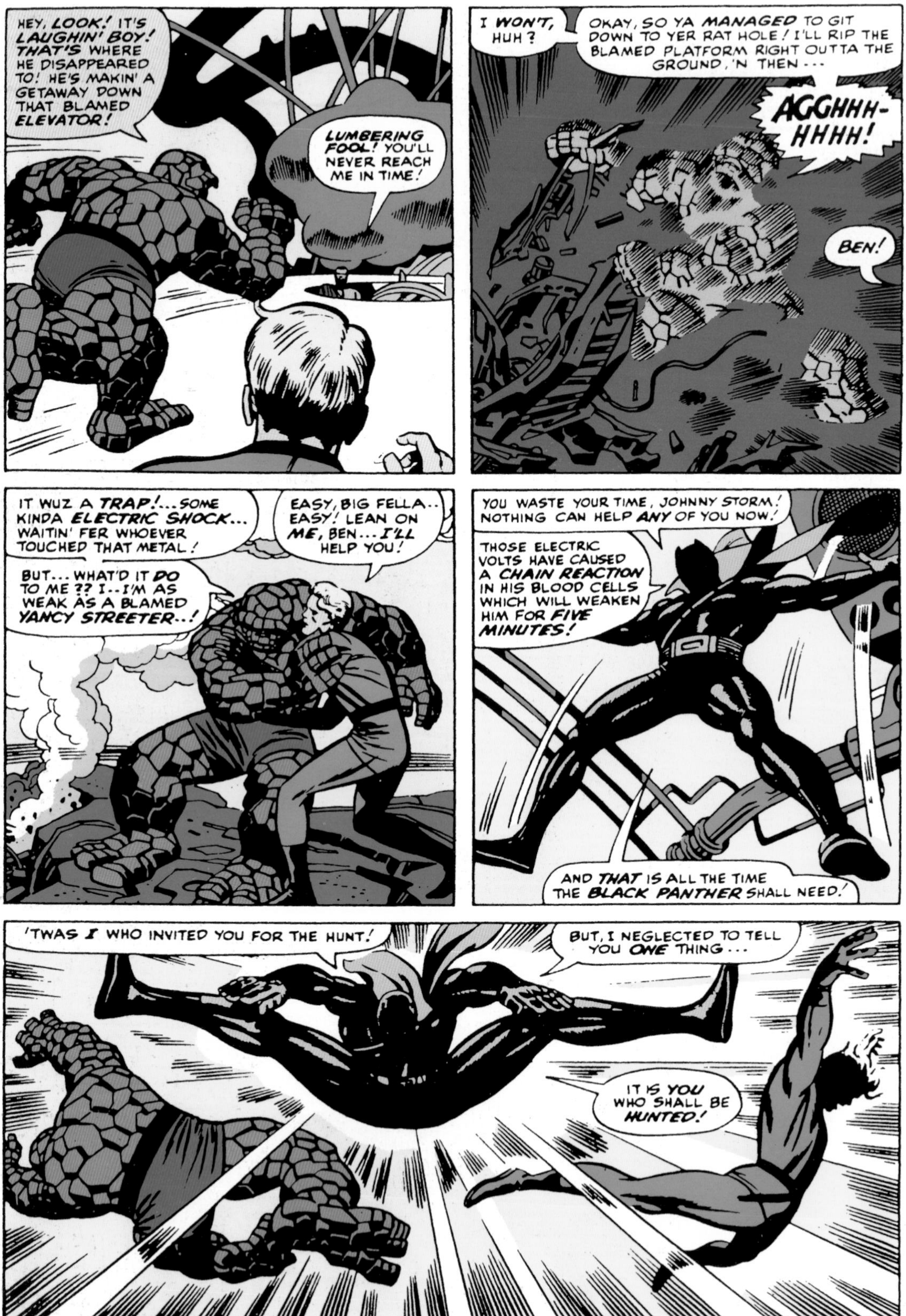
HEY, LOOK! IT'S LAUGHIN' BOY! THAT'S WHERE HE DISAPPEARED TO! HE'S MAKIN' A GETAWAY DOWN THAT BLAMED ELEVATOR!
LUMBERING FOOL! YOU'LL NEVER REACH ME IN TIME!
I WON'T, HUH?
OKAY, SO YA MANAGED TO GIT DOWN TO YER RAT HOLE! I'LL RIP THE BLAMED PLATFORM RIGHT OUTTA THE GROUND, 'N THEN ---
AGGHHH-HHHH!
BEN!
IT WUZ A TRAP!...SOME KINDA ELECTRIC SHOCK... WAITIN' FER WHOEVER TOUCHED THAT METAL!
BUT... WHAT'D IT DO TO ME?? I--I'M AS WEAK AS A BLAMED YANCY STREETER--!
EASY, BIG FELLA.. EASY! LEAN ON ME, BEN... I'LL HELP YOU!
YOU WASTE YOUR TIME, JOHNNY STORM! NOTHING CAN HELP ANY OF YOU NOW!
THOSE ELECTRIC VOLTS HAVE CAUSED A CHAIN REACTION IN HIS BLOOD CELLS WHICH WILL WEAKEN HIM FOR FIVE MINUTES!
AND THAT IS ALL THE TIME THE BLACK PANTHER SHALL NEED!
'TWAS I WHO INVITED YOU FOR THE HUNT!
BUT, I NEGLECTED TO TELL YOU ONE THING...
IT IS YOU WHO SHALL BE HUNTED!

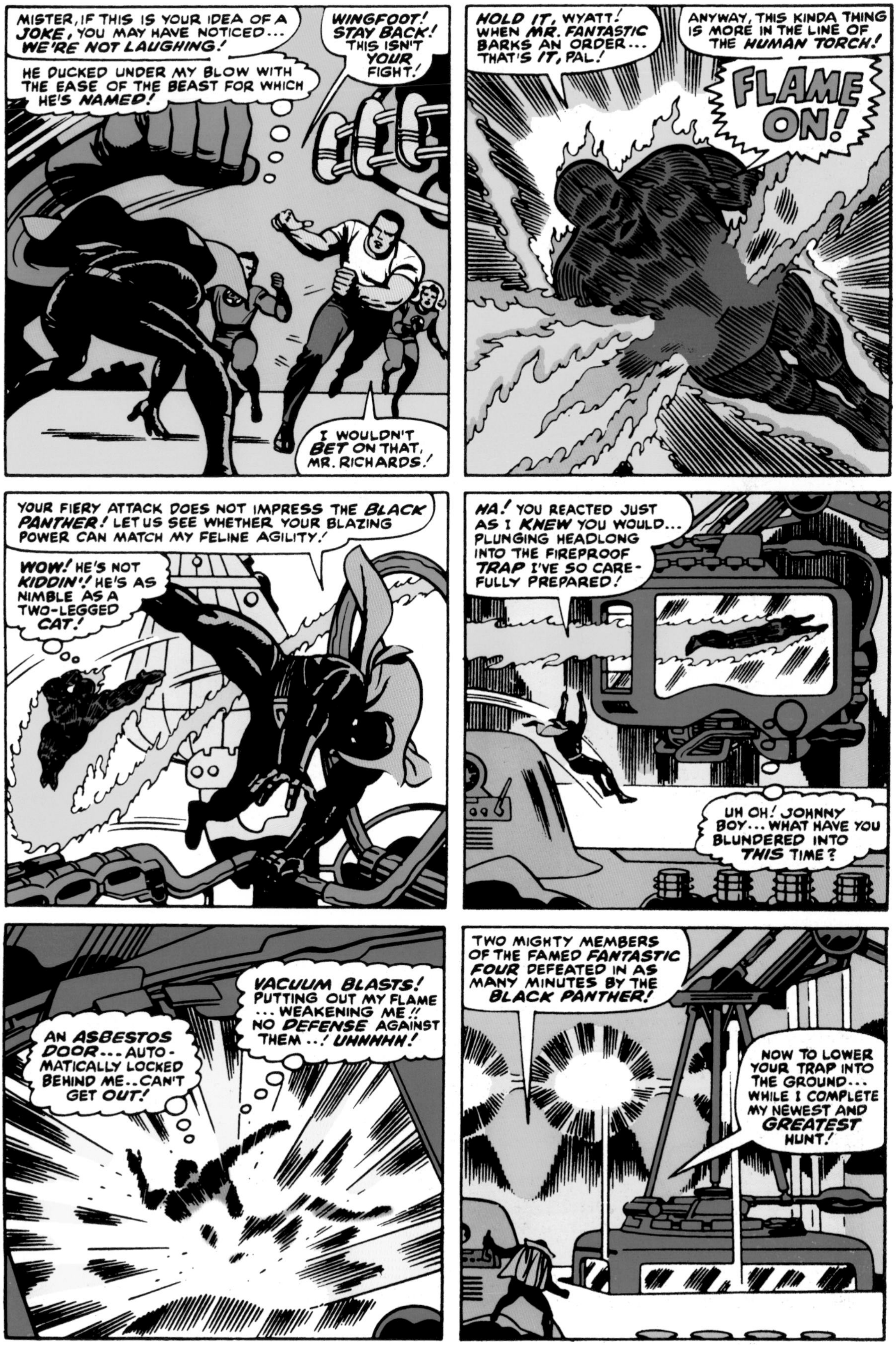
MISTER, IF THIS IS YOUR IDEA OF A JOKE, YOU MAY HAVE NOTICED... WE'RE NOT LAUGHING!
HE DUCKED UNDER MY BLOW WITH THE EASE OF THE BEAST FOR WHICH HE'S NAMED!
WINGFOOT! STAY BACK! THIS ISN'T YOUR FIGHT!
I WOULDN'T BET ON THAT, MR. RICHARDS!
HOLD IT, WYATT! WHEN MR. FANTASTIC BARKS AN ORDER... THAT'S IT, PAL!
ANYWAY, THIS KINDA THING IS MORE IN THE LINE OF THE HUMAN TORCH!
FLAME ON!
YOUR FIERY ATTACK DOES NOT IMPRESS THE BLACK PANTHER! LET US SEE WHETHER YOUR BLAZING POWER CAN MATCH MY FELINE AGILITY!
WOW! HE'S NOT KIDDIN'! HE'S AS NIMBLE AS A TWO-LEGGED CAT!
HA! YOU REACTED JUST AS I KNEW YOU WOULD... PLUNGING HEADLONG INTO THE FIREPROOF TRAP I'VE SO CAREFULLY PREPARED!
UH OH! JOHNNY BOY... WHAT HAVE YOU BLUNDERED INTO THIS TIME?
VACUUM BLASTS! PUTTING OUT MY FLAME ... WEAKENING ME!! NO DEFENSE AGAINST THEM...! UNHHHH!
AN ASBESTOS DOOR... AUTOMATICALLY LOCKED BEHIND ME.. CAN'T GET OUT!
TWO MIGHTY MEMBERS OF THE FAMED FANTASTIC FOUR DEFEATED IN AS MANY MINUTES BY THE BLACK PANTHER!
NOW TO LOWER YOUR TRAP INTO THE GROUND... WHILE I COMPLETE MY NEWEST AND GREATEST HUNT!

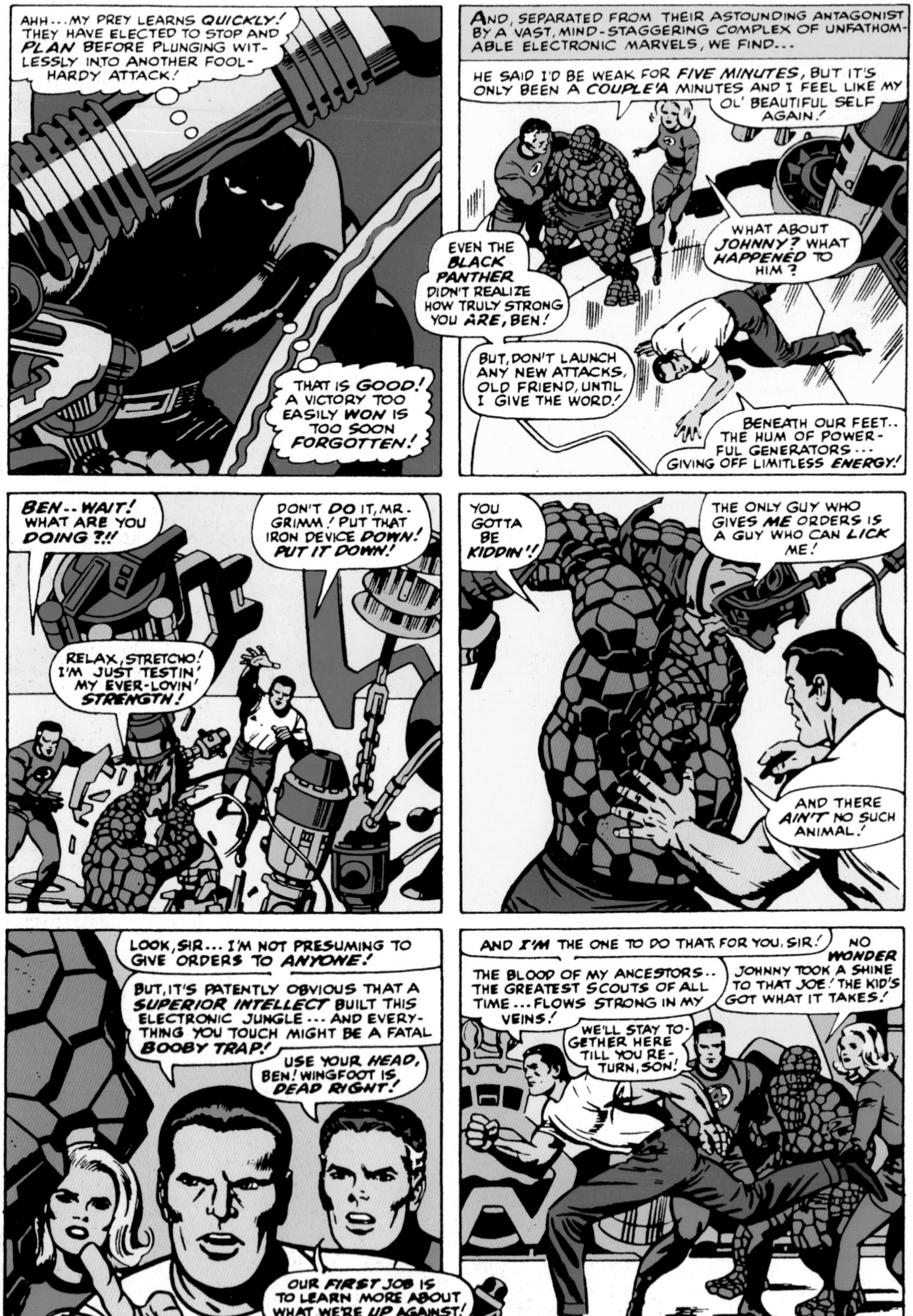
AHH... MY PREY LEARNS QUICKLY! THEY HAVE ELECTED TO STOP AND PLAN BEFORE PLUNGING WITLESSLY INTO ANOTHER FOOLHARDY ATTACK!
THAT IS GOOD! A VICTORY TOO EASILY WON IS TOO SOON FORGOTTEN!
AND, SEPARATED FROM THEIR ASTOUNDING ANTAGONIST BY A VAST, MIND-STAGGERING COMPLEX OF UNFATHOMABLE ELECTRONIC MARVELS, WE FIND...
HE SAID I'D BE WEAK FOR FIVE MINUTES, BUT IT'S ONLY BEEN A COUPLE'A MINUTES AND I FEEL LIKE MY OL' BEAUTIFUL SELF AGAIN!
WHAT ABOUT JOHNNY? WHAT HAPPENED TO HIM?
EVEN THE BLACK PANTHER DIDN'T REALIZE HOW TRULY STRONG YOU ARE, BEN!
BUT, DON'T LAUNCH ANY NEW ATTACKS, OLD FRIEND, UNTIL I GIVE THE WORD!
BENEATH OUR FEET.. THE HUM OF POWERFUL GENERATORS... GIVING OFF LIMITLESS ENERGY!
BEN--WAIT! WHAT ARE YOU DOING?!!
DON'T DO IT, MR. GRIMM! PUT THAT IRON DEVICE DOWN! PUT IT DOWN!
RELAX, STRETCHO! I'M JUST TESTIN' MY EVER-LOVIN' STRENGTH!
YOU GOTTA BE KIDDIN'!
THE ONLY GUY WHO GIVES ME ORDERS IS A GUY WHO CAN LICK ME!
AND THERE AIN'T NO SUCH ANIMAL!
LOOK, SIR... I'M NOT PRESUMING TO GIVE ORDERS TO ANYONE!
BUT, IT'S PATENTLY OBVIOUS THAT A SUPERIOR INTELLECT BUILT THIS ELECTRONIC JUNGLE... AND EVERYTHING YOU TOUCH MIGHT BE A FATAL BOOBY TRAP!
USE YOUR HEAD, BEN! WINGFOOT IS DEAD RIGHT!
OUR FIRST JOB IS TO LEARN MORE ABOUT WHAT WE'RE UP AGAINST!
AND I'M THE ONE TO DO THAT FOR YOU, SIR!
THE BLOOD OF MY ANCESTORS.. THE GREATEST SCOUTS OF ALL TIME... FLOWS STRONG IN MY VEINS!
WE'LL STAY TOGETHER HERE TILL YOU RETURN, SON!
NO WONDER JOHNNY TOOK A SHINE TO THAT JOE! THE KID'S GOT WHAT IT TAKES!

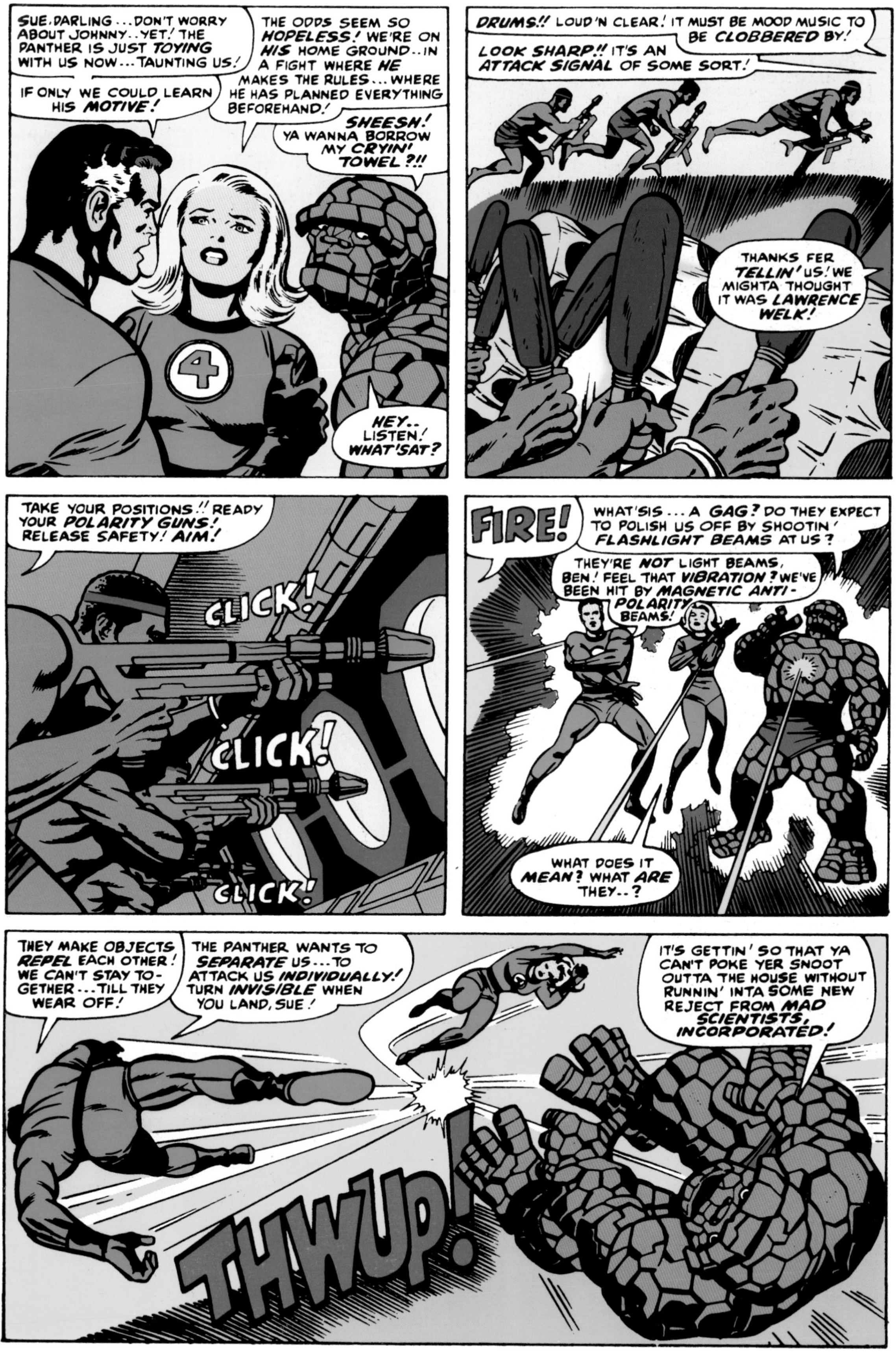
SUE, DARLING... DON'T WORRY ABOUT JOHNNY.. YET! THE PANTHER IS JUST TOYING WITH US NOW... TAUNTING US!
IF ONLY WE COULD LEARN HIS MOTIVE!
THE ODDS SEEM SO HOPELESS! WE'RE ON HIS HOME GROUND.. IN A FIGHT WHERE HE MAKES THE RULES... WHERE HE HAS PLANNED EVERYTHING BEFOREHAND!
SHEESH! YA WANNA BORROW MY CRYIN' TOWEL?!!
HEY.. LISTEN! WHAT'SAT?
DRUMS!! LOUD 'N CLEAR! IT MUST BE MOOD MUSIC TO BE CLOBBERED BY!
LOOK SHARP!! IT'S AN ATTACK SIGNAL OF SOME SORT!
THANKS FER TELLIN' US! WE MIGHTA THOUGHT IT WAS LAWRENCE WELK!
TAKE YOUR POSITIONS!! READY YOUR POLARITY GUNS! RELEASE SAFETY! AIM!
CLICK!
CLICK!
CLICK!
FIRE!
WHAT'SIS... A GAG? DO THEY EXPECT TO POLISH US OFF BY SHOOTIN' FLASHLIGHT BEAMS AT US?
THEY'RE NOT LIGHT BEAMS, BEN! FEEL THAT VIBRATION? WE'VE BEEN HIT BY MAGNETIC ANTI-POLARITY BEAMS!
WHAT DOES IT MEAN? WHAT ARE THEY..?
THEY MAKE OBJECTS REPEL EACH OTHER! WE CAN'T STAY TO-GETHER... TILL THEY WEAR OFF!
THE PANTHER WANTS TO SEPARATE US... TO ATTACK US INDIVIDUALLY! TURN INVISIBLE WHEN YOU LAND, SUE!
IT'S GETTIN' SO THAT YA CAN'T POKE YER SNOOT OUTTA THE HOUSE WITHOUT RUNNIN' INTA SOME NEW REJECT FROM MAD SCIENTISTS, INCORPORATED!
THWUP!

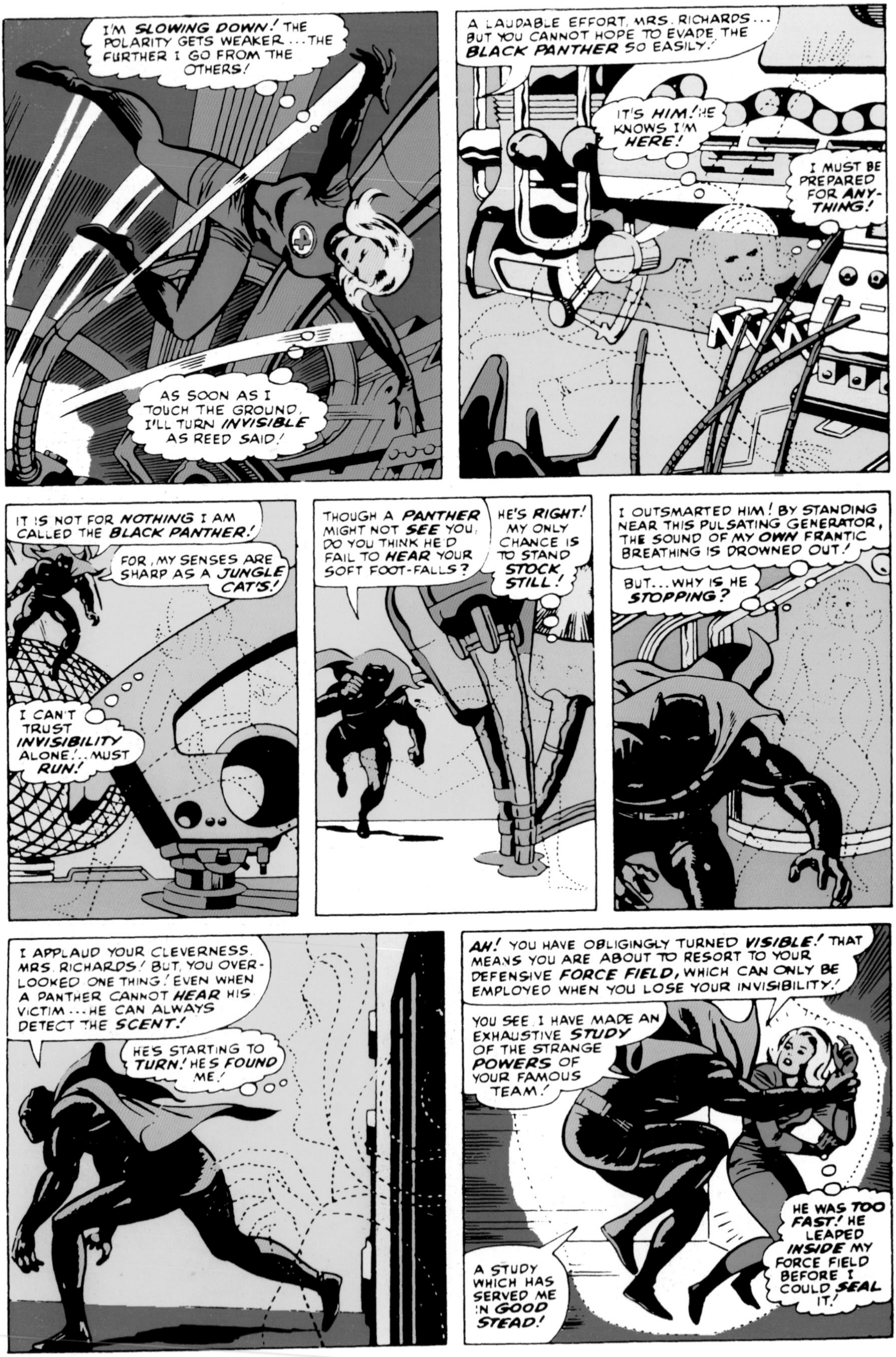
I'M SLOWING DOWN! THE POLARITY GETS WEAKER ... THE FURTHER I GO FROM THE OTHERS!
AS SOON AS I TOUCH THE GROUND, I'LL TURN INVISIBLE AS REED SAID!
A LAUDABLE EFFORT, MRS. RICHARDS ... BUT YOU CANNOT HOPE TO EVADE THE BLACK PANTHER SO EASILY!
IT'S HIM! HE KNOWS I'M HERE!
I MUST BE PREPARED FOR ANY-THING!
IT IS NOT FOR NOTHING I AM CALLED THE BLACK PANTHER!
FOR, MY SENSES ARE SHARP AS A JUNGLE CAT'S!
I CAN'T TRUST INVISIBILITY ALONE!.. MUST RUN!
THOUGH A PANTHER MIGHT NOT SEE YOU, DO YOU THINK HE'D FAIL TO HEAR YOUR SOFT FOOT-FALLS?
HE'S RIGHT! MY ONLY CHANCE IS TO STAND STOCK STILL!
I OUTSMARTED HIM! BY STANDING NEAR THIS PULSATING GENERATOR, THE SOUND OF MY OWN FRANTIC BREATHING IS DROWNED OUT!
BUT... WHY IS HE STOPPING?
I APPLAUD YOUR CLEVERNESS, MRS. RICHARDS! BUT, YOU OVER-LOOKED ONE THING! EVEN WHEN A PANTHER CANNOT HEAR HIS VICTIM ... HE CAN ALWAYS DETECT THE SCENT!
HE'S STARTING TO TURN! HE'S FOUND ME!
AH! YOU HAVE OBLIGINGLY TURNED VISIBLE! THAT MEANS YOU ARE ABOUT TO RESORT TO YOUR DEFENSIVE FORCE FIELD, WHICH CAN ONLY BE EMPLOYED WHEN YOU LOSE YOUR INVISIBILITY!
YOU SEE, I HAVE MADE AN EXHAUSTIVE STUDY OF THE STRANGE POWERS OF YOUR FAMOUS TEAM!
A STUDY WHICH HAS SERVED ME IN GOOD STEAD!
HE WAS TOO FAST! HE LEAPED INSIDE MY FORCE FIELD BEFORE I COULD SEAL IT!

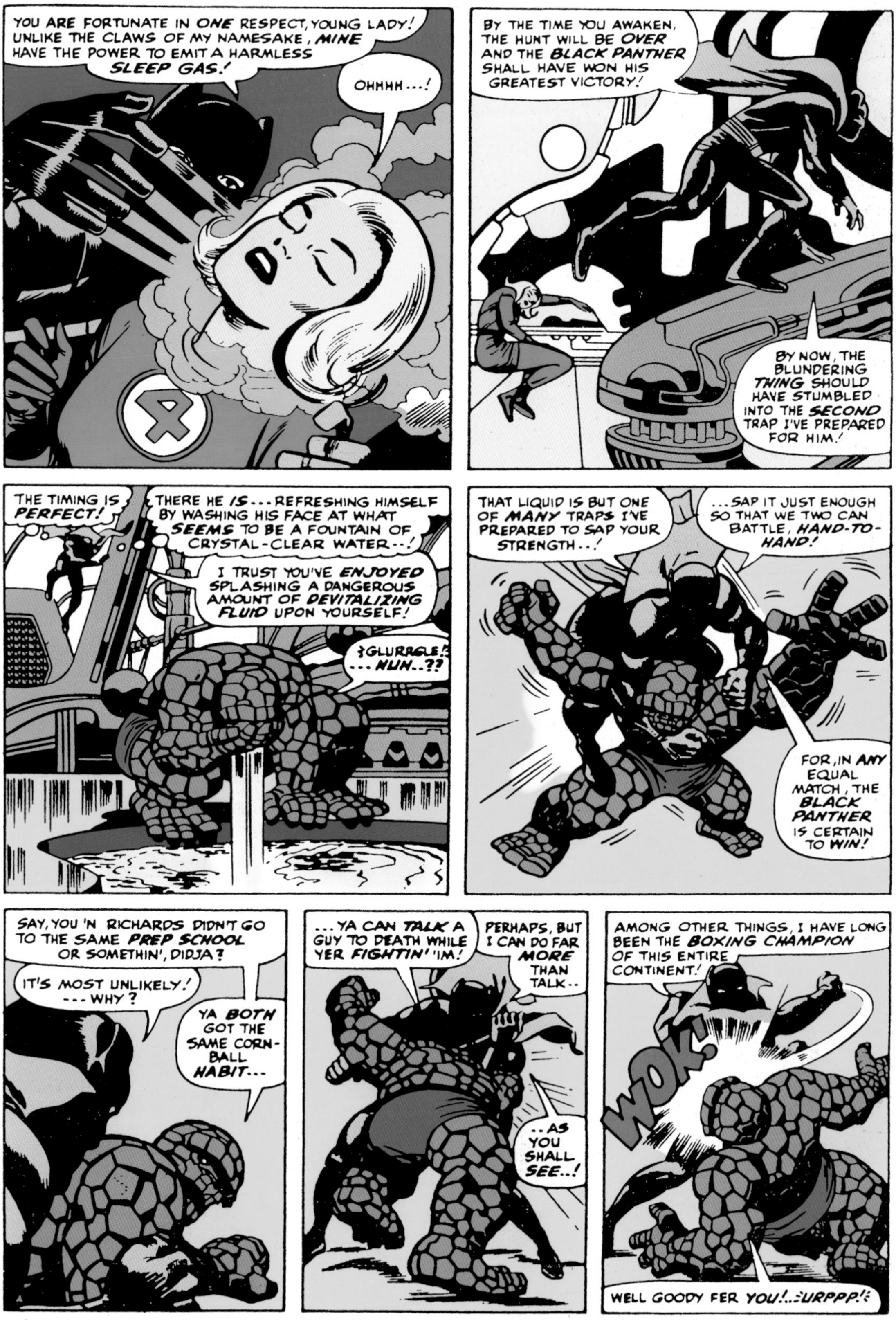
YOU ARE FORTUNATE IN ONE RESPECT, YOUNG LADY! UNLIKE THE CLAWS OF MY NAMESAKE, MINE HAVE THE POWER TO EMIT A HARMLESS SLEEP GAS!
OHHHH...!
BY THE TIME YOU AWAKEN, THE HUNT WILL BE OVER AND THE BLACK PANTHER SHALL HAVE WON HIS GREATEST VICTORY!
BY NOW, THE BLUNDERING THING SHOULD HAVE STUMBLED INTO THE SECOND TRAP I'VE PREPARED FOR HIM!
THE TIMING IS PERFECT!
THERE HE IS... REFRESHING HIMSELF BY WASHING HIS FACE AT WHAT SEEMS TO BE A FOUNTAIN OF CRYSTAL-CLEAR WATER--!
I TRUST YOU'VE ENJOYED SPLASHING A DANGEROUS AMOUNT OF DEVITALIZING FLUID UPON YOURSELF!
GLURRGLE! ...HUH..??
THAT LIQUID IS BUT ONE OF MANY TRAPS I'VE PREPARED TO SAP YOUR STRENGTH--!
...SAP IT JUST ENOUGH SO THAT WE TWO CAN BATTLE, HAND-TO-HAND!
FOR, IN ANY EQUAL MATCH, THE BLACK PANTHER IS CERTAIN TO WIN!
SAY, YOU 'N RICHARDS DIDN'T GO TO THE SAME PREP SCHOOL OR SOMETHIN', DIDJA?
IT'S MOST UNLIKELY! ---WHY?
YA BOTH GOT THE SAME CORN-BALL HABIT...
...YA CAN TALK A GUY TO DEATH WHILE YER FIGHTIN' 'IM!
PERHAPS, BUT I CAN DO FAR MORE THAN TALK--
..AS YOU SHALL SEE..!
AMONG OTHER THINGS, I HAVE LONG BEEN THE BOXING CHAMPION OF THIS ENTIRE CONTINENT!
WOK!
WELL GOODY FER YOU!..URPPP!

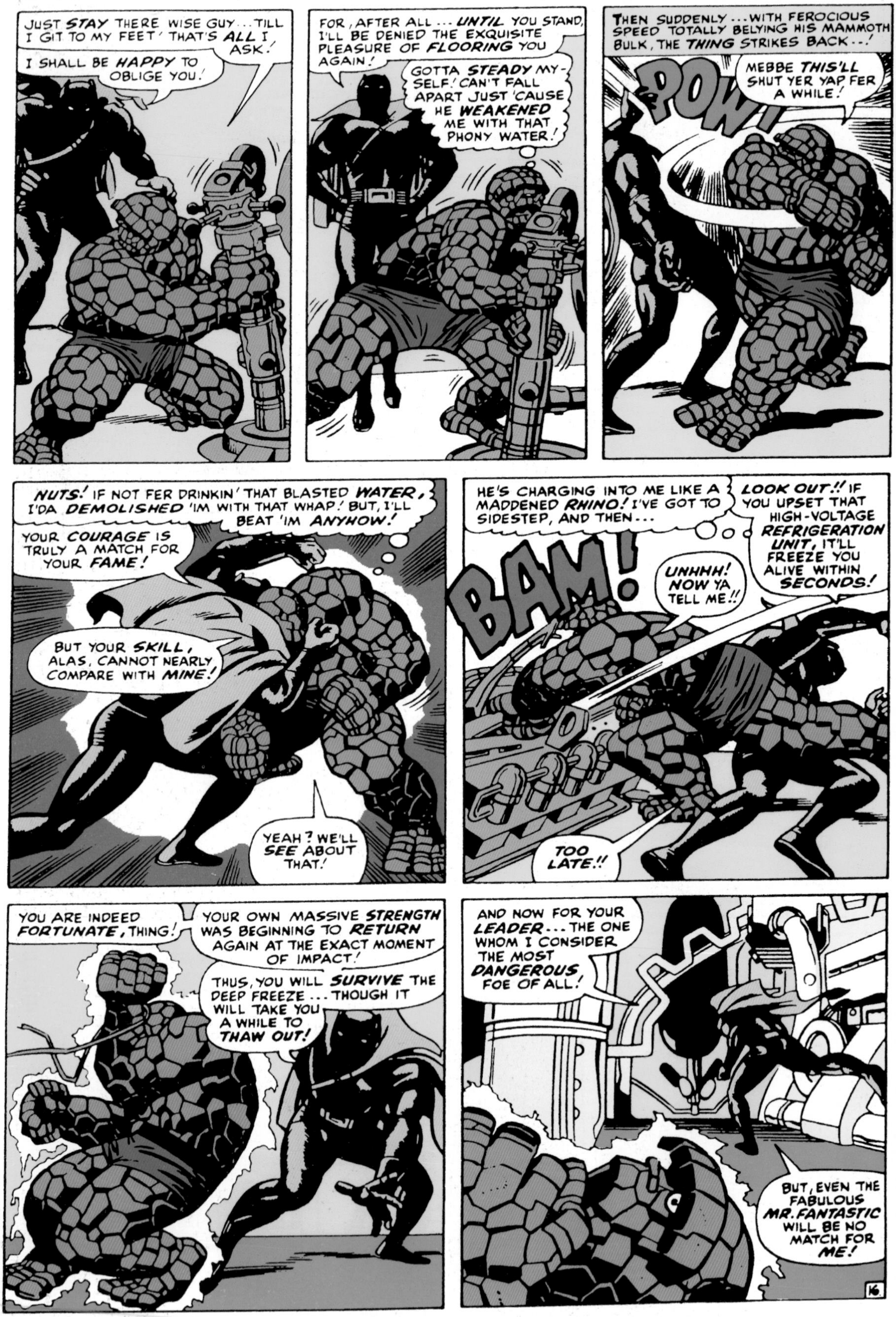
JUST STAY THERE WISE GUY... TILL I GIT TO MY FEET! THAT'S ALL I ASK!
I SHALL BE HAPPY TO OBLIGE YOU!
FOR, AFTER ALL... UNTIL YOU STAND, I'LL BE DENIED THE EXQUISITE PLEASURE OF FLOORING YOU AGAIN!
GOTTA STEADY MY-SELF! CAN'T FALL APART JUST 'CAUSE HE WEAKENED ME WITH THAT PHONY WATER!
THEN SUDDENLY... WITH FEROCIOUS SPEED TOTALLY BELYING HIS MAMMOTH BULK, THE THING STRIKES BACK..!
POW!
MEBBE THIS'LL SHUT YER YAP FER A WHILE!
NUTS! IF NOT FER DRINKIN' THAT BLASTED WATER, I'DA DEMOLISHED 'IM WITH THAT WHAP! BUT, I'LL BEAT 'IM ANYHOW!
YOUR COURAGE IS TRULY A MATCH FOR YOUR FAME!
BUT YOUR SKILL, ALAS, CANNOT NEARLY COMPARE WITH MINE!
YEAH? WE'LL SEE ABOUT THAT!
HE'S CHARGING INTO ME LIKE A MADDENED RHINO! I'VE GOT TO SIDESTEP, AND THEN...
LOOK OUT!! IF YOU UPSET THAT HIGH-VOLTAGE REFRIGERATION UNIT, IT'LL FREEZE YOU ALIVE WITHIN SECONDS!
BAM!
UNHHH! NOW YA TELL ME!!
TOO LATE!!
YOU ARE INDEED FORTUNATE, THING!
YOUR OWN MASSIVE STRENGTH WAS BEGINNING TO RETURN AGAIN AT THE EXACT MOMENT OF IMPACT!
THUS, YOU WILL SURVIVE THE DEEP FREEZE... THOUGH IT WILL TAKE YOU A WHILE TO THAW OUT!
AND NOW FOR YOUR LEADER... THE ONE WHOM I CONSIDER THE MOST DANGEROUS FOE OF ALL!
BUT, EVEN THE FABULOUS MR. FANTASTIC WILL BE NO MATCH FOR ME!
16

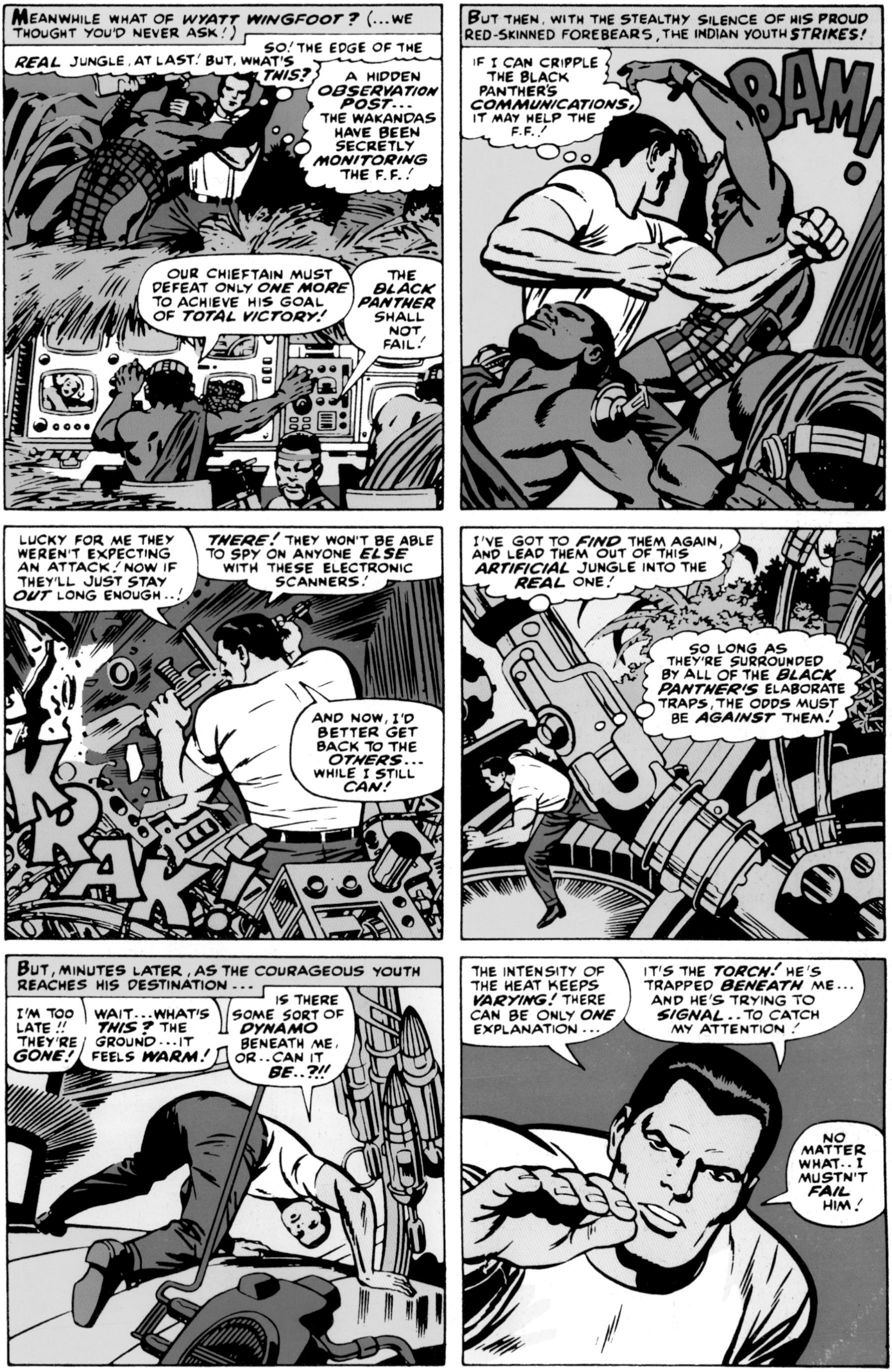

MEANWHILE WHAT OF WYATT WINGFOOT? (...WE THOUGHT YOU'D NEVER ASK!)
SO! THE EDGE OF THE REAL JUNGLE, AT LAST! BUT, WHAT'S THIS?
A HIDDEN OBSERVATION POST... THE WAKANDAS HAVE BEEN SECRETLY MONITORING THE F.F.!
OUR CHIEFTAIN MUST DEFEAT ONLY ONE MORE TO ACHIEVE HIS GOAL OF TOTAL VICTORY!
THE BLACK PANTHER SHALL NOT FAIL!
BUT THEN, WITH THE STEALTHY SILENCE OF HIS PROUD RED-SKINNED FOREBEARS, THE INDIAN YOUTH STRIKES!
IF I CAN CRIPPLE THE BLACK PANTHER'S COMMUNICATIONS, IT MAY HELP THE F.F.!
BAM!
LUCKY FOR ME THEY WEREN'T EXPECTING AN ATTACK! NOW IF THEY'LL JUST STAY OUT LONG ENOUGH..!
THERE! THEY WON'T BE ABLE TO SPY ON ANYONE ELSE WITH THESE ELECTRONIC SCANNERS!
AND NOW, I'D BETTER GET BACK TO THE OTHERS... WHILE I STILL CAN!
KRAK!
I'VE GOT TO FIND THEM AGAIN, AND LEAD THEM OUT OF THIS ARTIFICIAL JUNGLE INTO THE REAL ONE!
SO LONG AS THEY'RE SURROUNDED BY ALL OF THE BLACK PANTHER'S ELABORATE TRAPS, THE ODDS MUST BE AGAINST THEM!
BUT, MINUTES LATER, AS THE COURAGEOUS YOUTH REACHES HIS DESTINATION...
I'M TOO LATE!! THEY'RE GONE!
WAIT...WHAT'S THIS? THE GROUND...IT FEELS WARM!
IS THERE SOME SORT OF DYNAMO BENEATH ME, OR..CAN IT BE..?!!
THE INTENSITY OF THE HEAT KEEPS VARYING! THERE CAN BE ONLY ONE EXPLANATION...
IT'S THE TORCH! HE'S TRAPPED BENEATH ME... AND HE'S TRYING TO SIGNAL..TO CATCH MY ATTENTION!
NO MATTER WHAT..I MUSTN'T FAIL HIM!

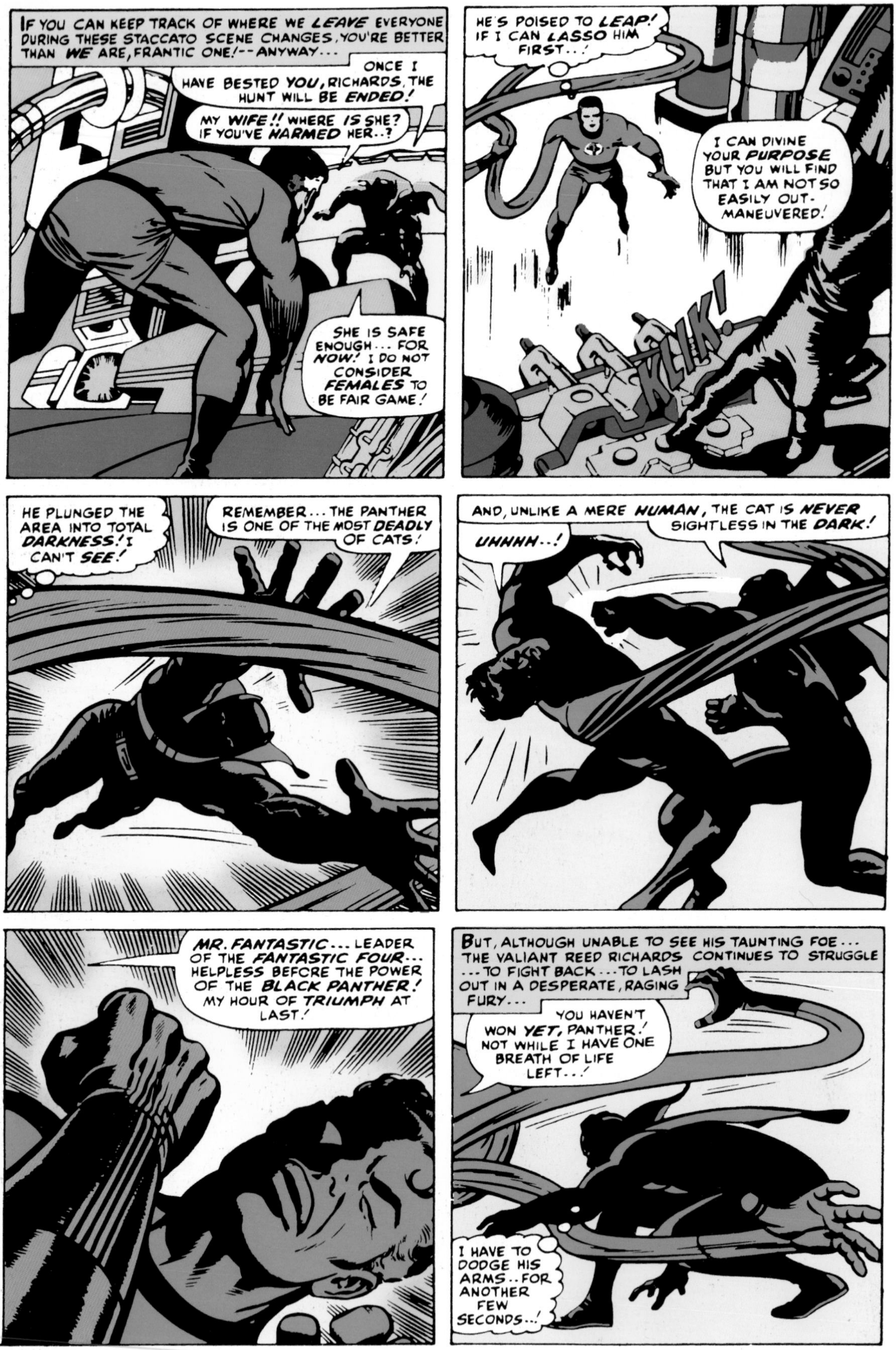
IF YOU CAN KEEP TRACK OF WHERE WE LEAVE EVERYONE DURING THESE STACCATO SCENE CHANGES, YOU'RE BETTER THAN WE ARE, FRANTIC ONE!--ANYWAY...
ONCE I HAVE BESTED YOU, RICHARDS, THE HUNT WILL BE ENDED!
MY WIFE!! WHERE IS SHE? IF YOU'VE HARMED HER..?
SHE IS SAFE ENOUGH... FOR NOW! I DO NOT CONSIDER FEMALES TO BE FAIR GAME!
HE'S POISED TO LEAP! IF I CAN LASSO HIM FIRST...!
I CAN DIVINE YOUR PURPOSE BUT YOU WILL FIND THAT I AM NOT SO EASILY OUT-MANEUVERED!
KLIK!
HE PLUNGED THE AREA INTO TOTAL DARKNESS! I CAN'T SEE!
REMEMBER... THE PANTHER IS ONE OF THE MOST DEADLY OF CATS!
AND, UNLIKE A MERE HUMAN, THE CAT IS NEVER SIGHTLESS IN THE DARK!
UHHHH..!
MR. FANTASTIC... LEADER OF THE FANTASTIC FOUR... HELPLESS BEFORE THE POWER OF THE BLACK PANTHER! MY HOUR OF TRIUMPH AT LAST!
BUT, ALTHOUGH UNABLE TO SEE HIS TAUNTING FOE... THE VALIANT REED RICHARDS CONTINUES TO STRUGGLE ...TO FIGHT BACK...TO LASH OUT IN A DESPERATE, RAGING FURY...
YOU HAVEN'T WON YET, PANTHER! NOT WHILE I HAVE ONE BREATH OF LIFE LEFT..!
I HAVE TO DODGE HIS ARMS..FOR ANOTHER FEW SECONDS..!

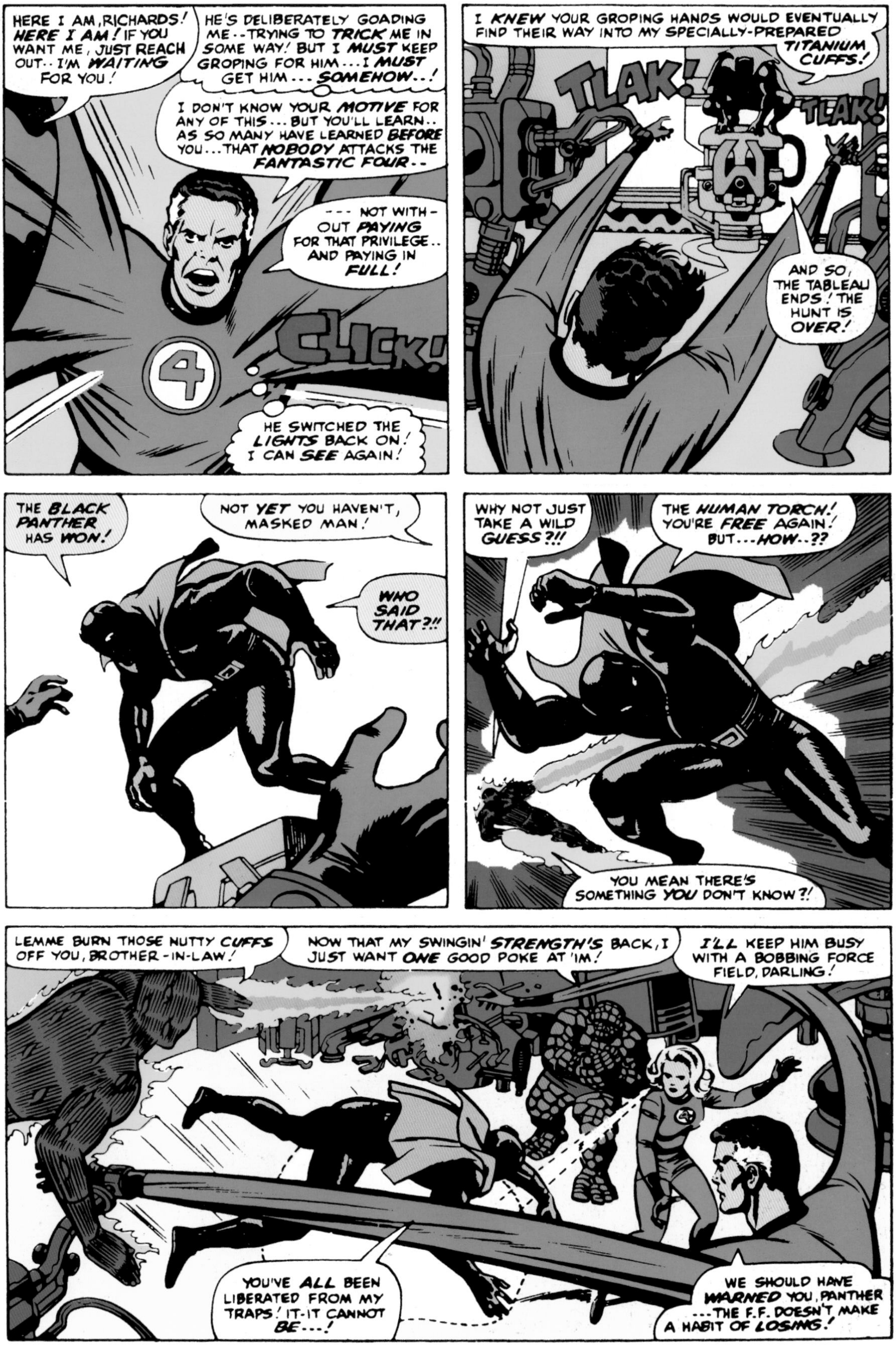
HERE I AM, RICHARDS! HERE I AM! IF YOU WANT ME, JUST REACH OUT-- I'M WAITING FOR YOU!
HE'S DELIBERATELY GOADING ME--TRYING TO TRICK ME IN SOME WAY! BUT I MUST KEEP GROPING FOR HIM...I MUST GET HIM...SOMEHOW..!
I DON'T KNOW YOUR MOTIVE FOR ANY OF THIS... BUT YOU'LL LEARN.. AS SO MANY HAVE LEARNED BEFORE YOU...THAT NOBODY ATTACKS THE FANTASTIC FOUR--
---NOT WITH-OUT PAYING FOR THAT PRIVILEGE.. AND PAYING IN FULL!
CLICK!!
HE SWITCHED THE LIGHTS BACK ON! I CAN SEE AGAIN!
I KNEW YOUR GROPING HANDS WOULD EVENTUALLY FIND THEIR WAY INTO MY SPECIALLY-PREPARED TITANIUM CUFFS!
TLAK!
TLAK!
AND SO, THE TABLEAU ENDS! THE HUNT IS OVER!
THE BLACK PANTHER HAS WON!
NOT YET YOU HAVEN'T, MASKED MAN!
WHO SAID THAT?!!
WHY NOT JUST TAKE A WILD GUESS?!!
THE HUMAN TORCH! YOU'RE FREE AGAIN! BUT...HOW..??
YOU MEAN THERE'S SOMETHING YOU DON'T KNOW?!
LEMME BURN THOSE NUTTY CUFFS OFF YOU, BROTHER-IN-LAW!
NOW THAT MY SWINGIN' STRENGTH'S BACK, I JUST WANT ONE GOOD POKE AT 'IM!
I'LL KEEP HIM BUSY WITH A BOBBING FORCE FIELD, DARLING!
YOU'VE ALL BEEN LIBERATED FROM MY TRAPS! IT-IT CANNOT BE--!
WE SHOULD HAVE WARNED YOU, PANTHER ---THE F.F. DOESN'T MAKE A HABIT OF LOSING!

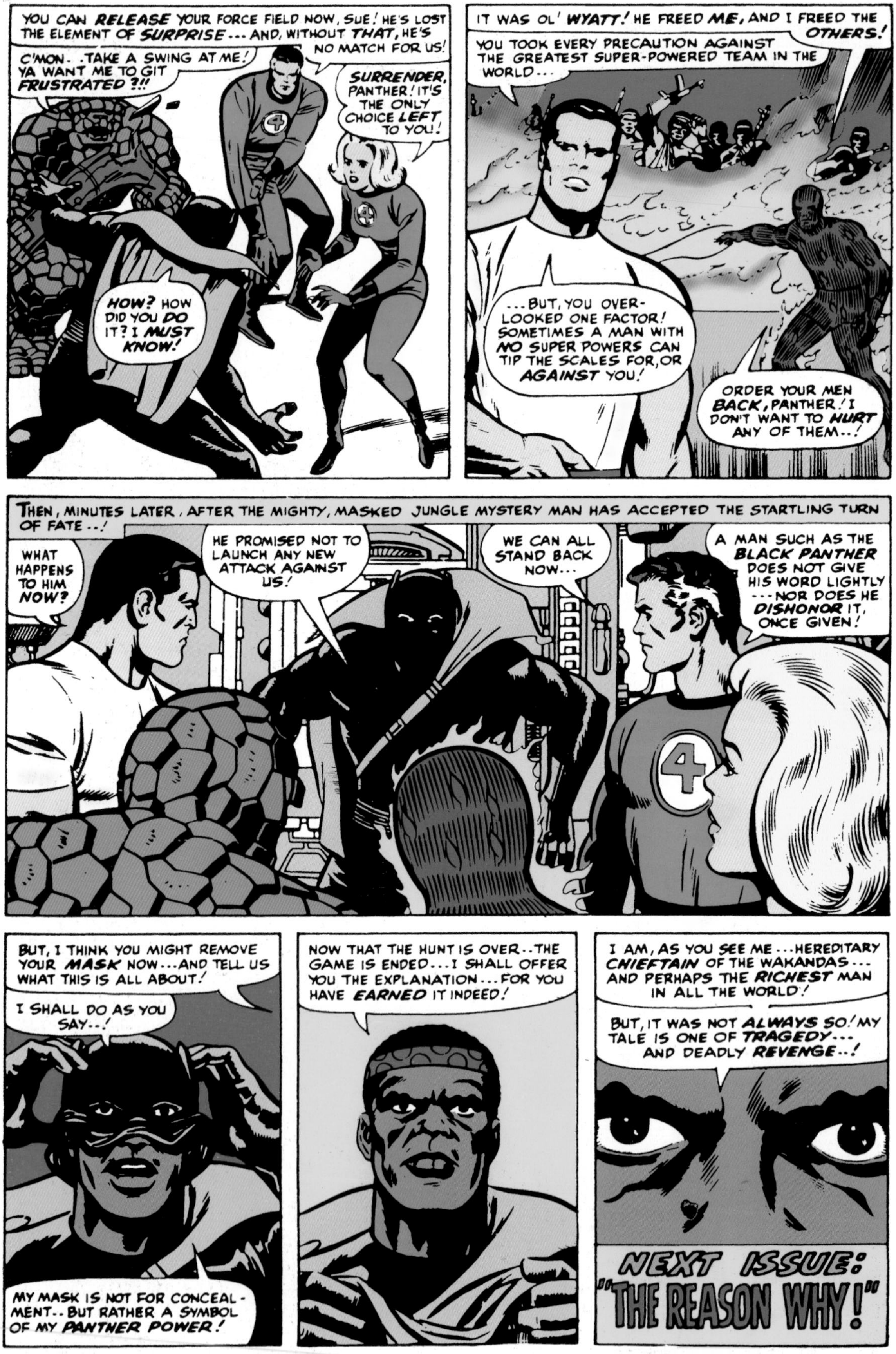
YOU CAN RELEASE YOUR FORCE FIELD NOW, SUE! HE'S LOST THE ELEMENT OF SURPRISE --- AND, WITHOUT THAT, HE'S NO MATCH FOR US!
C'MON - - TAKE A SWING AT ME! YA WANT ME TO GIT FRUSTRATED ?!!
SURRENDER, PANTHER! IT'S THE ONLY CHOICE LEFT TO YOU!
HOW? HOW DID YOU DO IT? I MUST KNOW!
IT WAS OL' WYATT! HE FREED ME, AND I FREED THE OTHERS!
YOU TOOK EVERY PRECAUTION AGAINST THE GREATEST SUPER-POWERED TEAM IN THE WORLD...
...BUT, YOU OVER-LOOKED ONE FACTOR! SOMETIMES A MAN WITH NO SUPER POWERS CAN TIP THE SCALES FOR, OR AGAINST YOU!
ORDER YOUR MEN BACK, PANTHER! I DON'T WANT TO HURT ANY OF THEM..!
THEN, MINUTES LATER, AFTER THE MIGHTY, MASKED JUNGLE MYSTERY MAN HAS ACCEPTED THE STARTLING TURN OF FATE..!
WHAT HAPPENS TO HIM NOW?
HE PROMISED NOT TO LAUNCH ANY NEW ATTACK AGAINST US!
WE CAN ALL STAND BACK NOW...
A MAN SUCH AS THE BLACK PANTHER DOES NOT GIVE HIS WORD LIGHTLY ---NOR DOES HE DISHONOR IT, ONCE GIVEN!
BUT, I THINK YOU MIGHT REMOVE YOUR MASK NOW... AND TELL US WHAT THIS IS ALL ABOUT!
I SHALL DO AS YOU SAY..!
MY MASK IS NOT FOR CONCEAL-MENT.. BUT RATHER A SYMBOL OF MY PANTHER POWER!
NOW THAT THE HUNT IS OVER..THE GAME IS ENDED... I SHALL OFFER YOU THE EXPLANATION... FOR YOU HAVE EARNED IT INDEED!
I AM, AS YOU SEE ME ... HEREDITARY CHIEFTAIN OF THE WAKANDAS... AND PERHAPS THE RICHEST MAN IN ALL THE WORLD!
BUT, IT WAS NOT ALWAYS SO! MY TALE IS ONE OF TRAGEDY--- AND DEADLY REVENGE..!
NEXT ISSUE:
"THE REASON WHY!"

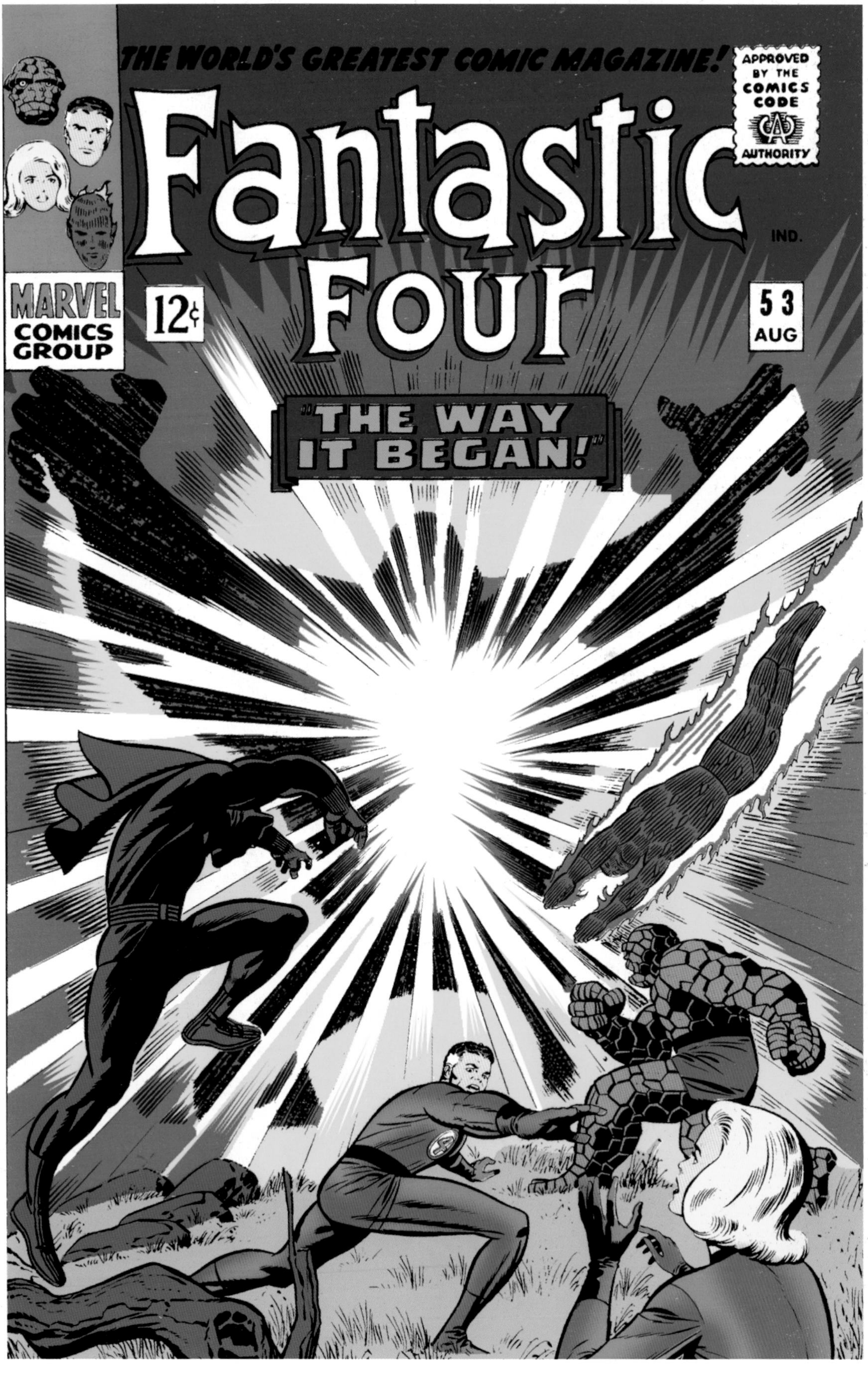
THE WORLD'S GREATEST COMIC MAGAZINE!
APPROVED BY THE COMICS CODE AUTHORITY
Fantastic Four
IND.
MARVEL COMICS GROUP
12¢
53 AUG
"THE WAY IT BEGAN!"

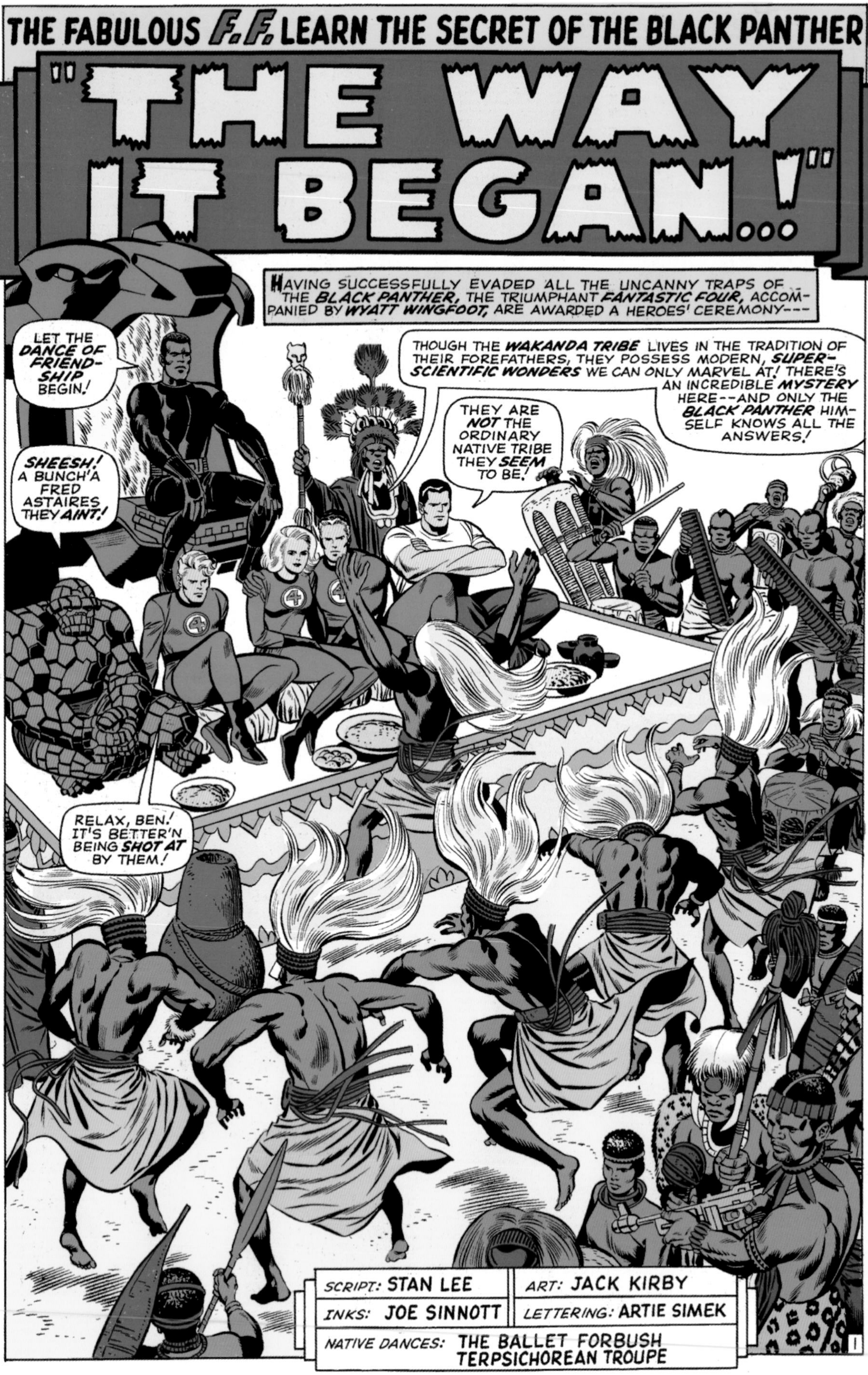
THE FABULOUS F.F. LEARN THE SECRET OF THE BLACK PANTHER
"THE WAY IT BEGAN!"...
HAVING SUCCESSFULLY EVADED ALL THE UNCANNY TRAPS OF THE BLACK PANTHER, THE TRIUMPHANT FANTASTIC FOUR, ACCOMPANIED BY WYATT WINGFOOT, ARE AWARDED A HEROES' CEREMONY---
LET THE DANCE OF FRIENDSHIP BEGIN!
THOUGH THE WAKANDA TRIBE LIVES IN THE TRADITION OF THEIR FOREFATHERS, THEY POSSESS MODERN, SUPER-SCIENTIFIC WONDERS WE CAN ONLY MARVEL AT! THERE'S AN INCREDIBLE MYSTERY HERE--AND ONLY THE BLACK PANTHER HIMSELF KNOWS ALL THE ANSWERS!
THEY ARE NOT THE ORDINARY NATIVE TRIBE THEY SEEM TO BE!
SHEESH! A BUNCH'A FRED ASTAIRES THEY AIN'T!
RELAX, BEN! IT'S BETTER'N BEING SHOT AT BY THEM!
SCRIPT: STAN LEE
ART: JACK KIRBY
INKS: JOE SINNOTT
LETTERING: ARTIE SIMEK
NATIVE DANCES: THE BALLET FORBUSH TERPSICHOREAN TROUPE
1

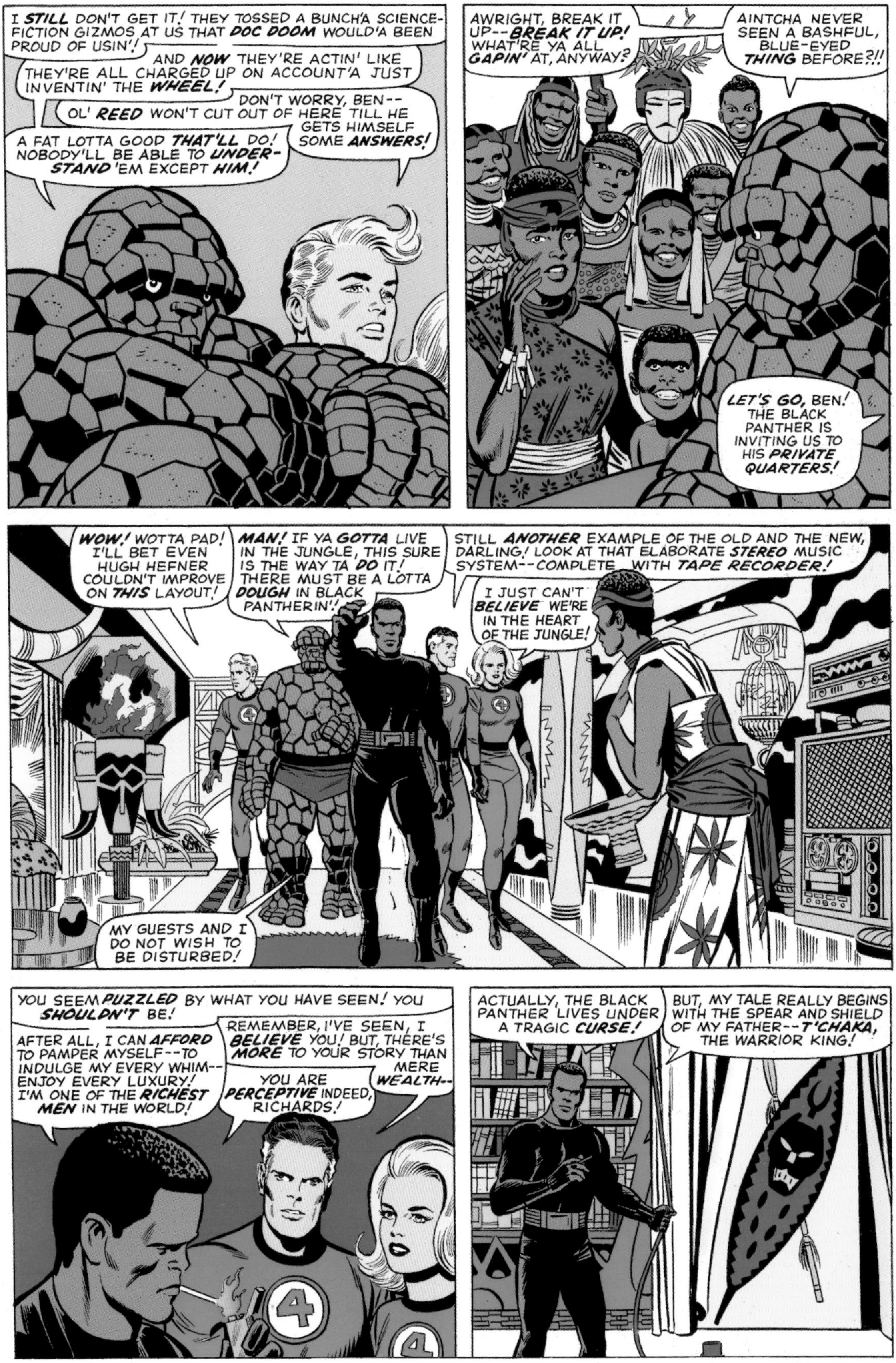

I STILL DON'T GET IT! THEY TOSSED A BUNCH'A SCIENCE-FICTION GIZMOS AT US THAT DOC DOOM WOULD'A BEEN PROUD OF USIN'!
AND NOW THEY'RE ACTIN' LIKE THEY'RE ALL CHARGED UP ON ACCOUNT'A JUST INVENTIN' THE WHEEL!
DON'T WORRY, BEN-- OL' REED WON'T CUT OUT OF HERE TILL HE GETS HIMSELF SOME ANSWERS!
A FAT LOTTA GOOD THAT'LL DO! NOBODY'LL BE ABLE TO UNDER-STAND 'EM EXCEPT HIM!
AWRIGHT, BREAK IT UP--BREAK IT UP! WHAT'RE YA ALL GAPIN' AT, ANYWAY?
AINTCHA NEVER SEEN A BASHFUL, BLUE-EYED THING BEFORE?!!
LET'S GO, BEN! THE BLACK PANTHER IS INVITING US TO HIS PRIVATE QUARTERS!
WOW! WOTTA PAD! I'LL BET EVEN HUGH HEFNER COULDN'T IMPROVE ON THIS LAYOUT!
MAN! IF YA GOTTA LIVE IN THE JUNGLE, THIS SURE IS THE WAY TA DO IT! THERE MUST BE A LOTTA DOUGH IN BLACK PANTHERIN'!
STILL ANOTHER EXAMPLE OF THE OLD AND THE NEW, DARLING! LOOK AT THAT ELABORATE STEREO MUSIC SYSTEM--COMPLETE WITH TAPE RECORDER!
I JUST CAN'T BELIEVE WE'RE IN THE HEART OF THE JUNGLE!
MY GUESTS AND I DO NOT WISH TO BE DISTURBED!
YOU SEEM PUZZLED BY WHAT YOU HAVE SEEN! YOU SHOULDN'T BE!
AFTER ALL, I CAN AFFORD TO PAMPER MYSELF--TO INDULGE MY EVERY WHIM--ENJOY EVERY LUXURY! I'M ONE OF THE RICHEST MEN IN THE WORLD!
REMEMBER, I'VE SEEN, I BELIEVE YOU! BUT, THERE'S MORE TO YOUR STORY THAN MERE WEALTH--
YOU ARE PERCEPTIVE INDEED, RICHARDS!
ACTUALLY, THE BLACK PANTHER LIVES UNDER A TRAGIC CURSE!
BUT, MY TALE REALLY BEGINS WITH THE SPEAR AND SHIELD OF MY FATHER--T'CHAKA, THE WARRIOR KING!

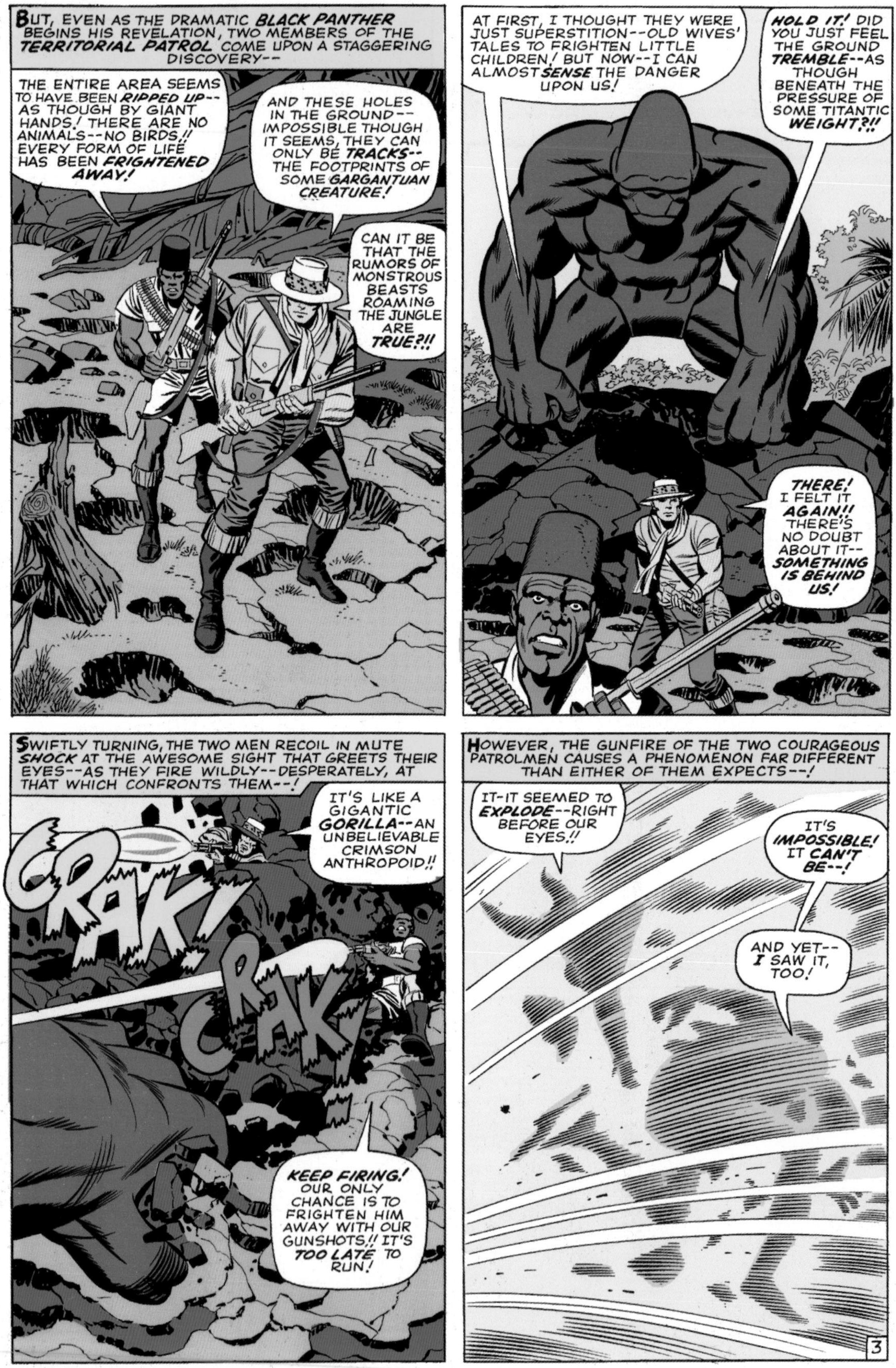
BUT, EVEN AS THE DRAMATIC BLACK PANTHER BEGINS HIS REVELATION, TWO MEMBERS OF THE TERRITORIAL PATROL COME UPON A STAGGERING DISCOVERY--
THE ENTIRE AREA SEEMS TO HAVE BEEN RIPPED UP--AS THOUGH BY GIANT HANDS! THERE ARE NO ANIMALS--NO BIRDS!! EVERY FORM OF LIFE HAS BEEN FRIGHTENED AWAY!
AND THESE HOLES IN THE GROUND--IMPOSSIBLE THOUGH IT SEEMS, THEY CAN ONLY BE TRACKS--THE FOOTPRINTS OF SOME GARGANTUAN CREATURE!
CAN IT BE THAT THE RUMORS OF MONSTROUS BEASTS ROAMING THE JUNGLE ARE TRUE?!!
AT FIRST, I THOUGHT THEY WERE JUST SUPERSTITION--OLD WIVES' TALES TO FRIGHTEN LITTLE CHILDREN! BUT NOW--I CAN ALMOST SENSE THE DANGER UPON US!
HOLD IT! DID YOU JUST FEEL THE GROUND TREMBLE--AS THOUGH BENEATH THE PRESSURE OF SOME TITANTIC WEIGHT?!!
THERE! I FELT IT AGAIN!! THERE'S NO DOUBT ABOUT IT--SOMETHING IS BEHIND US!
SWIFTLY TURNING, THE TWO MEN RECOIL IN MUTE SHOCK AT THE AWESOME SIGHT THAT GREETS THEIR EYES--AS THEY FIRE WILDLY--DESPERATELY, AT THAT WHICH CONFRONTS THEM--!
IT'S LIKE A GIGANTIC GORILLA--AN UNBELIEVABLE CRIMSON ANTHROPOID!!
CRAK!
CRAK!
KEEP FIRING! OUR ONLY CHANCE IS TO FRIGHTEN HIM AWAY WITH OUR GUNSHOTS!! IT'S TOO LATE TO RUN!
HOWEVER, THE GUNFIRE OF THE TWO COURAGEOUS PATROLMEN CAUSES A PHENOMENON FAR DIFFERENT THAN EITHER OF THEM EXPECTS--!
IT-IT SEEMED TO EXPLODE--RIGHT BEFORE OUR EYES!!
IT'S IMPOSSIBLE! IT CAN'T BE--!
AND YET--I SAW IT, TOO!
3

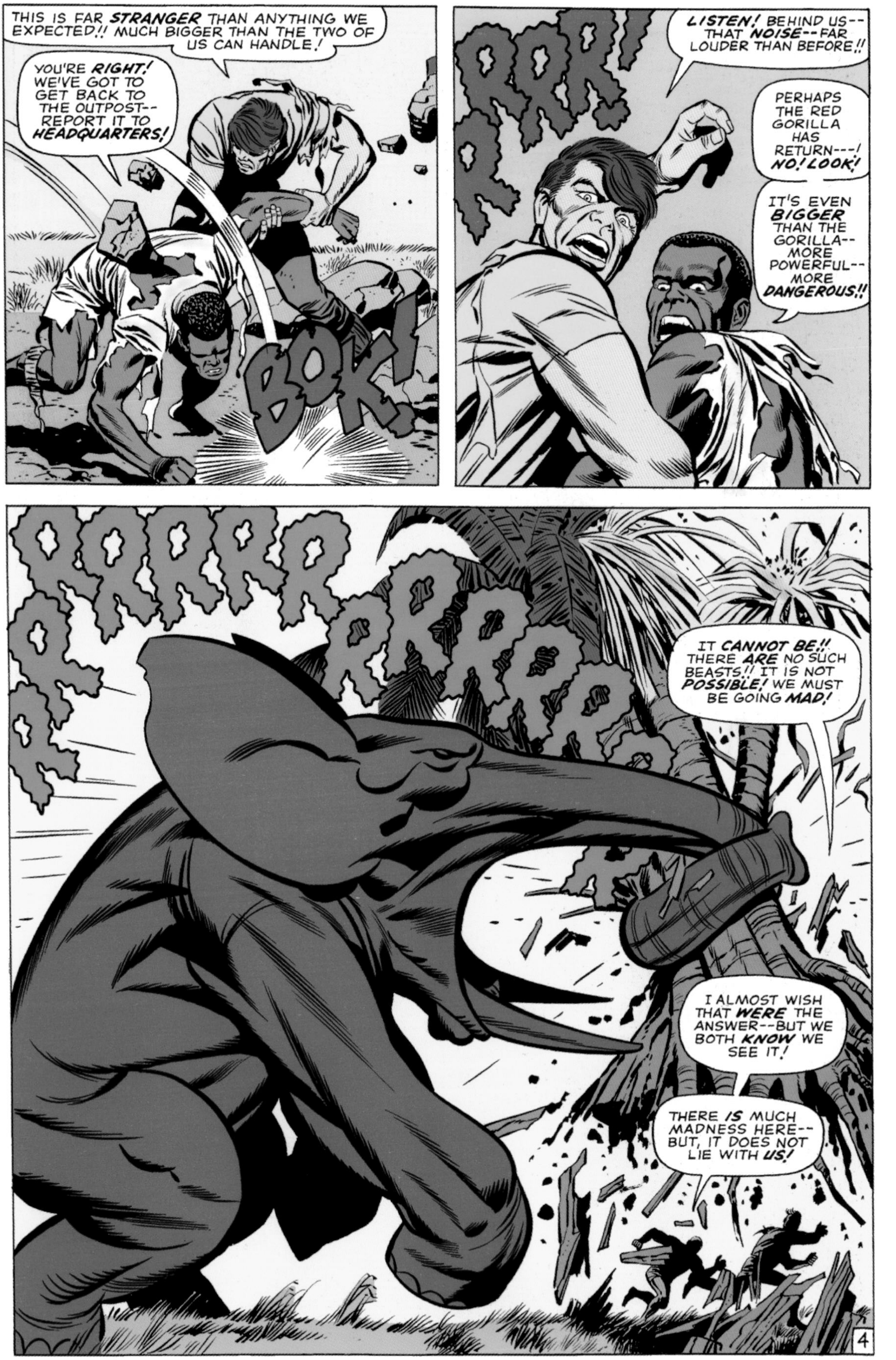

THIS IS FAR STRANGER THAN ANYTHING WE EXPECTED!! MUCH BIGGER THAN THE TWO OF US CAN HANDLE!
YOU'RE RIGHT! WE'VE GOT TO GET BACK TO THE OUTPOST--REPORT IT TO HEADQUARTERS!
BOK!
RRR!
LISTEN! BEHIND US--THAT NOISE--FAR LOUDER THAN BEFORE!!
PERHAPS THE RED GORILLA HAS RETURN---! NO! LOOK!
IT'S EVEN BIGGER THAN THE GORILLA--MORE POWERFUL--MORE DANGEROUS!!
RRRRRR
RRRRRR
IT CANNOT BE!! THERE ARE NO SUCH BEASTS!! IT IS NOT POSSIBLE! WE MUST BE GOING MAD!
I ALMOST WISH THAT WERE THE ANSWER--BUT WE BOTH KNOW WE SEE IT!
THERE IS MUCH MADNESS HERE--BUT, IT DOES NOT LIE WITH US!
4

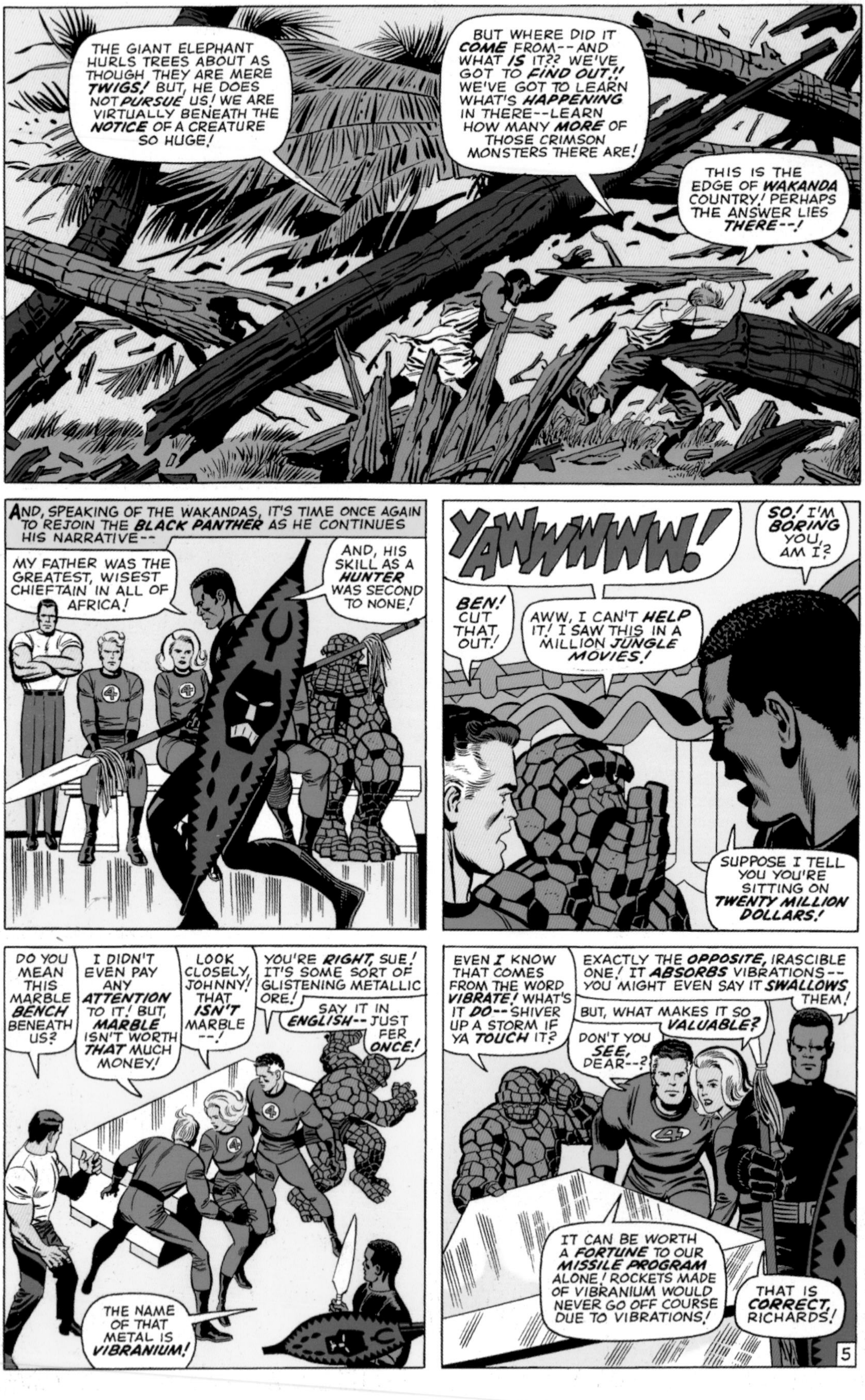
THE GIANT ELEPHANT HURLS TREES ABOUT AS THOUGH THEY ARE MERE TWIGS! BUT, HE DOES NOT PURSUE US! WE ARE VIRTUALLY BENEATH THE NOTICE OF A CREATURE SO HUGE!
BUT WHERE DID IT COME FROM--AND WHAT IS IT?? WE'VE GOT TO FIND OUT!! WE'VE GOT TO LEARN WHAT'S HAPPENING IN THERE--LEARN HOW MANY MORE OF THOSE CRIMSON MONSTERS THERE ARE!
THIS IS THE EDGE OF WAKANDA COUNTRY! PERHAPS THE ANSWER LIES THERE--!
AND, SPEAKING OF THE WAKANDAS, IT'S TIME ONCE AGAIN TO REJOIN THE BLACK PANTHER AS HE CONTINUES HIS NARRATIVE--
MY FATHER WAS THE GREATEST, WISEST CHIEFTAIN IN ALL OF AFRICA!
AND, HIS SKILL AS A HUNTER WAS SECOND TO NONE!
YAWWWWW!
SO! I'M BORING YOU, AM I?
BEN! CUT THAT OUT!
AWW, I CAN'T HELP IT! I SAW THIS IN A MILLION JUNGLE MOVIES!
SUPPOSE I TELL YOU YOU'RE SITTING ON TWENTY MILLION DOLLARS!
DO YOU MEAN THIS MARBLE BENCH BENEATH US?
I DIDN'T EVEN PAY ANY ATTENTION TO IT! BUT, MARBLE ISN'T WORTH THAT MUCH MONEY!
LOOK CLOSELY, JOHNNY! THAT ISN'T MARBLE--!
YOU'RE RIGHT, SUE! IT'S SOME SORT OF GLISTENING METALLIC ORE!
SAY IT IN ENGLISH--JUST FER ONCE!
THE NAME OF THAT METAL IS VIBRANIUM!
EVEN I KNOW THAT COMES FROM THE WORD VIBRATE! WHAT'S IT DO--SHIVER UP A STORM IF YA TOUCH IT?
EXACTLY THE OPPOSITE, IRASCIBLE ONE! IT ABSORBS VIBRATIONS--YOU MIGHT EVEN SAY IT SWALLOWS THEM!
BUT, WHAT MAKES IT SO VALUABLE?
DON'T YOU SEE, DEAR--?
IT CAN BE WORTH A FORTUNE TO OUR MISSILE PROGRAM ALONE! ROCKETS MADE OF VIBRANIUM WOULD NEVER GO OFF COURSE DUE TO VIBRATIONS!
THAT IS CORRECT, RICHARDS!
5

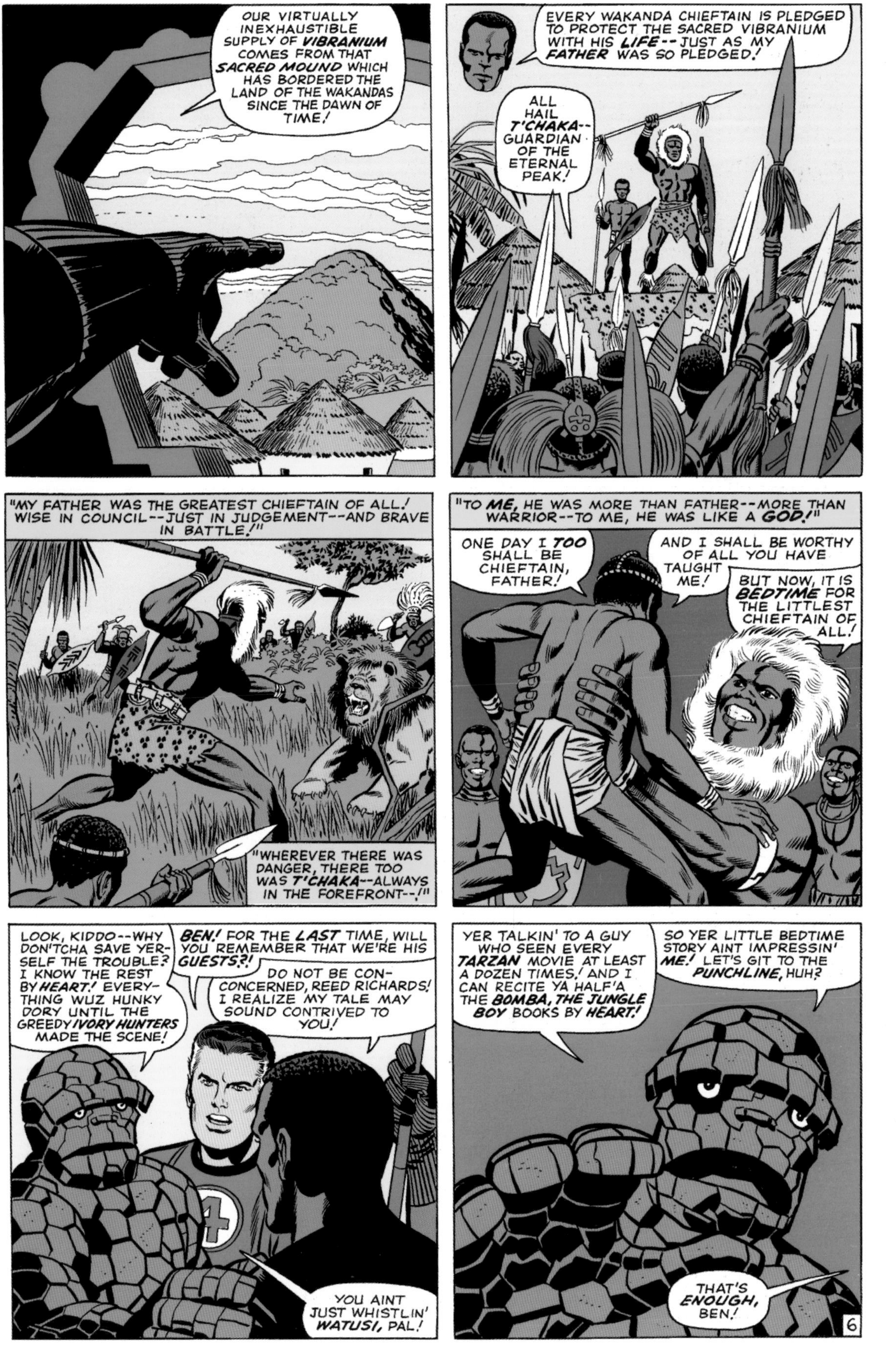
OUR VIRTUALLY INEXHAUSTIBLE SUPPLY OF VIBRANIUM COMES FROM THAT SACRED MOUND WHICH HAS BORDERED THE LAND OF THE WAKANDAS SINCE THE DAWN OF TIME!
EVERY WAKANDA CHIEFTAIN IS PLEDGED TO PROTECT THE SACRED VIBRANIUM WITH HIS LIFE -- JUST AS MY FATHER WAS SO PLEDGED!
ALL HAIL T'CHAKA-- GUARDIAN OF THE ETERNAL PEAK!
"MY FATHER WAS THE GREATEST CHIEFTAIN OF ALL! WISE IN COUNCIL--JUST IN JUDGEMENT--AND BRAVE IN BATTLE!"
"WHEREVER THERE WAS DANGER, THERE TOO WAS T'CHAKA--ALWAYS IN THE FOREFRONT--!"
"TO ME, HE WAS MORE THAN FATHER--MORE THAN WARRIOR--TO ME, HE WAS LIKE A GOD!"
ONE DAY I TOO SHALL BE CHIEFTAIN, FATHER!
AND I SHALL BE WORTHY OF ALL YOU HAVE TAUGHT ME!
BUT NOW, IT IS BEDTIME FOR THE LITTLEST CHIEFTAIN OF ALL!
LOOK, KIDDO--WHY DON'TCHA SAVE YERSELF THE TROUBLE? I KNOW THE REST BY HEART! EVERYTHING WUZ HUNKY DORY UNTIL THE GREEDY IVORY HUNTERS MADE THE SCENE!
BEN! FOR THE LAST TIME, WILL YOU REMEMBER THAT WE'RE HIS GUESTS?!
DO NOT BE CONCONCERNED, REED RICHARDS! I REALIZE MY TALE MAY SOUND CONTRIVED TO YOU!
YOU AINT JUST WHISTLIN' WATUSI, PAL!
YER TALKIN' TO A GUY WHO SEEN EVERY TARZAN MOVIE AT LEAST A DOZEN TIMES! AND I CAN RECITE YA HALF'A THE BOMBA, THE JUNGLE BOY BOOKS BY HEART!
SO YER LITTLE BEDTIME STORY AINT IMPRESSIN' ME! LET'S GIT TO THE PUNCHLINE, HUH?
THAT'S ENOUGH, BEN!

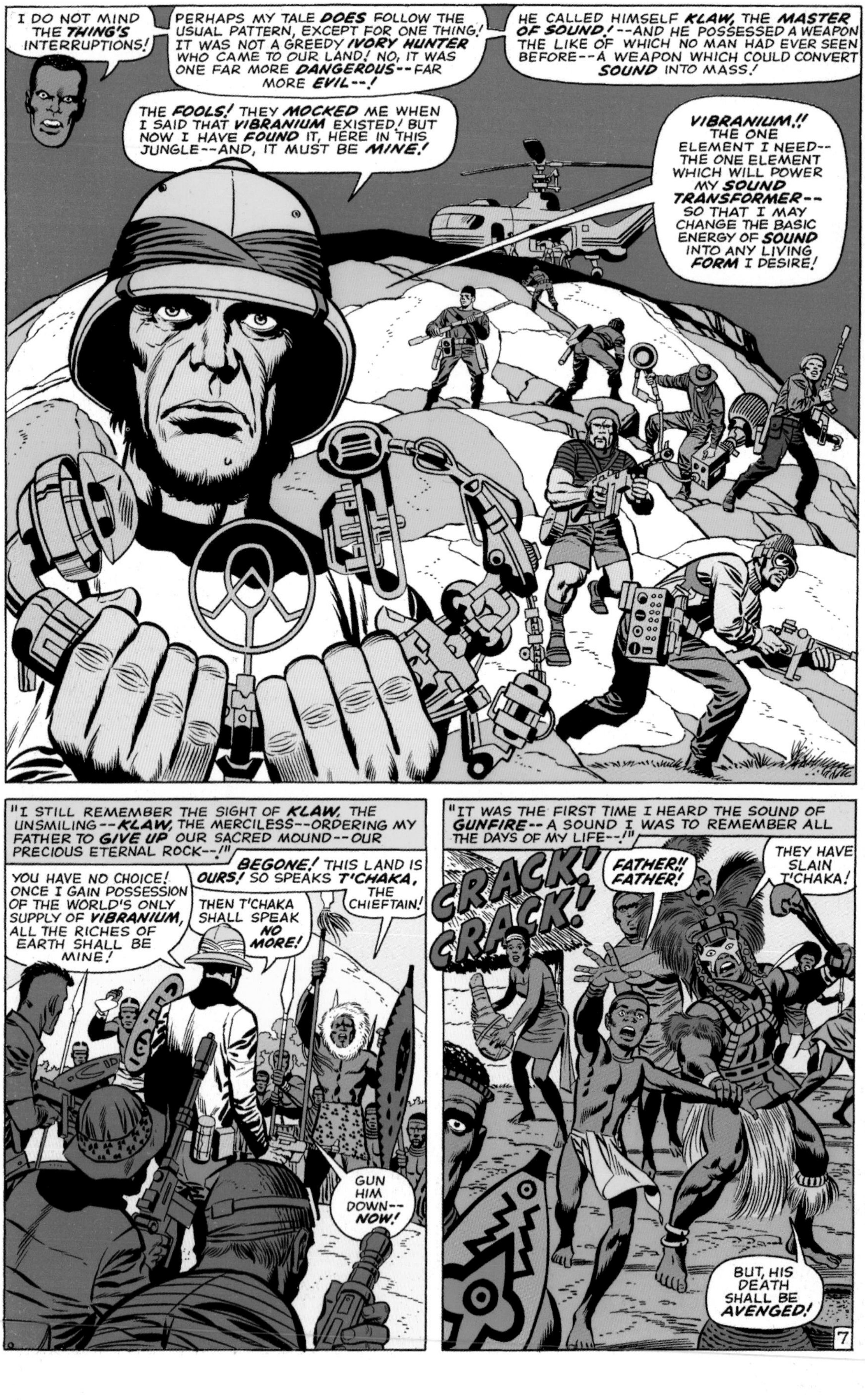
I DO NOT MIND THE THING'S INTERRUPTIONS!
PERHAPS MY TALE DOES FOLLOW THE USUAL PATTERN, EXCEPT FOR ONE THING! IT WAS NOT A GREEDY IVORY HUNTER WHO CAME TO OUR LAND! NO, IT WAS ONE FAR MORE DANGEROUS--FAR MORE EVIL--!
HE CALLED HIMSELF KLAW, THE MASTER OF SOUND! --AND HE POSSESSED A WEAPON THE LIKE OF WHICH NO MAN HAD EVER SEEN BEFORE--A WEAPON WHICH COULD CONVERT SOUND INTO MASS!
THE FOOLS! THEY MOCKED ME WHEN I SAID THAT VIBRANIUM EXISTED! BUT NOW I HAVE FOUND IT, HERE IN THIS JUNGLE--AND, IT MUST BE MINE!
VIBRANIUM!! THE ONE ELEMENT I NEED--THE ONE ELEMENT WHICH WILL POWER MY SOUND TRANSFORMER--SO THAT I MAY CHANGE THE BASIC ENERGY OF SOUND INTO ANY LIVING FORM I DESIRE!
"I STILL REMEMBER THE SIGHT OF KLAW, THE UNSMILING--KLAW, THE MERCILESS--ORDERING MY FATHER TO GIVE UP OUR SACRED MOUND--OUR PRECIOUS ETERNAL ROCK--!"
YOU HAVE NO CHOICE! ONCE I GAIN POSSESSION OF THE WORLD'S ONLY SUPPLY OF VIBRANIUM, ALL THE RICHES OF EARTH SHALL BE MINE!
BEGONE! THIS LAND IS OURS! SO SPEAKS T'CHAKA, THE CHIEFTAIN!
THEN T'CHAKA SHALL SPEAK NO MORE!
GUN HIM DOWN--NOW!
"IT WAS THE FIRST TIME I HEARD THE SOUND OF GUNFIRE--A SOUND I WAS TO REMEMBER ALL THE DAYS OF MY LIFE--!"
CRACK! CRACK!
FATHER!! FATHER!
THEY HAVE SLAIN T'CHAKA!
BUT, HIS DEATH SHALL BE AVENGED!

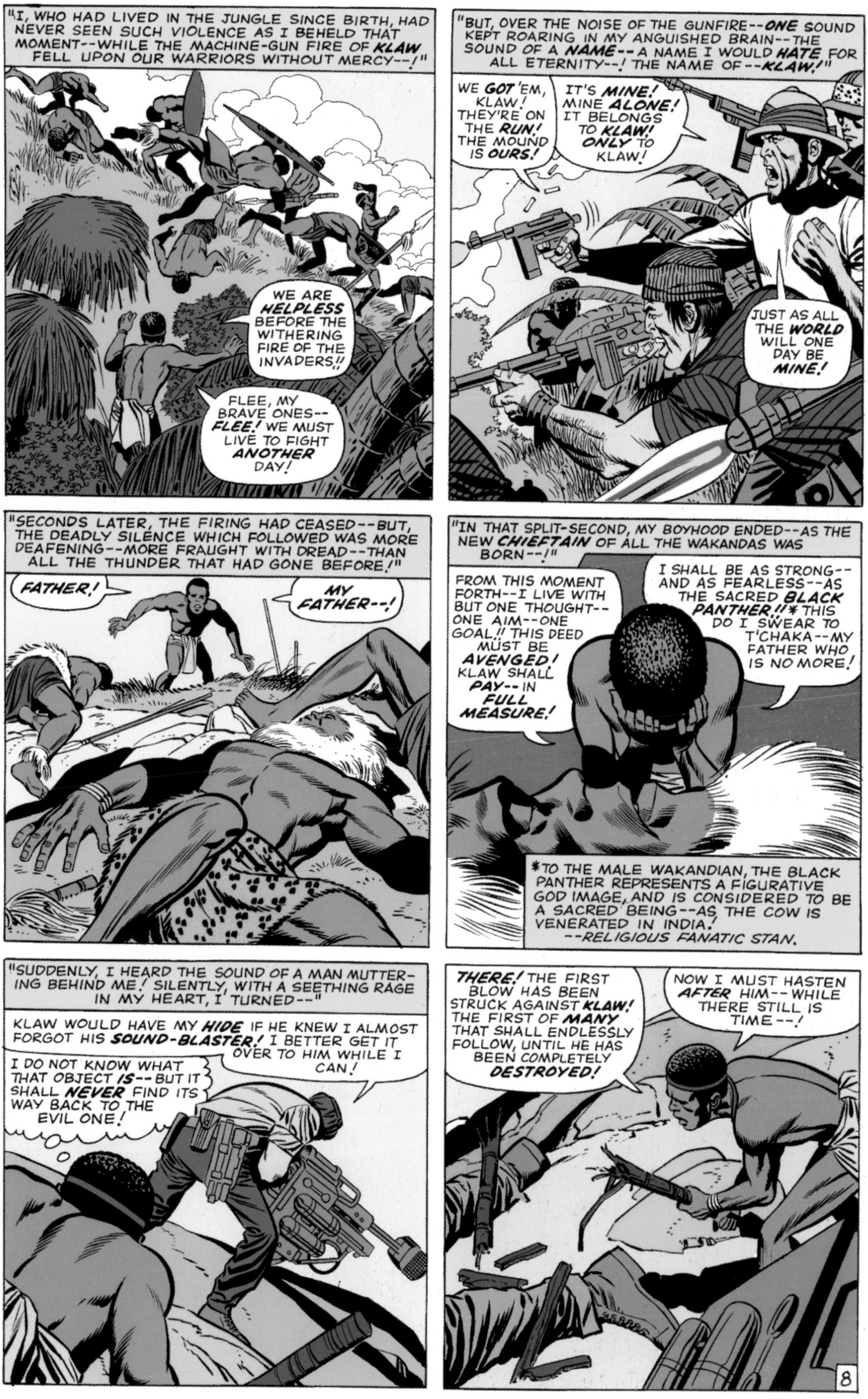
"I, WHO HAD LIVED IN THE JUNGLE SINCE BIRTH, HAD NEVER SEEN SUCH VIOLENCE AS I BEHELD THAT MOMENT--WHILE THE MACHINE-GUN FIRE OF KLAW FELL UPON OUR WARRIORS WITHOUT MERCY--!"
WE ARE HELPLESS BEFORE THE WITHERING FIRE OF THE INVADERS!!
FLEE, MY BRAVE ONES--FLEE! WE MUST LIVE TO FIGHT ANOTHER DAY!
"BUT, OVER THE NOISE OF THE GUNFIRE--ONE SOUND KEPT ROARING IN MY ANGUISHED BRAIN--THE SOUND OF A NAME--A NAME I WOULD HATE FOR ALL ETERNITY--! THE NAME OF--KLAW!"
WE GOT 'EM, KLAW! THEY'RE ON THE RUN! THE MOUND IS OURS!
IT'S MINE! MINE ALONE! IT BELONGS TO KLAW! ONLY TO KLAW!
JUST AS ALL THE WORLD WILL ONE DAY BE MINE!
"SECONDS LATER, THE FIRING HAD CEASED--BUT, THE DEADLY SILENCE WHICH FOLLOWED WAS MORE DEAFENING--MORE FRAUGHT WITH DREAD--THAN ALL THE THUNDER THAT HAD GONE BEFORE!"
FATHER!
MY FATHER--!
"IN THAT SPLIT-SECOND, MY BOYHOOD ENDED--AS THE NEW CHIEFTAIN OF ALL THE WAKANDAS WAS BORN--!"
FROM THIS MOMENT FORTH--I LIVE WITH BUT ONE THOUGHT--ONE AIM--ONE GOAL!! THIS DEED MUST BE AVENGED! KLAW SHALL PAY--IN FULL MEASURE!
I SHALL BE AS STRONG--AND AS FEARLESS--AS THE SACRED BLACK PANTHER!!* THIS DO I SWEAR TO T'CHAKA--MY FATHER WHO IS NO MORE!
*TO THE MALE WAKANDIAN, THE BLACK PANTHER REPRESENTS A FIGURATIVE GOD IMAGE, AND IS CONSIDERED TO BE A SACRED BEING--AS THE COW IS VENERATED IN INDIA! --RELIGIOUS FANATIC STAN.
"SUDDENLY, I HEARD THE SOUND OF A MAN MUTTERING BEHIND ME! SILENTLY, WITH A SEETHING RAGE IN MY HEART, I TURNED--"
KLAW WOULD HAVE MY HIDE IF HE KNEW I ALMOST FORGOT HIS SOUND-BLASTER! I BETTER GET IT OVER TO HIM WHILE I CAN!
I DO NOT KNOW WHAT THAT OBJECT IS--BUT IT SHALL NEVER FIND ITS WAY BACK TO THE EVIL ONE!
THERE! THE FIRST BLOW HAS BEEN STRUCK AGAINST KLAW! THE FIRST OF MANY THAT SHALL ENDLESSLY FOLLOW, UNTIL HE HAS BEEN COMPLETELY DESTROYED!
NOW I MUST HASTEN AFTER HIM--WHILE THERE STILL IS TIME--!
8

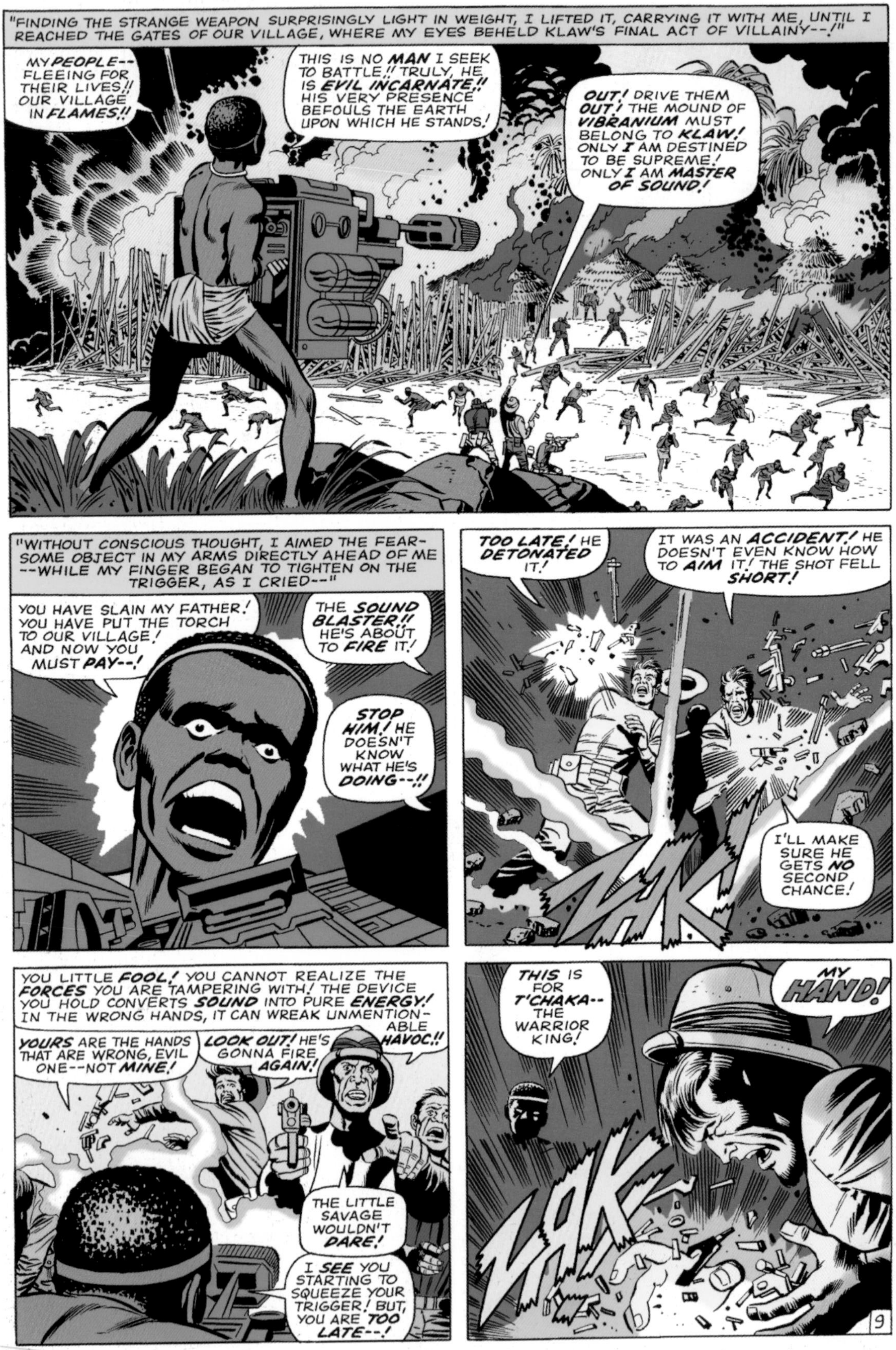
"FINDING THE STRANGE WEAPON SURPRISINGLY LIGHT IN WEIGHT, I LIFTED IT, CARRYING IT WITH ME, UNTIL I REACHED THE GATES OF OUR VILLAGE, WHERE MY EYES BEHELD KLAW'S FINAL ACT OF VILLAINY--!"
MY PEOPLE-- FLEEING FOR THEIR LIVES!! OUR VILLAGE IN FLAMES!!
THIS IS NO MAN I SEEK TO BATTLE!! TRULY, HE IS EVIL INCARNATE!! HIS VERY PRESENCE BEFOULS THE EARTH UPON WHICH HE STANDS!
OUT! DRIVE THEM OUT! THE MOUND OF VIBRANIUM MUST BELONG TO KLAW! ONLY I AM DESTINED TO BE SUPREME! ONLY I AM MASTER OF SOUND!
"WITHOUT CONSCIOUS THOUGHT, I AIMED THE FEARSOME OBJECT IN MY ARMS DIRECTLY AHEAD OF ME --WHILE MY FINGER BEGAN TO TIGHTEN ON THE TRIGGER, AS I CRIED--"
YOU HAVE SLAIN MY FATHER! YOU HAVE PUT THE TORCH TO OUR VILLAGE! AND NOW YOU MUST PAY--!
THE SOUND BLASTER!! HE'S ABOUT TO FIRE IT!
STOP HIM! HE DOESN'T KNOW WHAT HE'S DOING--!!
TOO LATE! HE DETONATED IT!
IT WAS AN ACCIDENT! HE DOESN'T EVEN KNOW HOW TO AIM IT! THE SHOT FELL SHORT!
I'LL MAKE SURE HE GETS NO SECOND CHANCE!
ZAK
YOU LITTLE FOOL! YOU CANNOT REALIZE THE FORCES YOU ARE TAMPERING WITH! THE DEVICE YOU HOLD CONVERTS SOUND INTO PURE ENERGY! IN THE WRONG HANDS, IT CAN WREAK UNMENTIONABLE HAVOC!!
YOURS ARE THE HANDS THAT ARE WRONG, EVIL ONE--NOT MINE!
LOOK OUT! HE'S GONNA FIRE AGAIN!
THE LITTLE SAVAGE WOULDN'T DARE!
I SEE YOU STARTING TO SQUEEZE YOUR TRIGGER! BUT, YOU ARE TOO LATE--!
THIS IS FOR T'CHAKA-- THE WARRIOR KING!
MY HAND!
ZAK

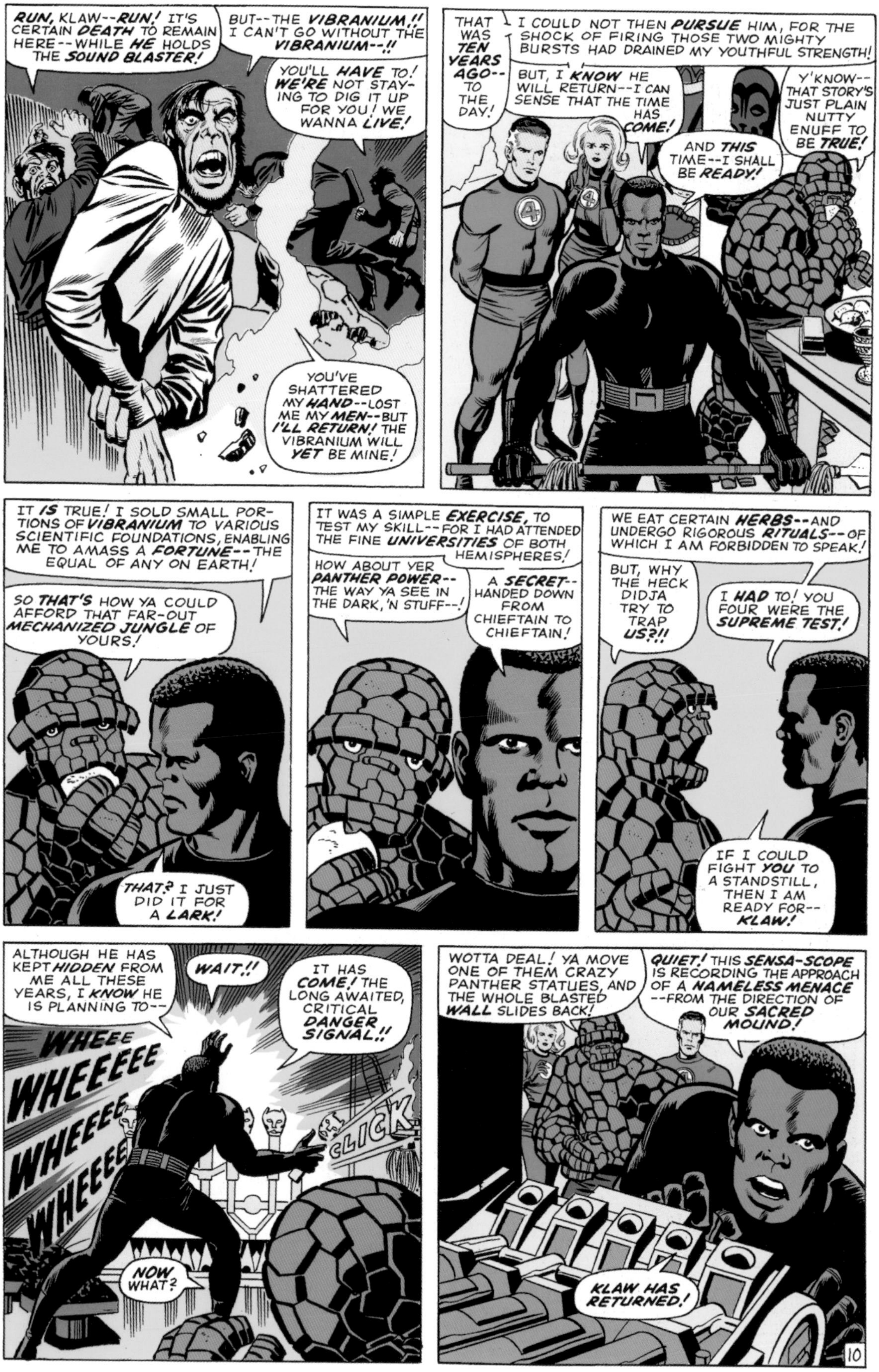
RUN, KLAW--RUN! IT'S CERTAIN DEATH TO REMAIN HERE--WHILE HE HOLDS THE SOUND BLASTER!
BUT--THE VIBRANIUM!! I CAN'T GO WITHOUT THE VIBRANIUM--!!
YOU'LL HAVE TO! WE'RE NOT STAYING TO DIG IT UP FOR YOU! WE WANNA LIVE!
YOU'VE SHATTERED MY HAND--LOST ME MY MEN--BUT I'LL RETURN! THE VIBRANIUM WILL YET BE MINE!
THAT WAS TEN YEARS AGO--TO THE DAY!
I COULD NOT THEN PURSUE HIM, FOR THE SHOCK OF FIRING THOSE TWO MIGHTY BURSTS HAD DRAINED MY YOUTHFUL STRENGTH!
BUT, I KNOW HE WILL RETURN--I CAN SENSE THAT THE TIME HAS COME!
AND THIS TIME--I SHALL BE READY!
Y'KNOW--THAT STORY'S JUST PLAIN NUTTY ENUFF TO BE TRUE!
IT IS TRUE! I SOLD SMALL PORTIONS OF VIBRANIUM TO VARIOUS SCIENTIFIC FOUNDATIONS, ENABLING ME TO AMASS A FORTUNE--THE EQUAL OF ANY ON EARTH!
SO THAT'S HOW YA COULD AFFORD THAT FAR-OUT MECHANIZED JUNGLE OF YOURS!
THAT? I JUST DID IT FOR A LARK!
IT WAS A SIMPLE EXERCISE, TO TEST MY SKILL--FOR I HAD ATTENDED THE FINE UNIVERSITIES OF BOTH HEMISPHERES!
HOW ABOUT YER PANTHER POWER--THE WAY YA SEE IN THE DARK, 'N STUFF--!
A SECRET--HANDED DOWN FROM CHIEFTAIN TO CHIEFTAIN!
WE EAT CERTAIN HERBS--AND UNDERGO RIGOROUS RITUALS--OF WHICH I AM FORBIDDEN TO SPEAK!
BUT, WHY THE HECK DIDJA TRY TO TRAP US?!!
I HAD TO! YOU FOUR WERE THE SUPREME TEST!
IF I COULD FIGHT YOU TO A STANDSTILL, THEN I AM READY FOR--KLAW!
ALTHOUGH HE HAS KEPT HIDDEN FROM ME ALL THESE YEARS, I KNOW HE IS PLANNING TO--
WAIT!!
IT HAS COME! THE LONG AWAITED, CRITICAL DANGER SIGNAL!!
WHEEEE
WHEEEEE
WHEEEEE
WHEEEEE
WHEEEEE
CLICK
NOW WHAT?
WOTTA DEAL! YA MOVE ONE OF THEM CRAZY PANTHER STATUES, AND THE WHOLE BLASTED WALL SLIDES BACK!
QUIET! THIS SENSA-SCOPE IS RECORDING THE APPROACH OF A NAMELESS MENACE--FROM THE DIRECTION OF OUR SACRED MOUND!
KLAW HAS RETURNED!
10

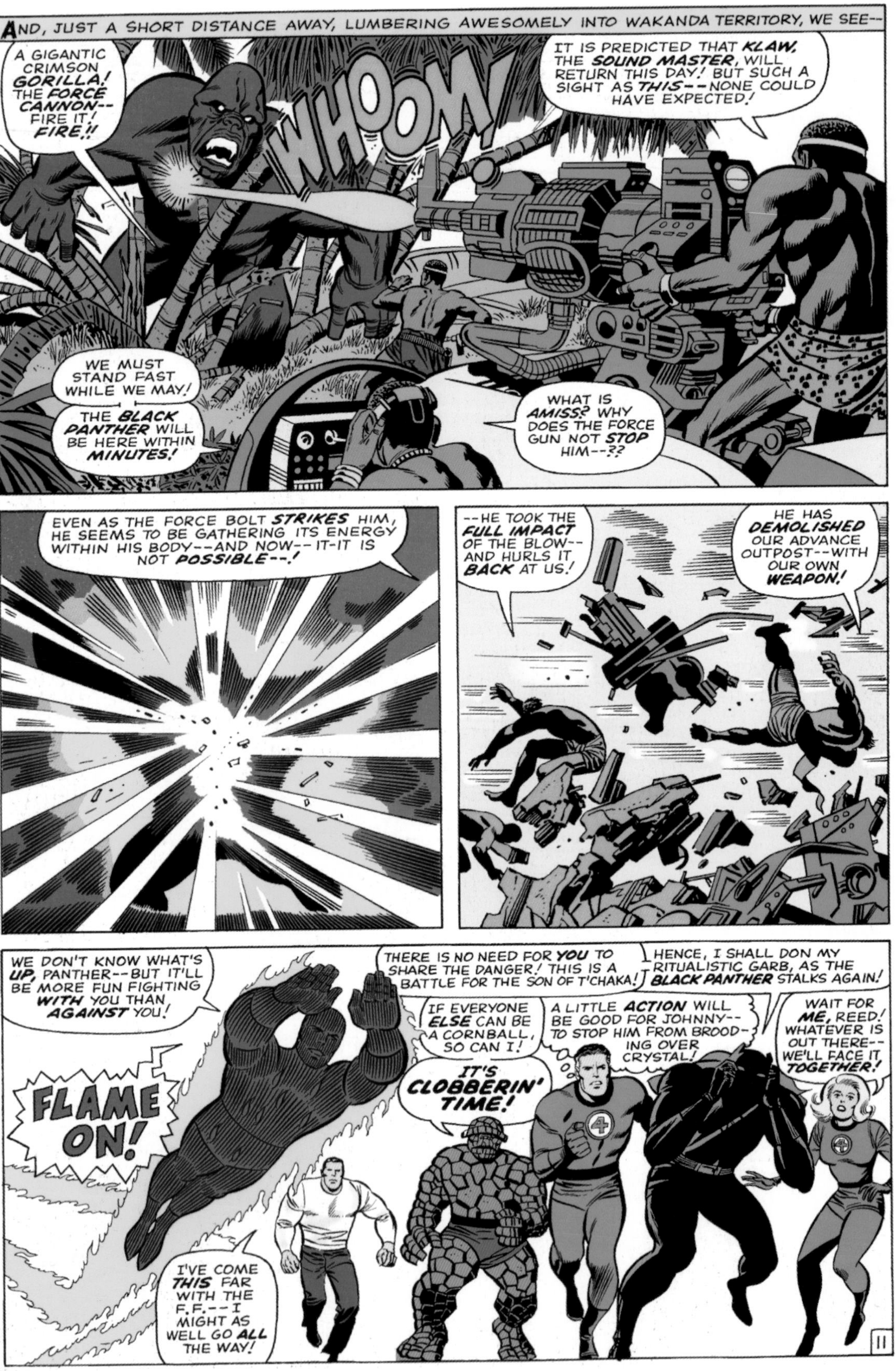
AND, JUST A SHORT DISTANCE AWAY, LUMBERING AWESOMELY INTO WAKANDA TERRITORY, WE SEE--
A GIGANTIC CRIMSON GORILLA! THE FORCE CANNON-- FIRE IT! FIRE!!
WHOOM!
IT IS PREDICTED THAT KLAW, THE SOUND MASTER, WILL RETURN THIS DAY! BUT SUCH A SIGHT AS THIS--NONE COULD HAVE EXPECTED!
WE MUST STAND FAST WHILE WE MAY!
THE BLACK PANTHER WILL BE HERE WITHIN MINUTES!
WHAT IS AMISS? WHY DOES THE FORCE GUN NOT STOP HIM--??
EVEN AS THE FORCE BOLT STRIKES HIM, HE SEEMS TO BE GATHERING ITS ENERGY WITHIN HIS BODY--AND NOW--IT-IT IS NOT POSSIBLE--!
--HE TOOK THE FULL IMPACT OF THE BLOW--AND HURLS IT BACK AT US!
HE HAS DEMOLISHED OUR ADVANCE OUTPOST--WITH OUR OWN WEAPON!
WE DON'T KNOW WHAT'S UP, PANTHER--BUT IT'LL BE MORE FUN FIGHTING WITH YOU THAN AGAINST YOU!
THERE IS NO NEED FOR YOU TO SHARE THE DANGER! THIS IS A BATTLE FOR THE SON OF T'CHAKA!
HENCE, I SHALL DON MY RITUALISTIC GARB, AS THE BLACK PANTHER STALKS AGAIN!
FLAME ON!
IF EVERYONE ELSE CAN BE A CORNBALL, SO CAN I!
IT'S CLOBBERIN' TIME!
A LITTLE ACTION WILL BE GOOD FOR JOHNNY--TO STOP HIM FROM BROODING OVER CRYSTAL!
WAIT FOR ME, REED! WHATEVER IS OUT THERE--WE'LL FACE IT TOGETHER!
I'VE COME THIS FAR WITH THE F.F.--I MIGHT AS WELL GO ALL THE WAY!
11

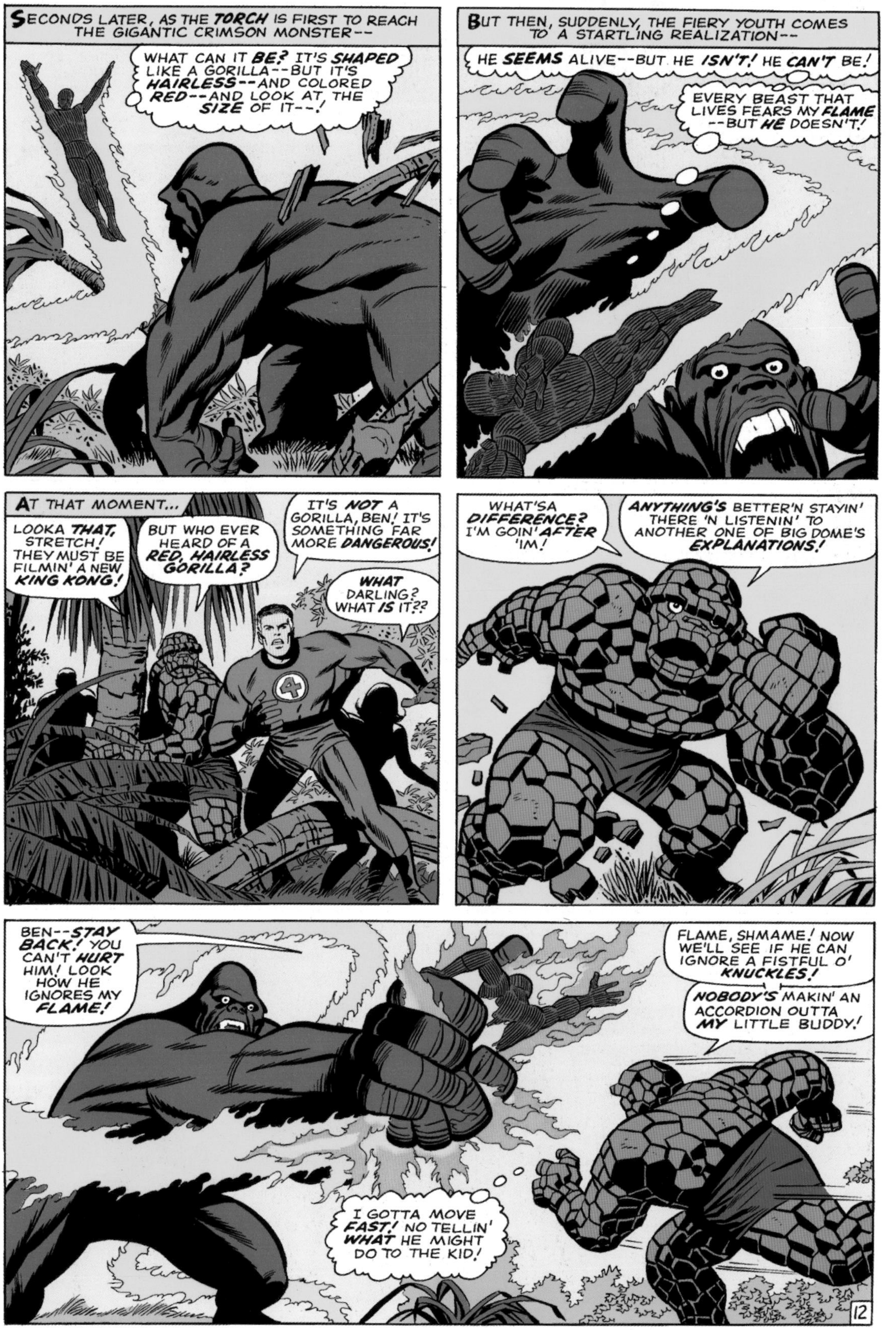
SECONDS LATER, AS THE TORCH IS FIRST TO REACH THE GIGANTIC CRIMSON MONSTER--
WHAT CAN IT BE? IT'S SHAPED LIKE A GORILLA--BUT IT'S HAIRLESS--AND COLORED RED--AND LOOK AT, THE SIZE OF IT--!
BUT THEN, SUDDENLY, THE FIERY YOUTH COMES TO A STARTLING REALIZATION--
HE SEEMS ALIVE--BUT HE ISN'T! HE CAN'T BE!
EVERY BEAST THAT LIVES FEARS MY FLAME --BUT HE DOESN'T!
AT THAT MOMENT...
LOOKA THAT, STRETCH! THEY MUST BE FILMIN' A NEW KING KONG!
BUT WHO EVER HEARD OF A RED, HAIRLESS GORILLA?
IT'S NOT A GORILLA, BEN! IT'S SOMETHING FAR MORE DANGEROUS!
WHAT DARLING? WHAT IS IT??
WHAT'SA DIFFERENCE? I'M GOIN' AFTER 'IM!
ANYTHING'S BETTER'N STAYIN' THERE 'N LISTENIN' TO ANOTHER ONE OF BIG DOME'S EXPLANATIONS!
BEN--STAY BACK! YOU CAN'T HURT HIM! LOOK HOW HE IGNORES MY FLAME!
FLAME, SHMAME! NOW WE'LL SEE IF HE CAN IGNORE A FISTFUL O' KNUCKLES!
NOBODY'S MAKIN' AN ACCORDION OUTTA MY LITTLE BUDDY!
I GOTTA MOVE FAST! NO TELLIN' WHAT HE MIGHT DO TO THE KID!
12

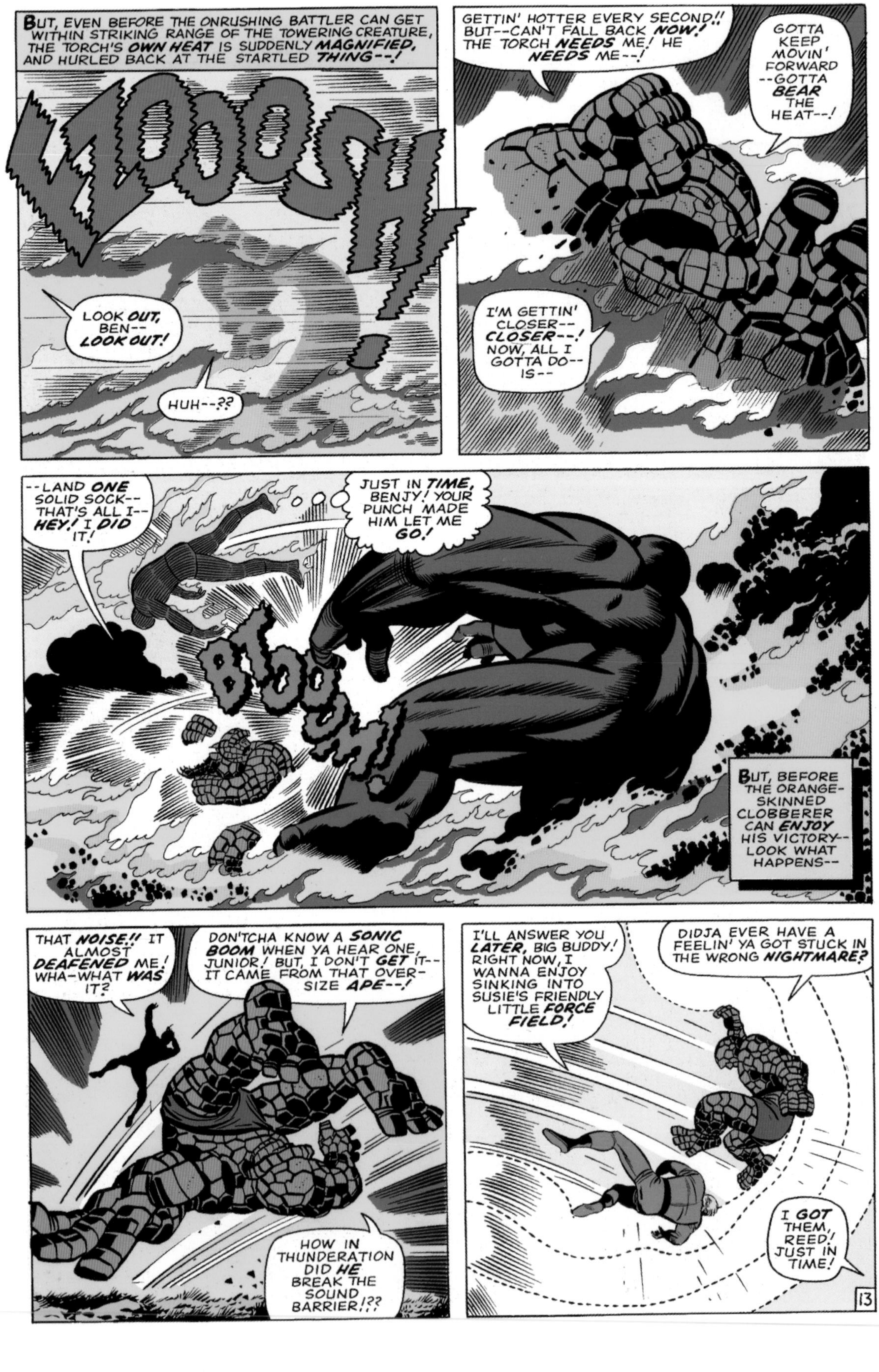
BUT, EVEN BEFORE THE ONRUSHING BATTLER CAN GET WITHIN STRIKING RANGE OF THE TOWERING CREATURE, THE TORCH'S OWN HEAT IS SUDDENLY MAGNIFIED, AND HURLED BACK AT THE STARTLED THING--!
ZZOOOSH!
LOOK OUT, BEN-- LOOK OUT!
HUH--??
GETTIN' HOTTER EVERY SECOND!! BUT--CAN'T FALL BACK NOW! THE TORCH NEEDS ME! HE NEEDS ME--!
GOTTA KEEP MOVIN' FORWARD --GOTTA BEAR THE HEAT--!
I'M GETTIN' CLOSER-- CLOSER--! NOW, ALL I GOTTA DO-- IS--
--LAND ONE SOLID SOCK-- THAT'S ALL I-- HEY! I DID IT!
JUST IN TIME, BENJY! YOUR PUNCH MADE HIM LET ME GO!
BTOOOM!
BUT, BEFORE THE ORANGE-SKINNED CLOBBERER CAN ENJOY HIS VICTORY-- LOOK WHAT HAPPENS--
THAT NOISE!! IT ALMOST DEAFENED ME! WHA-WHAT WAS IT?
DON'TCHA KNOW A SONIC BOOM WHEN YA HEAR ONE, JUNIOR! BUT, I DON'T GET IT-- IT CAME FROM THAT OVER-SIZE APE--!
HOW IN THUNDERATION DID HE BREAK THE SOUND BARRIER!??
I'LL ANSWER YOU LATER, BIG BUDDY! RIGHT NOW, I WANNA ENJOY SINKING INTO SUSIE'S FRIENDLY LITTLE FORCE FIELD!
DIDJA EVER HAVE A FEELIN' YA GOT STUCK IN THE WRONG NIGHTMARE?
I GOT THEM, REED! JUST IN TIME!
13

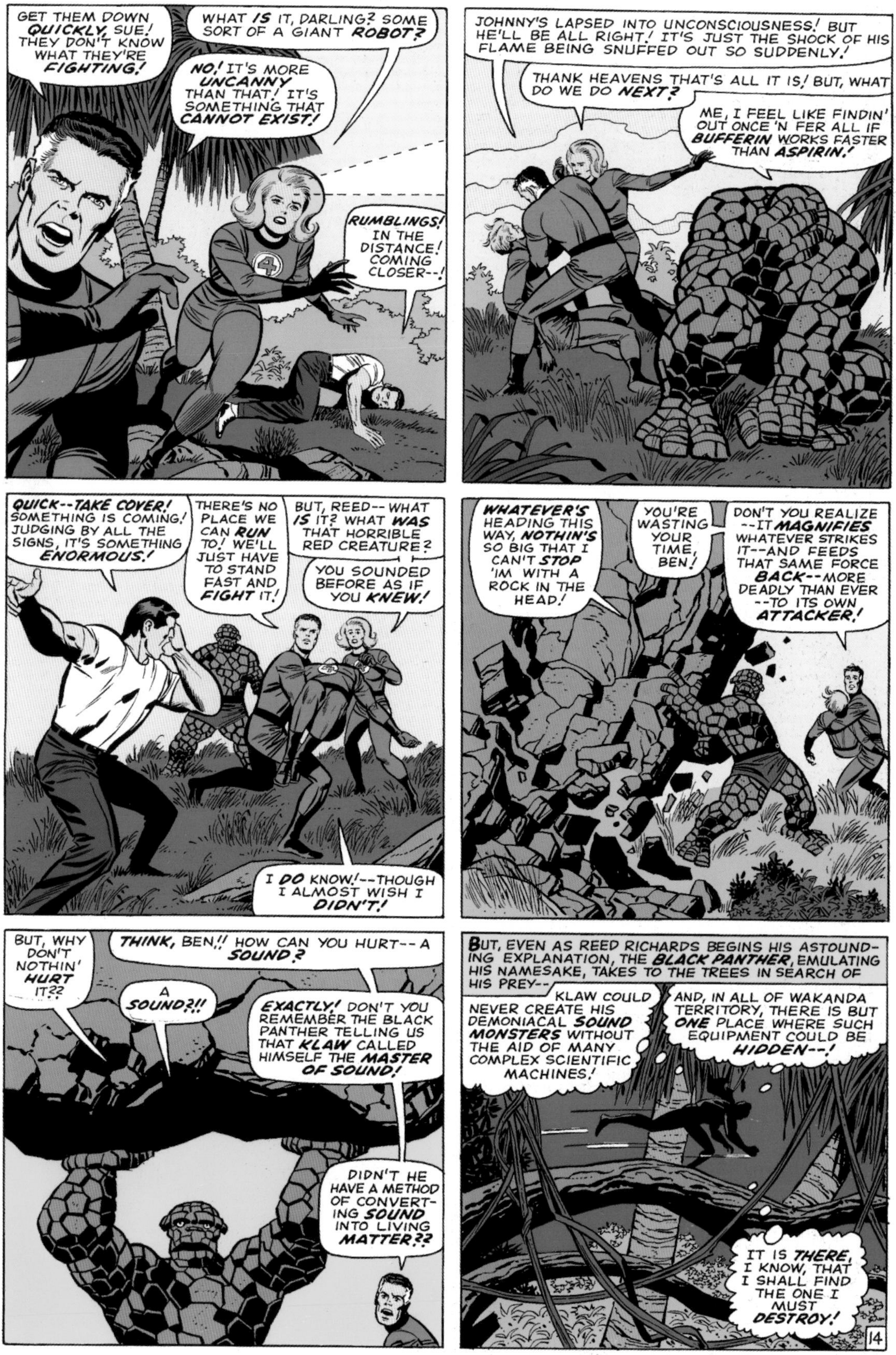
GET THEM DOWN QUICKLY, SUE! THEY DON'T KNOW WHAT THEY'RE FIGHTING!
WHAT IS IT, DARLING? SOME SORT OF A GIANT ROBOT?
NO! IT'S MORE UNCANNY THAN THAT! IT'S SOMETHING THAT CANNOT EXIST!
RUMBLINGS! IN THE DISTANCE! COMING CLOSER--!
JOHNNY'S LAPSED INTO UNCONSCIOUSNESS! BUT HE'LL BE ALL RIGHT! IT'S JUST THE SHOCK OF HIS FLAME BEING SNUFFED OUT SO SUDDENLY!
THANK HEAVENS THAT'S ALL IT IS! BUT, WHAT DO WE DO NEXT?
ME, I FEEL LIKE FINDIN' OUT ONCE 'N FER ALL IF BUFFERIN WORKS FASTER THAN ASPIRIN!
QUICK--TAKE COVER! SOMETHING IS COMING! JUDGING BY ALL THE SIGNS, IT'S SOMETHING ENORMOUS!
THERE'S NO PLACE WE CAN RUN TO! WE'LL JUST HAVE TO STAND FAST AND FIGHT IT!
BUT, REED-- WHAT IS IT? WHAT WAS THAT HORRIBLE RED CREATURE?
YOU SOUNDED BEFORE AS IF YOU KNEW!
I DO KNOW!--THOUGH I ALMOST WISH I DIDN'T!
WHATEVER'S HEADING THIS WAY, NOTHIN'S SO BIG THAT I CAN'T STOP 'IM WITH A ROCK IN THE HEAD!
YOU'RE WASTING YOUR TIME, BEN!
DON'T YOU REALIZE --IT MAGNIFIES WHATEVER STRIKES IT--AND FEEDS THAT SAME FORCE BACK--MORE DEADLY THAN EVER --TO ITS OWN ATTACKER!
BUT, WHY DON'T NOTHIN' HURT IT??
THINK, BEN!! HOW CAN YOU HURT-- A SOUND?
A SOUND?!!
EXACTLY! DON'T YOU REMEMBER THE BLACK PANTHER TELLING US THAT KLAW CALLED HIMSELF THE MASTER OF SOUND!
DIDN'T HE HAVE A METHOD OF CONVERTING SOUND INTO LIVING MATTER??
BUT, EVEN AS REED RICHARDS BEGINS HIS ASTOUNDING EXPLANATION, THE BLACK PANTHER, EMULATING HIS NAMESAKE, TAKES TO THE TREES IN SEARCH OF HIS PREY--
KLAW COULD NEVER CREATE HIS DEMONIACAL SOUND MONSTERS WITHOUT THE AID OF MANY COMPLEX SCIENTIFIC MACHINES!
AND, IN ALL OF WAKANDA TERRITORY, THERE IS BUT ONE PLACE WHERE SUCH EQUIPMENT COULD BE HIDDEN--!
IT IS THERE, I KNOW, THAT I SHALL FIND THE ONE I MUST DESTROY!
14

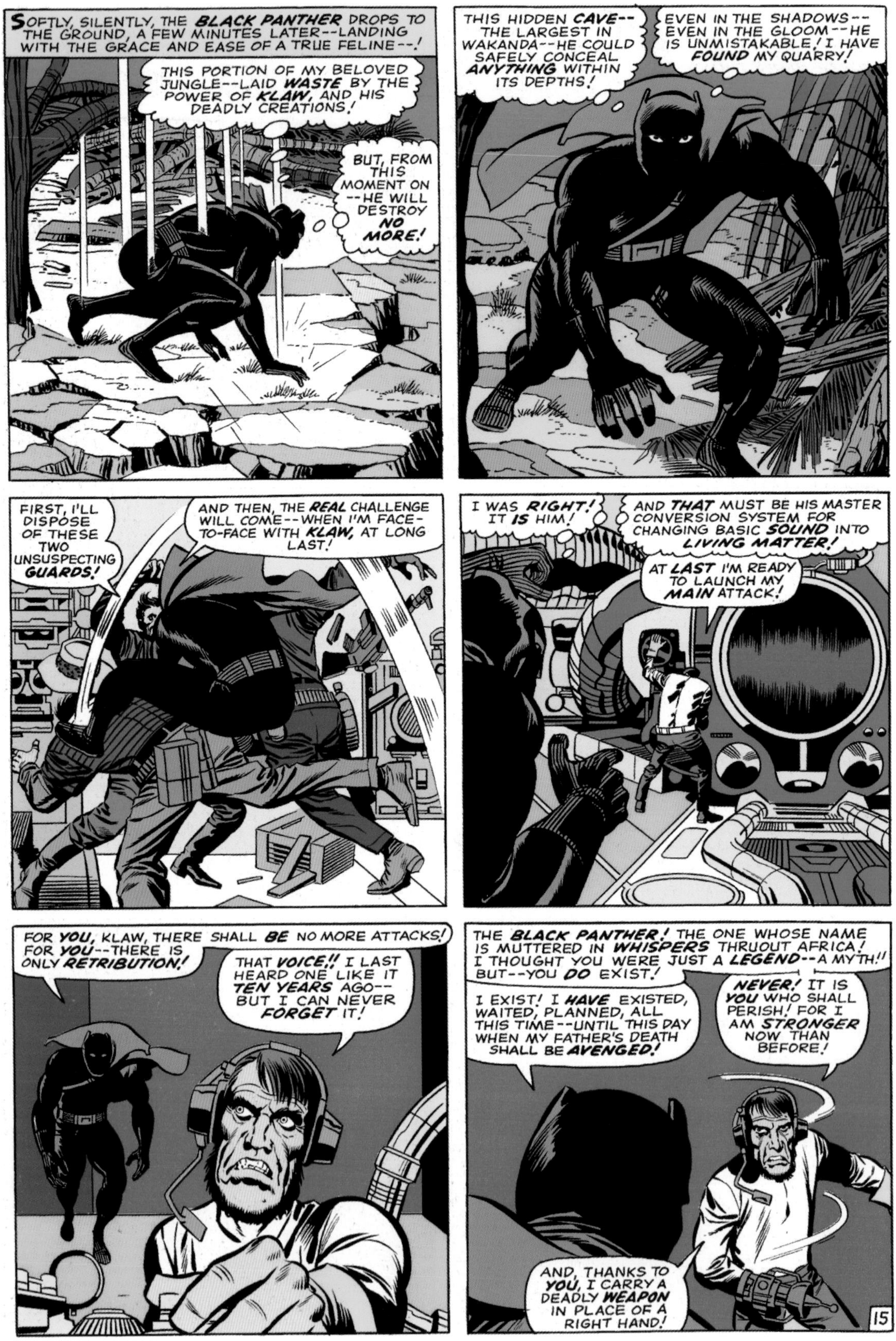

SOFTLY, SILENTLY, THE BLACK PANTHER DROPS TO THE GROUND, A FEW MINUTES LATER--LANDING WITH THE GRACE AND EASE OF A TRUE FELINE--!
THIS PORTION OF MY BELOVED JUNGLE--LAID WASTE BY THE POWER OF KLAW, AND HIS DEADLY CREATIONS!
BUT, FROM THIS MOMENT ON --HE WILL DESTROY NO MORE!
THIS HIDDEN CAVE-- THE LARGEST IN WAKANDA--HE COULD SAFELY CONCEAL ANYTHING WITHIN ITS DEPTHS!
EVEN IN THE SHADOWS-- EVEN IN THE GLOOM--HE IS UNMISTAKABLE! I HAVE FOUND MY QUARRY!
FIRST, I'LL DISPOSE OF THESE TWO UNSUSPECTING GUARDS!
AND THEN, THE REAL CHALLENGE WILL COME--WHEN I'M FACE-TO-FACE WITH KLAW, AT LONG LAST!
I WAS RIGHT! IT IS HIM!
AND THAT MUST BE HIS MASTER CONVERSION SYSTEM FOR CHANGING BASIC SOUND INTO LIVING MATTER!
AT LAST I'M READY TO LAUNCH MY MAIN ATTACK!
FOR YOU, KLAW, THERE SHALL BE NO MORE ATTACKS! FOR YOU--THERE IS ONLY RETRIBUTION!
THAT VOICE!! I LAST HEARD ONE LIKE IT TEN YEARS AGO-- BUT I CAN NEVER FORGET IT!
THE BLACK PANTHER! THE ONE WHOSE NAME IS MUTTERED IN WHISPERS THRUOUT AFRICA! I THOUGHT YOU WERE JUST A LEGEND--A MYTH!! BUT--YOU DO EXIST!
I EXIST! I HAVE EXISTED, WAITED, PLANNED, ALL THIS TIME--UNTIL THIS DAY WHEN MY FATHER'S DEATH SHALL BE AVENGED!
NEVER! IT IS YOU WHO SHALL PERISH! FOR I AM STRONGER NOW THAN BEFORE!
AND, THANKS TO YOU, I CARRY A DEADLY WEAPON IN PLACE OF A RIGHT HAND!
15

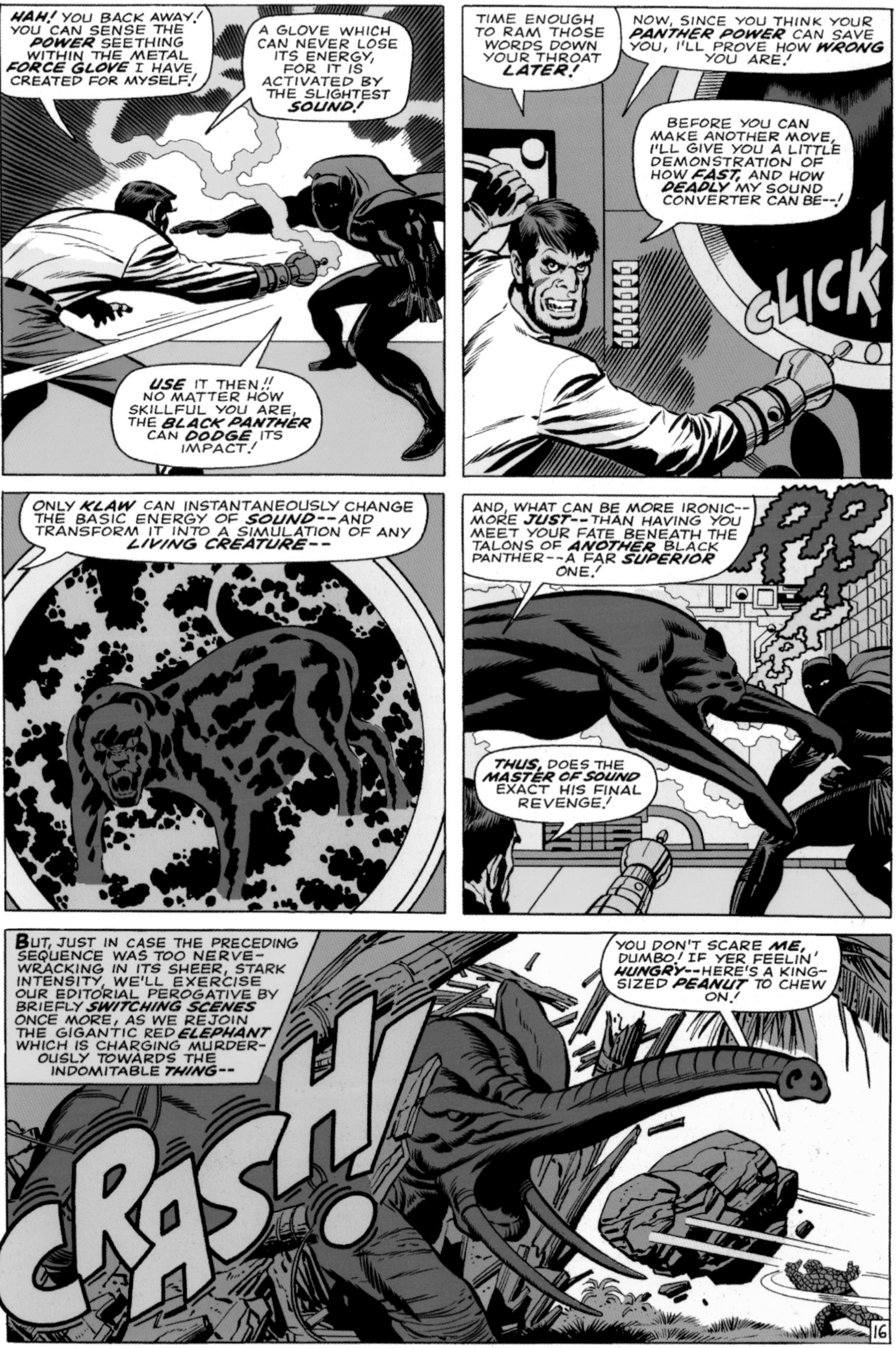
HAH! YOU BACK AWAY! YOU CAN SENSE THE POWER SEETHING WITHIN THE METAL FORCE GLOVE I HAVE CREATED FOR MYSELF!
A GLOVE WHICH CAN NEVER LOSE ITS ENERGY, FOR IT IS ACTIVATED BY THE SLIGHTEST SOUND!
USE IT THEN!! NO MATTER HOW SKILLFUL YOU ARE, THE BLACK PANTHER CAN DODGE ITS IMPACT!
TIME ENOUGH TO RAM THOSE WORDS DOWN YOUR THROAT LATER!
NOW, SINCE YOU THINK YOUR PANTHER POWER CAN SAVE YOU, I'LL PROVE HOW WRONG YOU ARE!
BEFORE YOU CAN MAKE ANOTHER MOVE, I'LL GIVE YOU A LITTLE DEMONSTRATION OF HOW FAST, AND HOW DEADLY MY SOUND CONVERTER CAN BE--!
CLICK!
ONLY KLAW CAN INSTANTANEOUSLY CHANGE THE BASIC ENERGY OF SOUND--AND TRANSFORM IT INTO A SIMULATION OF ANY LIVING CREATURE--
AND, WHAT CAN BE MORE IRONIC--MORE JUST--THAN HAVING YOU MEET YOUR FATE BENEATH THE TALONS OF ANOTHER BLACK PANTHER--A FAR SUPERIOR ONE!
RRR
THUS, DOES THE MASTER OF SOUND EXACT HIS FINAL REVENGE!
BUT, JUST IN CASE THE PRECEDING SEQUENCE WAS TOO NERVE-WRACKING IN ITS SHEER, STARK INTENSITY, WE'LL EXERCISE OUR EDITORIAL PEROGATIVE BY BRIEFLY SWITCHING SCENES ONCE MORE, AS WE REJOIN THE GIGANTIC RED ELEPHANT WHICH IS CHARGING MURDEROUSLY TOWARDS THE INDOMITABLE THING--
YOU DON'T SCARE ME, DUMBO! IF YER FEELIN' HUNGRY--HERE'S A KING-SIZED PEANUT TO CHEW ON!
CRASH!
16

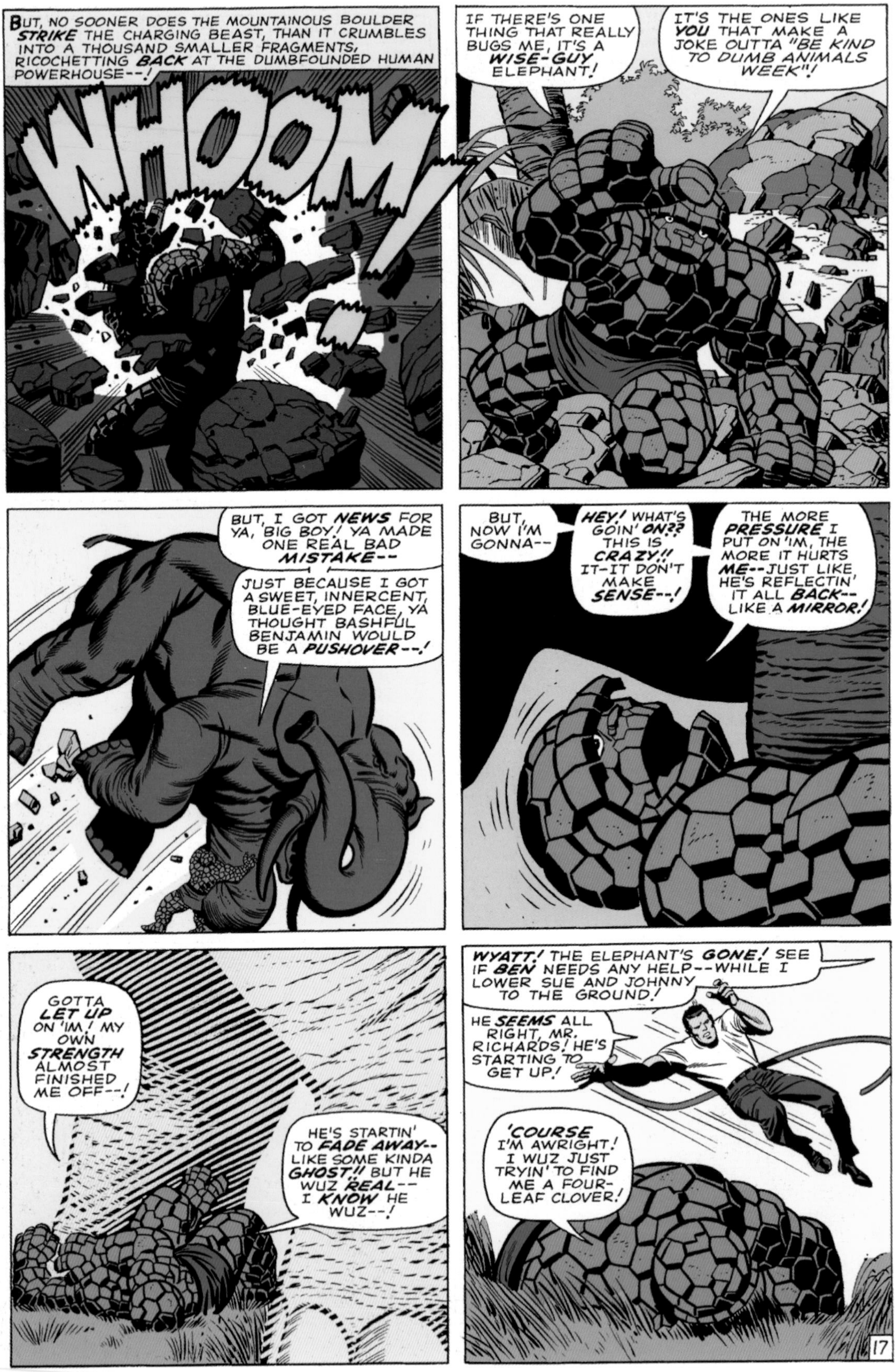
BUT, NO SOONER DOES THE MOUNTAINOUS BOULDER STRIKE THE CHARGING BEAST, THAN IT CRUMBLES INTO A THOUSAND SMALLER FRAGMENTS, RICOCHETTING BACK AT THE DUMBFOUNDED HUMAN POWERHOUSE--!
WHOOM!
IF THERE'S ONE THING THAT REALLY BUGS ME, IT'S A WISE-GUY ELEPHANT!
IT'S THE ONES LIKE YOU THAT MAKE A JOKE OUTTA "BE KIND TO DUMB ANIMALS WEEK"!
BUT, I GOT NEWS FOR YA, BIG BOY! YA MADE ONE REAL BAD MISTAKE--
JUST BECAUSE I GOT A SWEET, INNERCENT, BLUE-EYED FACE, YA THOUGHT BASHFUL BENJAMIN WOULD BE A PUSHOVER--!
BUT, NOW I'M GONNA--
HEY! WHAT'S GOIN' ON?? THIS IS CRAZY!! IT-IT DON'T MAKE SENSE--!
THE MORE PRESSURE I PUT ON 'IM, THE MORE IT HURTS ME--JUST LIKE HE'S REFLECTIN' IT ALL BACK--LIKE A MIRROR!
GOTTA LET UP ON 'IM! MY OWN STRENGTH ALMOST FINISHED ME OFF--!
HE'S STARTIN' TO FADE AWAY--LIKE SOME KINDA GHOST!! BUT HE WUZ REAL--I KNOW HE WUZ--!
WYATT! THE ELEPHANT'S GONE! SEE IF BEN NEEDS ANY HELP--WHILE I LOWER SUE AND JOHNNY TO THE GROUND!
HE SEEMS ALL RIGHT, MR. RICHARDS! HE'S STARTING TO GET UP!
'COURSE I'M AWRIGHT! I WUZ JUST TRYIN' TO FIND ME A FOUR-LEAF CLOVER!
17

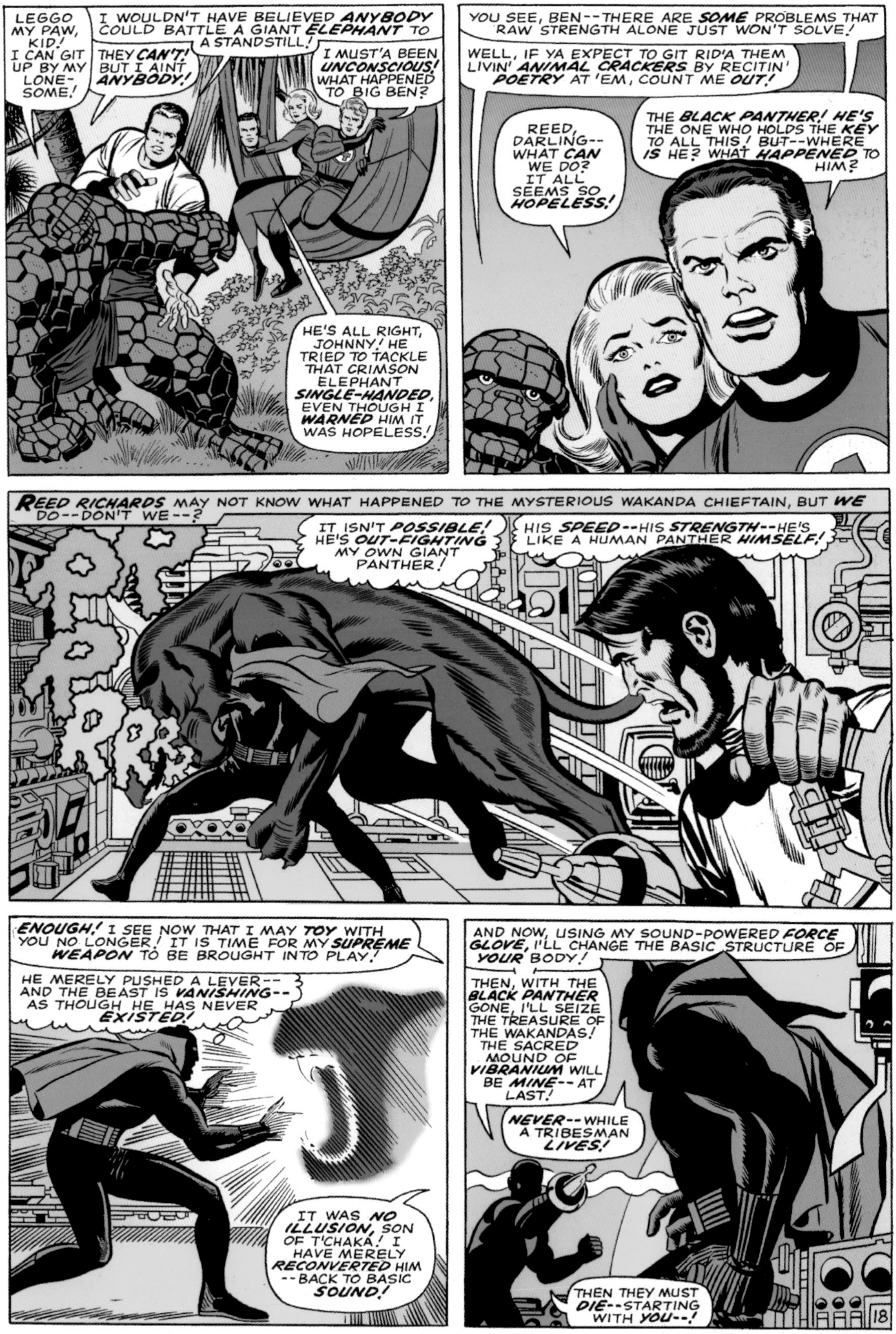

LEGGO MY PAW, KID! I CAN GIT UP BY MY LONESOME!
I WOULDN'T HAVE BELIEVED ANYBODY COULD BATTLE A GIANT ELEPHANT TO A STANDSTILL!
THEY CAN'T! BUT I AINT ANYBODY!
I MUST'A BEEN UNCONSCIOUS! WHAT HAPPENED TO BIG BEN?
HE'S ALL RIGHT, JOHNNY! HE TRIED TO TACKLE THAT CRIMSON ELEPHANT SINGLE-HANDED, EVEN THOUGH I WARNED HIM IT WAS HOPELESS!
YOU SEE, BEN--THERE ARE SOME PROBLEMS THAT RAW STRENGTH ALONE JUST WON'T SOLVE!
WELL, IF YA EXPECT TO GIT RID'A THEM LIVIN' ANIMAL CRACKERS BY RECITIN' POETRY AT 'EM, COUNT ME OUT!
REED, DARLING--WHAT CAN WE DO? IT ALL SEEMS SO HOPELESS!
THE BLACK PANTHER! HE'S THE ONE WHO HOLDS THE KEY TO ALL THIS! BUT--WHERE IS HE? WHAT HAPPENED TO HIM?
REED RICHARDS MAY NOT KNOW WHAT HAPPENED TO THE MYSTERIOUS WAKANDA CHIEFTAIN, BUT WE DO--DON'T WE--?
IT ISN'T POSSIBLE! HE'S OUT-FIGHTING MY OWN GIANT PANTHER!
HIS SPEED--HIS STRENGTH--HE'S LIKE A HUMAN PANTHER HIMSELF!
ENOUGH! I SEE NOW THAT I MAY TOY WITH YOU NO LONGER! IT IS TIME FOR MY SUPREME WEAPON TO BE BROUGHT INTO PLAY!
HE MERELY PUSHED A LEVER--AND THE BEAST IS VANISHING--AS THOUGH HE HAS NEVER EXISTED!
IT WAS NO ILLUSION, SON OF T'CHAKA! I HAVE MERELY RECONVERTED HIM--BACK TO BASIC SOUND!
AND NOW, USING MY SOUND-POWERED FORCE GLOVE, I'LL CHANGE THE BASIC STRUCTURE OF YOUR BODY!
THEN, WITH THE BLACK PANTHER GONE, I'LL SEIZE THE TREASURE OF THE WAKANDAS! THE SACRED MOUND OF VIBRANIUM WILL BE MINE--AT LAST!
NEVER--WHILE A TRIBESMAN LIVES!
THEN THEY MUST DIE--STARTING WITH YOU--!
18

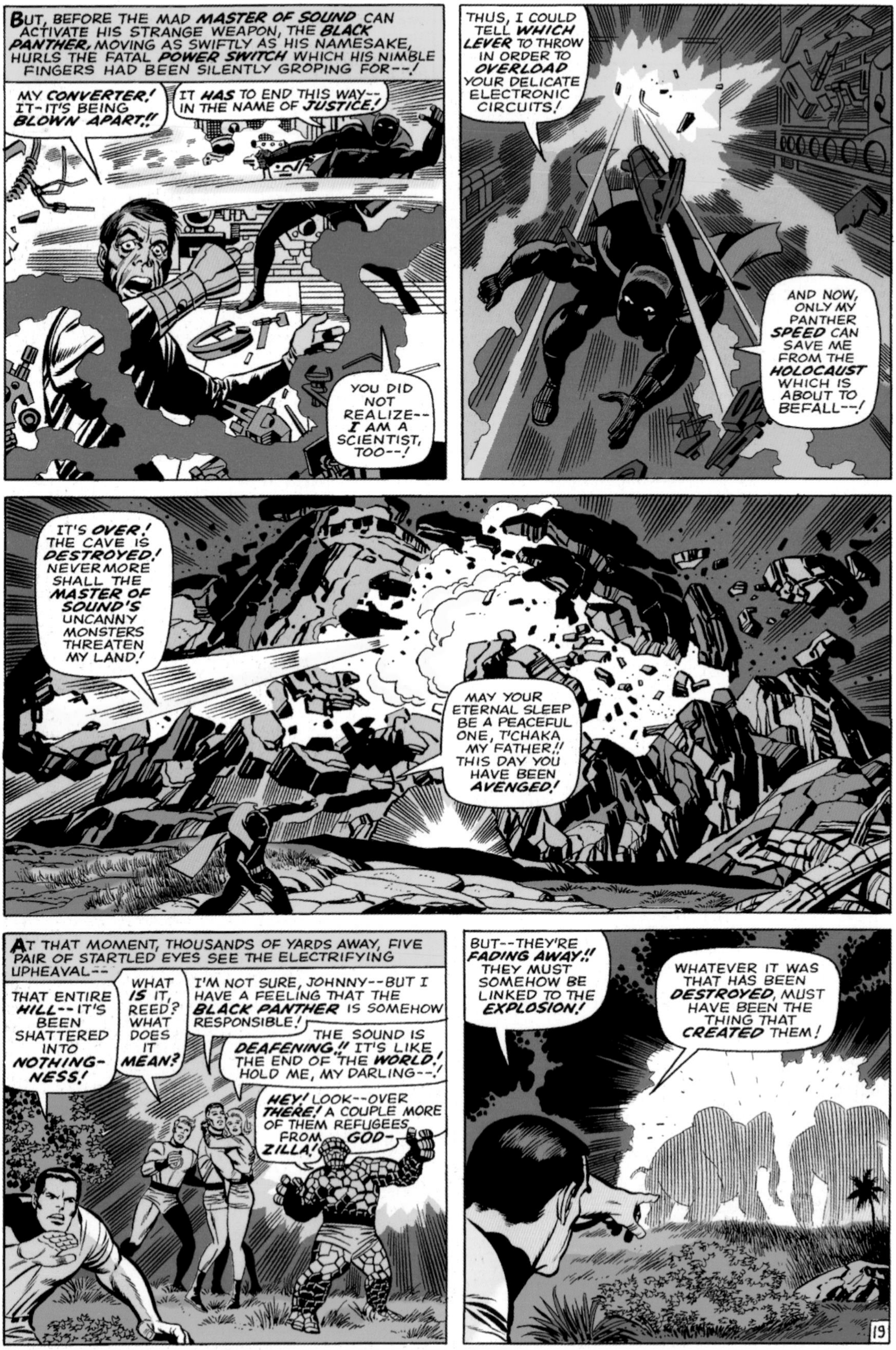
BUT, BEFORE THE MAD MASTER OF SOUND CAN ACTIVATE HIS STRANGE WEAPON, THE BLACK PANTHER, MOVING AS SWIFTLY AS HIS NAMESAKE, HURLS THE FATAL POWER SWITCH WHICH HIS NIMBLE FINGERS HAD BEEN SILENTLY GROPING FOR--!
MY CONVERTER! IT-IT'S BEING BLOWN APART!!
IT HAS TO END THIS WAY-- IN THE NAME OF JUSTICE!
YOU DID NOT REALIZE-- I AM A SCIENTIST, TOO--!
THUS, I COULD TELL WHICH LEVER TO THROW IN ORDER TO OVERLOAD YOUR DELICATE ELECTRONIC CIRCUITS!
AND NOW, ONLY MY PANTHER SPEED CAN SAVE ME FROM THE HOLOCAUST WHICH IS ABOUT TO BEFALL--!
IT'S OVER! THE CAVE IS DESTROYED! NEVERMORE SHALL THE MASTER OF SOUND'S UNCANNY MONSTERS THREATEN MY LAND!
MAY YOUR ETERNAL SLEEP BE A PEACEFUL ONE, T'CHAKA MY FATHER!! THIS DAY YOU HAVE BEEN AVENGED!
AT THAT MOMENT, THOUSANDS OF YARDS AWAY, FIVE PAIR OF STARTLED EYES SEE THE ELECTRIFYING UPHEAVAL--
THAT ENTIRE HILL--IT'S BEEN SHATTERED INTO NOTHING-NESS!
WHAT IS IT, REED? WHAT DOES IT MEAN?
I'M NOT SURE, JOHNNY--BUT I HAVE A FEELING THAT THE BLACK PANTHER IS SOMEHOW RESPONSIBLE!
THE SOUND IS DEAFENING!! IT'S LIKE THE END OF THE WORLD! HOLD ME, MY DARLING--!
HEY! LOOK--OVER THERE! A COUPLE MORE OF THEM REFUGEES FROM GOD-ZILLA!
BUT--THEY'RE FADING AWAY!! THEY MUST SOMEHOW BE LINKED TO THE EXPLOSION!
WHATEVER IT WAS THAT HAS BEEN DESTROYED, MUST HAVE BEEN THE THING THAT CREATED THEM!
19

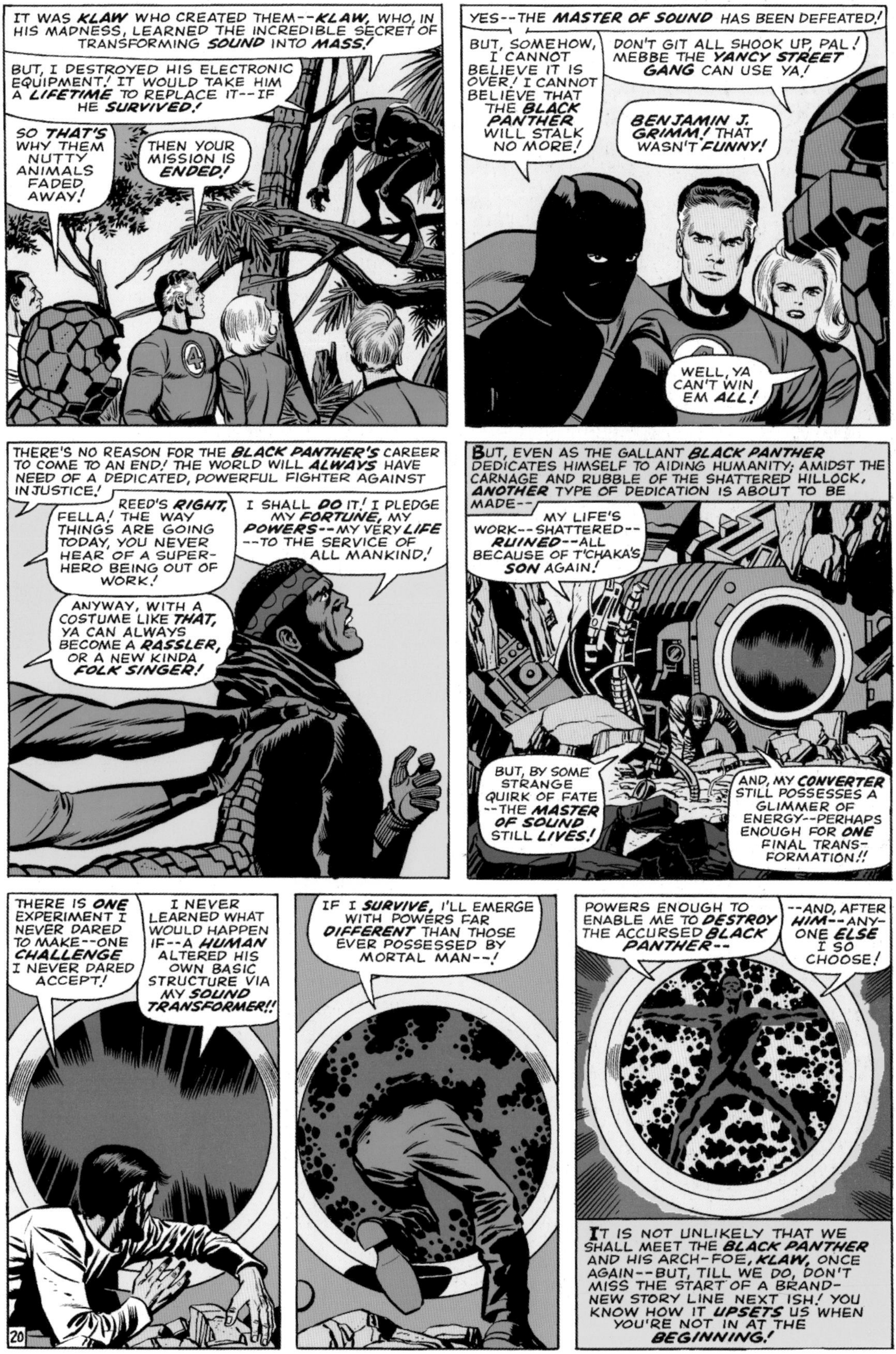

IT WAS KLAW WHO CREATED THEM--KLAW, WHO, IN HIS MADNESS, LEARNED THE INCREDIBLE SECRET OF TRANSFORMING SOUND INTO MASS!
BUT, I DESTROYED HIS ELECTRONIC EQUIPMENT! IT WOULD TAKE HIM A LIFETIME TO REPLACE IT--IF HE SURVIVED!
SO THAT'S WHY THEM NUTTY ANIMALS FADED AWAY!
THEN YOUR MISSION IS ENDED!
YES--THE MASTER OF SOUND HAS BEEN DEFEATED!
BUT, SOMEHOW, I CANNOT BELIEVE IT IS OVER! I CANNOT BELIEVE THAT THE BLACK PANTHER WILL STALK NO MORE!
DON'T GIT ALL SHOOK UP, PAL! MEBBE THE YANCY STREET GANG CAN USE YA!
BENJAMIN J. GRIMM! THAT WASN'T FUNNY!
WELL, YA CAN'T WIN EM ALL!
THERE'S NO REASON FOR THE BLACK PANTHER'S CAREER TO COME TO AN END! THE WORLD WILL ALWAYS HAVE NEED OF A DEDICATED, POWERFUL FIGHTER AGAINST INJUSTICE!
REED'S RIGHT, FELLA! THE WAY THINGS ARE GOING TODAY, YOU NEVER HEAR OF A SUPER-HERO BEING OUT OF WORK!
I SHALL DO IT! I PLEDGE MY FORTUNE, MY POWERS--MY VERY LIFE--TO THE SERVICE OF ALL MANKIND!
ANYWAY, WITH A COSTUME LIKE THAT, YA CAN ALWAYS BECOME A RASSLER, OR A NEW KINDA FOLK SINGER!
BUT, EVEN AS THE GALLANT BLACK PANTHER DEDICATES HIMSELF TO AIDING HUMANITY; AMIDST THE CARNAGE AND RUBBLE OF THE SHATTERED HILLOCK, ANOTHER TYPE OF DEDICATION IS ABOUT TO BE MADE--
MY LIFE'S WORK--SHATTERED--RUINED--ALL BECAUSE OF T'CHAKA'S SON AGAIN!
BUT, BY SOME STRANGE QUIRK OF FATE --THE MASTER OF SOUND STILL LIVES!
AND, MY CONVERTER STILL POSSESSES A GLIMMER OF ENERGY--PERHAPS ENOUGH FOR ONE FINAL TRANS-FORMATION!!
THERE IS ONE EXPERIMENT I NEVER DARED TO MAKE--ONE CHALLENGE I NEVER DARED ACCEPT!
I NEVER LEARNED WHAT WOULD HAPPEN IF--A HUMAN ALTERED HIS OWN BASIC STRUCTURE VIA MY SOUND TRANSFORMER!!
20
IF I SURVIVE, I'LL EMERGE WITH POWERS FAR DIFFERENT THAN THOSE EVER POSSESSED BY MORTAL MAN--!
POWERS ENOUGH TO ENABLE ME TO DESTROY THE ACCURSED BLACK PANTHER--
--AND, AFTER HIM--ANYONE ELSE I SO CHOOSE!
IT IS NOT UNLIKELY THAT WE SHALL MEET THE BLACK PANTHER AND HIS ARCH-FOE, KLAW, ONCE AGAIN--BUT, TILL WE DO, DON'T MISS THE START OF A BRAND-NEW STORY LINE NEXT ISH! YOU KNOW HOW IT UPSETS US WHEN YOU'RE NOT IN AT THE BEGINNING!

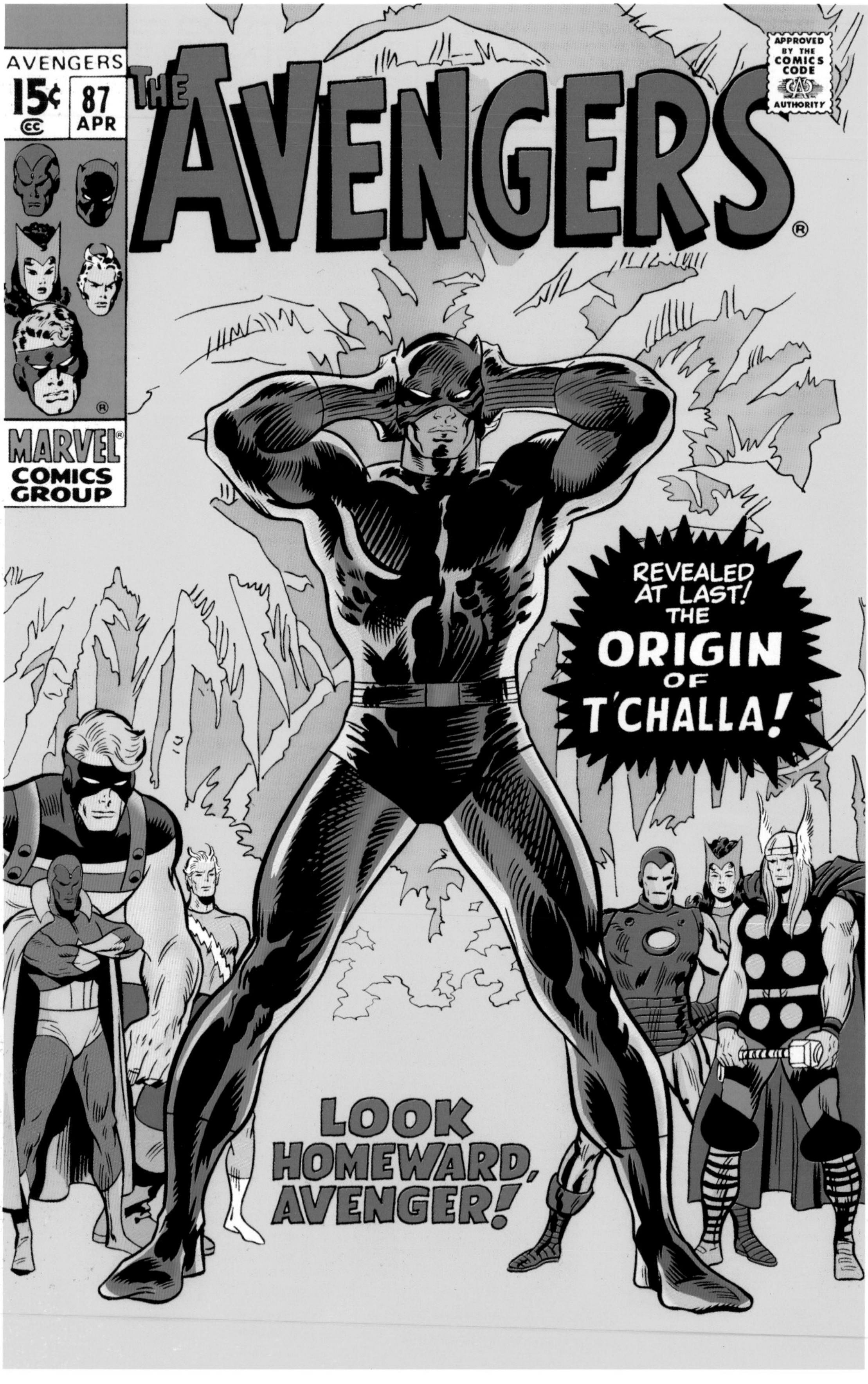
AVENGERS
15¢
87
APR
THE AVENGERS®
APPROVED BY THE COMICS CODE AUTHORITY
MARVEL® COMICS GROUP
REVEALED AT LAST! THE ORIGIN OF T'CHALLA!
LOOK HOMEWARD, AVENGER!

THE MIGHTY AVENGERS!®

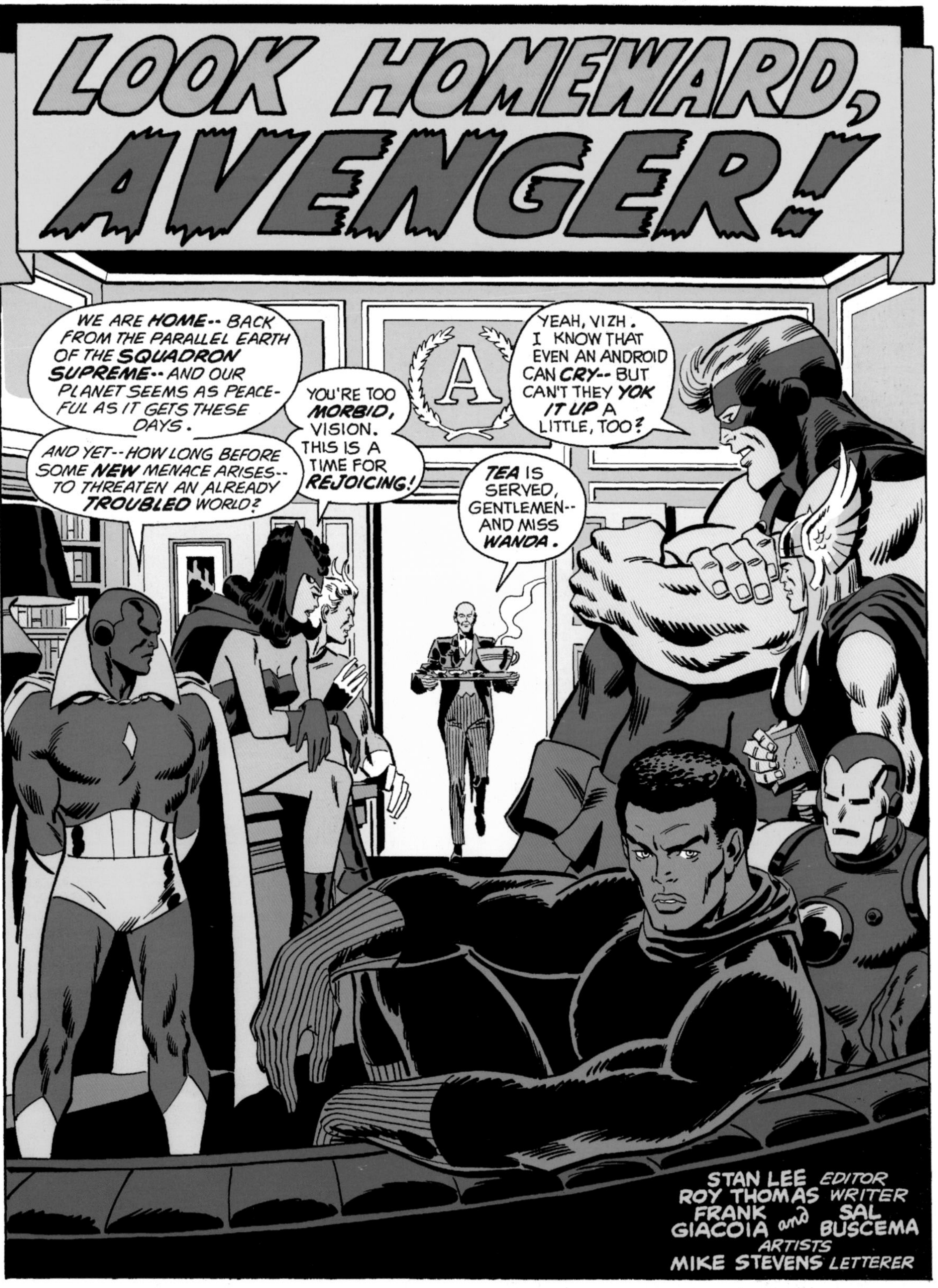
LOOK HOMEWARD, AVENGER!
WE ARE HOME-- BACK FROM THE PARALLEL EARTH OF THE SQUADRON SUPREME-- AND OUR PLANET SEEMS AS PEACE-FUL AS IT GETS THESE DAYS.
AND YET-- HOW LONG BEFORE SOME NEW MENACE ARISES-- TO THREATEN AN ALREADY TROUBLED WORLD?
YOU'RE TOO MORBID, VISION. THIS IS A TIME FOR REJOICING!
YEAH, VIZH. I KNOW THAT EVEN AN ANDROID CAN CRY-- BUT CAN'T THEY YOK IT UP A LITTLE, TOO?
TEA IS SERVED, GENTLEMEN-- AND MISS WANDA.
A
STAN LEE EDITOR
ROY THOMAS WRITER
FRANK GIACOIA and SAL BUSCEMA ARTISTS
MIKE STEVENS LETTERER

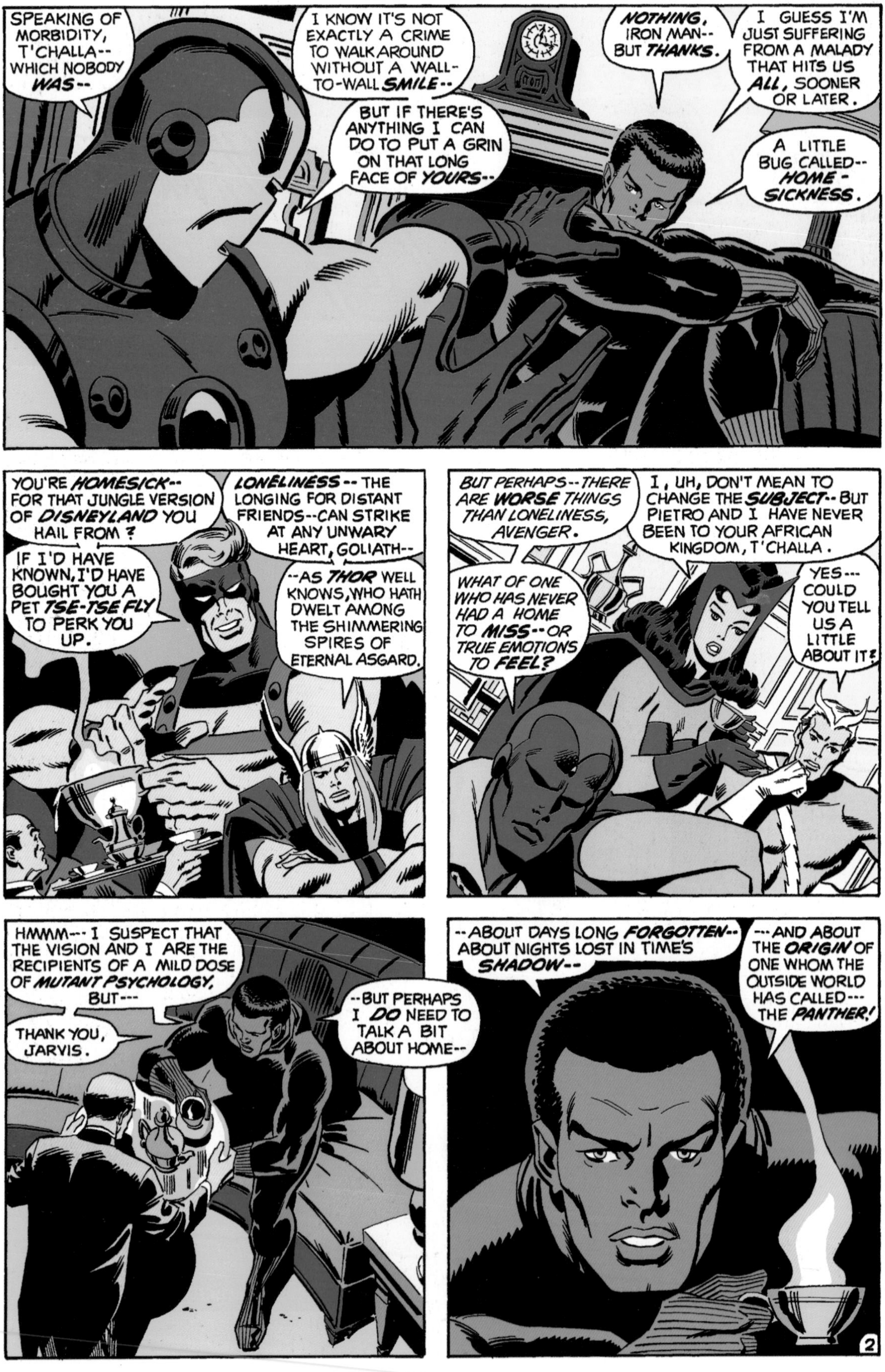
SPEAKING OF MORBIDITY, T'CHALLA-- WHICH NOBODY WAS--
I KNOW IT'S NOT EXACTLY A CRIME TO WALK AROUND WITHOUT A WALL-TO-WALL SMILE--
BUT IF THERE'S ANYTHING I CAN DO TO PUT A GRIN ON THAT LONG FACE OF YOURS--
NOTHING, IRON MAN-- BUT THANKS.
I GUESS I'M JUST SUFFERING FROM A MALADY THAT HITS US ALL, SOONER OR LATER.
A LITTLE BUG CALLED-- HOME-SICKNESS.
YOU'RE HOMESICK-- FOR THAT JUNGLE VERSION OF DISNEYLAND YOU HAIL FROM?
IF I'D HAVE KNOWN, I'D HAVE BOUGHT YOU A PET TSE-TSE FLY TO PERK YOU UP.
LONELINESS -- THE LONGING FOR DISTANT FRIENDS--CAN STRIKE AT ANY UNWARY HEART, GOLIATH--
--AS THOR WELL KNOWS, WHO HATH DWELT AMONG THE SHIMMERING SPIRES OF ETERNAL ASGARD.
BUT PERHAPS--THERE ARE WORSE THINGS THAN LONELINESS, AVENGER.
WHAT OF ONE WHO HAS NEVER HAD A HOME TO MISS--OR TRUE EMOTIONS TO FEEL?
I, UH, DON'T MEAN TO CHANGE THE SUBJECT--BUT PIETRO AND I HAVE NEVER BEEN TO YOUR AFRICAN KINGDOM, T'CHALLA.
YES--- COULD YOU TELL US A LITTLE ABOUT IT?
HMMM--- I SUSPECT THAT THE VISION AND I ARE THE RECIPIENTS OF A MILD DOSE OF MUTANT PSYCHOLOGY. BUT---
THANK YOU, JARVIS.
--BUT PERHAPS I DO NEED TO TALK A BIT ABOUT HOME--
--ABOUT DAYS LONG FORGOTTEN-- ABOUT NIGHTS LOST IN TIME'S SHADOW--
---AND ABOUT THE ORIGIN OF ONE WHOM THE OUTSIDE WORLD HAS CALLED--- THE PANTHER!
2

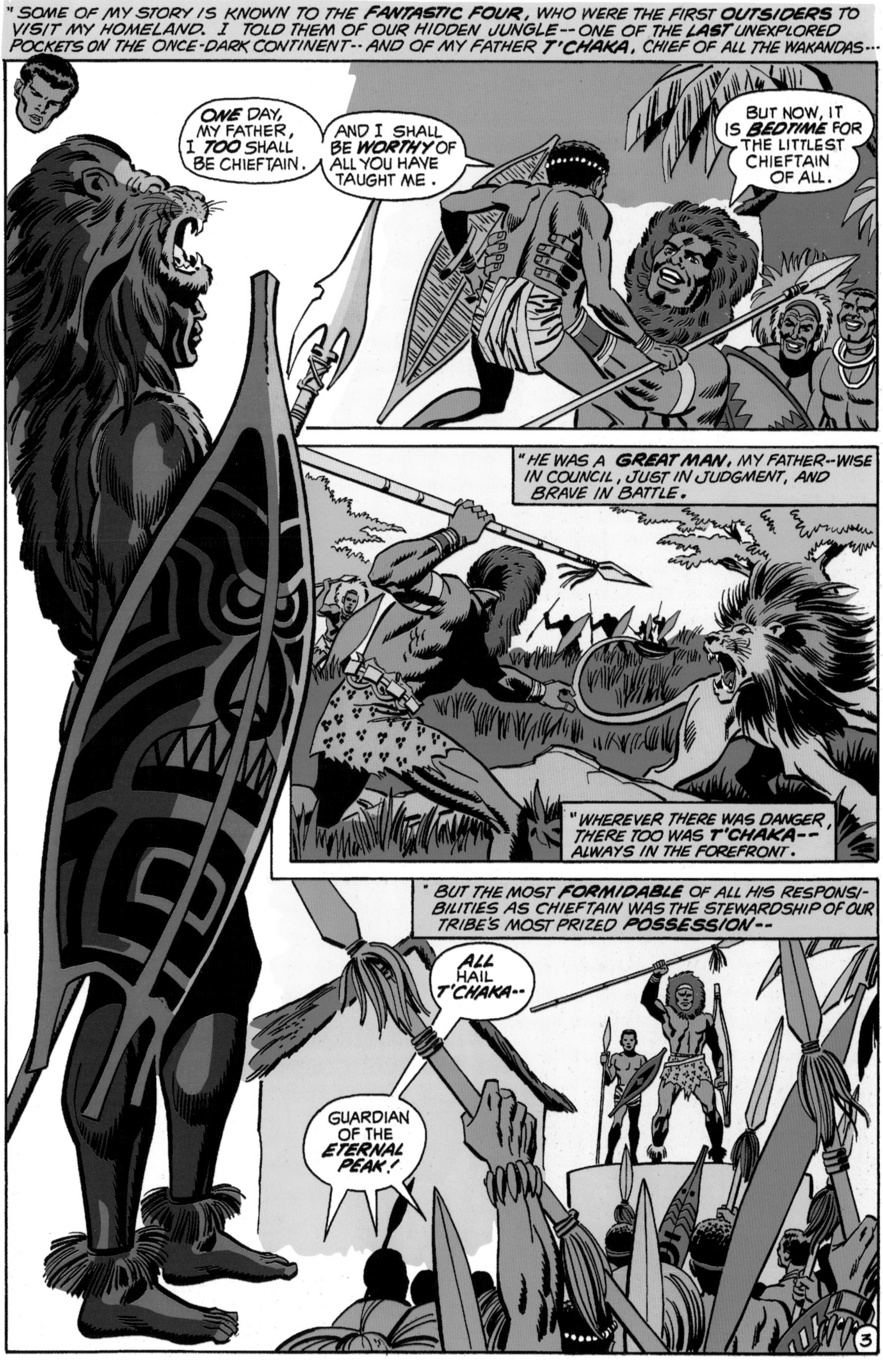
"SOME OF MY STORY IS KNOWN TO THE FANTASTIC FOUR, WHO WERE THE FIRST OUTSIDERS TO VISIT MY HOMELAND. I TOLD THEM OF OUR HIDDEN JUNGLE -- ONE OF THE LAST UNEXPLORED POCKETS ON THE ONCE-DARK CONTINENT -- AND OF MY FATHER T'CHAKA, CHIEF OF ALL THE WAKANDAS --
ONE DAY, MY FATHER, I TOO SHALL BE CHIEFTAIN.
AND I SHALL BE WORTHY OF ALL YOU HAVE TAUGHT ME.
BUT NOW, IT IS BEDTIME FOR THE LITTLEST CHIEFTAIN OF ALL.
"HE WAS A GREAT MAN, MY FATHER -- WISE IN COUNCIL, JUST IN JUDGMENT, AND BRAVE IN BATTLE.
"WHEREVER THERE WAS DANGER, THERE TOO WAS T'CHAKA -- ALWAYS IN THE FOREFRONT.
"BUT THE MOST FORMIDABLE OF ALL HIS RESPONSIBILITIES AS CHIEFTAIN WAS THE STEWARDSHIP OF OUR TRIBE'S MOST PRIZED POSSESSION --
ALL HAIL T'CHAKA --
GUARDIAN OF THE ETERNAL PEAK!
3

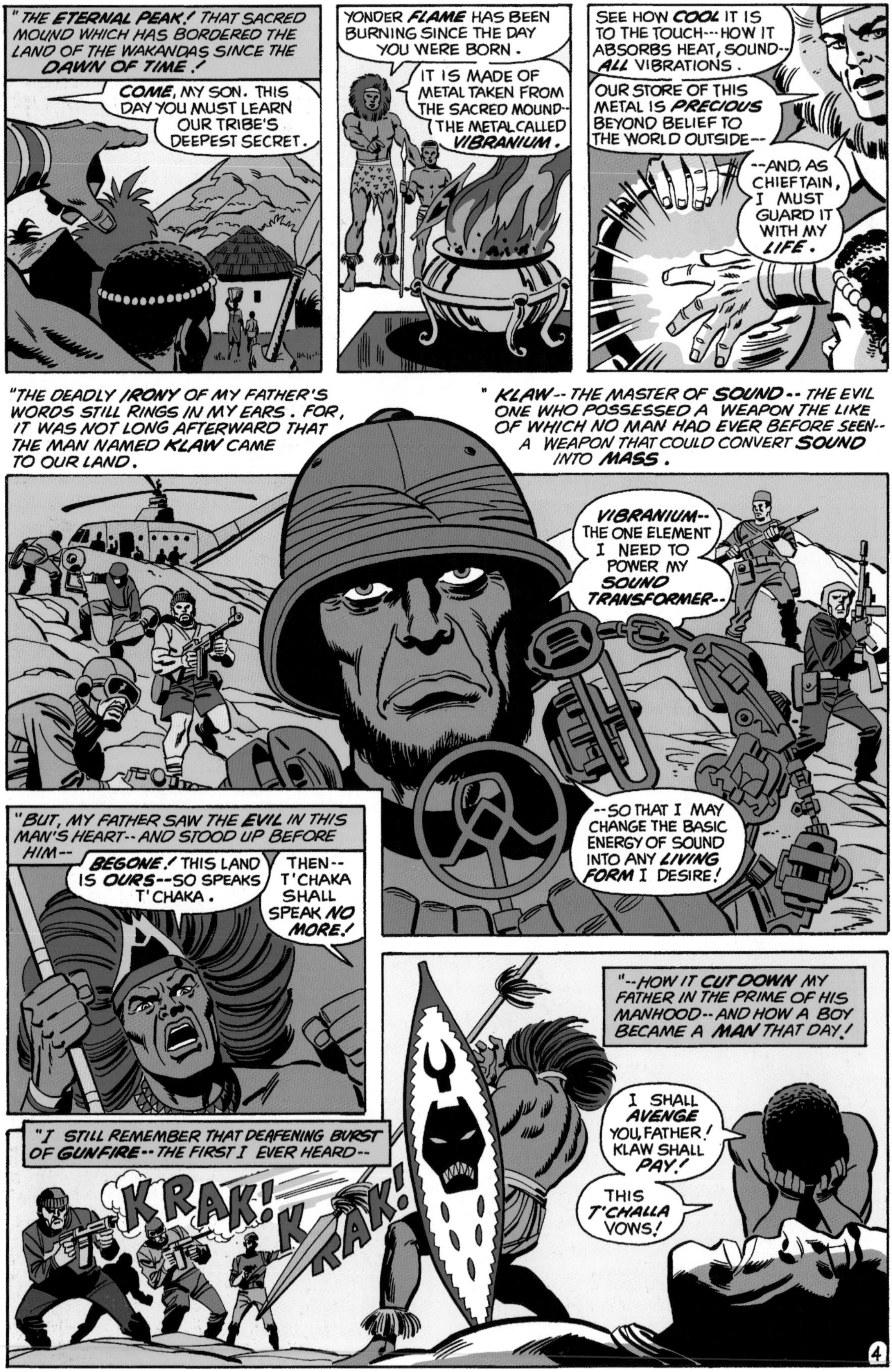
"THE ETERNAL PEAK! THAT SACRED MOUND WHICH HAS BORDERED THE LAND OF THE WAKANDAS SINCE THE DAWN OF TIME!
COME, MY SON. THIS DAY YOU MUST LEARN OUR TRIBE'S DEEPEST SECRET.
YONDER FLAME HAS BEEN BURNING SINCE THE DAY YOU WERE BORN.
IT IS MADE OF METAL TAKEN FROM THE SACRED MOUND--THE METAL CALLED VIBRANIUM.
SEE HOW COOL IT IS TO THE TOUCH---HOW IT ABSORBS HEAT, SOUND--ALL VIBRATIONS.
OUR STORE OF THIS METAL IS PRECIOUS BEYOND BELIEF TO THE WORLD OUTSIDE--
--AND, AS CHIEFTAIN, I MUST GUARD IT WITH MY LIFE.
"THE DEADLY IRONY OF MY FATHER'S WORDS STILL RINGS IN MY EARS. FOR, IT WAS NOT LONG AFTERWARD THAT THE MAN NAMED KLAW CAME TO OUR LAND.
" KLAW--THE MASTER OF SOUND--THE EVIL ONE WHO POSSESSED A WEAPON THE LIKE OF WHICH NO MAN HAD EVER BEFORE SEEN--A WEAPON THAT COULD CONVERT SOUND INTO MASS.
VIBRANIUM--THE ONE ELEMENT I NEED TO POWER MY SOUND TRANSFORMER--
--SO THAT I MAY CHANGE THE BASIC ENERGY OF SOUND INTO ANY LIVING FORM I DESIRE!
"BUT, MY FATHER SAW THE EVIL IN THIS MAN'S HEART--AND STOOD UP BEFORE HIM--
BEGONE! THIS LAND IS OURS--SO SPEAKS T'CHAKA.
THEN--T'CHAKA SHALL SPEAK NO MORE!
"--HOW IT CUT DOWN MY FATHER IN THE PRIME OF HIS MANHOOD--AND HOW A BOY BECAME A MAN THAT DAY!
"I STILL REMEMBER THAT DEAFENING BURST OF GUNFIRE--THE FIRST I EVER HEARD--
KRAK! KRAK!
I SHALL AVENGE YOU, FATHER! KLAW SHALL PAY!
THIS T'CHALLA VOWS!

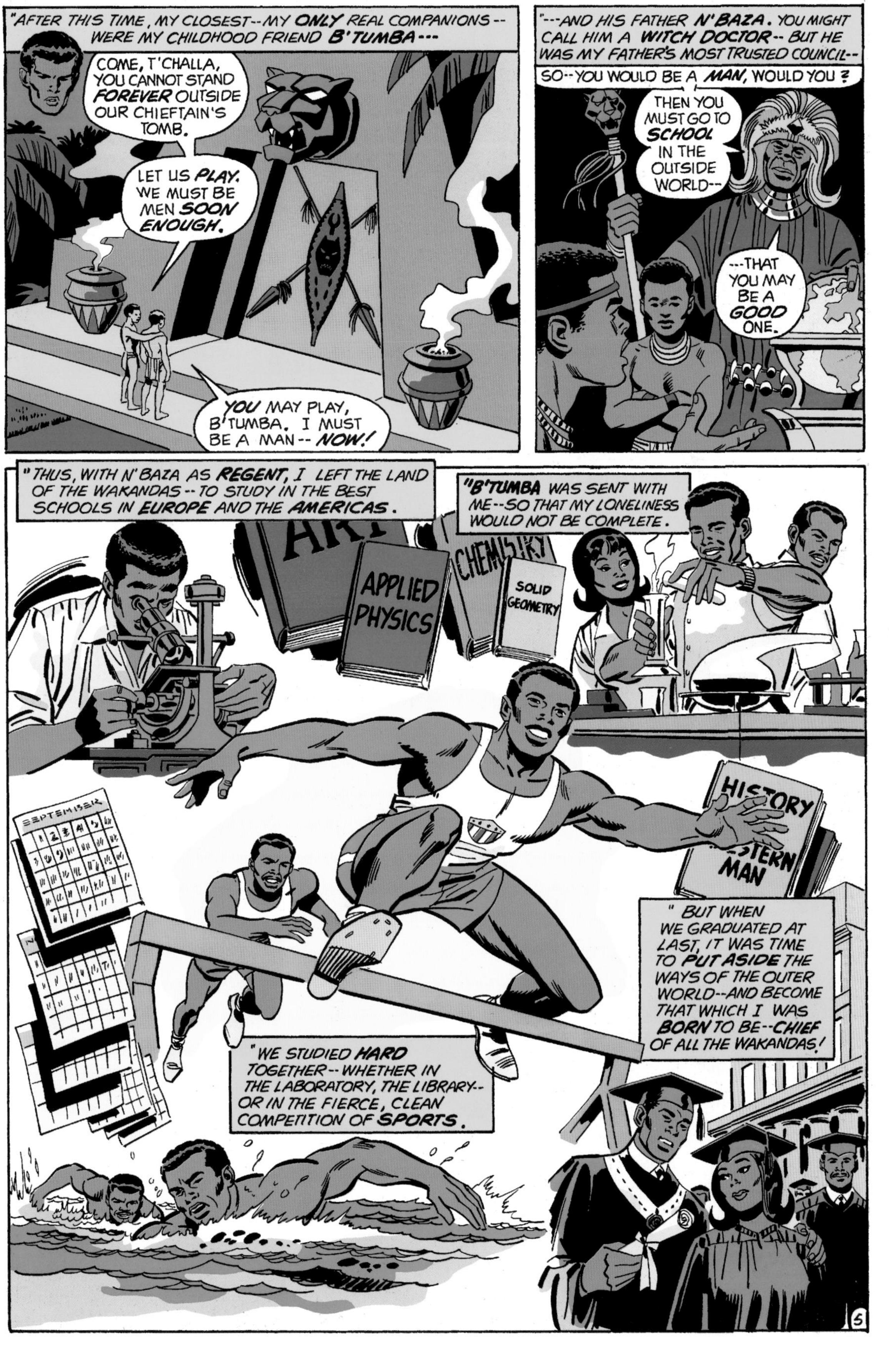

"AFTER THIS TIME, MY CLOSEST--MY ONLY REAL COMPANIONS--WERE MY CHILDHOOD FRIEND B'TUMBA---
COME, T'CHALLA, YOU CANNOT STAND FOREVER OUTSIDE OUR CHIEFTAIN'S TOMB.
LET US PLAY. WE MUST BE MEN SOON ENOUGH.
YOU MAY PLAY, B'TUMBA. I MUST BE A MAN--NOW!
"---AND HIS FATHER N'BAZA. YOU MIGHT CALL HIM A WITCH DOCTOR--BUT HE WAS MY FATHER'S MOST TRUSTED COUNCIL--
SO--YOU WOULD BE A MAN, WOULD YOU?
THEN YOU MUST GO TO SCHOOL IN THE OUTSIDE WORLD--
--THAT YOU MAY BE A GOOD ONE.
"THUS, WITH N'BAZA AS REGENT, I LEFT THE LAND OF THE WAKANDAS--TO STUDY IN THE BEST SCHOOLS IN EUROPE AND THE AMERICAS.
"B'TUMBA WAS SENT WITH ME--SO THAT MY LONELINESS WOULD NOT BE COMPLETE.
APPLIED PHYSICS
SOLID GEOMETRY
"WE STUDIED HARD TOGETHER--WHETHER IN THE LABORATORY, THE LIBRARY--OR IN THE FIERCE, CLEAN COMPETITION OF SPORTS.
" BUT WHEN WE GRADUATED AT LAST, IT WAS TIME TO PUT ASIDE THE WAYS OF THE OUTER WORLD--AND BECOME THAT WHICH I WAS BORN TO BE--CHIEF OF ALL THE WAKANDAS!
5

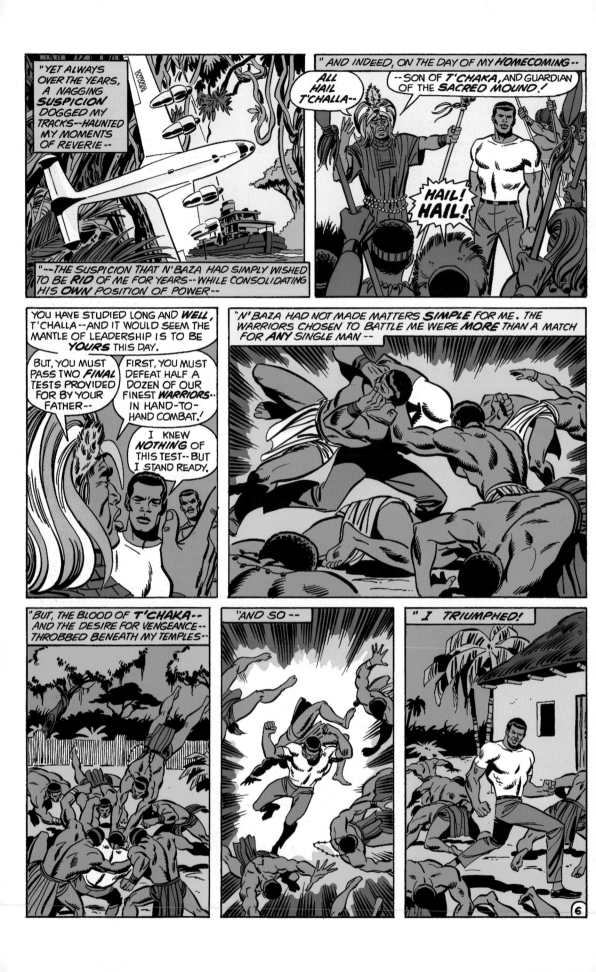

"YET ALWAYS OVER THE YEARS, A NAGGING *SUSPICION* DOGGED MY TRACKS--HAUNTED MY MOMENTS OF REVERIE--

"--THE SUSPICION THAT N'BAZA HAD SIMPLY WISHED TO BE *RID* OF ME FOR YEARS--WHILE CONSOLIDATING HIS *OWN* POSITION OF POWER--

" AND INDEED, ON THE DAY OF MY *HOMECOMING*--

ALL HAIL T'CHALLA--

--SON OF *T'CHAKA*, AND GUARDIAN OF THE *SACRED MOUND!*

HAIL! HAIL!

YOU HAVE STUDIED LONG AND *WELL*, T'CHALLA--AND IT WOULD SEEM THE MANTLE OF LEADERSHIP IS TO BE *YOURS* THIS DAY.

BUT, YOU MUST PASS TWO *FINAL* TESTS PROVIDED FOR BY YOUR FATHER--

FIRST, YOU MUST DEFEAT HALF A DOZEN OF OUR FINEST *WARRIORS*-- IN HAND-TO-HAND COMBAT!

I KNEW *NOTHING* OF THIS TEST-- BUT I STAND READY.

"N'BAZA HAD NOT MADE MATTERS *SIMPLE* FOR ME. THE WARRIORS CHOSEN TO BATTLE ME WERE *MORE* THAN A MATCH FOR *ANY* SINGLE MAN --

"BUT, THE BLOOD OF *T'CHAKA*-- AND THE DESIRE FOR VENGEANCE-- THROBBED BENEATH MY TEMPLES--

"AND SO --

" *I TRIUMPHED!*

6

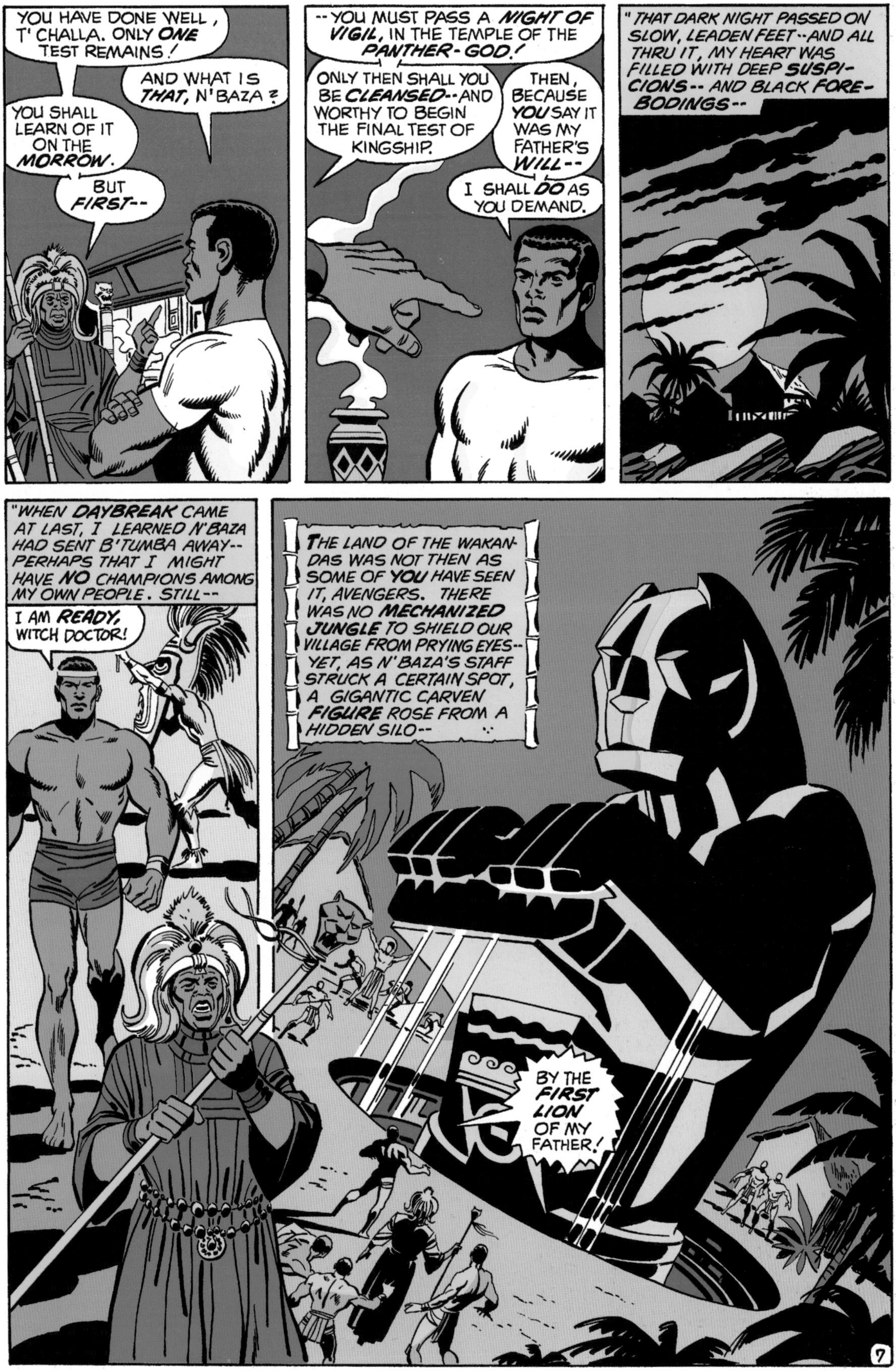

YOU HAVE DONE WELL, T'CHALLA. ONLY ONE TEST REMAINS!
AND WHAT IS THAT, N'BAZA?
YOU SHALL LEARN OF IT ON THE MORROW.
BUT FIRST--
--YOU MUST PASS A NIGHT OF VIGIL, IN THE TEMPLE OF THE PANTHER-GOD!
ONLY THEN SHALL YOU BE CLEANSED--AND WORTHY TO BEGIN THE FINAL TEST OF KINGSHIP.
THEN, BECAUSE YOU SAY IT WAS MY FATHER'S WILL--
I SHALL DO AS YOU DEMAND.
"THAT DARK NIGHT PASSED ON SLOW, LEADEN FEET--AND ALL THRU IT, MY HEART WAS FILLED WITH DEEP SUSPICIONS-- AND BLACK FOREBODINGS--
"WHEN DAYBREAK CAME AT LAST, I LEARNED N'BAZA HAD SENT B'TUMBA AWAY--PERHAPS THAT I MIGHT HAVE NO CHAMPIONS AMONG MY OWN PEOPLE. STILL--
I AM READY, WITCH DOCTOR!
THE LAND OF THE WAKANDAS WAS NOT THEN AS SOME OF YOU HAVE SEEN IT, AVENGERS. THERE WAS NO MECHANIZED JUNGLE TO SHIELD OUR VILLAGE FROM PRYING EYES--YET, AS N'BAZA'S STAFF STRUCK A CERTAIN SPOT, A GIGANTIC CARVEN FIGURE ROSE FROM A HIDDEN SILO--
BY THE FIRST LION OF MY FATHER!
7

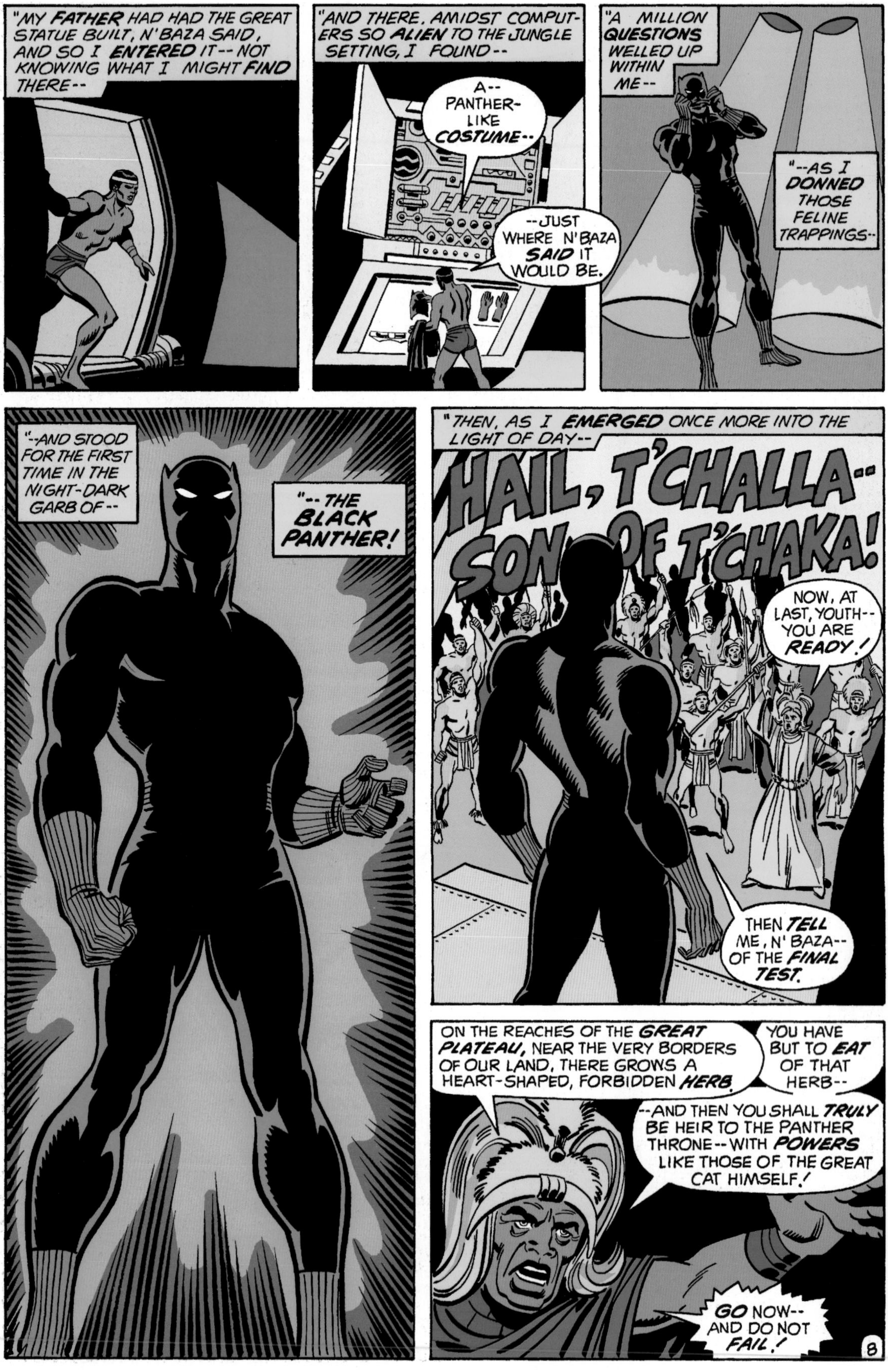

"MY FATHER HAD HAD THE GREAT STATUE BUILT, N'BAZA SAID, AND SO I ENTERED IT -- NOT KNOWING WHAT I MIGHT FIND THERE--
"AND THERE, AMIDST COMPUTERS SO ALIEN TO THE JUNGLE SETTING, I FOUND--
A-- PANTHER-LIKE COSTUME--
--JUST WHERE N'BAZA SAID IT WOULD BE.
"A MILLION QUESTIONS WELLED UP WITHIN ME--
"--AS I DONNED THOSE FELINE TRAPPINGS--
"--AND STOOD FOR THE FIRST TIME IN THE NIGHT-DARK GARB OF--
"-- THE BLACK PANTHER!
"THEN, AS I EMERGED ONCE MORE INTO THE LIGHT OF DAY--
HAIL, T'CHALLA-- SON OF T'CHAKA!
NOW, AT LAST, YOUTH-- YOU ARE READY!
THEN TELL ME, N'BAZA-- OF THE FINAL TEST.
ON THE REACHES OF THE GREAT PLATEAU, NEAR THE VERY BORDERS OF OUR LAND, THERE GROWS A HEART-SHAPED, FORBIDDEN HERB.
YOU HAVE BUT TO EAT OF THAT HERB--
--AND THEN YOU SHALL TRULY BE HEIR TO THE PANTHER THRONE-- WITH POWERS LIKE THOSE OF THE GREAT CAT HIMSELF!
GO NOW-- AND DO NOT FAIL!
8

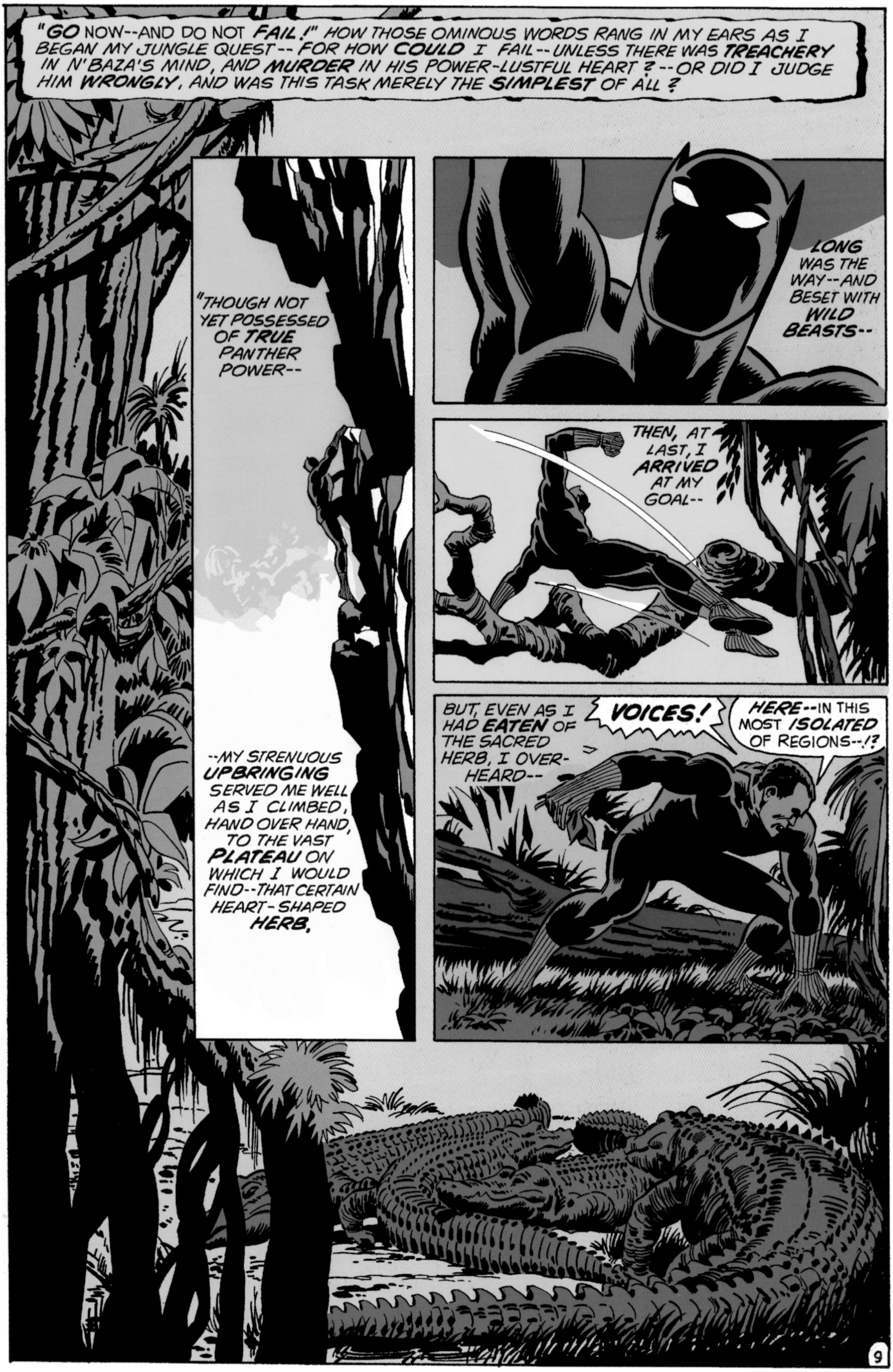
"GO NOW--AND DO NOT FAIL!" HOW THOSE OMINOUS WORDS RANG IN MY EARS AS I BEGAN MY JUNGLE QUEST-- FOR HOW COULD I FAIL--UNLESS THERE WAS TREACHERY IN N'BAZA'S MIND, AND MURDER IN HIS POWER-LUSTFUL HEART? --OR DID I JUDGE HIM WRONGLY, AND WAS THIS TASK MERELY THE SIMPLEST OF ALL?
"THOUGH NOT YET POSSESSED OF TRUE PANTHER POWER--
--MY STRENUOUS UPBRINGING SERVED ME WELL AS I CLIMBED, HAND OVER HAND, TO THE VAST PLATEAU ON WHICH I WOULD FIND--THAT CERTAIN HEART-SHAPED HERB.
LONG WAS THE WAY--AND BESET WITH WILD BEASTS--
THEN, AT LAST, I ARRIVED AT MY GOAL--
BUT, EVEN AS I HAD EATEN OF THE SACRED HERB, I OVER-HEARD--
VOICES!
HERE--IN THIS MOST ISOLATED OF REGIONS--!?

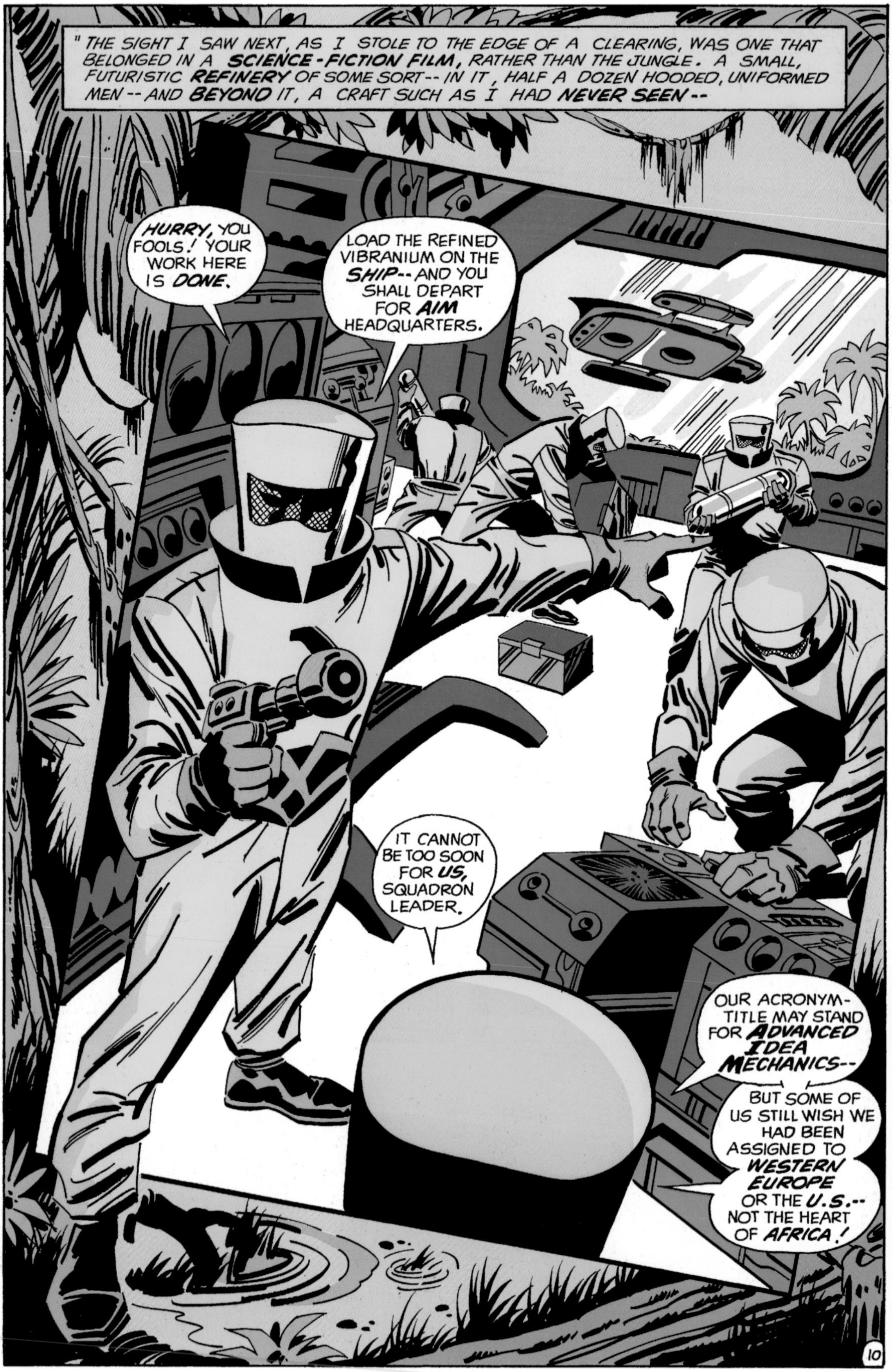
"THE SIGHT I SAW NEXT, AS I STOLE TO THE EDGE OF A CLEARING, WAS ONE THAT BELONGED IN A SCIENCE-FICTION FILM, RATHER THAN THE JUNGLE. A SMALL, FUTURISTIC REFINERY OF SOME SORT-- IN IT, HALF A DOZEN HOODED, UNIFORMED MEN -- AND BEYOND IT, A CRAFT SUCH AS I HAD NEVER SEEN --
HURRY, YOU FOOLS! YOUR WORK HERE IS DONE.
LOAD THE REFINED VIBRANIUM ON THE SHIP-- AND YOU SHALL DEPART FOR AIM HEADQUARTERS.
IT CANNOT BE TOO SOON FOR US, SQUADRON LEADER.
OUR ACRONYM-TITLE MAY STAND FOR ADVANCED IDEA MECHANICS--
BUT SOME OF US STILL WISH WE HAD BEEN ASSIGNED TO WESTERN EUROPE OR THE U.S.-- NOT THE HEART OF AFRICA!
10

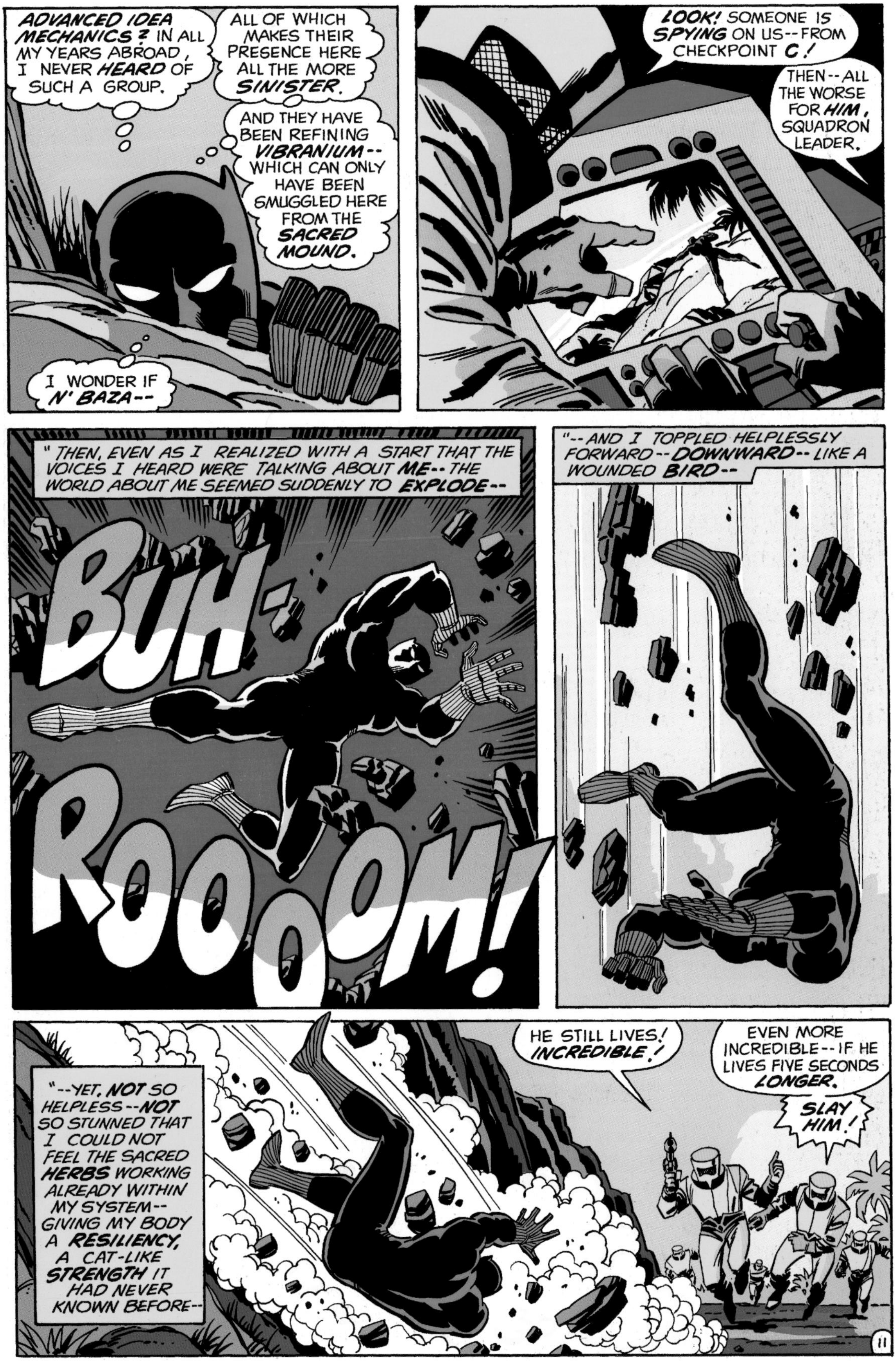
ADVANCED IDEA MECHANICS? IN ALL MY YEARS ABROAD, I NEVER HEARD OF SUCH A GROUP.
ALL OF WHICH MAKES THEIR PRESENCE HERE ALL THE MORE SINISTER.
AND THEY HAVE BEEN REFINING VIBRANIUM-- WHICH CAN ONLY HAVE BEEN SMUGGLED HERE FROM THE SACRED MOUND.
I WONDER IF N' BAZA--
LOOK! SOMEONE IS SPYING ON US--FROM CHECKPOINT C!
THEN--ALL THE WORSE FOR HIM, SQUADRON LEADER.
"THEN, EVEN AS I REALIZED WITH A START THAT THE VOICES I HEARD WERE TALKING ABOUT ME--THE WORLD ABOUT ME SEEMED SUDDENLY TO EXPLODE--
BUH-ROOOOM!
"--AND I TOPPLED HELPLESSLY FORWARD--DOWNWARD--LIKE A WOUNDED BIRD--
"--YET, NOT SO HELPLESS--NOT SO STUNNED THAT I COULD NOT FEEL THE SACRED HERBS WORKING ALREADY WITHIN MY SYSTEM--GIVING MY BODY A RESILIENCY, A CAT-LIKE STRENGTH IT HAD NEVER KNOWN BEFORE--
HE STILL LIVES! INCREDIBLE!
EVEN MORE INCREDIBLE--IF HE LIVES FIVE SECONDS LONGER.
SLAY HIM!

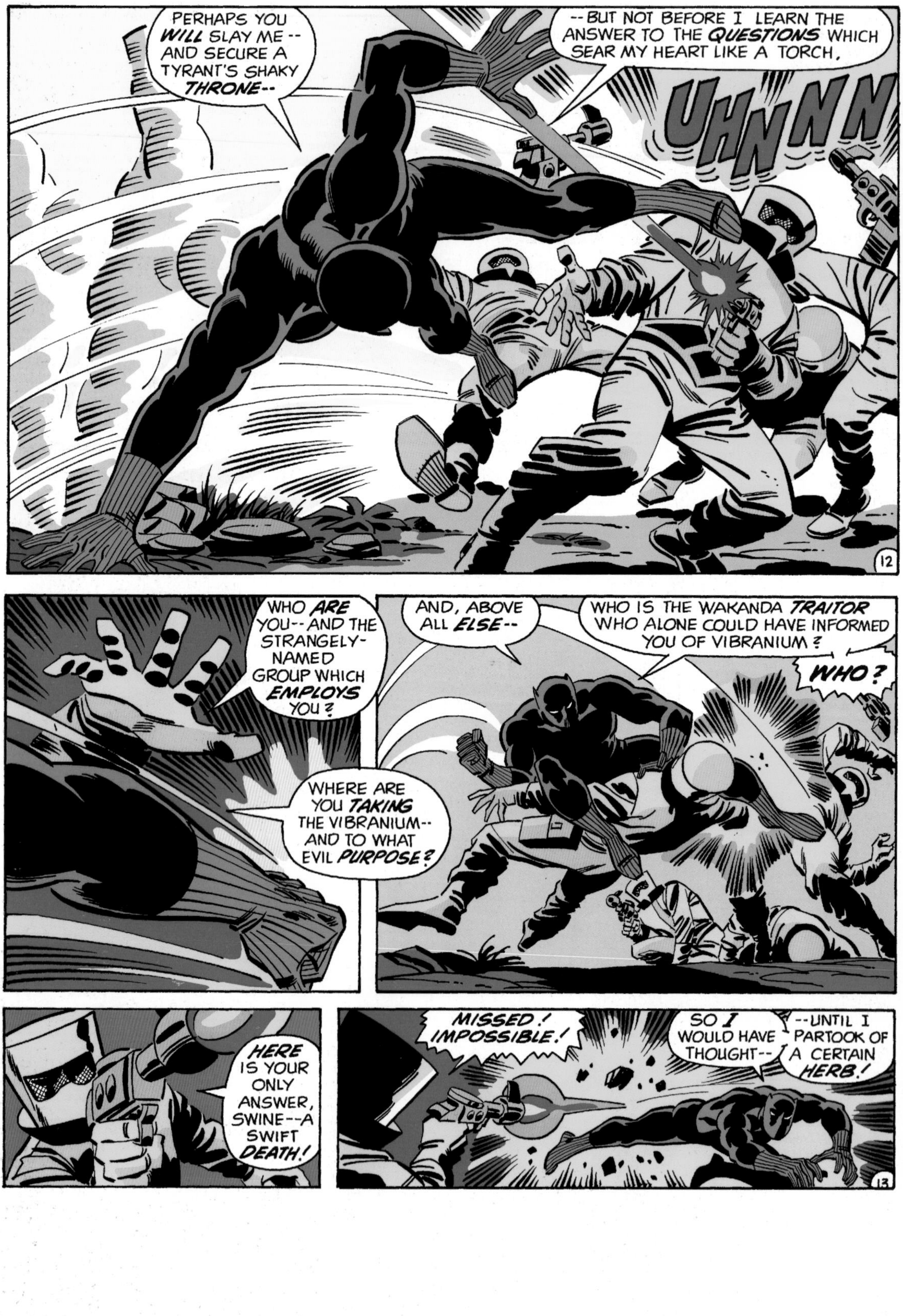
PERHAPS YOU WILL SLAY ME -- AND SECURE A TYRANT'S SHAKY THRONE--
-- BUT NOT BEFORE I LEARN THE ANSWER TO THE QUESTIONS WHICH SEAR MY HEART LIKE A TORCH,
UHNNN
12
WHO ARE YOU-- AND THE STRANGELY-NAMED GROUP WHICH EMPLOYS YOU?
WHERE ARE YOU TAKING THE VIBRANIUM-- AND TO WHAT EVIL PURPOSE?
AND, ABOVE ALL ELSE--
WHO IS THE WAKANDA TRAITOR WHO ALONE COULD HAVE INFORMED YOU OF VIBRANIUM?
WHO?
HERE IS YOUR ONLY ANSWER, SWINE--A SWIFT DEATH!
MISSED! IMPOSSIBLE!
SO I WOULD HAVE THOUGHT--
--UNTIL I PARTOOK OF A CERTAIN HERB!
13

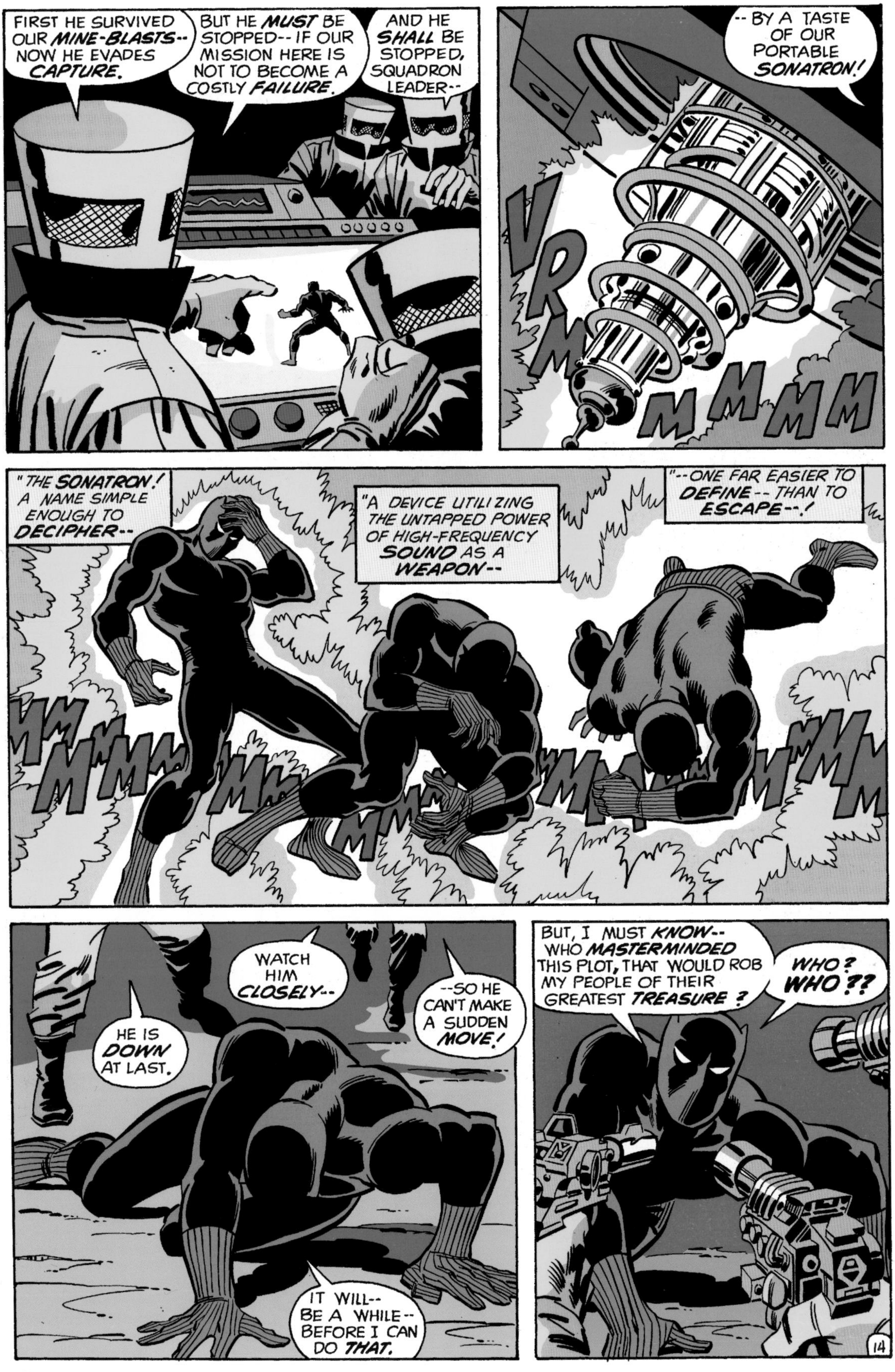
FIRST HE SURVIVED OUR MINE-BLASTS-- NOW HE EVADES CAPTURE.
BUT HE MUST BE STOPPED-- IF OUR MISSION HERE IS NOT TO BECOME A COSTLY FAILURE.
AND HE SHALL BE STOPPED, SQUADRON LEADER--
-- BY A TASTE OF OUR PORTABLE SONATRON!
VRMMMMMM
"THE SONATRON! A NAME SIMPLE ENOUGH TO DECIPHER--
"A DEVICE UTILIZING THE UNTAPPED POWER OF HIGH-FREQUENCY SOUND AS A WEAPON--
"--ONE FAR EASIER TO DEFINE -- THAN TO ESCAPE--!
HE IS DOWN AT LAST.
WATCH HIM CLOSELY--
--SO HE CAN'T MAKE A SUDDEN MOVE!
IT WILL-- BE A WHILE-- BEFORE I CAN DO THAT.
BUT, I MUST KNOW-- WHO MASTERMINDED THIS PLOT, THAT WOULD ROB MY PEOPLE OF THEIR GREATEST TREASURE ?
WHO? WHO??
14

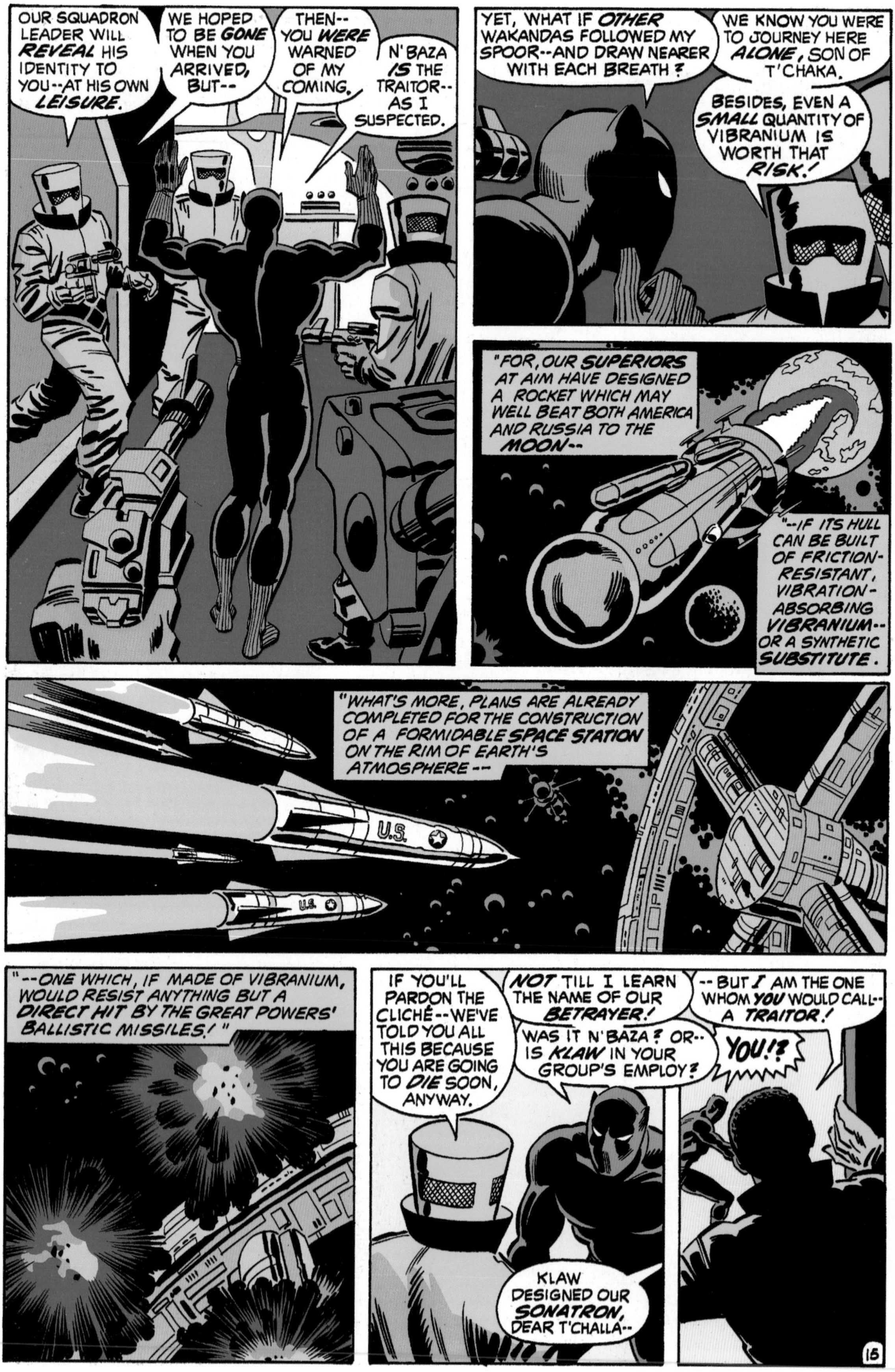
OUR SQUADRON LEADER WILL REVEAL HIS IDENTITY TO YOU--AT HIS OWN LEISURE.
WE HOPED TO BE GONE WHEN YOU ARRIVED, BUT--
THEN--YOU WERE WARNED OF MY COMING.
N'BAZA IS THE TRAITOR--AS I SUSPECTED.
YET, WHAT IF OTHER WAKANDAS FOLLOWED MY SPOOR--AND DRAW NEARER WITH EACH BREATH?
WE KNOW YOU WERE TO JOURNEY HERE ALONE, SON OF T'CHAKA.
BESIDES, EVEN A SMALL QUANTITY OF VIBRANIUM IS WORTH THAT RISK!
"FOR, OUR SUPERIORS AT AIM HAVE DESIGNED A ROCKET WHICH MAY WELL BEAT BOTH AMERICA AND RUSSIA TO THE MOON--
"--IF ITS HULL CAN BE BUILT OF FRICTION-RESISTANT, VIBRATION-ABSORBING VIBRANIUM--OR A SYNTHETIC SUBSTITUTE.
"WHAT'S MORE, PLANS ARE ALREADY COMPLETED FOR THE CONSTRUCTION OF A FORMIDABLE SPACE STATION ON THE RIM OF EARTH'S ATMOSPHERE--
U.S.
U.S.
"--ONE WHICH, IF MADE OF VIBRANIUM, WOULD RESIST ANYTHING BUT A DIRECT HIT BY THE GREAT POWERS' BALLISTIC MISSILES!"
IF YOU'LL PARDON THE CLICHÉ--WE'VE TOLD YOU ALL THIS BECAUSE YOU ARE GOING TO DIE SOON, ANYWAY.
NOT TILL I LEARN THE NAME OF OUR BETRAYER!
WAS IT N'BAZA? OR--IS KLAW IN YOUR GROUP'S EMPLOY?
KLAW DESIGNED OUR SONATRON, DEAR T'CHALLA--
--BUT I AM THE ONE WHOM YOU WOULD CALL--A TRAITOR!
YOU!?

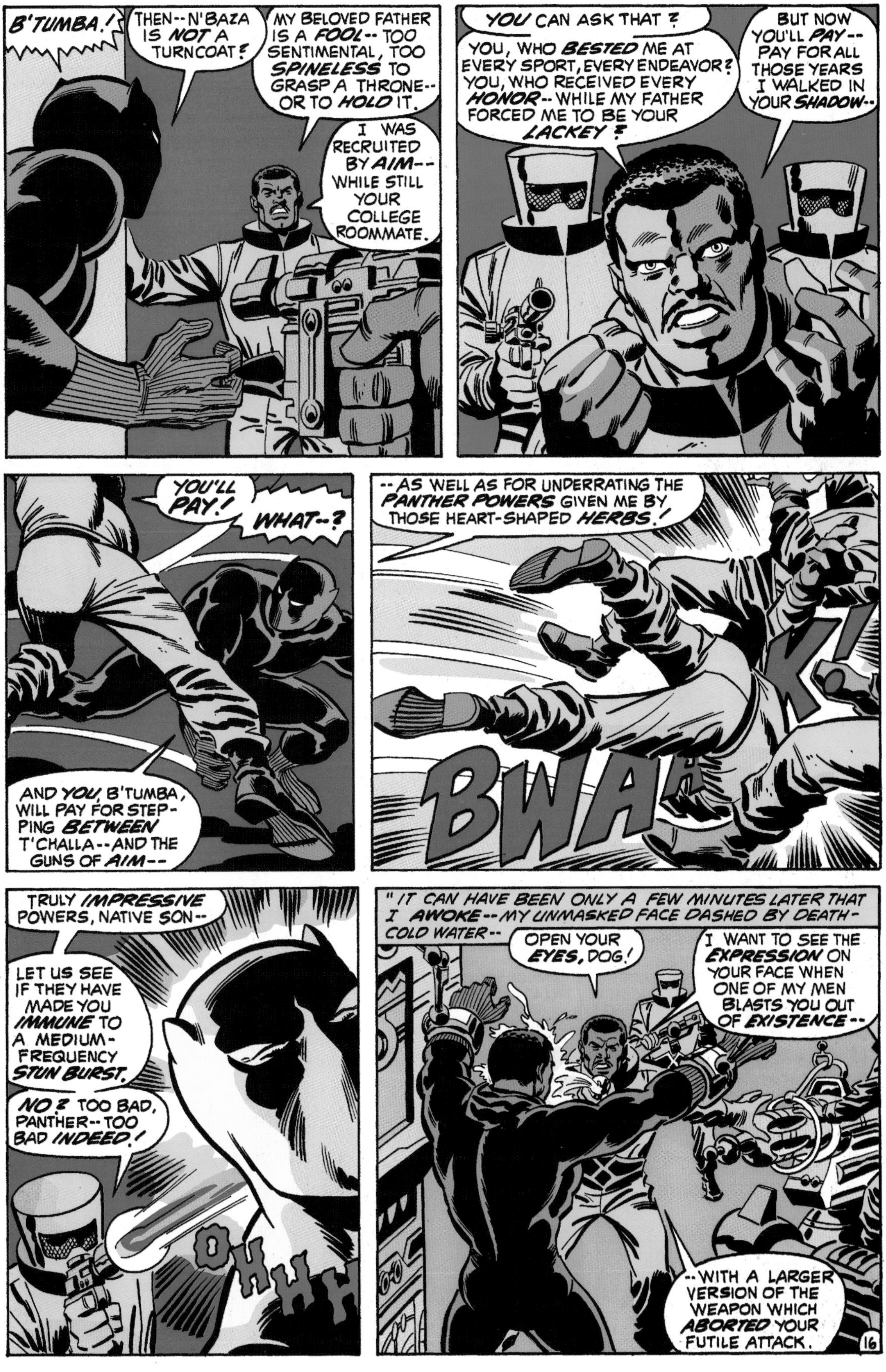

B'TUMBA.!
THEN--N'BAZA IS NOT A TURNCOAT?
MY BELOVED FATHER IS A FOOL--TOO SENTIMENTAL, TOO SPINELESS TO GRASP A THRONE--OR TO HOLD IT.
I WAS RECRUITED BY AIM--WHILE STILL YOUR COLLEGE ROOMMATE.
YOU CAN ASK THAT?
YOU, WHO BESTED ME AT EVERY SPORT, EVERY ENDEAVOR? YOU, WHO RECEIVED EVERY HONOR--WHILE MY FATHER FORCED ME TO BE YOUR LACKEY?
BUT NOW YOU'LL PAY--PAY FOR ALL THOSE YEARS I WALKED IN YOUR SHADOW--
YOU'LL PAY!
WHAT--?
AND YOU, B'TUMBA, WILL PAY FOR STEPPING BETWEEN T'CHALLA--AND THE GUNS OF AIM--
--AS WELL AS FOR UNDERRATING THE PANTHER POWERS GIVEN ME BY THOSE HEART-SHAPED HERBS!
BWAK!
TRULY IMPRESSIVE POWERS, NATIVE SON--
LET US SEE IF THEY HAVE MADE YOU IMMUNE TO A MEDIUM-FREQUENCY STUN BURST.
NO? TOO BAD, PANTHER--TOO BAD INDEED!
OHHH
"IT CAN HAVE BEEN ONLY A FEW MINUTES LATER THAT I AWOKE--MY UNMASKED FACE DASHED BY DEATH-COLD WATER--
OPEN YOUR EYES, DOG!
I WANT TO SEE THE EXPRESSION ON YOUR FACE WHEN ONE OF MY MEN BLASTS YOU OUT OF EXISTENCE--
--WITH A LARGER VERSION OF THE WEAPON WHICH ABORTED YOUR FUTILE ATTACK.
16

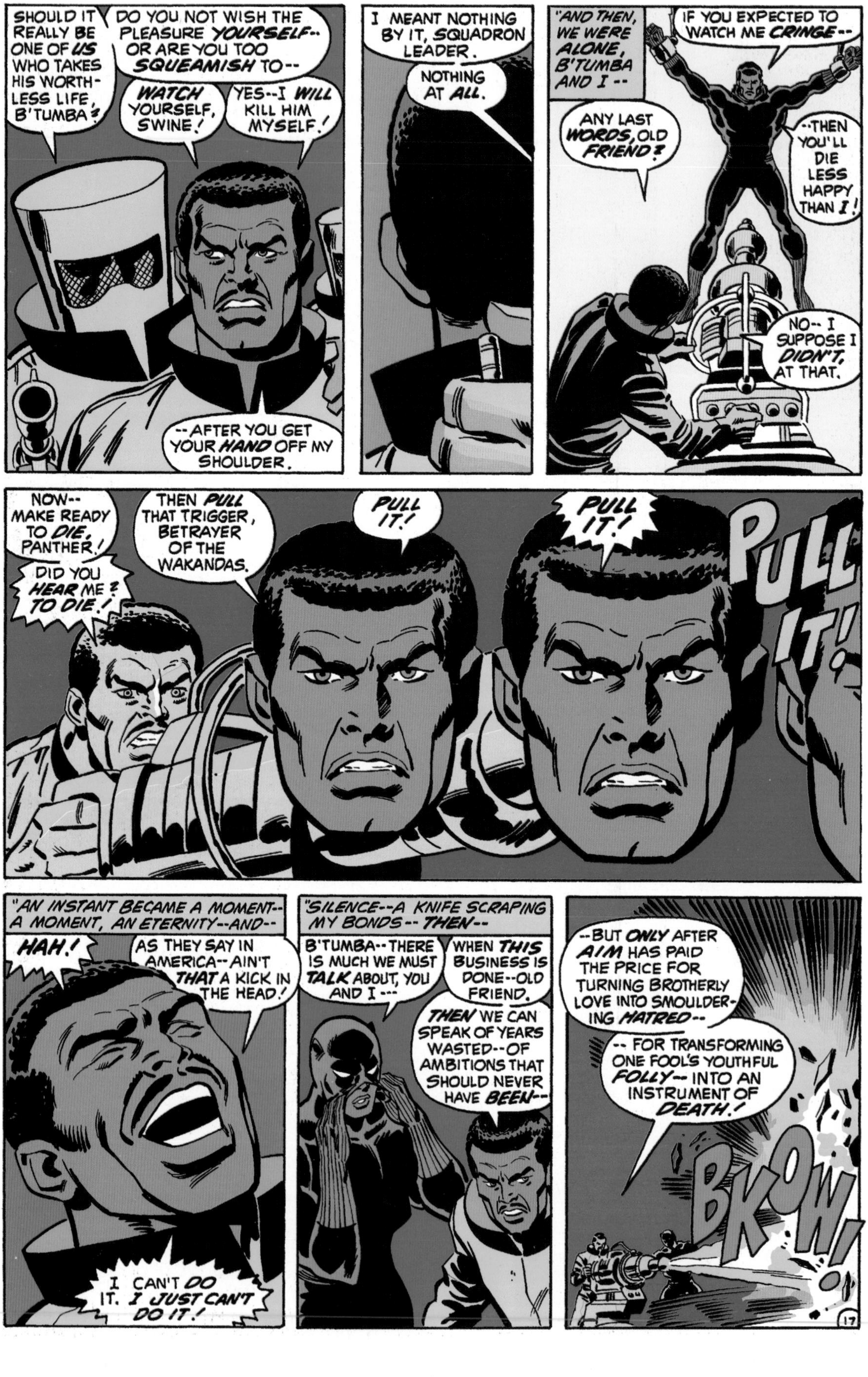
SHOULD IT REALLY BE ONE OF US WHO TAKES HIS WORTHLESS LIFE, B'TUMBA?
DO YOU NOT WISH THE PLEASURE YOURSELF-- OR ARE YOU TOO SQUEAMISH TO--
WATCH YOURSELF, SWINE!
YES--I WILL KILL HIM MYSELF!
--AFTER YOU GET YOUR HAND OFF MY SHOULDER.
I MEANT NOTHING BY IT, SQUADRON LEADER.
NOTHING AT ALL.
"AND THEN, WE WERE ALONE, B'TUMBA AND I --
IF YOU EXPECTED TO WATCH ME CRINGE--
ANY LAST WORDS, OLD FRIEND?
--THEN YOU'LL DIE LESS HAPPY THAN I!
NO-- I SUPPOSE I DIDN'T, AT THAT.
NOW-- MAKE READY TO DIE, PANTHER!
DID YOU HEAR ME? TO DIE!
THEN PULL THAT TRIGGER, BETRAYER OF THE WAKANDAS.
PULL IT!
PULL IT!
PULL IT!
"AN INSTANT BECAME A MOMENT-- A MOMENT, AN ETERNITY--AND--
HAH!
AS THEY SAY IN AMERICA--AIN'T THAT A KICK IN THE HEAD!
I CAN'T DO IT. I JUST CAN'T DO IT!
"SILENCE--A KNIFE SCRAPING MY BONDS-- THEN--
B'TUMBA--THERE IS MUCH WE MUST TALK ABOUT, YOU AND I---
WHEN THIS BUSINESS IS DONE--OLD FRIEND.
THEN WE CAN SPEAK OF YEARS WASTED--OF AMBITIONS THAT SHOULD NEVER HAVE BEEN--
--BUT ONLY AFTER AIM HAS PAID THE PRICE FOR TURNING BROTHERLY LOVE INTO SMOULDERING HATRED--
-- FOR TRANSFORMING ONE FOOL'S YOUTHFUL FOLLY-- INTO AN INSTRUMENT OF DEATH!
BKOW!
17

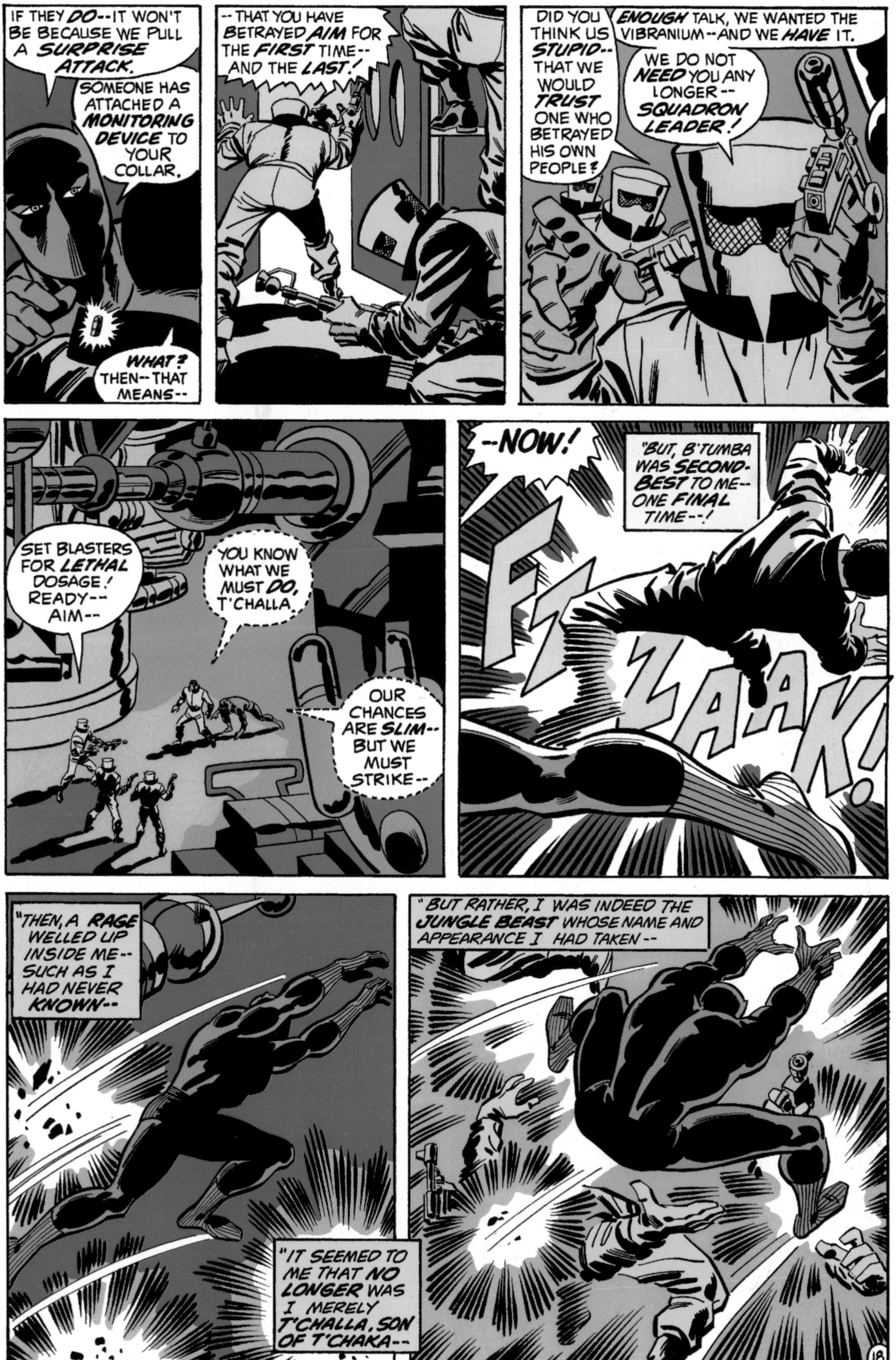
IF THEY DO--IT WON'T BE BECAUSE WE PULL A SURPRISE ATTACK.
SOMEONE HAS ATTACHED A MONITORING DEVICE TO YOUR COLLAR.
WHAT? THEN--THAT MEANS--
--THAT YOU HAVE BETRAYED AIM FOR THE FIRST TIME--AND THE LAST!
DID YOU THINK US STUPID--THAT WE WOULD TRUST ONE WHO BETRAYED HIS OWN PEOPLE?
ENOUGH TALK, WE WANTED THE VIBRANIUM--AND WE HAVE IT.
WE DO NOT NEED YOU ANY LONGER--SQUADRON LEADER!
SET BLASTERS FOR LETHAL DOSAGE! READY--AIM--
YOU KNOW WHAT WE MUST DO, T'CHALLA.
OUR CHANCES ARE SLIM--BUT WE MUST STRIKE--
--NOW!
"BUT, B'TUMBA WAS SECOND-BEST TO ME--ONE FINAL TIME--!
FTZAAK!
"THEN, A RAGE WELLED UP INSIDE ME--SUCH AS I HAD NEVER KNOWN--
"IT SEEMED TO ME THAT NO LONGER WAS I MERELY T'CHALLA, SON OF T'CHAKA--
"BUT RATHER, I WAS INDEED THE JUNGLE BEAST WHOSE NAME AND APPEARANCE I HAD TAKEN--
18

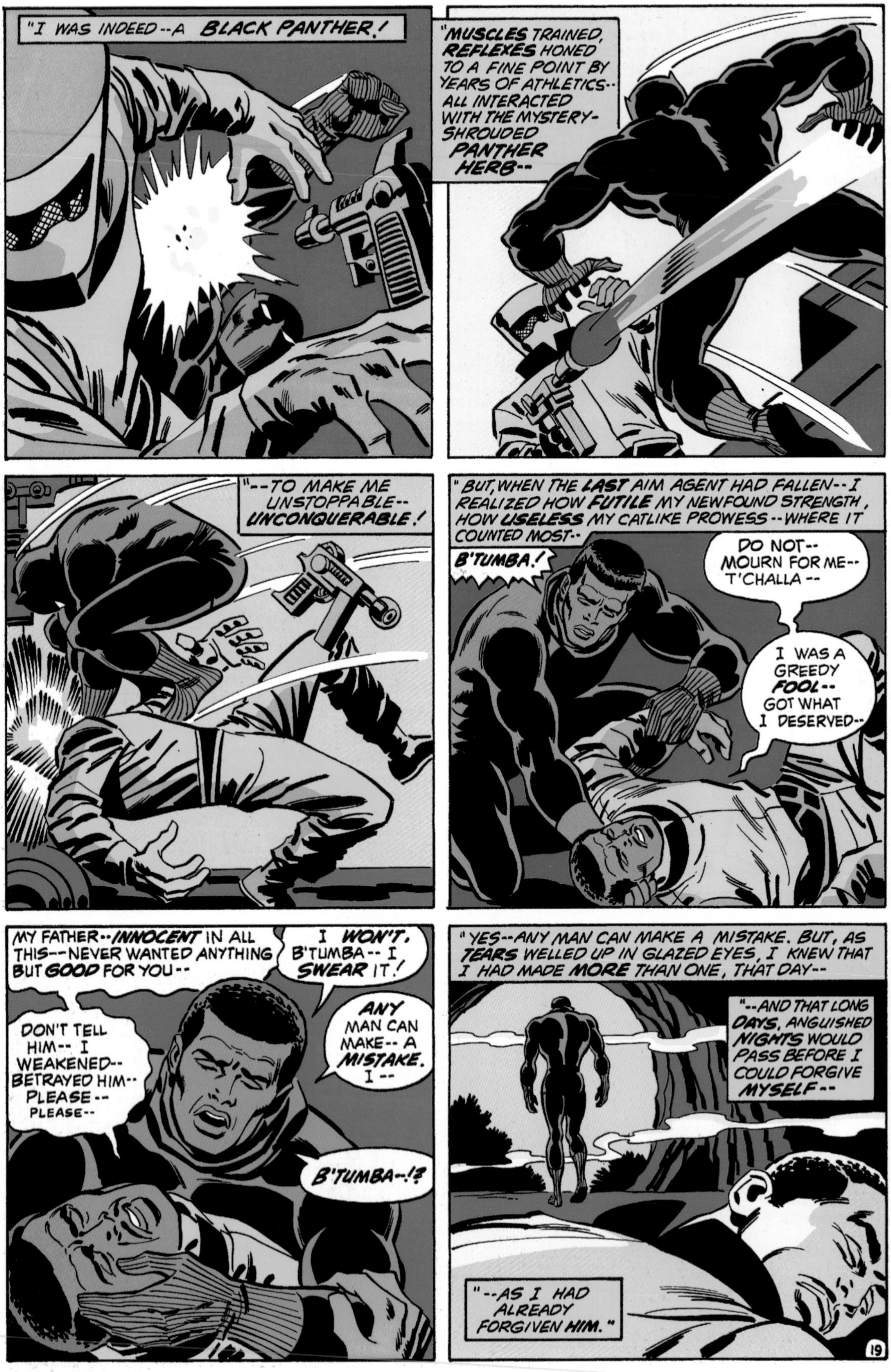
"I WAS INDEED--A BLACK PANTHER!
"MUSCLES TRAINED, REFLEXES HONED TO A FINE POINT BY YEARS OF ATHLETICS--ALL INTERACTED WITH THE MYSTERY-SHROUDED PANTHER HERB--
"--TO MAKE ME UNSTOPPABLE--UNCONQUERABLE!
"BUT, WHEN THE LAST AIM AGENT HAD FALLEN--I REALIZED HOW FUTILE MY NEWFOUND STRENGTH, HOW USELESS MY CATLIKE PROWESS--WHERE IT COUNTED MOST--
B'TUMBA!
DO NOT--MOURN FOR ME--T'CHALLA--
I WAS A GREEDY FOOL--GOT WHAT I DESERVED--
MY FATHER--INNOCENT IN ALL THIS--NEVER WANTED ANYTHING BUT GOOD FOR YOU--
I WON'T, B'TUMBA--I SWEAR IT!
DON'T TELL HIM--I WEAKENED--BETRAYED HIM--PLEASE--PLEASE--
ANY MAN CAN MAKE--A MISTAKE. I--
B'TUMBA--!?
"YES--ANY MAN CAN MAKE A MISTAKE. BUT, AS TEARS WELLED UP IN GLAZED EYES, I KNEW THAT I HAD MADE MORE THAN ONE, THAT DAY--
"--AND THAT LONG DAYS, ANGUISHED NIGHTS WOULD PASS BEFORE I COULD FORGIVE MYSELF--
"--AS I HAD ALREADY FORGIVEN HIM."
19

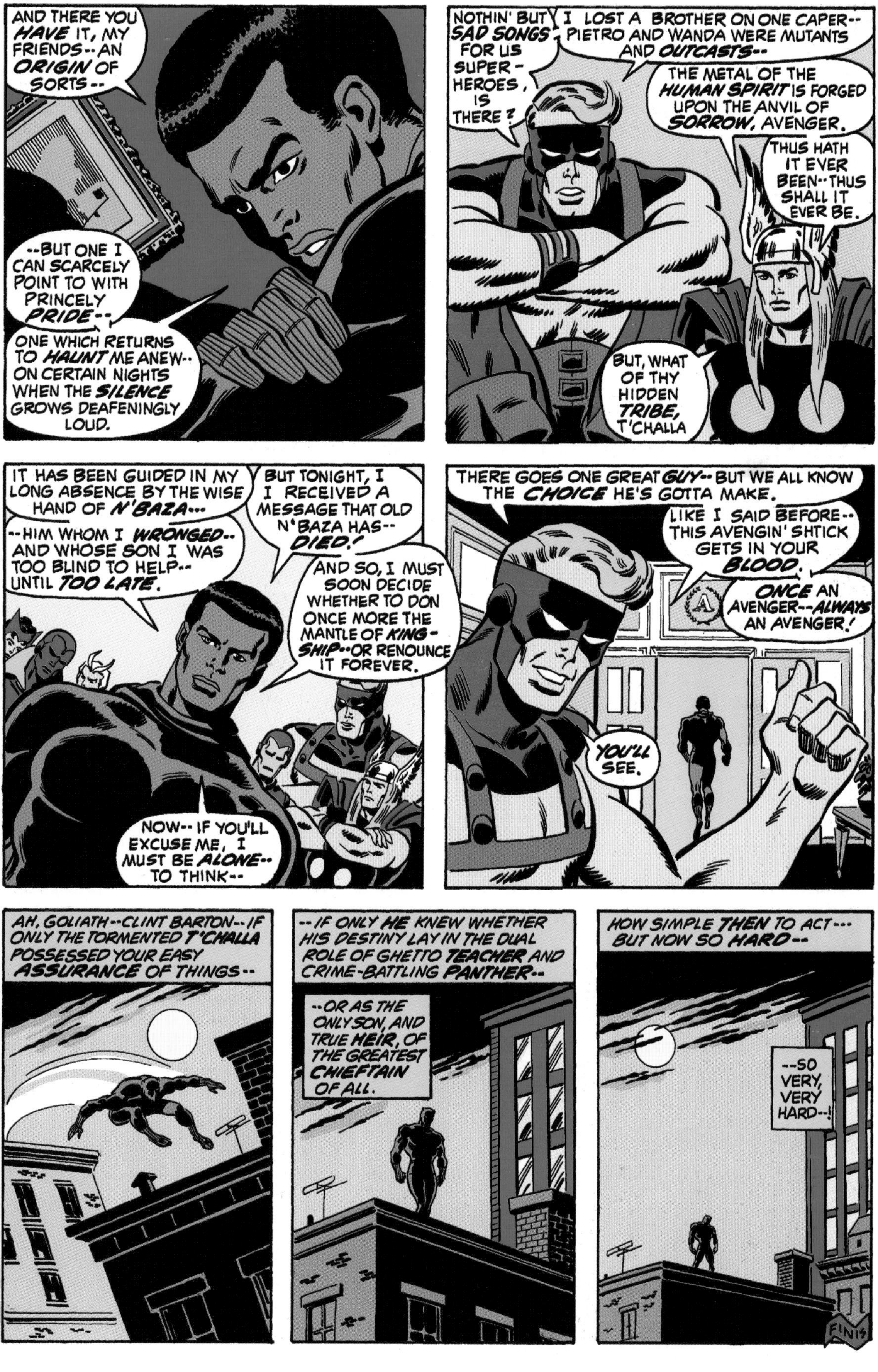
AND THERE YOU HAVE IT, MY FRIENDS--AN ORIGIN OF SORTS--
--BUT ONE I CAN SCARCELY POINT TO WITH PRINCELY PRIDE--
ONE WHICH RETURNS TO HAUNT ME ANEW--ON CERTAIN NIGHTS WHEN THE SILENCE GROWS DEAFENINGLY LOUD.
NOTHIN' BUT SAD SONGS FOR US SUPER-HEROES, IS THERE?
I LOST A BROTHER ON ONE CAPER--PIETRO AND WANDA WERE MUTANTS AND OUTCASTS--
THE METAL OF THE HUMAN SPIRIT IS FORGED UPON THE ANVIL OF SORROW, AVENGER.
THUS HATH IT EVER BEEN--THUS SHALL IT EVER BE.
BUT, WHAT OF THY HIDDEN TRIBE, T'CHALLA
IT HAS BEEN GUIDED IN MY LONG ABSENCE BY THE WISE HAND OF N'BAZA--
--HIM WHOM I WRONGED--AND WHOSE SON I WAS TOO BLIND TO HELP--UNTIL TOO LATE.
BUT TONIGHT, I RECEIVED A MESSAGE THAT OLD N'BAZA HAS--DIED!
AND SO, I MUST SOON DECIDE WHETHER TO DON ONCE MORE THE MANTLE OF KING-SHIP--OR RENOUNCE IT FOREVER.
NOW--IF YOU'LL EXCUSE ME, I MUST BE ALONE--TO THINK--
THERE GOES ONE GREAT GUY--BUT WE ALL KNOW THE CHOICE HE'S GOTTA MAKE.
LIKE I SAID BEFORE--THIS AVENGIN' SHTICK GETS IN YOUR BLOOD.
ONCE AN AVENGER--ALWAYS AN AVENGER!
YOU'LL SEE.
AH, GOLIATH--CLINT BARTON--IF ONLY THE TORMENTED T'CHALLA POSSESSED YOUR EASY ASSURANCE OF THINGS--
--IF ONLY HE KNEW WHETHER HIS DESTINY LAY IN THE DUAL ROLE OF GHETTO TEACHER AND CRIME-BATTLING PANTHER--
--OR AS THE ONLY SON, AND TRUE HEIR, OF THE GREATEST CHIEFTAIN OF ALL.
HOW SIMPLE THEN TO ACT--BUT NOW SO HARD--
--SO VERY, VERY HARD--!
FINIS

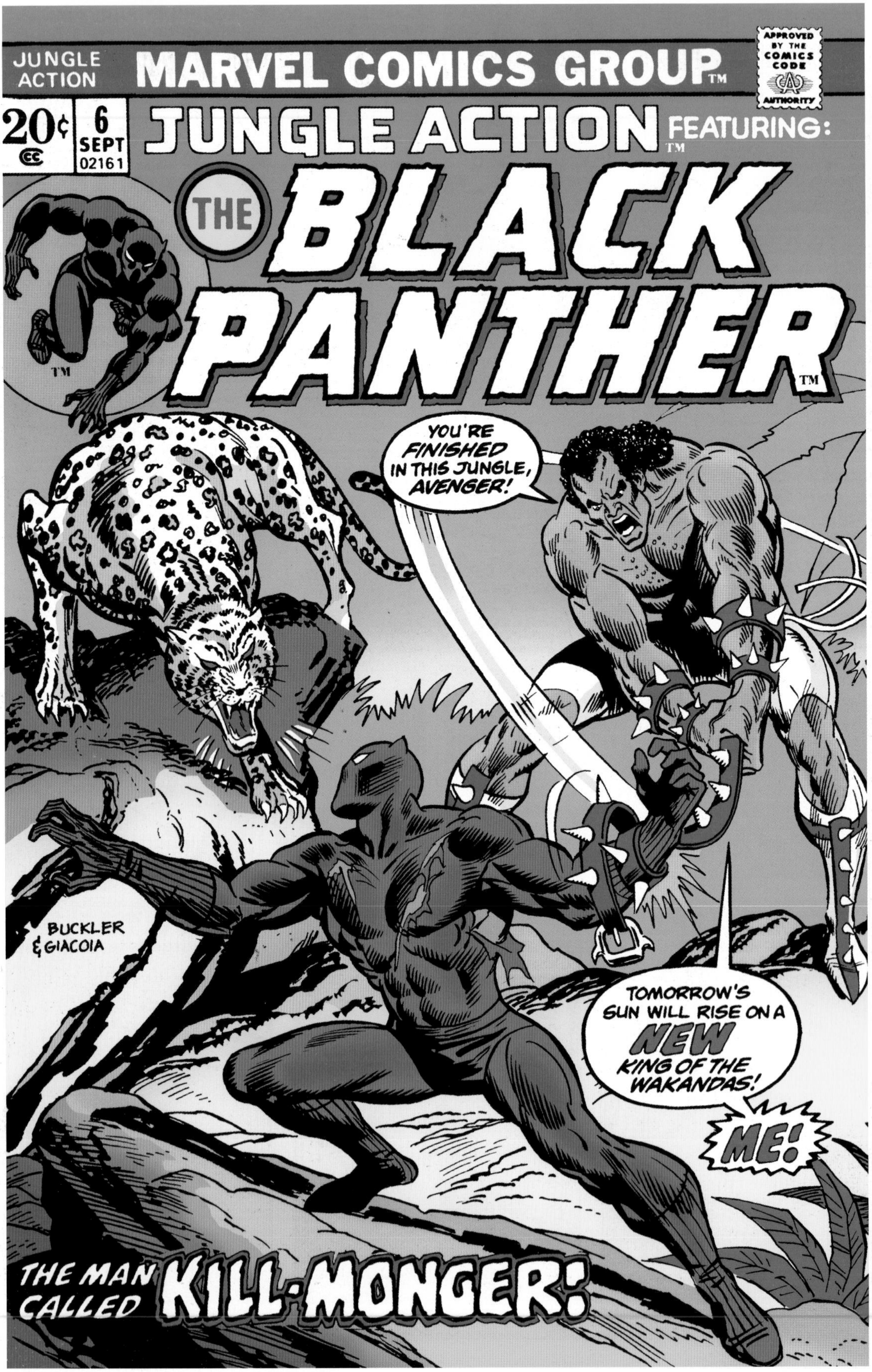
JUNGLE ACTION
MARVEL COMICS GROUP™
APPROVED BY THE COMICS CODE AUTHORITY
20¢
6 SEPT 02161
JUNGLE ACTION FEATURING: ™
THE BLACK PANTHER™
™
YOU'RE FINISHED IN THIS JUNGLE, AVENGER!
BUCKLER & GIACOIA
TOMORROW'S SUN WILL RISE ON A NEW KING OF THE WAKANDAS!
ME!
THE MAN CALLED KILL-MONGER!

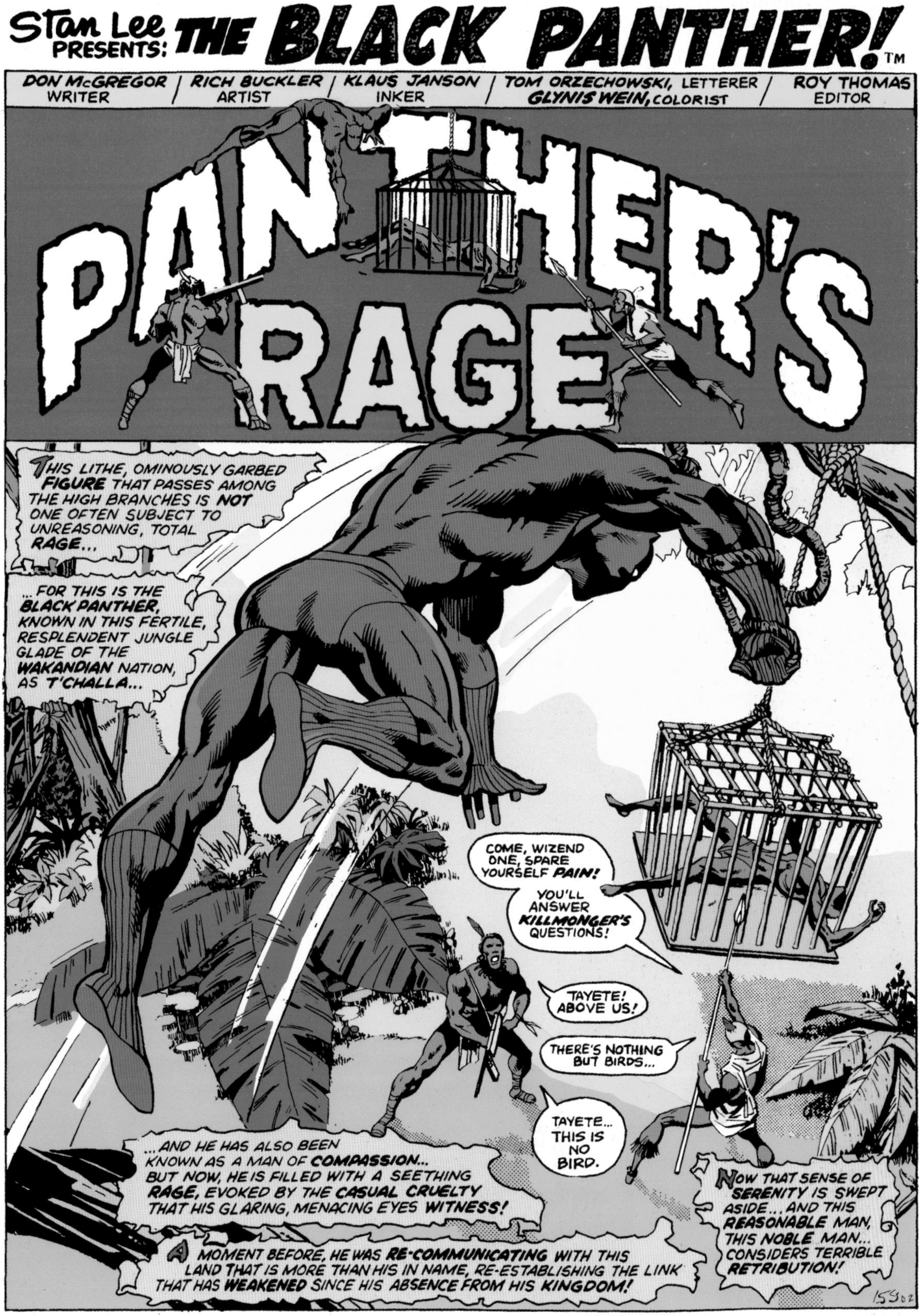

Stan Lee PRESENTS: THE BLACK PANTHER!™
DON McGREGOR WRITER | RICH BUCKLER ARTIST | KLAUS JANSON INKER | TOM ORZECHOWSKI, LETTERER GLYNIS WEIN, COLORIST | ROY THOMAS EDITOR
PANTHER'S RAGE
THIS LITHE, OMINOUSLY GARBED FIGURE THAT PASSES AMONG THE HIGH BRANCHES IS NOT ONE OFTEN SUBJECT TO UNREASONING, TOTAL RAGE...
...FOR THIS IS THE BLACK PANTHER, KNOWN IN THIS FERTILE, RESPLENDENT JUNGLE GLADE OF THE WAKANDIAN NATION, AS T'CHALLA...
COME, WIZEND ONE, SPARE YOURSELF PAIN!
YOU'LL ANSWER KILLMONGER'S QUESTIONS!
TAYETE! ABOVE US!
THERE'S NOTHING BUT BIRDS...
TAYETE... THIS IS NO BIRD.
...AND HE HAS ALSO BEEN KNOWN AS A MAN OF COMPASSION... BUT NOW, HE IS FILLED WITH A SEETHING RAGE, EVOKED BY THE CASUAL CRUELTY THAT HIS GLARING, MENACING EYES WITNESS!
NOW THAT SENSE OF SERENITY IS SWEPT ASIDE... AND THIS REASONABLE MAN, THIS NOBLE MAN... CONSIDERS TERRIBLE RETRIBUTION!
A MOMENT BEFORE, HE WAS RE-COMMUNICATING WITH THIS LAND THAT IS MORE THAN HIS IN NAME, RE-ESTABLISHING THE LINK THAT HAS WEAKENED SINCE HIS ABSENCE FROM HIS KINGDOM!

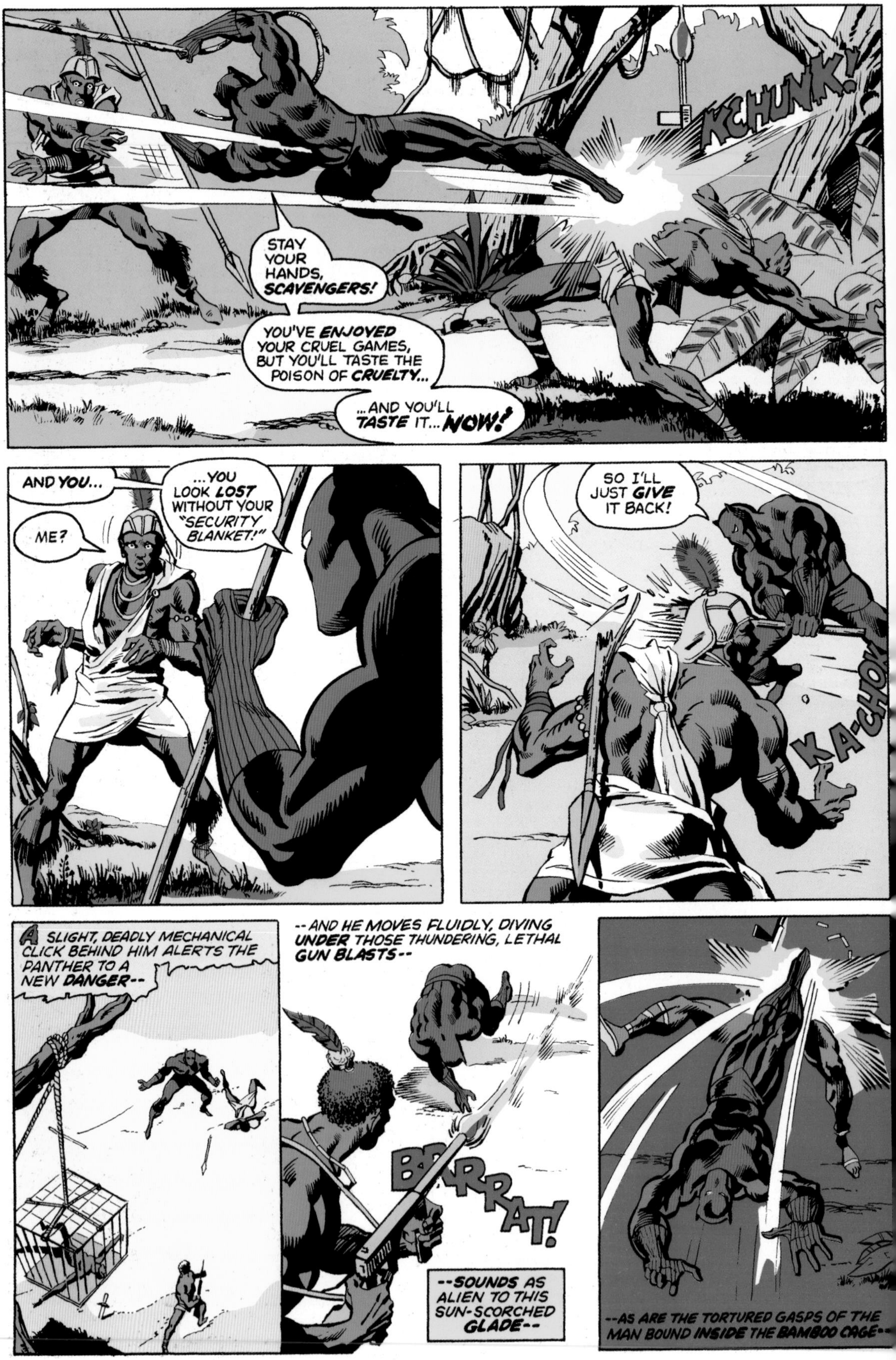

KCHUNK!
STAY YOUR HANDS, SCAVENGERS!
YOU'VE ENJOYED YOUR CRUEL GAMES, BUT YOU'LL TASTE THE POISON OF CRUELTY...
...AND YOU'LL TASTE IT... NOW!
AND YOU...
...YOU LOOK LOST WITHOUT YOUR "SECURITY BLANKET!"
ME?
SO I'LL JUST GIVE IT BACK!
KA-CHOK
A SLIGHT, DEADLY MECHANICAL CLICK BEHIND HIM ALERTS THE PANTHER TO A NEW DANGER--
--AND HE MOVES FLUIDLY, DIVING UNDER THOSE THUNDERING, LETHAL GUN BLASTS--
BRRRAT!
--SOUNDS AS ALIEN TO THIS SUN-SCORCHED GLADE--
--AS ARE THE TORTURED GASPS OF THE MAN BOUND INSIDE THE BAMBOO CAGE--

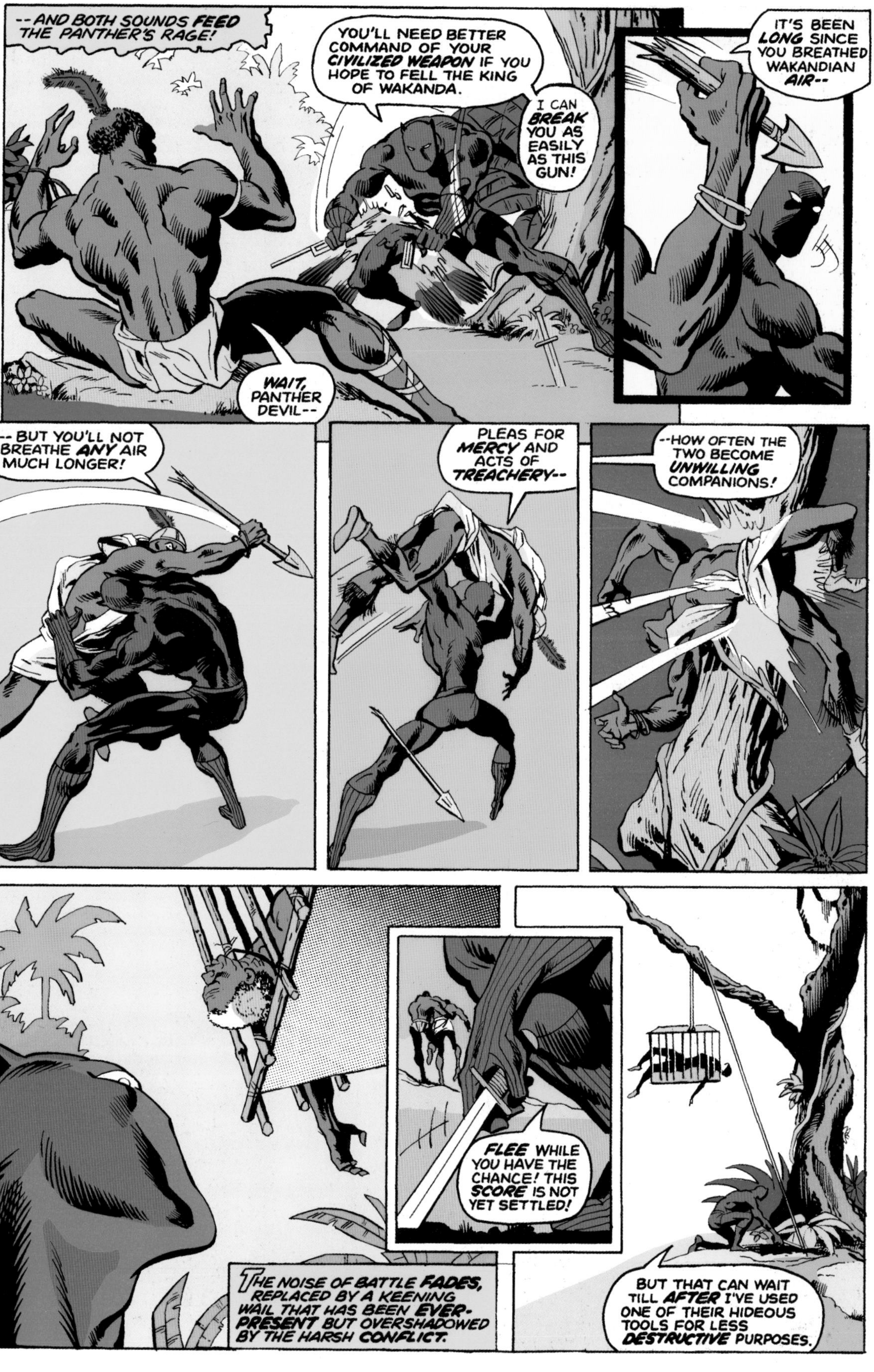
--AND BOTH SOUNDS FEED THE PANTHER'S RAGE!
YOU'LL NEED BETTER COMMAND OF YOUR CIVILIZED WEAPON IF YOU HOPE TO FELL THE KING OF WAKANDA.
I CAN BREAK YOU AS EASILY AS THIS GUN!
WAIT, PANTHER DEVIL--
IT'S BEEN LONG SINCE YOU BREATHED WAKANDIAN AIR--
--BUT YOU'LL NOT BREATHE ANY AIR MUCH LONGER!
PLEAS FOR MERCY AND ACTS OF TREACHERY--
--HOW OFTEN THE TWO BECOME UNWILLING COMPANIONS!
FLEE WHILE YOU HAVE THE CHANCE! THIS SCORE IS NOT YET SETTLED!
THE NOISE OF BATTLE FADES, REPLACED BY A KEENING WAIL THAT HAS BEEN EVER-PRESENT BUT OVERSHADOWED BY THE HARSH CONFLICT.
BUT THAT CAN WAIT TILL AFTER I'VE USED ONE OF THEIR HIDEOUS TOOLS FOR LESS DESTRUCTIVE PURPOSES.

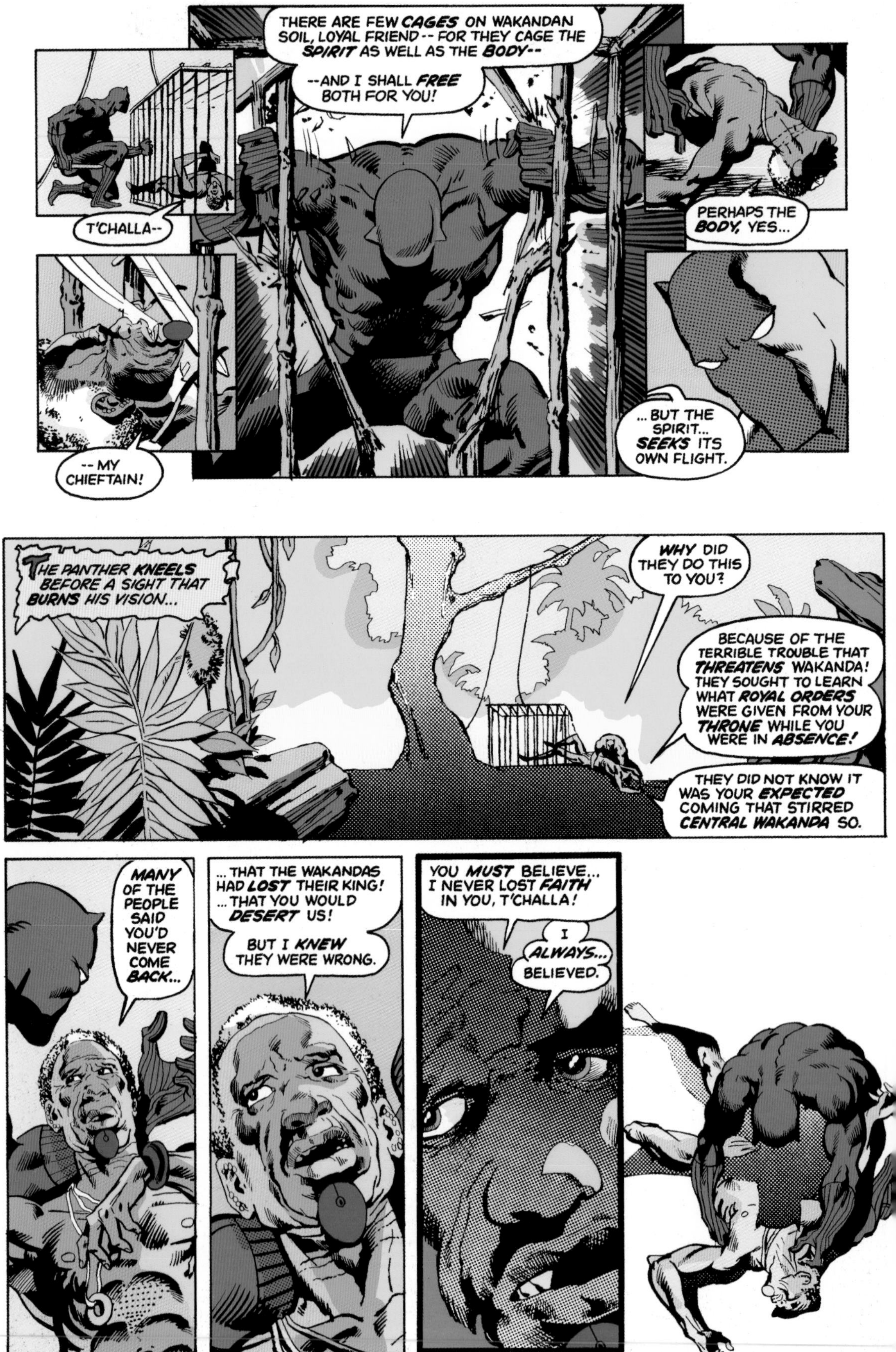
T'CHALLA--
-- MY CHIEFTAIN!
THERE ARE FEW CAGES ON WAKANDAN SOIL, LOYAL FRIEND -- FOR THEY CAGE THE SPIRIT AS WELL AS THE BODY--
--AND I SHALL FREE BOTH FOR YOU!
PERHAPS THE BODY, YES...
... BUT THE SPIRIT... SEEKS ITS OWN FLIGHT.
THE PANTHER KNEELS BEFORE A SIGHT THAT BURNS HIS VISION...
WHY DID THEY DO THIS TO YOU?
BECAUSE OF THE TERRIBLE TROUBLE THAT THREATENS WAKANDA! THEY SOUGHT TO LEARN WHAT ROYAL ORDERS WERE GIVEN FROM YOUR THRONE WHILE YOU WERE IN ABSENCE!
THEY DID NOT KNOW IT WAS YOUR EXPECTED COMING THAT STIRRED CENTRAL WAKANDA SO.
MANY OF THE PEOPLE SAID YOU'D NEVER COME BACK...
... THAT THE WAKANDAS HAD LOST THEIR KING! ... THAT YOU WOULD DESERT US!
BUT I KNEW THEY WERE WRONG.
YOU MUST BELIEVE... I NEVER LOST FAITH IN YOU, T'CHALLA!
I ALWAYS... BELIEVED.

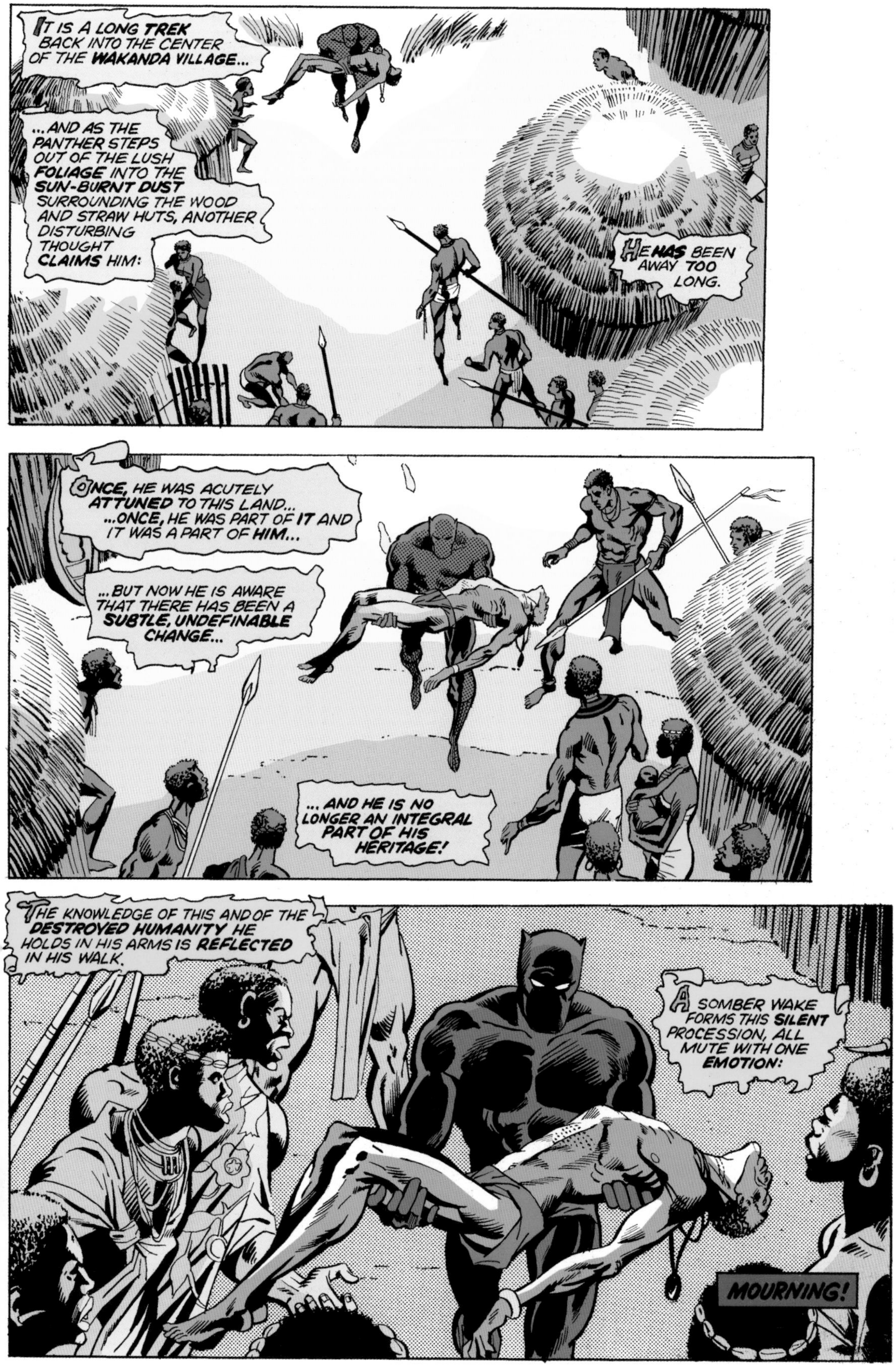
IT IS A LONG TREK BACK INTO THE CENTER OF THE WAKANDA VILLAGE...
...AND AS THE PANTHER STEPS OUT OF THE LUSH FOLIAGE INTO THE SUN-BURNT DUST SURROUNDING THE WOOD AND STRAW HUTS, ANOTHER DISTURBING THOUGHT CLAIMS HIM:
HE HAS BEEN AWAY TOO LONG.
ONCE, HE WAS ACUTELY ATTUNED TO THIS LAND... ...ONCE, HE WAS PART OF IT AND IT WAS A PART OF HIM...
...BUT NOW HE IS AWARE THAT THERE HAS BEEN A SUBTLE, UNDEFINABLE CHANGE...
...AND HE IS NO LONGER AN INTEGRAL PART OF HIS HERITAGE!
THE KNOWLEDGE OF THIS AND OF THE DESTROYED HUMANITY HE HOLDS IN HIS ARMS IS REFLECTED IN HIS WALK.
A SOMBER WAKE FORMS THIS SILENT PROCESSION, ALL MUTE WITH ONE EMOTION:
MOURNING!

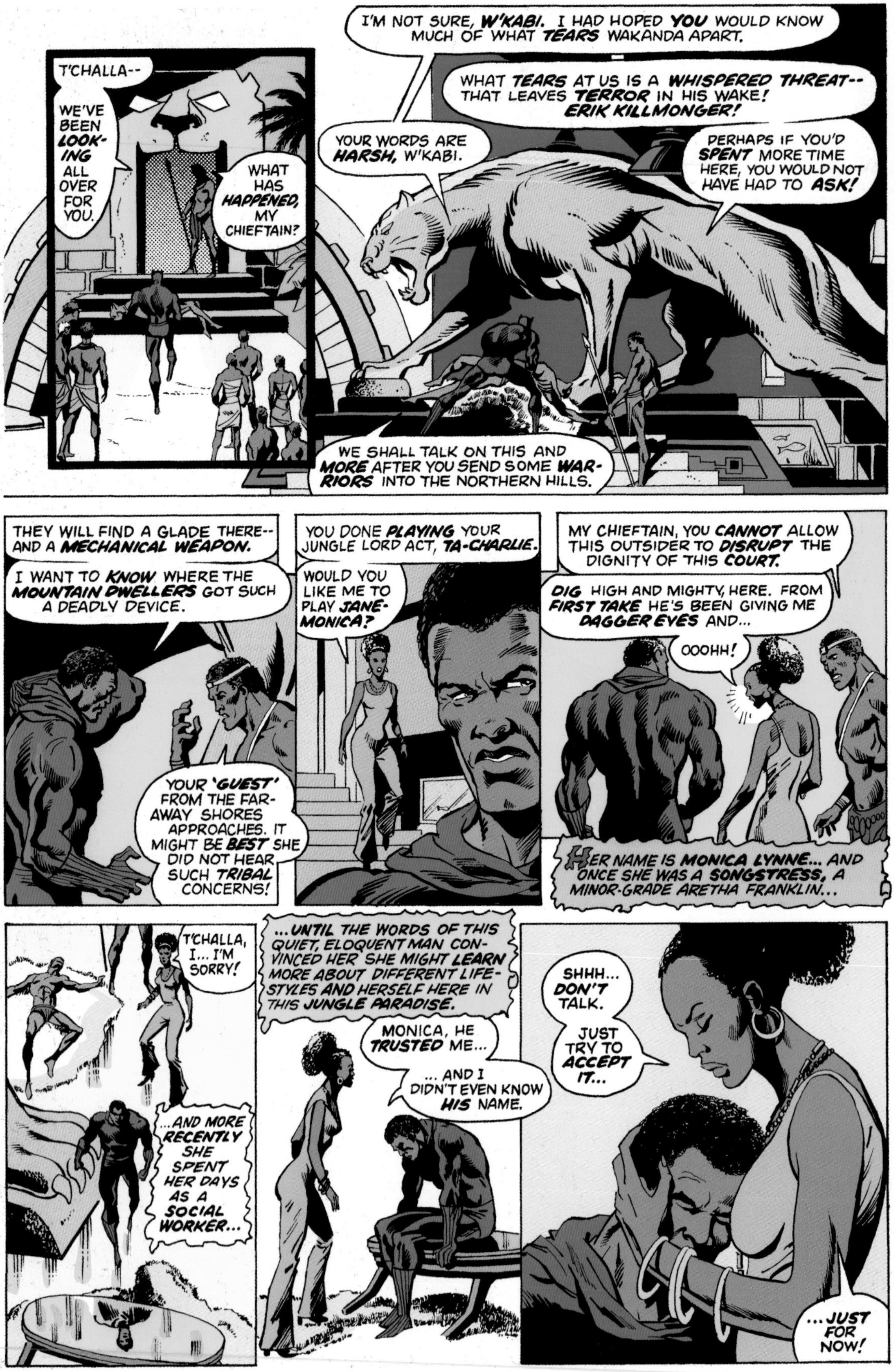
T'CHALLA--
WE'VE BEEN LOOKING ALL OVER FOR YOU.
WHAT HAS HAPPENED, MY CHIEFTAIN?
I'M NOT SURE, W'KABI. I HAD HOPED YOU WOULD KNOW MUCH OF WHAT TEARS WAKANDA APART.
WHAT TEARS AT US IS A WHISPERED THREAT-- THAT LEAVES TERROR IN HIS WAKE! ERIK KILLMONGER!
YOUR WORDS ARE HARSH, W'KABI.
PERHAPS IF YOU'D SPENT MORE TIME HERE, YOU WOULD NOT HAVE HAD TO ASK!
WE SHALL TALK ON THIS AND MORE AFTER YOU SEND SOME WARRIORS INTO THE NORTHERN HILLS.
THEY WILL FIND A GLADE THERE-- AND A MECHANICAL WEAPON.
I WANT TO KNOW WHERE THE MOUNTAIN DWELLERS GOT SUCH A DEADLY DEVICE.
YOUR 'GUEST' FROM THE FAR-AWAY SHORES APPROACHES. IT MIGHT BE BEST SHE DID NOT HEAR SUCH TRIBAL CONCERNS!
YOU DONE PLAYING YOUR JUNGLE LORD ACT, TA-CHARLIE.
WOULD YOU LIKE ME TO PLAY JANE-MONICA?
MY CHIEFTAIN, YOU CANNOT ALLOW THIS OUTSIDER TO DISRUPT THE DIGNITY OF THIS COURT.
DIG HIGH AND MIGHTY, HERE. FROM FIRST TAKE HE'S BEEN GIVING ME DAGGER EYES AND...
OOOHH!
HER NAME IS MONICA LYNNE... AND ONCE SHE WAS A SONGSTRESS, A MINOR-GRADE ARETHA FRANKLIN...
T'CHALLA, I... I'M SORRY!
...AND MORE RECENTLY SHE SPENT HER DAYS AS A SOCIAL WORKER...
...UNTIL THE WORDS OF THIS QUIET, ELOQUENT MAN CONVINCED HER SHE MIGHT LEARN MORE ABOUT DIFFERENT LIFE-STYLES AND HERSELF HERE IN THIS JUNGLE PARADISE.
MONICA, HE TRUSTED ME...
... AND I DIDN'T EVEN KNOW HIS NAME.
SHHH... DON'T TALK.
JUST TRY TO ACCEPT IT...
...JUST FOR NOW!

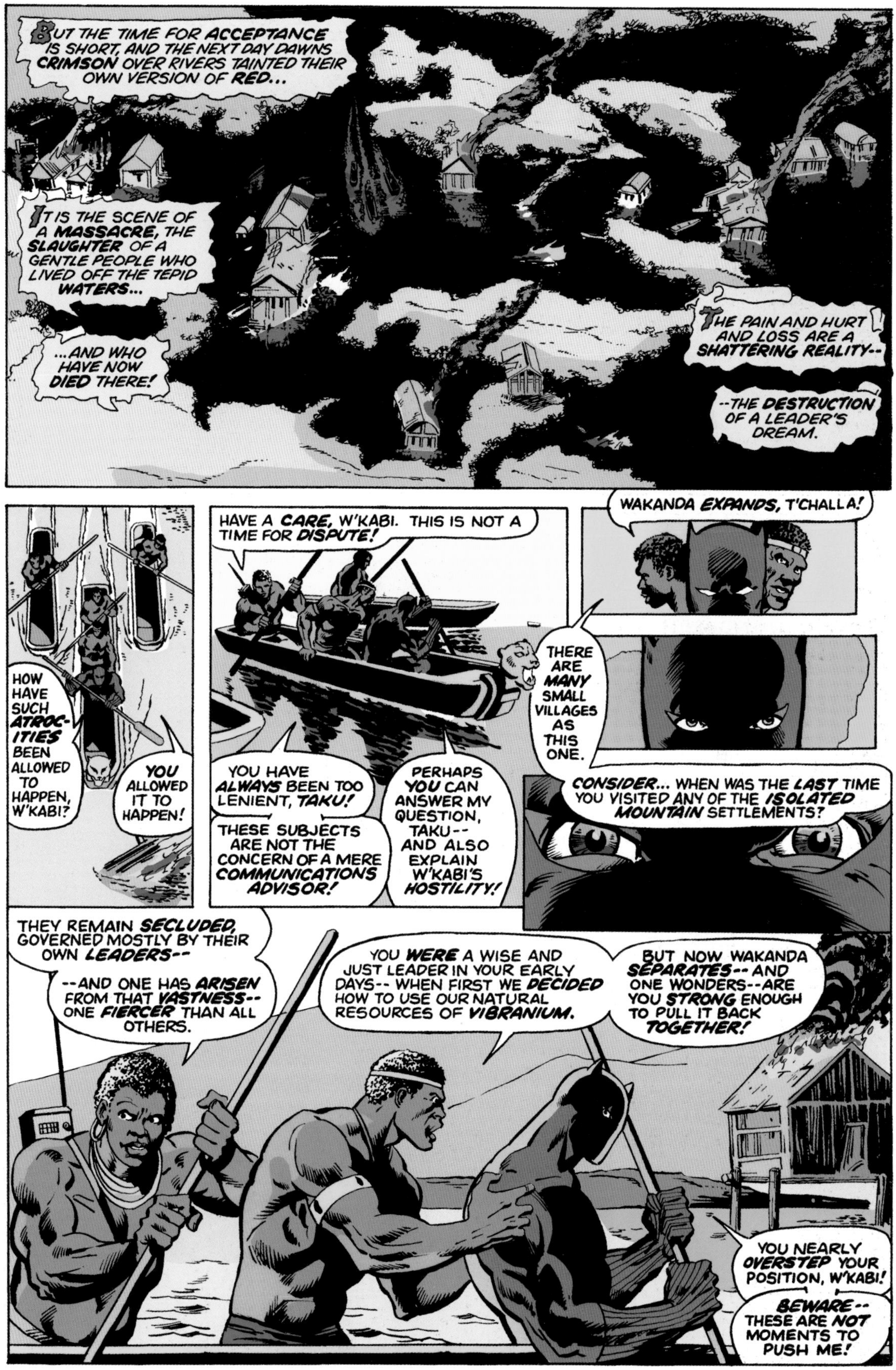
BUT THE TIME FOR ACCEPTANCE IS SHORT, AND THE NEXT DAY DAWNS CRIMSON OVER RIVERS TAINTED THEIR OWN VERSION OF RED...
IT IS THE SCENE OF A MASSACRE, THE SLAUGHTER OF A GENTLE PEOPLE WHO LIVED OFF THE TEPID WATERS...
...AND WHO HAVE NOW DIED THERE!
THE PAIN AND HURT AND LOSS ARE A SHATTERING REALITY--
--THE DESTRUCTION OF A LEADER'S DREAM.
HOW HAVE SUCH ATROC-ITIES BEEN ALLOWED TO HAPPEN, W'KABI?
YOU ALLOWED IT TO HAPPEN!
HAVE A CARE, W'KABI. THIS IS NOT A TIME FOR DISPUTE!
YOU HAVE ALWAYS BEEN TOO LENIENT, TAKU!
THESE SUBJECTS ARE NOT THE CONCERN OF A MERE COMMUNICATIONS ADVISOR!
PERHAPS YOU CAN ANSWER MY QUESTION, TAKU-- AND ALSO EXPLAIN W'KABI'S HOSTILITY!
WAKANDA EXPANDS, T'CHALLA!
THERE ARE MANY SMALL VILLAGES AS THIS ONE.
CONSIDER... WHEN WAS THE LAST TIME YOU VISITED ANY OF THE ISOLATED MOUNTAIN SETTLEMENTS?
THEY REMAIN SECLUDED, GOVERNED MOSTLY BY THEIR OWN LEADERS--
--AND ONE HAS ARISEN FROM THAT VASTNESS-- ONE FIERCER THAN ALL OTHERS.
YOU WERE A WISE AND JUST LEADER IN YOUR EARLY DAYS-- WHEN FIRST WE DECIDED HOW TO USE OUR NATURAL RESOURCES OF VIBRANIUM.
BUT NOW WAKANDA SEPARATES-- AND ONE WONDERS--ARE YOU STRONG ENOUGH TO PULL IT BACK TOGETHER!
YOU NEARLY OVERSTEP YOUR POSITION, W'KABI!
BEWARE-- THESE ARE NOT MOMENTS TO PUSH ME!

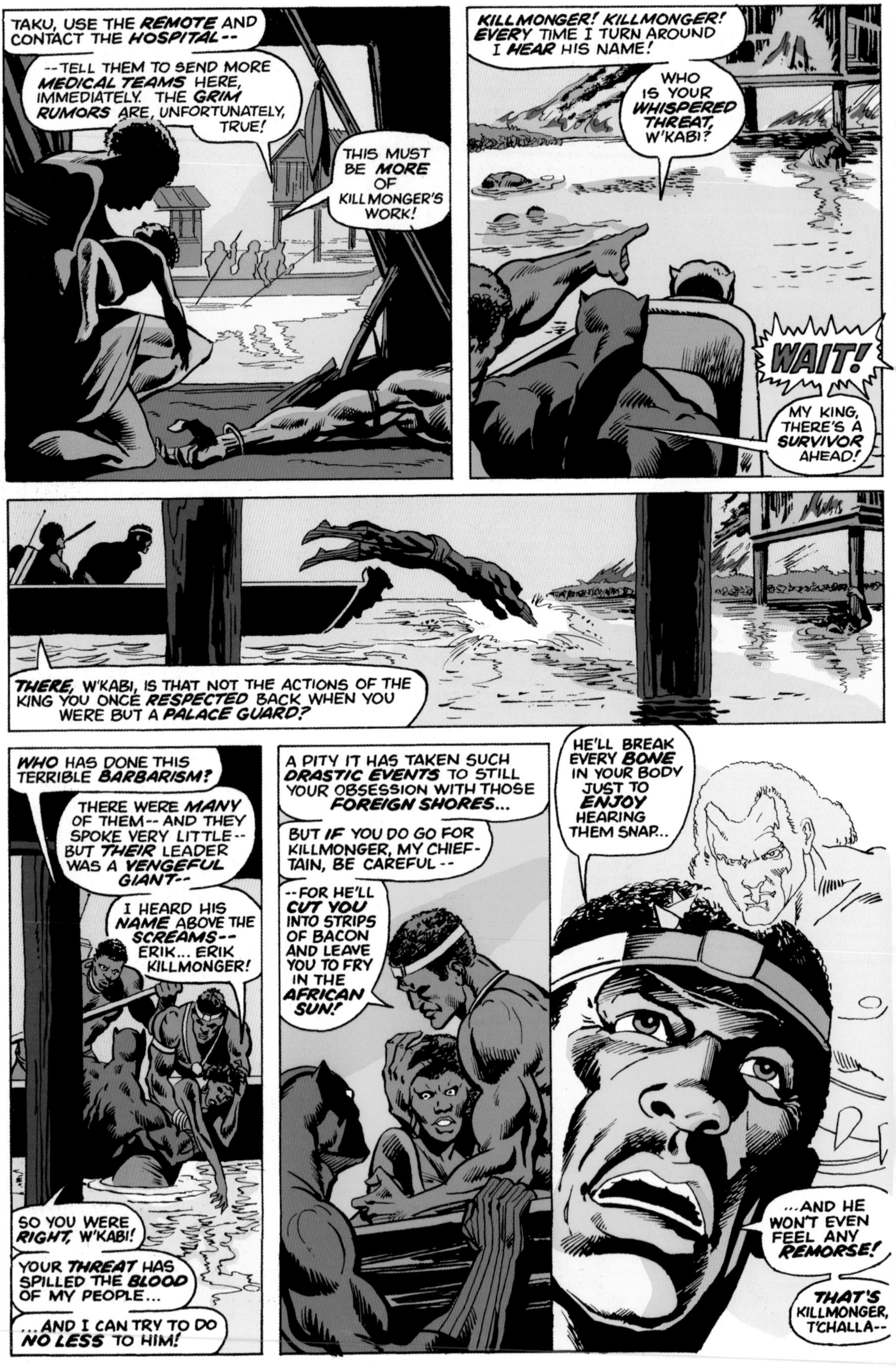

TAKU, USE THE REMOTE AND CONTACT THE HOSPITAL--
--TELL THEM TO SEND MORE MEDICAL TEAMS HERE, IMMEDIATELY. THE GRIM RUMORS ARE, UNFORTUNATELY, TRUE!
THIS MUST BE MORE OF KILLMONGER'S WORK!
KILLMONGER! KILLMONGER! EVERY TIME I TURN AROUND I HEAR HIS NAME!
WHO IS YOUR WHISPERED THREAT, W'KABI?
WAIT!
MY KING, THERE'S A SURVIVOR AHEAD!
THERE, W'KABI, IS THAT NOT THE ACTIONS OF THE KING YOU ONCE RESPECTED BACK WHEN YOU WERE BUT A PALACE GUARD?
WHO HAS DONE THIS TERRIBLE BARBARISM?
THERE WERE MANY OF THEM-- AND THEY SPOKE VERY LITTLE-- BUT THEIR LEADER WAS A VENGEFUL GIANT--
I HEARD HIS NAME ABOVE THE SCREAMS-- ERIK... ERIK KILLMONGER!
SO YOU WERE RIGHT, W'KABI!
YOUR THREAT HAS SPILLED THE BLOOD OF MY PEOPLE...
...AND I CAN TRY TO DO NO LESS TO HIM!
A PITY IT HAS TAKEN SUCH DRASTIC EVENTS TO STILL YOUR OBSESSION WITH THOSE FOREIGN SHORES...
BUT IF YOU DO GO FOR KILLMONGER, MY CHIEFTAIN, BE CAREFUL--
--FOR HE'LL CUT YOU INTO STRIPS OF BACON AND LEAVE YOU TO FRY IN THE AFRICAN SUN!
HE'LL BREAK EVERY BONE IN YOUR BODY JUST TO ENJOY HEARING THEM SNAP...
...AND HE WON'T EVEN FEEL ANY REMORSE!
THAT'S KILLMONGER, T'CHALLA--

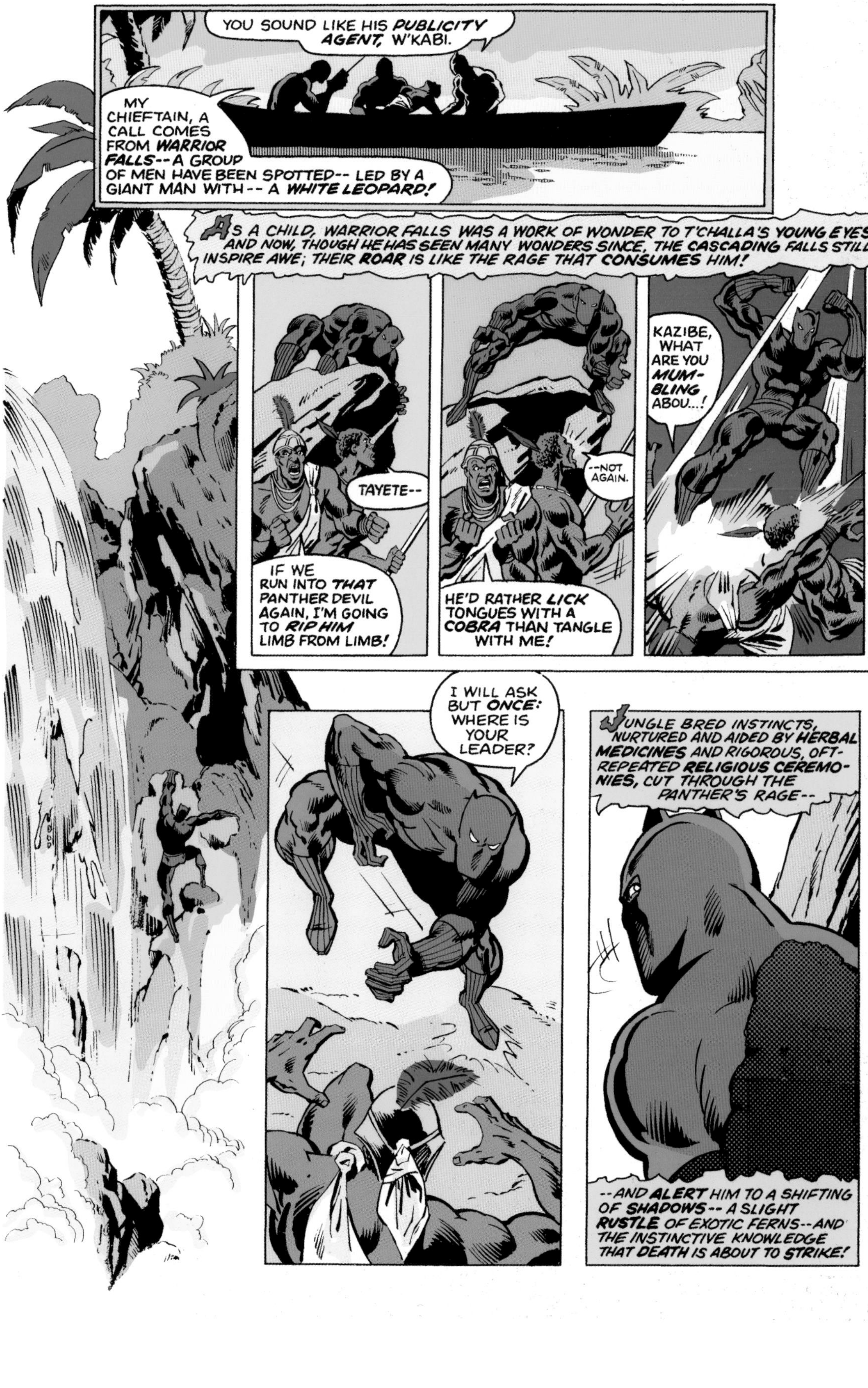
YOU SOUND LIKE HIS PUBLICITY AGENT, W'KABI.
MY CHIEFTAIN, A CALL COMES FROM WARRIOR FALLS-- A GROUP OF MEN HAVE BEEN SPOTTED-- LED BY A GIANT MAN WITH -- A WHITE LEOPARD!
AS A CHILD, WARRIOR FALLS WAS A WORK OF WONDER TO T'CHALLA'S YOUNG EYES-- AND NOW, THOUGH HE HAS SEEN MANY WONDERS SINCE, THE CASCADING FALLS STILL INSPIRE AWE; THEIR ROAR IS LIKE THE RAGE THAT CONSUMES HIM!
TAYETE--
IF WE RUN INTO THAT PANTHER DEVIL AGAIN, I'M GOING TO RIP HIM LIMB FROM LIMB!
--NOT AGAIN.
HE'D RATHER LICK TONGUES WITH A COBRA THAN TANGLE WITH ME!
KAZIBE, WHAT ARE YOU MUM-BLING ABOU...!
I WILL ASK BUT ONCE: WHERE IS YOUR LEADER?
JUNGLE BRED INSTINCTS, NURTURED AND AIDED BY HERBAL MEDICINES AND RIGOROUS, OFT-REPEATED RELIGIOUS CEREMO-NIES, CUT THROUGH THE PANTHER'S RAGE--
--AND ALERT HIM TO A SHIFTING OF SHADOWS-- A SLIGHT RUSTLE OF EXOTIC FERNS--AND THE INSTINCTIVE KNOWLEDGE THAT DEATH IS ABOUT TO STRIKE!

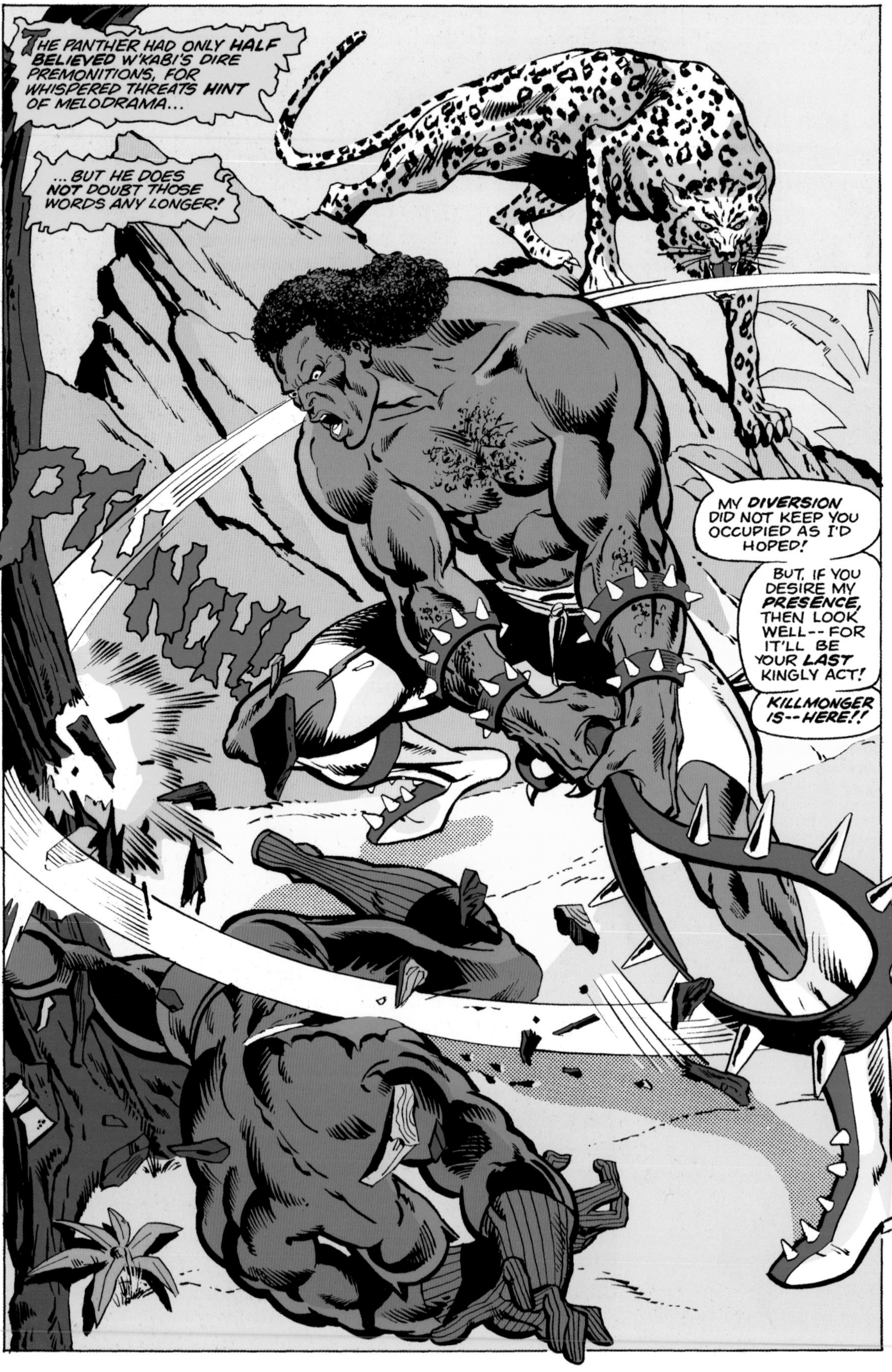

THE PANTHER HAD ONLY HALF BELIEVED W'KABI'S DIRE PREMONITIONS, FOR WHISPERED THREATS HINT OF MELODRAMA...
...BUT HE DOES NOT DOUBT THOSE WORDS ANY LONGER!
PTANCH!
MY DIVERSION DID NOT KEEP YOU OCCUPIED AS I'D HOPED!
BUT, IF YOU DESIRE MY PRESENCE, THEN LOOK WELL--FOR IT'LL BE YOUR LAST KINGLY ACT!
KILLMONGER IS--HERE!!

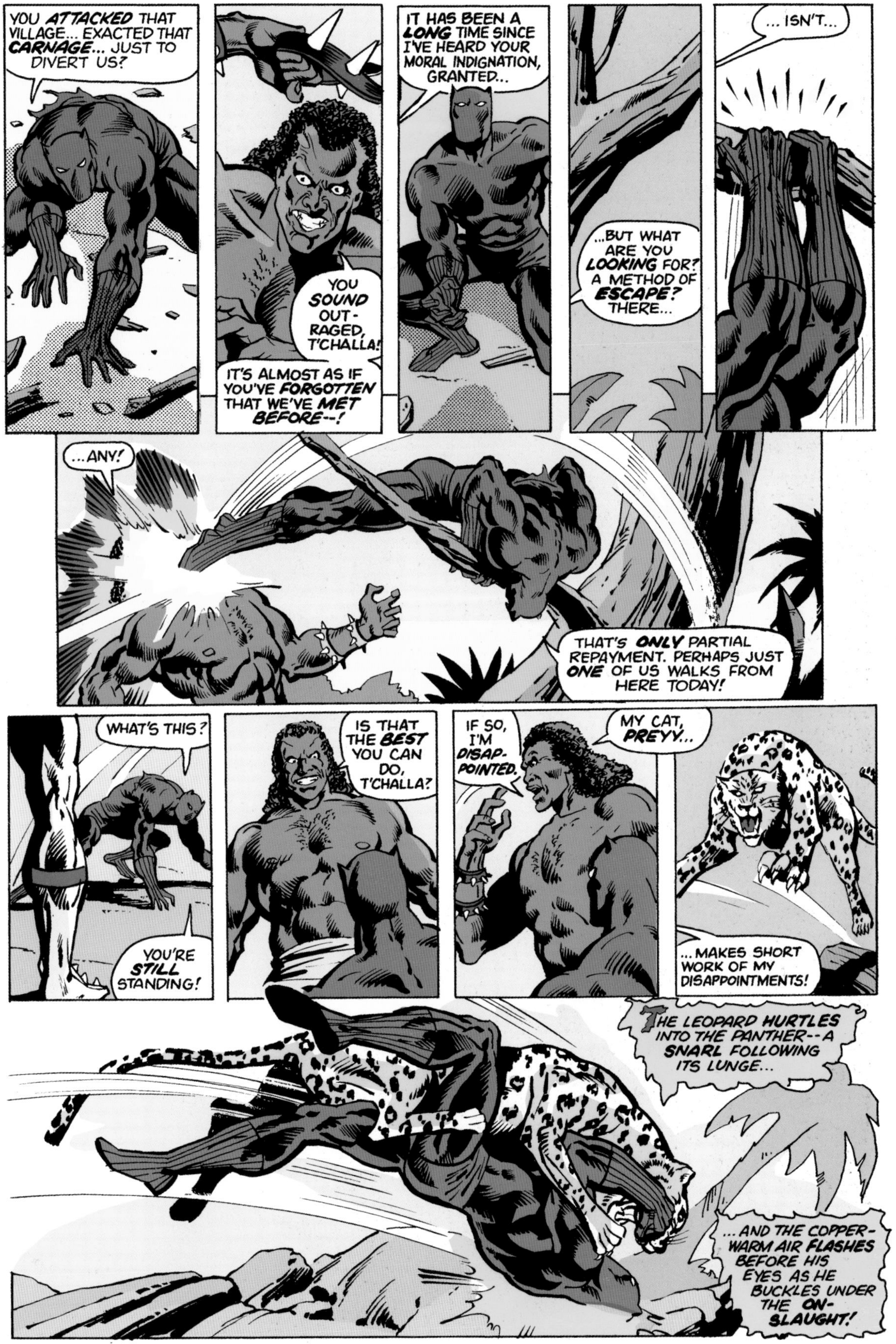
YOU ATTACKED THAT VILLAGE... EXACTED THAT CARNAGE... JUST TO DIVERT US?
YOU SOUND OUT-RAGED, T'CHALLA!
IT'S ALMOST AS IF YOU'VE FORGOTTEN THAT WE'VE MET BEFORE--!
IT HAS BEEN A LONG TIME SINCE I'VE HEARD YOUR MORAL INDIGNATION, GRANTED...
...BUT WHAT ARE YOU LOOKING FOR? A METHOD OF ESCAPE? THERE...
... ISN'T...
...ANY!
THAT'S ONLY PARTIAL REPAYMENT. PERHAPS JUST ONE OF US WALKS FROM HERE TODAY!
WHAT'S THIS?
YOU'RE STILL STANDING!
IS THAT THE BEST YOU CAN DO, T'CHALLA?
IF SO, I'M DISAP-POINTED.
MY CAT, PREYY...
...MAKES SHORT WORK OF MY DISAPPOINTMENTS!
THE LEOPARD HURTLES INTO THE PANTHER--A SNARL FOLLOWING ITS LUNGE...
...AND THE COPPER-WARM AIR FLASHES BEFORE HIS EYES AS HE BUCKLES UNDER THE ON-SLAUGHT!

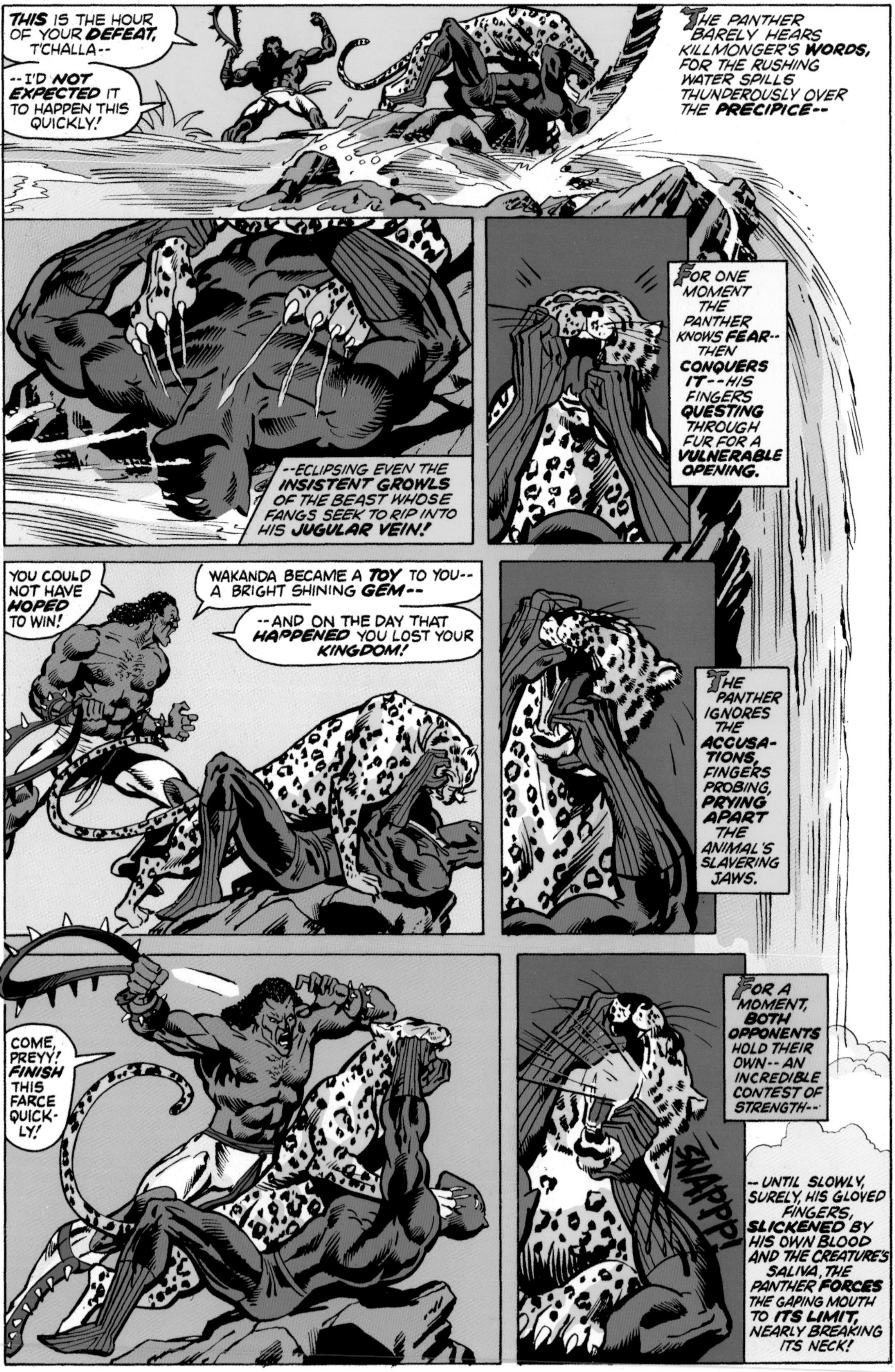
THIS IS THE HOUR OF YOUR DEFEAT, T'CHALLA--
--I'D NOT EXPECTED IT TO HAPPEN THIS QUICKLY!
THE PANTHER BARELY HEARS KILLMONGER'S WORDS, FOR THE RUSHING WATER SPILLS THUNDEROUSLY OVER THE PRECIPICE--
--ECLIPSING EVEN THE INSISTENT GROWLS OF THE BEAST WHOSE FANGS SEEK TO RIP INTO HIS JUGULAR VEIN!
FOR ONE MOMENT THE PANTHER KNOWS FEAR-- THEN CONQUERS IT--HIS FINGERS QUESTING THROUGH FUR FOR A VULNERABLE OPENING.
YOU COULD NOT HAVE HOPED TO WIN!
WAKANDA BECAME A TOY TO YOU-- A BRIGHT SHINING GEM--
--AND ON THE DAY THAT HAPPENED YOU LOST YOUR KINGDOM!
THE PANTHER IGNORES THE ACCUSATIONS, FINGERS PROBING, PRYING APART THE ANIMAL'S SLAVERING JAWS.
COME, PREYY! FINISH THIS FARCE QUICKLY!
FOR A MOMENT, BOTH OPPONENTS HOLD THEIR OWN-- AN INCREDIBLE CONTEST OF STRENGTH--
SNAPPP!
--UNTIL SLOWLY, SURELY, HIS GLOVED FINGERS, SLICKENED BY HIS OWN BLOOD AND THE CREATURE'S SALIVA, THE PANTHER FORCES THE GAPING MOUTH TO ITS LIMIT, NEARLY BREAKING ITS NECK!

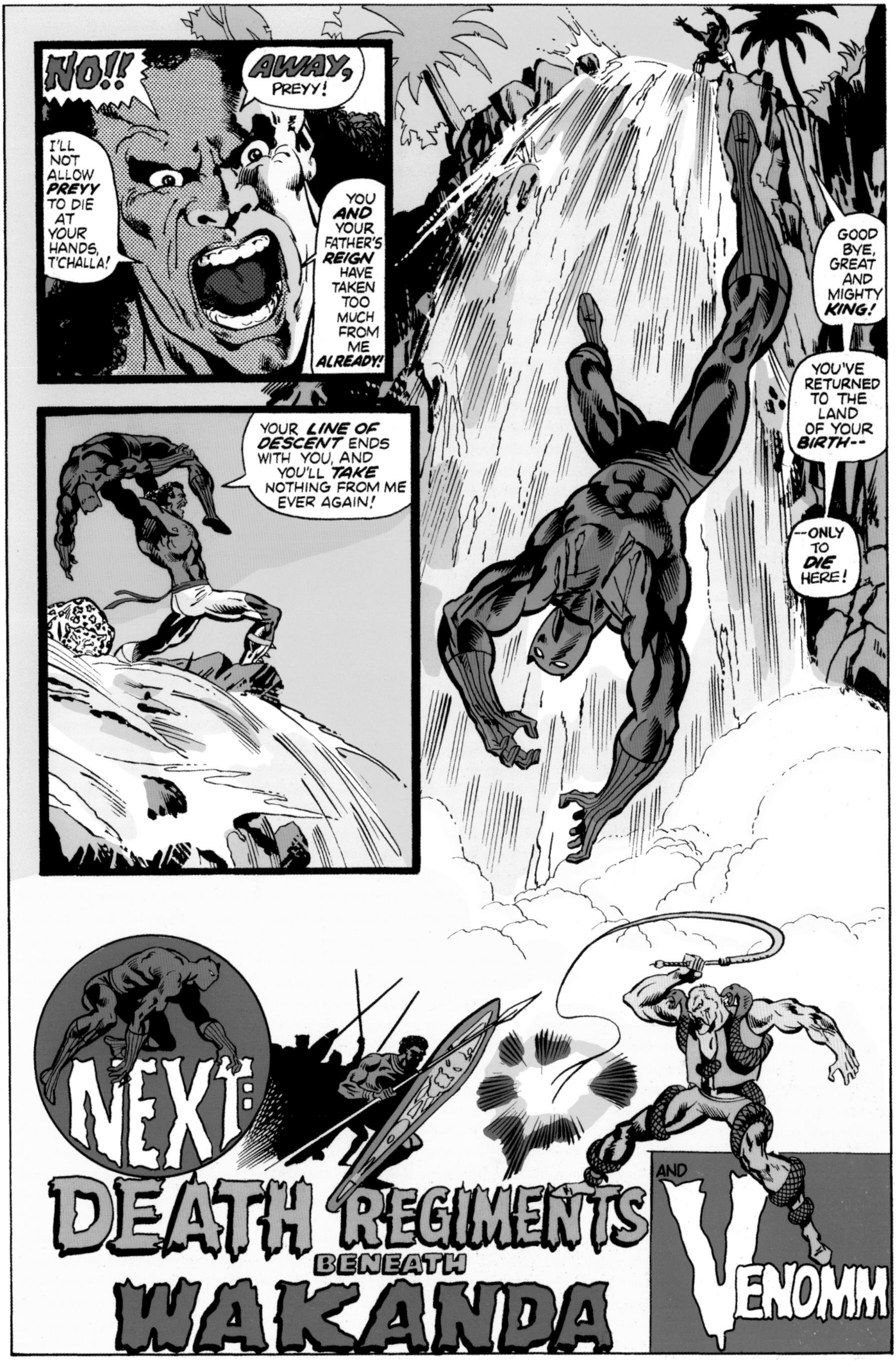
NO!!
AWAY, PREYY!
I'LL NOT ALLOW PREYY TO DIE AT YOUR HANDS, T'CHALLA!
YOU AND YOUR FATHER'S REIGN HAVE TAKEN TOO MUCH FROM ME ALREADY!
YOUR LINE OF DESCENT ENDS WITH YOU, AND YOU'LL TAKE NOTHING FROM ME EVER AGAIN!
GOOD BYE, GREAT AND MIGHTY KING!
YOU'VE RETURNED TO THE LAND OF YOUR BIRTH--
--ONLY TO DIE HERE!
NEXT:
DEATH REGIMENTS BENEATH WAKANDA
AND VENOMM

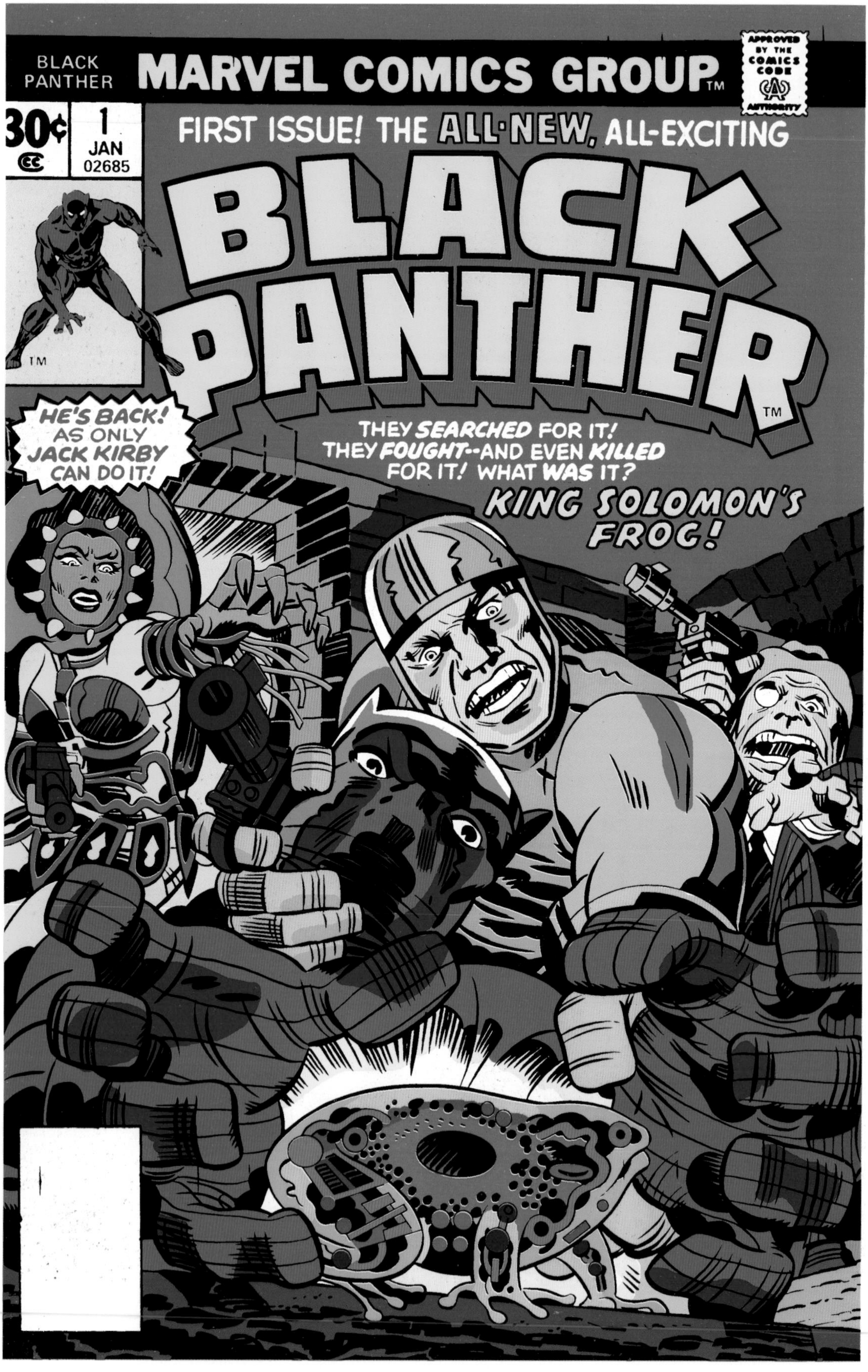
BLACK PANTHER
MARVEL COMICS GROUP
APPROVED BY THE COMICS CODE AUTHORITY
30¢
1 JAN 02685
FIRST ISSUE! THE ALL-NEW, ALL-EXCITING
BLACK PANTHER
HE'S BACK! AS ONLY JACK KIRBY CAN DO IT!
THEY SEARCHED FOR IT! THEY FOUGHT--AND EVEN KILLED FOR IT! WHAT WAS IT?
KING SOLOMON'S FROG!

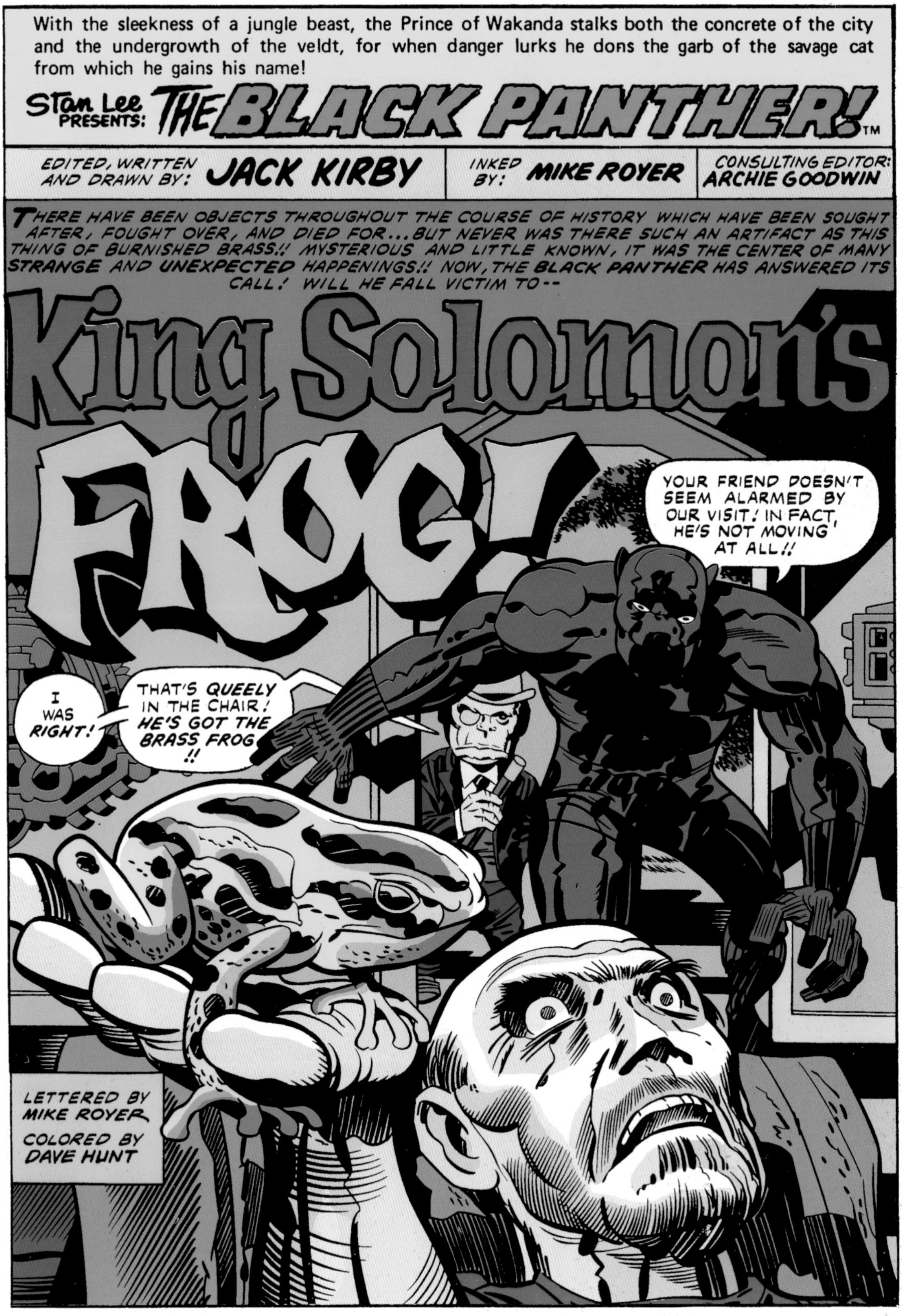

With the sleekness of a jungle beast, the Prince of Wakanda stalks both the concrete of the city and the undergrowth of the veldt, for when danger lurks he dons the garb of the savage cat from which he gains his name!
STAN LEE PRESENTS: THE BLACK PANTHER! TM
EDITED, WRITTEN AND DRAWN BY: JACK KIRBY
INKED BY: MIKE ROYER
CONSULTING EDITOR: ARCHIE GOODWIN
THERE HAVE BEEN OBJECTS THROUGHOUT THE COURSE OF HISTORY WHICH HAVE BEEN SOUGHT AFTER, FOUGHT OVER, AND DIED FOR... BUT NEVER WAS THERE SUCH AN ARTIFACT AS THIS THING OF BURNISHED BRASS!! MYSTERIOUS AND LITTLE KNOWN, IT WAS THE CENTER OF MANY STRANGE AND UNEXPECTED HAPPENINGS!! NOW, THE BLACK PANTHER HAS ANSWERED ITS CALL! WILL HE FALL VICTIM TO--
King Solomon's FROG!
YOUR FRIEND DOESN'T SEEM ALARMED BY OUR VISIT! IN FACT, HE'S NOT MOVING AT ALL!!
I WAS RIGHT!
THAT'S QUEELY IN THE CHAIR! HE'S GOT THE BRASS FROG!!
LETTERED BY MIKE ROYER
COLORED BY DAVE HUNT

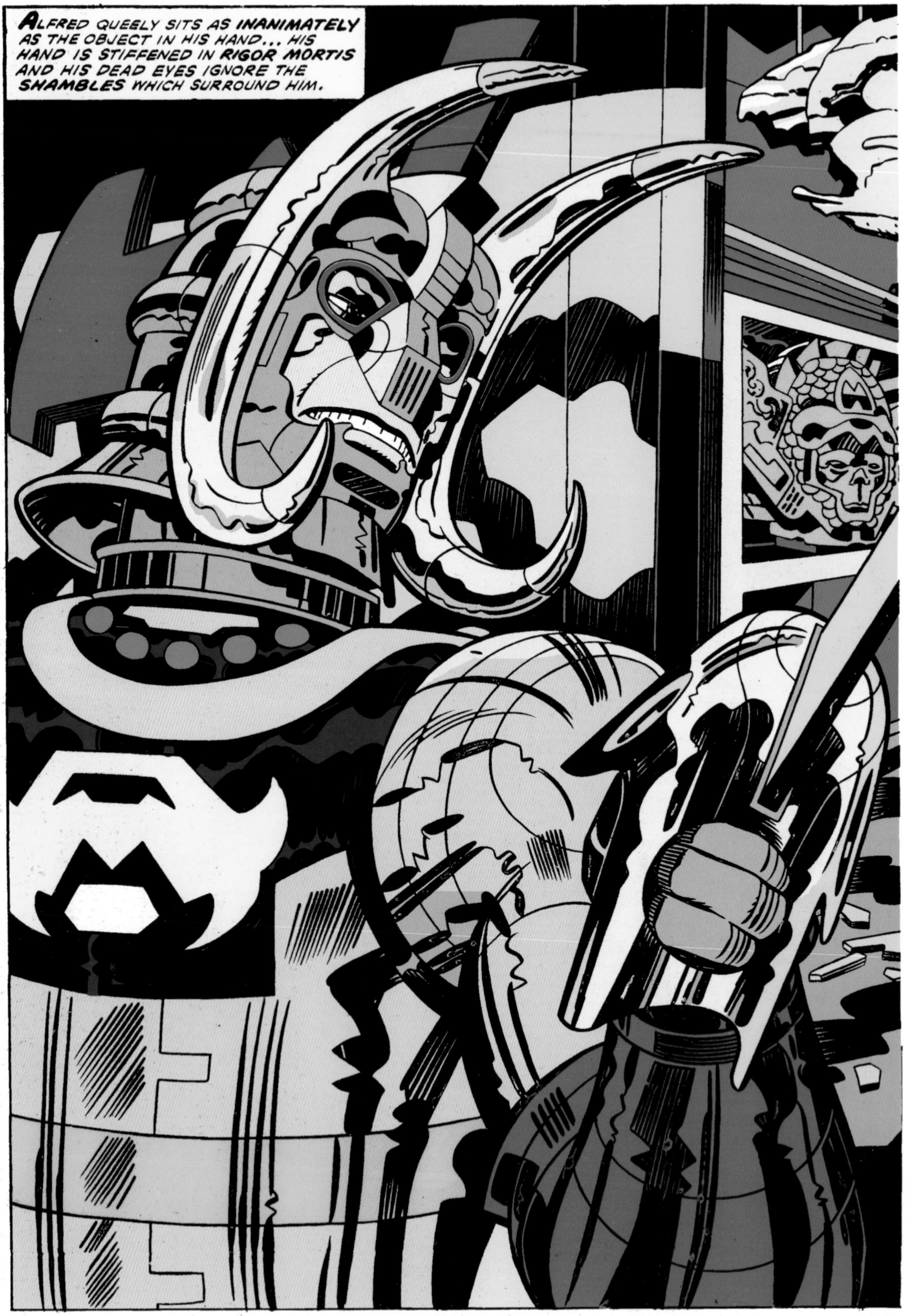
ALFRED QUEELY SITS AS INANIMATELY AS THE OBJECT IN HIS HAND... HIS HAND IS STIFFENED IN RIGOR MORTIS AND HIS DEAD EYES IGNORE THE SHAMBLES WHICH SURROUND HIM.

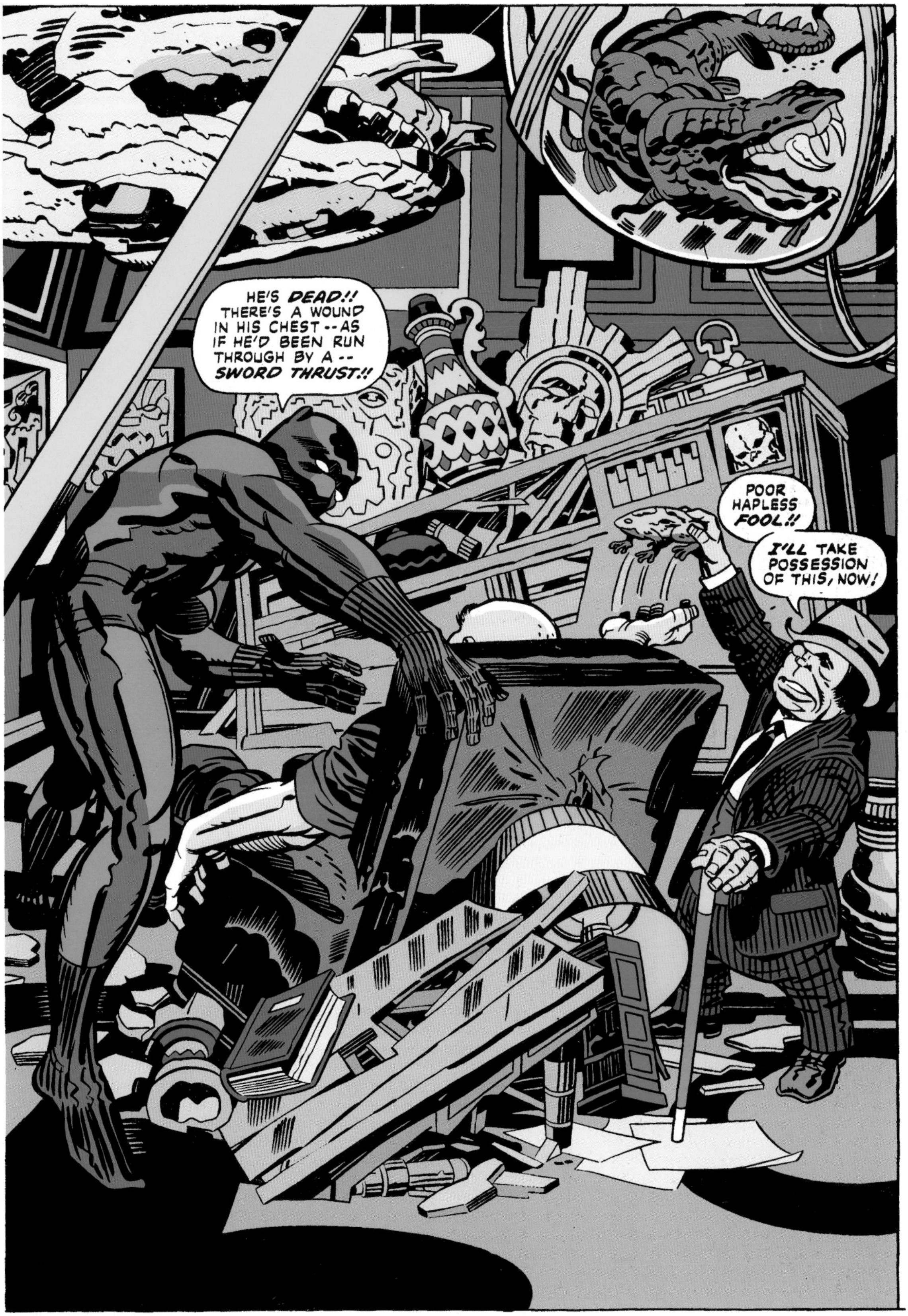
HE'S DEAD!! THERE'S A WOUND IN HIS CHEST--AS IF HE'D BEEN RUN THROUGH BY A--SWORD THRUST!!
POOR HAPLESS FOOL!!
I'LL TAKE POSSESSION OF THIS, NOW!

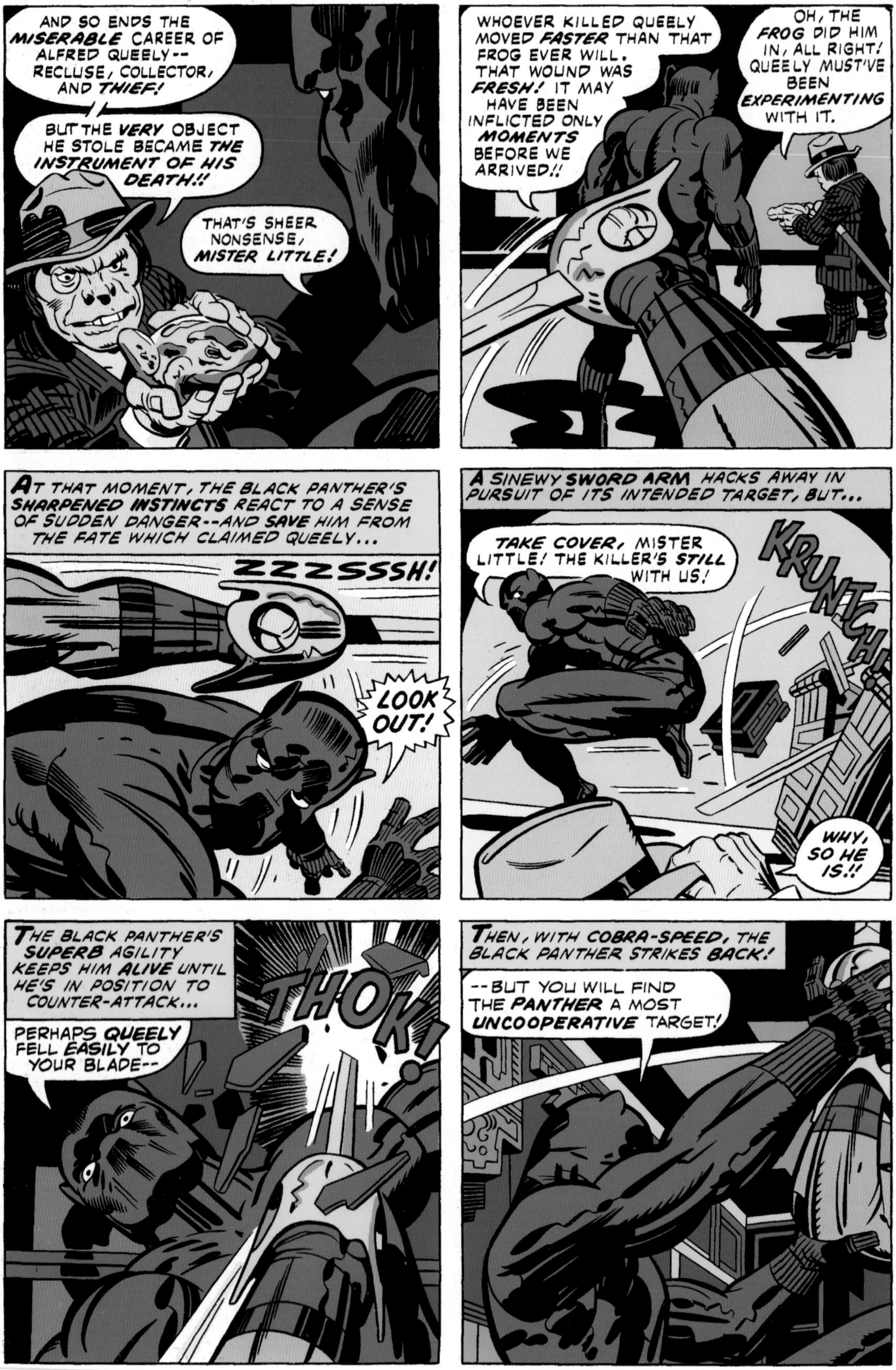
AND SO ENDS THE MISERABLE CAREER OF ALFRED QUEELY-- RECLUSE, COLLECTOR, AND THIEF!
BUT THE VERY OBJECT HE STOLE BECAME THE INSTRUMENT OF HIS DEATH!!
THAT'S SHEER NONSENSE, MISTER LITTLE!
WHOEVER KILLED QUEELY MOVED FASTER THAN THAT FROG EVER WILL. THAT WOUND WAS FRESH! IT MAY HAVE BEEN INFLICTED ONLY MOMENTS BEFORE WE ARRIVED!!
OH, THE FROG DID HIM IN, ALL RIGHT! QUEELY MUST'VE BEEN EXPERIMENTING WITH IT.
AT THAT MOMENT, THE BLACK PANTHER'S SHARPENED INSTINCTS REACT TO A SENSE OF SUDDEN DANGER--AND SAVE HIM FROM THE FATE WHICH CLAIMED QUEELY...
ZZZSSSH!
LOOK OUT!
A SINEWY SWORD ARM HACKS AWAY IN PURSUIT OF ITS INTENDED TARGET, BUT...
TAKE COVER, MISTER LITTLE! THE KILLER'S STILL WITH US!
KRUNTCH!
WHY, SO HE IS!!
THE BLACK PANTHER'S SUPERB AGILITY KEEPS HIM ALIVE UNTIL HE'S IN POSITION TO COUNTER-ATTACK...
PERHAPS QUEELY FELL EASILY TO YOUR BLADE--
THOK!
THEN, WITH COBRA-SPEED, THE BLACK PANTHER STRIKES BACK!
--BUT YOU WILL FIND THE PANTHER A MOST UNCOOPERATIVE TARGET!

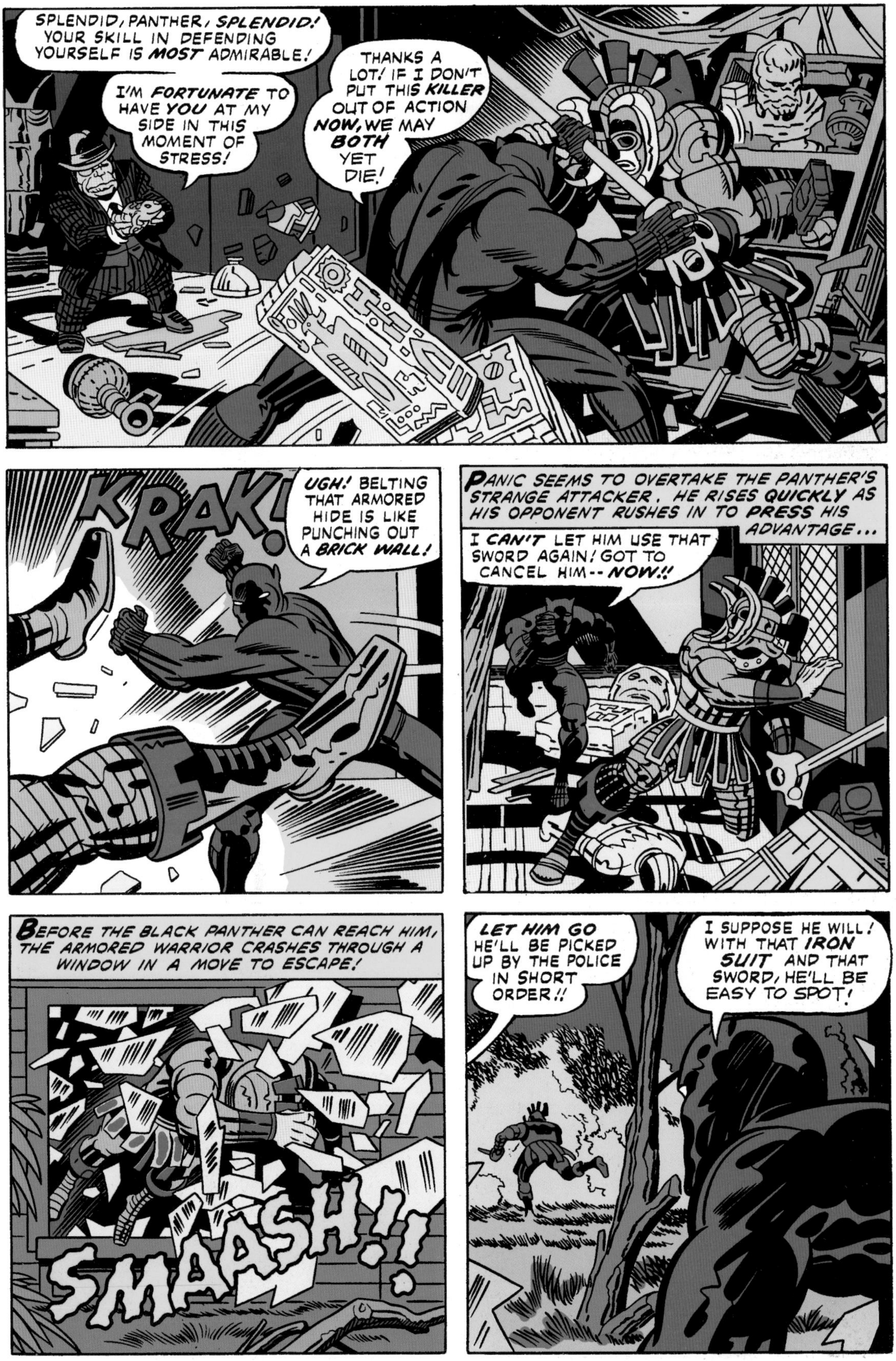
SPLENDID, PANTHER, SPLENDID! YOUR SKILL IN DEFENDING YOURSELF IS MOST ADMIRABLE!
I'M FORTUNATE TO HAVE YOU AT MY SIDE IN THIS MOMENT OF STRESS!
THANKS A LOT! IF I DON'T PUT THIS KILLER OUT OF ACTION NOW, WE MAY BOTH YET DIE!
KRAK!
UGH! BELTING THAT ARMORED HIDE IS LIKE PUNCHING OUT A BRICK WALL!
PANIC SEEMS TO OVERTAKE THE PANTHER'S STRANGE ATTACKER. HE RISES QUICKLY AS HIS OPPONENT RUSHES IN TO PRESS HIS ADVANTAGE...
I CAN'T LET HIM USE THAT SWORD AGAIN! GOT TO CANCEL HIM--NOW!!
BEFORE THE BLACK PANTHER CAN REACH HIM, THE ARMORED WARRIOR CRASHES THROUGH A WINDOW IN A MOVE TO ESCAPE!
SMAASH!!
LET HIM GO HE'LL BE PICKED UP BY THE POLICE IN SHORT ORDER!!
I SUPPOSE HE WILL! WITH THAT IRON SUIT AND THAT SWORD, HE'LL BE EASY TO SPOT!

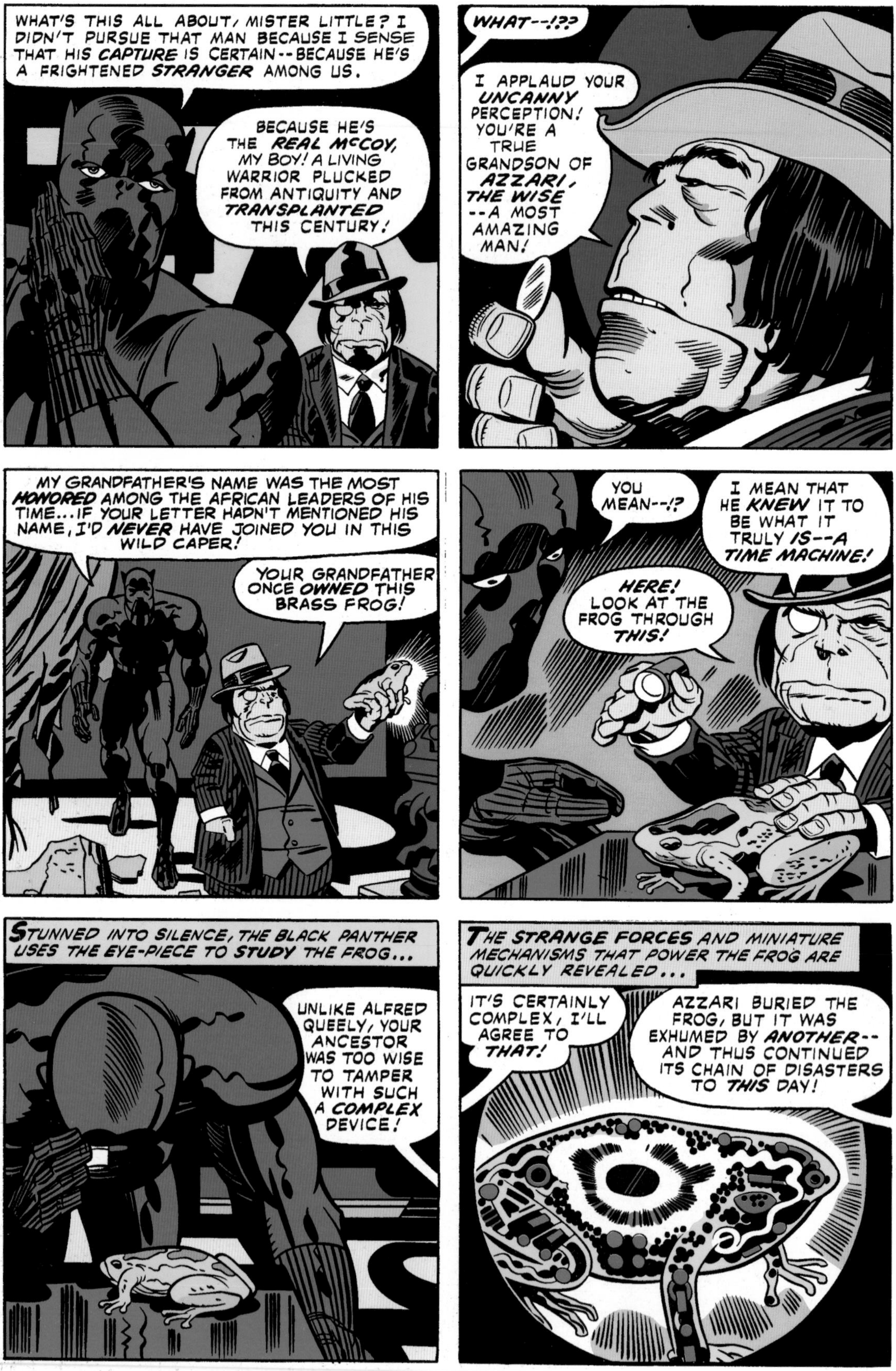
WHAT'S THIS ALL ABOUT, MISTER LITTLE? I DIDN'T PURSUE THAT MAN BECAUSE I SENSE THAT HIS CAPTURE IS CERTAIN--BECAUSE HE'S A FRIGHTENED STRANGER AMONG US.
BECAUSE HE'S THE REAL McCOY, MY BOY! A LIVING WARRIOR PLUCKED FROM ANTIQUITY AND TRANSPLANTED THIS CENTURY!
WHAT--!??
I APPLAUD YOUR UNCANNY PERCEPTION! YOU'RE A TRUE GRANDSON OF AZZARI, THE WISE--A MOST AMAZING MAN!
MY GRANDFATHER'S NAME WAS THE MOST HONORED AMONG THE AFRICAN LEADERS OF HIS TIME...IF YOUR LETTER HADN'T MENTIONED HIS NAME, I'D NEVER HAVE JOINED YOU IN THIS WILD CAPER!
YOUR GRANDFATHER ONCE OWNED THIS BRASS FROG!
YOU MEAN--!?
I MEAN THAT HE KNEW IT TO BE WHAT IT TRULY IS--A TIME MACHINE!
HERE! LOOK AT THE FROG THROUGH THIS!
STUNNED INTO SILENCE, THE BLACK PANTHER USES THE EYE-PIECE TO STUDY THE FROG...
UNLIKE ALFRED QUEELY, YOUR ANCESTOR WAS TOO WISE TO TAMPER WITH SUCH A COMPLEX DEVICE!
THE STRANGE FORCES AND MINIATURE MECHANISMS THAT POWER THE FROG ARE QUICKLY REVEALED...
IT'S CERTAINLY COMPLEX, I'LL AGREE TO THAT!
AZZARI BURIED THE FROG, BUT IT WAS EXHUMED BY ANOTHER--AND THUS CONTINUED ITS CHAIN OF DISASTERS TO THIS DAY!

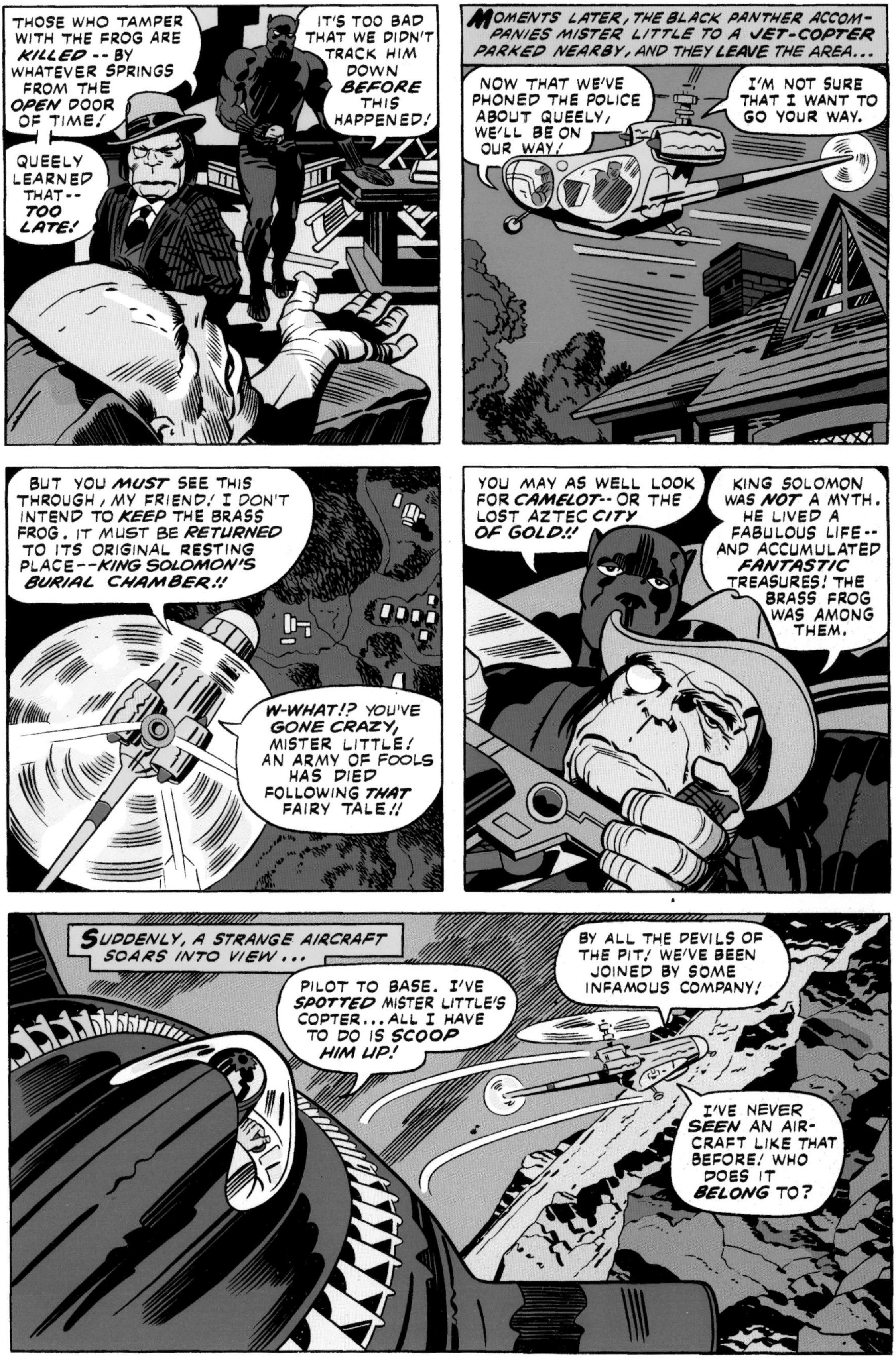
THOSE WHO TAMPER WITH THE FROG ARE KILLED -- BY WHATEVER SPRINGS FROM THE OPEN DOOR OF TIME!
QUEELY LEARNED THAT -- TOO LATE!
IT'S TOO BAD THAT WE DIDN'T TRACK HIM DOWN BEFORE THIS HAPPENED!
MOMENTS LATER, THE BLACK PANTHER ACCOMPANIES MISTER LITTLE TO A JET-COPTER PARKED NEARBY, AND THEY LEAVE THE AREA...
NOW THAT WE'VE PHONED THE POLICE ABOUT QUEELY, WE'LL BE ON OUR WAY!
I'M NOT SURE THAT I WANT TO GO YOUR WAY.
BUT YOU MUST SEE THIS THROUGH, MY FRIEND! I DON'T INTEND TO KEEP THE BRASS FROG. IT MUST BE RETURNED TO ITS ORIGINAL RESTING PLACE--KING SOLOMON'S BURIAL CHAMBER!!
W-WHAT!? YOU'VE GONE CRAZY, MISTER LITTLE! AN ARMY OF FOOLS HAS DIED FOLLOWING THAT FAIRY TALE!!
YOU MAY AS WELL LOOK FOR CAMELOT-- OR THE LOST AZTEC CITY OF GOLD!!
KING SOLOMON WAS NOT A MYTH. HE LIVED A FABULOUS LIFE -- AND ACCUMULATED FANTASTIC TREASURES! THE BRASS FROG WAS AMONG THEM.
SUDDENLY, A STRANGE AIRCRAFT SOARS INTO VIEW...
PILOT TO BASE. I'VE SPOTTED MISTER LITTLE'S COPTER... ALL I HAVE TO DO IS SCOOP HIM UP!
BY ALL THE DEVILS OF THE PIT! WE'VE BEEN JOINED BY SOME INFAMOUS COMPANY!
I'VE NEVER SEEN AN AIRCRAFT LIKE THAT BEFORE! WHO DOES IT BELONG TO?

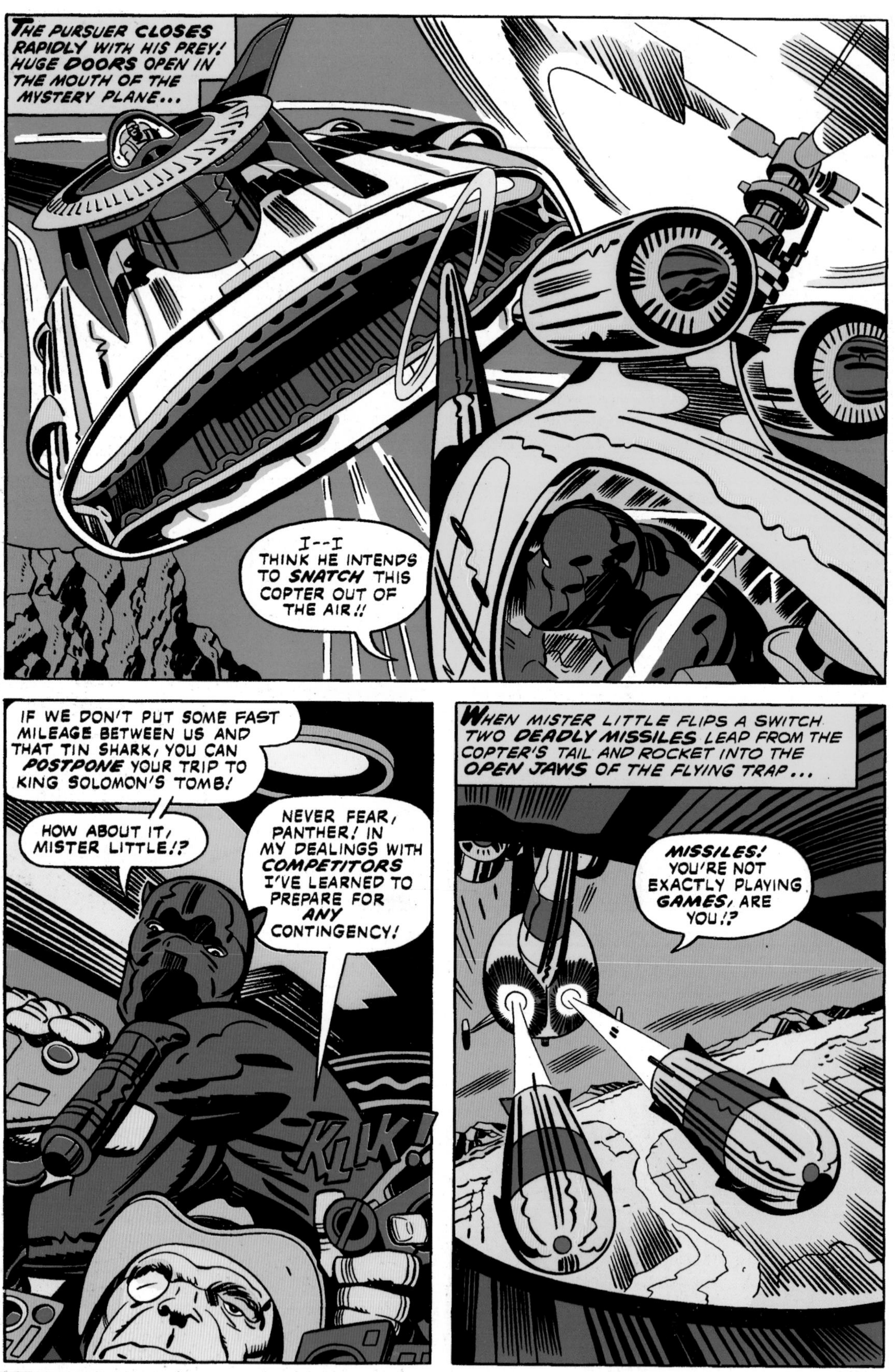
THE PURSUER CLOSES RAPIDLY WITH HIS PREY! HUGE DOORS OPEN IN THE MOUTH OF THE MYSTERY PLANE...
I--I THINK HE INTENDS TO SNATCH THIS COPTER OUT OF THE AIR!!
IF WE DON'T PUT SOME FAST MILEAGE BETWEEN US AND THAT TIN SHARK, YOU CAN POSTPONE YOUR TRIP TO KING SOLOMON'S TOMB!
HOW ABOUT IT, MISTER LITTLE!?
NEVER FEAR, PANTHER! IN MY DEALINGS WITH COMPETITORS I'VE LEARNED TO PREPARE FOR ANY CONTINGENCY!
KLIK!
WHEN MISTER LITTLE FLIPS A SWITCH TWO DEADLY MISSILES LEAP FROM THE COPTER'S TAIL AND ROCKET INTO THE OPEN JAWS OF THE FLYING TRAP...
MISSILES! YOU'RE NOT EXACTLY PLAYING GAMES, ARE YOU!?

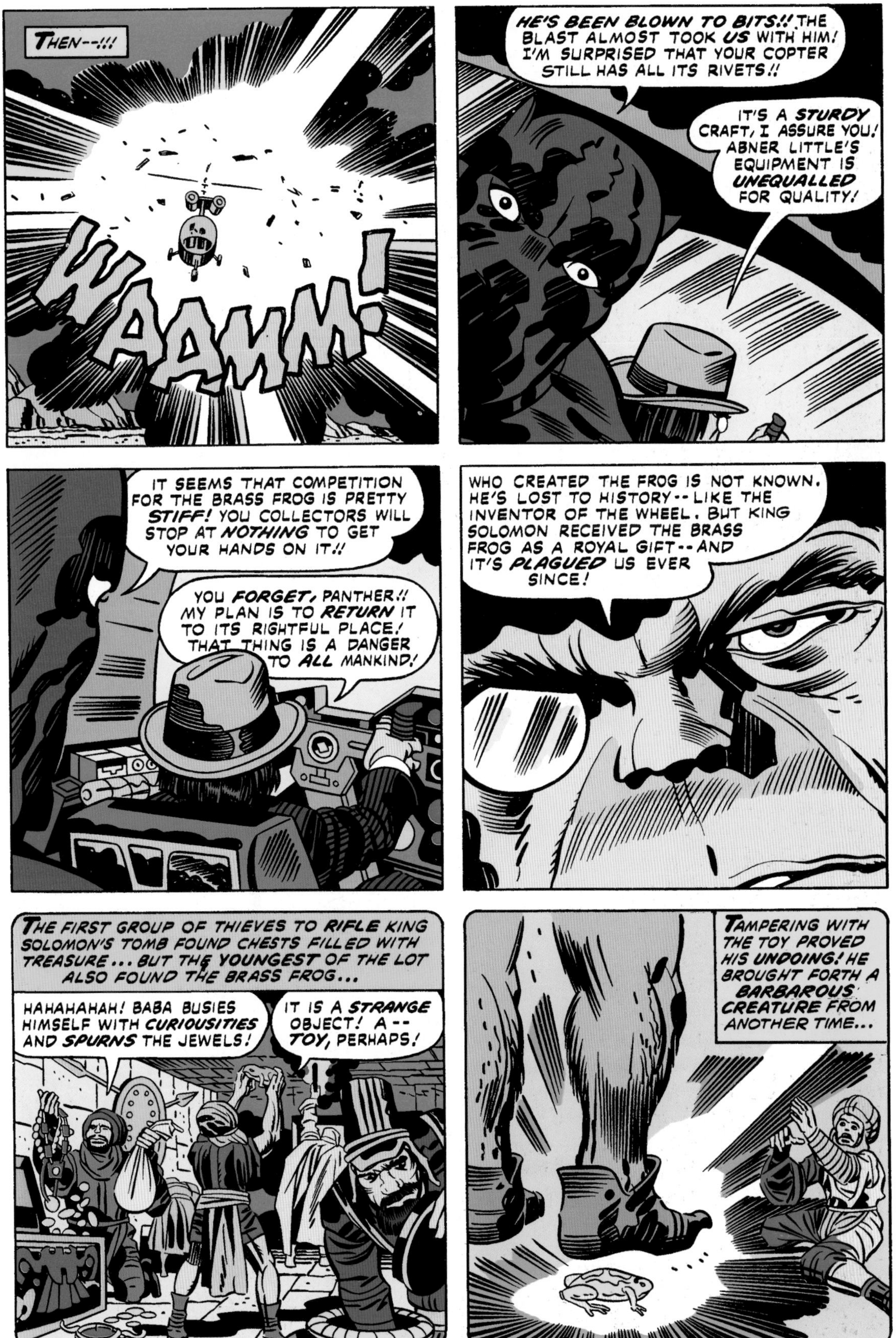
THEN--!!!
WAMM!
HE'S BEEN BLOWN TO BITS!! THE BLAST ALMOST TOOK US WITH HIM! I'M SURPRISED THAT YOUR COPTER STILL HAS ALL ITS RIVETS!!
IT'S A STURDY CRAFT, I ASSURE YOU! ABNER LITTLE'S EQUIPMENT IS UNEQUALLED FOR QUALITY!
IT SEEMS THAT COMPETITION FOR THE BRASS FROG IS PRETTY STIFF! YOU COLLECTORS WILL STOP AT NOTHING TO GET YOUR HANDS ON IT!!
YOU FORGET, PANTHER!! MY PLAN IS TO RETURN IT TO ITS RIGHTFUL PLACE! THAT THING IS A DANGER TO ALL MANKIND!
WHO CREATED THE FROG IS NOT KNOWN. HE'S LOST TO HISTORY--LIKE THE INVENTOR OF THE WHEEL. BUT KING SOLOMON RECEIVED THE BRASS FROG AS A ROYAL GIFT--AND IT'S PLAGUED US EVER SINCE!
THE FIRST GROUP OF THIEVES TO RIFLE KING SOLOMON'S TOMB FOUND CHESTS FILLED WITH TREASURE... BUT THE YOUNGEST OF THE LOT ALSO FOUND THE BRASS FROG...
HAHAHAHAH! BABA BUSIES HIMSELF WITH CURIOUSITIES AND SPURNS THE JEWELS!
IT IS A STRANGE OBJECT! A--TOY, PERHAPS!
TAMPERING WITH THE TOY PROVED HIS UNDOING! HE BROUGHT FORTH A BARBAROUS CREATURE FROM ANOTHER TIME...

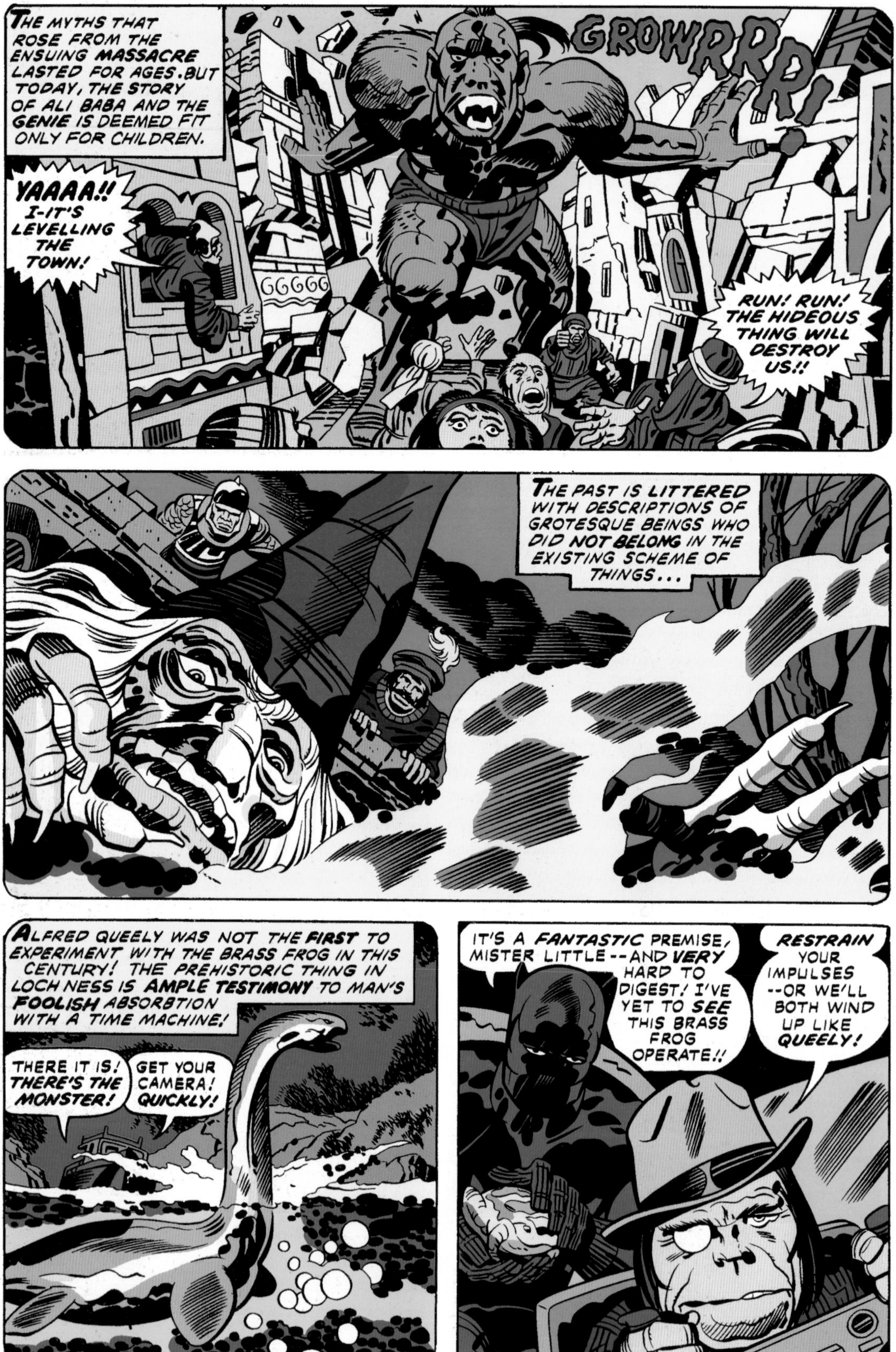

THE MYTHS THAT ROSE FROM THE ENSUING MASSACRE LASTED FOR AGES. BUT TODAY, THE STORY OF ALI BABA AND THE GENIE IS DEEMED FIT ONLY FOR CHILDREN.
GROWRRR!
YAAAA!! I-IT'S LEVELLING THE TOWN!
GGGGG
RUN! RUN! THE HIDEOUS THING WILL DESTROY US!!
THE PAST IS LITTERED WITH DESCRIPTIONS OF GROTESQUE BEINGS WHO DID NOT BELONG IN THE EXISTING SCHEME OF THINGS...
ALFRED QUEELY WAS NOT THE FIRST TO EXPERIMENT WITH THE BRASS FROG IN THIS CENTURY! THE PREHISTORIC THING IN LOCH NESS IS AMPLE TESTIMONY TO MAN'S FOOLISH ABSORBTION WITH A TIME MACHINE!
THERE IT IS! THERE'S THE MONSTER!
GET YOUR CAMERA! QUICKLY!
IT'S A FANTASTIC PREMISE, MISTER LITTLE--AND VERY HARD TO DIGEST! I'VE YET TO SEE THIS BRASS FROG OPERATE!!
RESTRAIN YOUR IMPULSES --OR WE'LL BOTH WIND UP LIKE QUEELY!

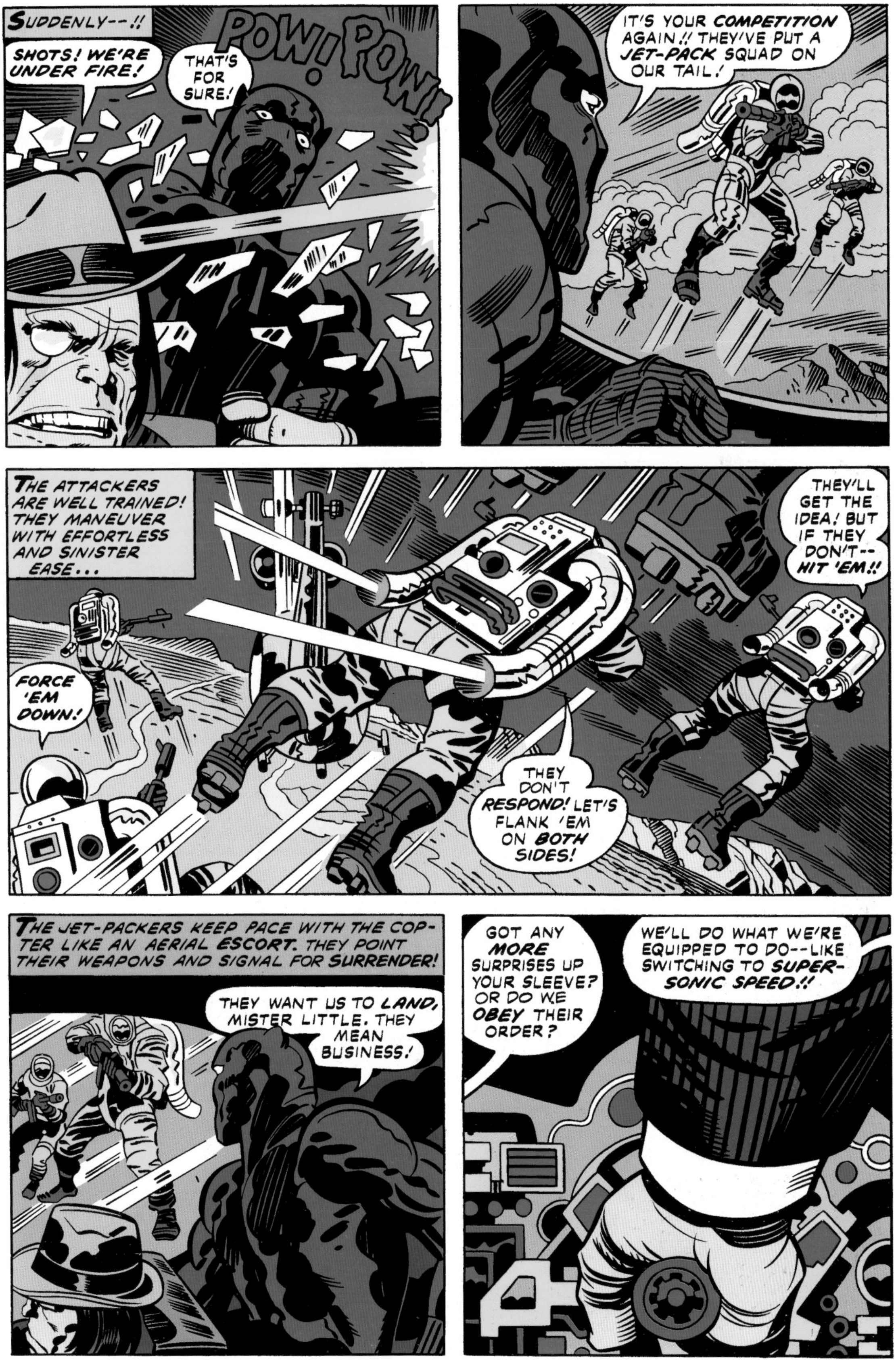
SUDDENLY--!!
SHOTS! WE'RE UNDER FIRE!
THAT'S FOR SURE!
POW! POW!!
IT'S YOUR COMPETITION AGAIN!! THEY'VE PUT A JET-PACK SQUAD ON OUR TAIL!
THE ATTACKERS ARE WELL TRAINED! THEY MANEUVER WITH EFFORTLESS AND SINISTER EASE...
FORCE 'EM DOWN!
THEY DON'T RESPOND! LET'S FLANK 'EM ON BOTH SIDES!
THEY'LL GET THE IDEA! BUT IF THEY DON'T-- HIT 'EM!!
THE JET-PACKERS KEEP PACE WITH THE COPTER LIKE AN AERIAL ESCORT. THEY POINT THEIR WEAPONS AND SIGNAL FOR SURRENDER!
THEY WANT US TO LAND, MISTER LITTLE. THEY MEAN BUSINESS!
GOT ANY MORE SURPRISES UP YOUR SLEEVE? OR DO WE OBEY THEIR ORDER?
WE'LL DO WHAT WE'RE EQUIPPED TO DO--LIKE SWITCHING TO SUPER-SONIC SPEED!!

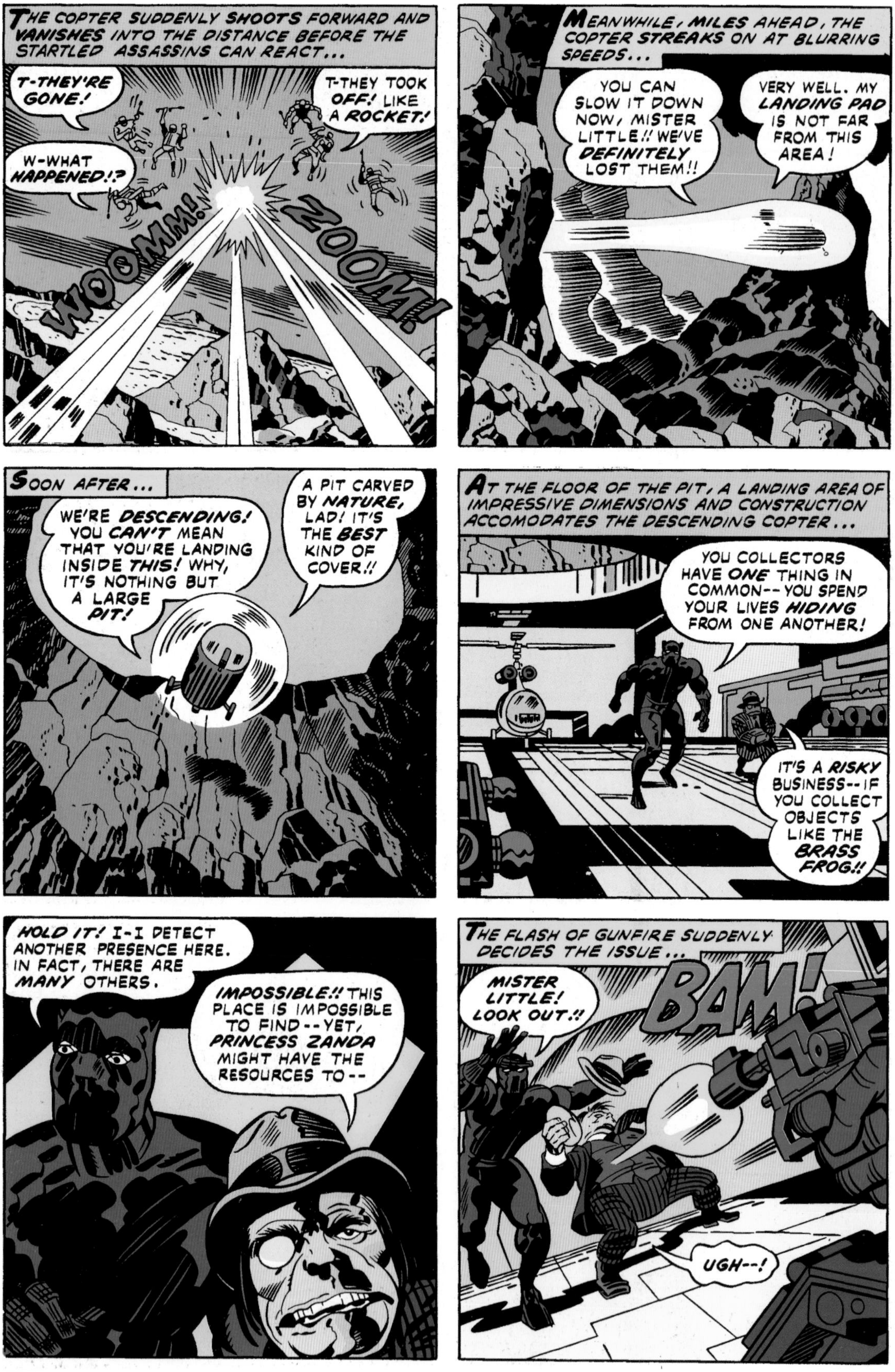
THE COPTER SUDDENLY SHOOTS FORWARD AND VANISHES INTO THE DISTANCE BEFORE THE STARTLED ASSASSINS CAN REACT...
T-THEY'RE GONE!
T-THEY TOOK OFF! LIKE A ROCKET!
W-WHAT HAPPENED!?
WOOMM!
ZOOM!
MEANWHILE, MILES AHEAD, THE COPTER STREAKS ON AT BLURRING SPEEDS...
YOU CAN SLOW IT DOWN NOW, MISTER LITTLE!! WE'VE DEFINITELY LOST THEM!!
VERY WELL. MY LANDING PAD IS NOT FAR FROM THIS AREA!
SOON AFTER...
WE'RE DESCENDING! YOU CAN'T MEAN THAT YOU'RE LANDING INSIDE THIS! WHY, IT'S NOTHING BUT A LARGE PIT!
A PIT CARVED BY NATURE, LAD! IT'S THE BEST KIND OF COVER!!
AT THE FLOOR OF THE PIT, A LANDING AREA OF IMPRESSIVE DIMENSIONS AND CONSTRUCTION ACCOMODATES THE DESCENDING COPTER...
YOU COLLECTORS HAVE ONE THING IN COMMON--YOU SPEND YOUR LIVES HIDING FROM ONE ANOTHER!
IT'S A RISKY BUSINESS--IF YOU COLLECT OBJECTS LIKE THE BRASS FROG!!
HOLD IT! I-I DETECT ANOTHER PRESENCE HERE. IN FACT, THERE ARE MANY OTHERS.
IMPOSSIBLE!! THIS PLACE IS IMPOSSIBLE TO FIND--YET, PRINCESS ZANDA MIGHT HAVE THE RESOURCES TO--
THE FLASH OF GUNFIRE SUDDENLY DECIDES THE ISSUE...
MISTER LITTLE! LOOK OUT!!
BAM!
UGH--!

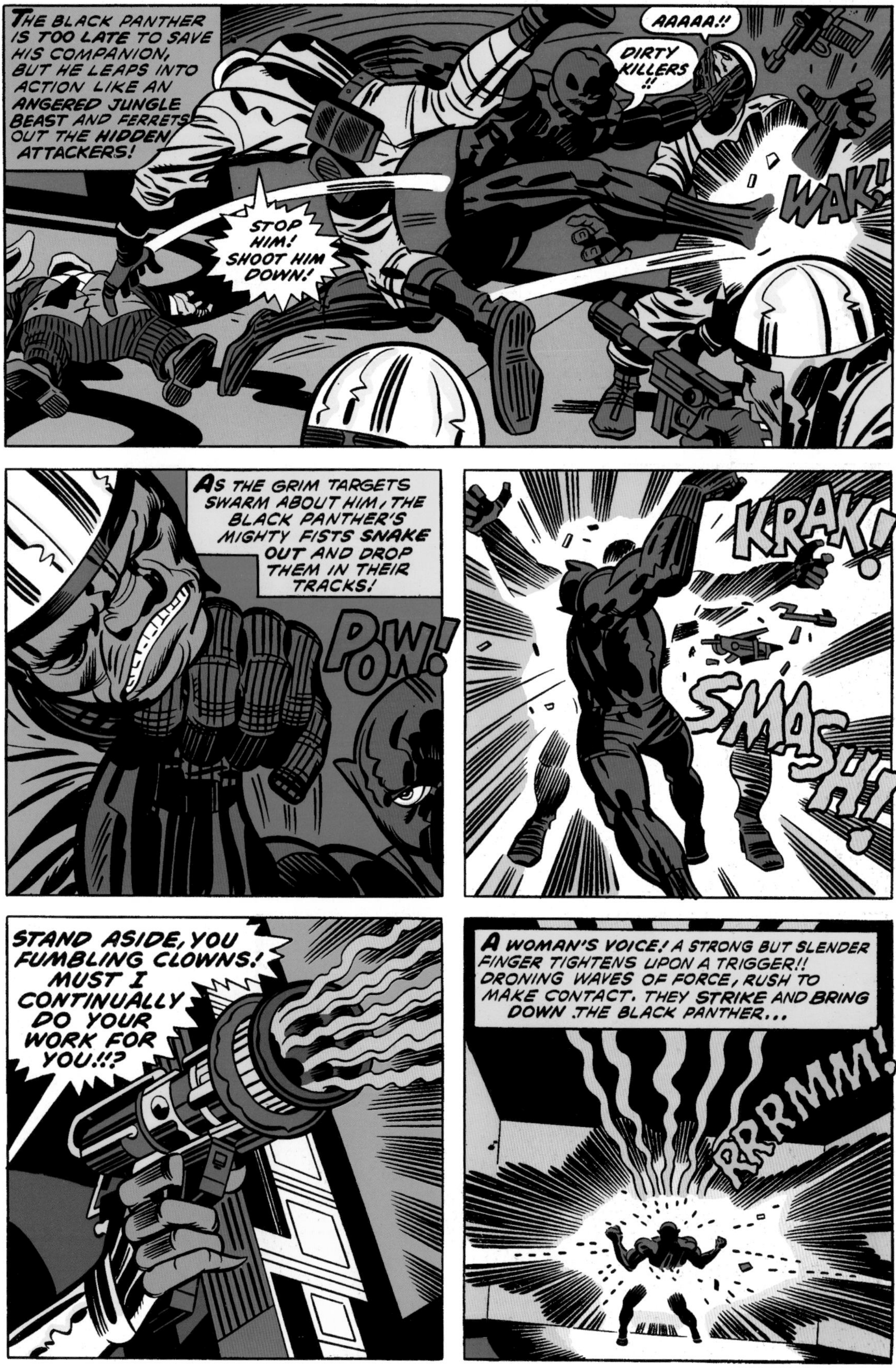
THE BLACK PANTHER IS TOO LATE TO SAVE HIS COMPANION, BUT HE LEAPS INTO ACTION LIKE AN ANGERED JUNGLE BEAST AND FERRETS OUT THE HIDDEN ATTACKERS!
AAAAA!!
DIRTY KILLERS!!
STOP HIM! SHOOT HIM DOWN!
WAK!
AS THE GRIM TARGETS SWARM ABOUT HIM, THE BLACK PANTHER'S MIGHTY FISTS SNAKE OUT AND DROP THEM IN THEIR TRACKS!
POW!
KRAK!
SMASH!!
STAND ASIDE, YOU FUMBLING CLOWNS! MUST I CONTINUALLY DO YOUR WORK FOR YOU!!?
A WOMAN'S VOICE! A STRONG BUT SLENDER FINGER TIGHTENS UPON A TRIGGER!! DRONING WAVES OF FORCE, RUSH TO MAKE CONTACT. THEY STRIKE AND BRING DOWN THE BLACK PANTHER...
RRRMMM!

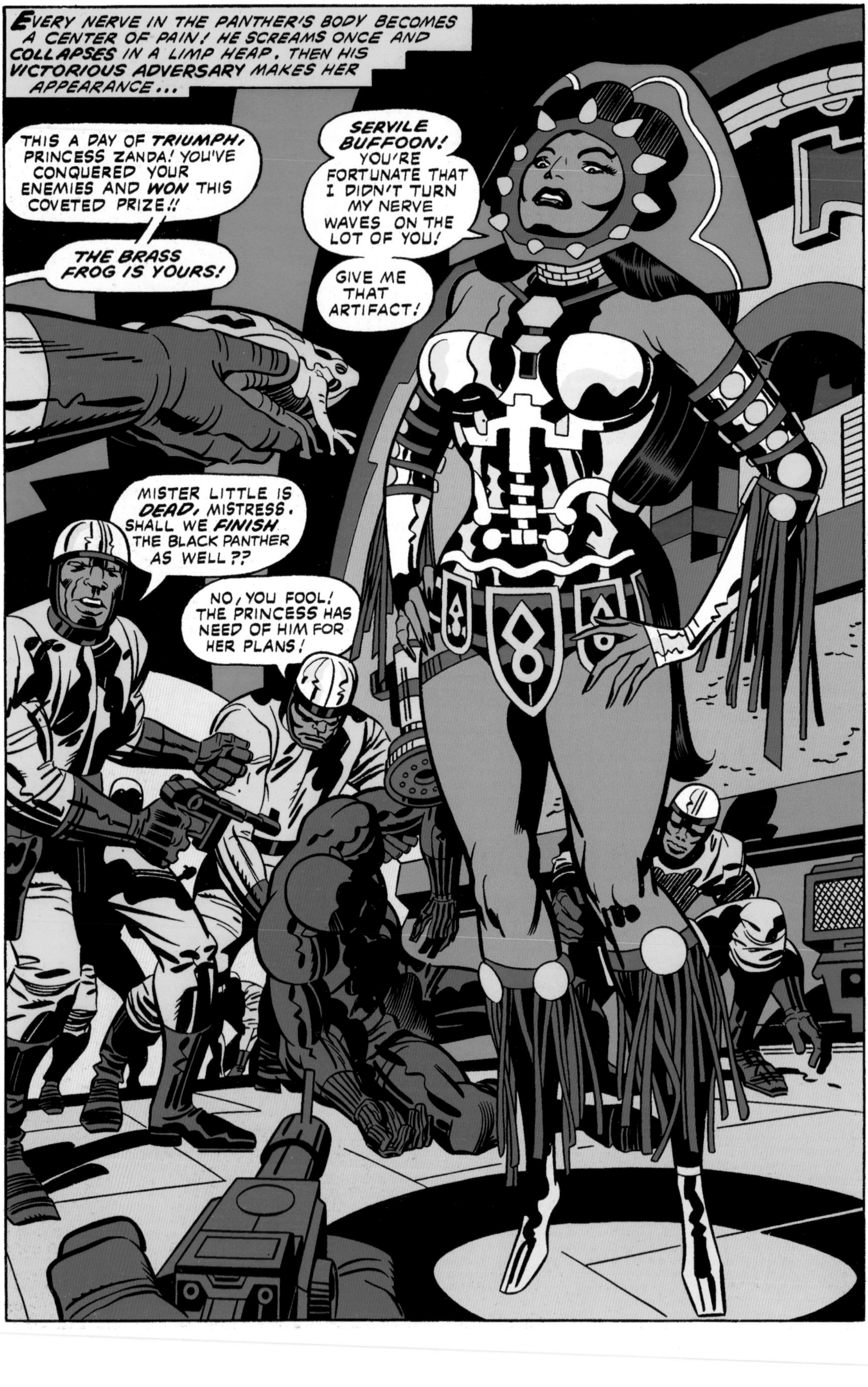

EVERY NERVE IN THE PANTHER'S BODY BECOMES A CENTER OF PAIN! HE SCREAMS ONCE AND COLLAPSES IN A LIMP HEAP. THEN HIS VICTORIOUS ADVERSARY MAKES HER APPEARANCE...
THIS A DAY OF TRIUMPH, PRINCESS ZANDA! YOU'VE CONQUERED YOUR ENEMIES AND WON THIS COVETED PRIZE!!
THE BRASS FROG IS YOURS!
SERVILE BUFFOON! YOU'RE FORTUNATE THAT I DIDN'T TURN MY NERVE WAVES ON THE LOT OF YOU!
GIVE ME THAT ARTIFACT!
MISTER LITTLE IS DEAD, MISTRESS. SHALL WE FINISH THE BLACK PANTHER AS WELL??
NO, YOU FOOL! THE PRINCESS HAS NEED OF HIM FOR HER PLANS!

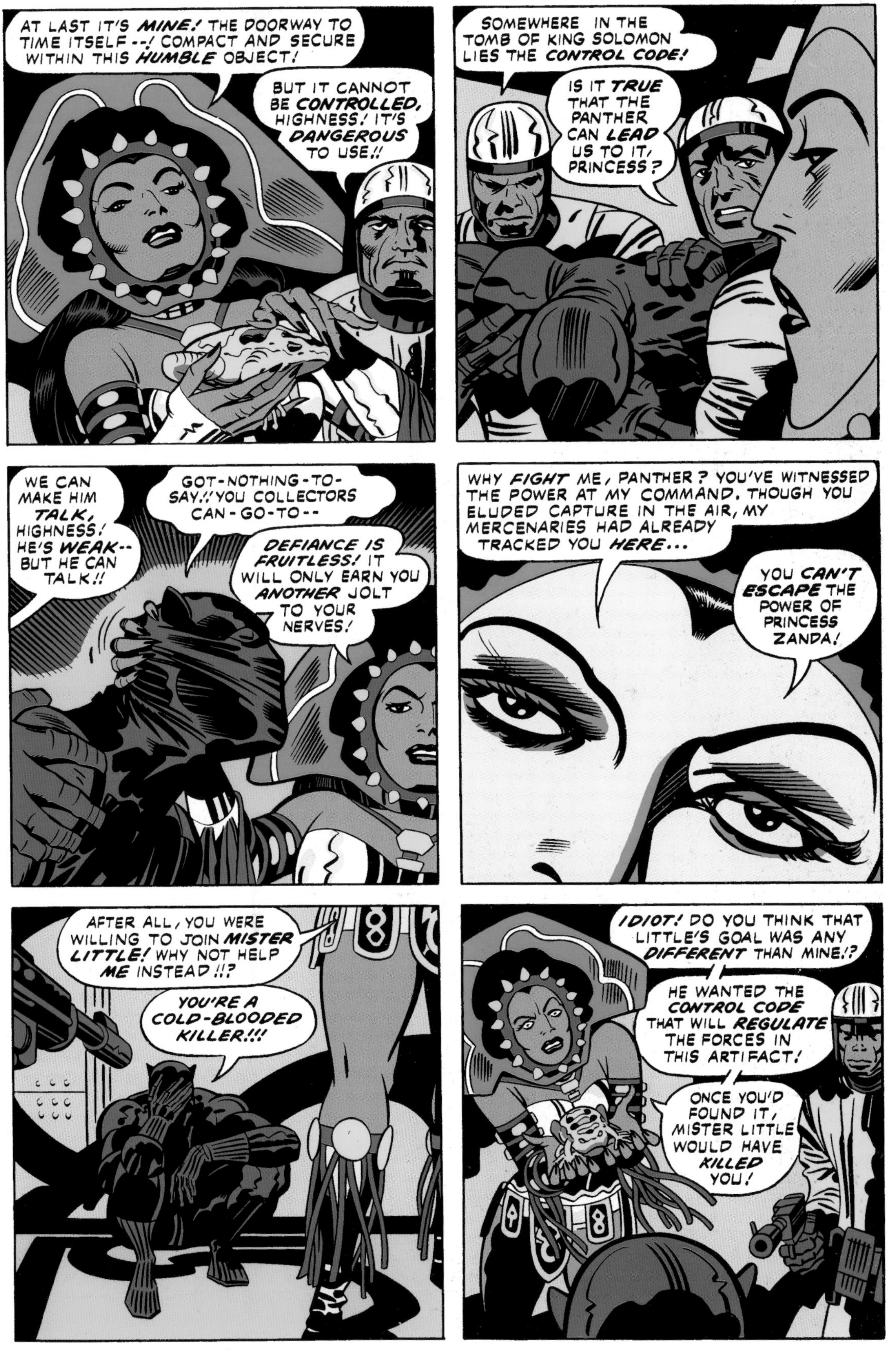
AT LAST IT'S MINE! THE DOORWAY TO TIME ITSELF --! COMPACT AND SECURE WITHIN THIS HUMBLE OBJECT!
BUT IT CANNOT BE CONTROLLED, HIGHNESS! IT'S DANGEROUS TO USE!!
SOMEWHERE IN THE TOMB OF KING SOLOMON LIES THE CONTROL CODE!
IS IT TRUE THAT THE PANTHER CAN LEAD US TO IT, PRINCESS?
WE CAN MAKE HIM TALK, HIGHNESS! HE'S WEAK-- BUT HE CAN TALK!!
GOT-NOTHING-TO-SAY!! YOU COLLECTORS CAN-GO-TO--
DEFIANCE IS FRUITLESS! IT WILL ONLY EARN YOU ANOTHER JOLT TO YOUR NERVES!
WHY FIGHT ME, PANTHER? YOU'VE WITNESSED THE POWER AT MY COMMAND. THOUGH YOU ELUDED CAPTURE IN THE AIR, MY MERCENARIES HAD ALREADY TRACKED YOU HERE...
YOU CAN'T ESCAPE THE POWER OF PRINCESS ZANDA!
AFTER ALL, YOU WERE WILLING TO JOIN MISTER LITTLE! WHY NOT HELP ME INSTEAD!!?
YOU'RE A COLD-BLOODED KILLER!!!
IDIOT! DO YOU THINK THAT LITTLE'S GOAL WAS ANY DIFFERENT THAN MINE!?
HE WANTED THE CONTROL CODE THAT WILL REGULATE THE FORCES IN THIS ARTIFACT!
ONCE YOU'D FOUND IT, MISTER LITTLE WOULD HAVE KILLED YOU!

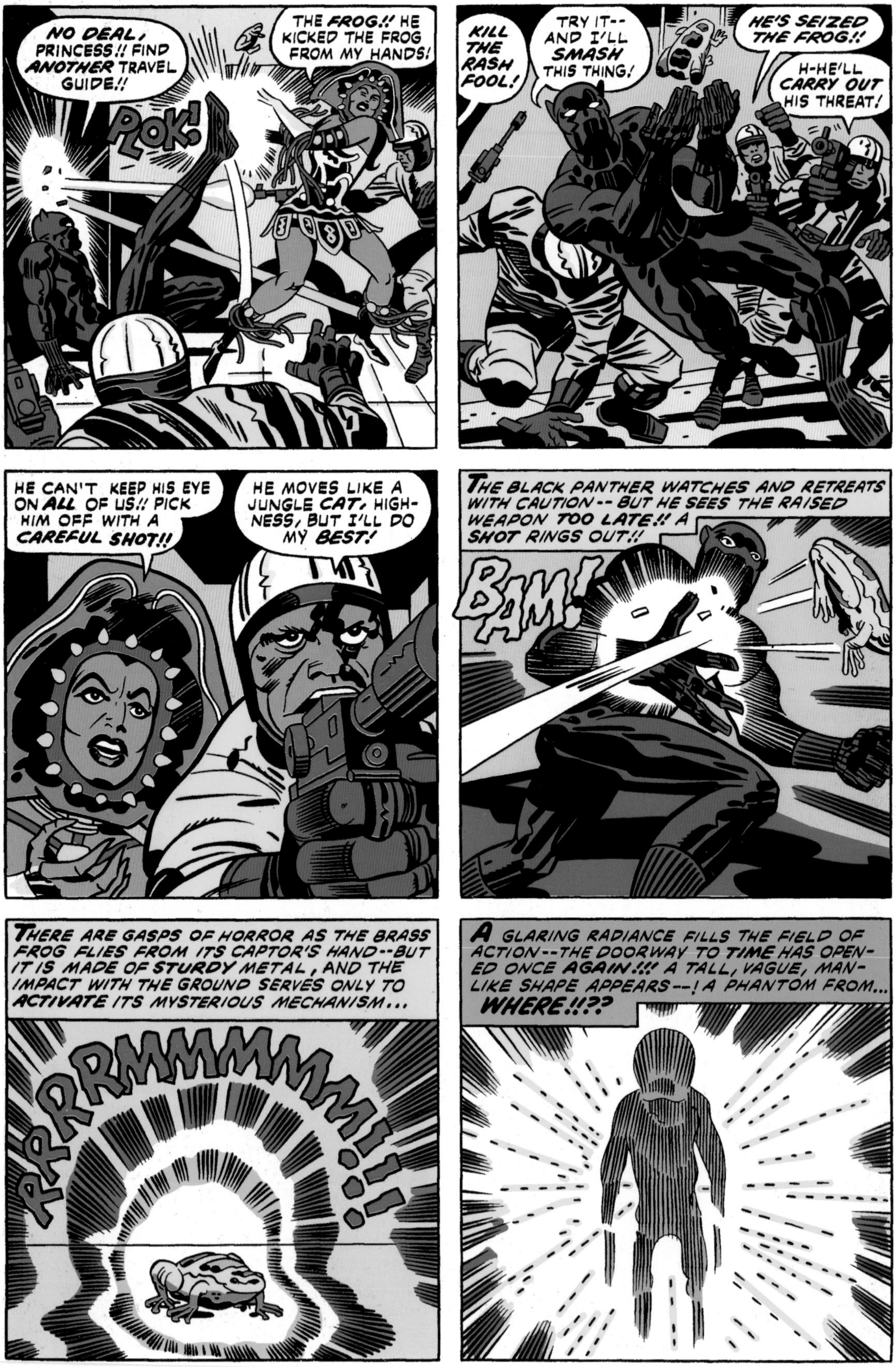
NO DEAL, PRINCESS!! FIND ANOTHER TRAVEL GUIDE!!
THE FROG!! HE KICKED THE FROG FROM MY HANDS!
PLOK!
KILL THE RASH FOOL!
TRY IT-- AND I'LL SMASH THIS THING!
HE'S SEIZED THE FROG!!
H-HE'LL CARRY OUT HIS THREAT!
HE CAN'T KEEP HIS EYE ON ALL OF US!! PICK HIM OFF WITH A CAREFUL SHOT!!
HE MOVES LIKE A JUNGLE CAT, HIGHNESS, BUT I'LL DO MY BEST!
THE BLACK PANTHER WATCHES AND RETREATS WITH CAUTION -- BUT HE SEES THE RAISED WEAPON TOO LATE!! A SHOT RINGS OUT!!
BAM!
THERE ARE GASPS OF HORROR AS THE BRASS FROG FLIES FROM ITS CAPTOR'S HAND--BUT IT IS MADE OF STURDY METAL, AND THE IMPACT WITH THE GROUND SERVES ONLY TO ACTIVATE ITS MYSTERIOUS MECHANISM...
RRRRMMMMMM!!!!
A GLARING RADIANCE FILLS THE FIELD OF ACTION--THE DOORWAY TO TIME HAS OPEN-ED ONCE AGAIN!!! A TALL, VAGUE, MAN-LIKE SHAPE APPEARS--! A PHANTOM FROM... WHERE!!??

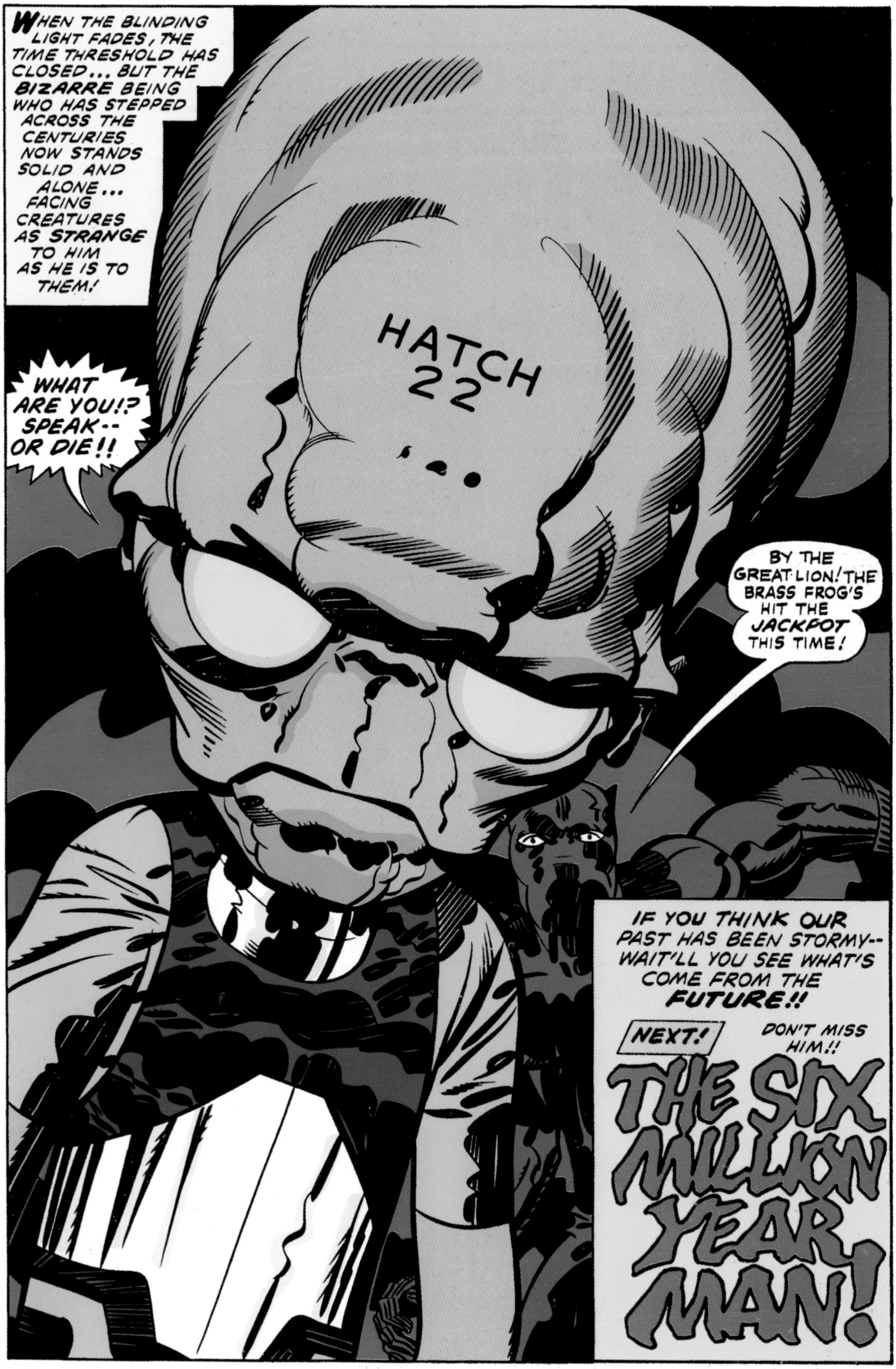
WHEN THE BLINDING LIGHT FADES, THE TIME THRESHOLD HAS CLOSED... BUT THE BIZARRE BEING WHO HAS STEPPED ACROSS THE CENTURIES NOW STANDS SOLID AND ALONE... FACING CREATURES AS STRANGE TO HIM AS HE IS TO THEM!
HATCH 22
WHAT ARE YOU!? SPEAK-- OR DIE!!
BY THE GREAT LION! THE BRASS FROG'S HIT THE JACKPOT THIS TIME!
IF YOU THINK OUR PAST HAS BEEN STORMY-- WAIT'LL YOU SEE WHAT'S COME FROM THE FUTURE!!
NEXT!
DON'T MISS HIM!!
THE SIX MILLION YEAR MAN!

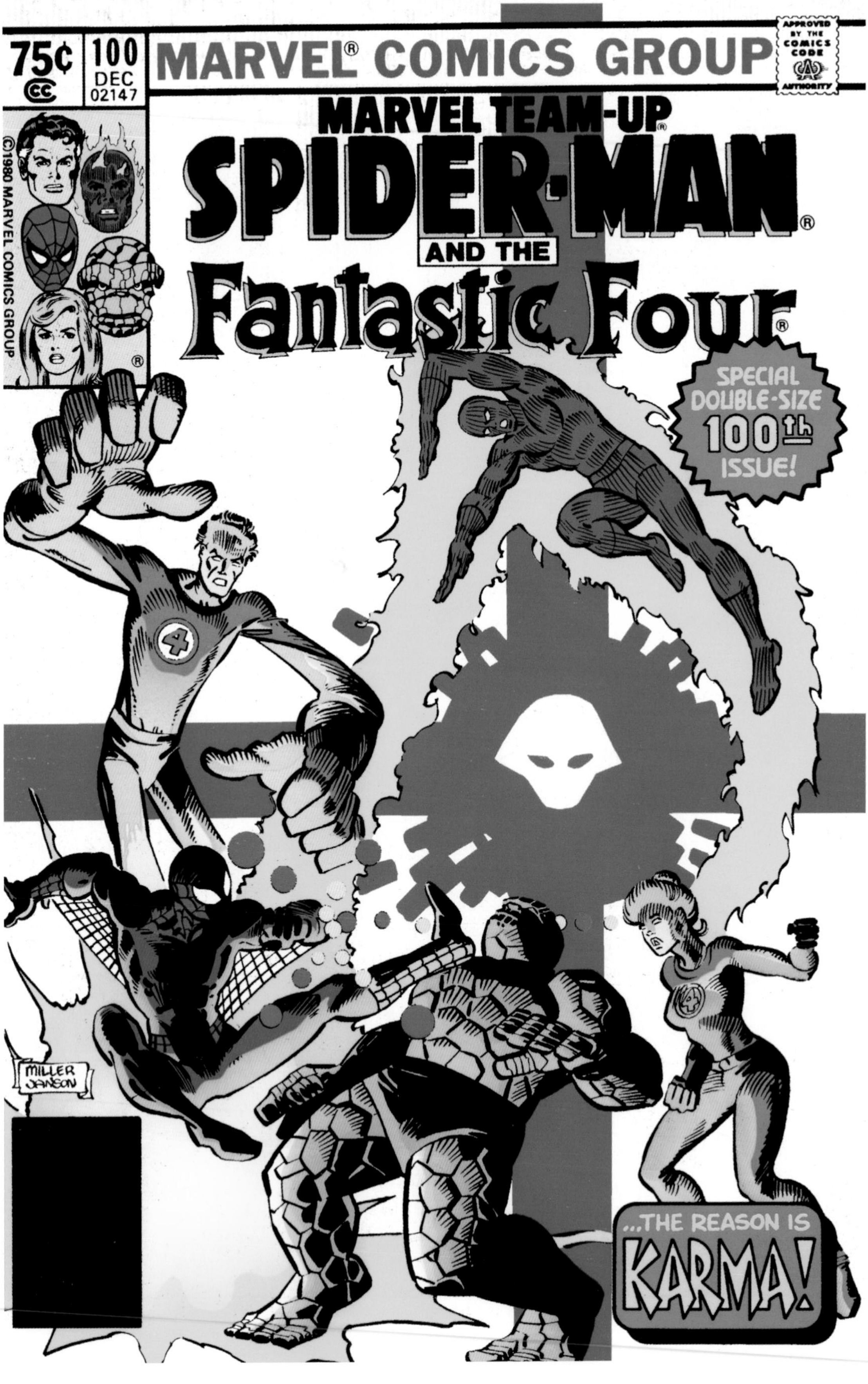
75¢
CC
100
DEC
02147
MARVEL® COMICS GROUP
APPROVED BY THE COMICS CODE AUTHORITY
©1980 MARVEL COMICS GROUP
MARVEL TEAM-UP®
SPIDER-MAN®
AND THE
Fantastic Four®
SPECIAL DOUBLE-SIZE 100th ISSUE!
MILLER JANSON
...THE REASON IS
KARMA!

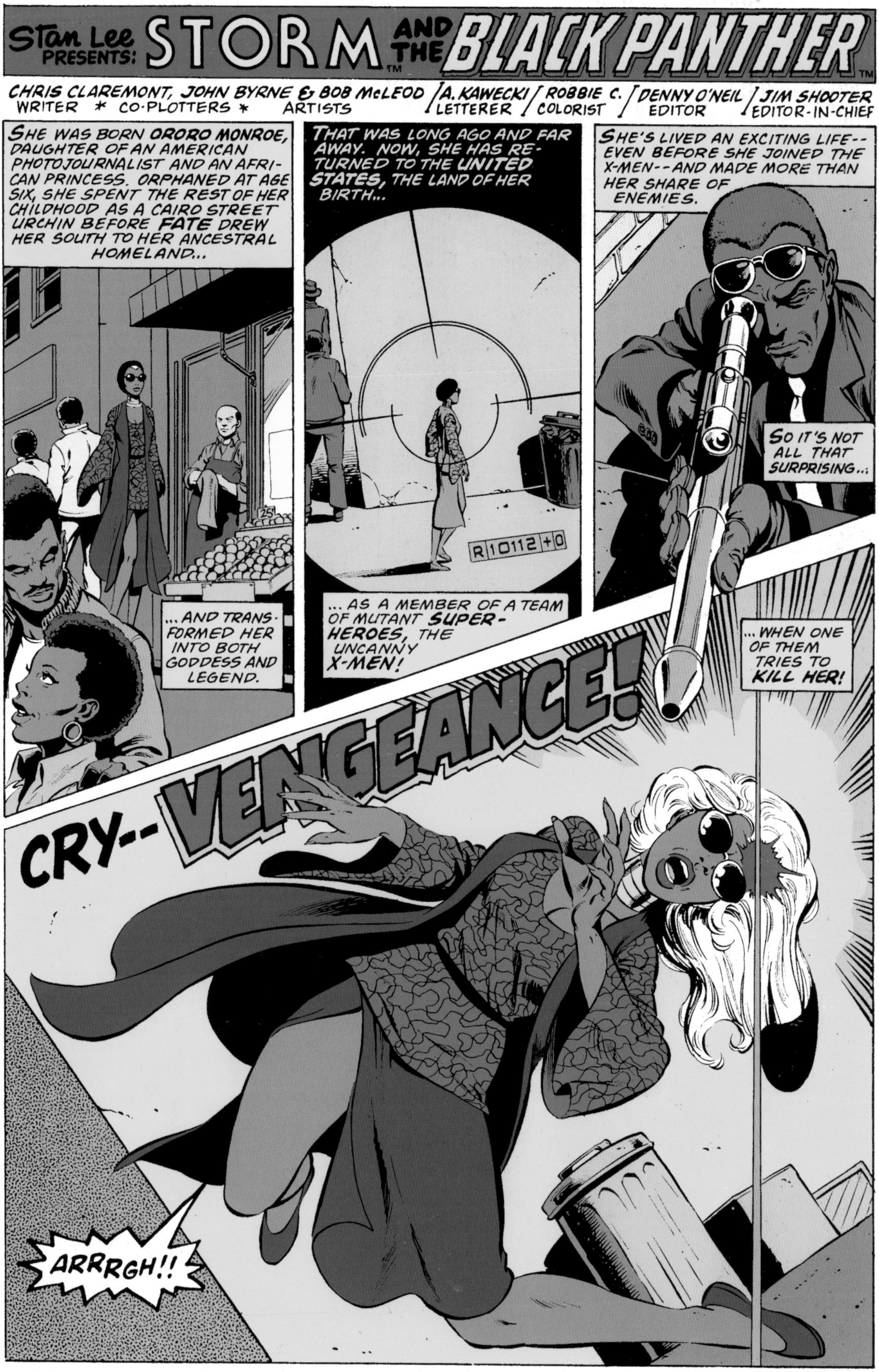

Stan Lee PRESENTS: STORM AND THE BLACK PANTHER
CHRIS CLAREMONT, JOHN BYRNE & BOB McLEOD / A. KAWECKI / ROBBIE C. / DENNY O'NEIL / JIM SHOOTER
WRITER * CO-PLOTTERS * ARTISTS / LETTERER / COLORIST / EDITOR / EDITOR-IN-CHIEF
SHE WAS BORN ORORO MONROE, DAUGHTER OF AN AMERICAN PHOTOJOURNALIST AND AN AFRICAN PRINCESS. ORPHANED AT AGE SIX, SHE SPENT THE REST OF HER CHILDHOOD AS A CAIRO STREET URCHIN BEFORE FATE DREW HER SOUTH TO HER ANCESTRAL HOMELAND...
...AND TRANSFORMED HER INTO BOTH GODDESS AND LEGEND.
THAT WAS LONG AGO AND FAR AWAY. NOW, SHE HAS RETURNED TO THE UNITED STATES, THE LAND OF HER BIRTH...
R 10112 +0
...AS A MEMBER OF A TEAM OF MUTANT SUPER-HEROES, THE UNCANNY X-MEN!
SHE'S LIVED AN EXCITING LIFE--EVEN BEFORE SHE JOINED THE X-MEN--AND MADE MORE THAN HER SHARE OF ENEMIES.
SO IT'S NOT ALL THAT SURPRISING...
...WHEN ONE OF THEM TRIES TO KILL HER!
CRY--VENGEANCE!
ARRRGH!!

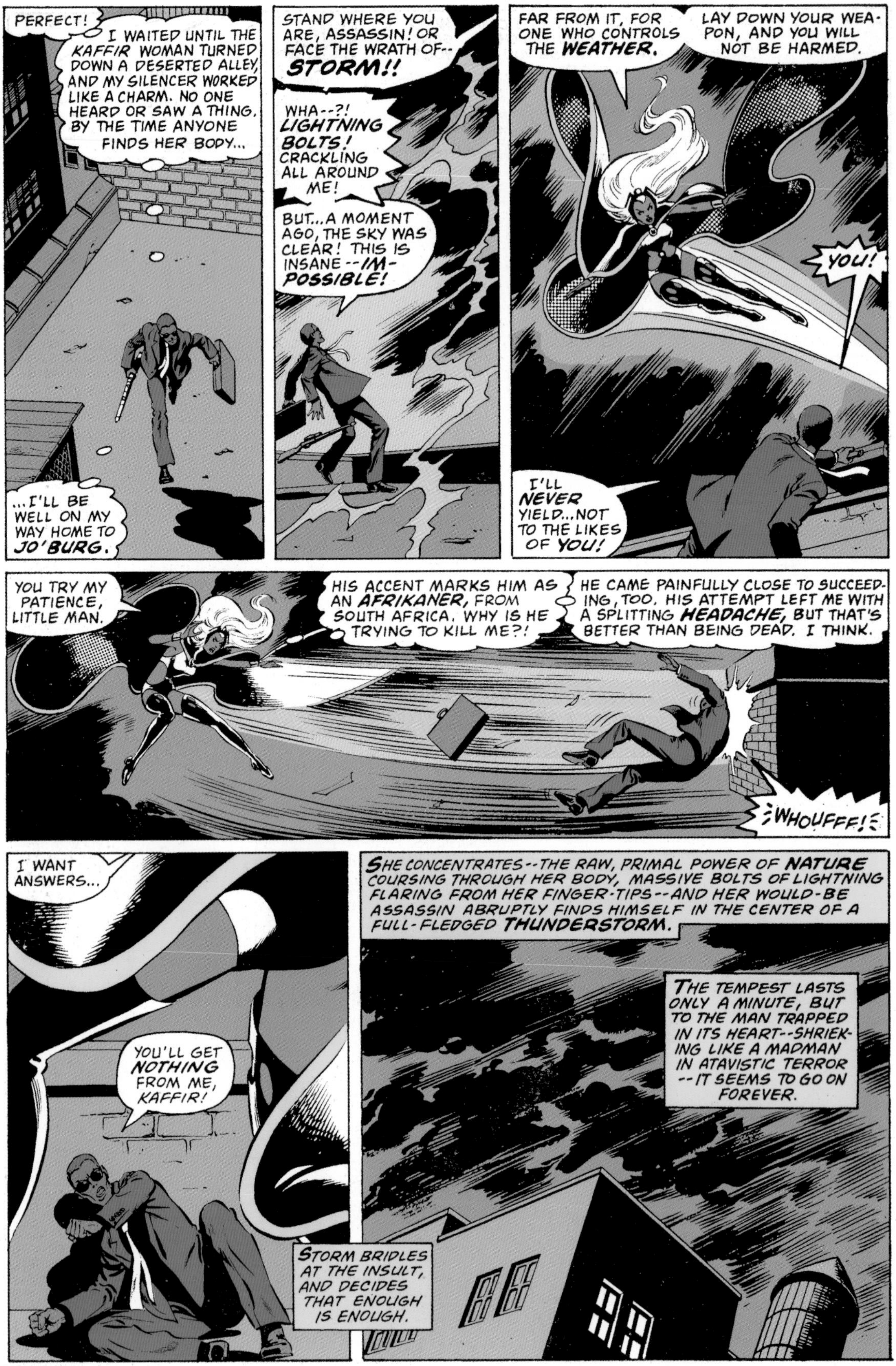
PERFECT!
I WAITED UNTIL THE KAFFIR WOMAN TURNED DOWN A DESERTED ALLEY, AND MY SILENCER WORKED LIKE A CHARM. NO ONE HEARD OR SAW A THING. BY THE TIME ANYONE FINDS HER BODY...
...I'LL BE WELL ON MY WAY HOME TO JO'BURG.
STAND WHERE YOU ARE, ASSASSIN! OR FACE THE WRATH OF-- STORM!!
WHA--?! LIGHTNING BOLTS! CRACKLING ALL AROUND ME!
BUT...A MOMENT AGO, THE SKY WAS CLEAR! THIS IS INSANE --IMPOSSIBLE!
FAR FROM IT, FOR ONE WHO CONTROLS THE WEATHER.
LAY DOWN YOUR WEAPON, AND YOU WILL NOT BE HARMED.
YOU!
I'LL NEVER YIELD...NOT TO THE LIKES OF YOU!
YOU TRY MY PATIENCE, LITTLE MAN.
HIS ACCENT MARKS HIM AS AN AFRIKANER, FROM SOUTH AFRICA. WHY IS HE TRYING TO KILL ME?!
HE CAME PAINFULLY CLOSE TO SUCCEEDING, TOO. HIS ATTEMPT LEFT ME WITH A SPLITTING HEADACHE, BUT THAT'S BETTER THAN BEING DEAD. I THINK.
WHOUFFF!
I WANT ANSWERS...
YOU'LL GET NOTHING FROM ME, KAFFIR!
STORM BRIDLES AT THE INSULT, AND DECIDES THAT ENOUGH IS ENOUGH.
SHE CONCENTRATES--THE RAW, PRIMAL POWER OF NATURE COURSING THROUGH HER BODY, MASSIVE BOLTS OF LIGHTNING FLARING FROM HER FINGER-TIPS--AND HER WOULD-BE ASSASSIN ABRUPTLY FINDS HIMSELF IN THE CENTER OF A FULL-FLEDGED THUNDERSTORM.
THE TEMPEST LASTS ONLY A MINUTE, BUT TO THE MAN TRAPPED IN ITS HEART--SHRIEKING LIKE A MADMAN IN ATAVISTIC TERROR --IT SEEMS TO GO ON FOREVER.

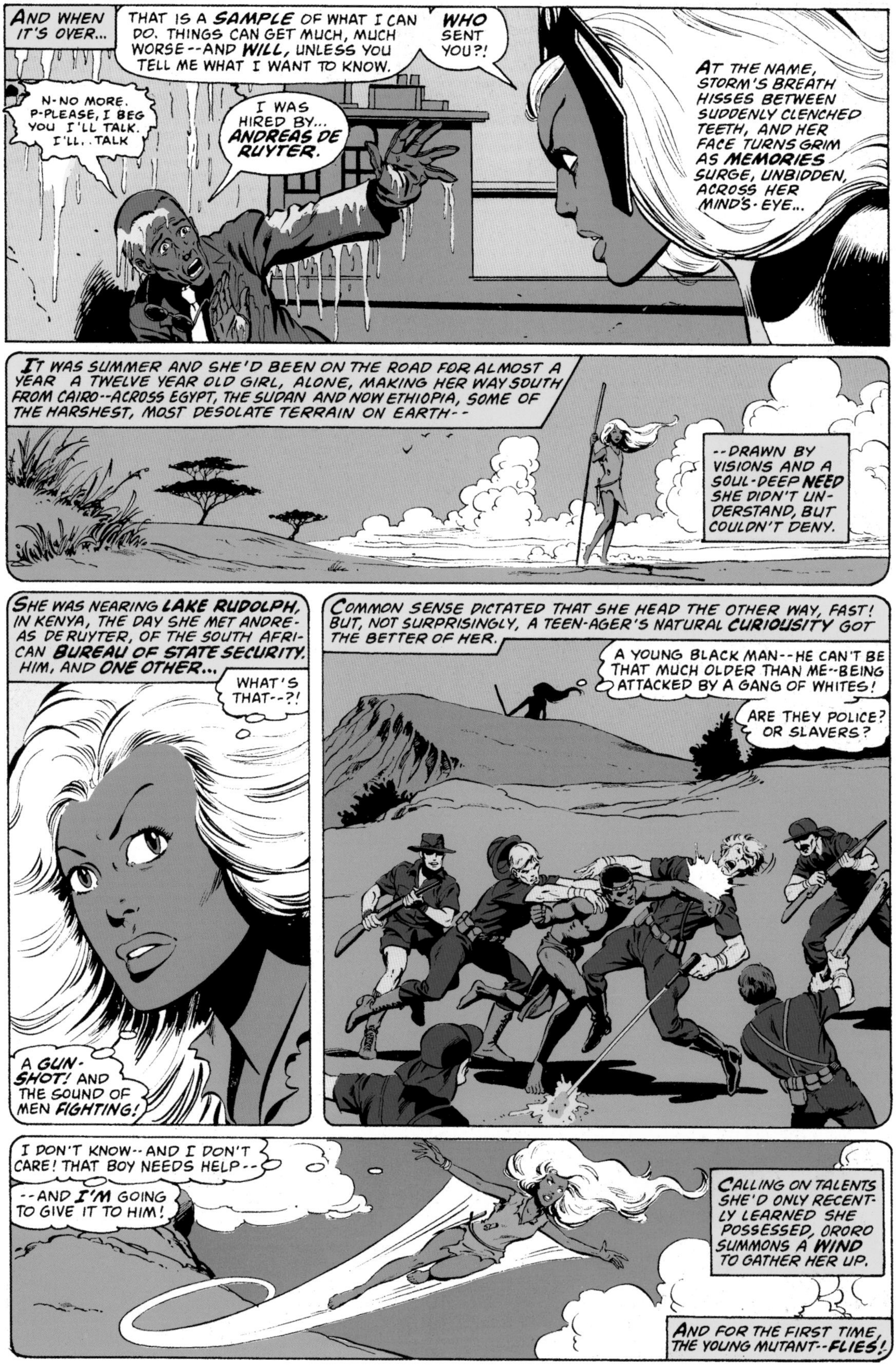
AND WHEN IT'S OVER...
THAT IS A SAMPLE OF WHAT I CAN DO. THINGS CAN GET MUCH, MUCH WORSE--AND WILL, UNLESS YOU TELL ME WHAT I WANT TO KNOW.
N-NO MORE. P-PLEASE, I BEG YOU I'LL TALK. I'LL.. TALK
WHO SENT YOU?!
I WAS HIRED BY... ANDREAS DE RUYTER.
AT THE NAME, STORM'S BREATH HISSES BETWEEN SUDDENLY CLENCHED TEETH, AND HER FACE TURNS GRIM AS MEMORIES SURGE, UNBIDDEN, ACROSS HER MIND'S-EYE...
IT WAS SUMMER AND SHE'D BEEN ON THE ROAD FOR ALMOST A YEAR A TWELVE YEAR OLD GIRL, ALONE, MAKING HER WAY SOUTH FROM CAIRO--ACROSS EGYPT, THE SUDAN AND NOW ETHIOPIA, SOME OF THE HARSHEST, MOST DESOLATE TERRAIN ON EARTH--
--DRAWN BY VISIONS AND A SOUL-DEEP NEED SHE DIDN'T UNDERSTAND, BUT COULDN'T DENY.
SHE WAS NEARING LAKE RUDOLPH, IN KENYA, THE DAY SHE MET ANDREAS DE RUYTER, OF THE SOUTH AFRICAN BUREAU OF STATE SECURITY. HIM, AND ONE OTHER...
WHAT'S THAT--?!
A GUNSHOT! AND THE SOUND OF MEN FIGHTING!
COMMON SENSE DICTATED THAT SHE HEAD THE OTHER WAY, FAST! BUT, NOT SURPRISINGLY, A TEEN-AGER'S NATURAL CURIOUSITY GOT THE BETTER OF HER.
A YOUNG BLACK MAN--HE CAN'T BE THAT MUCH OLDER THAN ME--BEING ATTACKED BY A GANG OF WHITES!
ARE THEY POLICE? OR SLAVERS?
I DON'T KNOW--AND I DON'T CARE! THAT BOY NEEDS HELP--
--AND I'M GOING TO GIVE IT TO HIM!
CALLING ON TALENTS SHE'D ONLY RECENTLY LEARNED SHE POSSESSED, ORORO SUMMONS A WIND TO GATHER HER UP.
AND FOR THE FIRST TIME, THE YOUNG MUTANT--FLIES!

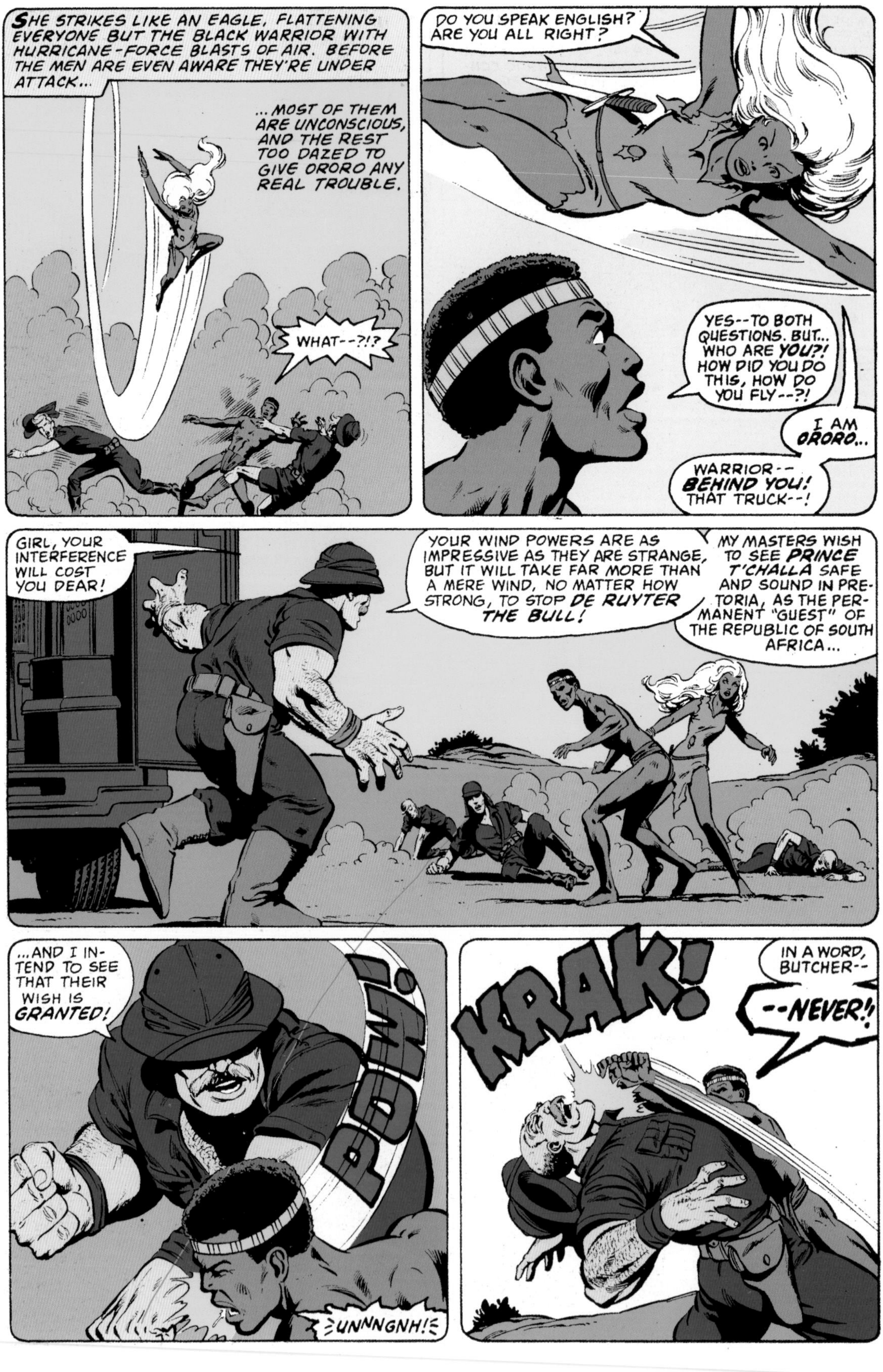
SHE STRIKES LIKE AN EAGLE, FLATTENING EVERYONE BUT THE BLACK WARRIOR WITH HURRICANE-FORCE BLASTS OF AIR. BEFORE THE MEN ARE EVEN AWARE THEY'RE UNDER ATTACK...
...MOST OF THEM ARE UNCONSCIOUS, AND THE REST TOO DAZED TO GIVE ORORO ANY REAL TROUBLE.
WHAT--?!?
DO YOU SPEAK ENGLISH? ARE YOU ALL RIGHT?
YES--TO BOTH QUESTIONS. BUT... WHO ARE YOU?! HOW DID YOU DO THIS, HOW DO YOU FLY--?!
I AM ORORO...
WARRIOR-- BEHIND YOU! THAT TRUCK--!
GIRL, YOUR INTERFERENCE WILL COST YOU DEAR!
YOUR WIND POWERS ARE AS IMPRESSIVE AS THEY ARE STRANGE, BUT IT WILL TAKE FAR MORE THAN A MERE WIND, NO MATTER HOW STRONG, TO STOP DE RUYTER THE BULL!
MY MASTERS WISH TO SEE PRINCE T'CHALLA SAFE AND SOUND IN PRETORIA, AS THE PERMANENT "GUEST" OF THE REPUBLIC OF SOUTH AFRICA...
...AND I INTEND TO SEE THAT THEIR WISH IS GRANTED!
POW!
UNNNGNH!
KRAK!
IN A WORD, BUTCHER--
--NEVER!

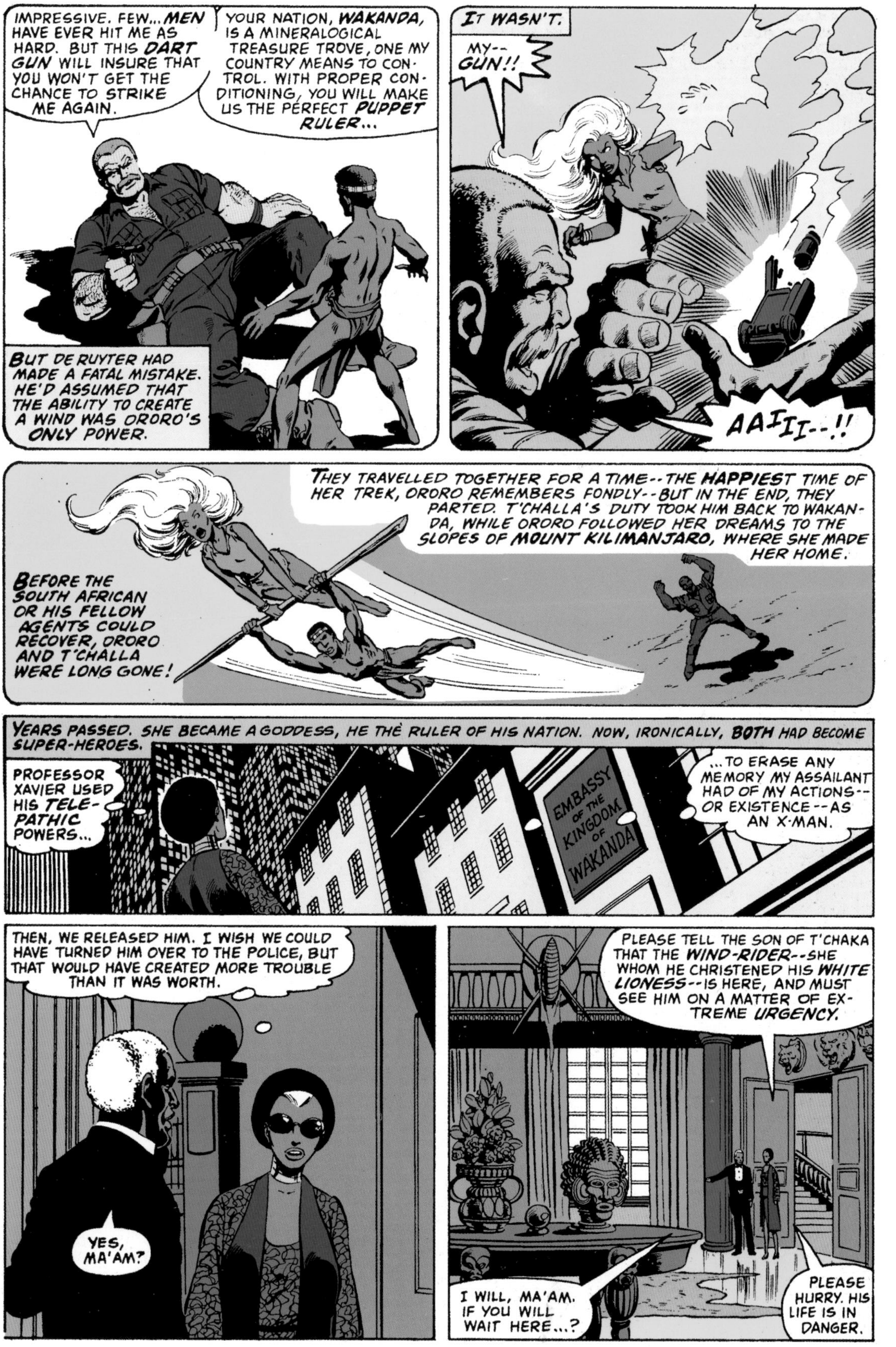
IMPRESSIVE. FEW... MEN HAVE EVER HIT ME AS HARD. BUT THIS DART GUN WILL INSURE THAT YOU WON'T GET THE CHANCE TO STRIKE ME AGAIN.
YOUR NATION, WAKANDA, IS A MINERALOGICAL TREASURE TROVE, ONE MY COUNTRY MEANS TO CONTROL. WITH PROPER CONDITIONING, YOU WILL MAKE US THE PERFECT PUPPET RULER...
BUT DE RUYTER HAD MADE A FATAL MISTAKE. HE'D ASSUMED THAT THE ABILITY TO CREATE A WIND WAS ORORO'S ONLY POWER.
IT WASN'T.
MY-- GUN!!
AAIII--!!
BEFORE THE SOUTH AFRICAN OR HIS FELLOW AGENTS COULD RECOVER, ORORO AND T'CHALLA WERE LONG GONE!
THEY TRAVELLED TOGETHER FOR A TIME--THE HAPPIEST TIME OF HER TREK, ORORO REMEMBERS FONDLY--BUT IN THE END, THEY PARTED. T'CHALLA'S DUTY TOOK HIM BACK TO WAKANDA, WHILE ORORO FOLLOWED HER DREAMS TO THE SLOPES OF MOUNT KILIMANJARO, WHERE SHE MADE HER HOME.
YEARS PASSED. SHE BECAME A GODDESS, HE THE RULER OF HIS NATION. NOW, IRONICALLY, BOTH HAD BECOME SUPER-HEROES.
PROFESSOR XAVIER USED HIS TELEPATHIC POWERS...
...TO ERASE ANY MEMORY MY ASSAILANT HAD OF MY ACTIONS--OR EXISTENCE--AS AN X-MAN.
EMBASSY OF THE KINGDOM OF WAKANDA
THEN, WE RELEASED HIM. I WISH WE COULD HAVE TURNED HIM OVER TO THE POLICE, BUT THAT WOULD HAVE CREATED MORE TROUBLE THAN IT WAS WORTH.
YES, MA'AM?
PLEASE TELL THE SON OF T'CHAKA THAT THE WIND-RIDER--SHE WHOM HE CHRISTENED HIS WHITE LIONESS--IS HERE, AND MUST SEE HIM ON A MATTER OF EXTREME URGENCY.
I WILL, MA'AM. IF YOU WILL WAIT HERE...?
PLEASE HURRY. HIS LIFE IS IN DANGER.

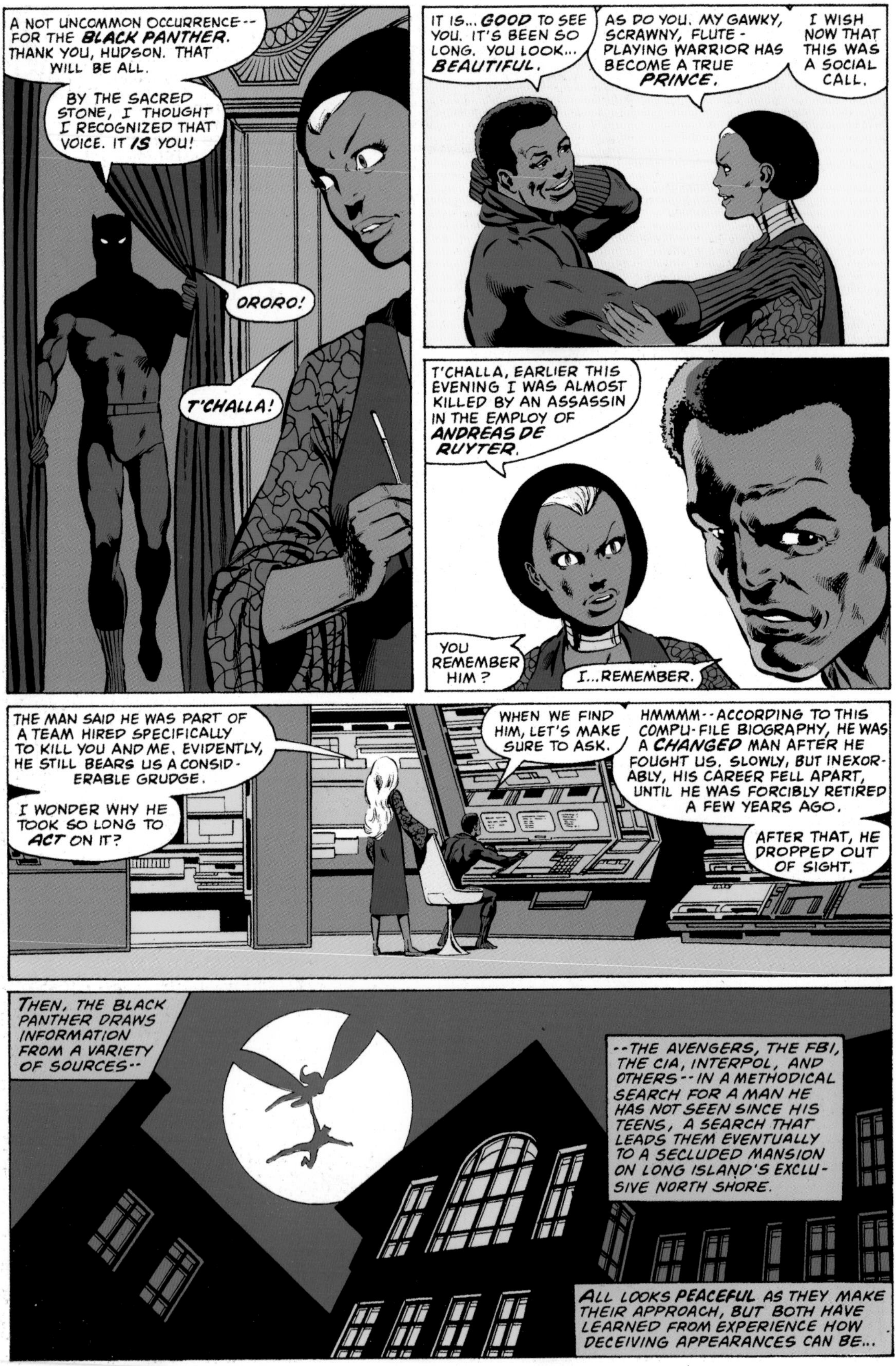
A NOT UNCOMMON OCCURRENCE-- FOR THE BLACK PANTHER. THANK YOU, HUDSON. THAT WILL BE ALL.
BY THE SACRED STONE, I THOUGHT I RECOGNIZED THAT VOICE. IT IS YOU!
ORORO!
T'CHALLA!
IT IS... GOOD TO SEE YOU. IT'S BEEN SO LONG. YOU LOOK... BEAUTIFUL.
AS DO YOU. MY GAWKY, SCRAWNY, FLUTE-PLAYING WARRIOR HAS BECOME A TRUE PRINCE.
I WISH NOW THAT THIS WAS A SOCIAL CALL.
T'CHALLA, EARLIER THIS EVENING I WAS ALMOST KILLED BY AN ASSASSIN IN THE EMPLOY OF ANDREAS DE RUYTER.
YOU REMEMBER HIM?
I...REMEMBER.
THE MAN SAID HE WAS PART OF A TEAM HIRED SPECIFICALLY TO KILL YOU AND ME. EVIDENTLY, HE STILL BEARS US A CONSIDERABLE GRUDGE.
I WONDER WHY HE TOOK SO LONG TO ACT ON IT?
WHEN WE FIND HIM, LET'S MAKE SURE TO ASK.
HMMMM--ACCORDING TO THIS COMPU-FILE BIOGRAPHY, HE WAS A CHANGED MAN AFTER HE FOUGHT US. SLOWLY, BUT INEXORABLY, HIS CAREER FELL APART, UNTIL HE WAS FORCIBLY RETIRED A FEW YEARS AGO.
AFTER THAT, HE DROPPED OUT OF SIGHT.
THEN, THE BLACK PANTHER DRAWS INFORMATION FROM A VARIETY OF SOURCES--
--THE AVENGERS, THE FBI, THE CIA, INTERPOL, AND OTHERS--IN A METHODICAL SEARCH FOR A MAN HE HAS NOT SEEN SINCE HIS TEENS, A SEARCH THAT LEADS THEM EVENTUALLY TO A SECLUDED MANSION ON LONG ISLAND'S EXCLUSIVE NORTH SHORE.
ALL LOOKS PEACEFUL AS THEY MAKE THEIR APPROACH, BUT BOTH HAVE LEARNED FROM EXPERIENCE HOW DECEIVING APPEARANCES CAN BE...

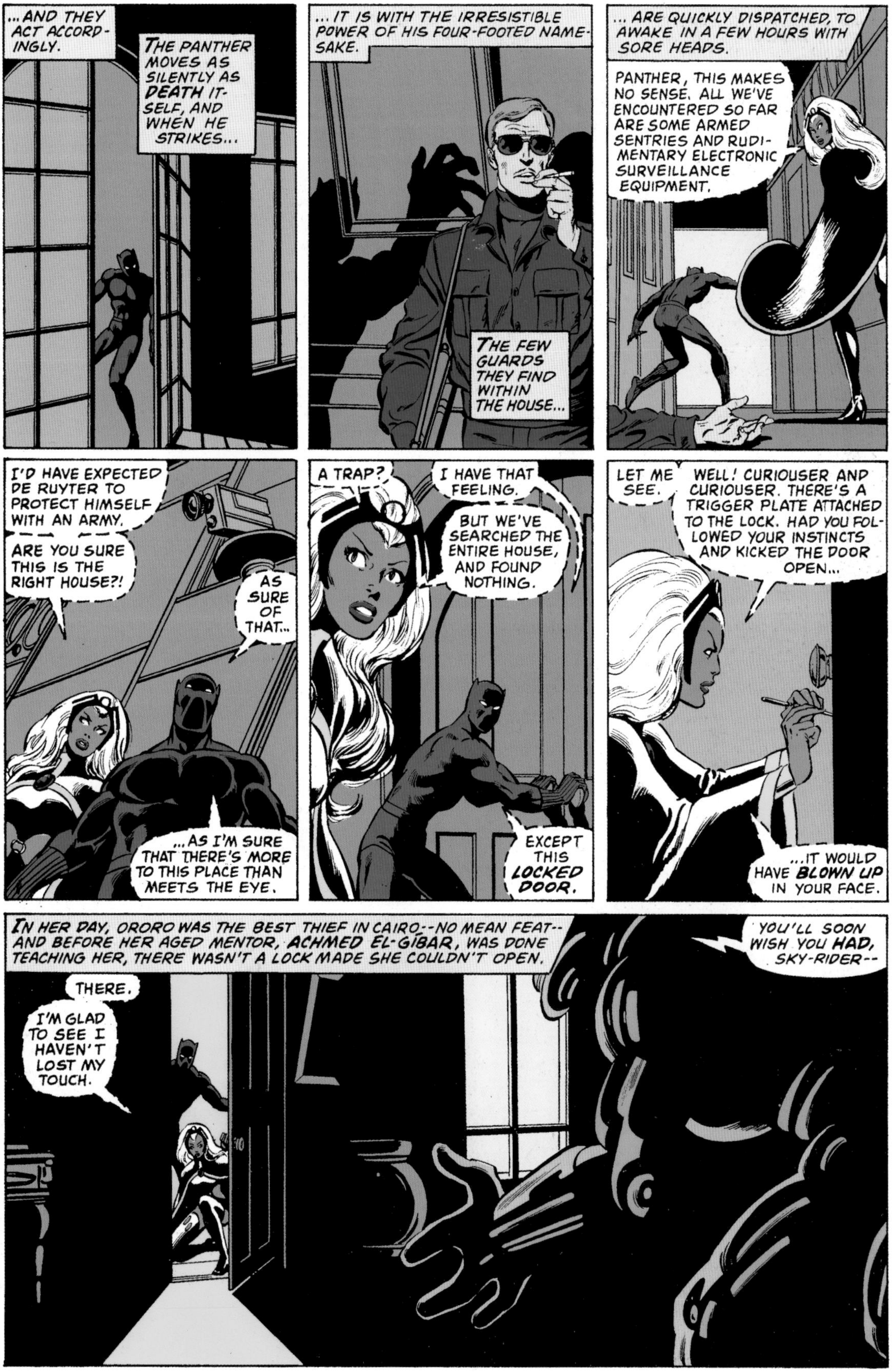
...AND THEY ACT ACCORDINGLY.
THE PANTHER MOVES AS SILENTLY AS DEATH ITSELF, AND WHEN HE STRIKES...
...IT IS WITH THE IRRESISTIBLE POWER OF HIS FOUR-FOOTED NAMESAKE.
THE FEW GUARDS THEY FIND WITHIN THE HOUSE...
...ARE QUICKLY DISPATCHED, TO AWAKE IN A FEW HOURS WITH SORE HEADS.
PANTHER, THIS MAKES NO SENSE. ALL WE'VE ENCOUNTERED SO FAR ARE SOME ARMED SENTRIES AND RUDIMENTARY ELECTRONIC SURVEILLANCE EQUIPMENT.
I'D HAVE EXPECTED DE RUYTER TO PROTECT HIMSELF WITH AN ARMY.
ARE YOU SURE THIS IS THE RIGHT HOUSE?!
AS SURE OF THAT...
...AS I'M SURE THAT THERE'S MORE TO THIS PLACE THAN MEETS THE EYE.
A TRAP?
I HAVE THAT FEELING.
BUT WE'VE SEARCHED THE ENTIRE HOUSE, AND FOUND NOTHING.
EXCEPT THIS LOCKED DOOR.
LET ME SEE.
WELL! CURIOUSER AND CURIOUSER. THERE'S A TRIGGER PLATE ATTACHED TO THE LOCK. HAD YOU FOLLOWED YOUR INSTINCTS AND KICKED THE DOOR OPEN...
...IT WOULD HAVE BLOWN UP IN YOUR FACE.
IN HER DAY, ORORO WAS THE BEST THIEF IN CAIRO--NO MEAN FEAT--AND BEFORE HER AGED MENTOR, ACHMED EL-GIBAR, WAS DONE TEACHING HER, THERE WASN'T A LOCK MADE SHE COULDN'T OPEN.
THERE.
I'M GLAD TO SEE I HAVEN'T LOST MY TOUCH.
YOU'LL SOON WISH YOU HAD, SKY-RIDER--

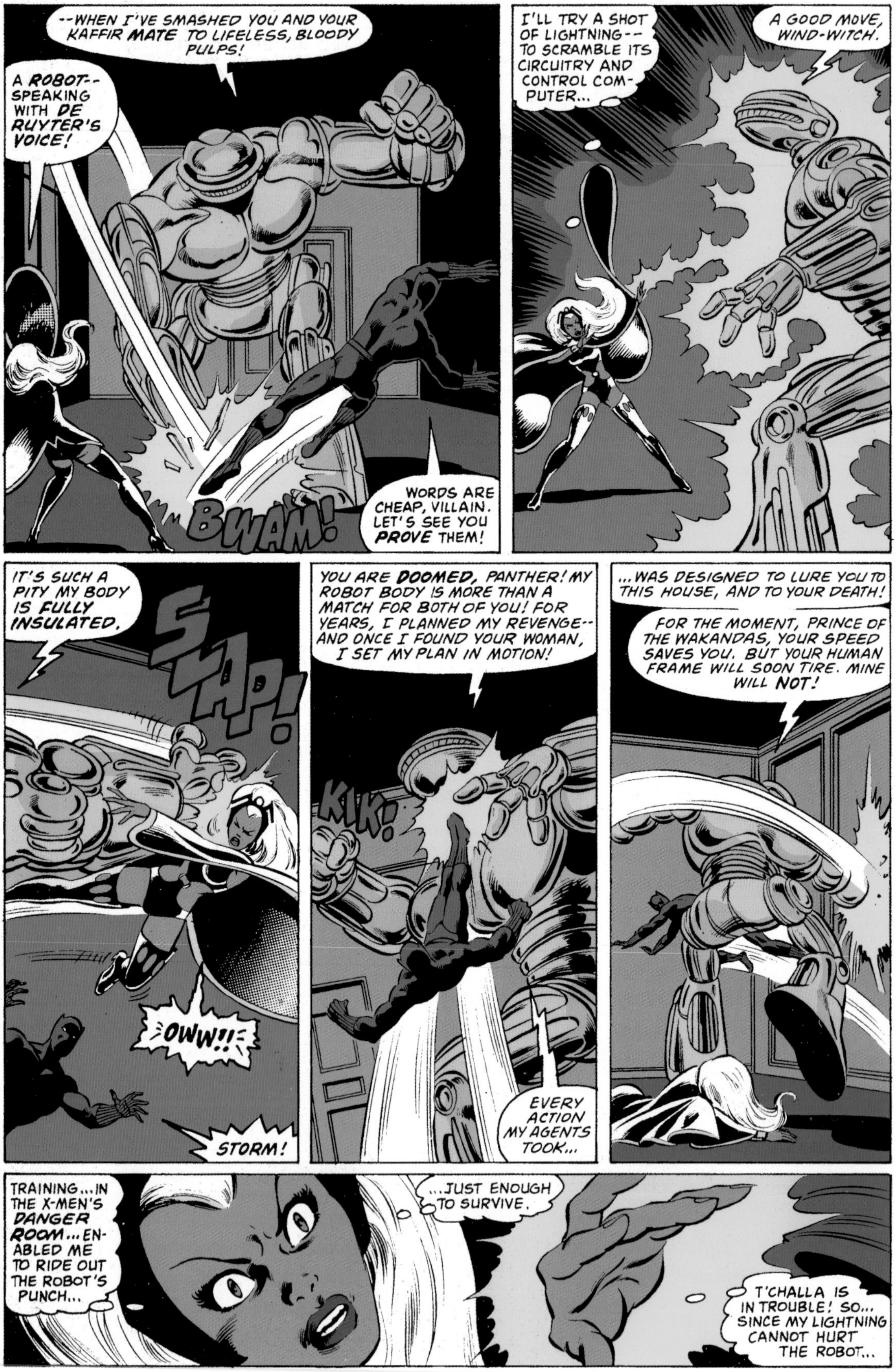

--WHEN I'VE SMASHED YOU AND YOUR KAFFIR MATE TO LIFELESS, BLOODY PULPS!
A ROBOT--SPEAKING WITH DE RUYTER'S VOICE!
WORDS ARE CHEAP, VILLAIN. LET'S SEE YOU PROVE THEM!
BWAM!
I'LL TRY A SHOT OF LIGHTNING--TO SCRAMBLE ITS CIRCUITRY AND CONTROL COMPUTER...
A GOOD MOVE, WIND-WITCH.
IT'S SUCH A PITY MY BODY IS FULLY INSULATED.
SNAP!
OWW!!
STORM!
YOU ARE DOOMED, PANTHER! MY ROBOT BODY IS MORE THAN A MATCH FOR BOTH OF YOU! FOR YEARS, I PLANNED MY REVENGE--AND ONCE I FOUND YOUR WOMAN, I SET MY PLAN IN MOTION!
KIK!
EVERY ACTION MY AGENTS TOOK...
...WAS DESIGNED TO LURE YOU TO THIS HOUSE, AND TO YOUR DEATH!
FOR THE MOMENT, PRINCE OF THE WAKANDAS, YOUR SPEED SAVES YOU. BUT YOUR HUMAN FRAME WILL SOON TIRE. MINE WILL NOT!
TRAINING...IN THE X-MEN'S DANGER ROOM...ENABLED ME TO RIDE OUT THE ROBOT'S PUNCH...
...JUST ENOUGH TO SURVIVE.
T'CHALLA IS IN TROUBLE! SO... SINCE MY LIGHTNING CANNOT HURT THE ROBOT...

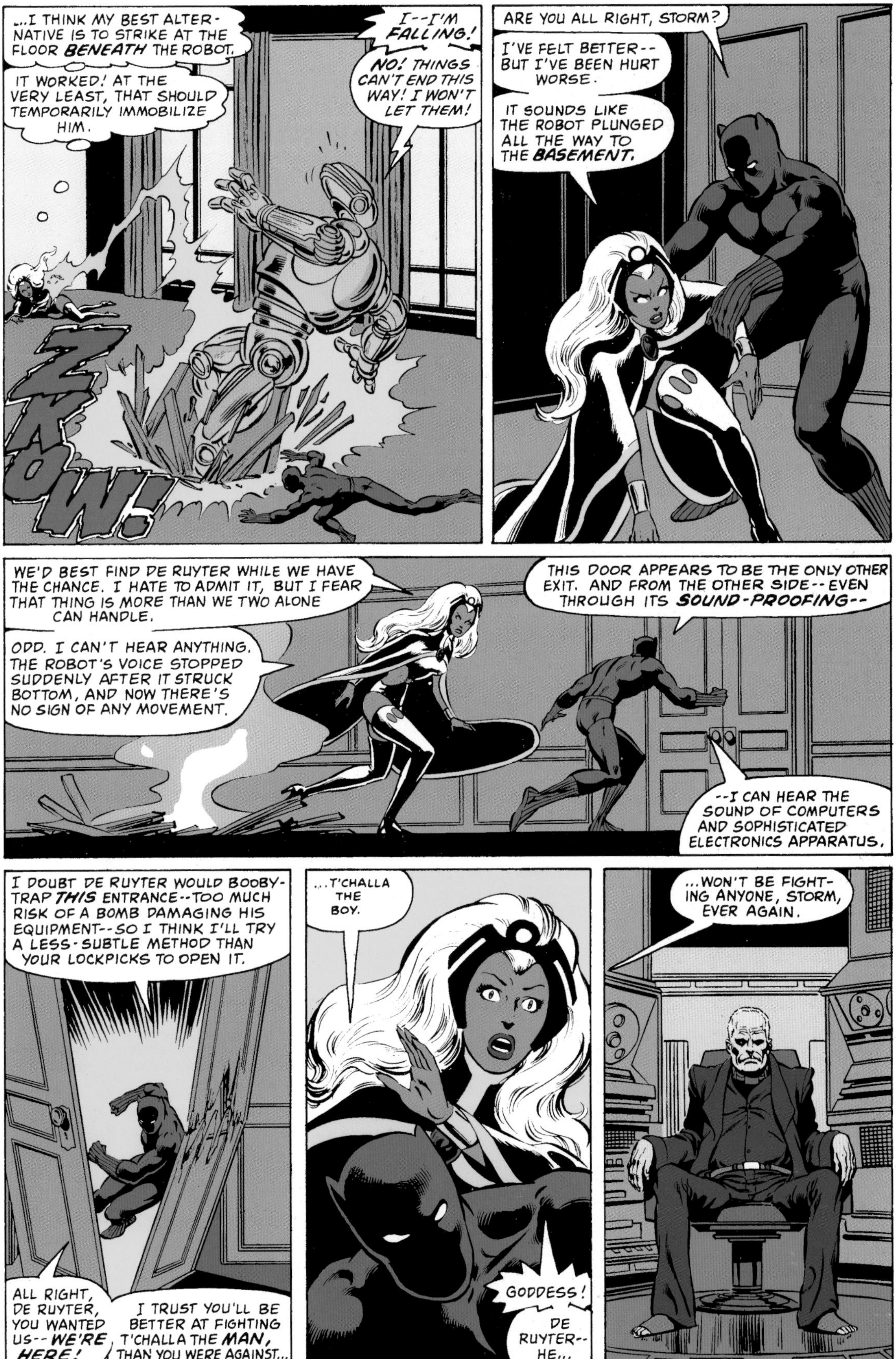
...I THINK MY BEST ALTERNATIVE IS TO STRIKE AT THE FLOOR BENEATH THE ROBOT.
IT WORKED! AT THE VERY LEAST, THAT SHOULD TEMPORARILY IMMOBILIZE HIM.
I--I'M FALLING!
NO! THINGS CAN'T END THIS WAY! I WON'T LET THEM!
ZZKROW!
ARE YOU ALL RIGHT, STORM?
I'VE FELT BETTER--BUT I'VE BEEN HURT WORSE.
IT SOUNDS LIKE THE ROBOT PLUNGED ALL THE WAY TO THE BASEMENT.
WE'D BEST FIND DE RUYTER WHILE WE HAVE THE CHANCE. I HATE TO ADMIT IT, BUT I FEAR THAT THING IS MORE THAN WE TWO ALONE CAN HANDLE.
ODD. I CAN'T HEAR ANYTHING. THE ROBOT'S VOICE STOPPED SUDDENLY AFTER IT STRUCK BOTTOM, AND NOW THERE'S NO SIGN OF ANY MOVEMENT.
THIS DOOR APPEARS TO BE THE ONLY OTHER EXIT. AND FROM THE OTHER SIDE--EVEN THROUGH ITS SOUND-PROOFING--
--I CAN HEAR THE SOUND OF COMPUTERS AND SOPHISTICATED ELECTRONICS APPARATUS.
I DOUBT DE RUYTER WOULD BOOBY-TRAP THIS ENTRANCE--TOO MUCH RISK OF A BOMB DAMAGING HIS EQUIPMENT--SO I THINK I'LL TRY A LESS-SUBTLE METHOD THAN YOUR LOCKPICKS TO OPEN IT.
ALL RIGHT, DE RUYTER, YOU WANTED US--WE'RE HERE!
I TRUST YOU'LL BE BETTER AT FIGHTING T'CHALLA THE MAN, THAN YOU WERE AGAINST...
...T'CHALLA THE BOY.
GODDESS!
DE RUYTER--HE...
...WON'T BE FIGHTING ANYONE, STORM, EVER AGAIN.

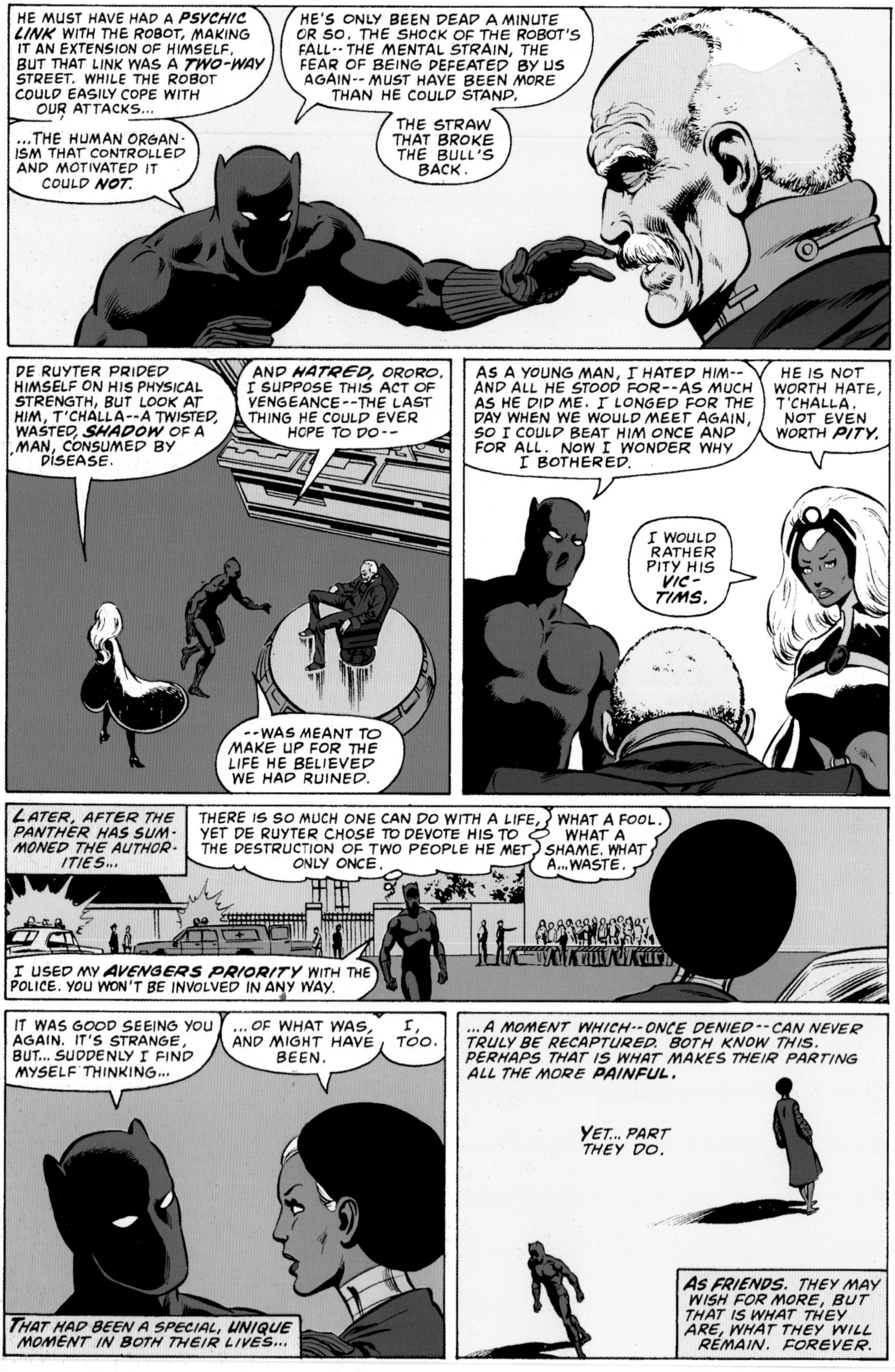
HE MUST HAVE HAD A PSYCHIC LINK WITH THE ROBOT, MAKING IT AN EXTENSION OF HIMSELF, BUT THAT LINK WAS A TWO-WAY STREET. WHILE THE ROBOT COULD EASILY COPE WITH OUR ATTACKS...
...THE HUMAN ORGANISM THAT CONTROLLED AND MOTIVATED IT COULD NOT.
HE'S ONLY BEEN DEAD A MINUTE OR SO. THE SHOCK OF THE ROBOT'S FALL--THE MENTAL STRAIN, THE FEAR OF BEING DEFEATED BY US AGAIN--MUST HAVE BEEN MORE THAN HE COULD STAND.
THE STRAW THAT BROKE THE BULL'S BACK.
DE RUYTER PRIDED HIMSELF ON HIS PHYSICAL STRENGTH, BUT LOOK AT HIM, T'CHALLA--A TWISTED, WASTED, SHADOW OF A MAN, CONSUMED BY DISEASE.
AND HATRED, ORORO. I SUPPOSE THIS ACT OF VENGEANCE--THE LAST THING HE COULD EVER HOPE TO DO--
--WAS MEANT TO MAKE UP FOR THE LIFE HE BELIEVED WE HAD RUINED.
AS A YOUNG MAN, I HATED HIM--AND ALL HE STOOD FOR--AS MUCH AS HE DID ME. I LONGED FOR THE DAY WHEN WE WOULD MEET AGAIN, SO I COULD BEAT HIM ONCE AND FOR ALL. NOW I WONDER WHY I BOTHERED.
HE IS NOT WORTH HATE, T'CHALLA. NOT EVEN WORTH PITY.
I WOULD RATHER PITY HIS VICTIMS.
LATER, AFTER THE PANTHER HAS SUMMONED THE AUTHORITIES...
THERE IS SO MUCH ONE CAN DO WITH A LIFE, YET DE RUYTER CHOSE TO DEVOTE HIS TO THE DESTRUCTION OF TWO PEOPLE HE MET ONLY ONCE.
WHAT A FOOL. WHAT A SHAME. WHAT A...WASTE.
I USED MY AVENGERS PRIORITY WITH THE POLICE. YOU WON'T BE INVOLVED IN ANY WAY.
IT WAS GOOD SEEING YOU AGAIN. IT'S STRANGE, BUT... SUDDENLY I FIND MYSELF THINKING...
...OF WHAT WAS, AND MIGHT HAVE BEEN.
I, TOO.
THAT HAD BEEN A SPECIAL, UNIQUE MOMENT IN BOTH THEIR LIVES...
...A MOMENT WHICH--ONCE DENIED--CAN NEVER TRULY BE RECAPTURED. BOTH KNOW THIS. PERHAPS THAT IS WHAT MAKES THEIR PARTING ALL THE MORE PAINFUL.
YET... PART THEY DO.
AS FRIENDS. THEY MAY WISH FOR MORE, BUT THAT IS WHAT THEY ARE, WHAT THEY WILL REMAIN. FOREVER.

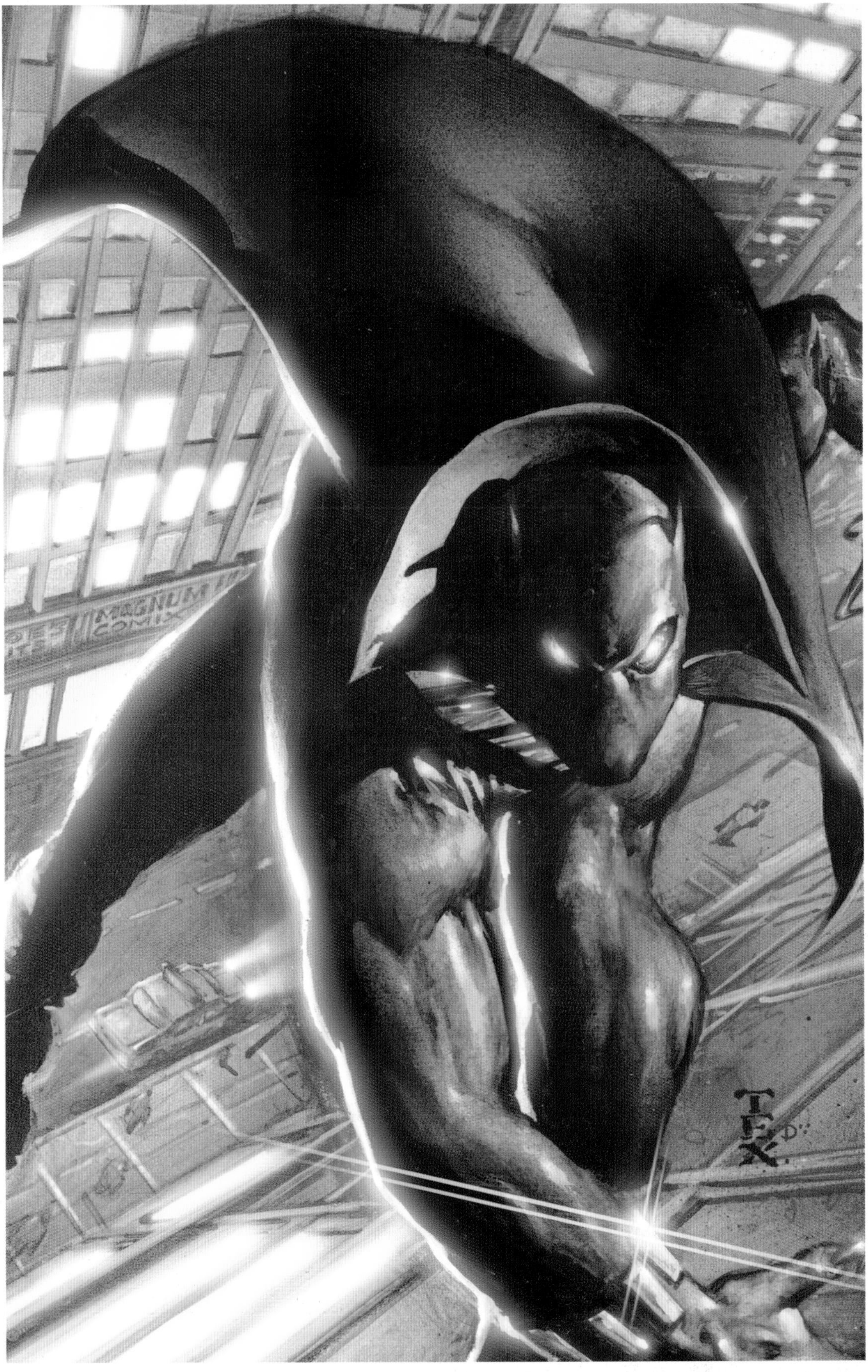
MAGNUM COMIX

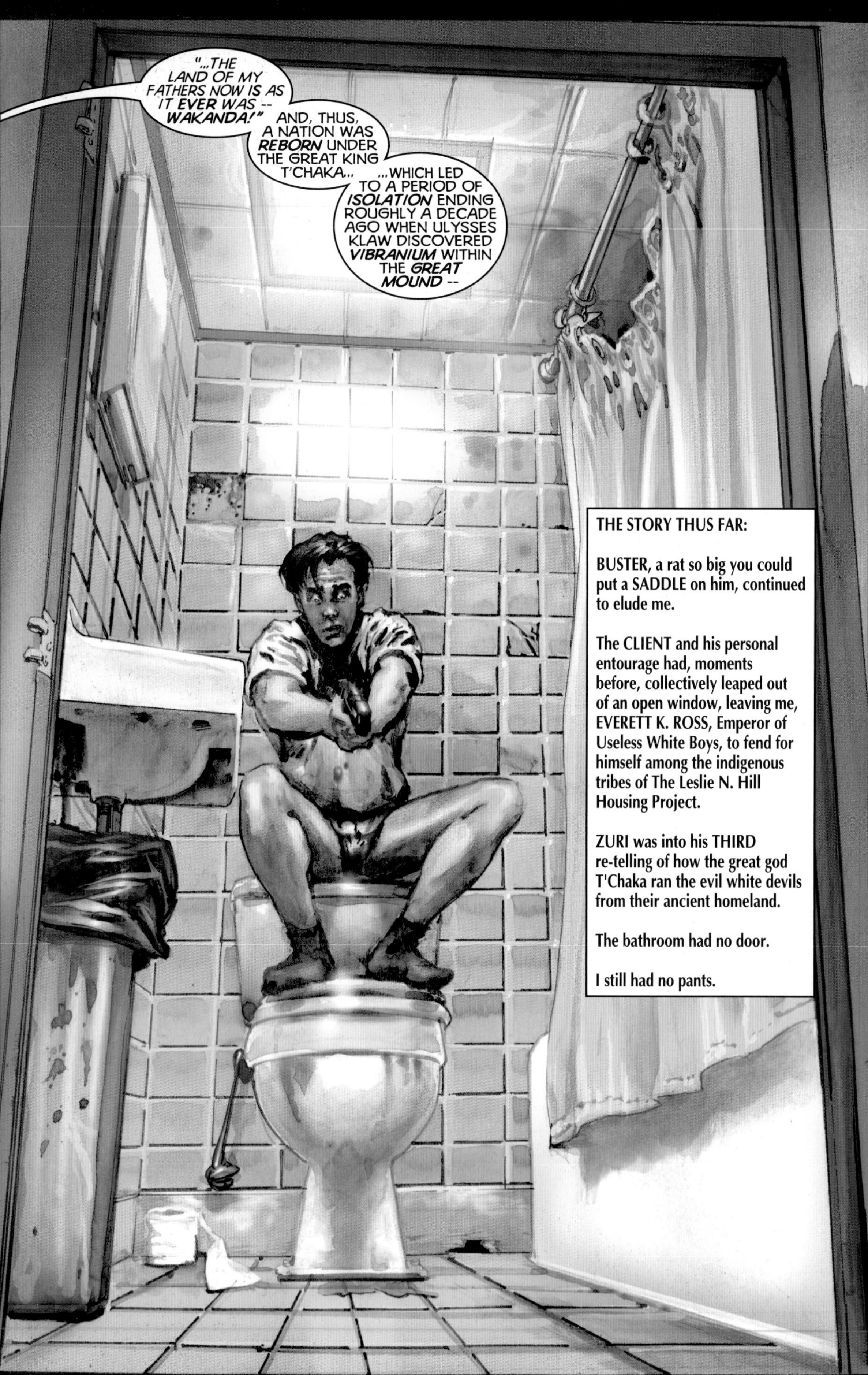
"...THE LAND OF MY FATHERS NOW IS AS IT EVER WAS -- WAKANDA!"
AND, THUS, A NATION WAS REBORN UNDER THE GREAT KING T'CHAKA...
...WHICH LED TO A PERIOD OF ISOLATION ENDING ROUGHLY A DECADE AGO WHEN ULYSSES KLAW DISCOVERED VIBRANIUM WITHIN THE GREAT MOUND --
THE STORY THUS FAR:
BUSTER, a rat so big you could put a SADDLE on him, continued to elude me.
The CLIENT and his personal entourage had, moments before, collectively leaped out of an open window, leaving me, EVERETT K. ROSS, Emperor of Useless White Boys, to fend for himself among the indigenous tribes of The Leslie N. Hill Housing Project.
ZURI was into his THIRD re-telling of how the great god T'Chaka ran the evil white devils from their ancient homeland.
The bathroom had no door.
I still had no pants.

CAT MAN DO

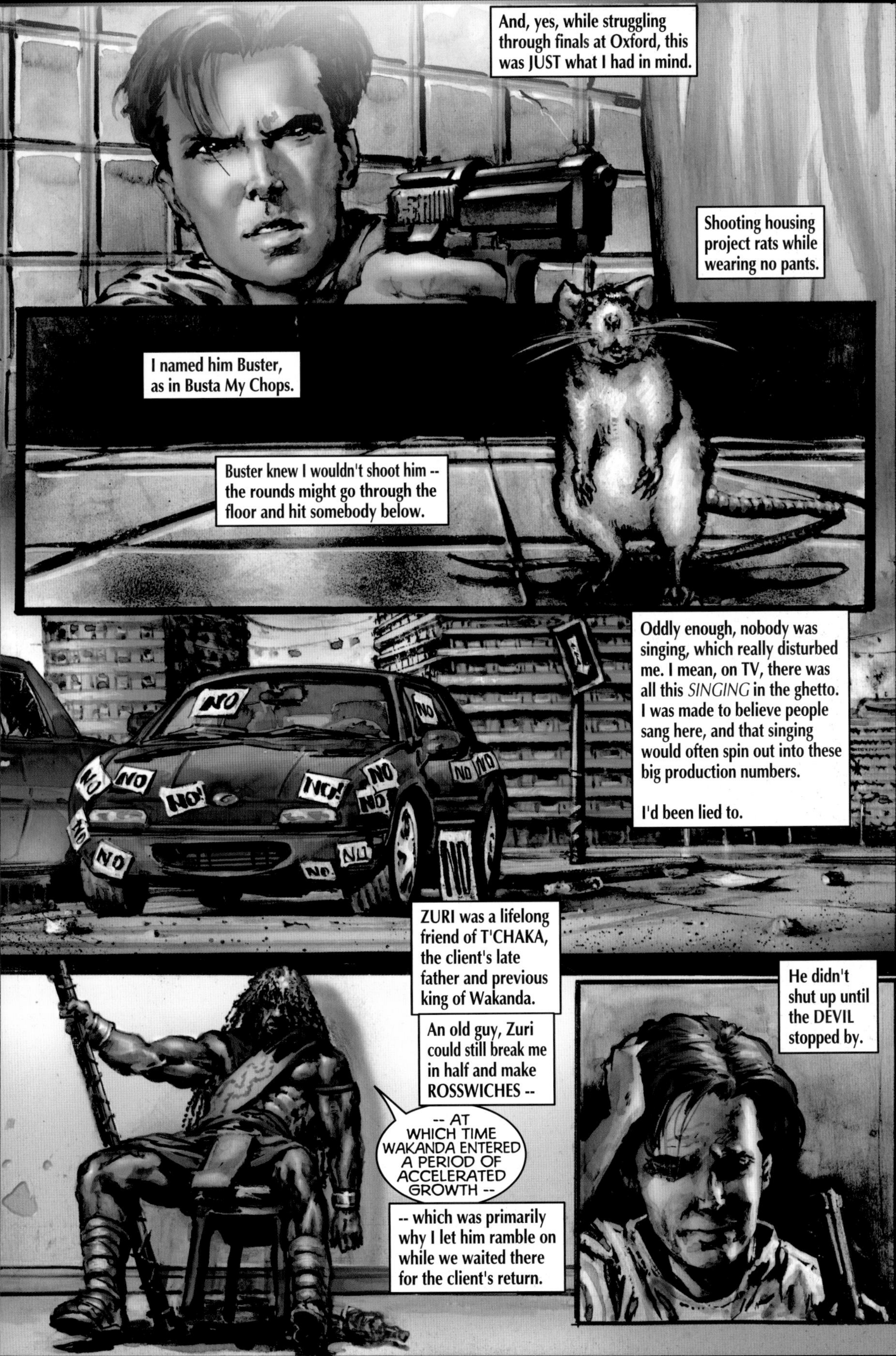

And, yes, while struggling through finals at Oxford, this was JUST what I had in mind.
Shooting housing project rats while wearing no pants.
I named him Buster, as in Busta My Chops.
Buster knew I wouldn't shoot him -- the rounds might go through the floor and hit somebody below.
Oddly enough, nobody was singing, which really disturbed me. I mean, on TV, there was all this *SINGING* in the ghetto. I was made to believe people sang here, and that singing would often spin out into these big production numbers.
I'd been lied to.
NO
NO
NO
NO
NO!
NO!
NO
NO
NO
NO
NO
ZURI was a lifelong friend of T'CHAKA, the client's late father and previous king of Wakanda.
An old guy, Zuri could still break me in half and make ROSSWICHES --
-- AT WHICH TIME WAKANDA ENTERED A PERIOD OF ACCELERATED GROWTH --
-- which was primarily why I let him ramble on while we waited there for the client's return.
He didn't shut up until the DEVIL stopped by.

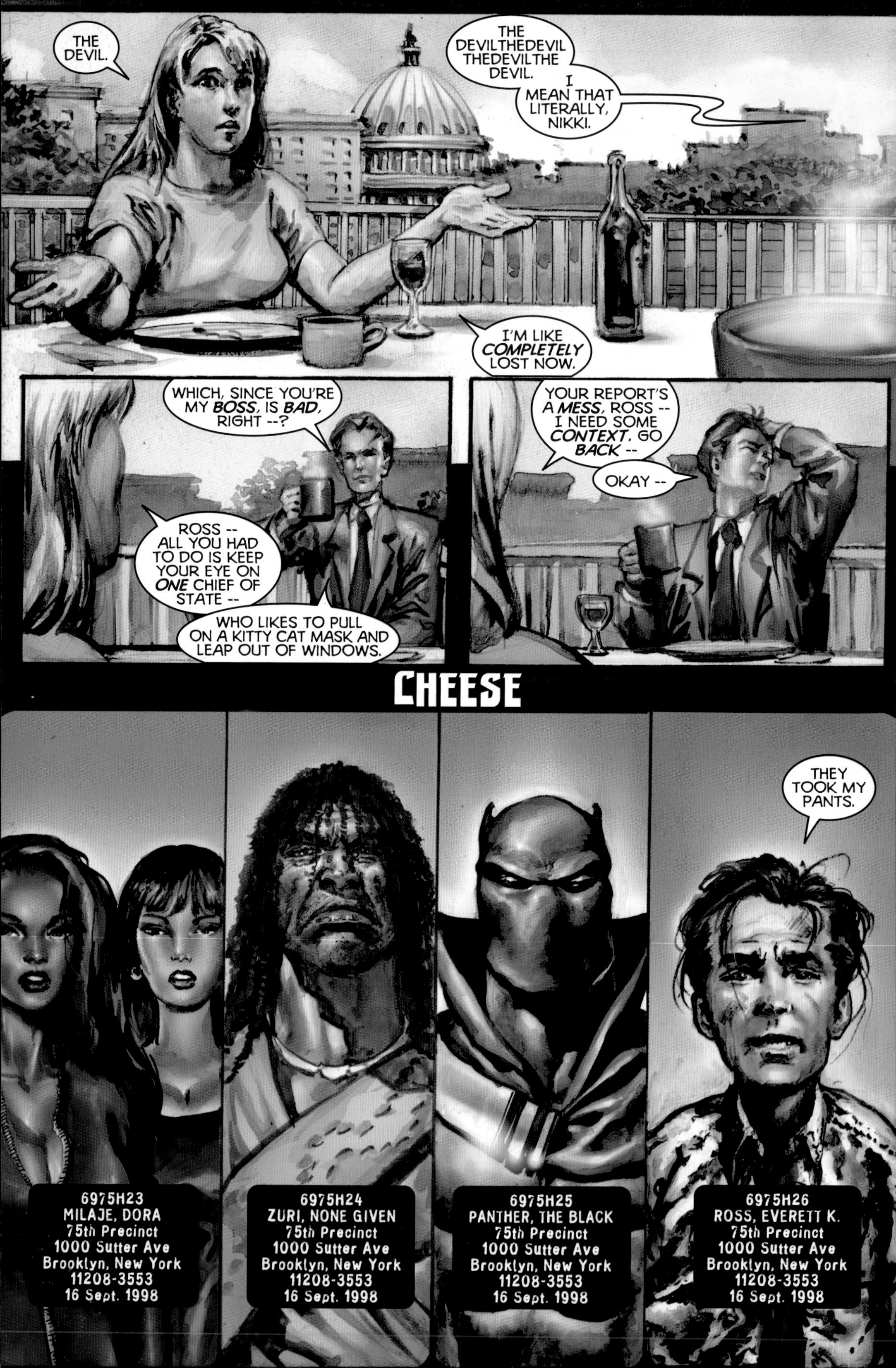
THE DEVIL.
THE DEVILTHEDEVIL THEDEVILTHE DEVIL.
I MEAN THAT LITERALLY, NIKKI.
I'M LIKE COMPLETELY LOST NOW.
WHICH, SINCE YOU'RE MY BOSS, IS BAD, RIGHT --?
ROSS -- ALL YOU HAD TO DO IS KEEP YOUR EYE ON ONE CHIEF OF STATE --
WHO LIKES TO PULL ON A KITTY CAT MASK AND LEAP OUT OF WINDOWS.
YOUR REPORT'S A MESS, ROSS -- I NEED SOME CONTEXT. GO BACK --
OKAY --
CHEESE
THEY TOOK MY PANTS.
6975H23
MILAJE, DORA
75th Precinct
1000 Sutter Ave
Brooklyn, New York
11208-3553
16 Sept. 1998
6975H24
ZURI, NONE GIVEN
75th Precinct
1000 Sutter Ave
Brooklyn, New York
11208-3553
16 Sept. 1998
6975H25
PANTHER, THE BLACK
75th Precinct
1000 Sutter Ave
Brooklyn, New York
11208-3553
16 Sept. 1998
6975H26
ROSS, EVERETT K.
75th Precinct
1000 Sutter Ave
Brooklyn, New York
11208-3553
16 Sept. 1998

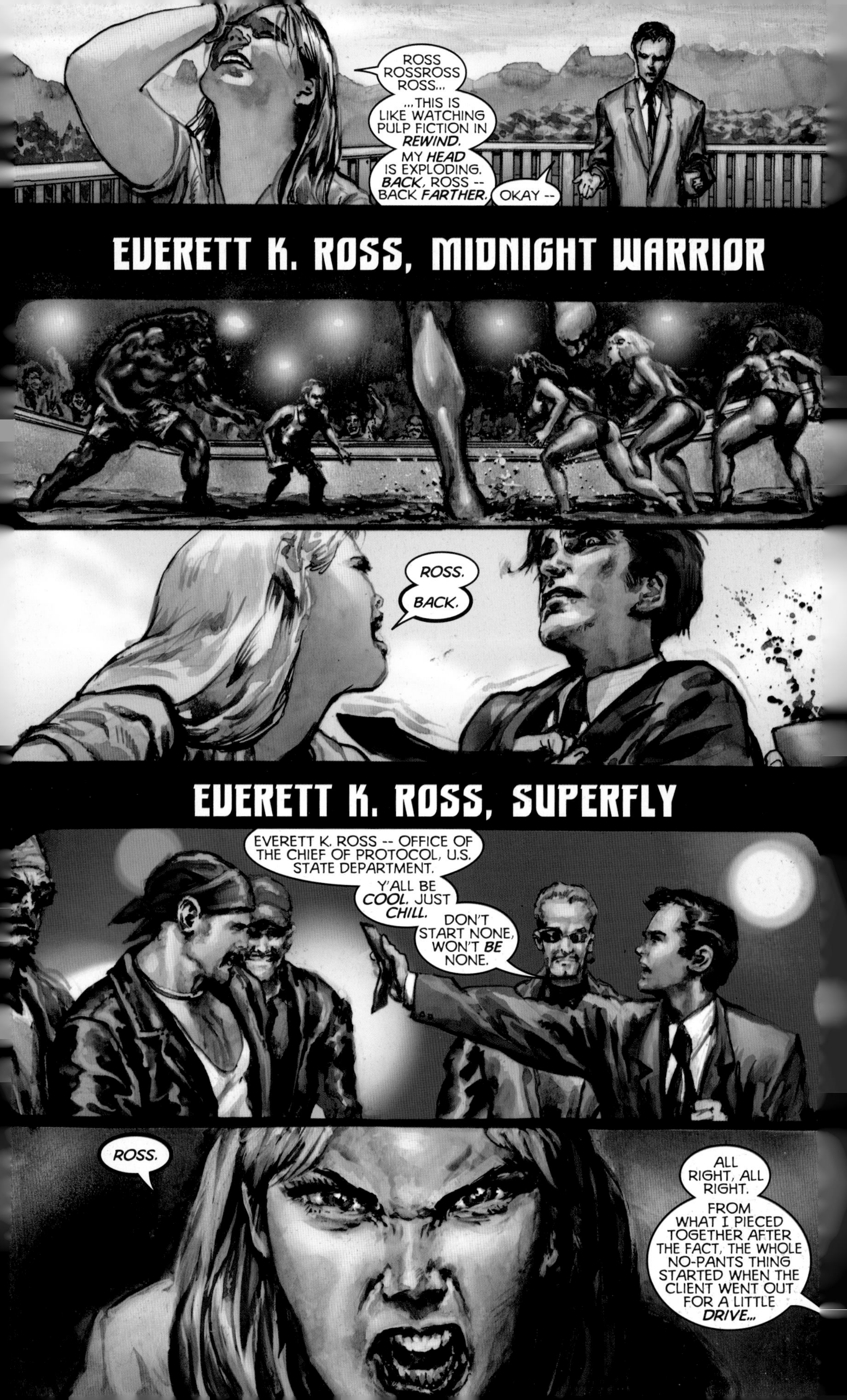
ROSS ROSSROSS ROSS...
...THIS IS LIKE WATCHING PULP FICTION IN REWIND.
MY HEAD IS EXPLODING.
BACK, ROSS -- BACK FARTHER.
OKAY --
EVERETT K. ROSS, MIDNIGHT WARRIOR
ROSS.
BACK.
EVERETT K. ROSS, SUPERFLY
EVERETT K. ROSS -- OFFICE OF THE CHIEF OF PROTOCOL, U.S. STATE DEPARTMENT.
Y'ALL BE COOL. JUST CHILL.
DON'T START NONE, WON'T BE NONE.
ROSS.
ALL RIGHT, ALL RIGHT.
FROM WHAT I PIECED TOGETHER AFTER THE FACT, THE WHOLE NO-PANTS THING STARTED WHEN THE CLIENT WENT OUT FOR A LITTLE DRIVE...

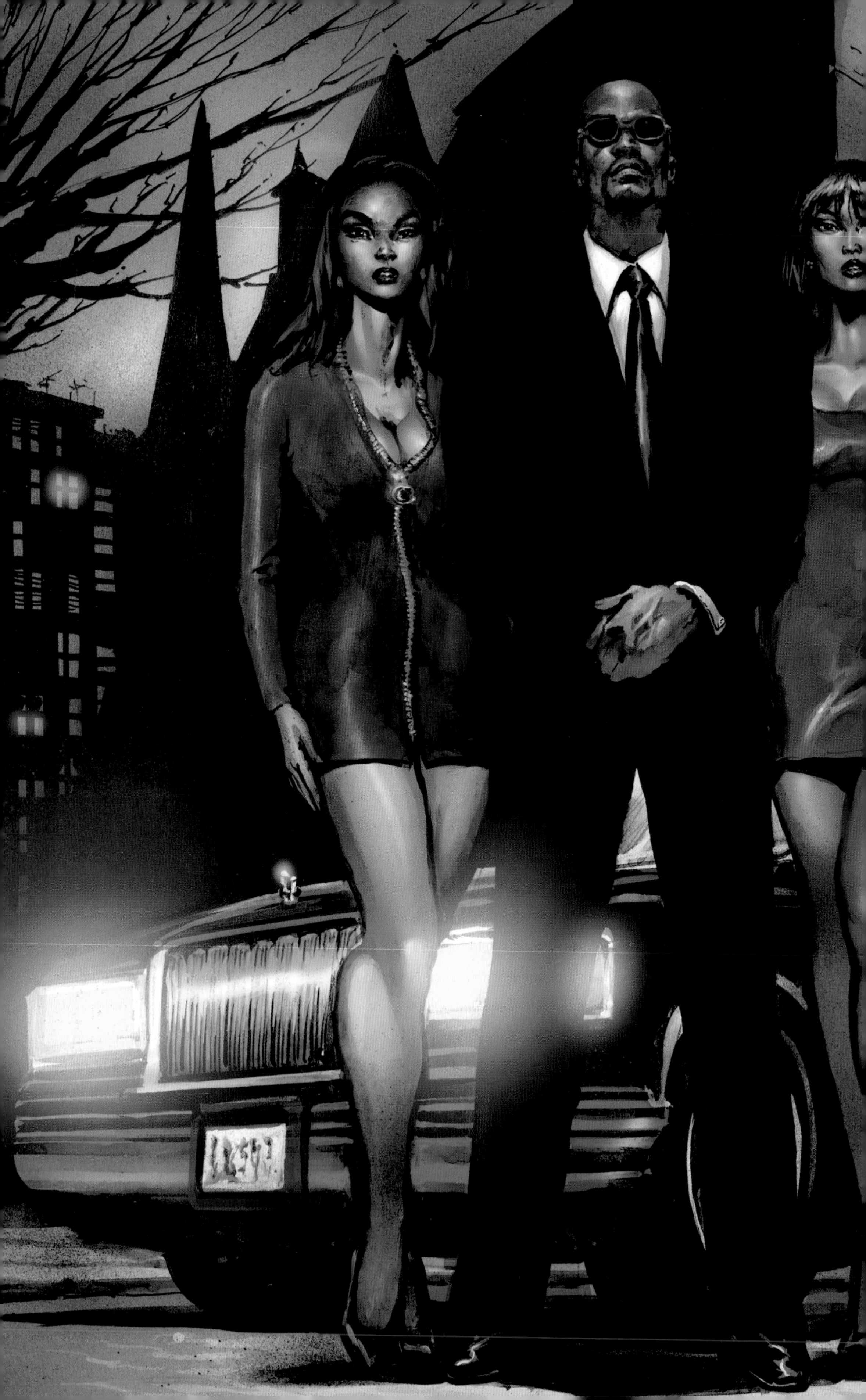

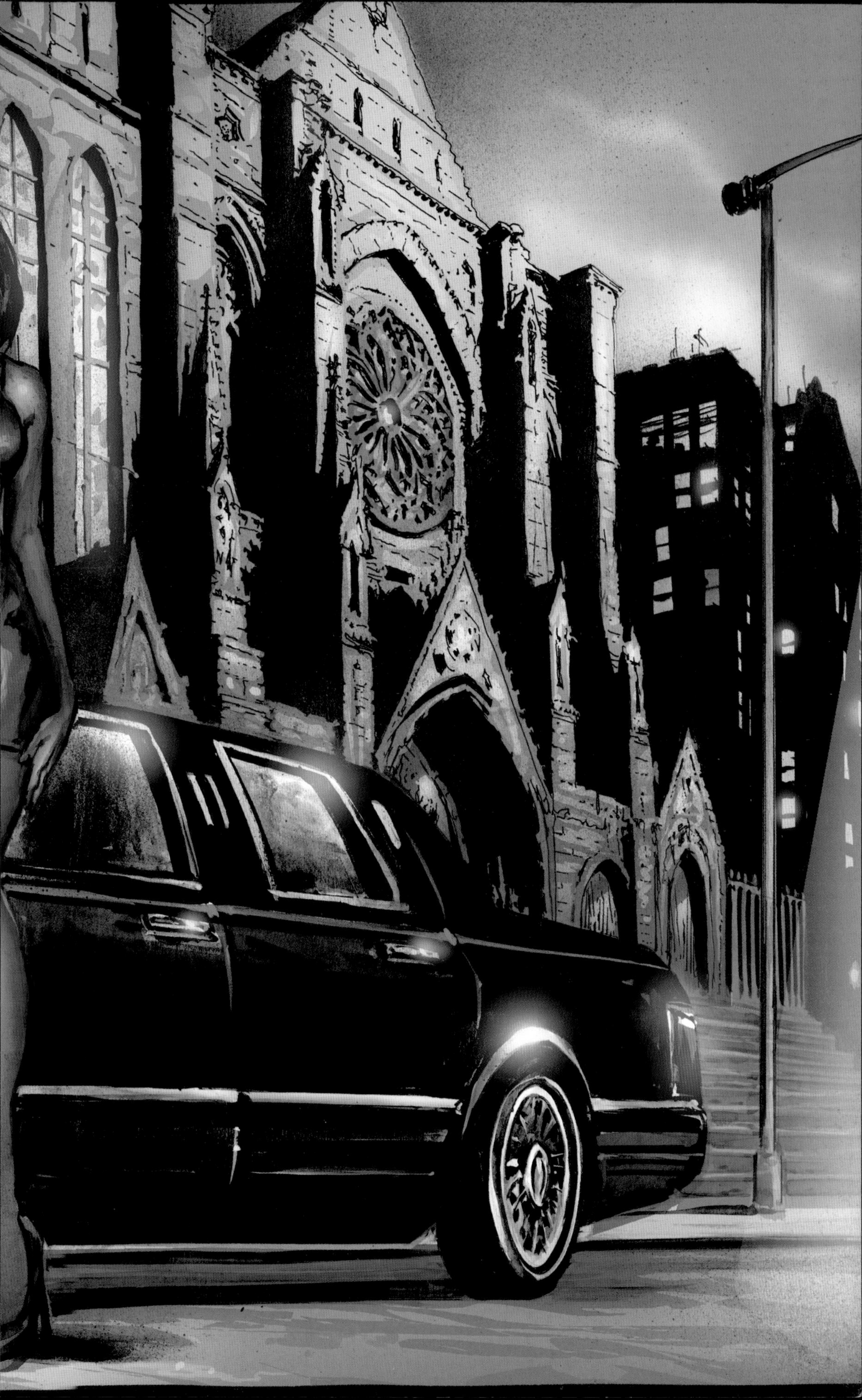

ME, MY AND MINE

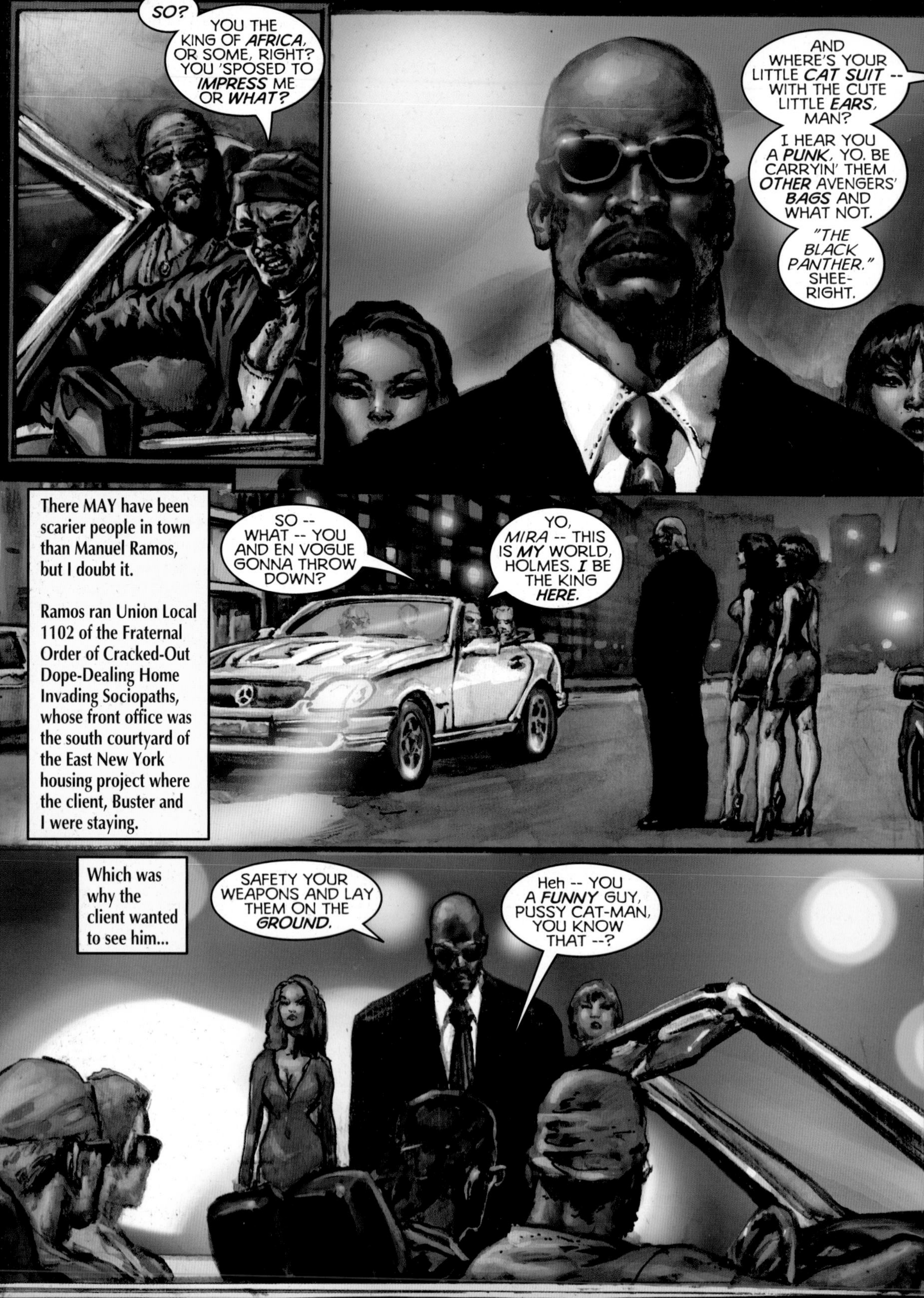

SO?
YOU THE KING OF *AFRICA*, OR SOME, RIGHT? YOU 'SPOSED TO *IMPRESS* ME OR *WHAT?*
AND WHERE'S YOUR LITTLE *CAT SUIT* -- WITH THE CUTE LITTLE *EARS*, MAN?
I HEAR YOU A *PUNK*, YO. BE CARRYIN' THEM *OTHER* AVENGERS' *BAGS* AND WHAT NOT.
"THE BLACK PANTHER." SHEE-RIGHT.
There MAY have been scarier people in town than Manuel Ramos, but I doubt it.
Ramos ran Union Local 1102 of the Fraternal Order of Cracked-Out Dope-Dealing Home Invading Sociopaths, whose front office was the south courtyard of the East New York housing project where the client, Buster and I were staying.
SO -- WHAT -- YOU AND EN VOGUE GONNA THROW DOWN?
YO, *MIRA* -- THIS IS *MY* WORLD, HOLMES. *I* BE THE KING *HERE*.
Which was why the client wanted to see him...
SAFETY YOUR WEAPONS AND LAY THEM ON THE *GROUND*.
Heh -- YOU A *FUNNY* GUY, PUSSY CAT-MAN, YOU KNOW THAT --?

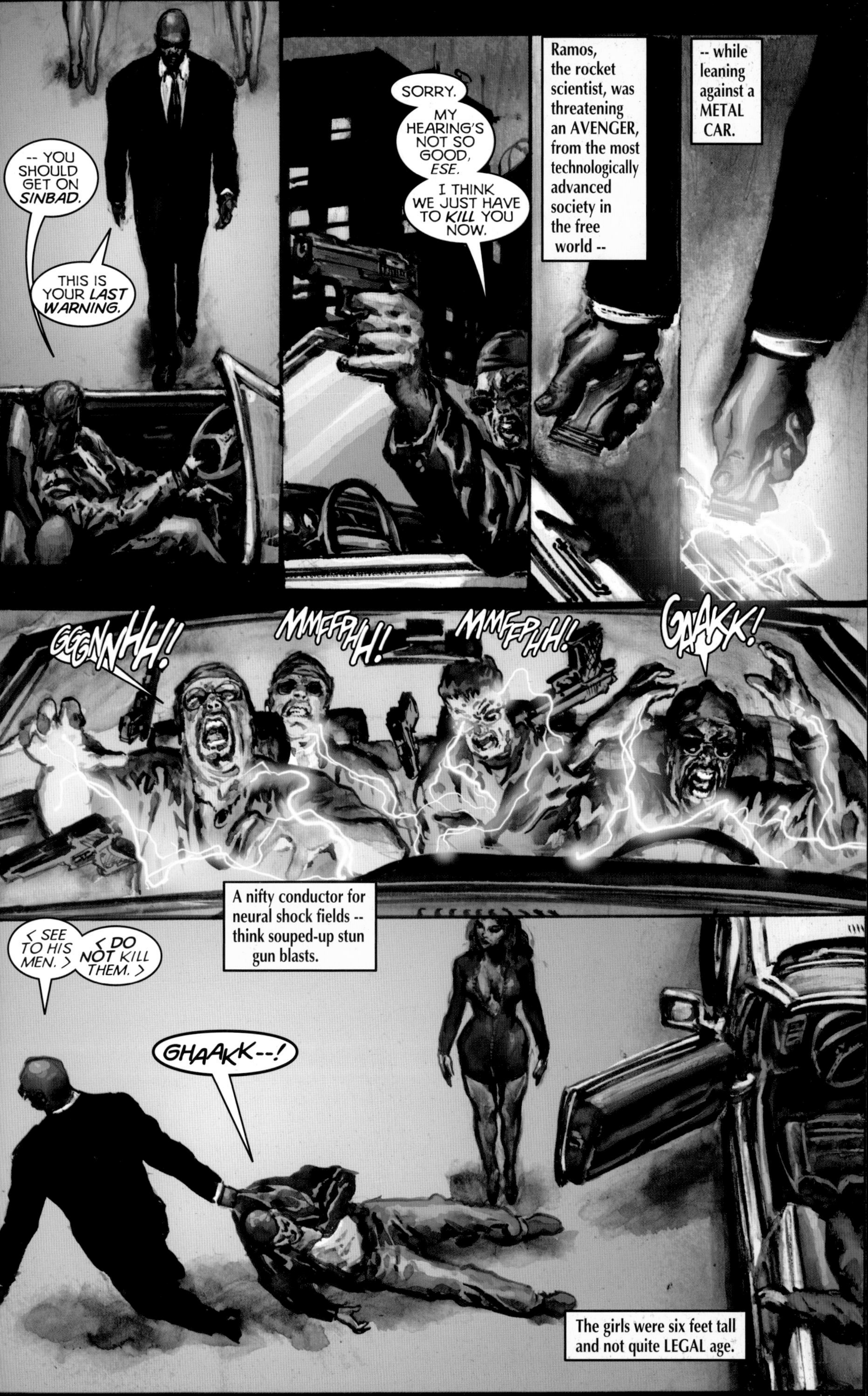
-- YOU SHOULD GET ON SINBAD.
THIS IS YOUR LAST WARNING.
SORRY.
MY HEARING'S NOT SO GOOD, ESE.
I THINK WE JUST HAVE TO KILL YOU NOW.
Ramos, the rocket scientist, was threatening an AVENGER, from the most technologically advanced society in the free world --
-- while leaning against a METAL CAR.
GGGNNHH!
MMFFPHH!
MMFFPHH!
GAAKK!
A nifty conductor for neural shock fields -- think souped-up stun gun blasts.
< SEE TO HIS MEN. >
< DO NOT KILL THEM. >
GHAAKK--!
The girls were six feet tall and not quite LEGAL age.

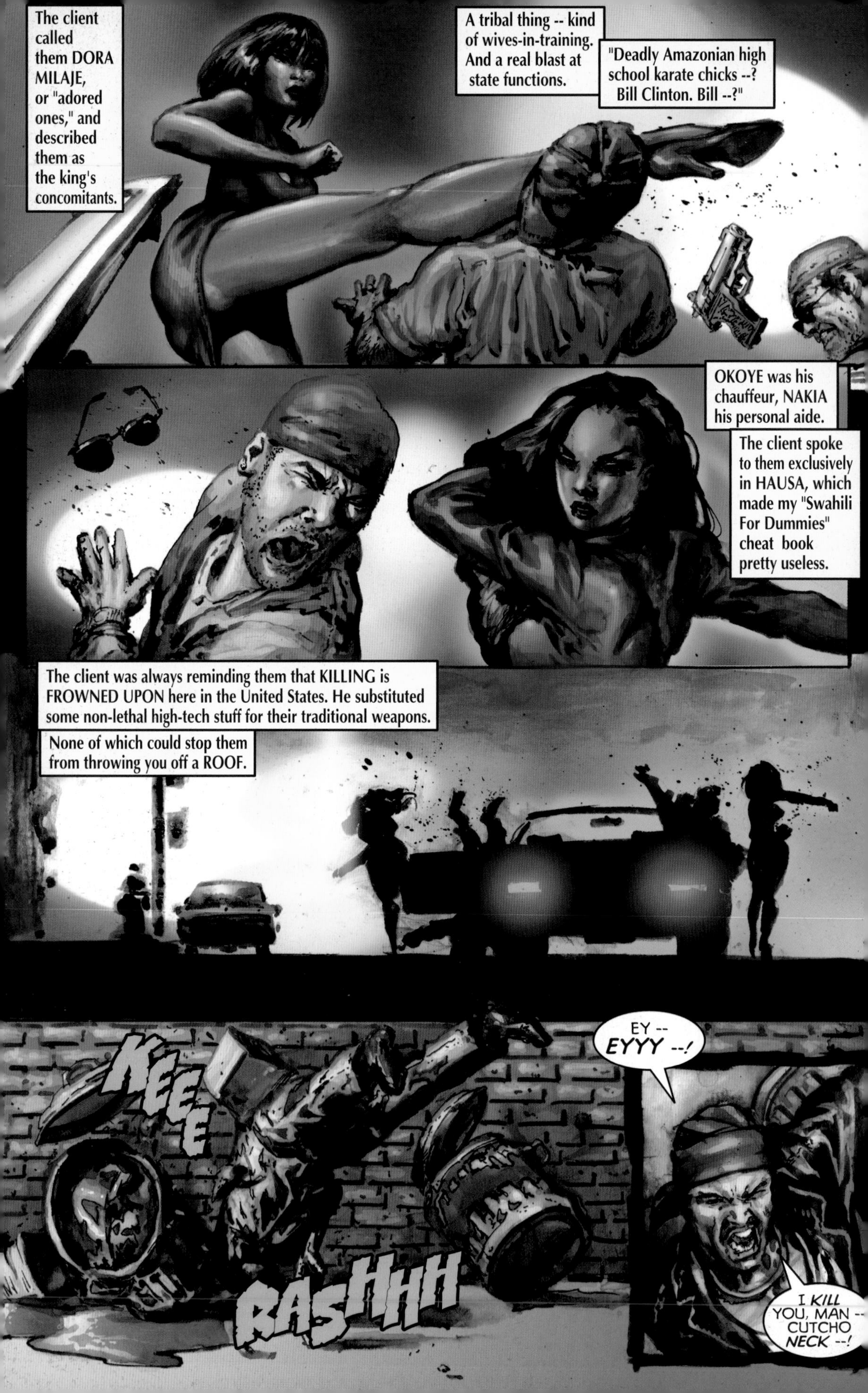

The client called them DORA MILAJE, or "adored ones," and described them as the king's concomitants.
A tribal thing -- kind of wives-in-training. And a real blast at state functions.
"Deadly Amazonian high school karate chicks --? Bill Clinton. Bill --?"
OKOYE was his chauffeur, NAKIA his personal aide.
The client spoke to them exclusively in HAUSA, which made my "Swahili For Dummies" cheat book pretty useless.
The client was always reminding them that KILLING is FROWNED UPON here in the United States. He substituted some non-lethal high-tech stuff for their traditional weapons.
None of which could stop them from throwing you off a ROOF.
KEEE
RASHHH
EY -- EYYY --!
I KILL YOU, MAN -- CUTCHO NECK --!

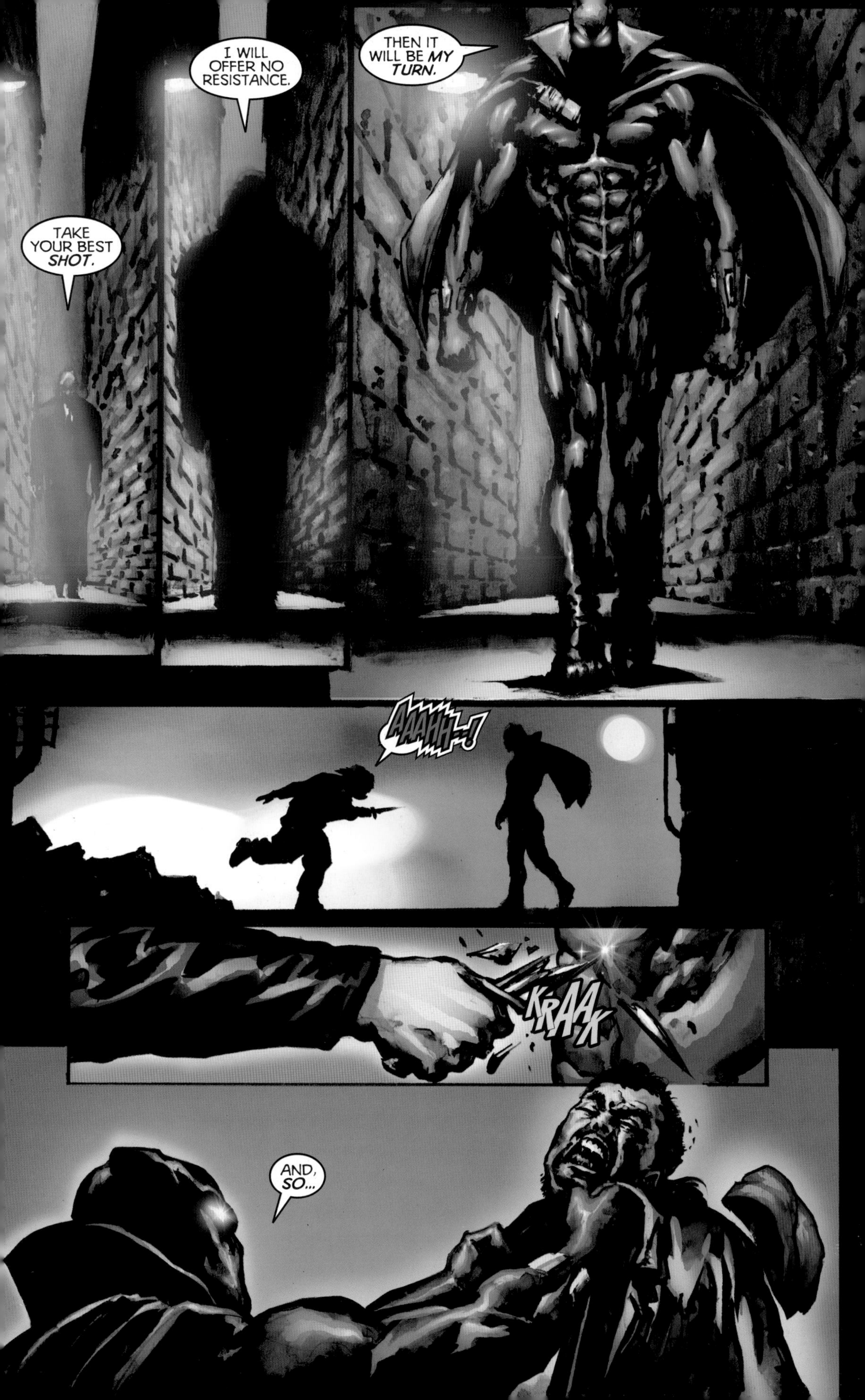
TAKE YOUR BEST SHOT.
I WILL OFFER NO RESISTANCE.
THEN IT WILL BE MY TURN.
AAAHH--!
KRAAK
AND, SO...

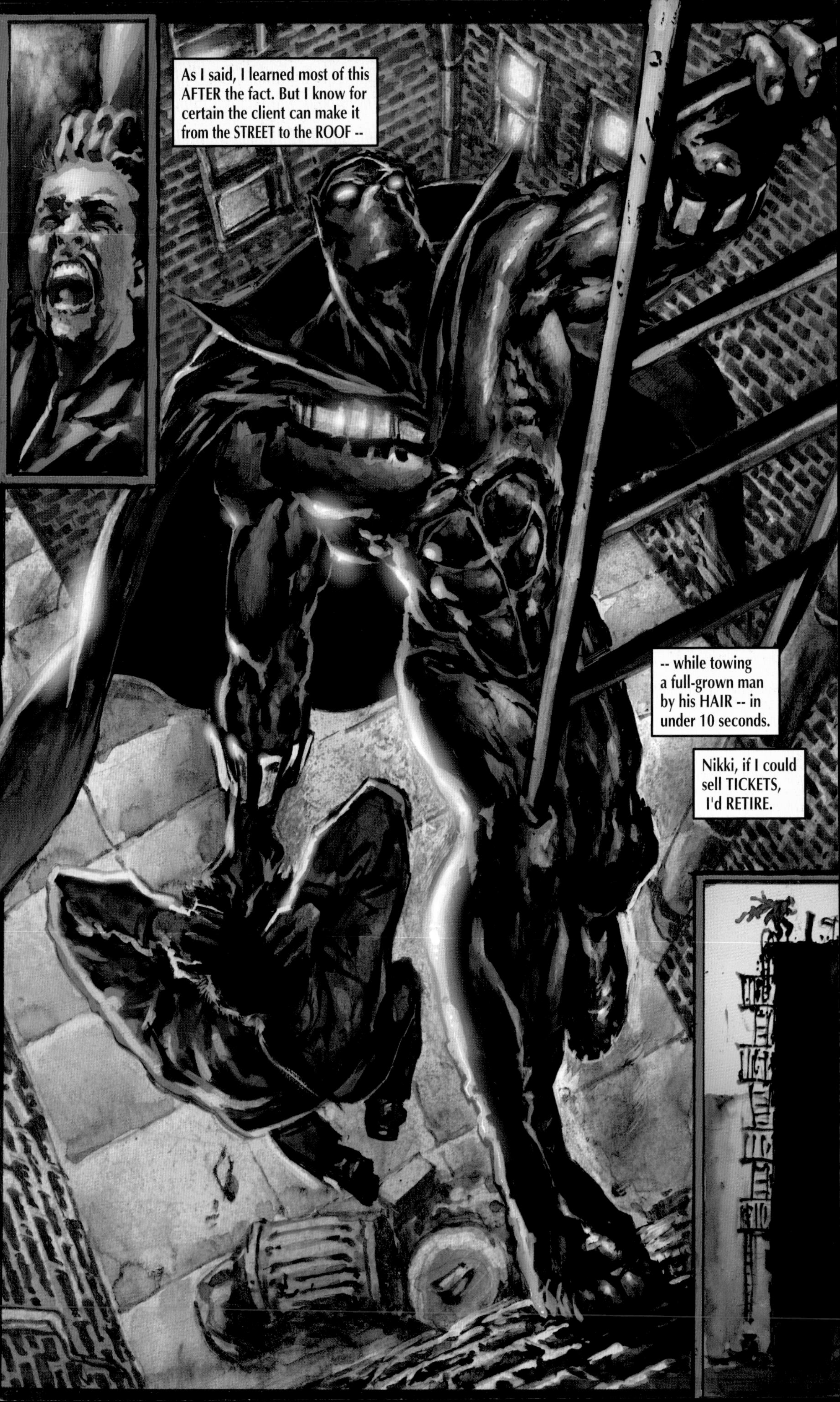
As I said, I learned most of this AFTER the fact. But I know for certain the client can make it from the STREET to the ROOF --
-- while towing a full-grown man by his HAIR -- in under 10 seconds.
Nikki, if I could sell TICKETS, I'd RETIRE.

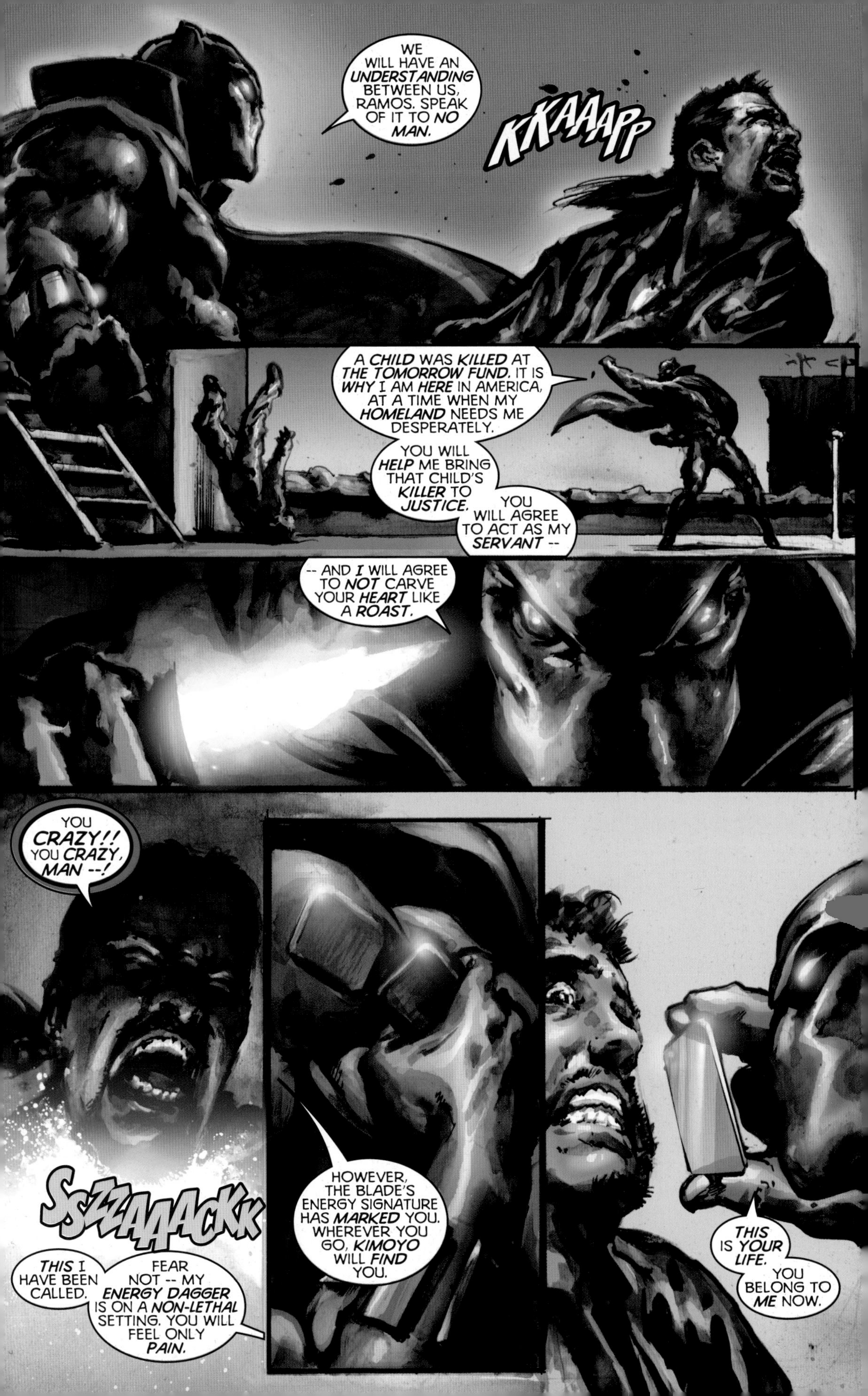
WE WILL HAVE AN UNDERSTANDING BETWEEN US, RAMOS. SPEAK OF IT TO NO MAN.
KKAAAPP
A CHILD WAS KILLED AT THE TOMORROW FUND. IT IS WHY I AM HERE IN AMERICA, AT A TIME WHEN MY HOMELAND NEEDS ME DESPERATELY.
YOU WILL HELP ME BRING THAT CHILD'S KILLER TO JUSTICE.
YOU WILL AGREE TO ACT AS MY SERVANT --
-- AND I WILL AGREE TO NOT CARVE YOUR HEART LIKE A ROAST.
YOU CRAZY!! YOU CRAZY, MAN --!
SSZZAAACKK
THIS I HAVE BEEN CALLED.
FEAR NOT -- MY ENERGY DAGGER IS ON A NON-LETHAL SETTING. YOU WILL FEEL ONLY PAIN.
HOWEVER, THE BLADE'S ENERGY SIGNATURE HAS MARKED YOU. WHEREVER YOU GO, KIMOYO WILL FIND YOU.
THIS IS YOUR LIFE.
YOU BELONG TO ME NOW.

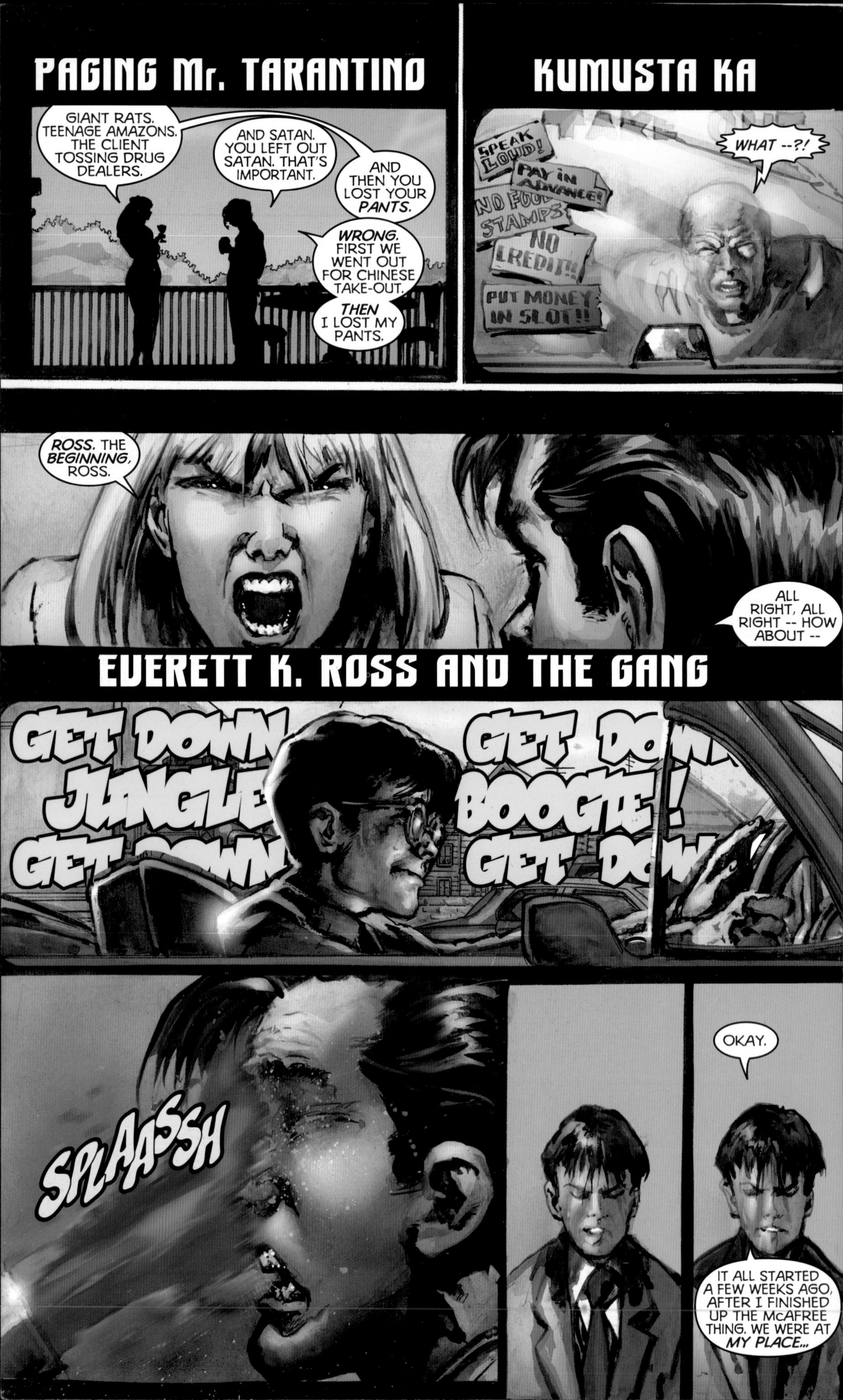
PAGING Mr. TARANTINO
GIANT RATS. TEENAGE AMAZONS. THE CLIENT TOSSING DRUG DEALERS.
AND SATAN. YOU LEFT OUT SATAN. THAT'S IMPORTANT.
AND THEN YOU LOST YOUR PANTS.
WRONG. FIRST WE WENT OUT FOR CHINESE TAKE-OUT.
THEN I LOST MY PANTS.
KUMUSTA KA
SPEAK LOUD!
PAY IN ADVANCE!
NO FOOD STAMPS
NO CREDIT!!
PUT MONEY IN SLOT!!
WHAT --?!
ROSS. THE BEGINNING, ROSS.
ALL RIGHT, ALL RIGHT -- HOW ABOUT --
EVERETT K. ROSS AND THE GANG
GET DOWN JUNGLE BOOGIE! GET DOWN GET DOWN
SPLAASSH
OKAY.
IT ALL STARTED A FEW WEEKS AGO, AFTER I FINISHED UP THE McAFREE THING. WE WERE AT MY PLACE...

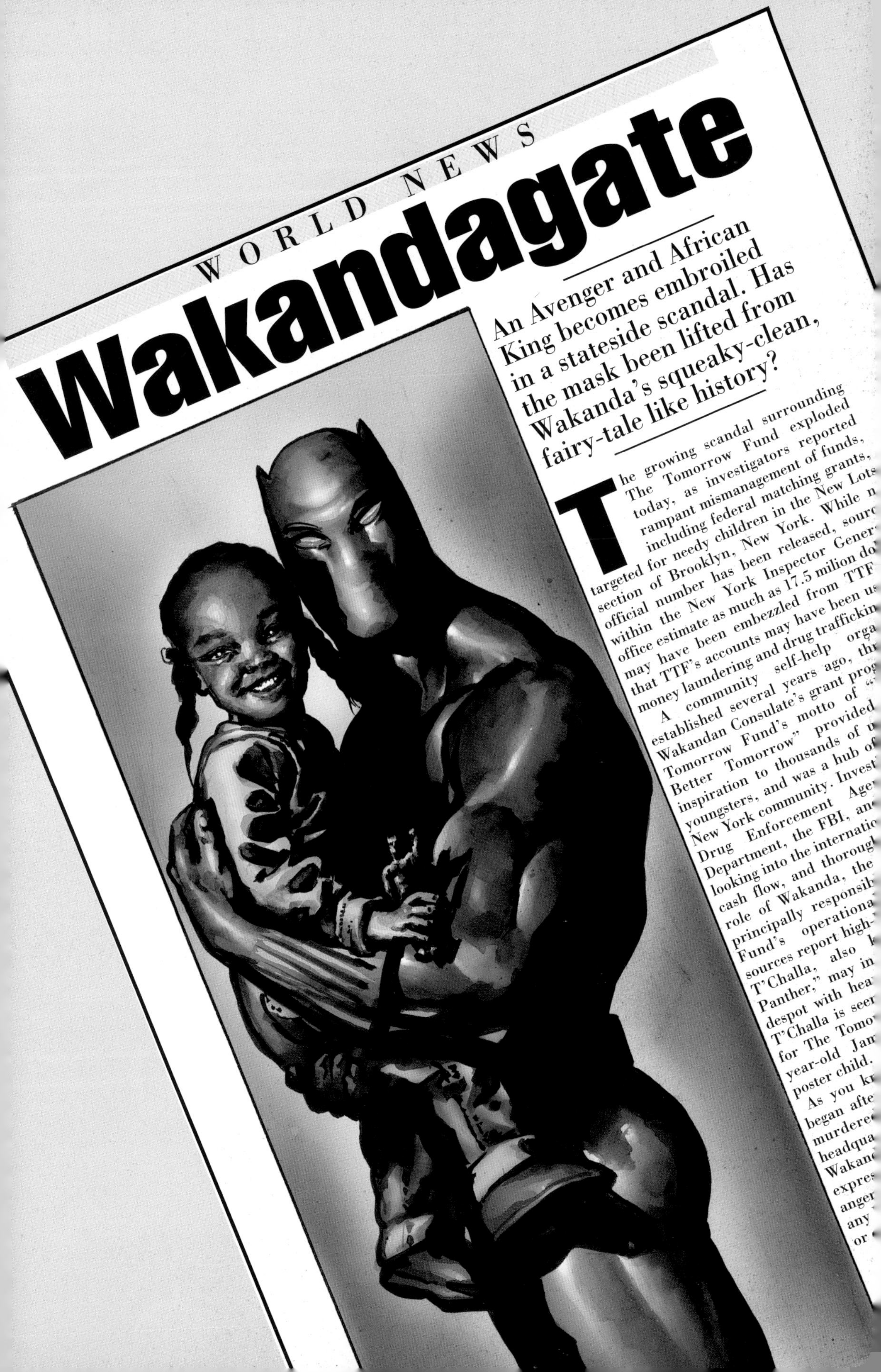

WORLD NEWS
Wakandagate
An Avenger and African King becomes embroiled in a stateside scandal. Has the mask been lifted from Wakanda's squeaky-clean, fairy-tale like history?
The growing scandal surrounding
The Tomorrow Fund exploded
today, as investigators reported
rampant mismanagement of funds,
including federal matching grants,
targeted for needy children in the New Lots
section of Brooklyn, New York. While n
official number has been released, sourc
within the New York Inspector Gener
office estimate as much as 17.5 milion do
may have been embezzled from TTF
that TTF's accounts may have been us
money laundering and drug traffickin
A community self-help orga
established several years ago, th
Wakandan Consulate's grant prog
Tomorrow Fund's motto of "
Better Tomorrow" provided
inspiration to thousands of u
youngsters, and was a hub of
New York community. Invest
Drug Enforcement Age
Department, the FBI, an
looking into the internatio
cash flow, and thoroug
role of Wakanda, the
principally responsib
Fund's operationa
sources report high-
T'Challa, also k
Panther," may in
despot with hea
T'Challa is seen
for The Tomo
year-old Jan
poster child.
As you kn
began afte
murdere
headqua
Wakan
expres
anger
any
or

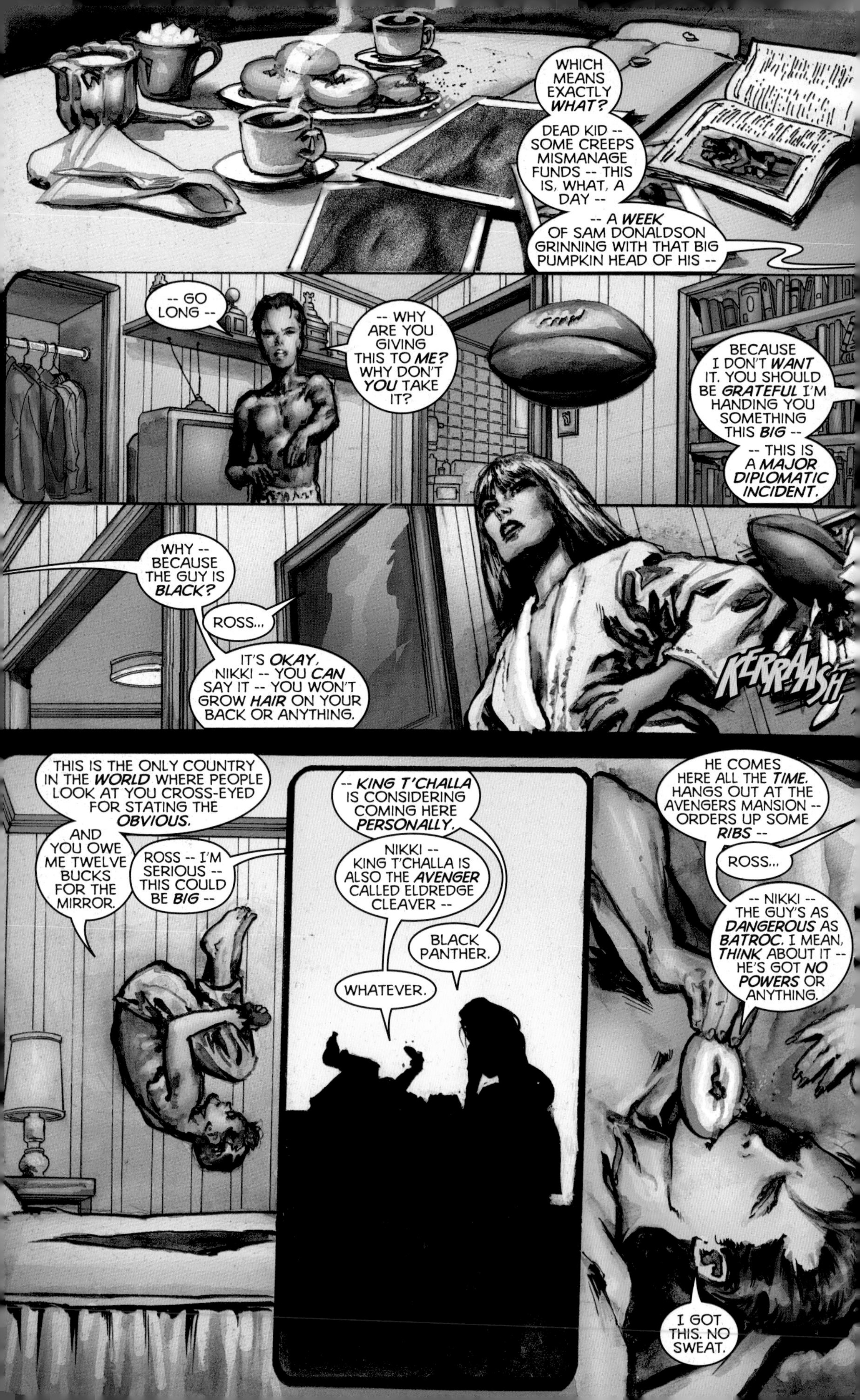
WHICH MEANS EXACTLY WHAT?
DEAD KID -- SOME CREEPS MISMANAGE FUNDS -- THIS IS, WHAT, A DAY --
-- A WEEK OF SAM DONALDSON GRINNING WITH THAT BIG PUMPKIN HEAD OF HIS --
-- GO LONG --
-- WHY ARE YOU GIVING THIS TO ME? WHY DON'T YOU TAKE IT?
BECAUSE I DON'T WANT IT. YOU SHOULD BE GRATEFUL I'M HANDING YOU SOMETHING THIS BIG --
-- THIS IS A MAJOR DIPLOMATIC INCIDENT.
WHY -- BECAUSE THE GUY IS BLACK?
ROSS...
IT'S OKAY, NIKKI -- YOU CAN SAY IT -- YOU WON'T GROW HAIR ON YOUR BACK OR ANYTHING.
KERRAASH
THIS IS THE ONLY COUNTRY IN THE WORLD WHERE PEOPLE LOOK AT YOU CROSS-EYED FOR STATING THE OBVIOUS.
AND YOU OWE ME TWELVE BUCKS FOR THE MIRROR.
ROSS -- I'M SERIOUS -- THIS COULD BE BIG --
-- KING T'CHALLA IS CONSIDERING COMING HERE PERSONALLY.
NIKKI -- KING T'CHALLA IS ALSO THE AVENGER CALLED ELDREDGE CLEAVER --
BLACK PANTHER.
WHATEVER.
HE COMES HERE ALL THE TIME. HANGS OUT AT THE AVENGERS MANSION -- ORDERS UP SOME RIBS --
ROSS...
-- NIKKI -- THE GUY'S AS DANGEROUS AS BATROC. I MEAN, THINK ABOUT IT -- HE'S GOT NO POWERS OR ANYTHING.
I GOT THIS. NO SWEAT.

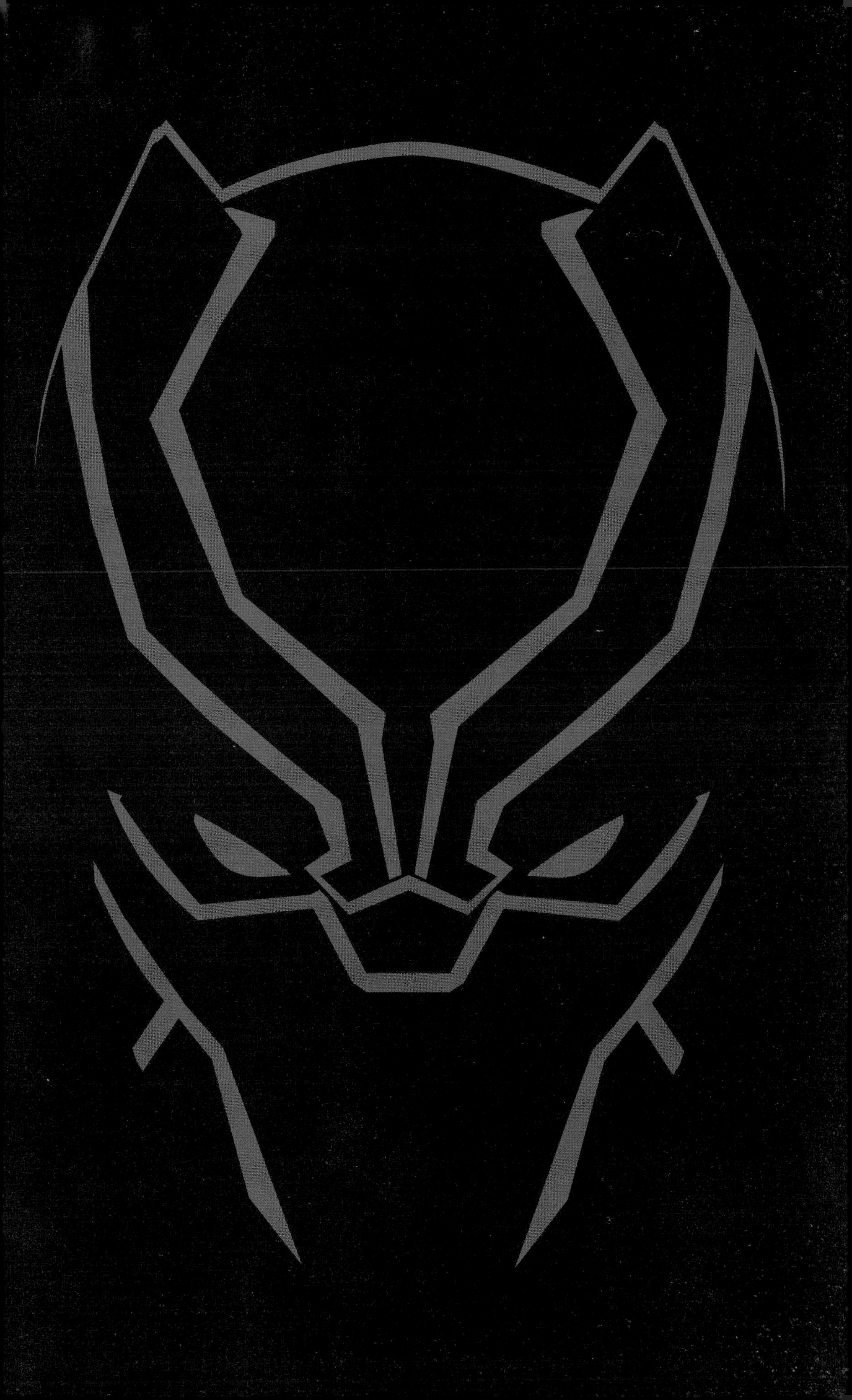

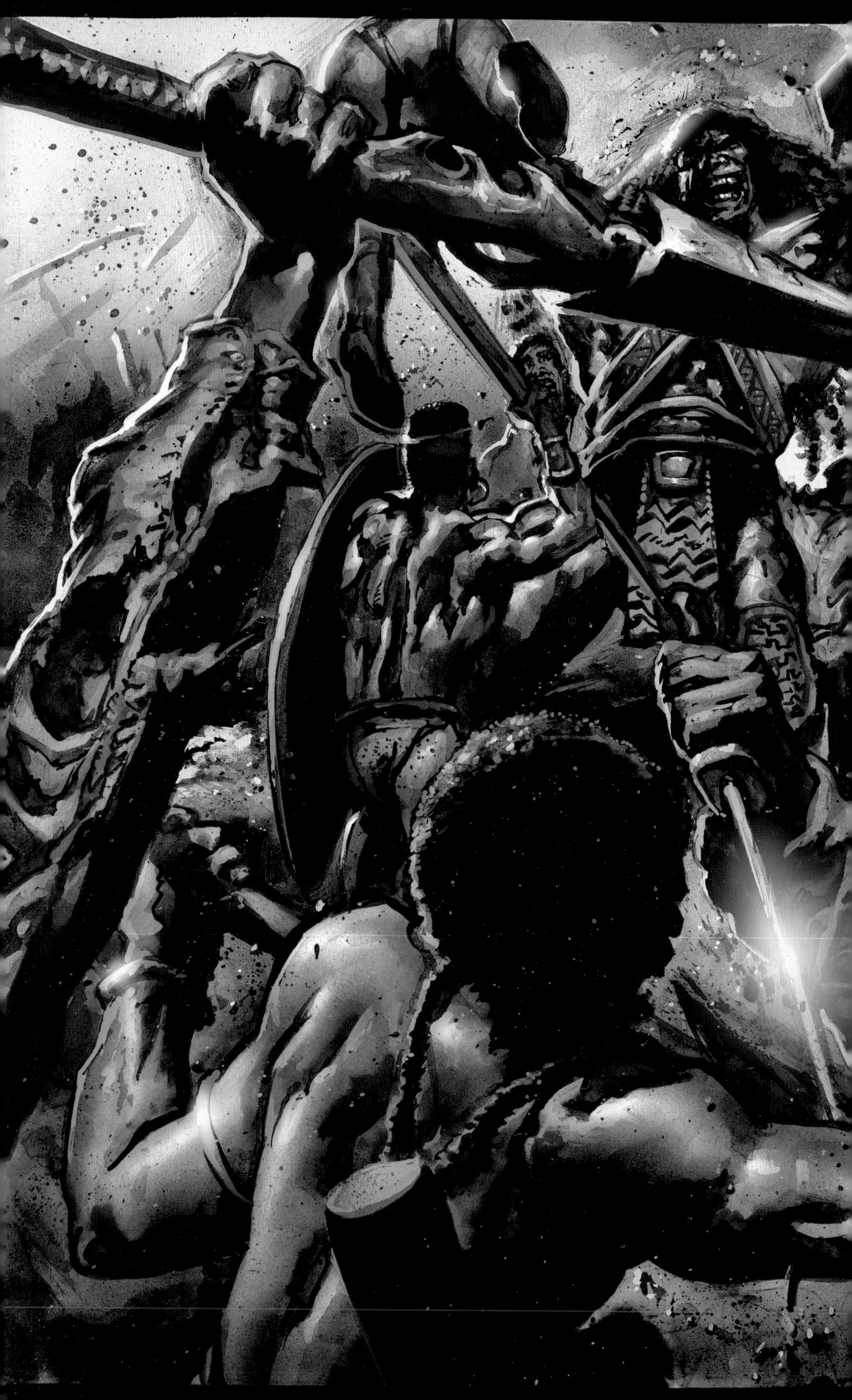

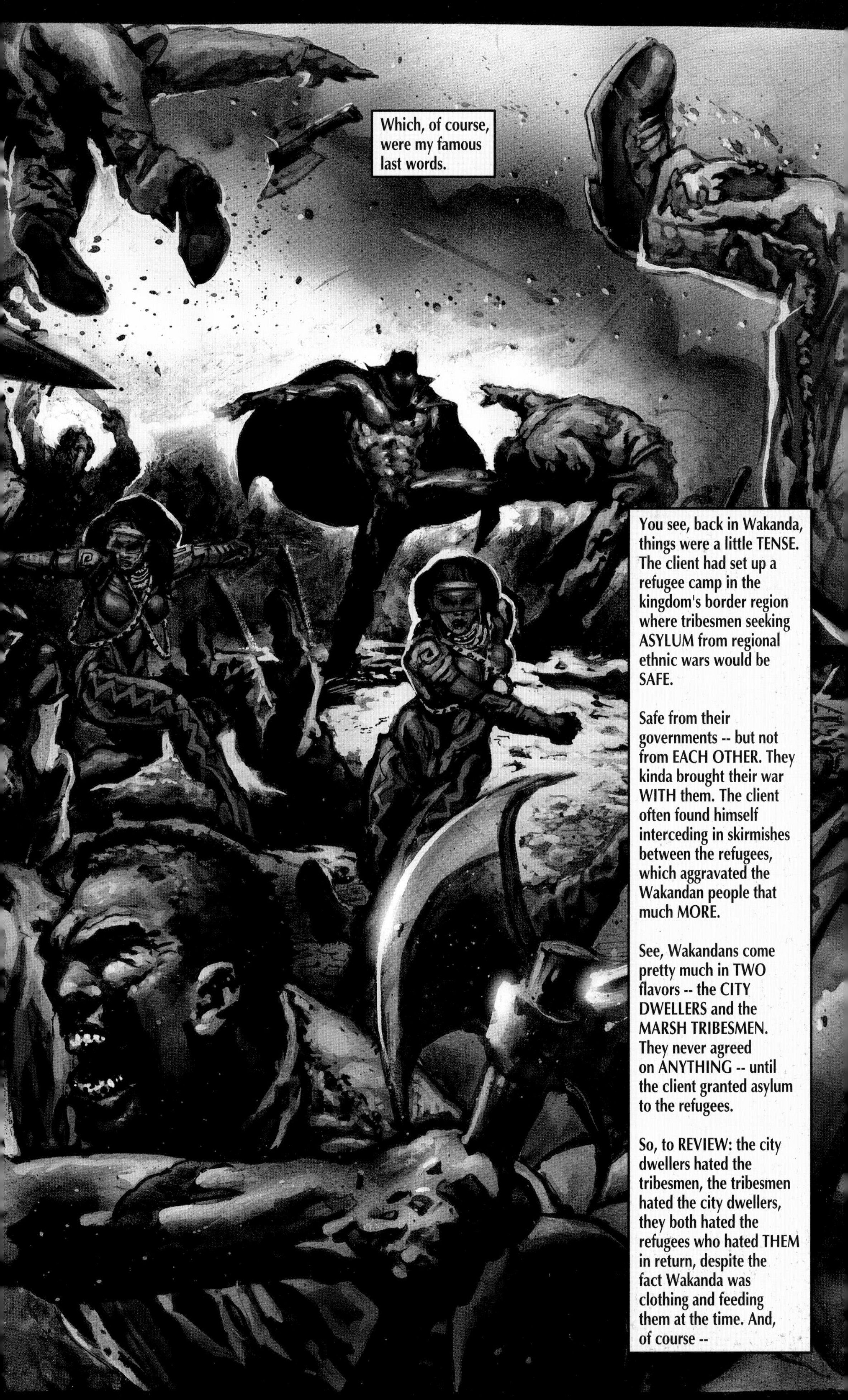
Which, of course, were my famous last words.
You see, back in Wakanda, things were a little TENSE. The client had set up a refugee camp in the kingdom's border region where tribesmen seeking ASYLUM from regional ethnic wars would be SAFE.
Safe from their governments -- but not from EACH OTHER. They kinda brought their war WITH them. The client often found himself interceding in skirmishes between the refugees, which aggravated the Wakandan people that much MORE.
See, Wakandans come pretty much in TWO flavors -- the CITY DWELLERS and the MARSH TRIBESMEN. They never agreed on ANYTHING -- until the client granted asylum to the refugees.
So, to REVIEW: the city dwellers hated the tribesmen, the tribesmen hated the city dwellers, they both hated the refugees who hated THEM in return, despite the fact Wakanda was clothing and feeding them at the time. And, of course --

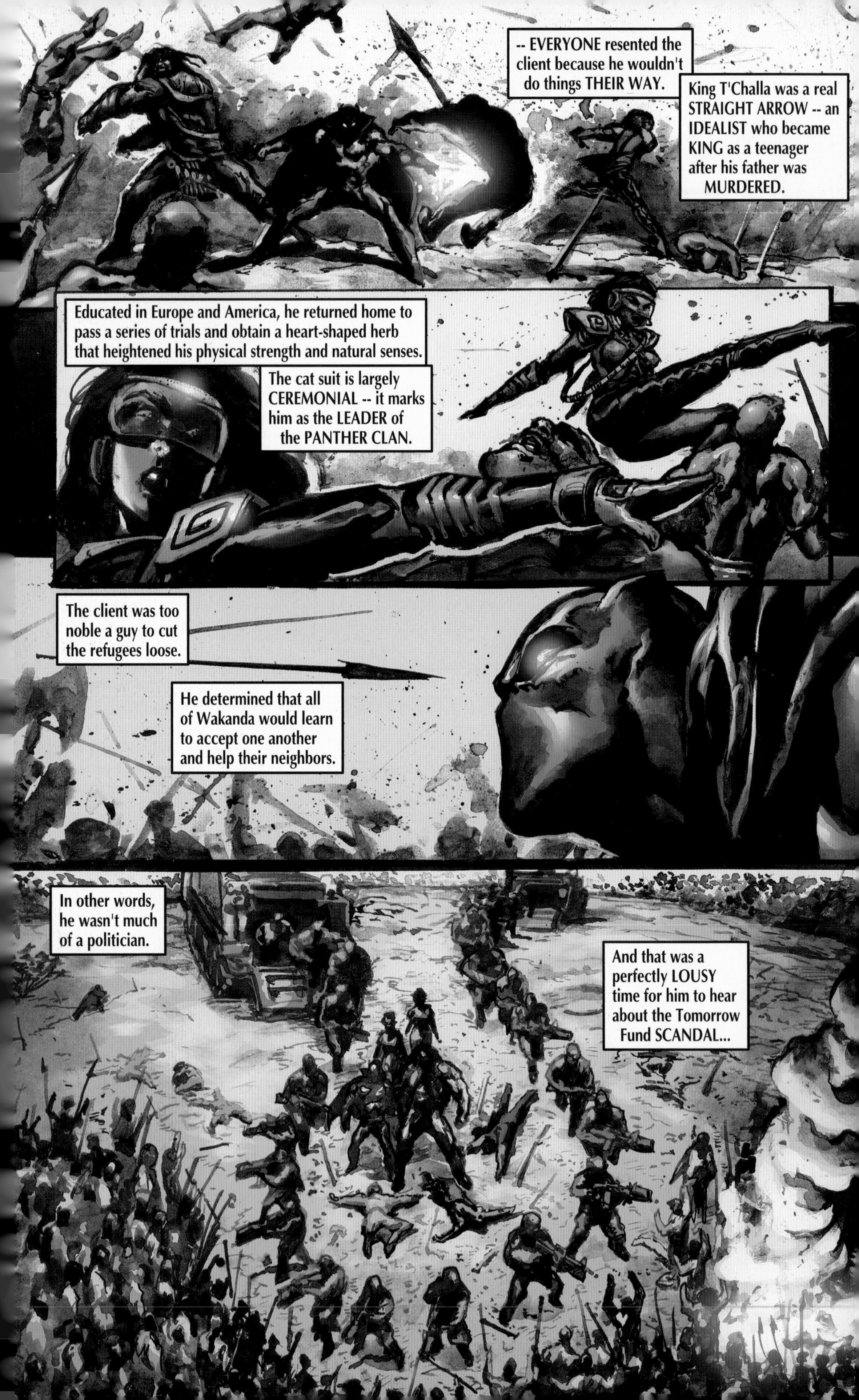

-- EVERYONE resented the client because he wouldn't do things THEIR WAY.
King T'Challa was a real STRAIGHT ARROW -- an IDEALIST who became KING as a teenager after his father was MURDERED.
Educated in Europe and America, he returned home to pass a series of trials and obtain a heart-shaped herb that heightened his physical strength and natural senses.
The cat suit is largely CEREMONIAL -- it marks him as the LEADER of the PANTHER CLAN.
The client was too noble a guy to cut the refugees loose.
He determined that all of Wakanda would learn to accept one another and help their neighbors.
In other words, he wasn't much of a politician.
And that was a perfectly LOUSY time for him to hear about the Tomorrow Fund SCANDAL...

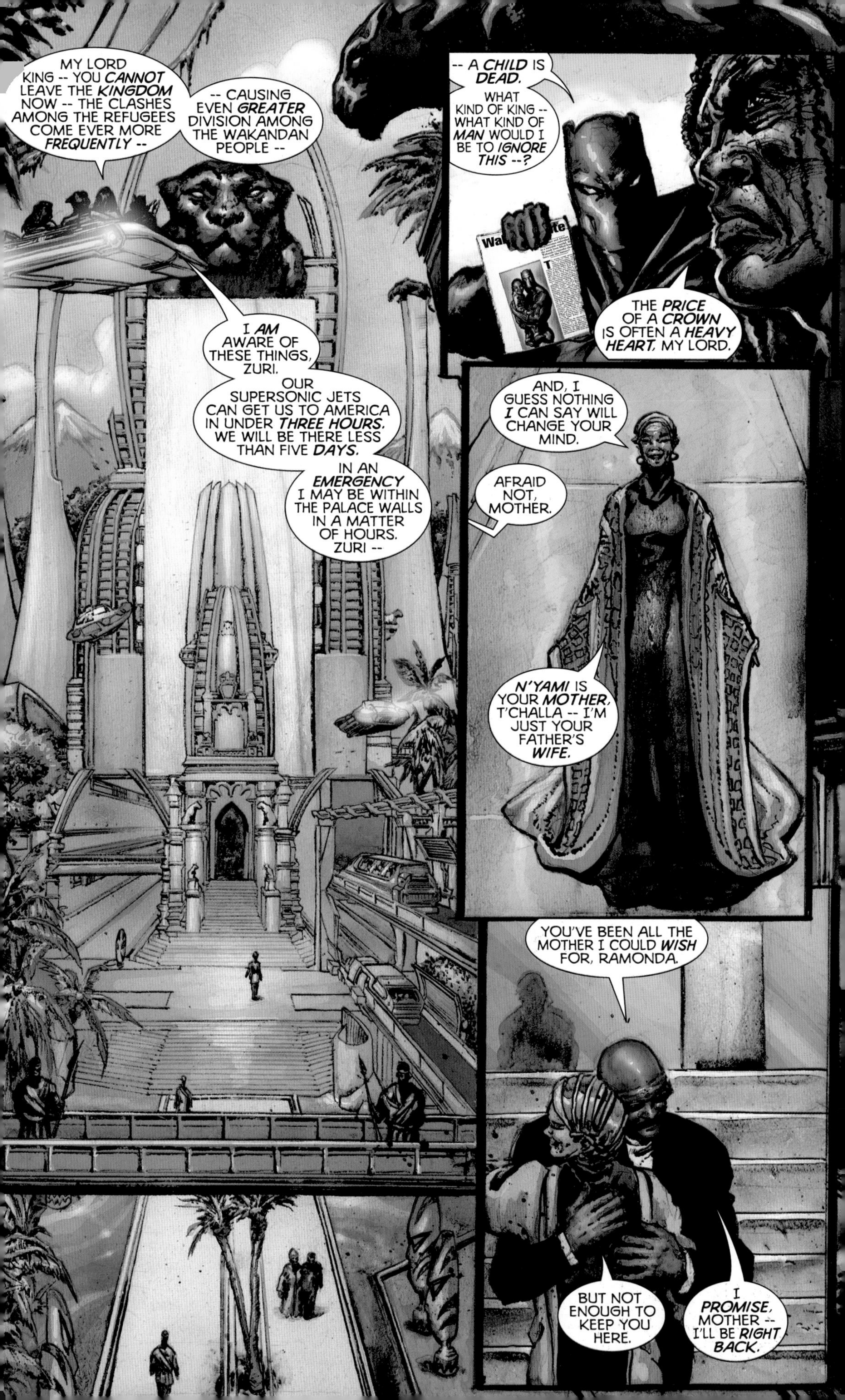
MY LORD KING -- YOU CANNOT LEAVE THE KINGDOM NOW -- THE CLASHES AMONG THE REFUGEES COME EVER MORE FREQUENTLY --
-- CAUSING EVEN GREATER DIVISION AMONG THE WAKANDAN PEOPLE --
I AM AWARE OF THESE THINGS, ZURI.
OUR SUPERSONIC JETS CAN GET US TO AMERICA IN UNDER THREE HOURS. WE WILL BE THERE LESS THAN FIVE DAYS.
IN AN EMERGENCY I MAY BE WITHIN THE PALACE WALLS IN A MATTER OF HOURS. ZURI --
-- A CHILD IS DEAD.
WHAT KIND OF KING -- WHAT KIND OF MAN WOULD I BE TO IGNORE THIS --?
THE PRICE OF A CROWN IS OFTEN A HEAVY HEART, MY LORD.
AND, I GUESS NOTHING I CAN SAY WILL CHANGE YOUR MIND.
AFRAID NOT, MOTHER.
N'YAMI IS YOUR MOTHER, T'CHALLA -- I'M JUST YOUR FATHER'S WIFE.
YOU'VE BEEN ALL THE MOTHER I COULD WISH FOR, RAMONDA.
BUT NOT ENOUGH TO KEEP YOU HERE.
I PROMISE, MOTHER -- I'LL BE RIGHT BACK.

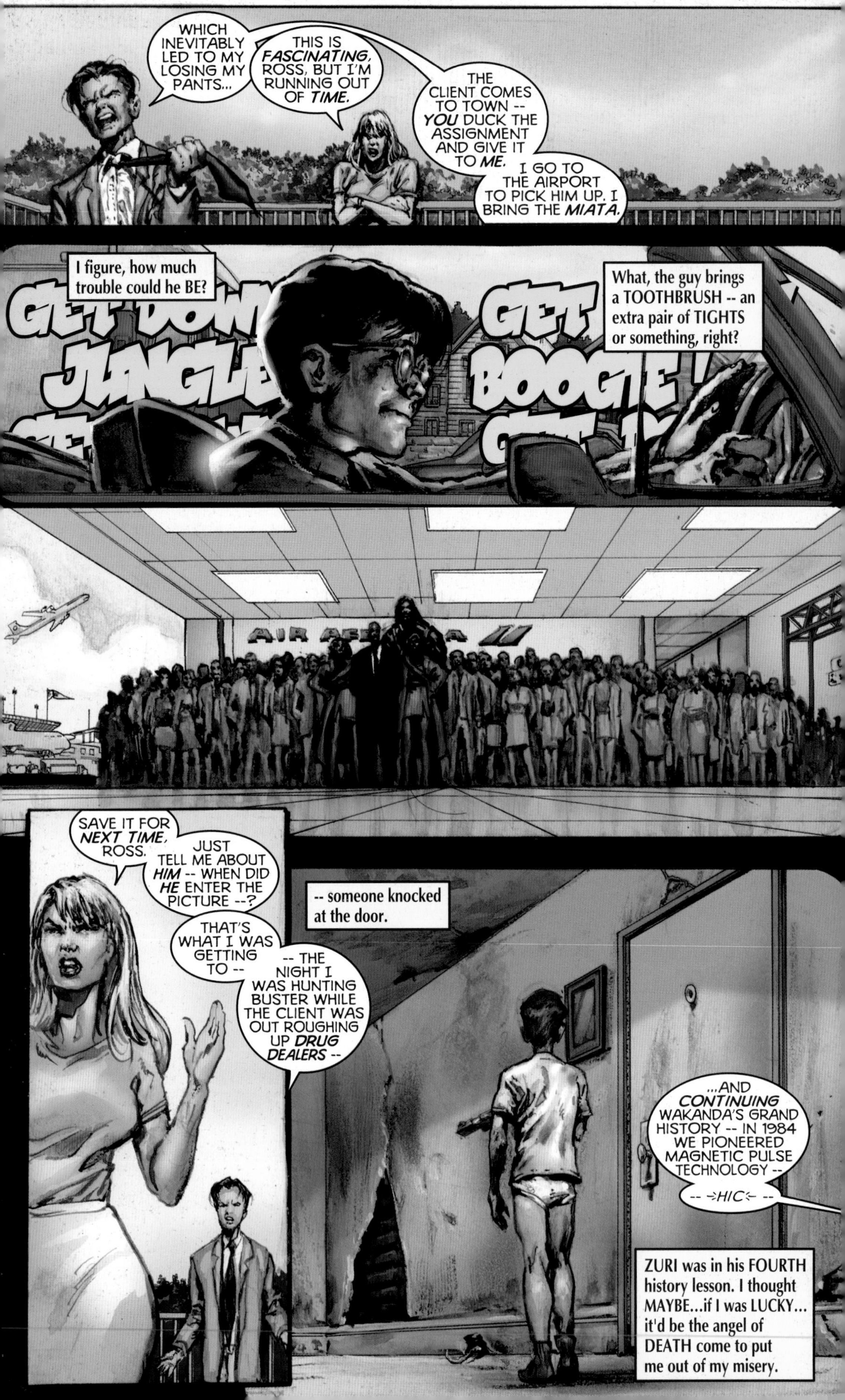
WHICH INEVITABLY LED TO MY LOSING MY PANTS...
THIS IS FASCINATING, ROSS, BUT I'M RUNNING OUT OF TIME.
THE CLIENT COMES TO TOWN -- YOU DUCK THE ASSIGNMENT AND GIVE IT TO ME.
I GO TO THE AIRPORT TO PICK HIM UP. I BRING THE MIATA.
I figure, how much trouble could he BE?
What, the guy brings a TOOTHBRUSH -- an extra pair of TIGHTS or something, right?
GET
JUNGLE
GET
BOOGIE!
SAVE IT FOR NEXT TIME, ROSS.
JUST TELL ME ABOUT HIM -- WHEN DID HE ENTER THE PICTURE --?
THAT'S WHAT I WAS GETTING TO --
-- THE NIGHT I WAS HUNTING BUSTER WHILE THE CLIENT WAS OUT ROUGHING UP DRUG DEALERS --
-- someone knocked at the door.
...AND CONTINUING WAKANDA'S GRAND HISTORY -- IN 1984 WE PIONEERED MAGNETIC PULSE TECHNOLOGY --
-- HIC --
ZURI was in his FOURTH history lesson. I thought MAYBE...if I was LUCKY... it'd be the angel of DEATH come to put me out of my misery.

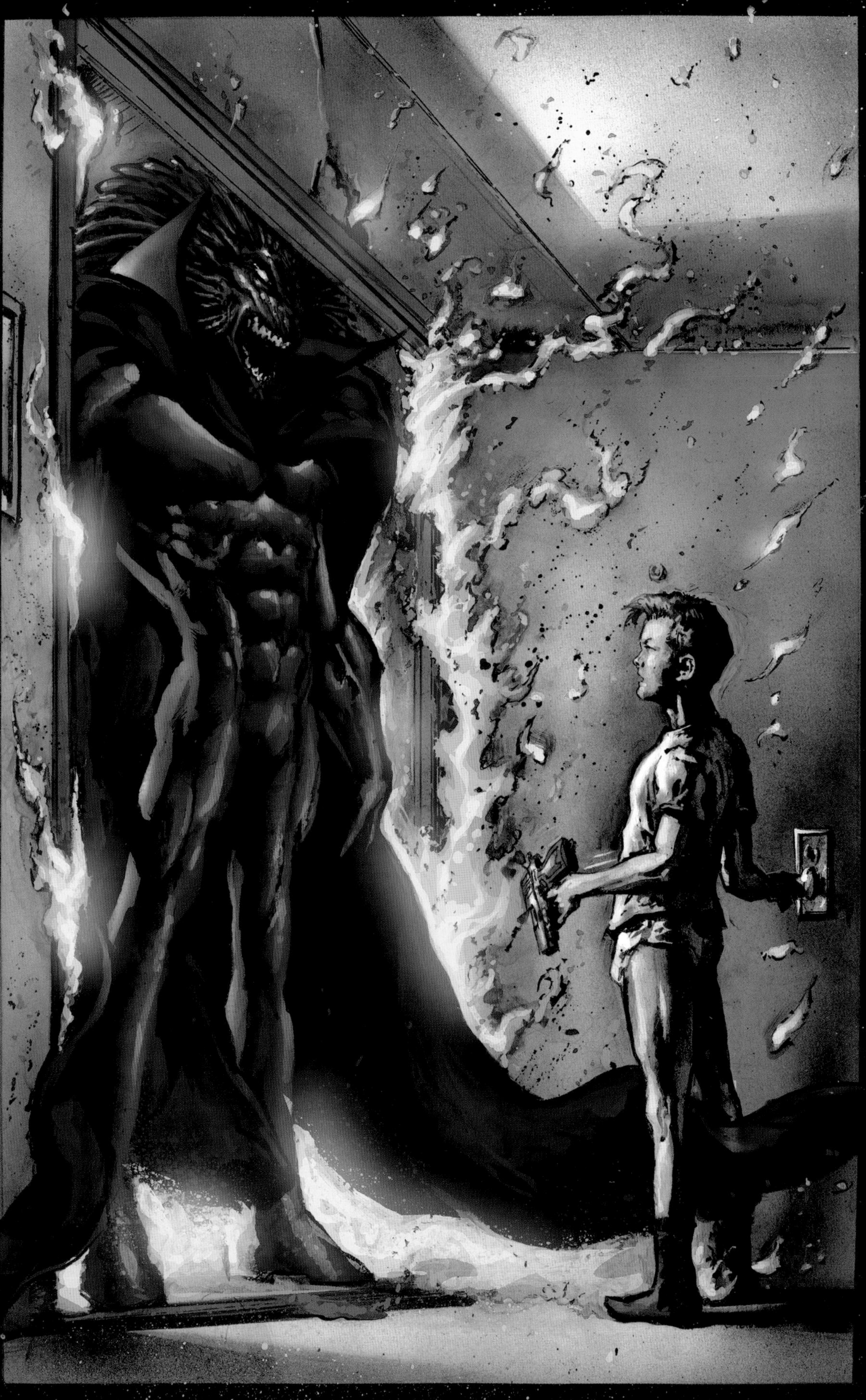

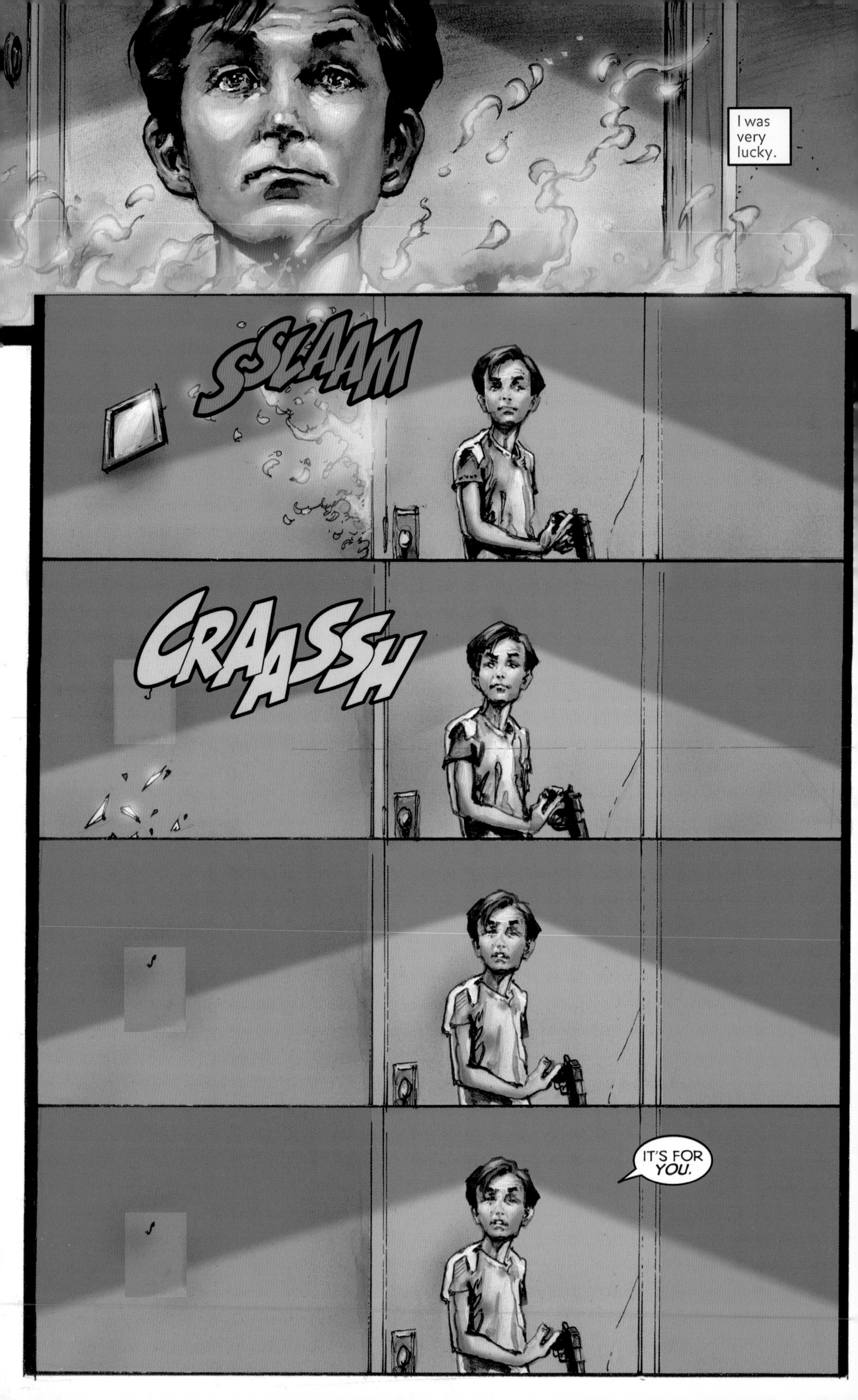
I was very lucky.
SSLAAM
CRAASSH
IT'S FOR YOU.

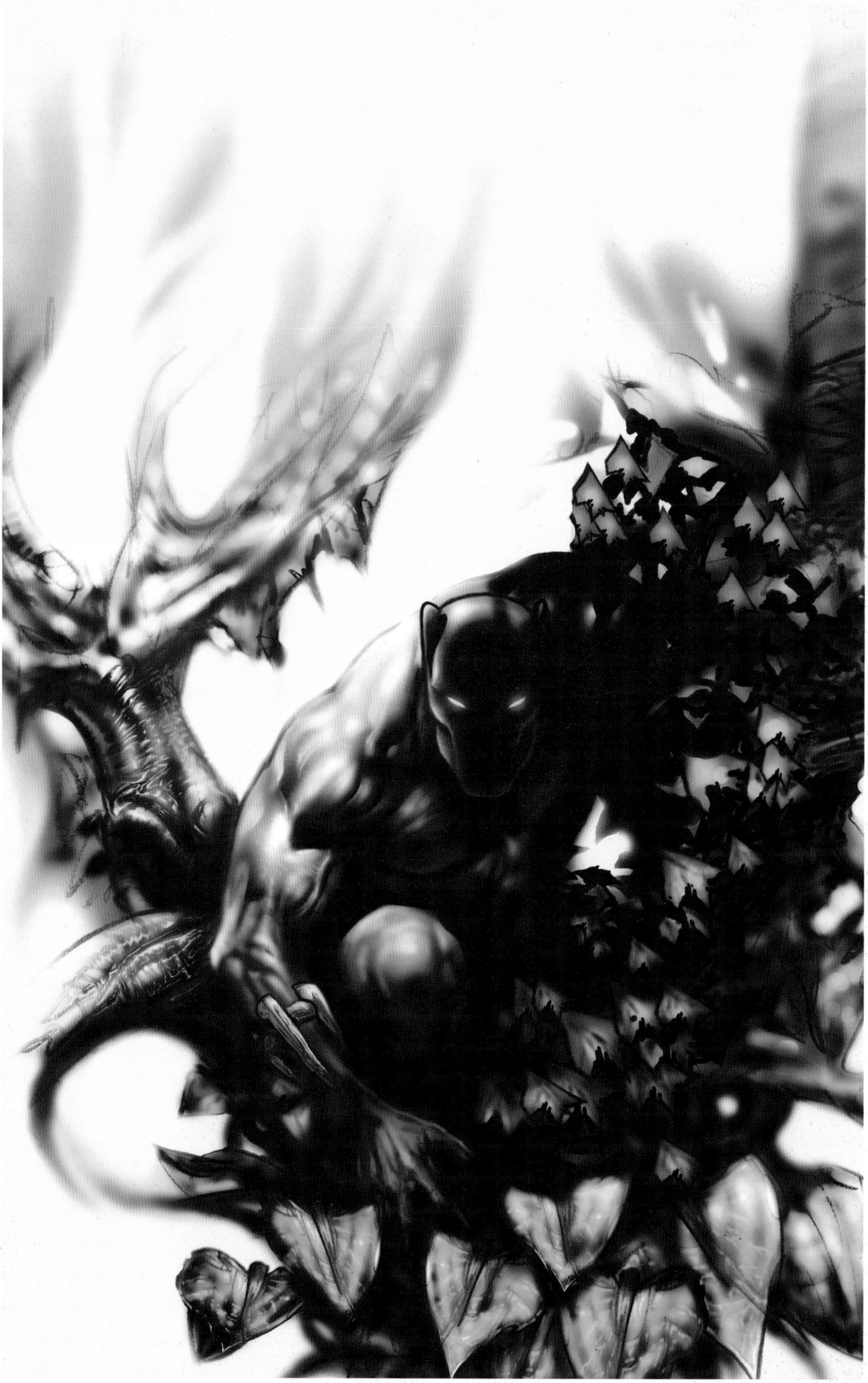

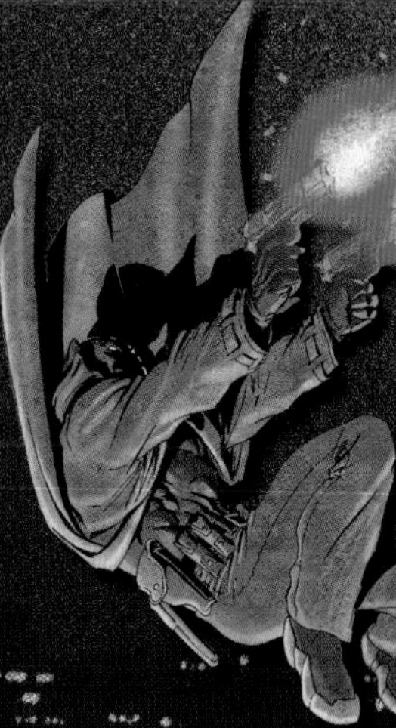

With the sleekness of the jungle cat whose name he bears, T'Challa — King of Wakanda — stalks both the concrete city and the undergrowth of the veldt. So it has been for countless generations of warrior kings, so it is today, and so it shall be, for the law dictates that only the swift, the smart, and the strong survive! Noble champion. Vigilant protector. Stan Lee presents

BLACK PANTHER

COMING TO AMERICA PART 1 OF 2

Previously...

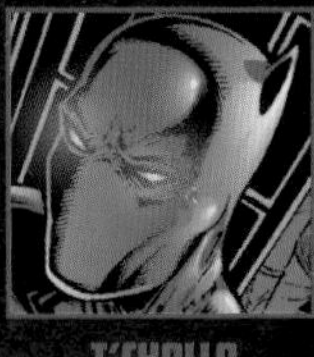

T'CHALLA
BLACK PANTHER

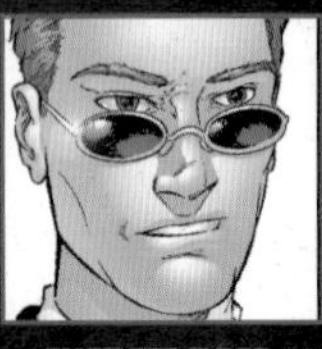

EVERETT ROSS
U.S. STATE DEPARTMENT

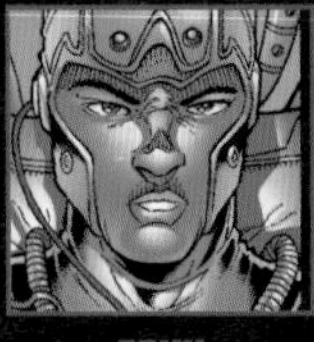

TAKU
AID TO T'CHALLA

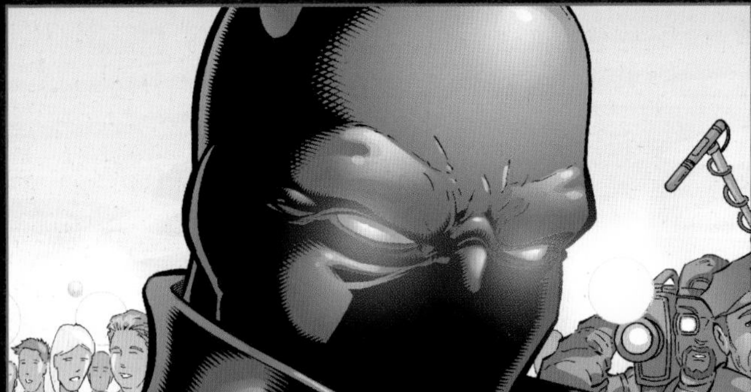

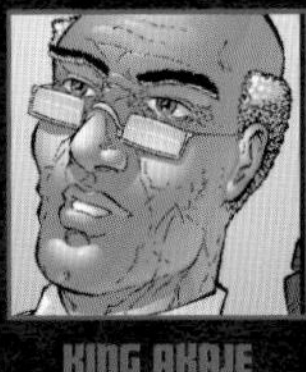

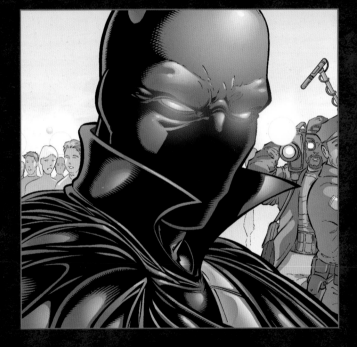

KING AKAJE
MONARCH OF DAKENIA

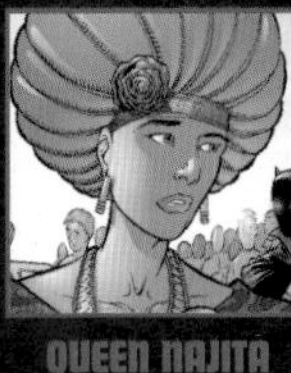

QUEEN NAJITA
AKAJE'S WIFE

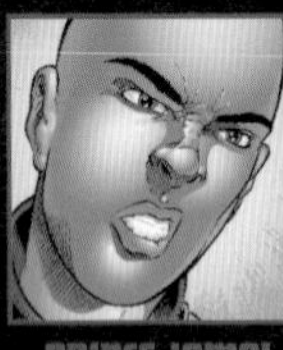

PRINCE JAMAL
AKAJE'S STEPSON

It is a year ago. The events of the past few months are the future and King T'Challa – THE BLACK PANTHER – still rules Wakanda.

T'Challa finds himself in the United States, aiding his old assistant Everett K. Ross with a new situation. Ross has been assigned by the U.S. State Department to serve as an escort to King Akaje and the Dakenian royal family as they visit America. And if we know anything about Ross and his track record with African royalty, things are about to go downhill very quickly...

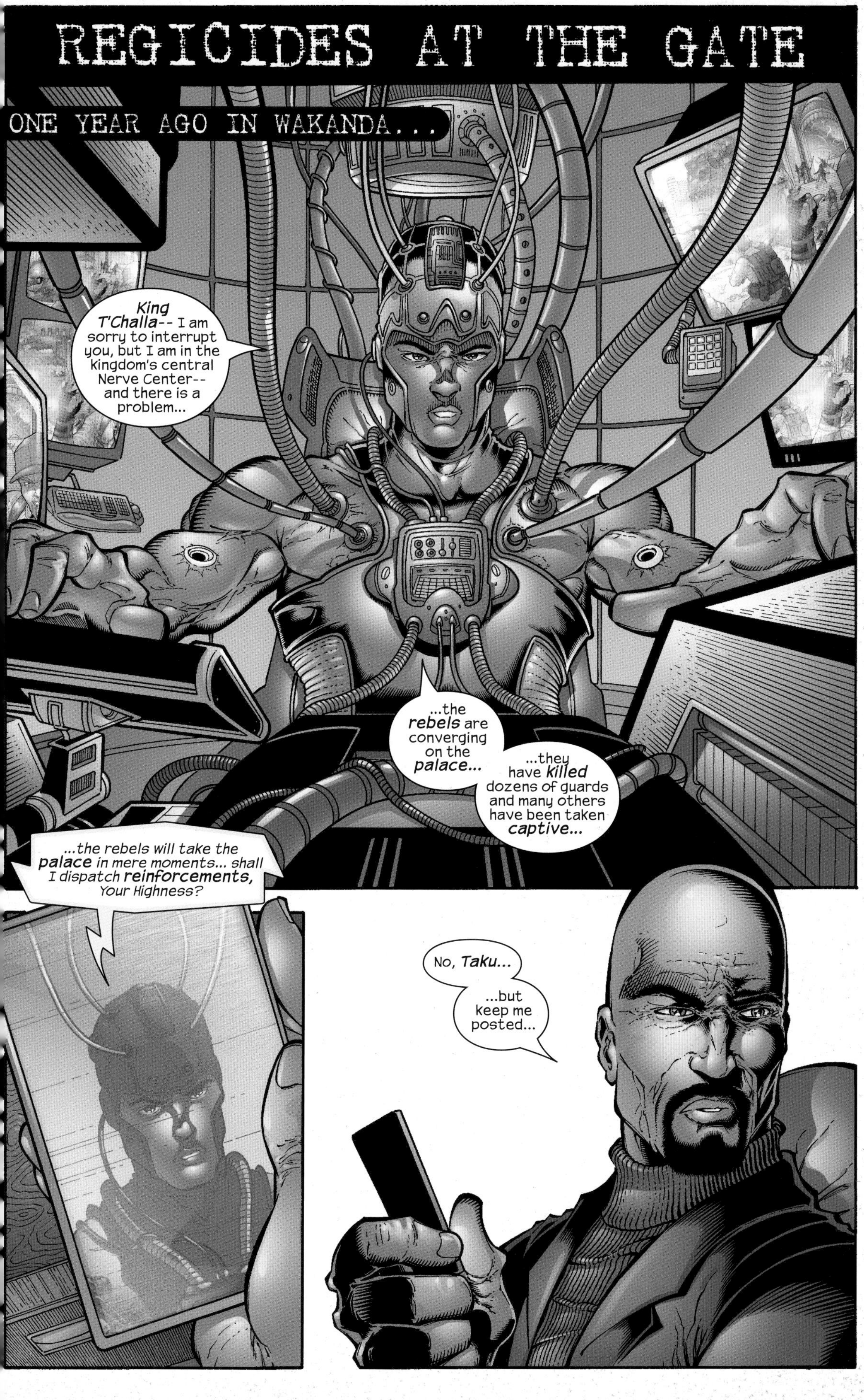
REGICIDES AT THE GATE
ONE YEAR AGO IN WAKANDA...
King T'Challa-- I am sorry to interrupt you, but I am in the kingdom's central Nerve Center-- and there is a problem...
...the rebels are converging on the palace...
...they have killed dozens of guards and many others have been taken captive...
...the rebels will take the palace in mere moments... shall I dispatch reinforcements, Your Highness?
No, Taku...
...but keep me posted...

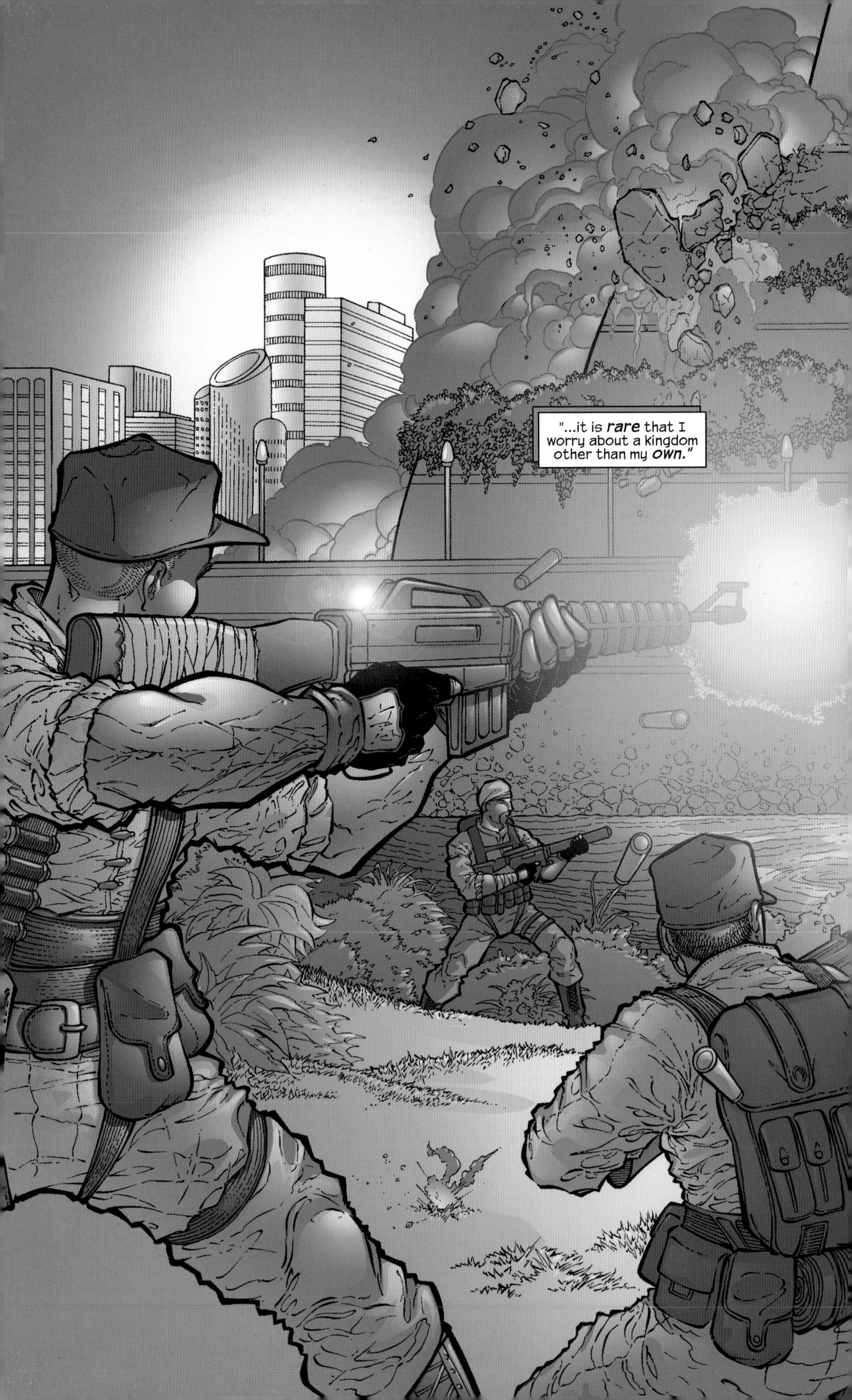
"...it is rare that I worry about a kingdom other than my own."

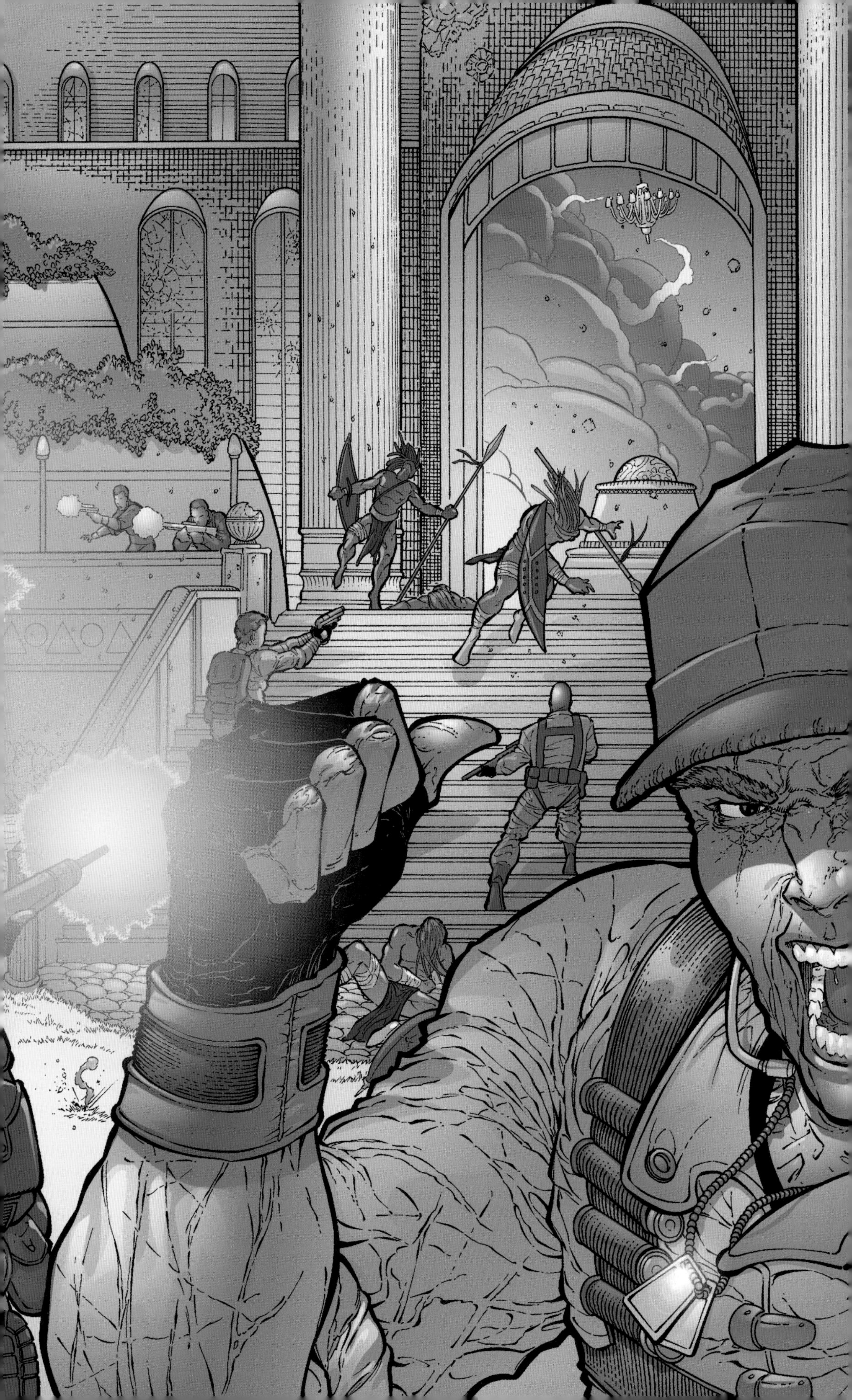

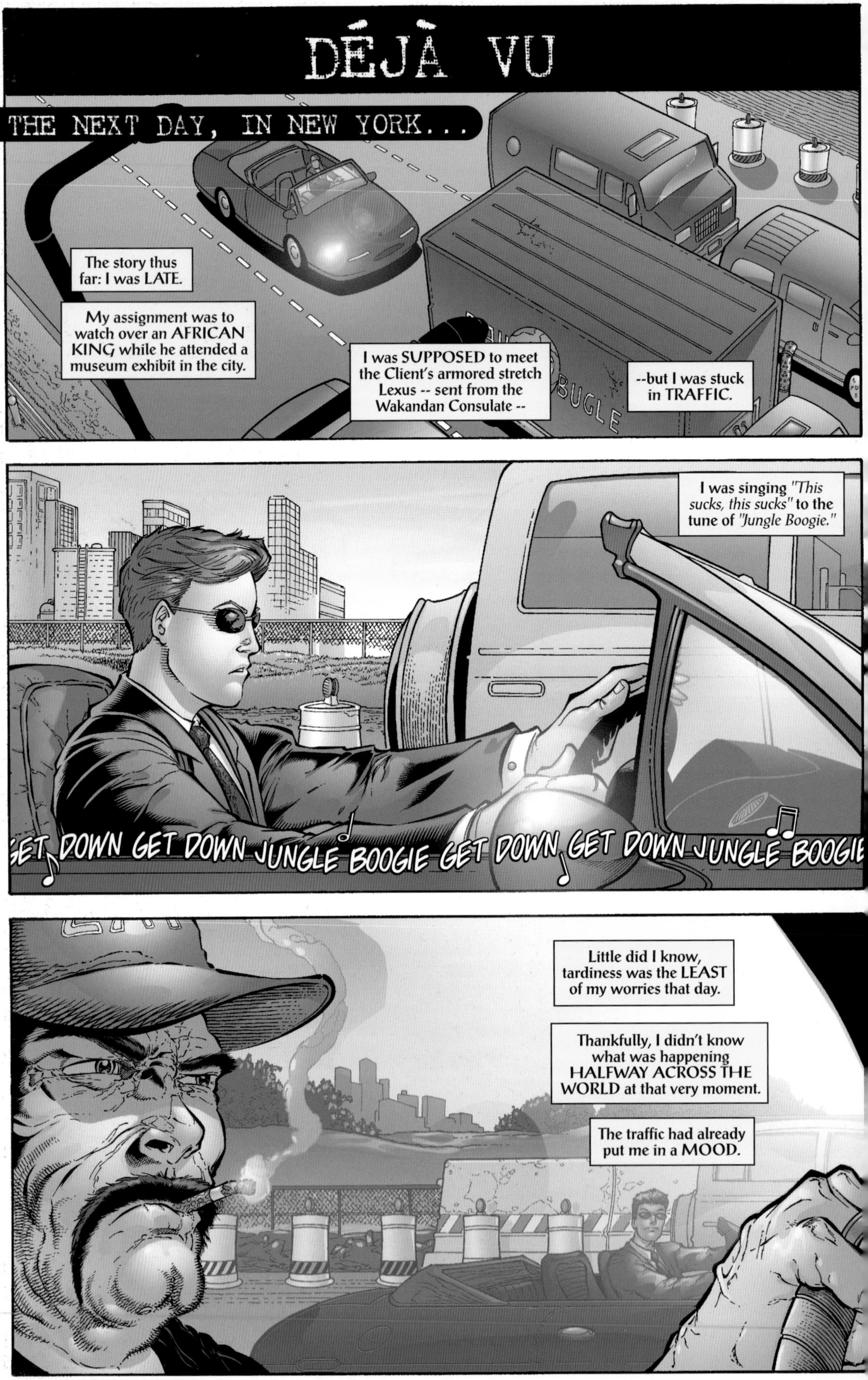
DÉJÀ VU
THE NEXT DAY, IN NEW YORK...
The story thus far: I was LATE.
My assignment was to watch over an AFRICAN KING while he attended a museum exhibit in the city.
I was SUPPOSED to meet the Client's armored stretch Lexus -- sent from the Wakandan Consulate --
--but I was stuck in TRAFFIC.
BUGLE
I was singing "This sucks, this sucks" to the tune of "Jungle Boogie."
GET DOWN GET DOWN JUNGLE BOOGIE GET DOWN GET DOWN JUNGLE BOOGIE
Little did I know, tardiness was the LEAST of my worries that day.
Thankfully, I didn't know what was happening HALFWAY ACROSS THE WORLD at that very moment.
The traffic had already put me in a MOOD.

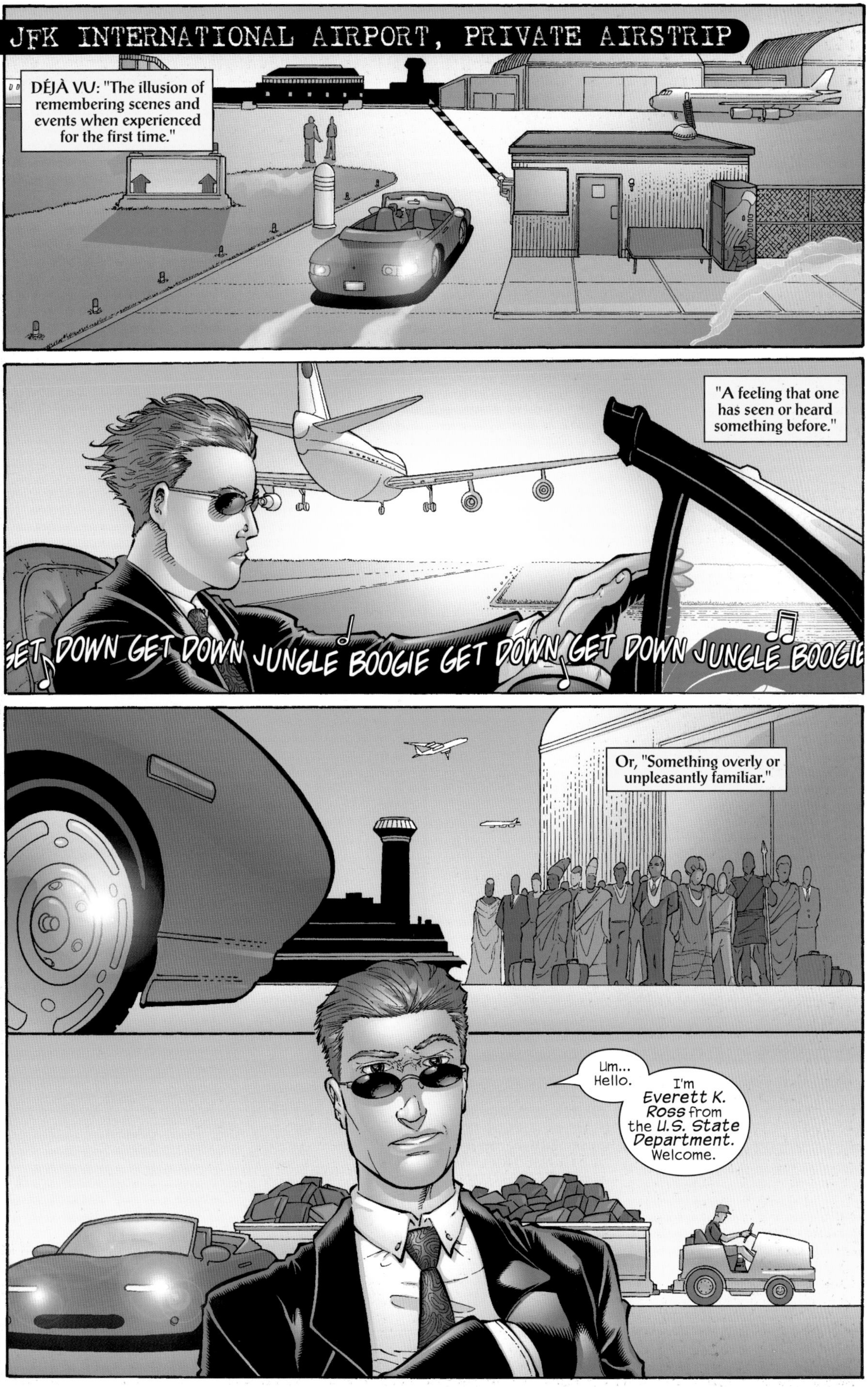
JFK INTERNATIONAL AIRPORT, PRIVATE AIRSTRIP
DÉJÀ VU: "The illusion of remembering scenes and events when experienced for the first time."
"A feeling that one has seen or heard something before."
GET DOWN GET DOWN JUNGLE BOOGIE GET DOWN GET DOWN JUNGLE BOOGIE
Or, "Something overly or unpleasantly familiar."
Um... Hello.
I'm Everett K. Ross from the U.S. State Department. Welcome.

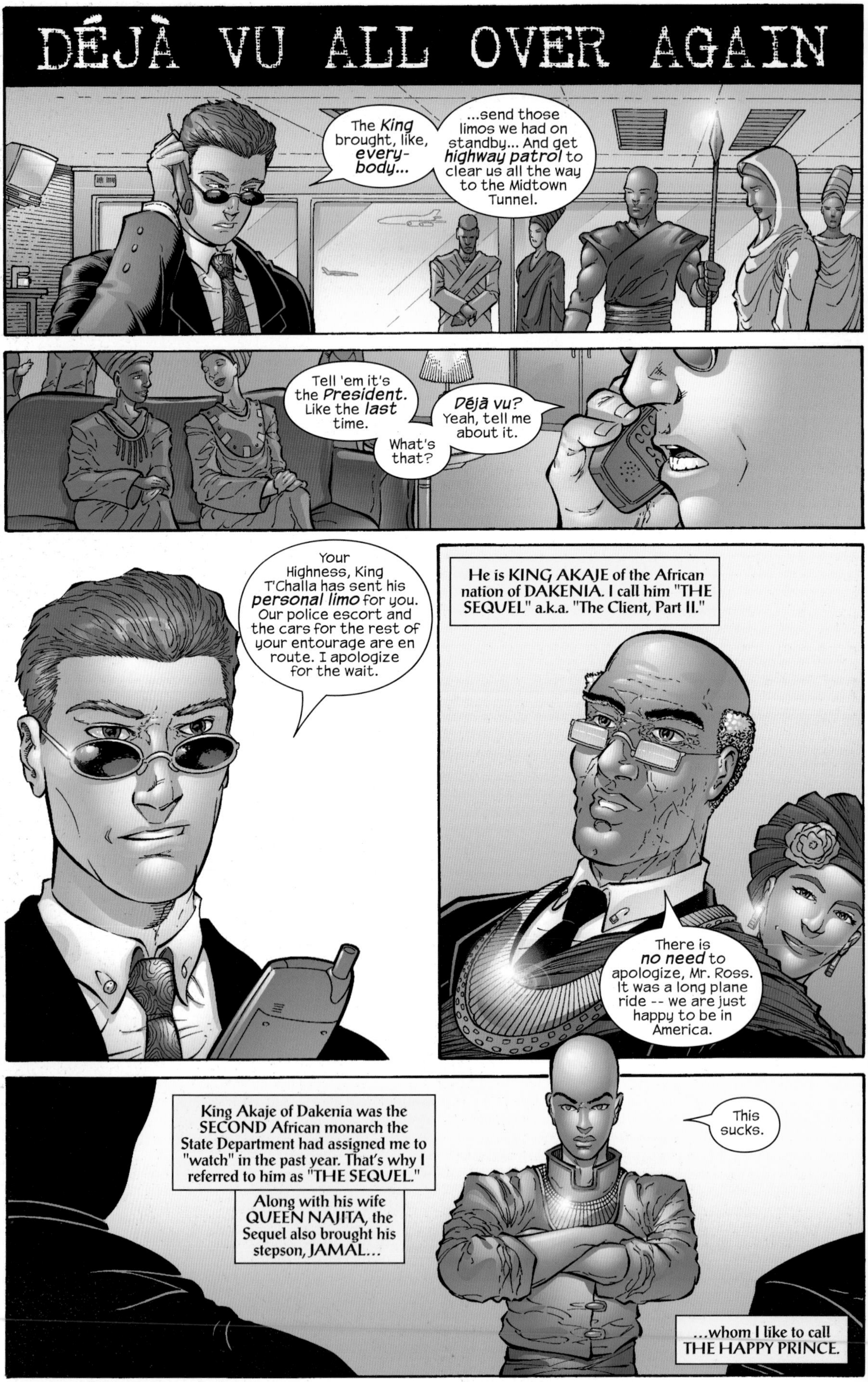
DÉJÀ VU ALL OVER AGAIN
The King brought, like, everybody...
...send those limos we had on standby... And get highway patrol to clear us all the way to the Midtown Tunnel.
Tell 'em it's the President. Like the last time.
What's that?
Déjà vu? Yeah, tell me about it.
Your Highness, King T'Challa has sent his personal limo for you. Our police escort and the cars for the rest of your entourage are en route. I apologize for the wait.
He is KING AKAJE of the African nation of DAKENIA. I call him "THE SEQUEL" a.k.a. "The Client, Part II."
There is no need to apologize, Mr. Ross. It was a long plane ride -- we are just happy to be in America.
King Akaje of Dakenia was the SECOND African monarch the State Department had assigned me to "watch" in the past year. That's why I referred to him as "THE SEQUEL."
Along with his wife QUEEN NAJITA, the Sequel also brought his stepson, JAMAL...
This sucks.
...whom I like to call THE HAPPY PRINCE.

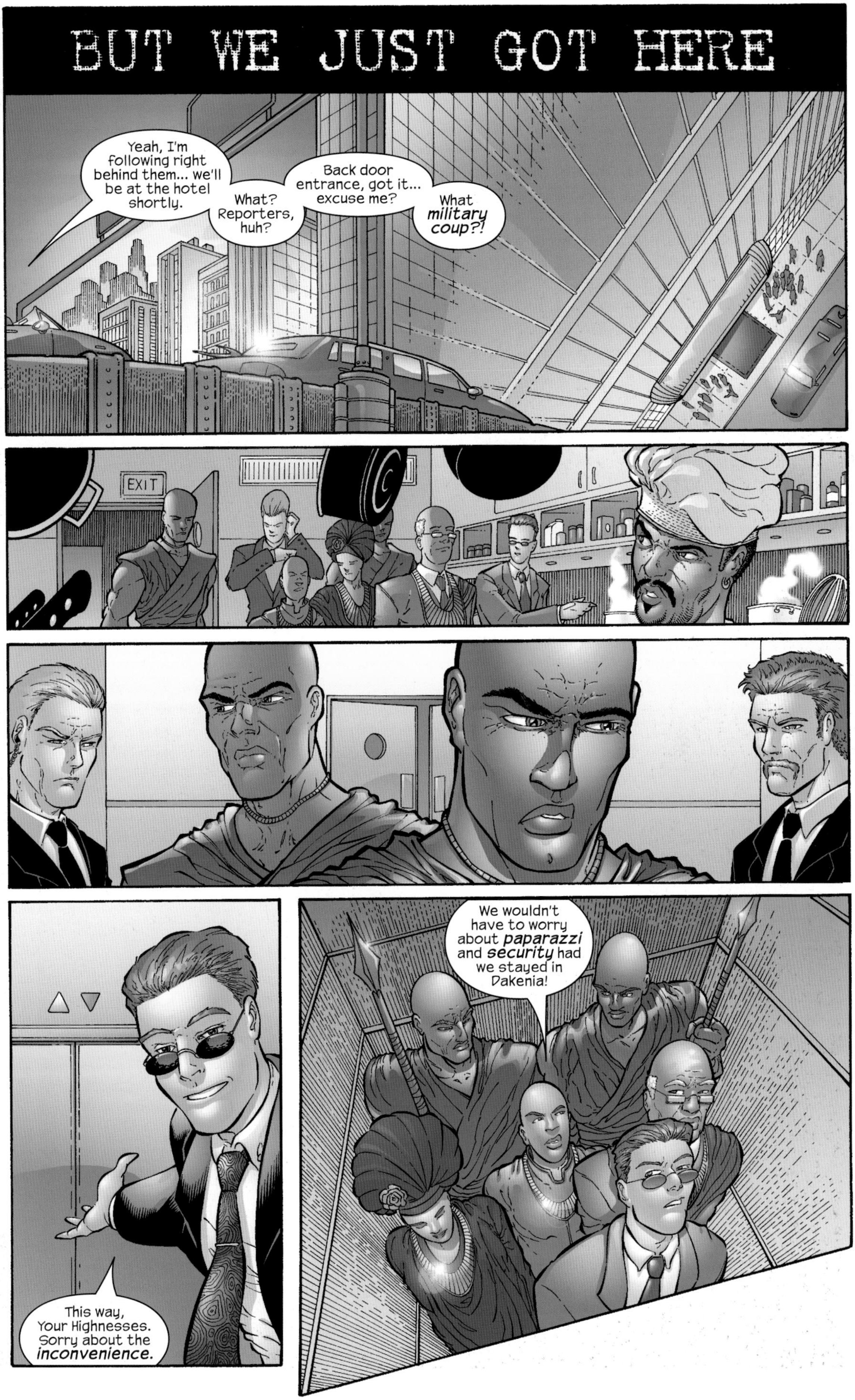
BUT WE JUST GOT HERE
Yeah, I'm following right behind them... we'll be at the hotel shortly.
What? Reporters, huh?
Back door entrance, got it... excuse me?
What military coup?!
EXIT
This way, Your Highnesses. Sorry about the inconvenience.
We wouldn't have to worry about paparazzi and security had we stayed in Dakenia!

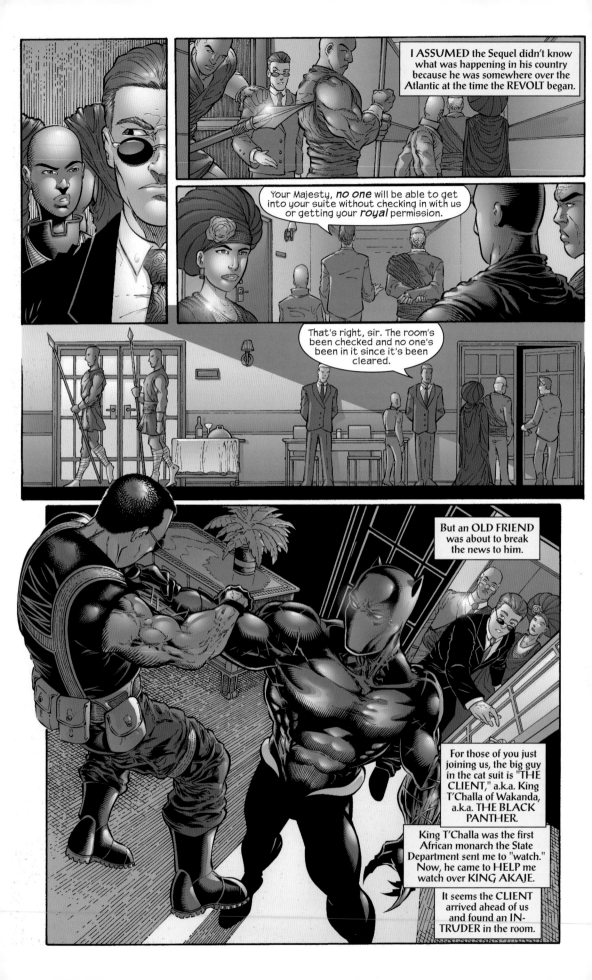

I ASSUMED the Sequel didn't know what was happening in his country because he was somewhere over the Atlantic at the time the REVOLT began.

Your Majesty, *no one* will be able to get into your suite without checking in with us or getting your *royal* permission.

That's right, sir. The room's been checked and no one's been in it since it's been cleared.

But an OLD FRIEND was about to break the news to him.

For those of you just joining us, the big guy in the cat suit is "THE CLIENT," a.k.a. King T'Challa of Wakanda, a.k.a. THE BLACK PANTHER.

King T'Challa was the first African monarch the State Department sent me to "watch." Now, he came to HELP me watch over KING AKAJE.

It seems the CLIENT arrived ahead of us and found an IN-TRUDER in the room.

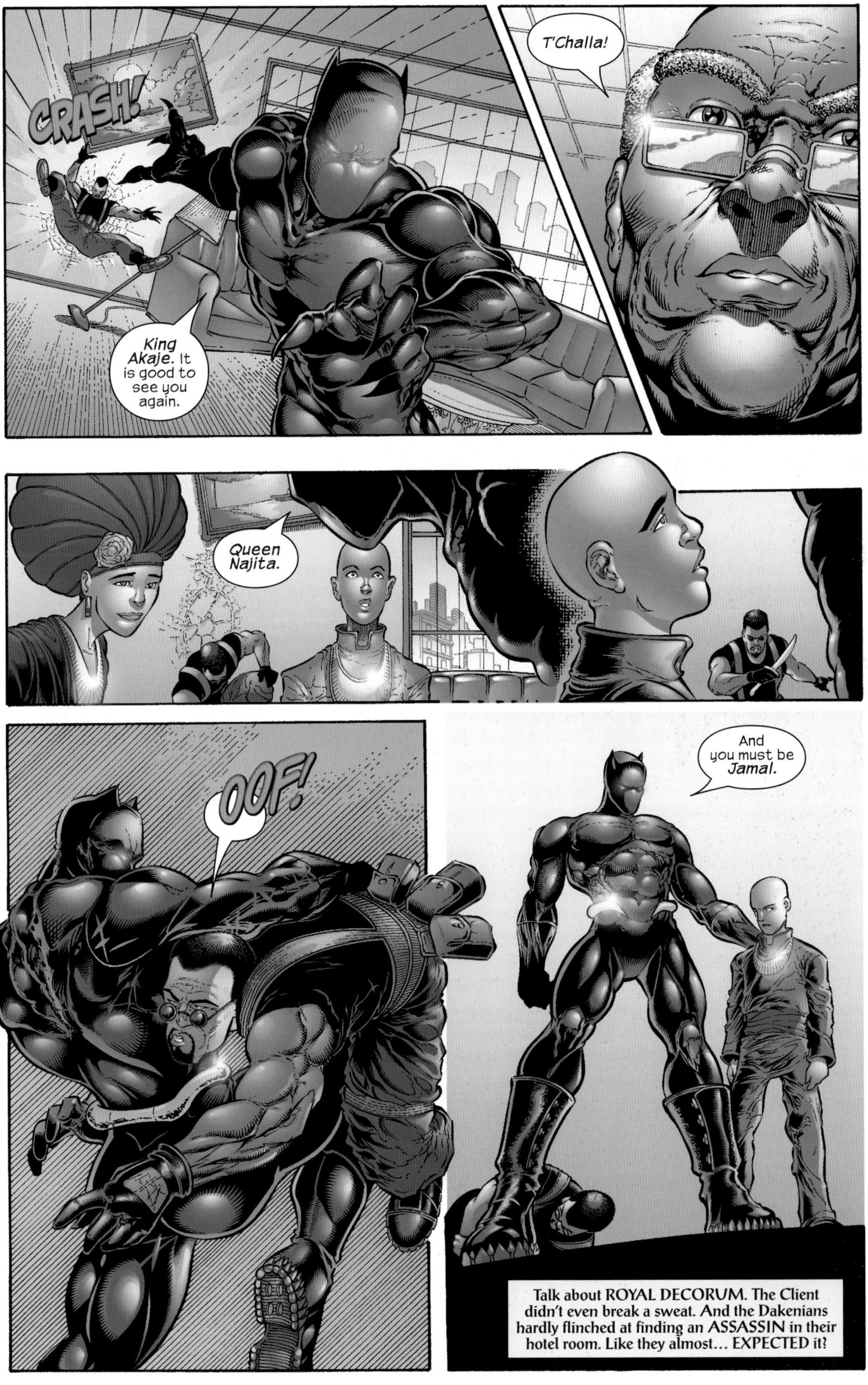
CRASH!
King Akaje. It is good to see you again.
T'Challa!
Queen Najita.
OOF!
And you must be Jamal.
Talk about ROYAL DECORUM. The Client didn't even break a sweat. And the Dakenians hardly flinched at finding an ASSASSIN in their hotel room. Like they almost… EXPECTED it?

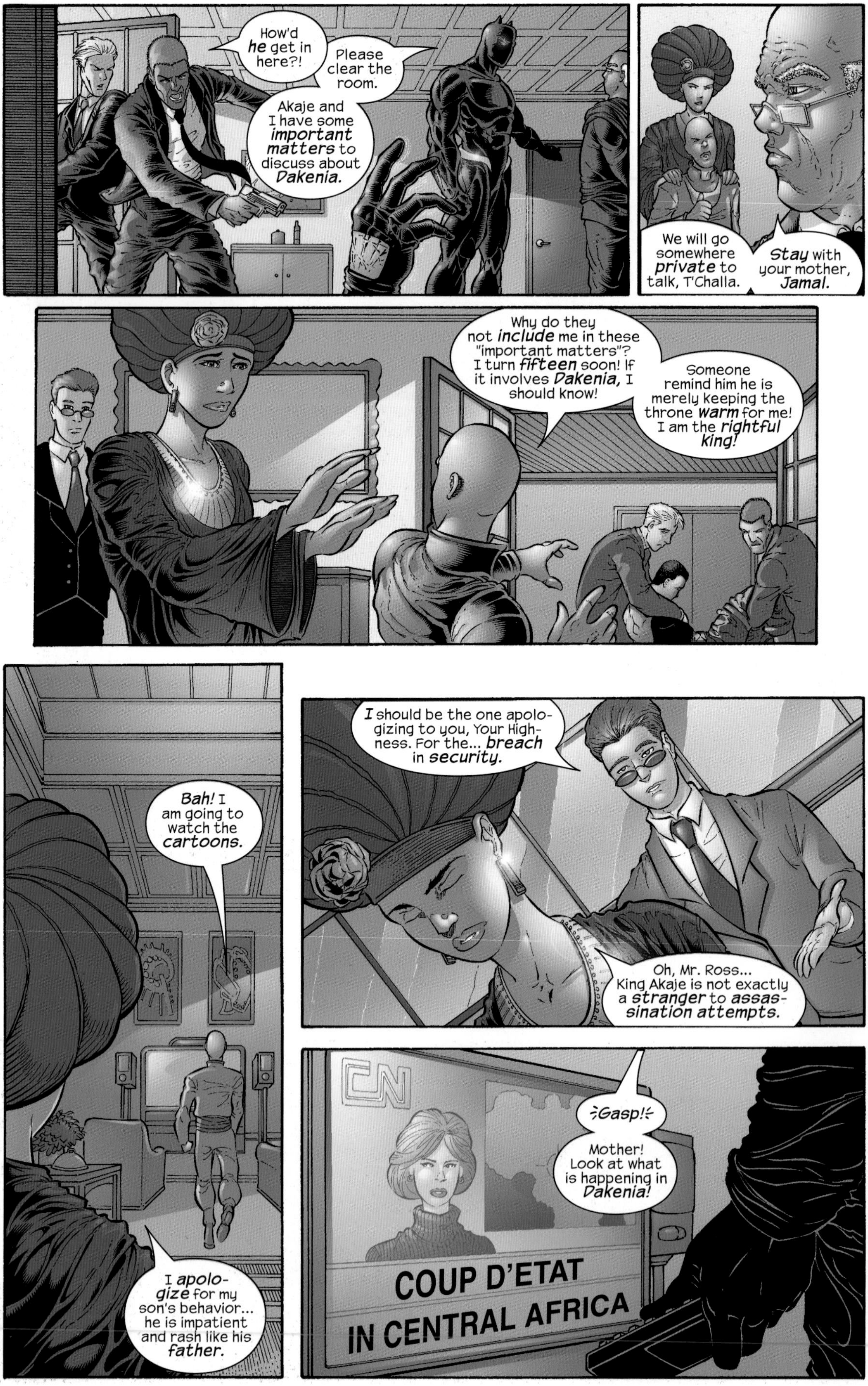
How'd he get in here?!
Please clear the room.
Akaje and I have some important matters to discuss about Dakenia.
We will go somewhere private to talk, T'Challa.
Stay with your mother, Jamal.
Why do they not include me in these "important matters"? I turn fifteen soon! If it involves Dakenia, I should know!
Someone remind him he is merely keeping the throne warm for me! I am the rightful king!
Bah! I am going to watch the cartoons.
I apologize for my son's behavior... he is impatient and rash like his father.
I should be the one apologizing to you, Your Highness. For the... breach in security.
Oh, Mr. Ross... King Akaje is not exactly a stranger to assassination attempts.
CN
COUP D'ETAT
IN CENTRAL AFRICA
Gasp!
Mother! Look at what is happening in Dakenia!

CAN WE GO HOME ALREADY?

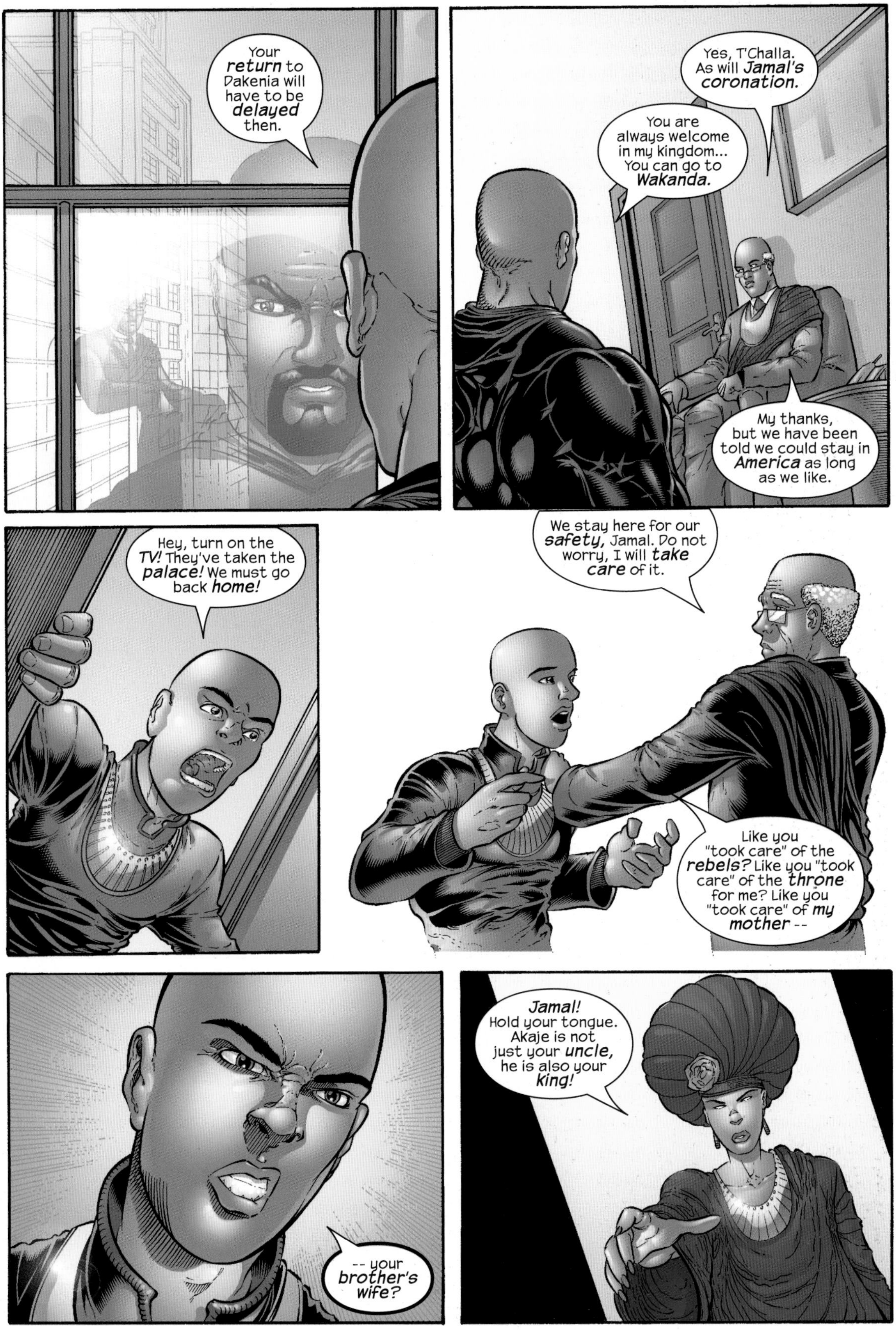

Your return to Dakenia will have to be delayed then.
Yes, T'Challa. As will Jamal's coronation.
You are always welcome in my kingdom... You can go to Wakanda.
My thanks, but we have been told we could stay in America as long as we like.
Hey, turn on the TV! They've taken the palace! We must go back home!
We stay here for our safety, Jamal. Do not worry, I will take care of it.
Like you "took care" of the rebels? Like you "took care" of the throne for me? Like you "took care" of my mother --
-- your brother's wife?
Jamal! Hold your tongue. Akaje is not just your uncle, he is also your king!

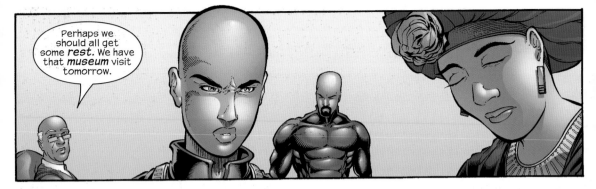

Perhaps we should all get some *rest.* We have that *museum* visit tomorrow.

The *museum?* But, Akaje--

Najita, we cannot hide like *cowards.* We must show our loyal subjects -- and *the world* -- that the royal family is alive and well during this *crisis.*

What better way to do that than by viewing the *exhibit* displaying the royal jewels and other treasures of Dakenia as *planned?*

Yes... *rest,* my friends. I will continue to monitor events for you --

-- and make sure the building is *secure* before I leave.

Akaje, you and I will talk more in the morning.

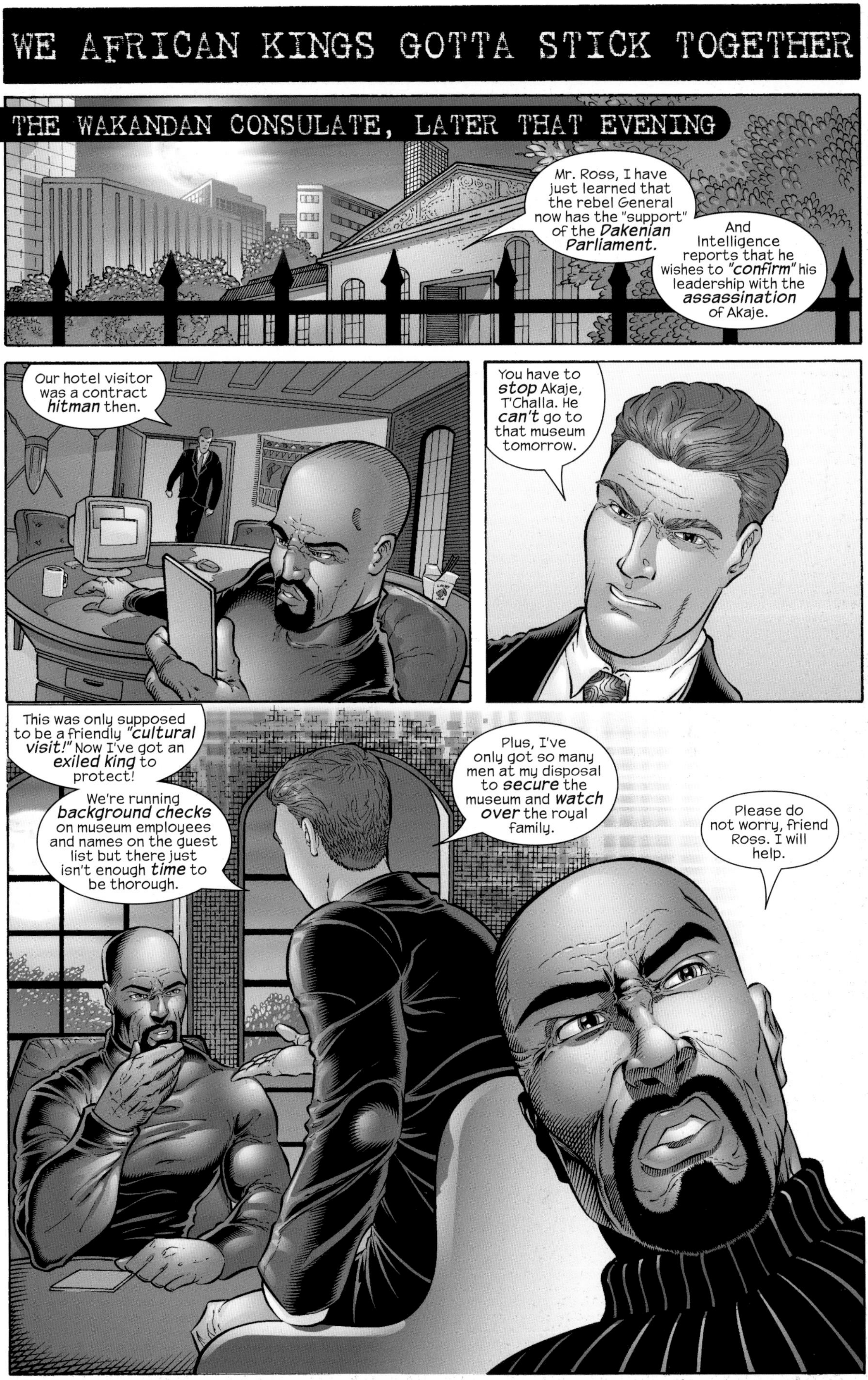
WE AFRICAN KINGS GOTTA STICK TOGETHER
THE WAKANDAN CONSULATE, LATER THAT EVENING
Mr. Ross, I have just learned that the rebel General now has the "support" of the Dakenian Parliament.
And Intelligence reports that he wishes to "confirm" his leadership with the assassination of Akaje.
Our hotel visitor was a contract hitman then.
You have to stop Akaje, T'Challa. He can't go to that museum tomorrow.
This was only supposed to be a friendly "cultural visit!" Now I've got an exiled king to protect!
We're running background checks on museum employees and names on the guest list but there just isn't enough time to be thorough.
Plus, I've only got so many men at my disposal to secure the museum and watch over the royal family.
Please do not worry, friend Ross. I will help.

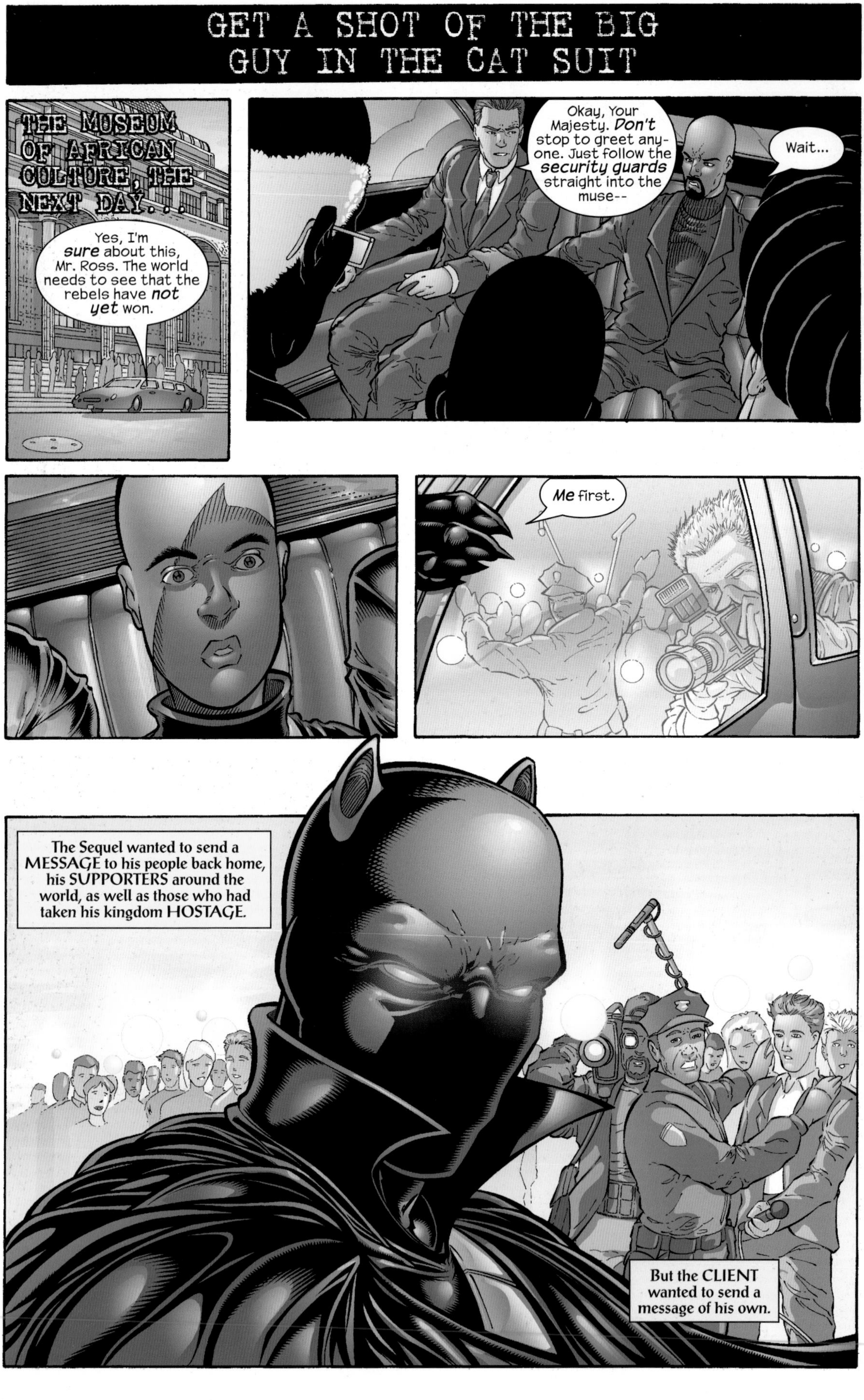
GET A SHOT OF THE BIG GUY IN THE CAT SUIT
THE MUSEUM OF AFRICAN CULTURE, THE NEXT DAY...
Yes, I'm *sure* about this, Mr. Ross. The world needs to see that the rebels have *not yet* won.
Okay, Your Majesty. *Don't* stop to greet any-one. Just follow the *security guards* straight into the muse--
Wait...
Me first.
The Sequel wanted to send a MESSAGE to his people back home, his SUPPORTERS around the world, as well as those who had taken his kingdom HOSTAGE.
But the CLIENT wanted to send a message of his own.

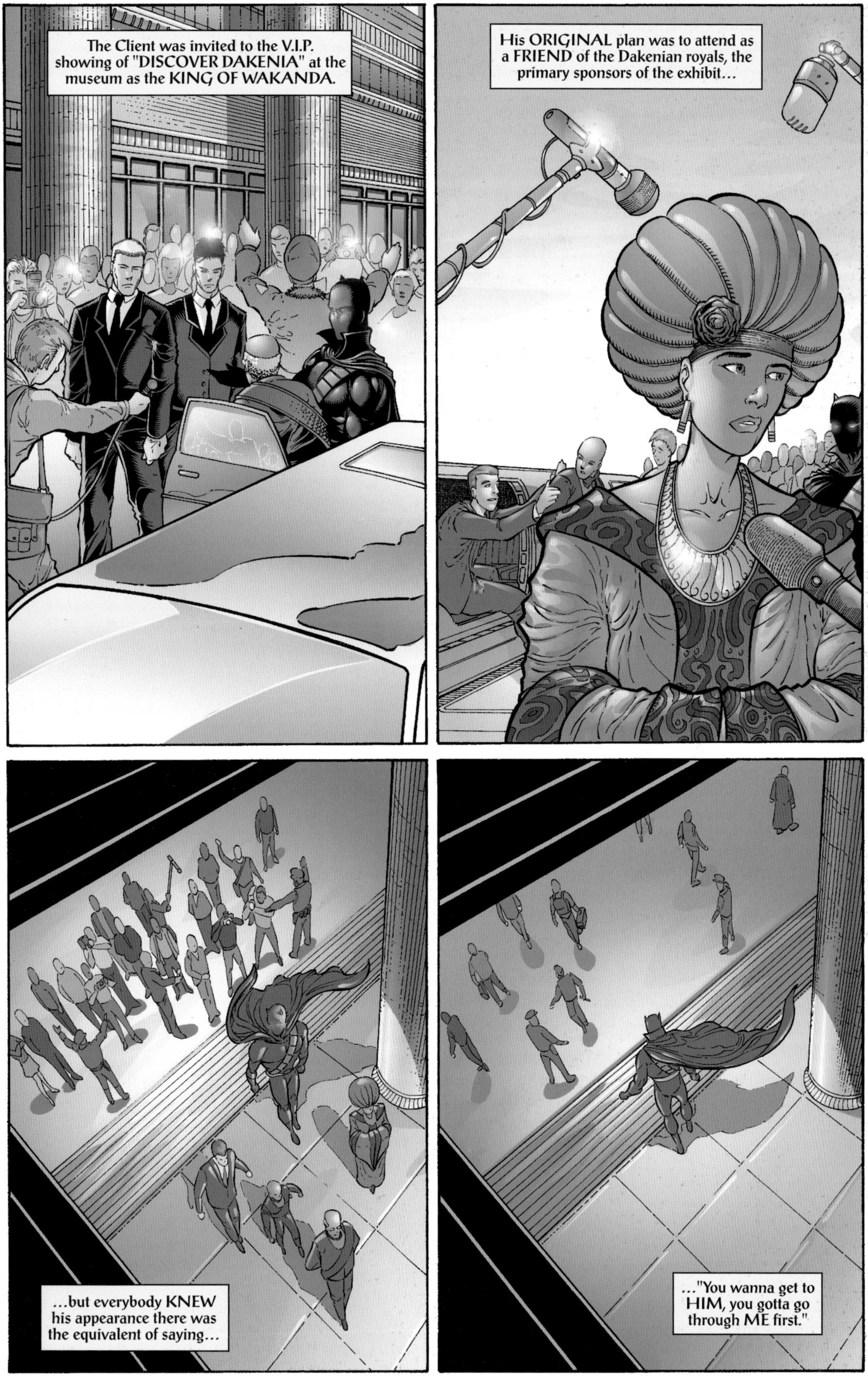
The Client was invited to the V.I.P. showing of "DISCOVER DAKENIA" at the museum as the KING OF WAKANDA.
His ORIGINAL plan was to attend as a FRIEND of the Dakenian royals, the primary sponsors of the exhibit...
...but everybody KNEW his appearance there was the equivalent of saying...
..."You wanna get to HIM, you gotta go through ME first."

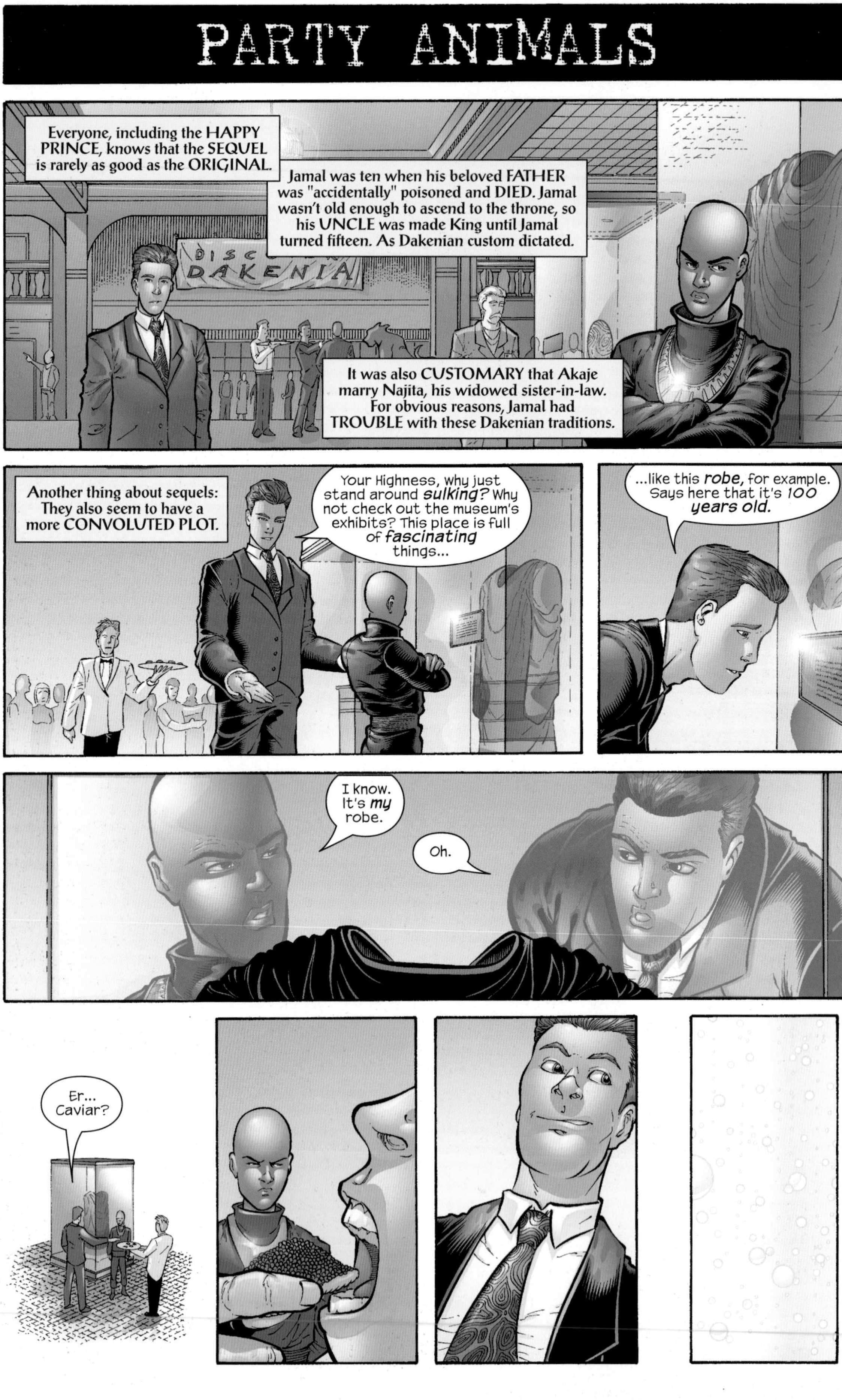
PARTY ANIMALS
Everyone, including the HAPPY PRINCE, knows that the SEQUEL is rarely as good as the ORIGINAL.
Jamal was ten when his beloved FATHER was "accidentally" poisoned and DIED. Jamal wasn't old enough to ascend to the throne, so his UNCLE was made King until Jamal turned fifteen. As Dakenian custom dictated.
DISCOVER DAKENIA
It was also CUSTOMARY that Akaje marry Najita, his widowed sister-in-law. For obvious reasons, Jamal had TROUBLE with these Dakenian traditions.
Another thing about sequels: They also seem to have a more CONVOLUTED PLOT.
Your Highness, why just stand around *sulking?* Why not check out the museum's exhibits? This place is full of *fascinating* things...
...like this *robe,* for example. Says here that it's *100 years old.*
I know. It's *my* robe.
Oh.
Er... Caviar?

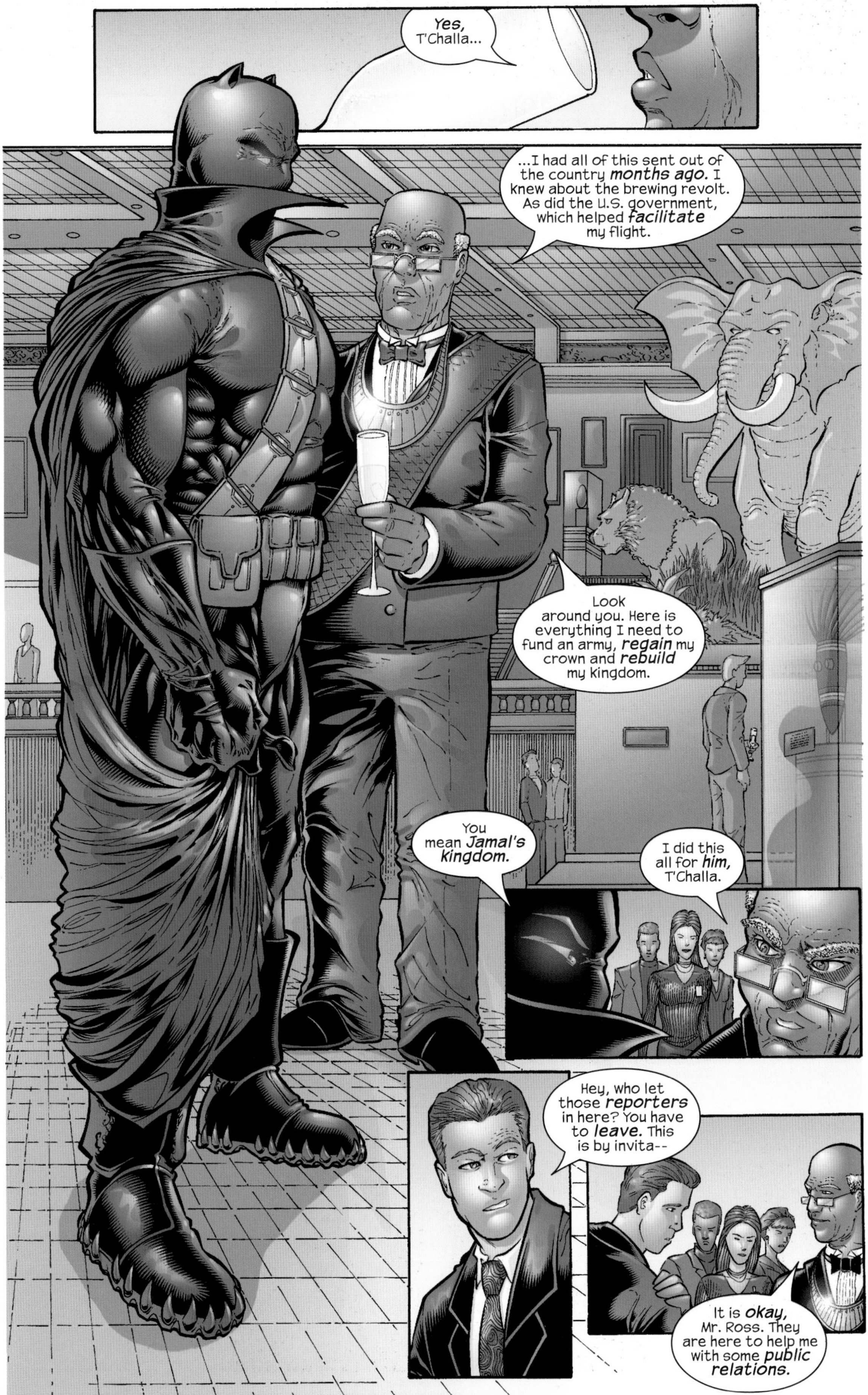
Yes, T'Challa...
...I had all of this sent out of the country months ago. I knew about the brewing revolt. As did the U.S. government, which helped facilitate my flight.
Look around you. Here is everything I need to fund an army, regain my crown and rebuild my kingdom.
You mean Jamal's kingdom.
I did this all for him, T'Challa.
Hey, who let those reporters in here? You have to leave. This is by invita--
It is okay, Mr. Ross. They are here to help me with some public relations.

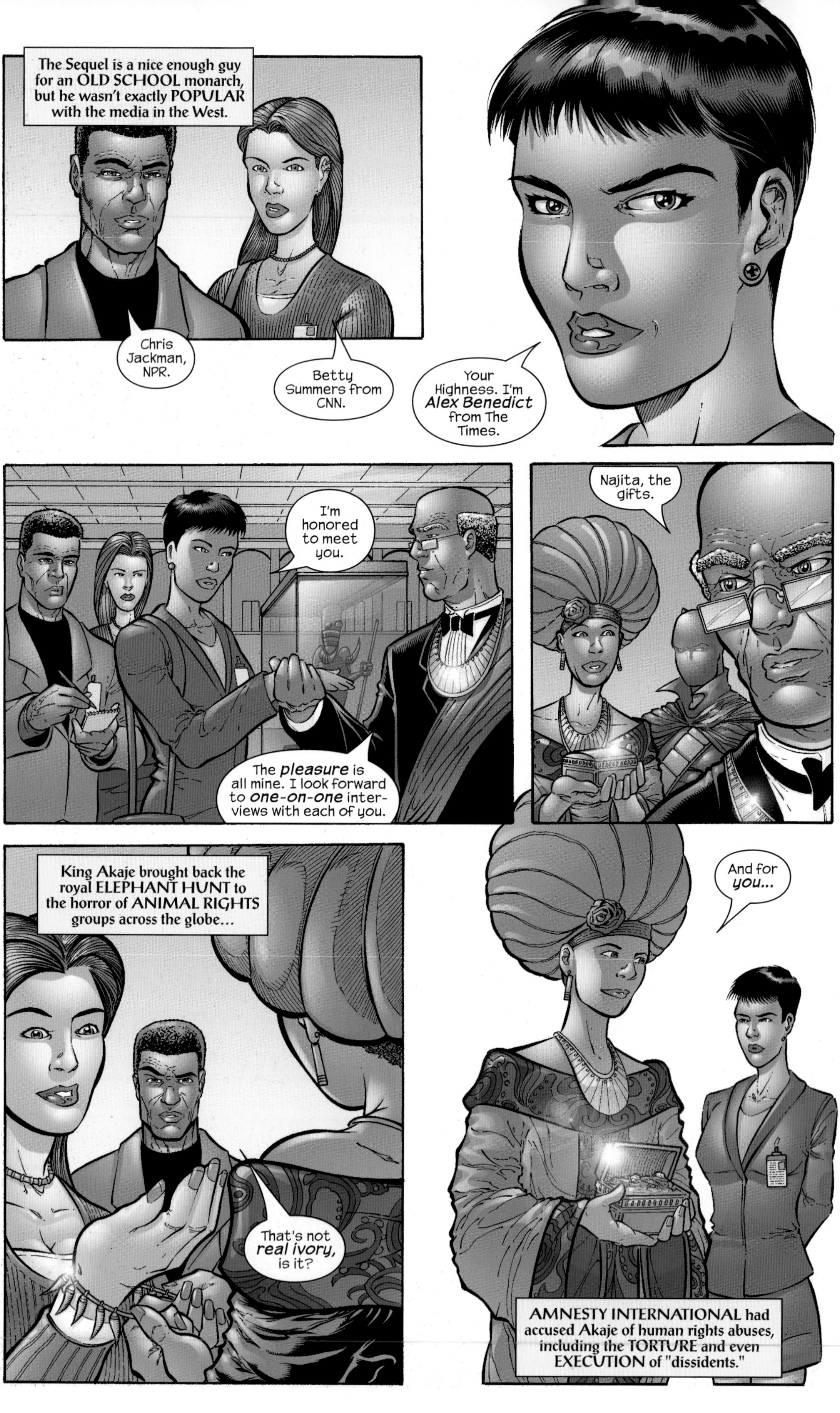

The Sequel is a nice enough guy for an OLD SCHOOL monarch, but he wasn't exactly POPULAR with the media in the West.
Chris Jackman, NPR.
Betty Summers from CNN.
Your Highness. I'm *Alex Benedict* from The Times.
I'm honored to meet you.
The *pleasure* is all mine. I look forward to *one-on-one* interviews with each of you.
Najita, the gifts.
King Akaje brought back the royal ELEPHANT HUNT to the horror of ANIMAL RIGHTS groups across the globe...
That's not *real ivory,* is it?
And for *you...*
AMNESTY INTERNATIONAL had accused Akaje of human rights abuses, including the TORTURE and even EXECUTION of "dissidents."

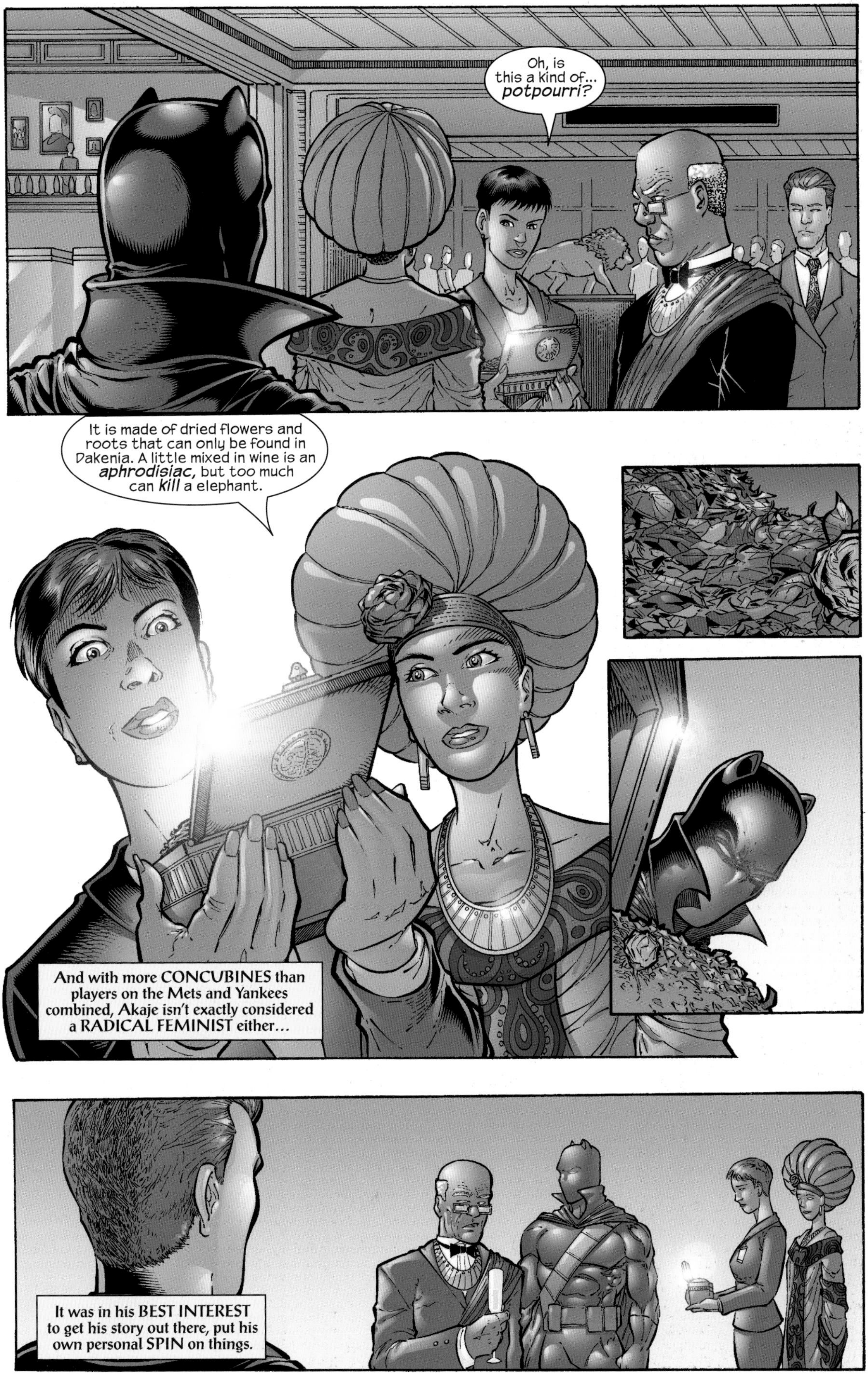

Oh, is this a kind of... *potpourri?*
It is made of dried flowers and roots that can only be found in Dakenia. A little mixed in wine is an *aphrodisiac,* but too much can *kill* a elephant.
And with more CONCUBINES than players on the Mets and Yankees combined, Akaje isn't exactly considered a RADICAL FEMINIST either...
It was in his BEST INTEREST to get his story out there, put his own personal SPIN on things.

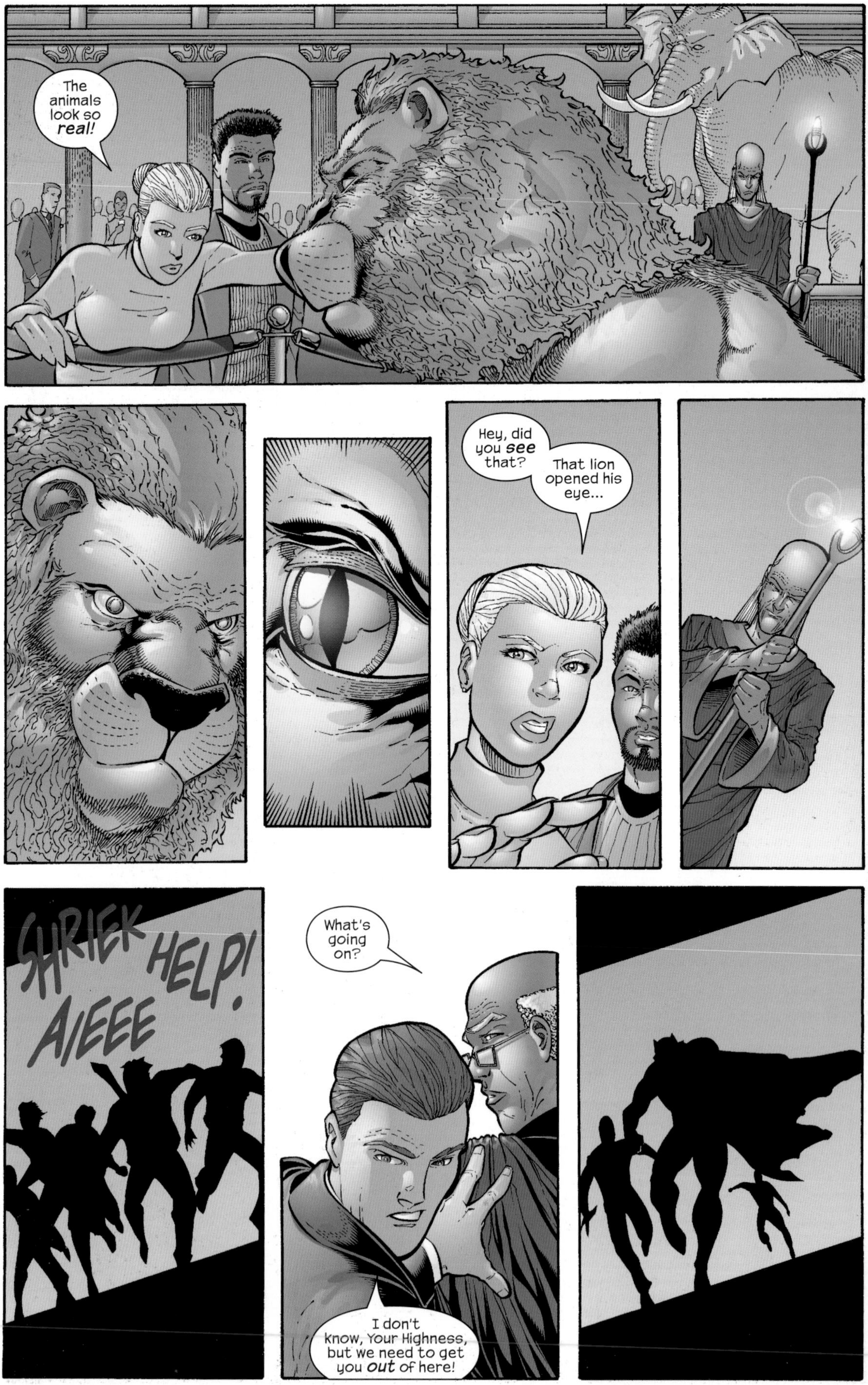
The animals look so *real!*
Hey, did you *see* that?
That lion opened his eye...
SHRIEK
HELP!
AIEEE
What's going on?
I don't know, Your Highness, but we need to get you *out* of here!

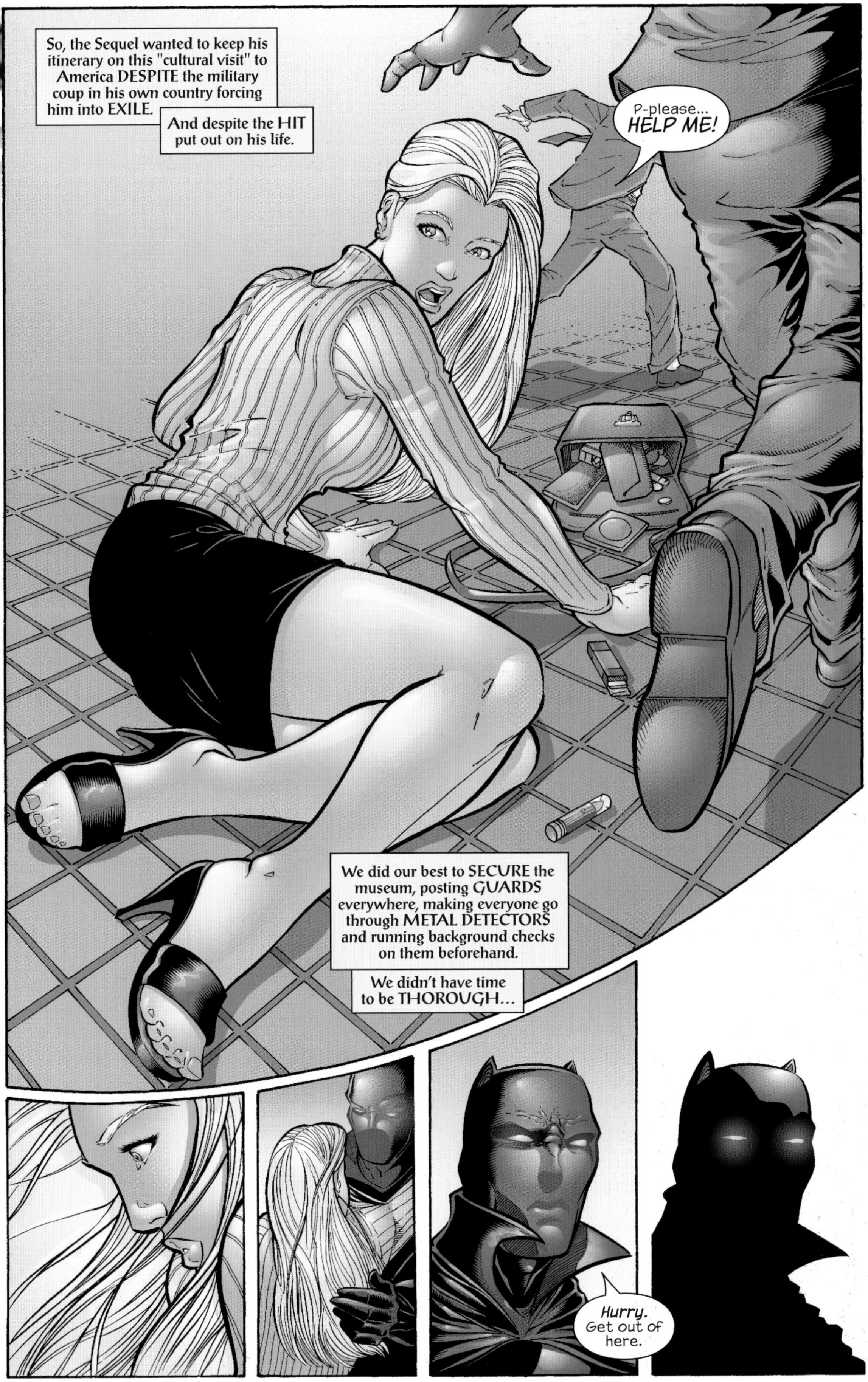

So, the Sequel wanted to keep his itinerary on this "cultural visit" to America DESPITE the military coup in his own country forcing him into EXILE.
And despite the HIT put out on his life.
P-please... HELP ME!
We did our best to SECURE the museum, posting GUARDS everywhere, making everyone go through METAL DETECTORS and running background checks on them beforehand.
We didn't have time to be THOROUGH...
Hurry. Get out of here.

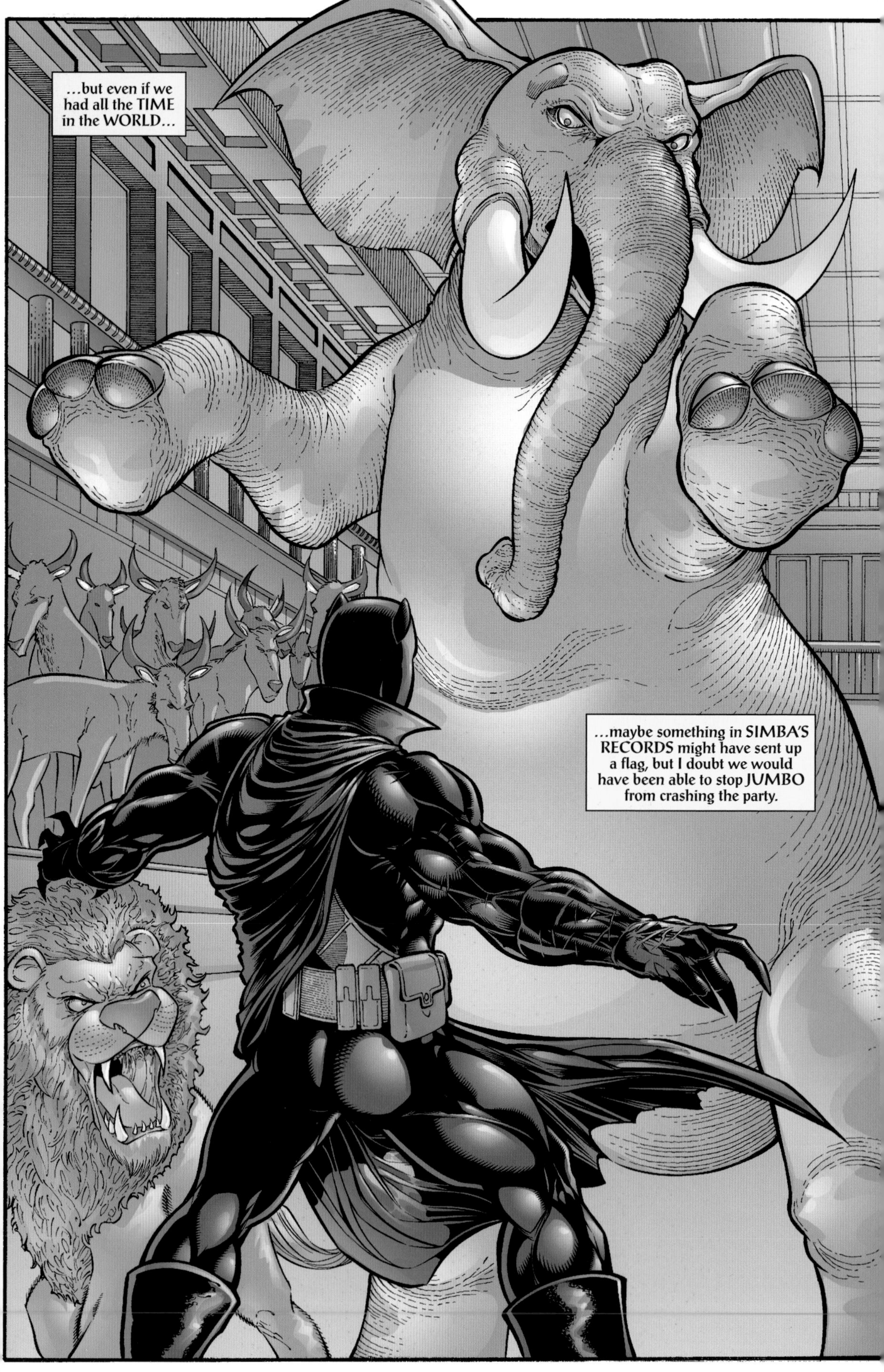
...but even if we had all the TIME in the WORLD...
...maybe something in SIMBA'S RECORDS might have sent up a flag, but I doubt we would have been able to stop JUMBO from crashing the party.

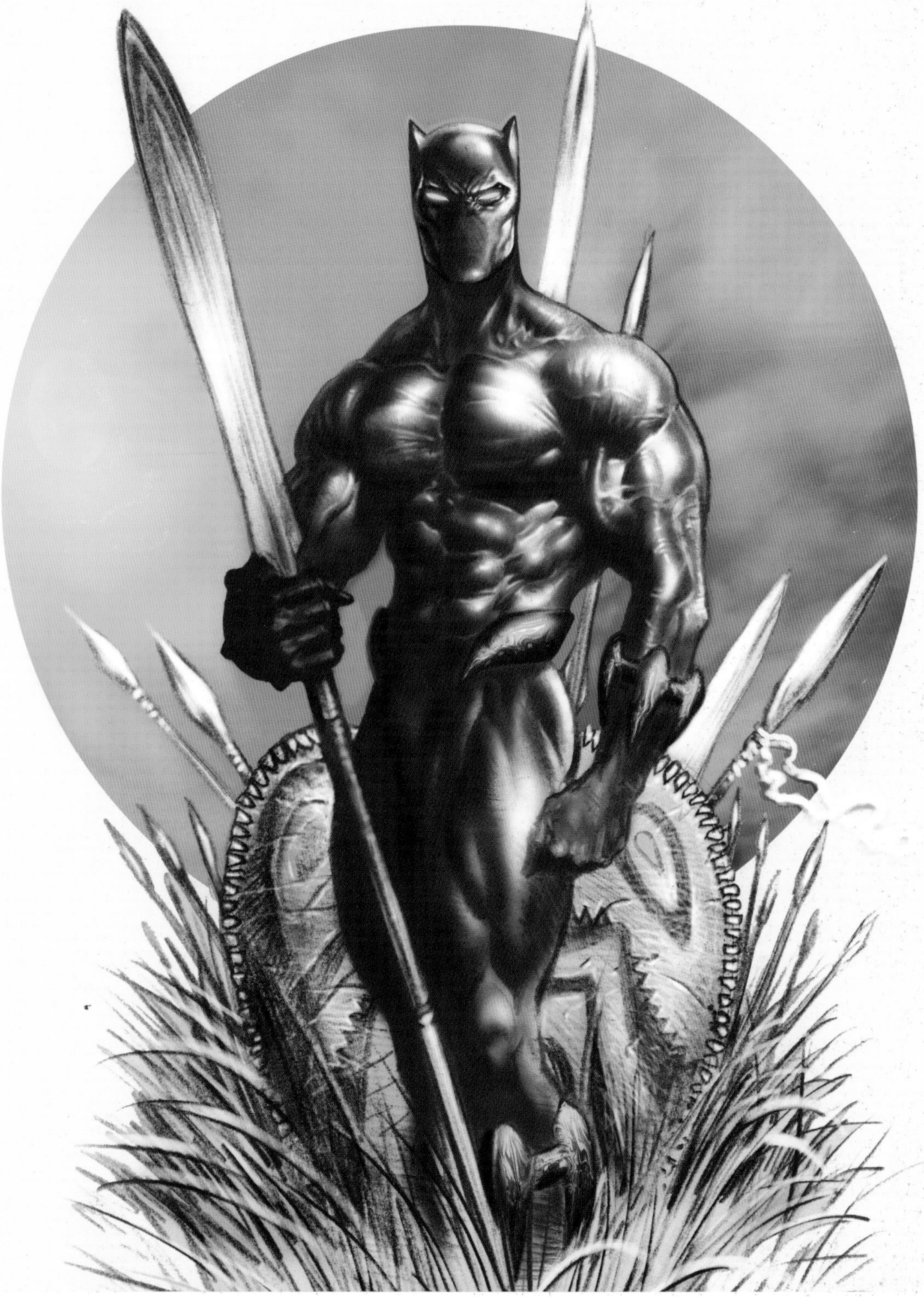

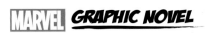

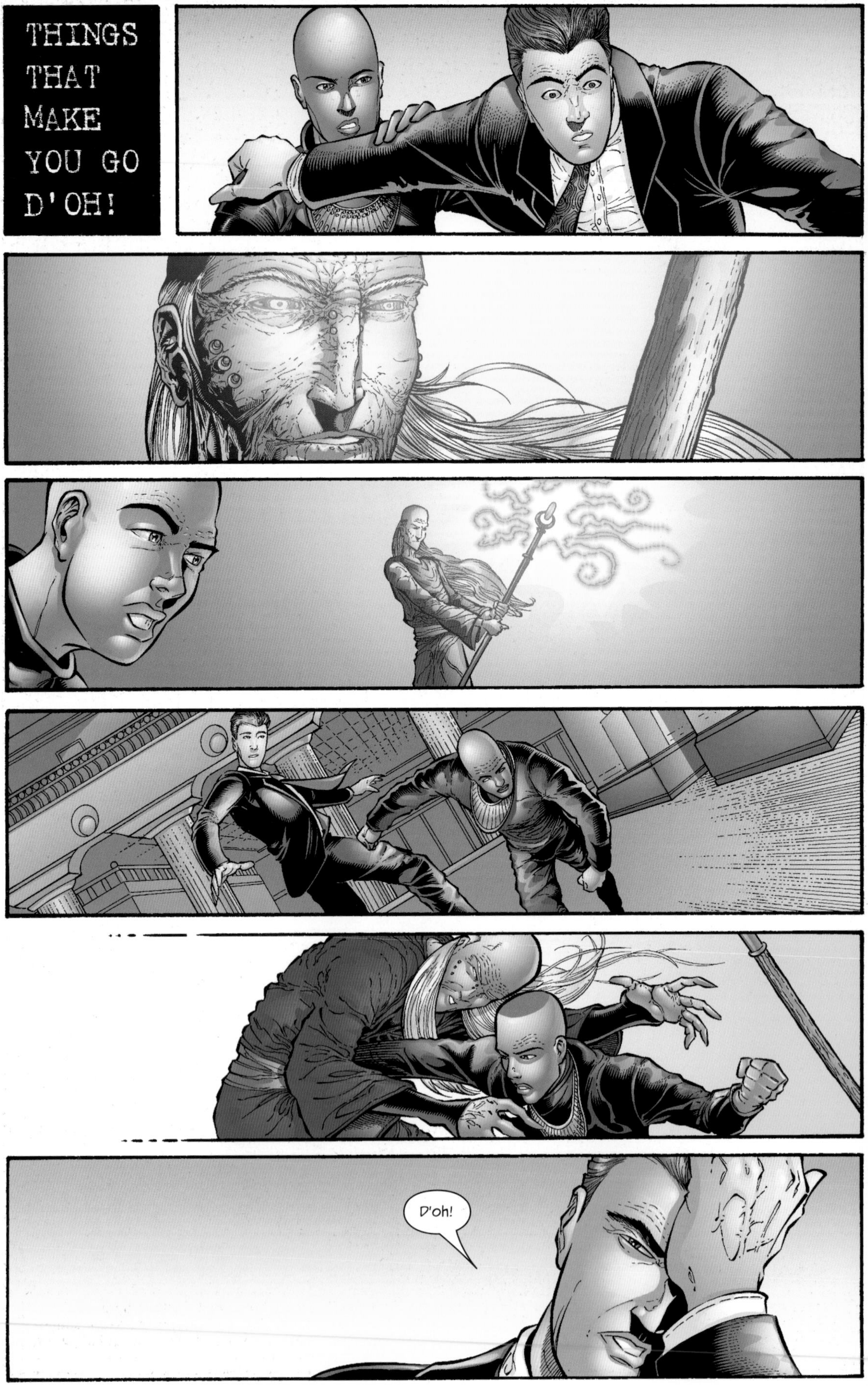
THINGS THAT MAKE YOU GO D'OH!
D'oh!

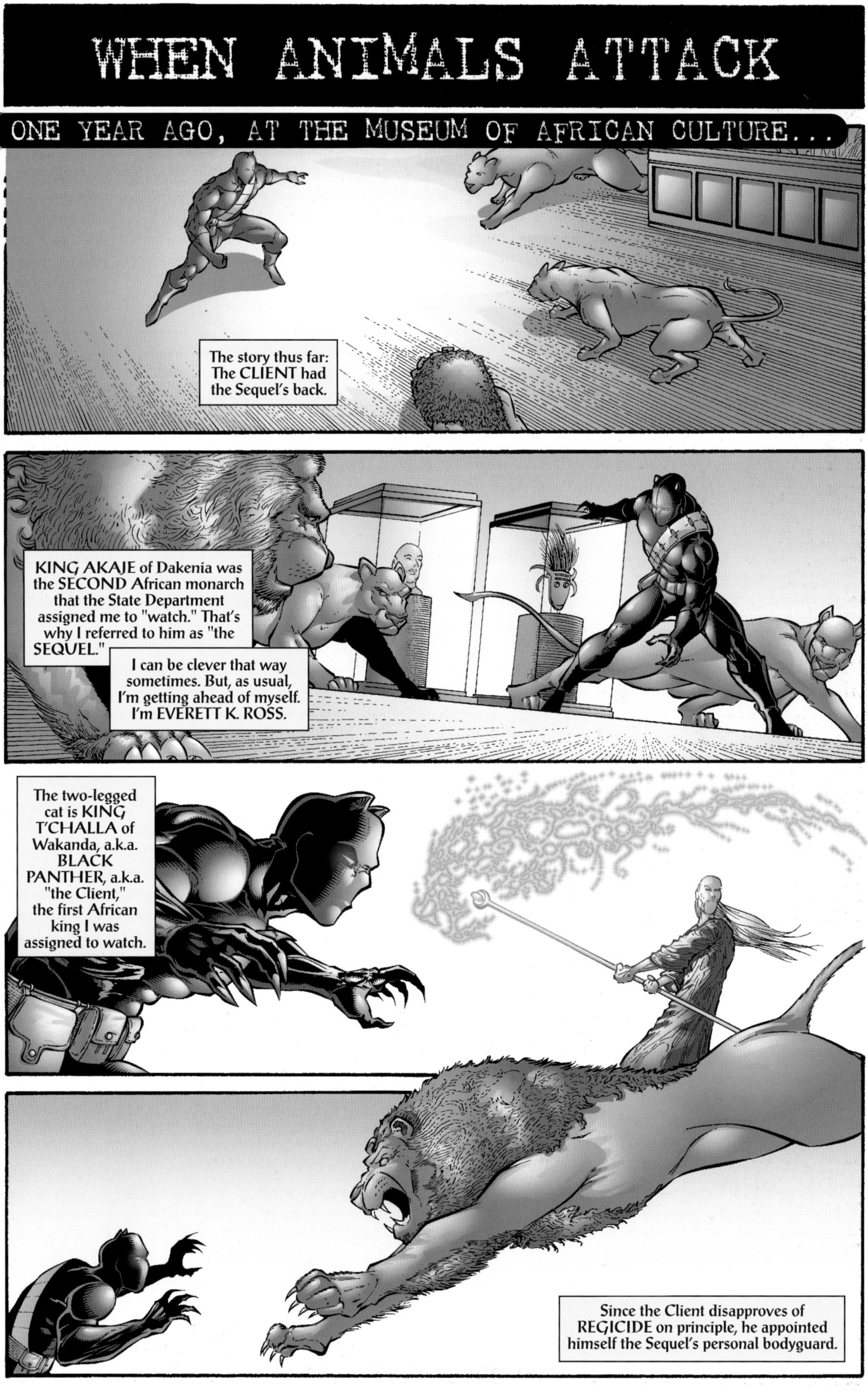
WHEN ANIMALS ATTACK
ONE YEAR AGO, AT THE MUSEUM OF AFRICAN CULTURE...
The story thus far: The CLIENT had the Sequel's back.
KING AKAJE of Dakenia was the SECOND African monarch that the State Department assigned me to "watch." That's why I referred to him as "the SEQUEL."
I can be clever that way sometimes. But, as usual, I'm getting ahead of myself. I'm EVERETT K. ROSS.
The two-legged cat is KING T'CHALLA of Wakanda, a.k.a. BLACK PANTHER, a.k.a. "the Client," the first African king I was assigned to watch.
Since the Client disapproves of REGICIDE on principle, he appointed himself the Sequel's personal bodyguard.

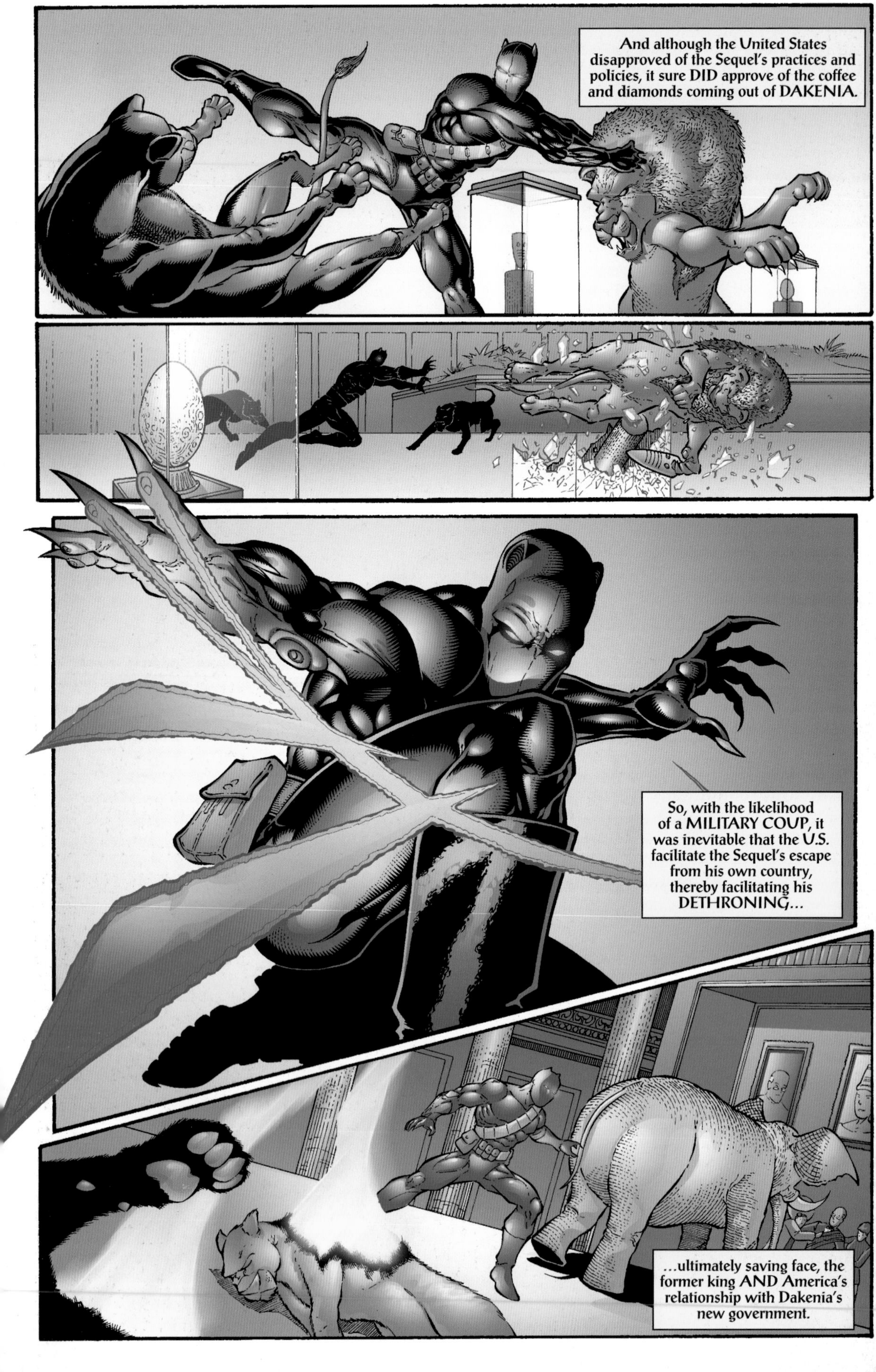
And although the United States disapproved of the Sequel's practices and policies, it sure DID approve of the coffee and diamonds coming out of DAKENIA.
So, with the likelihood of a MILITARY COUP, it was inevitable that the U.S. facilitate the Sequel's escape from his own country, thereby facilitating his DETHRONING...
...ultimately saving face, the former king AND America's relationship with Dakenia's new government.

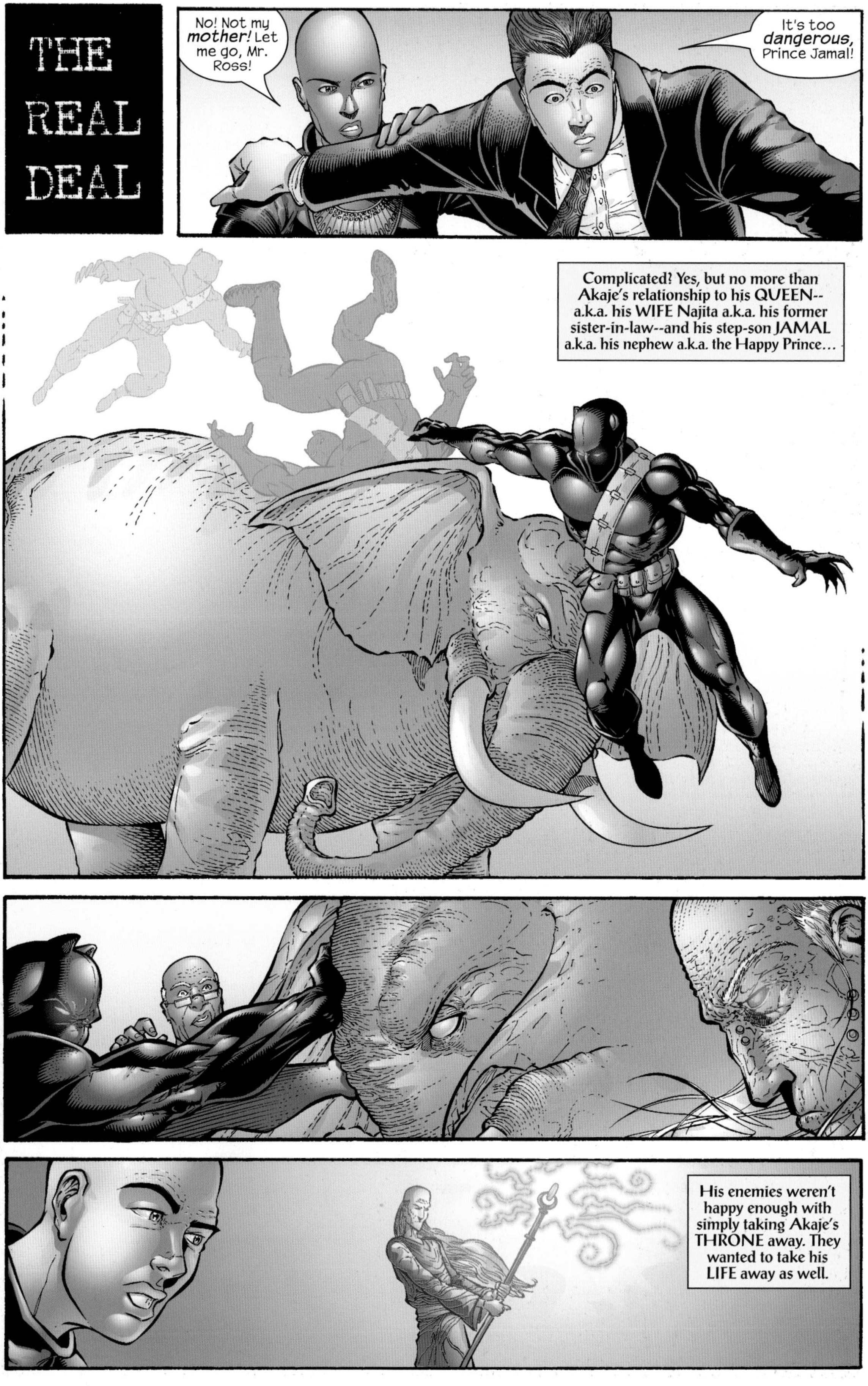
THE REAL DEAL
No! Not my mother! Let me go, Mr. Ross!
It's too dangerous, Prince Jamal!
Complicated? Yes, but no more than Akaje's relationship to his QUEEN--a.k.a. his WIFE Najita a.k.a. his former sister-in-law--and his step-son JAMAL a.k.a. his nephew a.k.a. the Happy Prince...
His enemies weren't happy enough with simply taking Akaje's THRONE away. They wanted to take his LIFE away as well.

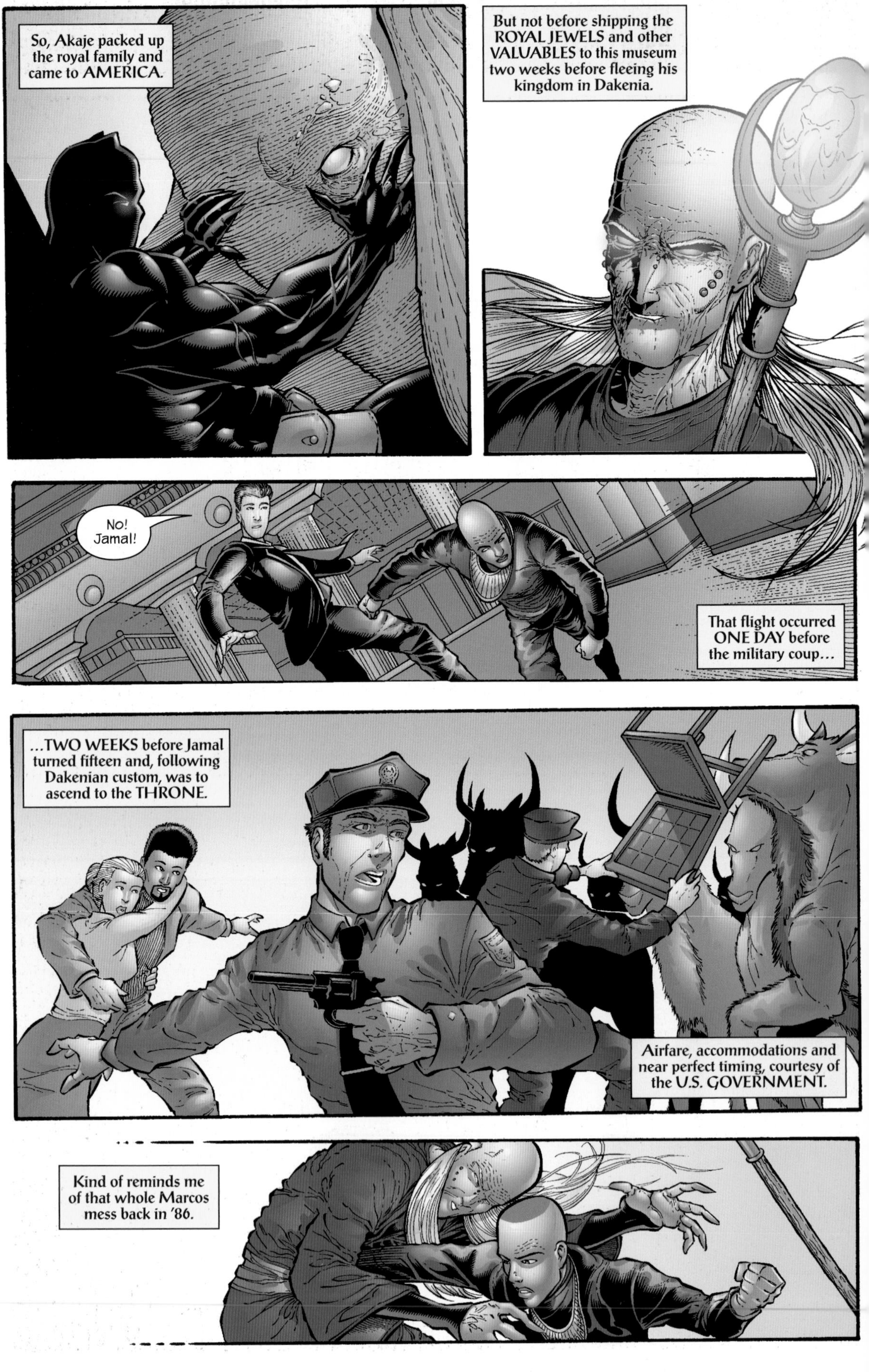
So, Akaje packed up the royal family and came to AMERICA.
But not before shipping the ROYAL JEWELS and other VALUABLES to this museum two weeks before fleeing his kingdom in Dakenia.
No! Jamal!
That flight occurred ONE DAY before the military coup...
...TWO WEEKS before Jamal turned fifteen and, following Dakenian custom, was to ascend to the THRONE.
Airfare, accommodations and near perfect timing, courtesy of the U.S. GOVERNMENT.
Kind of reminds me of that whole Marcos mess back in '86.

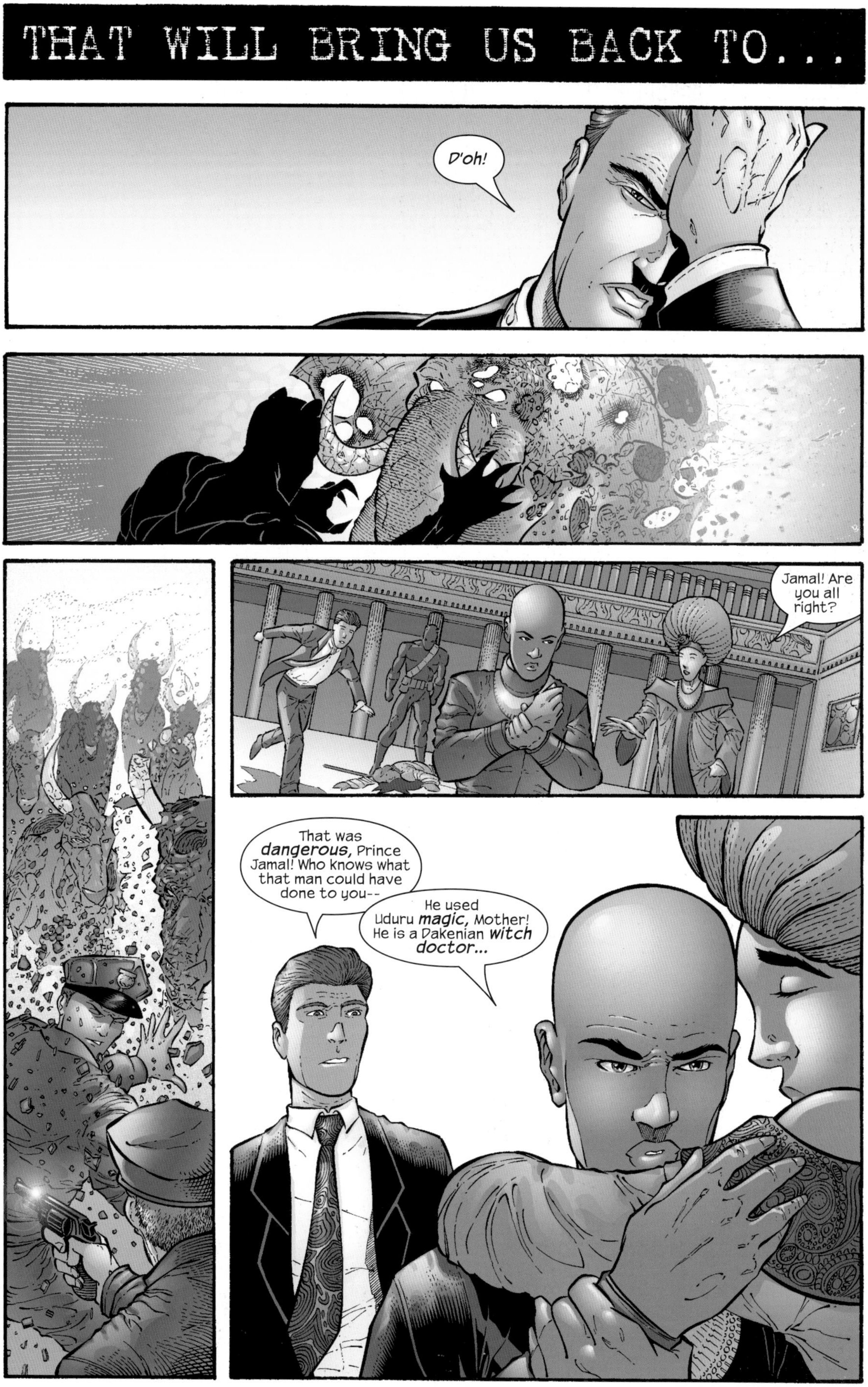
THAT WILL BRING US BACK TO...
D'oh!
Jamal! Are you all right?
That was dangerous, Prince Jamal! Who knows what that man could have done to you--
He used Uduru magic, Mother! He is a Dakenian witch doctor...

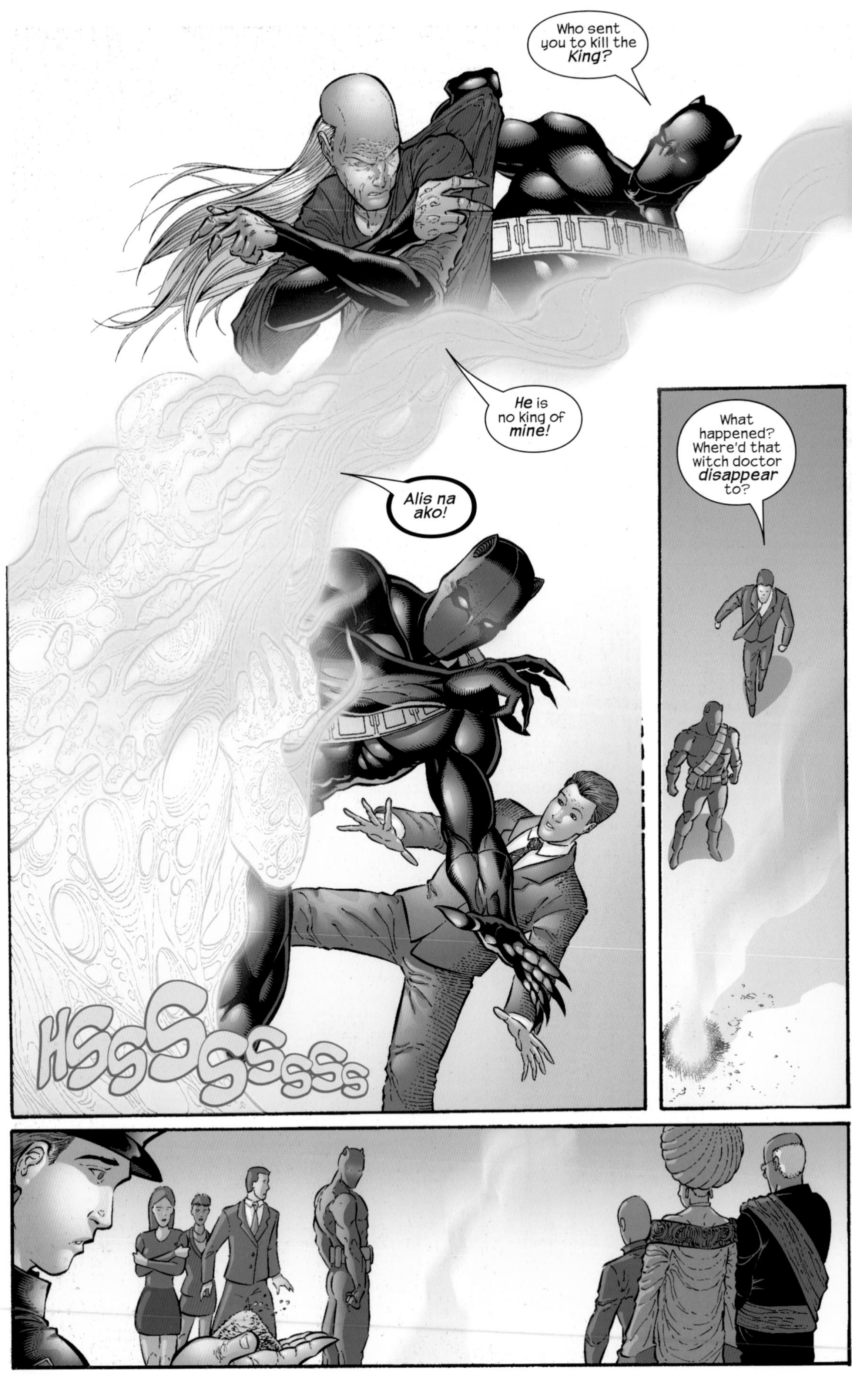
Who sent you to kill the *King?*
He is no king of *mine!*
Alis na ako!
HSSSSSSSSS
What happened? Where'd that witch doctor *disappear* to?

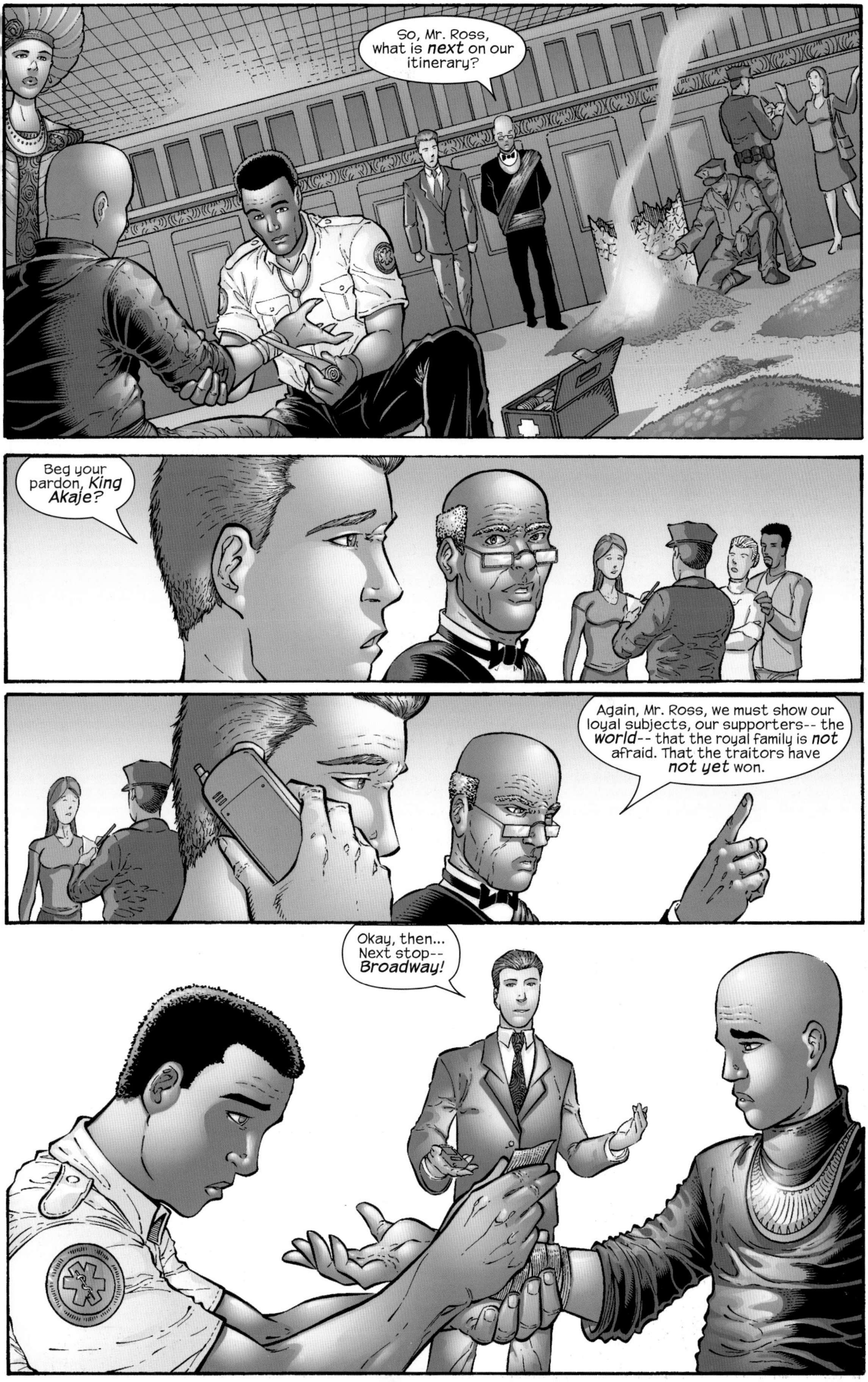
So, Mr. Ross, what is next on our itinerary?
Beg your pardon, King Akaje?
Again, Mr. Ross, we must show our loyal subjects, our supporters-- the world-- that the royal family is not afraid. That the traitors have not yet won.
Okay, then... Next stop-- Broadway!

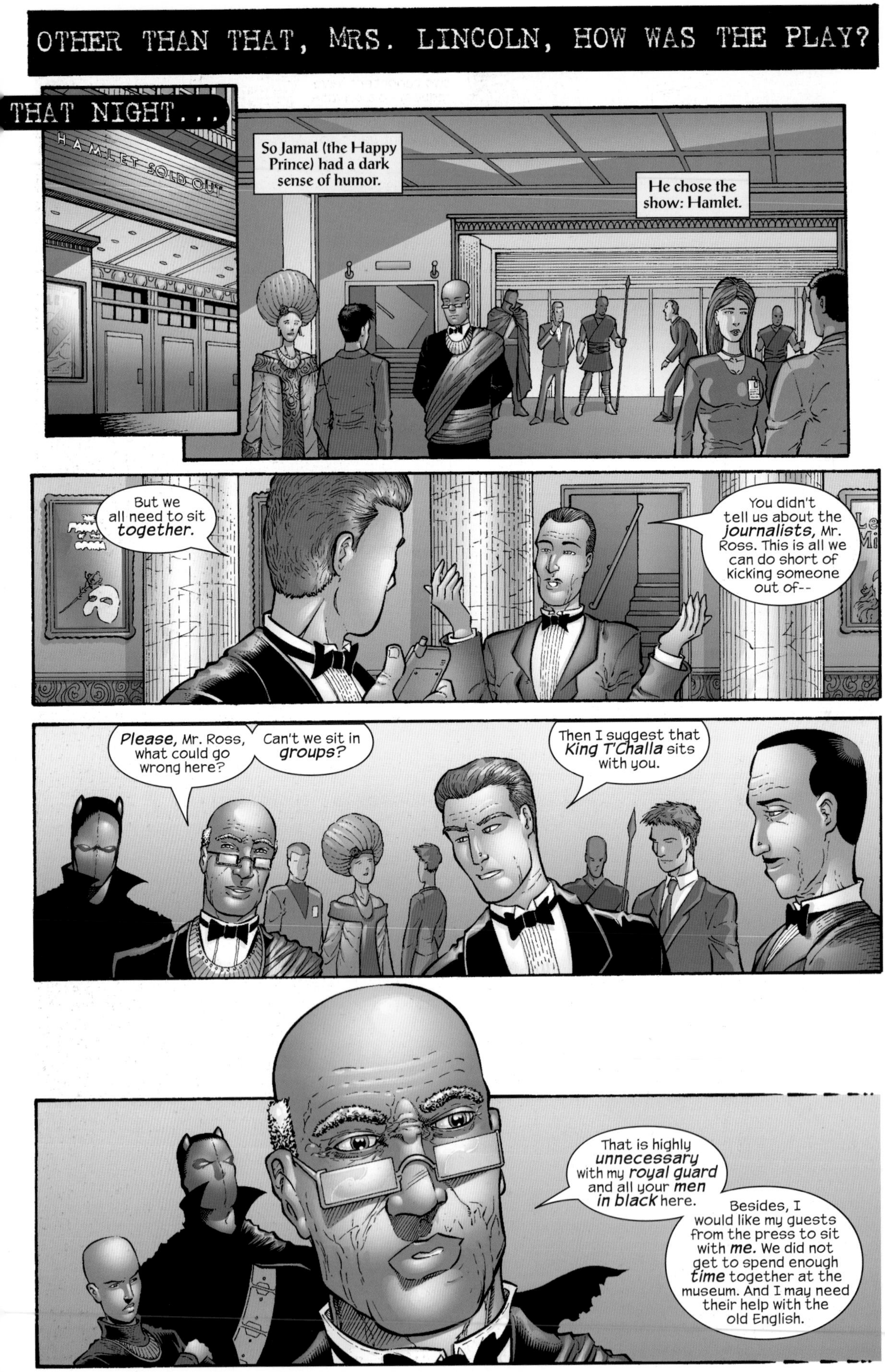
OTHER THAN THAT, MRS. LINCOLN, HOW WAS THE PLAY?
THAT NIGHT...
HAMLET SOLD OUT
So Jamal (the Happy Prince) had a dark sense of humor.
He chose the show: Hamlet.
But we all need to sit together.
You didn't tell us about the journalists, Mr. Ross. This is all we can do short of kicking someone out of--
Please, Mr. Ross, what could go wrong here?
Can't we sit in groups?
Then I suggest that King T'Challa sits with you.
That is highly unnecessary with my royal guard and all your men in black here.
Besides, I would like my guests from the press to sit with me. We did not get to spend enough time together at the museum. And I may need their help with the old English.

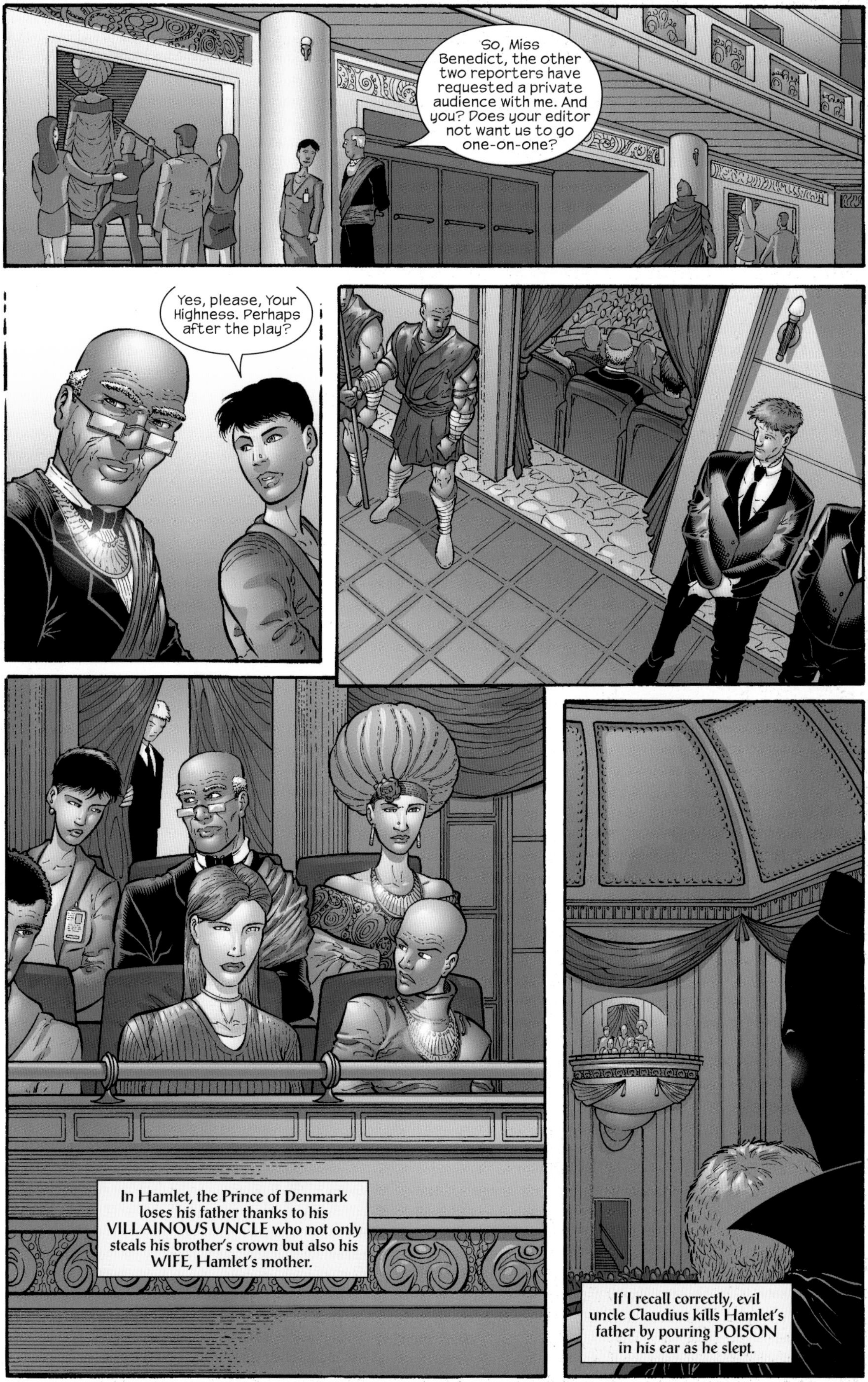
So, Miss Benedict, the other two reporters have requested a private audience with me. And you? Does your editor not want us to go one-on-one?
Yes, please, Your Highness. Perhaps after the play?
In Hamlet, the Prince of Denmark loses his father thanks to his VILLAINOUS UNCLE who not only steals his brother's crown but also his WIFE, Hamlet's mother.
If I recall correctly, evil uncle Claudius kills Hamlet's father by pouring POISON in his ear as he slept.

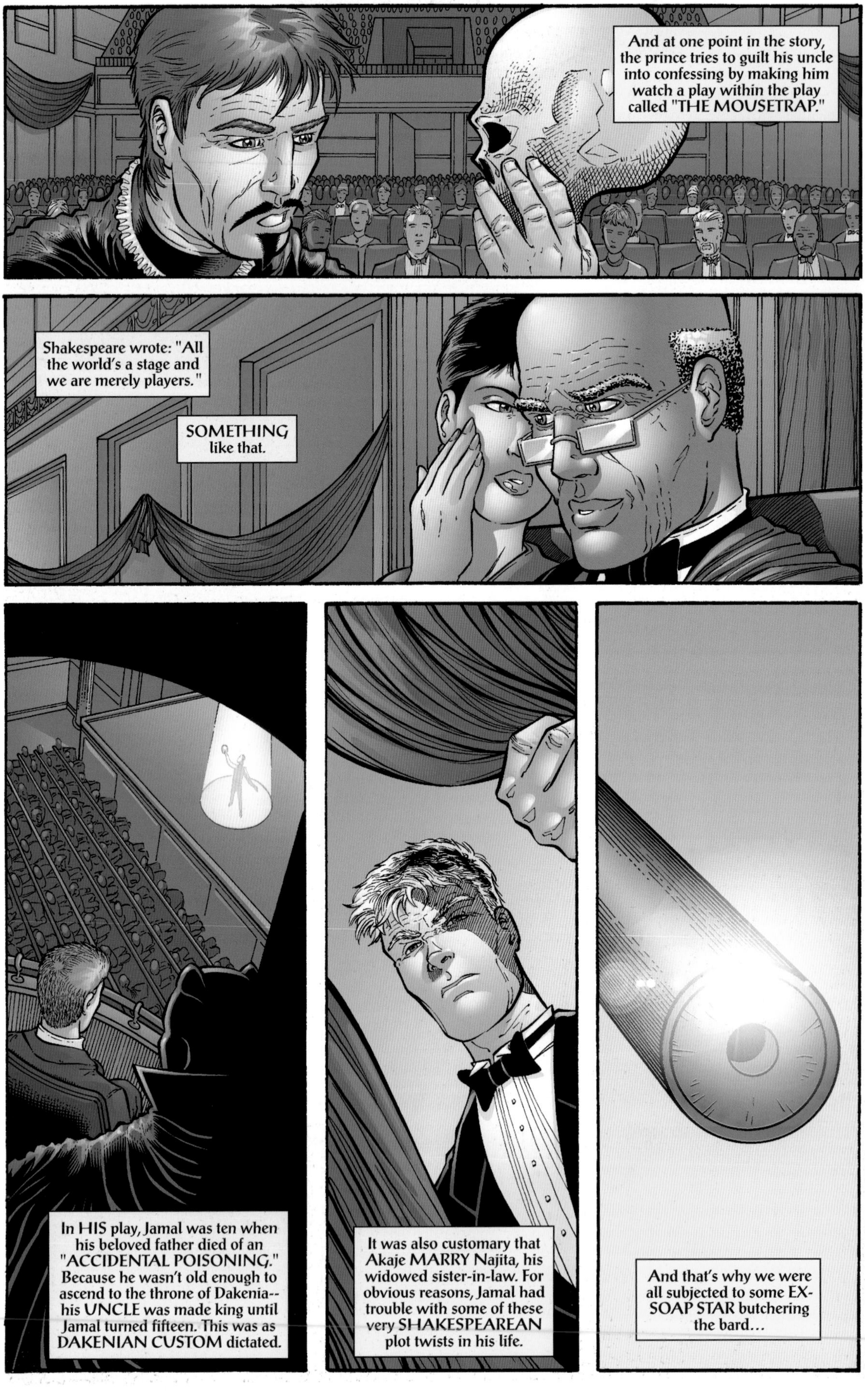

And at one point in the story, the prince tries to guilt his uncle into confessing by making him watch a play within the play called "THE MOUSETRAP."
Shakespeare wrote: "All the world's a stage and we are merely players."
SOMETHING like that.
In HIS play, Jamal was ten when his beloved father died of an "ACCIDENTAL POISONING." Because he wasn't old enough to ascend to the throne of Dakenia-- his UNCLE was made king until Jamal turned fifteen. This was as DAKENIAN CUSTOM dictated.
It was also customary that Akaje MARRY Najita, his widowed sister-in-law. For obvious reasons, Jamal had trouble with some of these very SHAKESPEAREAN plot twists in his life.
And that's why we were all subjected to some EX-SOAP STAR butchering the bard...

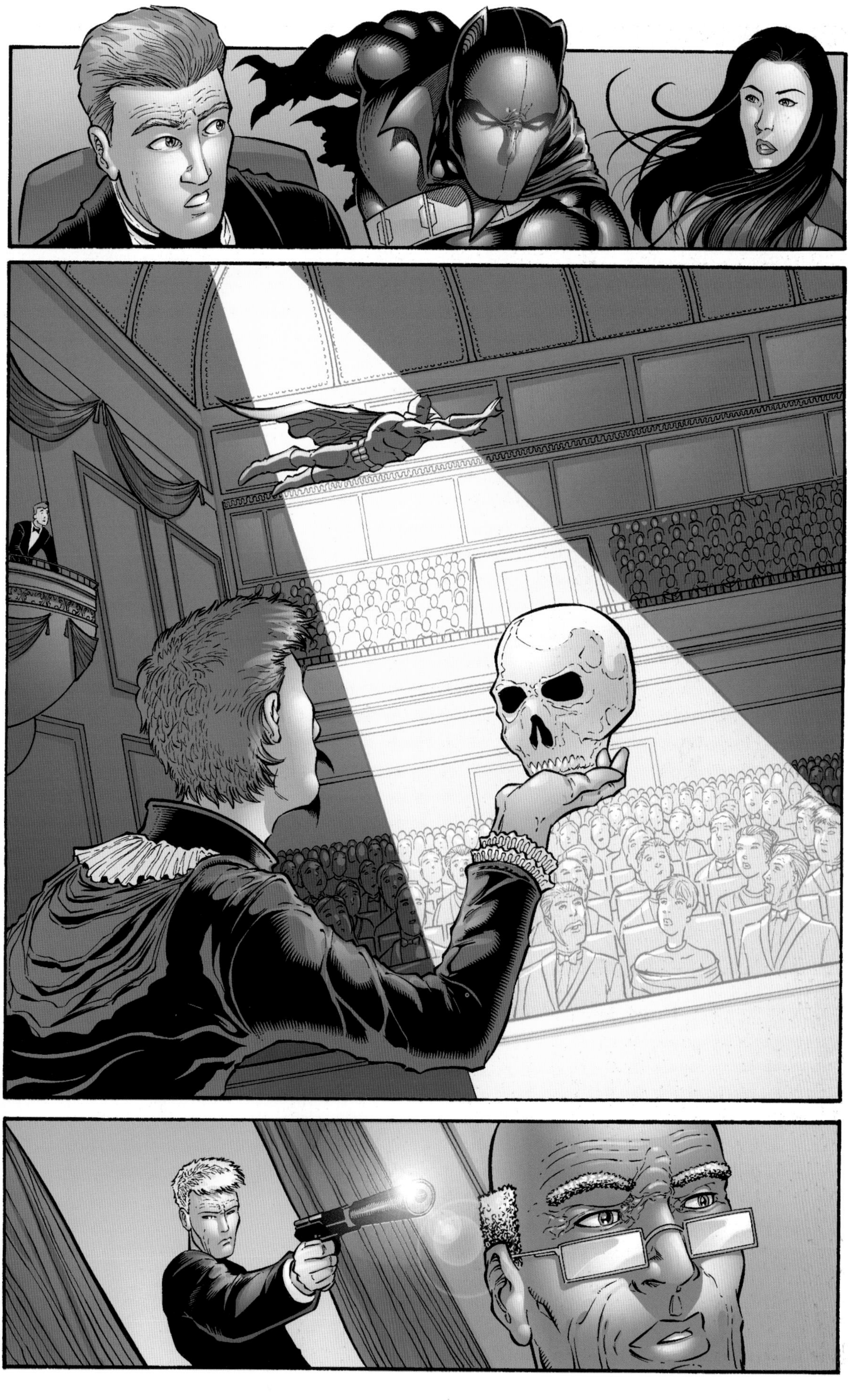

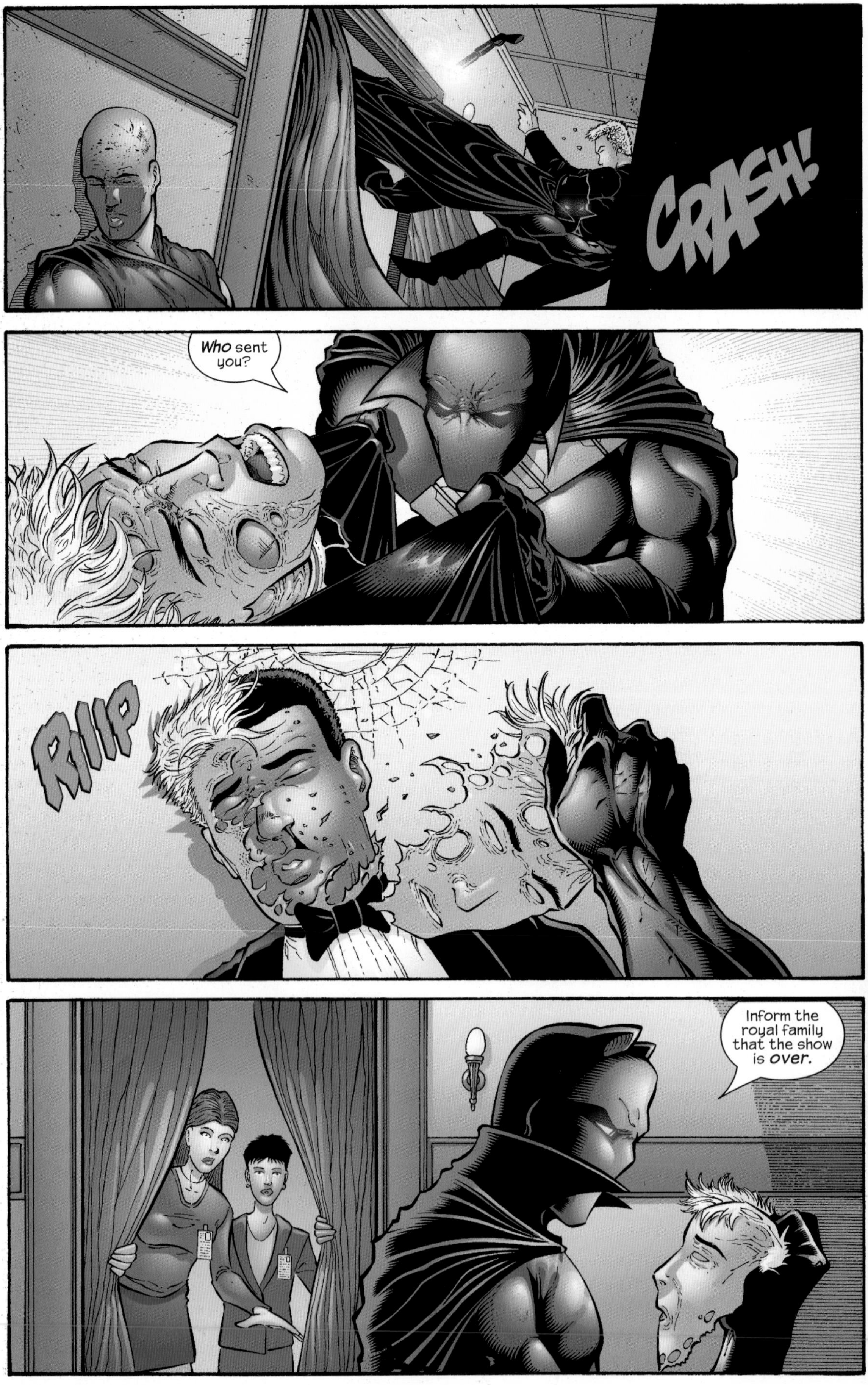
CRASH!
Who sent you?
RIIP
Inform the royal family that the show is over.

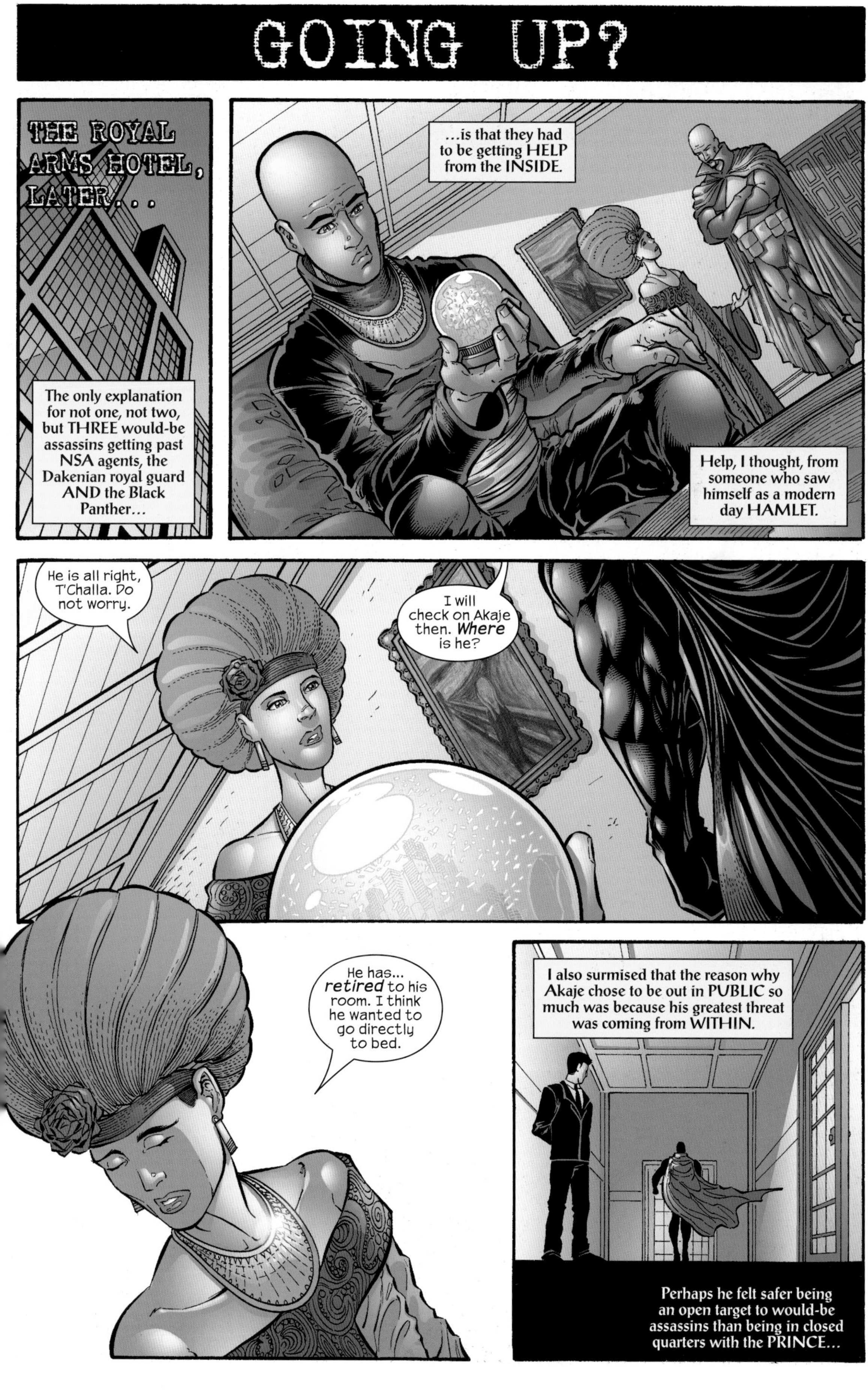
GOING UP?
THE ROYAL ARMS HOTEL, LATER...
The only explanation for not one, not two, but THREE would-be assassins getting past NSA agents, the Dakenian royal guard AND the Black Panther...
...is that they had to be getting HELP from the INSIDE.
Help, I thought, from someone who saw himself as a modern day HAMLET.
He is all right, T'Challa. Do not worry.
I will check on Akaje then. Where is he?
He has... retired to his room. I think he wanted to go directly to bed.
I also surmised that the reason why Akaje chose to be out in PUBLIC so much was because his greatest threat was coming from WITHIN.
Perhaps he felt safer being an open target to would-be assassins than being in closed quarters with the PRINCE...

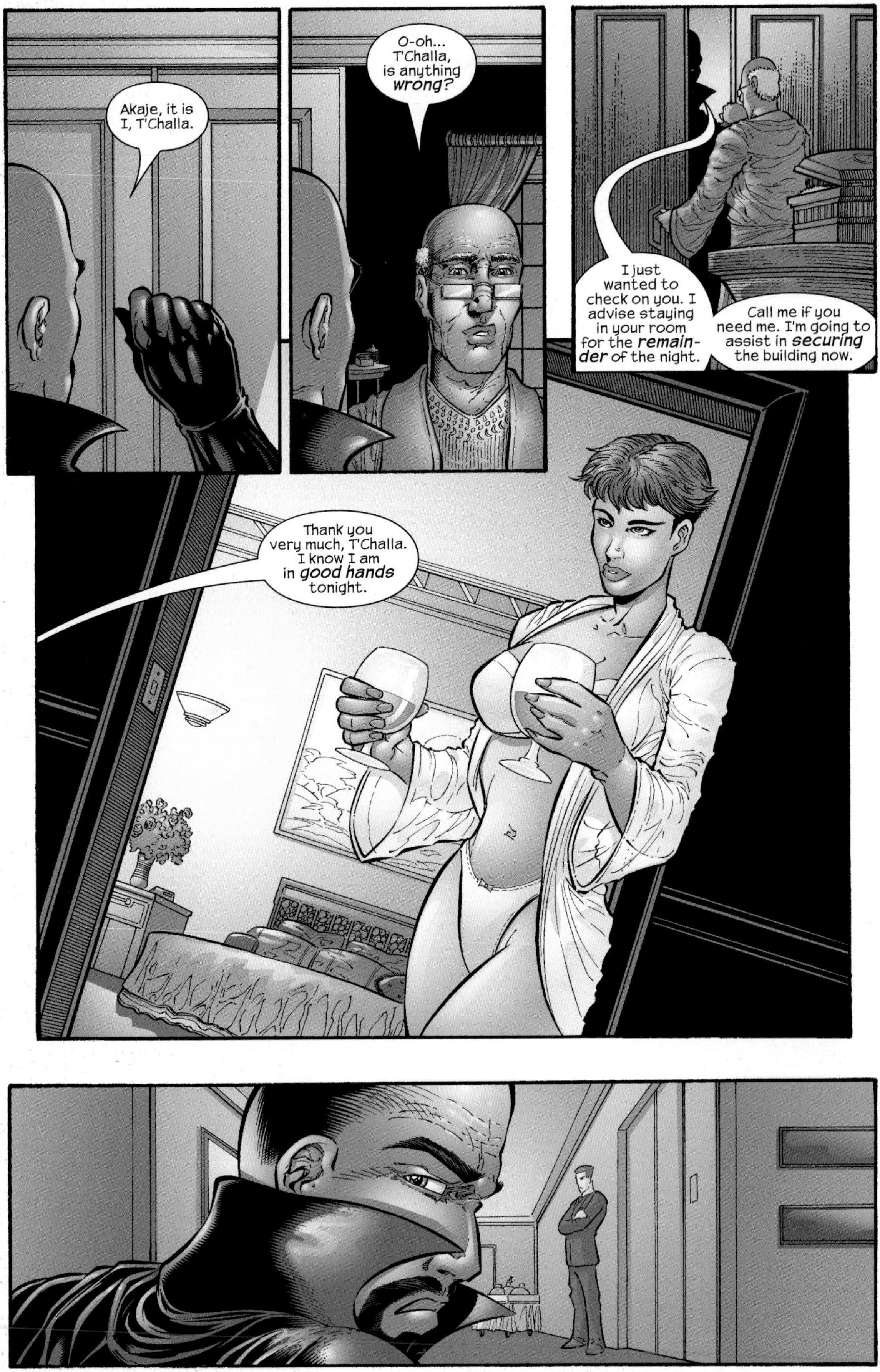

Akaje, it is I, T'Challa.
O-oh... T'Challa, is anything wrong?
I just wanted to check on you. I advise staying in your room for the remainder of the night.
Call me if you need me. I'm going to assist in securing the building now.
Thank you very much, T'Challa. I know I am in good hands tonight.

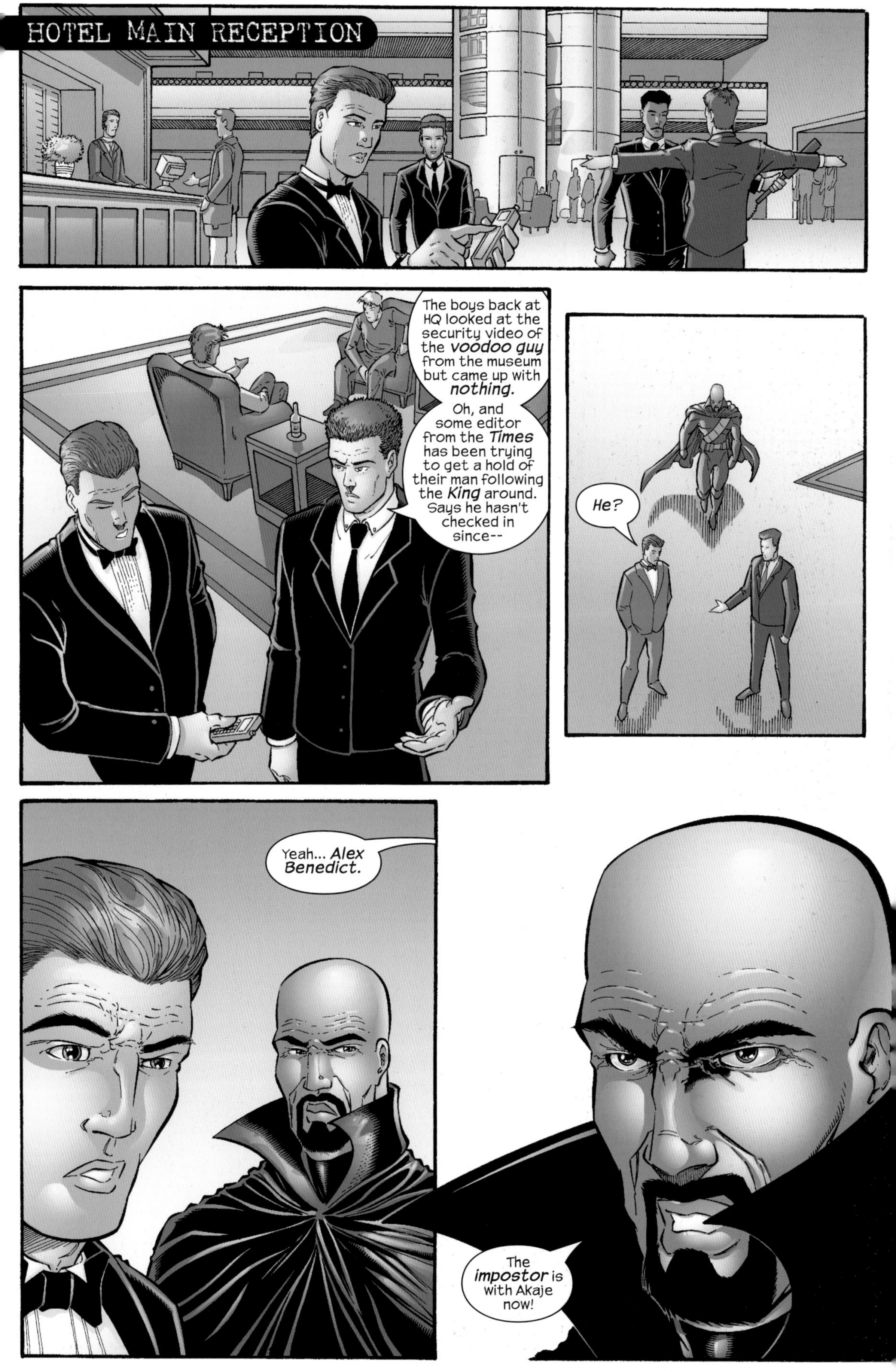
HOTEL MAIN RECEPTION
The boys back at HQ looked at the security video of the voodoo guy from the museum but came up with nothing.
Oh, and some editor from the Times has been trying to get a hold of their man following the King around. Says he hasn't checked in since--
He?
Yeah... Alex Benedict.
The impostor is with Akaje now!

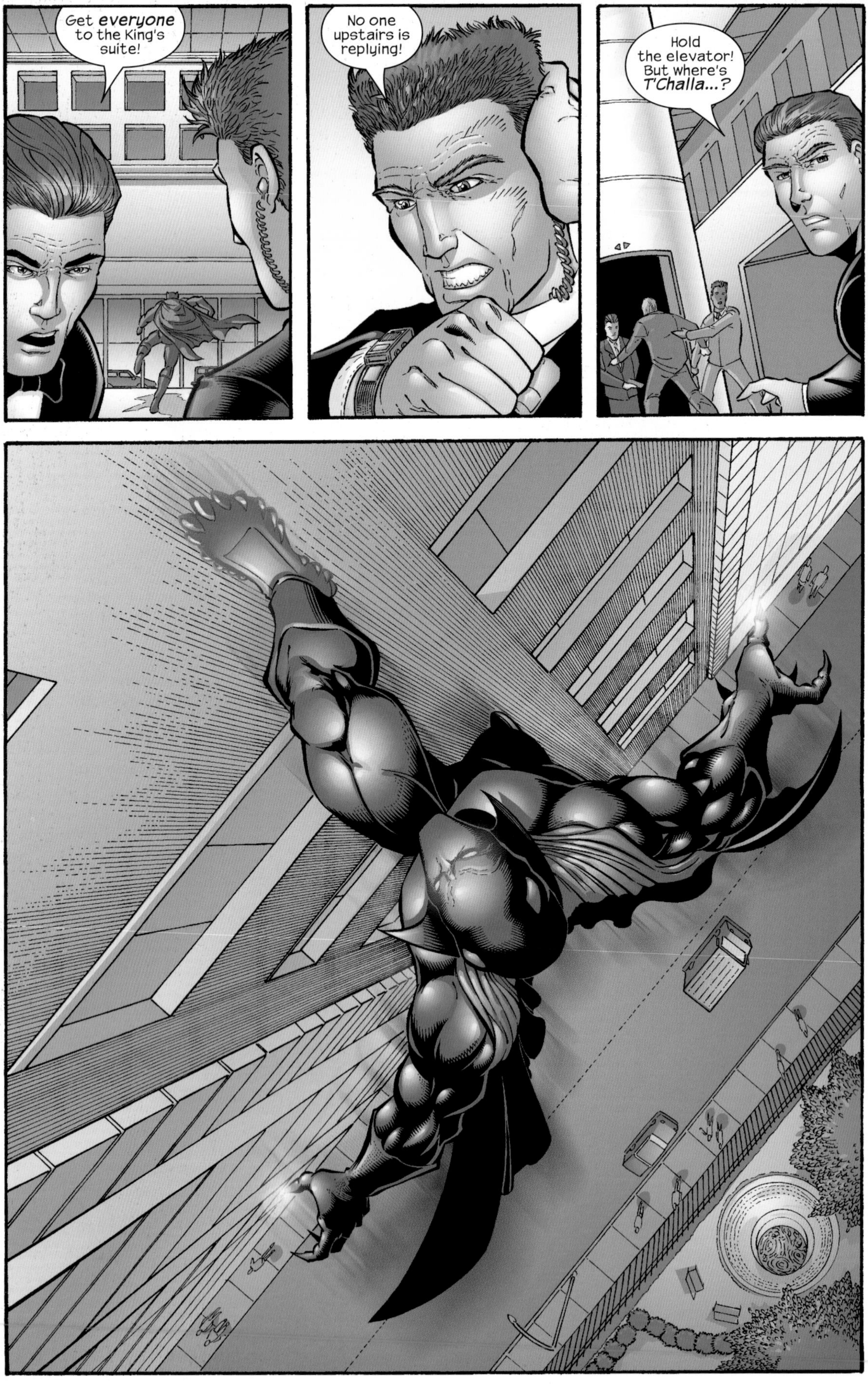
Get *everyone* to the King's suite!
No one upstairs is replying!
Hold the elevator! But where's *T'Challa...?*

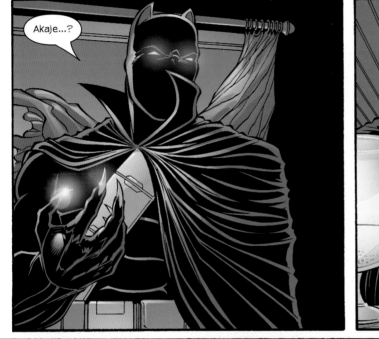

Akaje...?

You poison one king...

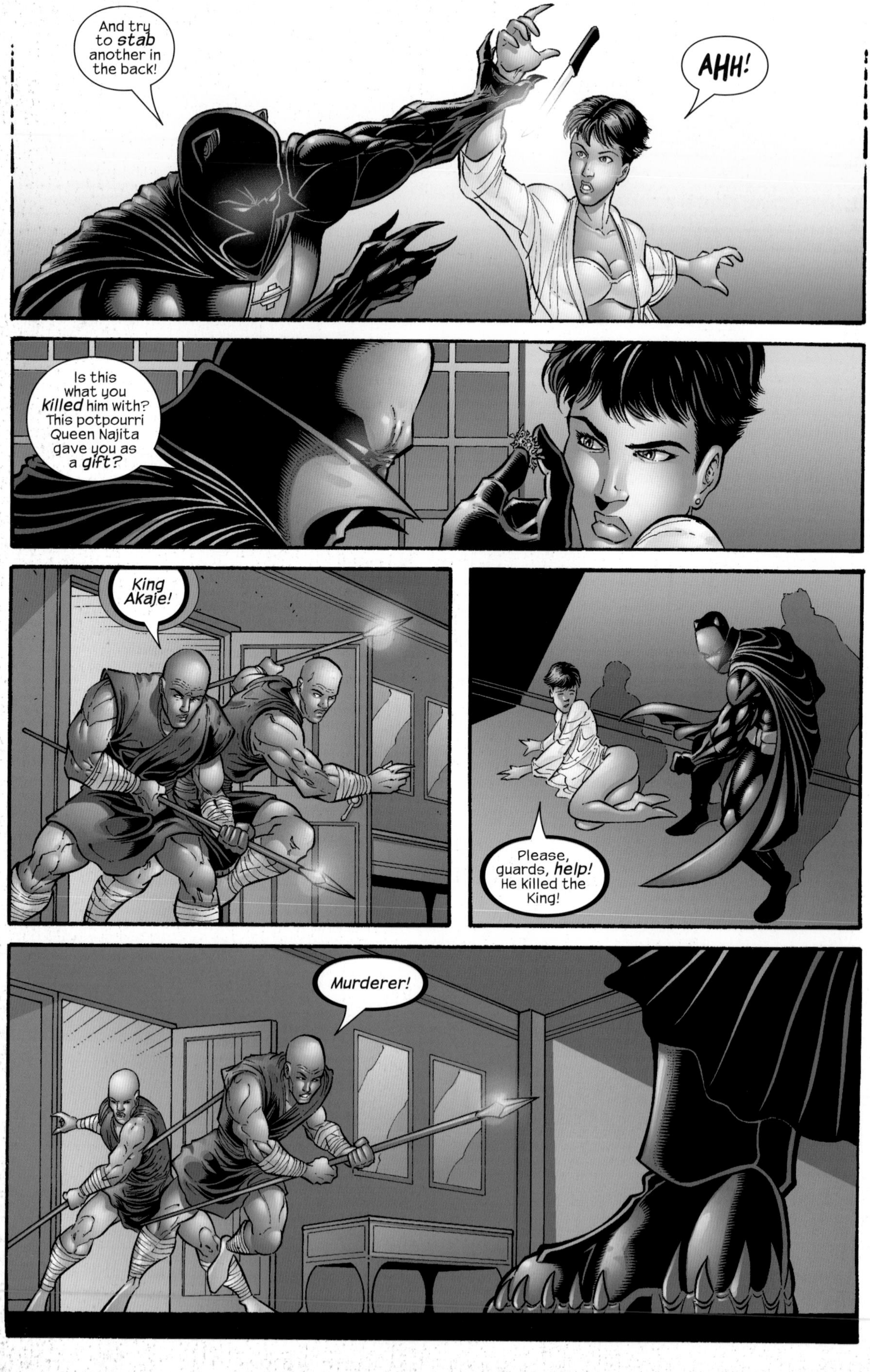
And try to stab another in the back!
AHH!
Is this what you killed him with? This potpourri Queen Najita gave you as a gift?
King Akaje!
Please, guards, help! He killed the King!
Murderer!

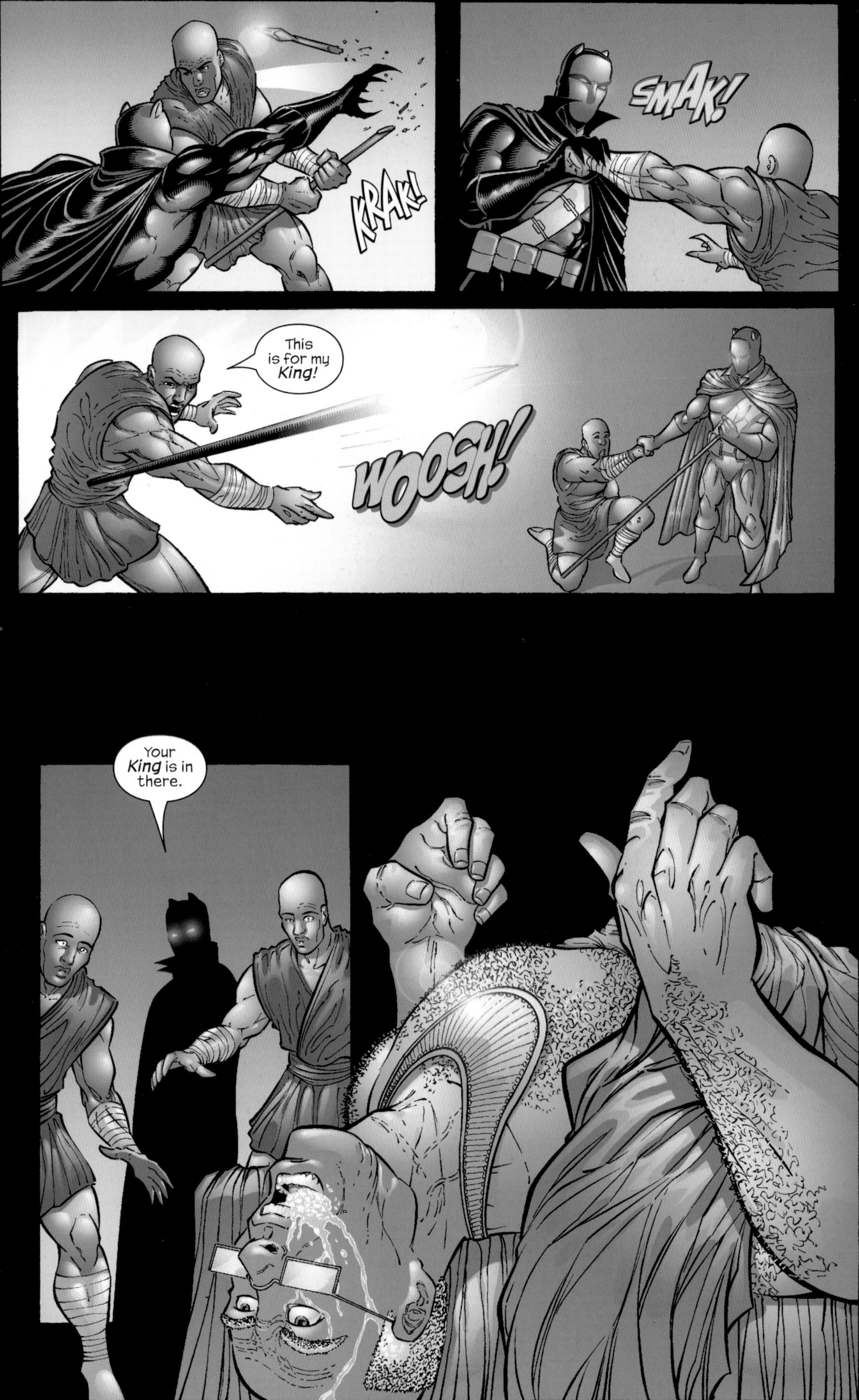
KRAK!
SMAK!
This is for my King!
WOOSH!
Your King is in there.

UNEASY LIES THE HEAD THAT WEARS THE CROWN

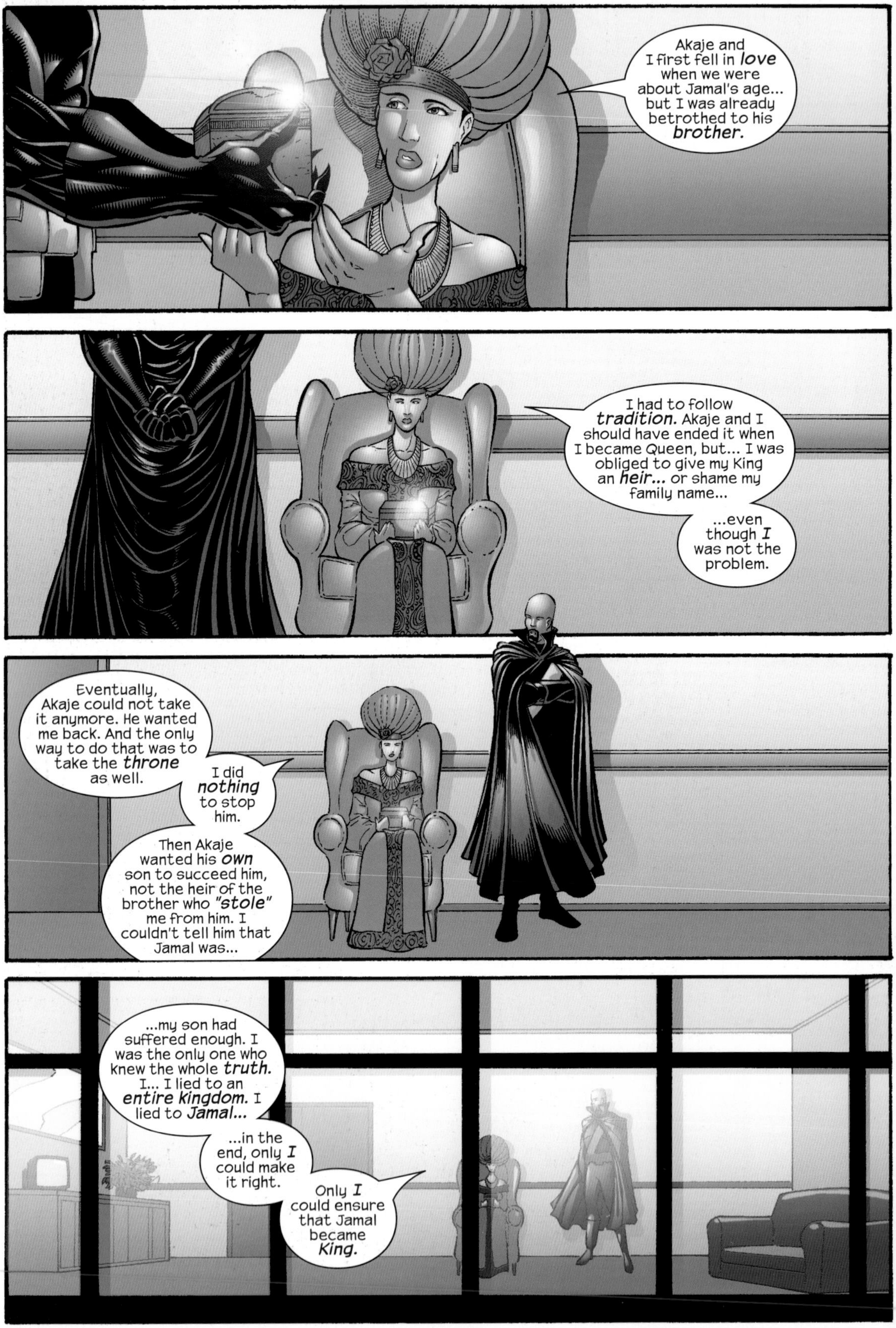

Akaje and I first fell in love when we were about Jamal's age... but I was already betrothed to his brother.
I had to follow tradition. Akaje and I should have ended it when I became Queen, but... I was obliged to give my King an heir... or shame my family name...
...even though I was not the problem.
Eventually, Akaje could not take it anymore. He wanted me back. And the only way to do that was to take the throne as well.
I did nothing to stop him.
Then Akaje wanted his own son to succeed him, not the heir of the brother who "stole" me from him. I couldn't tell him that Jamal was...
...my son had suffered enough. I was the only one who knew the whole truth. I... I lied to an entire kingdom. I lied to Jamal...
...in the end, only I could make it right.
Only I could ensure that Jamal became King.

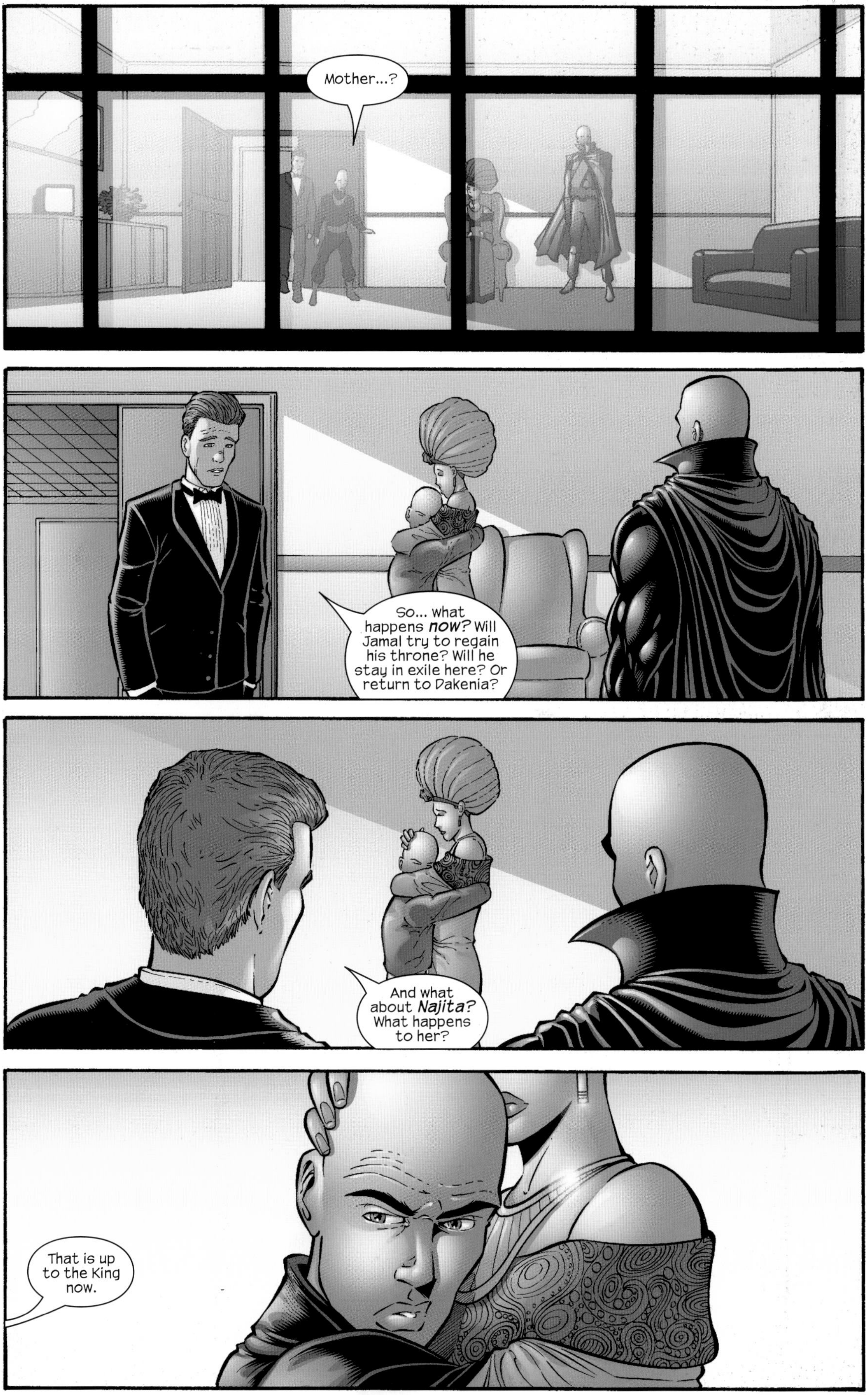
Mother...?
So... what happens NOW? Will Jamal try to regain his throne? Will he stay in exile here? Or return to Dakenia?
And what about Najita? What happens to her?
That is up to the King now.

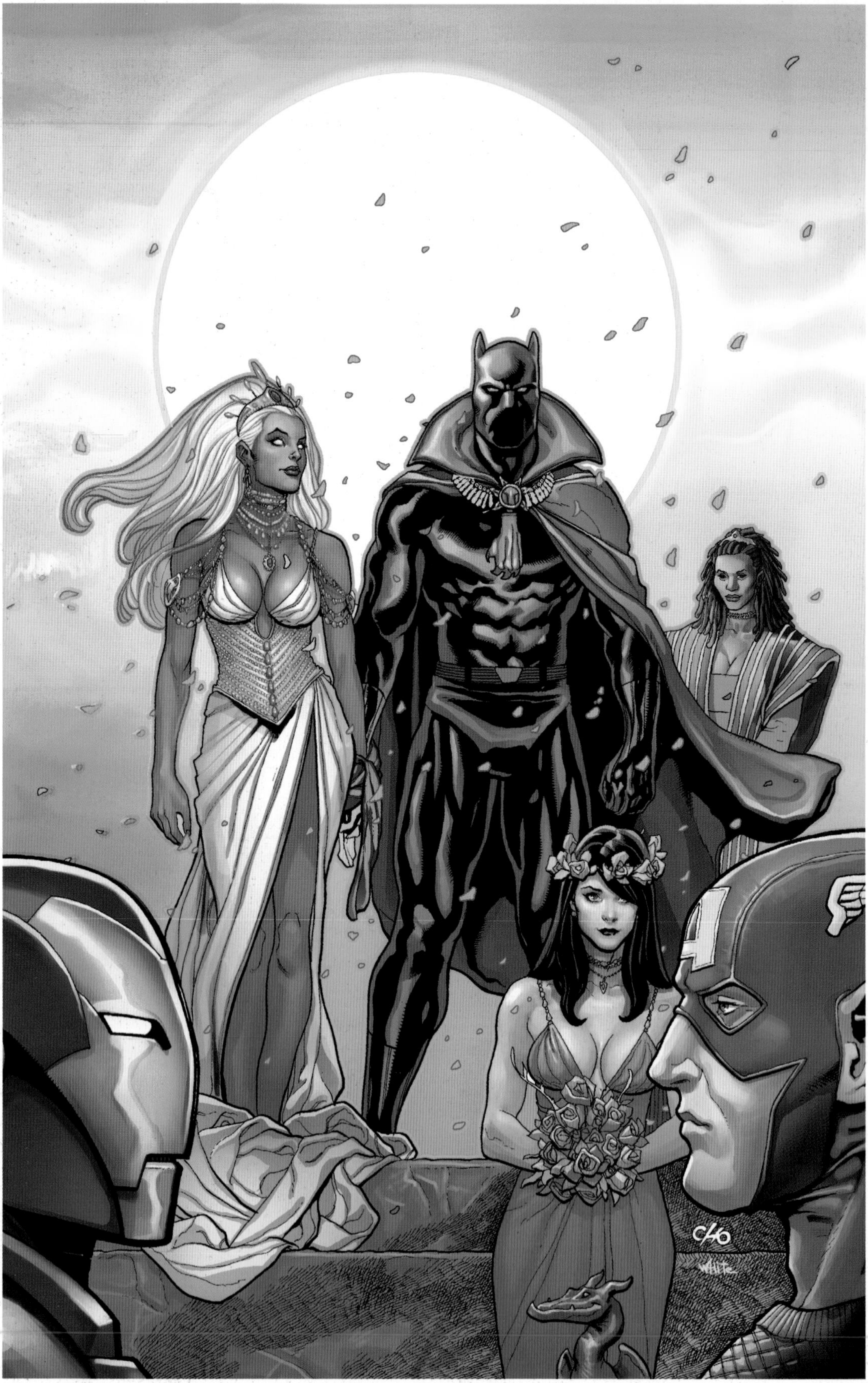

COUNTDOWN TO THE WEDDING OF THE CENTURY
BLACK PANTHER

LINSNER ·2006·

PREVIOUSLY

There are some places you just don't mess with. Since the dawn of time, that African warrior nation has been sending would-be conquerors home in body bags. While the rest of Africa got carved up like a Christmas turkey by the rest of the world, Wakanda's cultural evolution has gone unchecked for centuries, unfettered by the yoke of colonization. The result: a high-tech, resource-rich, ecologically-sound paradise that makes the rest of the world seem primitive by comparison.

Ruling over all of this is the Black Panther.

The Black Panther is more than just the embodiment of a warrior cult that's served as Wakanda's religious, political and military head since its inception. The Black Panther is the embodiment of the ideals of a people. Anyone who'd dare to make a move on Wakanda must go through him.

Now, the Panther is on the verge of fulfilling one of his duties as king: taking a queen. He has announced his engagement to Storm of the X-Men—a woman with whom he shares much love and history. The happy couple prepares for their union, unaware that conflict abroad and dark intentions at home may overshadow their joyous occasion...

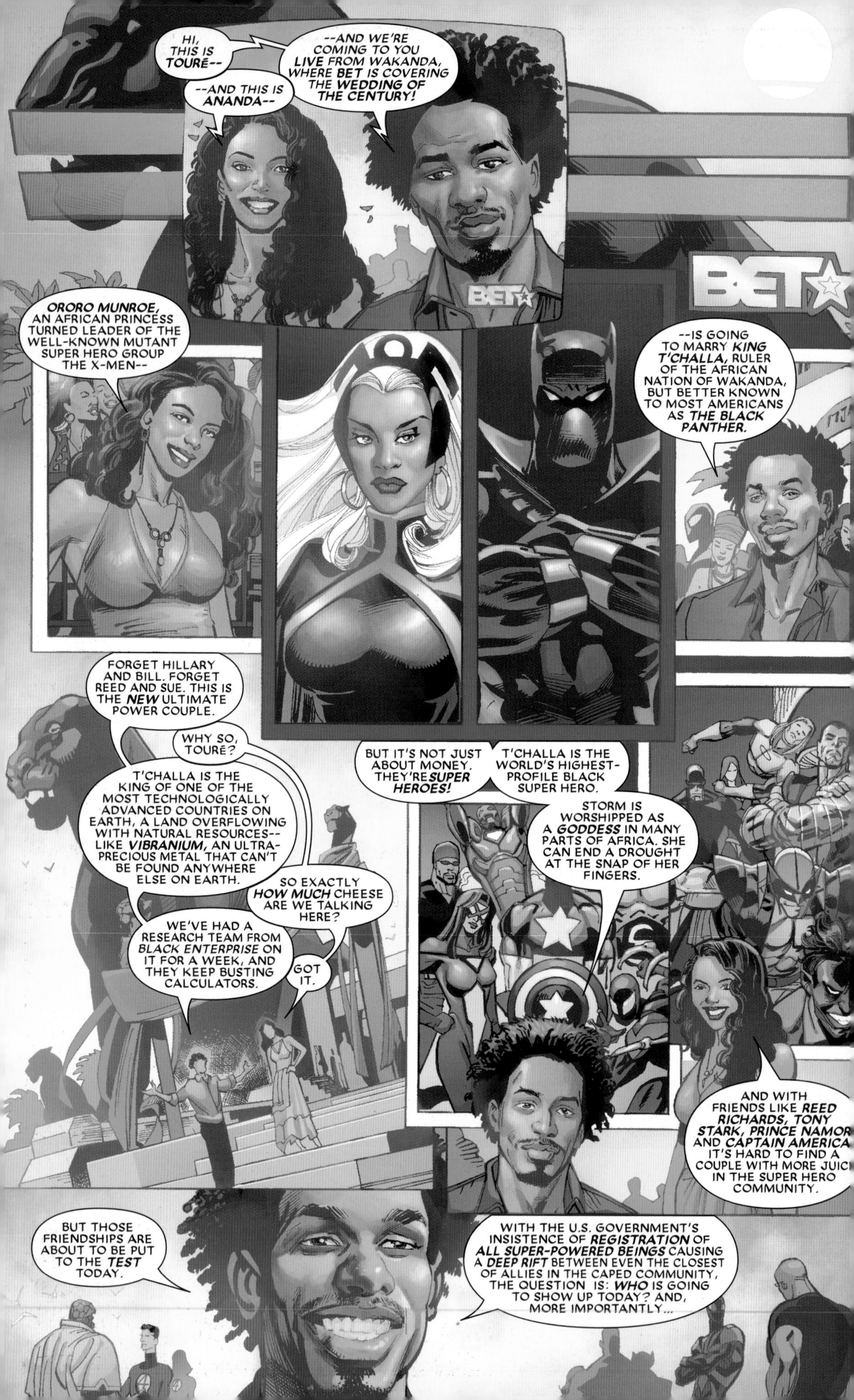
HI, THIS IS TOURÉ--
--AND WE'RE COMING TO YOU LIVE FROM WAKANDA, WHERE BET IS COVERING THE WEDDING OF THE CENTURY!
--AND THIS IS ANANDA--
ORORO MUNROE, AN AFRICAN PRINCESS TURNED LEADER OF THE WELL-KNOWN MUTANT SUPER HERO GROUP THE X-MEN--
--IS GOING TO MARRY KING T'CHALLA, RULER OF THE AFRICAN NATION OF WAKANDA, BUT BETTER KNOWN TO MOST AMERICANS AS THE BLACK PANTHER.
FORGET HILLARY AND BILL. FORGET REED AND SUE. THIS IS THE NEW ULTIMATE POWER COUPLE.
WHY SO, TOURÉ?
T'CHALLA IS THE KING OF ONE OF THE MOST TECHNOLOGICALLY ADVANCED COUNTRIES ON EARTH, A LAND OVERFLOWING WITH NATURAL RESOURCES--LIKE VIBRANIUM, AN ULTRA-PRECIOUS METAL THAT CAN'T BE FOUND ANYWHERE ELSE ON EARTH.
SO EXACTLY HOW MUCH CHEESE ARE WE TALKING HERE?
WE'VE HAD A RESEARCH TEAM FROM BLACK ENTERPRISE ON IT FOR A WEEK, AND THEY KEEP BUSTING CALCULATORS.
GOT IT.
BUT IT'S NOT JUST ABOUT MONEY. THEY'RE SUPER HEROES!
T'CHALLA IS THE WORLD'S HIGHEST-PROFILE BLACK SUPER HERO.
STORM IS WORSHIPPED AS A GODDESS IN MANY PARTS OF AFRICA. SHE CAN END A DROUGHT AT THE SNAP OF HER FINGERS.
AND WITH FRIENDS LIKE REED RICHARDS, TONY STARK, PRINCE NAMOR AND CAPTAIN AMERICA IT'S HARD TO FIND A COUPLE WITH MORE JUICE IN THE SUPER HERO COMMUNITY.
BUT THOSE FRIENDSHIPS ARE ABOUT TO BE PUT TO THE TEST TODAY.
WITH THE U.S. GOVERNMENT'S INSISTENCE OF REGISTRATION OF ALL SUPER-POWERED BEINGS CAUSING A DEEP RIFT BETWEEN EVEN THE CLOSEST OF ALLIES IN THE CAPED COMMUNITY, THE QUESTION IS: WHO IS GOING TO SHOW UP TODAY? AND, MORE IMPORTANTLY...

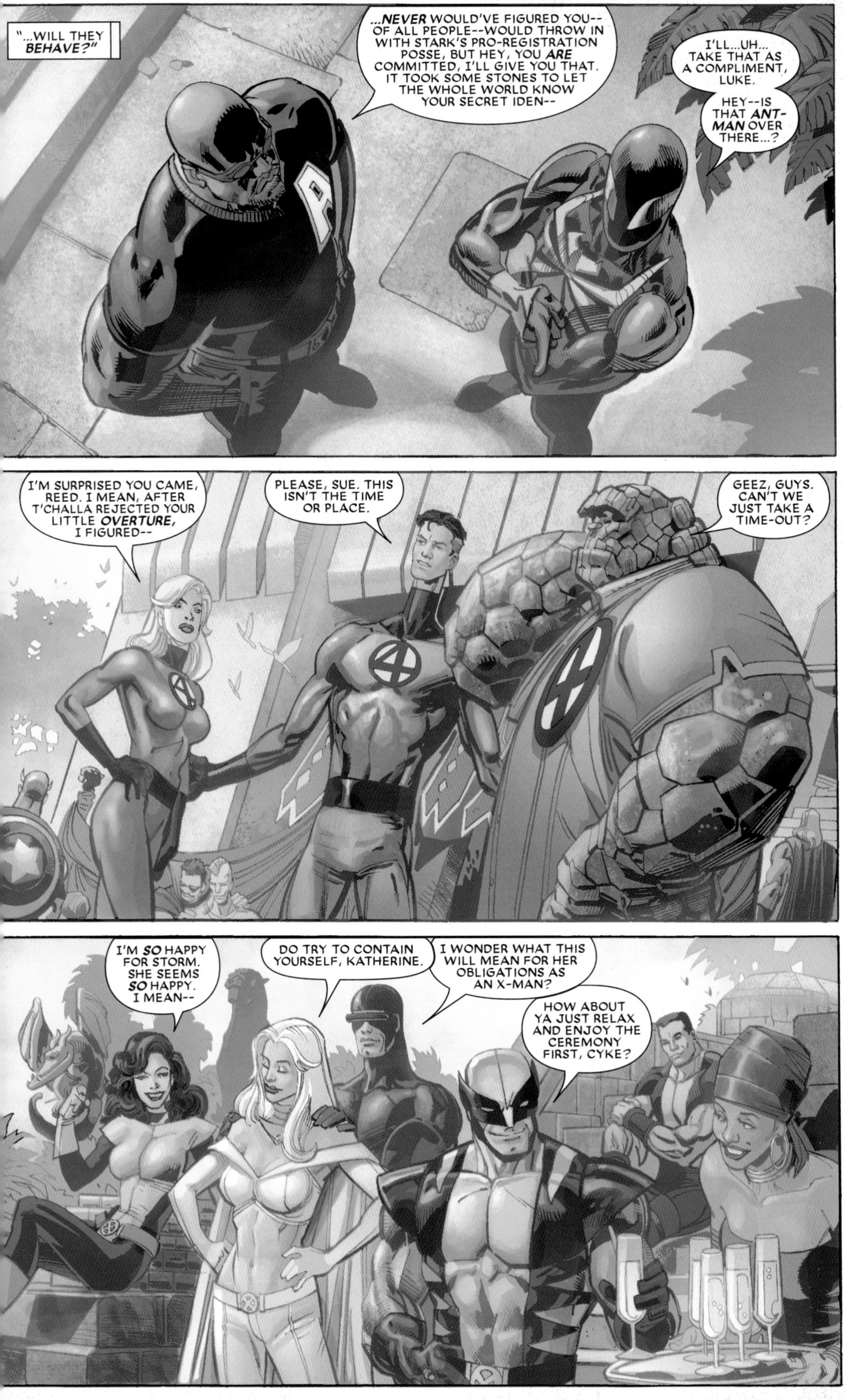
"...WILL THEY *BEHAVE?*"
...*NEVER* WOULD'VE FIGURED YOU--OF ALL PEOPLE--WOULD THROW IN WITH STARK'S PRO-REGISTRATION POSSE, BUT HEY, YOU *ARE* COMMITTED, I'LL GIVE YOU THAT. IT TOOK SOME STONES TO LET THE WHOLE WORLD KNOW YOUR SECRET IDEN--
I'LL...UH... TAKE THAT AS A COMPLIMENT, LUKE.
HEY--IS THAT *ANT-MAN* OVER THERE...?
I'M SURPRISED YOU CAME, REED. I MEAN, AFTER T'CHALLA REJECTED YOUR LITTLE *OVERTURE,* I FIGURED--
PLEASE, SUE. THIS ISN'T THE TIME OR PLACE.
GEEZ, GUYS. CAN'T WE JUST TAKE A TIME-OUT?
I'M *SO* HAPPY FOR STORM. SHE SEEMS *SO* HAPPY. I MEAN--
DO TRY TO CONTAIN YOURSELF, KATHERINE.
I WONDER WHAT THIS WILL MEAN FOR HER OBLIGATIONS AS AN X-MAN?
HOW ABOUT YA JUST RELAX AND ENJOY THE CEREMONY FIRST, CYKE?

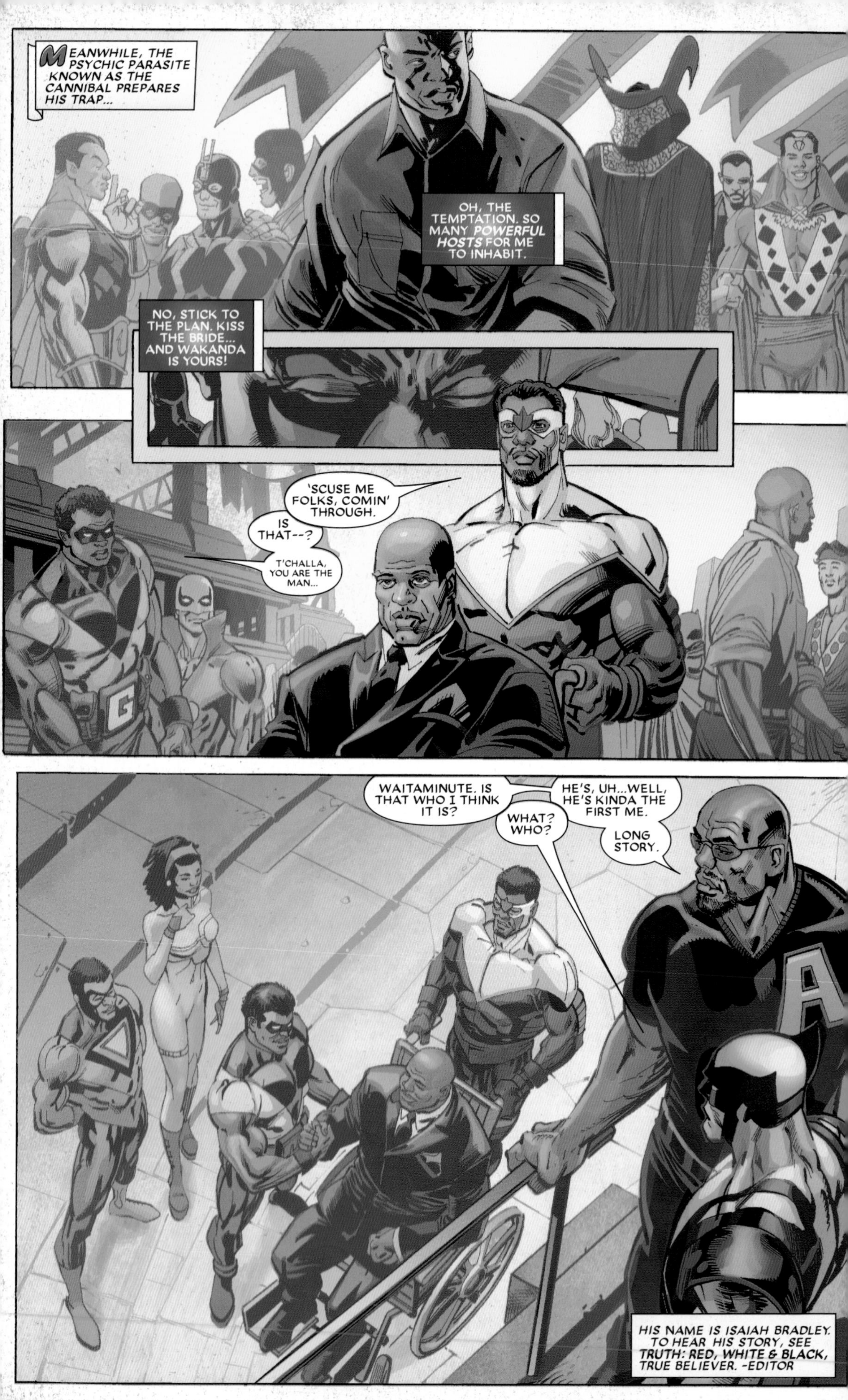
MEANWHILE, THE PSYCHIC PARASITE KNOWN AS THE CANNIBAL PREPARES HIS TRAP...
OH, THE TEMPTATION. SO MANY POWERFUL HOSTS FOR ME TO INHABIT.
NO, STICK TO THE PLAN. KISS THE BRIDE... AND WAKANDA IS YOURS!
'SCUSE ME FOLKS, COMIN' THROUGH.
IS THAT--?
T'CHALLA, YOU ARE THE MAN...
WAITAMINUTE. IS THAT WHO I THINK IT IS?
HE'S, UH...WELL, HE'S KINDA THE FIRST ME.
WHAT? WHO?
LONG STORY.
HIS NAME IS ISAIAH BRADLEY. TO HEAR HIS STORY, SEE TRUTH: RED, WHITE & BLACK, TRUE BELIEVER. -EDITOR

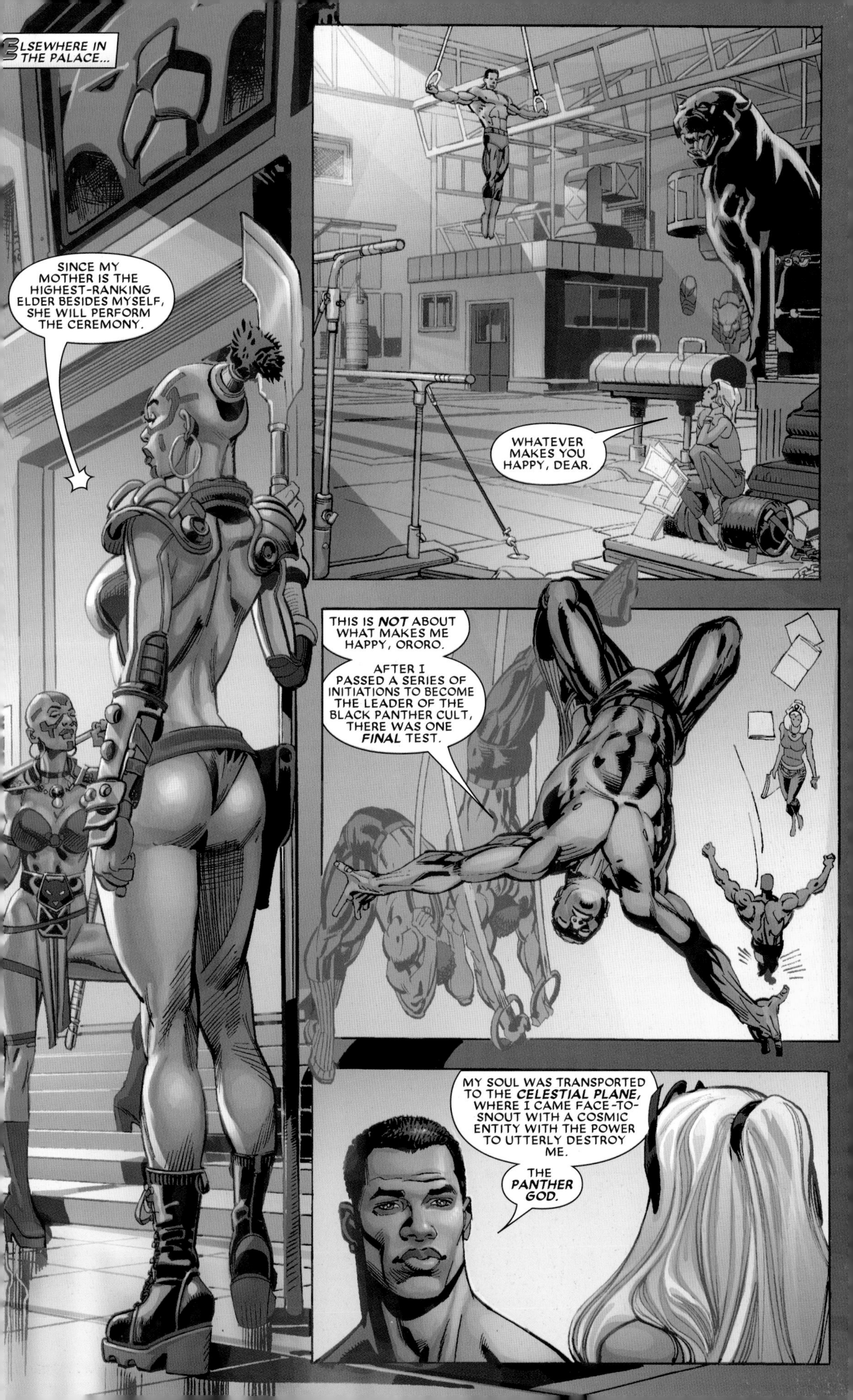
ELSEWHERE IN THE PALACE...
SINCE MY MOTHER IS THE HIGHEST-RANKING ELDER BESIDES MYSELF, SHE WILL PERFORM THE CEREMONY.
WHATEVER MAKES YOU HAPPY, DEAR.
THIS IS NOT ABOUT WHAT MAKES ME HAPPY, ORORO.
AFTER I PASSED A SERIES OF INITIATIONS TO BECOME THE LEADER OF THE BLACK PANTHER CULT, THERE WAS ONE FINAL TEST.
MY SOUL WAS TRANSPORTED TO THE CELESTIAL PLANE, WHERE I CAME FACE-TO-SNOUT WITH A COSMIC ENTITY WITH THE POWER TO UTTERLY DESTROY ME.
THE PANTHER GOD.

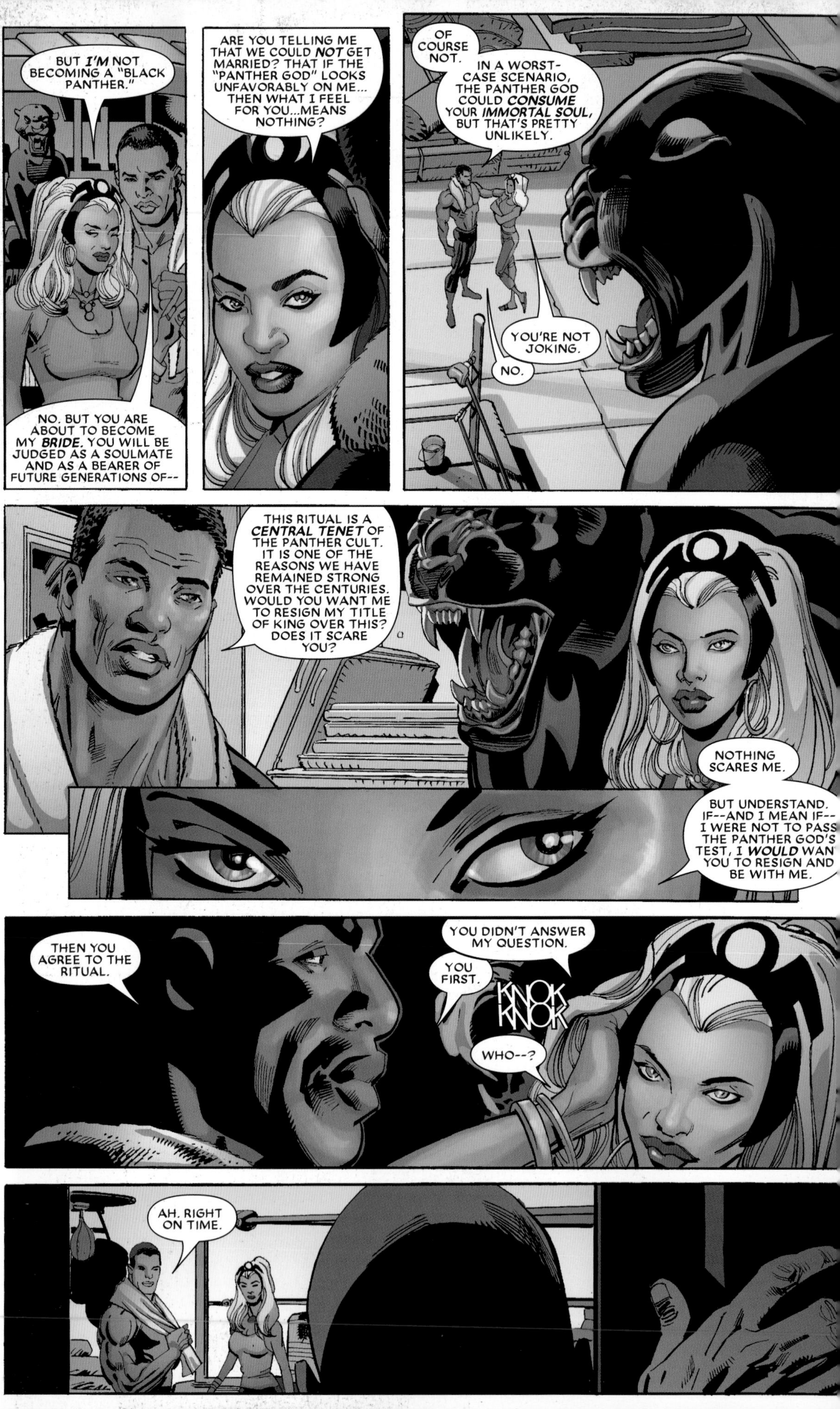
BUT I'M NOT BECOMING A "BLACK PANTHER."
NO. BUT YOU ARE ABOUT TO BECOME MY BRIDE. YOU WILL BE JUDGED AS A SOULMATE AND AS A BEARER OF FUTURE GENERATIONS OF--
ARE YOU TELLING ME THAT WE COULD NOT GET MARRIED? THAT IF THE "PANTHER GOD" LOOKS UNFAVORABLY ON ME... THEN WHAT I FEEL FOR YOU...MEANS NOTHING?
OF COURSE NOT.
IN A WORST-CASE SCENARIO, THE PANTHER GOD COULD CONSUME YOUR IMMORTAL SOUL, BUT THAT'S PRETTY UNLIKELY.
YOU'RE NOT JOKING.
NO.
THIS RITUAL IS A CENTRAL TENET OF THE PANTHER CULT. IT IS ONE OF THE REASONS WE HAVE REMAINED STRONG OVER THE CENTURIES. WOULD YOU WANT ME TO RESIGN MY TITLE OF KING OVER THIS? DOES IT SCARE YOU?
NOTHING SCARES ME.
BUT UNDERSTAND. IF--AND I MEAN IF-- I WERE NOT TO PASS THE PANTHER GOD'S TEST, I WOULD WANT YOU TO RESIGN AND BE WITH ME.
THEN YOU AGREE TO THE RITUAL.
YOU DIDN'T ANSWER MY QUESTION.
YOU FIRST.
KNOK KNOK
WHO--?
AH. RIGHT ON TIME.

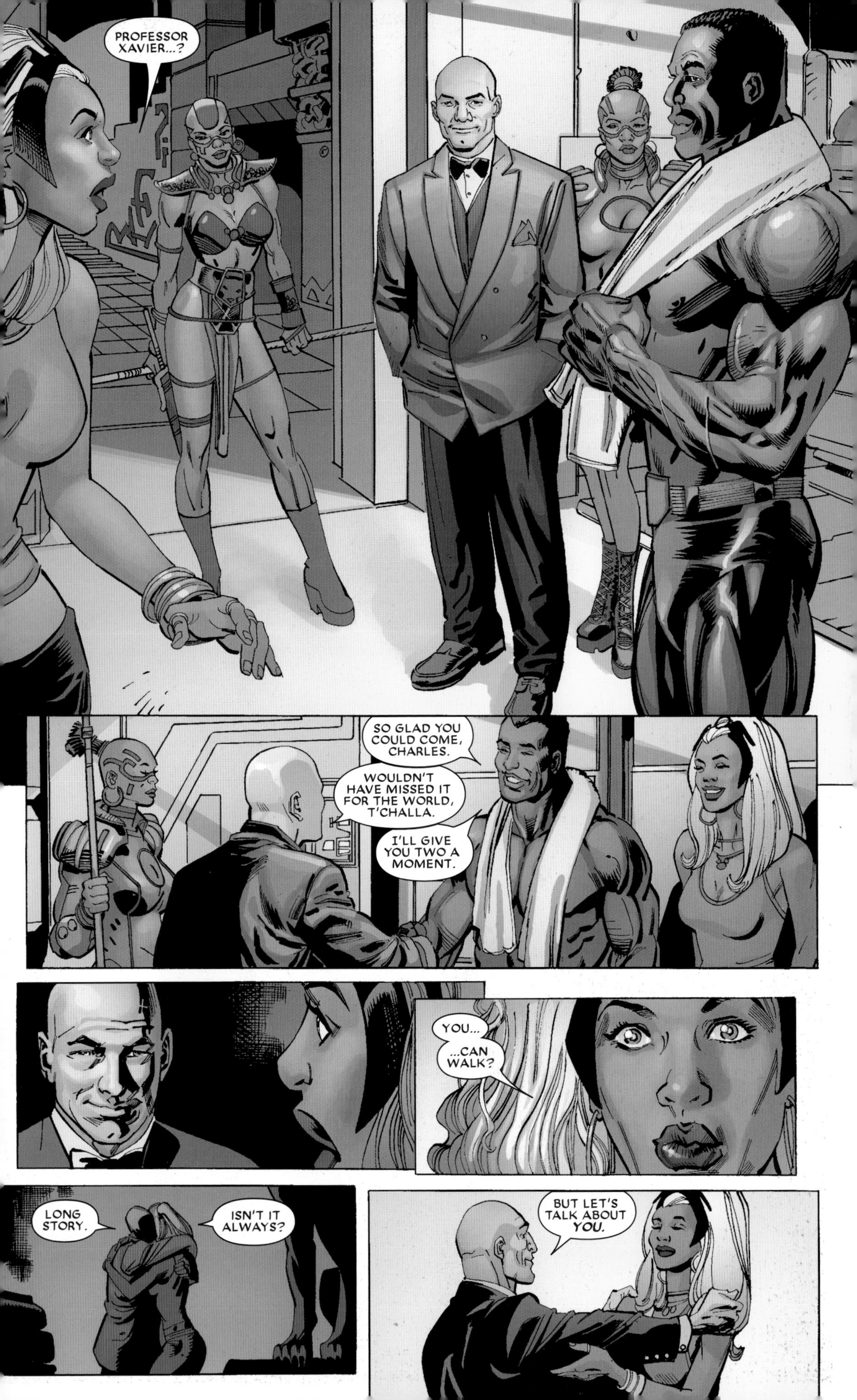
PROFESSOR XAVIER...?
SO GLAD YOU COULD COME, CHARLES.
WOULDN'T HAVE MISSED IT FOR THE WORLD, T'CHALLA.
I'LL GIVE YOU TWO A MOMENT.
YOU...
...CAN WALK?
LONG STORY.
ISN'T IT ALWAYS?
BUT LET'S TALK ABOUT *YOU.*

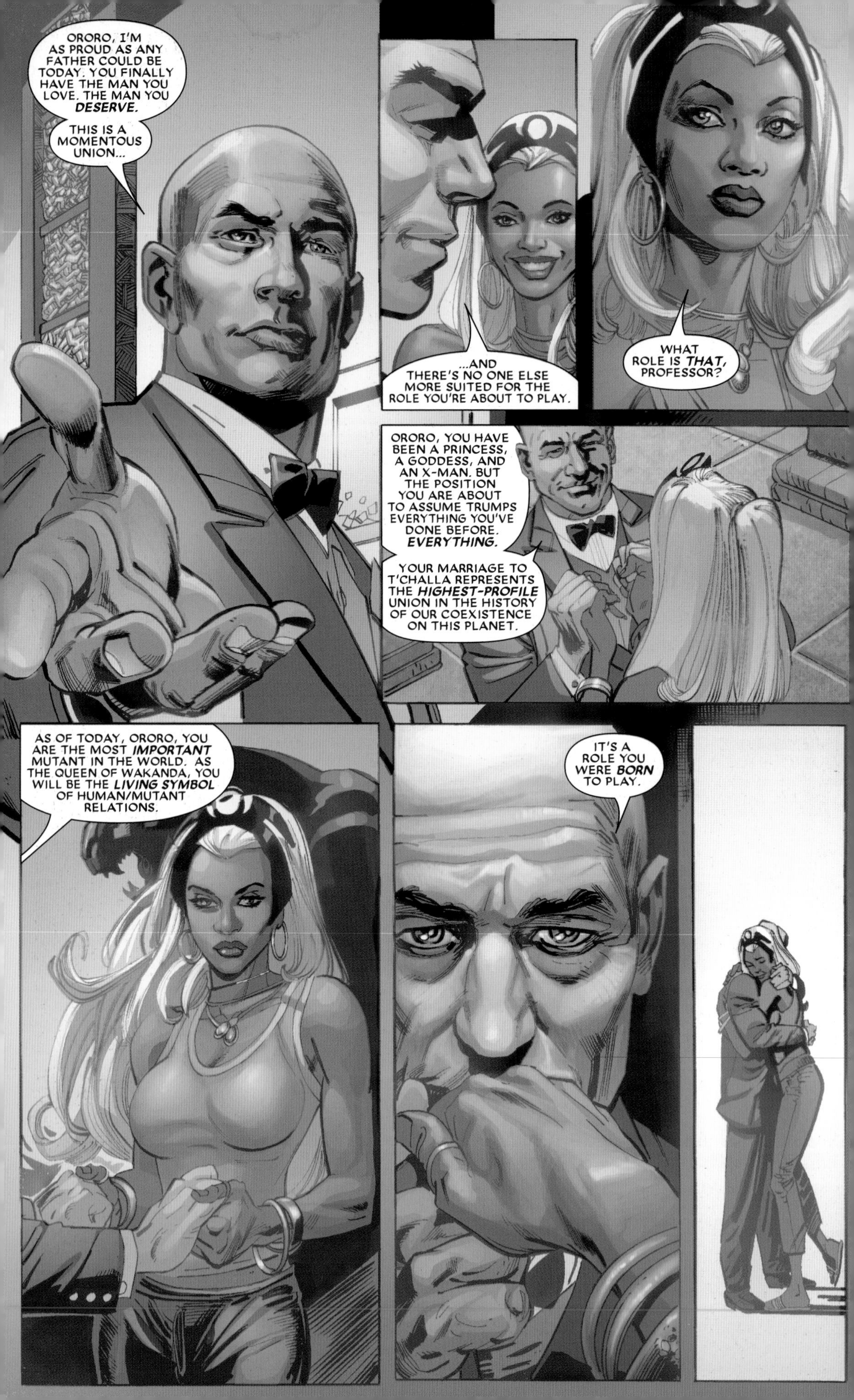
ORORO, I'M AS PROUD AS ANY FATHER COULD BE TODAY. YOU FINALLY HAVE THE MAN YOU LOVE. THE MAN YOU *DESERVE.*
THIS IS A MOMENTOUS UNION...
...AND THERE'S NO ONE ELSE MORE SUITED FOR THE ROLE YOU'RE ABOUT TO PLAY.
WHAT ROLE IS *THAT,* PROFESSOR?
ORORO, YOU HAVE BEEN A PRINCESS, A GODDESS, AND AN X-MAN. BUT THE POSITION YOU ARE ABOUT TO ASSUME TRUMPS EVERYTHING YOU'VE DONE BEFORE. *EVERYTHING.*
YOUR MARRIAGE TO T'CHALLA REPRESENTS THE *HIGHEST-PROFILE* UNION IN THE HISTORY OF OUR COEXISTENCE ON THIS PLANET.
AS OF TODAY, ORORO, YOU ARE THE MOST *IMPORTANT* MUTANT IN THE WORLD. AS THE QUEEN OF WAKANDA, YOU WILL BE THE *LIVING SYMBOL* OF HUMAN/MUTANT RELATIONS.
IT'S A ROLE YOU WERE *BORN* TO PLAY.

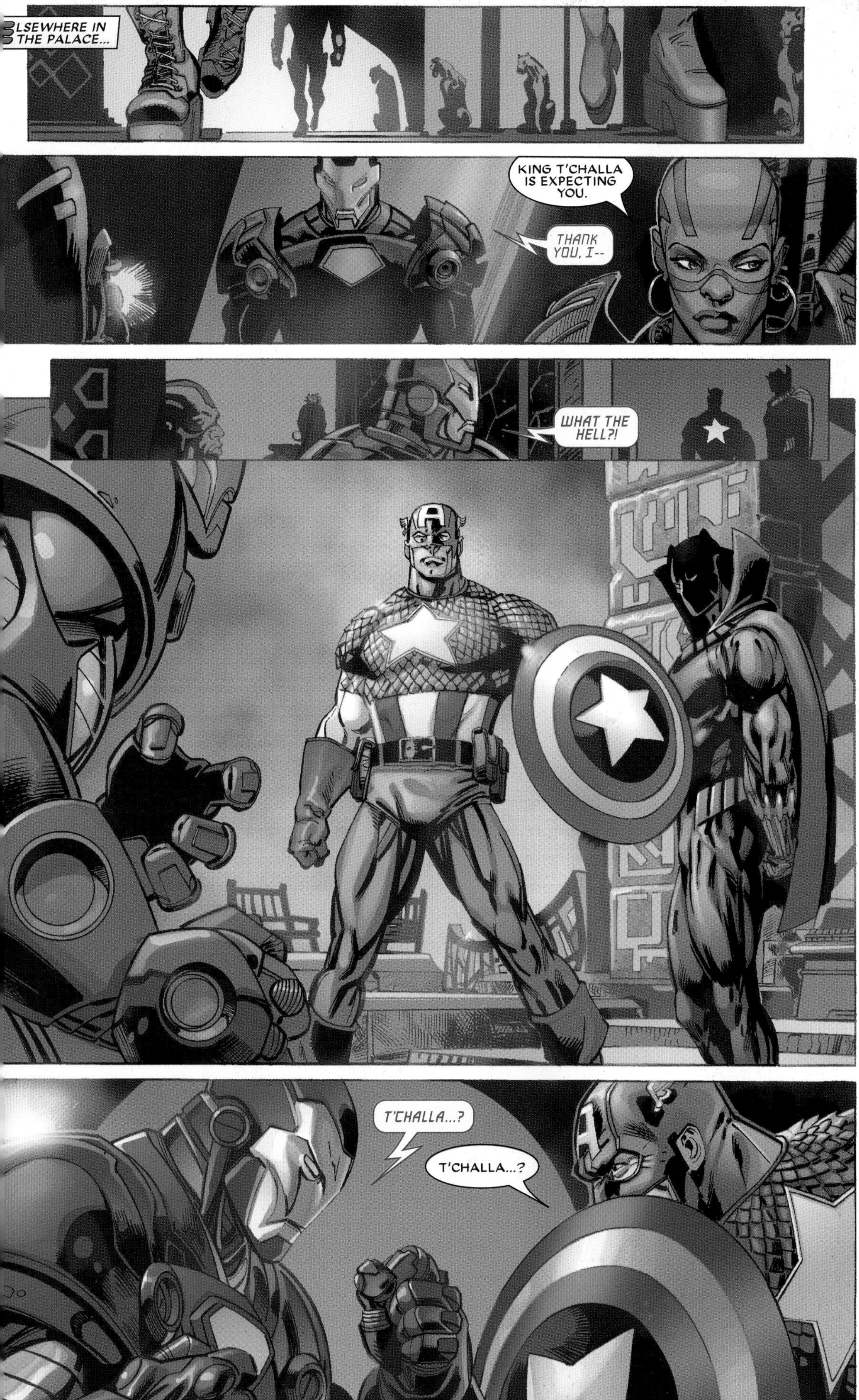
LSEWHERE IN THE PALACE...
KING T'CHALLA IS EXPECTING YOU.
THANK YOU, I--
WHAT THE HELL?!
T'CHALLA...?
T'CHALLA...?

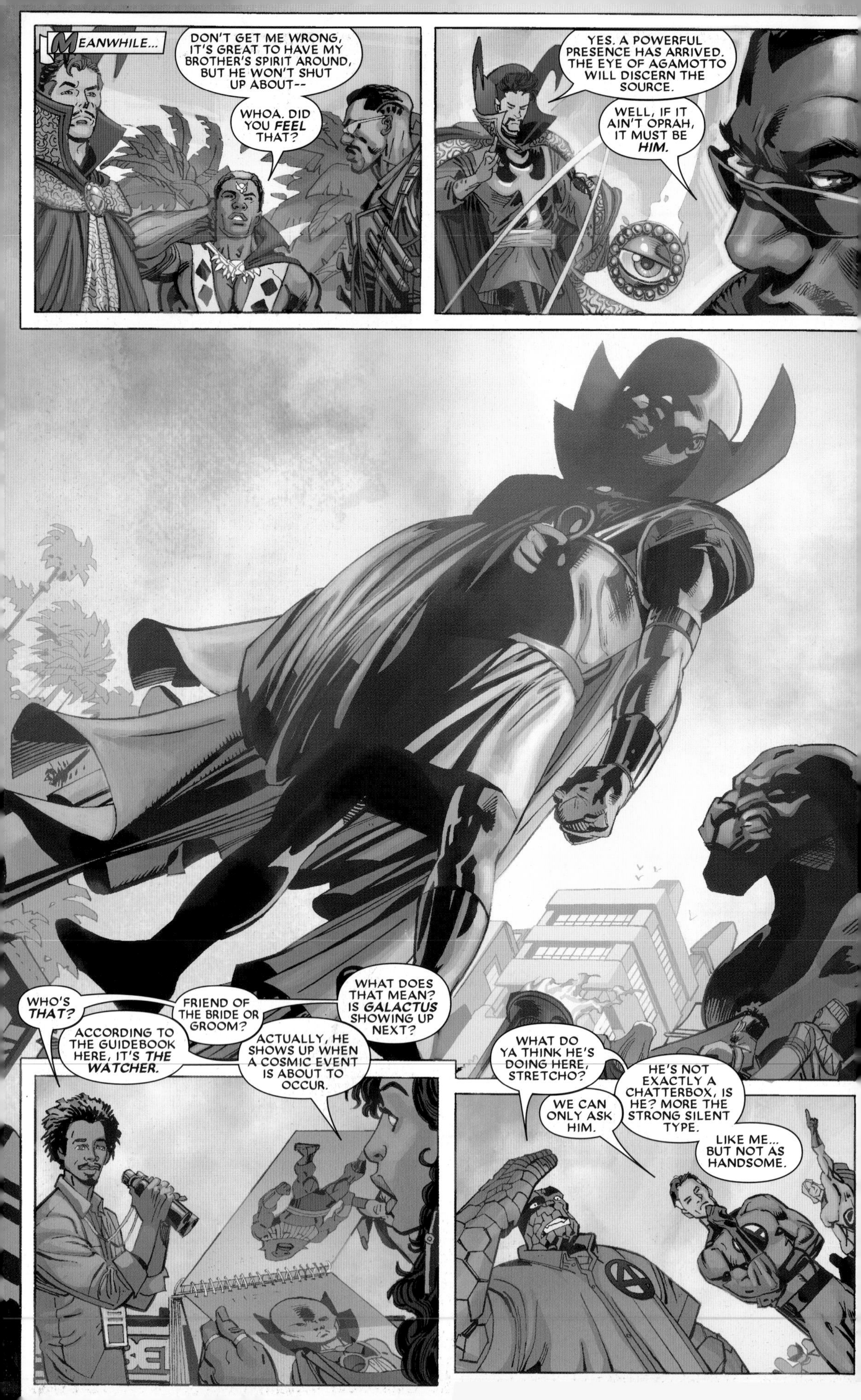
MEANWHILE...
DON'T GET ME WRONG, IT'S GREAT TO HAVE MY BROTHER'S SPIRIT AROUND, BUT HE WON'T SHUT UP ABOUT--
WHOA. DID YOU FEEL THAT?
YES. A POWERFUL PRESENCE HAS ARRIVED. THE EYE OF AGAMOTTO WILL DISCERN THE SOURCE.
WELL, IF IT AIN'T OPRAH, IT MUST BE HIM.
WHO'S THAT?
FRIEND OF THE BRIDE OR GROOM?
WHAT DOES THAT MEAN? IS GALACTUS SHOWING UP NEXT?
ACCORDING TO THE GUIDEBOOK HERE, IT'S THE WATCHER.
ACTUALLY, HE SHOWS UP WHEN A COSMIC EVENT IS ABOUT TO OCCUR.
WHAT DO YA THINK HE'S DOING HERE, STRETCHO?
WE CAN ONLY ASK HIM.
HE'S NOT EXACTLY A CHATTERBOX, IS HE? MORE THE STRONG SILENT TYPE.
LIKE ME... BUT NOT AS HANDSOME.

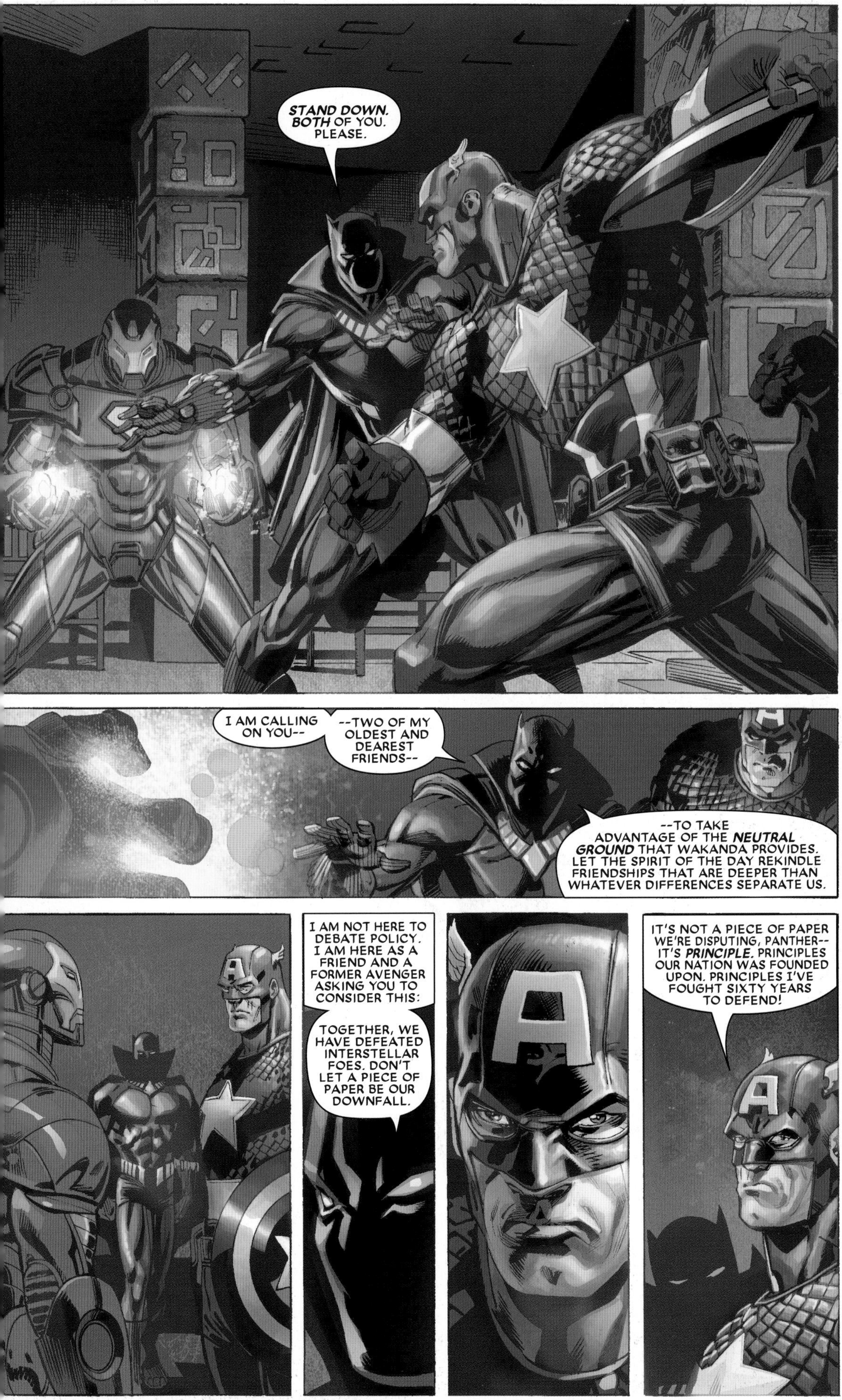
STAND DOWN. BOTH OF YOU. PLEASE.
I AM CALLING ON YOU--
--TWO OF MY OLDEST AND DEAREST FRIENDS--
--TO TAKE ADVANTAGE OF THE NEUTRAL GROUND THAT WAKANDA PROVIDES. LET THE SPIRIT OF THE DAY REKINDLE FRIENDSHIPS THAT ARE DEEPER THAN WHATEVER DIFFERENCES SEPARATE US.
I AM NOT HERE TO DEBATE POLICY. I AM HERE AS A FRIEND AND A FORMER AVENGER ASKING YOU TO CONSIDER THIS:
TOGETHER, WE HAVE DEFEATED INTERSTELLAR FOES. DON'T LET A PIECE OF PAPER BE OUR DOWNFALL.
IT'S NOT A PIECE OF PAPER WE'RE DISPUTING, PANTHER-- IT'S PRINCIPLE. PRINCIPLES OUR NATION WAS FOUNDED UPON. PRINCIPLES I'VE FOUGHT SIXTY YEARS TO DEFEND!

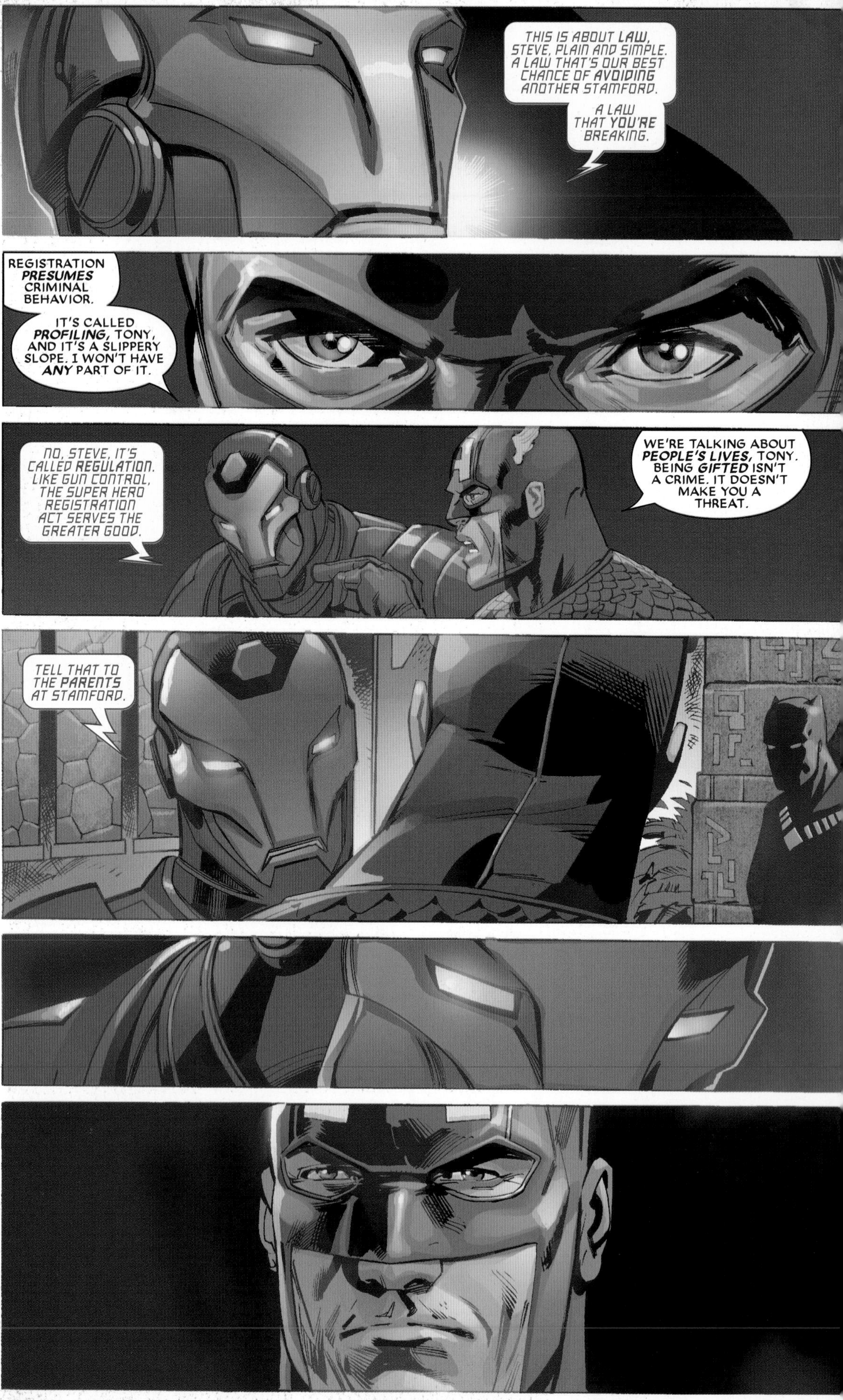
THIS IS ABOUT LAW, STEVE, PLAIN AND SIMPLE. A LAW THAT'S OUR BEST CHANCE OF AVOIDING ANOTHER STAMFORD.
A LAW THAT YOU'RE BREAKING.
REGISTRATION PRESUMES CRIMINAL BEHAVIOR.
IT'S CALLED PROFILING, TONY, AND IT'S A SLIPPERY SLOPE. I WON'T HAVE ANY PART OF IT.
NO, STEVE, IT'S CALLED REGULATION. LIKE GUN CONTROL, THE SUPER HERO REGISTRATION ACT SERVES THE GREATER GOOD.
WE'RE TALKING ABOUT PEOPLE'S LIVES, TONY. BEING GIFTED ISN'T A CRIME. IT DOESN'T MAKE YOU A THREAT.
TELL THAT TO THE PARENTS AT STAMFORD.

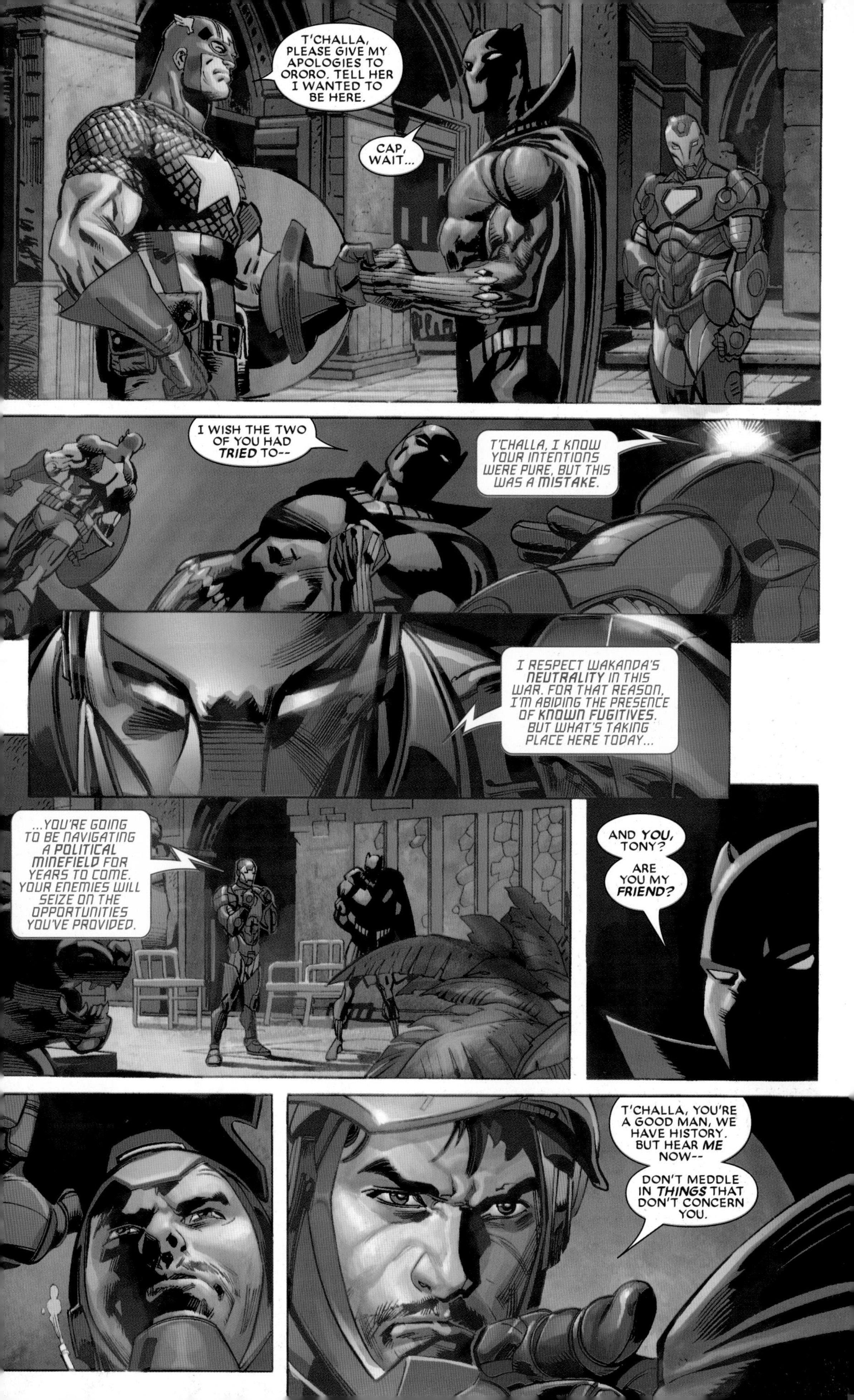

T'CHALLA, PLEASE GIVE MY APOLOGIES TO ORORO. TELL HER I WANTED TO BE HERE.
CAP, WAIT...
I WISH THE TWO OF YOU HAD TRIED TO--
T'CHALLA, I KNOW YOUR INTENTIONS WERE PURE, BUT THIS WAS A MISTAKE.
I RESPECT WAKANDA'S NEUTRALITY IN THIS WAR. FOR THAT REASON, I'M ABIDING THE PRESENCE OF KNOWN FUGITIVES. BUT WHAT'S TAKING PLACE HERE TODAY...
...YOU'RE GOING TO BE NAVIGATING A POLITICAL MINEFIELD FOR YEARS TO COME. YOUR ENEMIES WILL SEIZE ON THE OPPORTUNITIES YOU'VE PROVIDED.
AND YOU, TONY?
ARE YOU MY FRIEND?
T'CHALLA, YOU'RE A GOOD MAN, WE HAVE HISTORY. BUT HEAR ME NOW--
DON'T MEDDLE IN THINGS THAT DON'T CONCERN YOU.

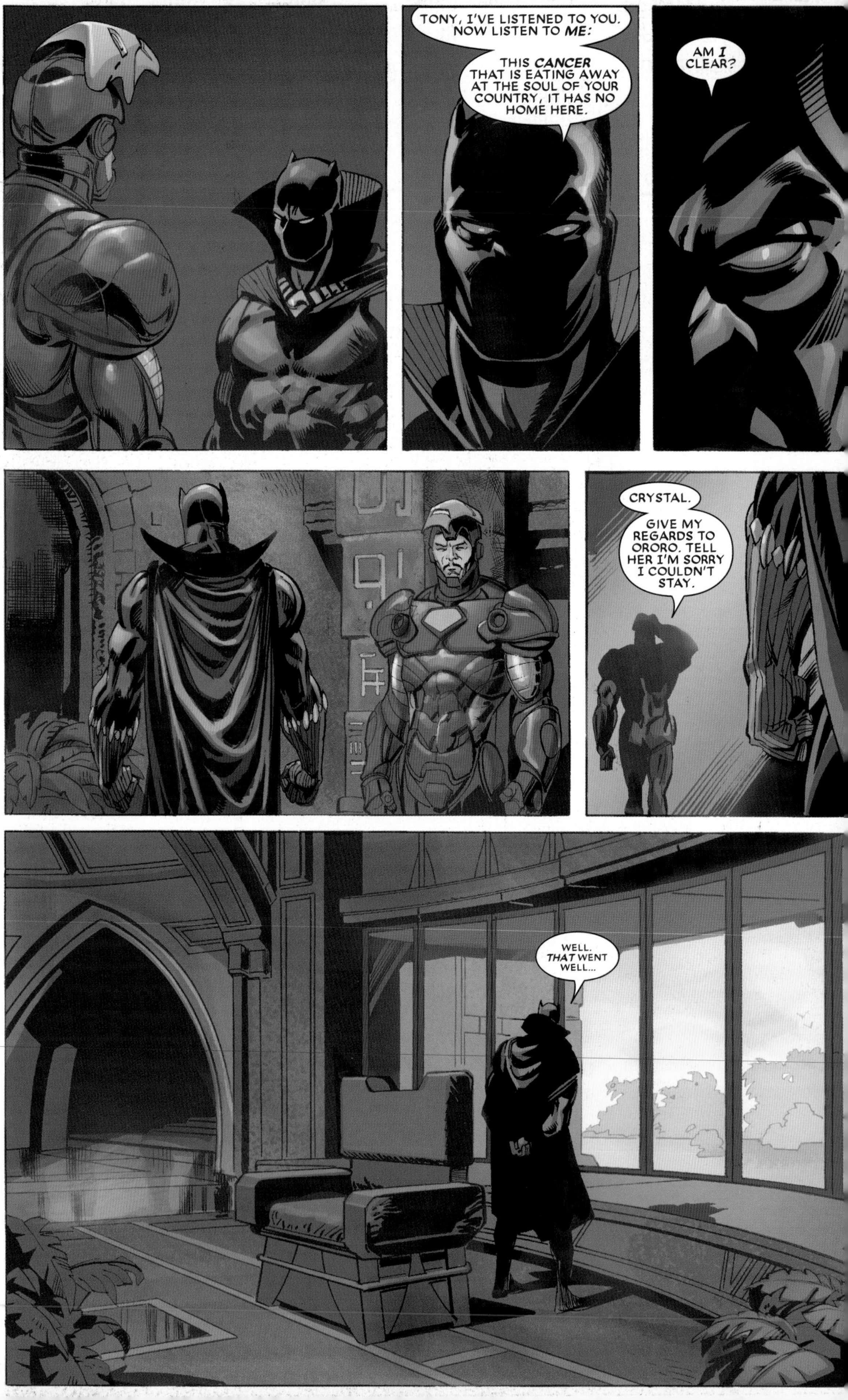
TONY, I'VE LISTENED TO YOU. NOW LISTEN TO *ME:*
THIS *CANCER* THAT IS EATING AWAY AT THE SOUL OF YOUR COUNTRY, IT HAS NO HOME HERE.
AM *I* CLEAR?
CRYSTAL.
GIVE MY REGARDS TO ORORO. TELL HER I'M SORRY I COULDN'T STAY.
WELL. *THAT* WENT WELL...

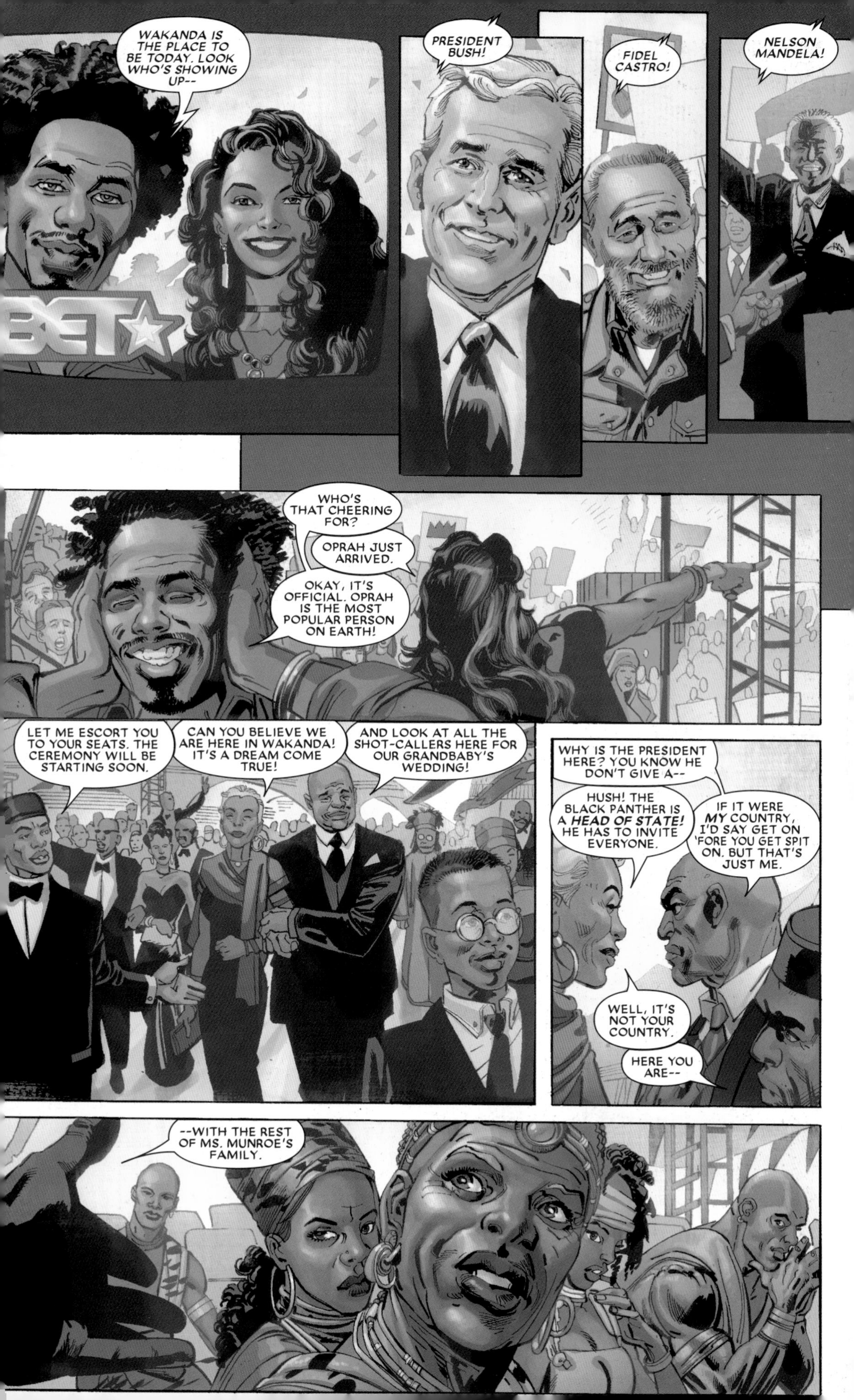

WAKANDA IS THE PLACE TO BE TODAY. LOOK WHO'S SHOWING UP--
PRESIDENT BUSH!
FIDEL CASTRO!
NELSON MANDELA!
WHO'S THAT CHEERING FOR?
OPRAH JUST ARRIVED.
OKAY, IT'S OFFICIAL. OPRAH IS THE MOST POPULAR PERSON ON EARTH!
LET ME ESCORT YOU TO YOUR SEATS. THE CEREMONY WILL BE STARTING SOON.
CAN YOU BELIEVE WE ARE HERE IN WAKANDA! IT'S A DREAM COME TRUE!
AND LOOK AT ALL THE SHOT-CALLERS HERE FOR OUR GRANDBABY'S WEDDING!
WHY IS THE PRESIDENT HERE? YOU KNOW HE DON'T GIVE A--
HUSH! THE BLACK PANTHER IS A HEAD OF STATE! HE HAS TO INVITE EVERYONE.
IF IT WERE MY COUNTRY, I'D SAY GET ON 'FORE YOU GET SPIT ON. BUT THAT'S JUST ME.
WELL, IT'S NOT YOUR COUNTRY.
HERE YOU ARE--
--WITH THE REST OF MS. MUNROE'S FAMILY.

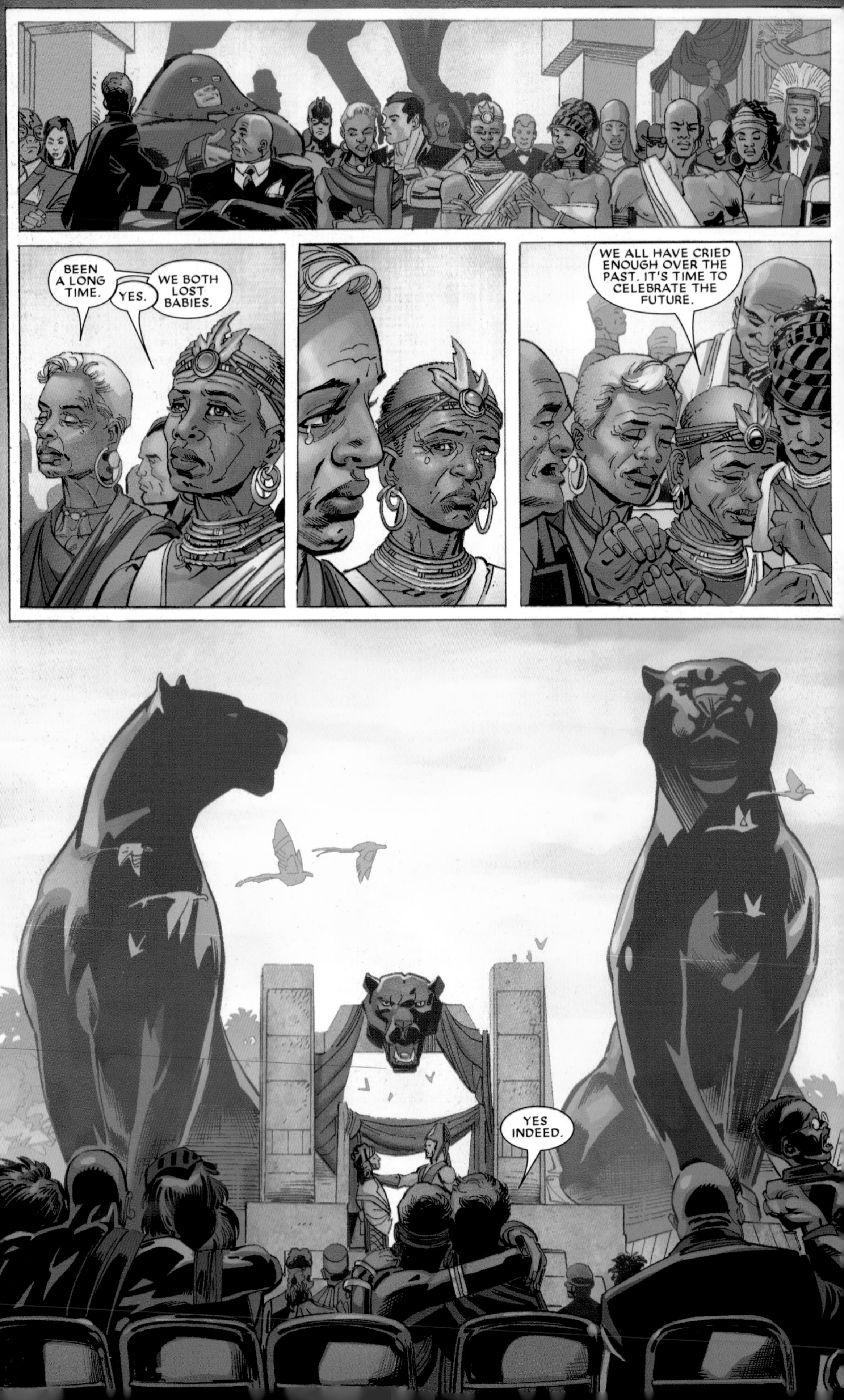
BEEN A LONG TIME.
YES.
WE BOTH LOST BABIES.
WE ALL HAVE CRIED ENOUGH OVER THE PAST. IT'S TIME TO CELEBRATE THE FUTURE.
YES INDEED.

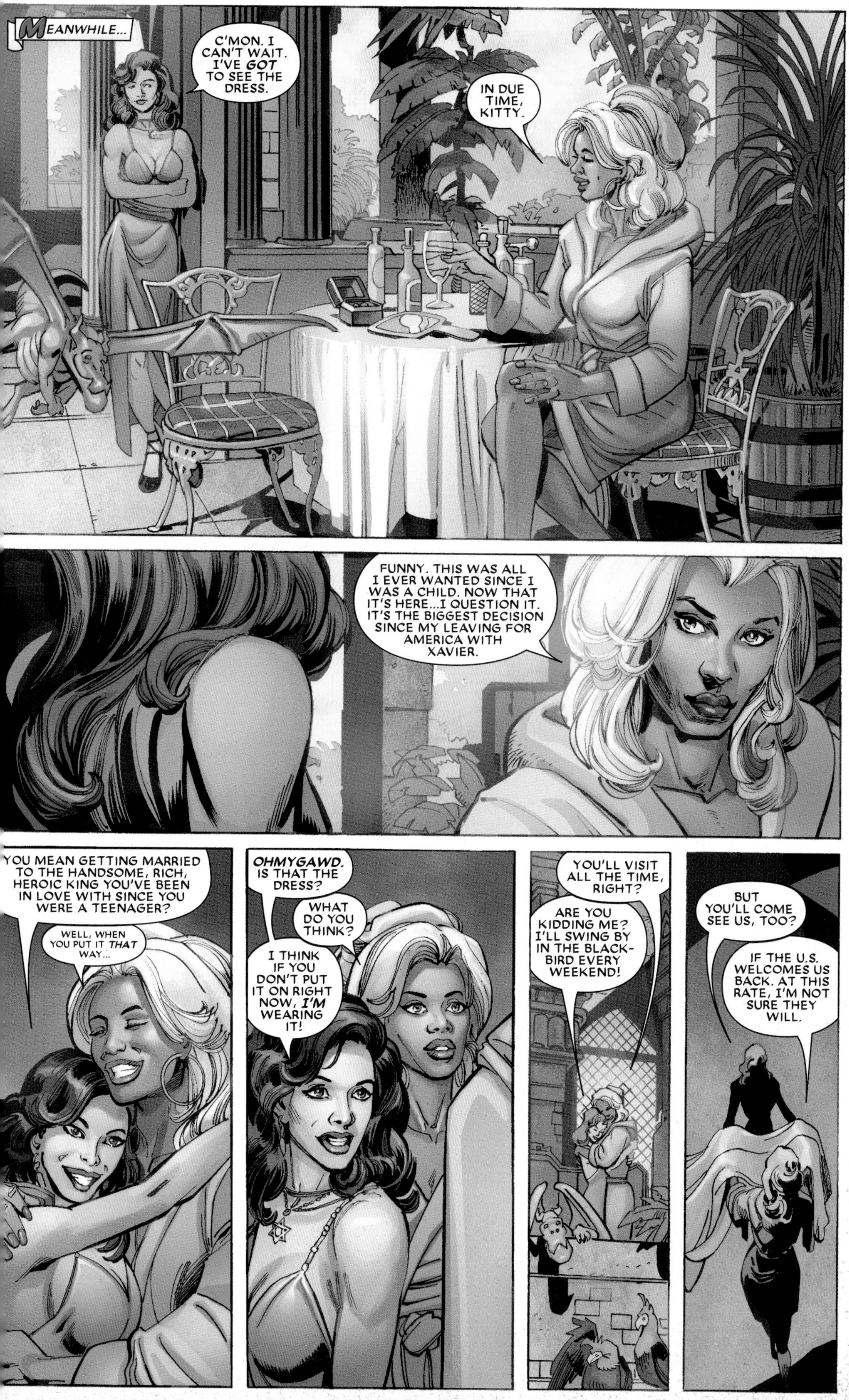
MEANWHILE...
C'MON. I CAN'T WAIT. I'VE GOT TO SEE THE DRESS.
IN DUE TIME, KITTY.
FUNNY. THIS WAS ALL I EVER WANTED SINCE I WAS A CHILD. NOW THAT IT'S HERE...I QUESTION IT. IT'S THE BIGGEST DECISION SINCE MY LEAVING FOR AMERICA WITH XAVIER.
YOU MEAN GETTING MARRIED TO THE HANDSOME, RICH, HEROIC KING YOU'VE BEEN IN LOVE WITH SINCE YOU WERE A TEENAGER?
WELL, WHEN YOU PUT IT THAT WAY...
OHMYGAWD. IS THAT THE DRESS?
WHAT DO YOU THINK?
I THINK IF YOU DON'T PUT IT ON RIGHT NOW, I'M WEARING IT!
YOU'LL VISIT ALL THE TIME, RIGHT?
ARE YOU KIDDING ME? I'LL SWING BY IN THE BLACK-BIRD EVERY WEEKEND!
BUT YOU'LL COME SEE US, TOO?
IF THE U.S. WELCOMES US BACK. AT THIS RATE, I'M NOT SURE THEY WILL.

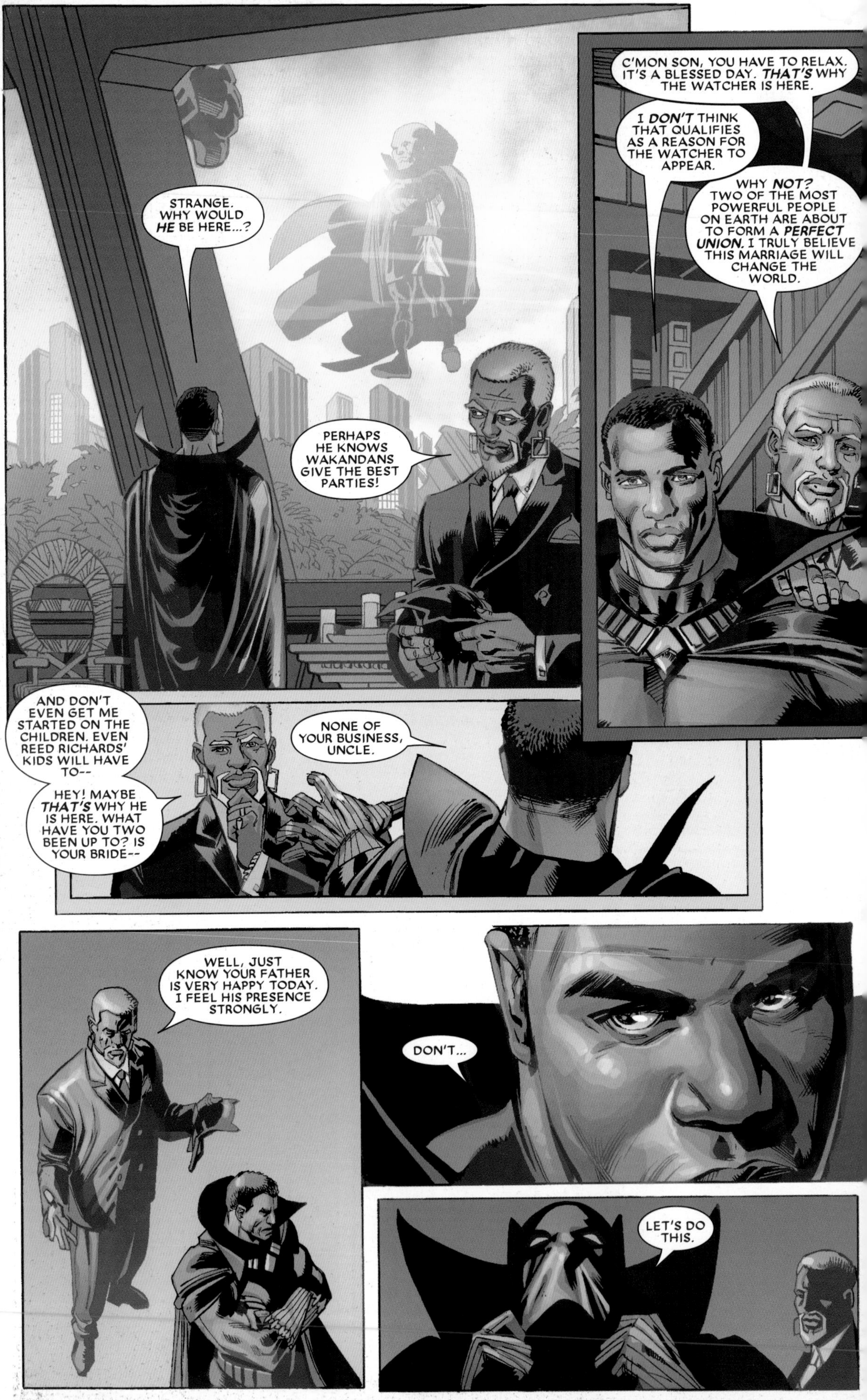
STRANGE. WHY WOULD HE BE HERE...?
PERHAPS HE KNOWS WAKANDANS GIVE THE BEST PARTIES!
C'MON SON, YOU HAVE TO RELAX. IT'S A BLESSED DAY. THAT'S WHY THE WATCHER IS HERE.
I DON'T THINK THAT QUALIFIES AS A REASON FOR THE WATCHER TO APPEAR.
WHY NOT? TWO OF THE MOST POWERFUL PEOPLE ON EARTH ARE ABOUT TO FORM A PERFECT UNION. I TRULY BELIEVE THIS MARRIAGE WILL CHANGE THE WORLD.
AND DON'T EVEN GET ME STARTED ON THE CHILDREN. EVEN REED RICHARDS' KIDS WILL HAVE TO--
HEY! MAYBE THAT'S WHY HE IS HERE. WHAT HAVE YOU TWO BEEN UP TO? IS YOUR BRIDE--
NONE OF YOUR BUSINESS, UNCLE.
WELL, JUST KNOW YOUR FATHER IS VERY HAPPY TODAY. I FEEL HIS PRESENCE STRONGLY.
DON'T...
LET'S DO THIS.

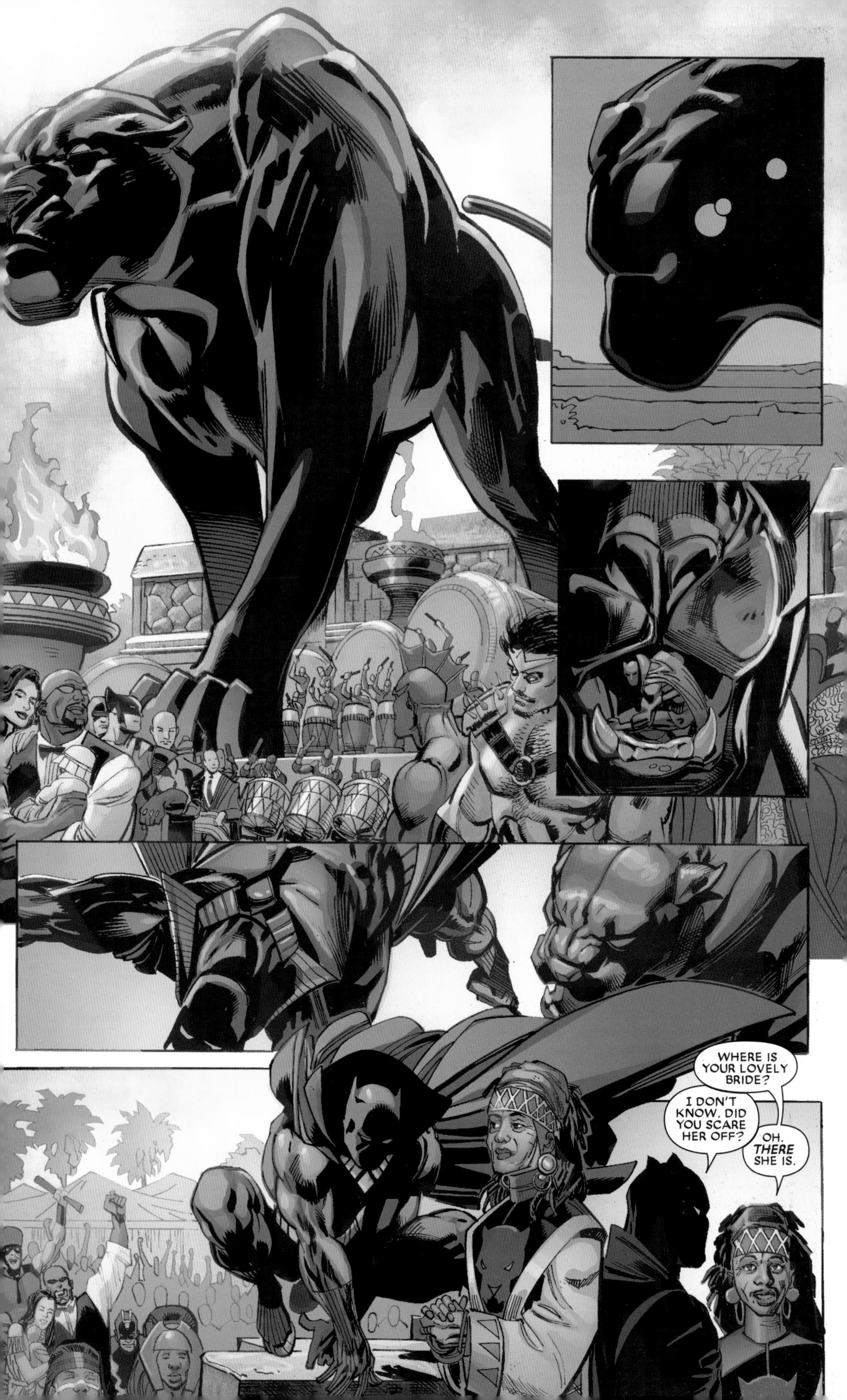
WHERE IS YOUR LOVELY BRIDE?
I DON'T KNOW. DID YOU SCARE HER OFF?
OH. *THERE* SHE IS.

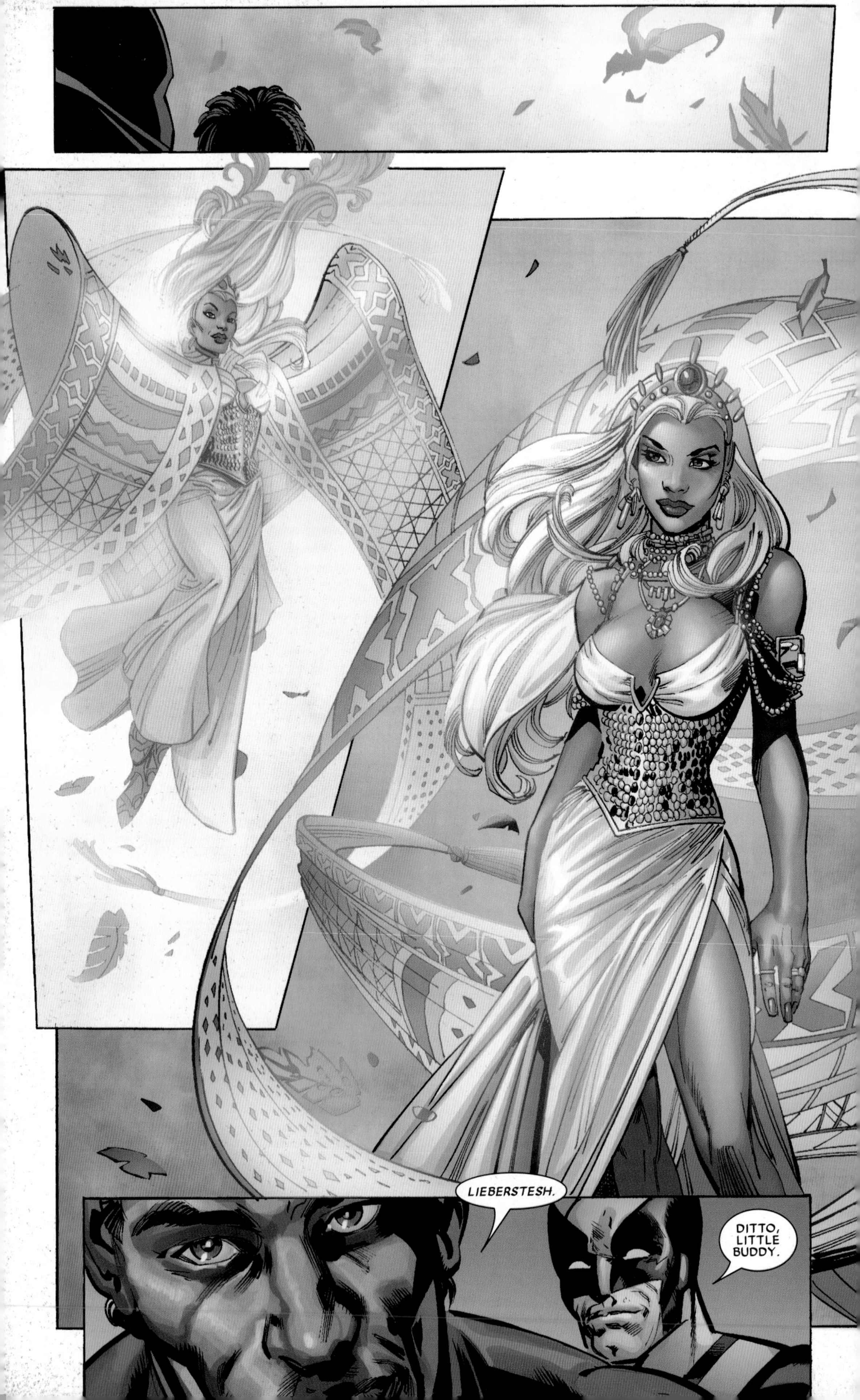
LIEBERSTESH.
DITTO, LITTLE BUDDY.

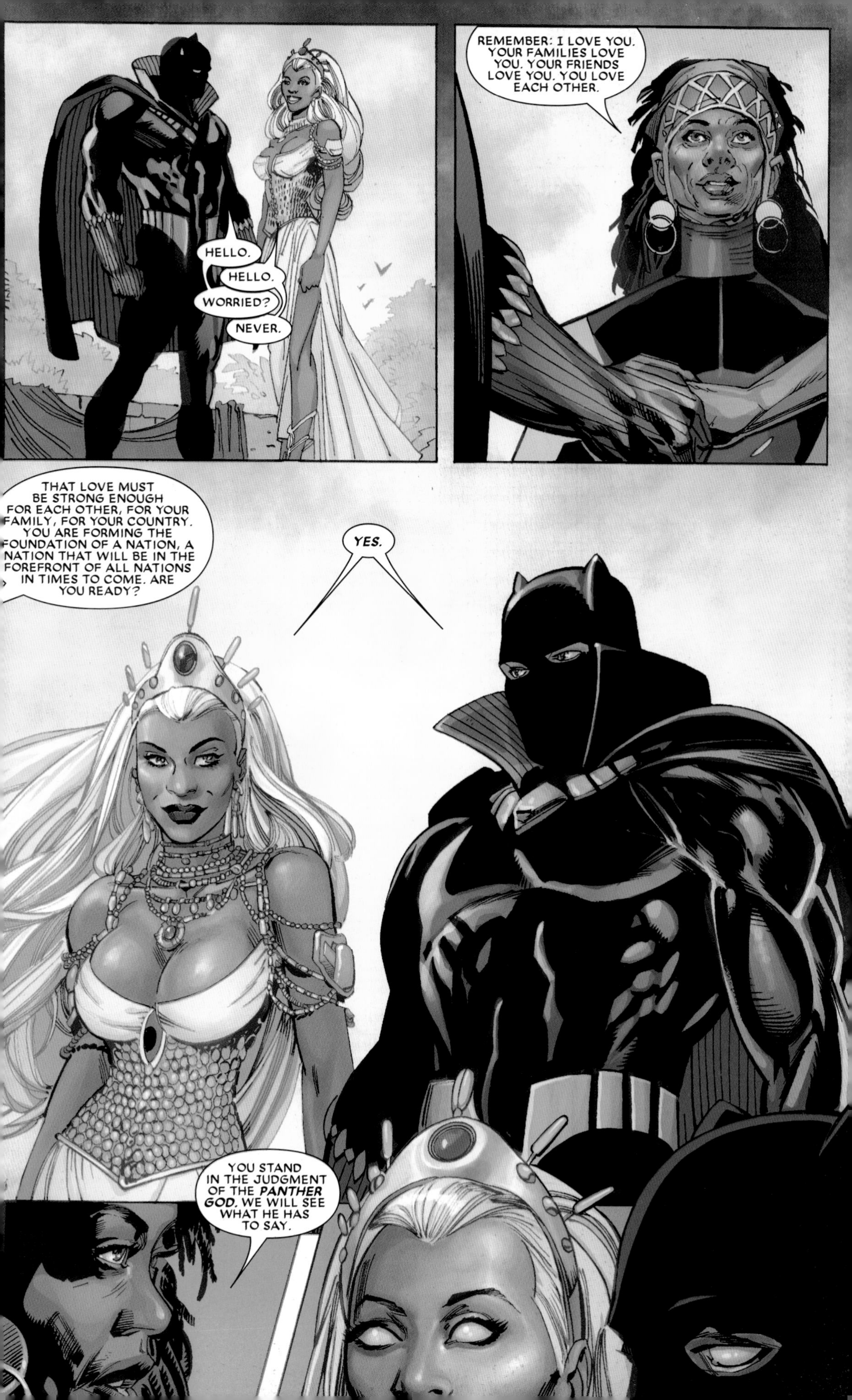
HELLO.
HELLO.
WORRIED?
NEVER.
REMEMBER: I LOVE YOU. YOUR FAMILIES LOVE YOU. YOUR FRIENDS LOVE YOU. YOU LOVE EACH OTHER.
THAT LOVE MUST BE STRONG ENOUGH FOR EACH OTHER, FOR YOUR FAMILY, FOR YOUR COUNTRY. YOU ARE FORMING THE FOUNDATION OF A NATION, A NATION THAT WILL BE IN THE FOREFRONT OF ALL NATIONS IN TIMES TO COME. ARE YOU READY?
YES.
YOU STAND IN THE JUDGMENT OF THE PANTHER GOD. WE WILL SEE WHAT HE HAS TO SAY.

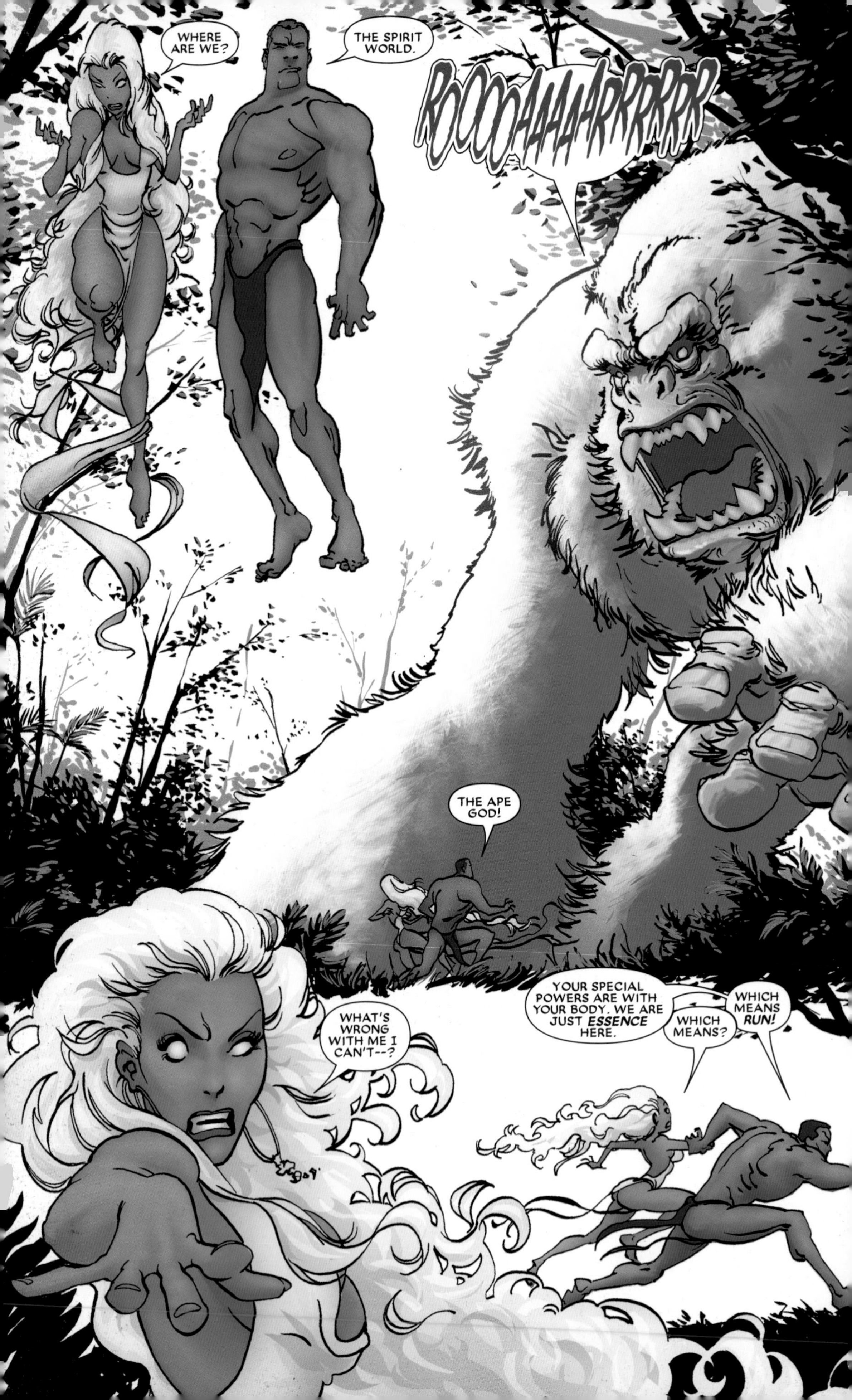
WHERE ARE WE?
THE SPIRIT WORLD.
ROOOOAAAAARRRRRR
THE APE GOD!
WHAT'S WRONG WITH ME I CAN'T--?
YOUR SPECIAL POWERS ARE WITH YOUR BODY. WE ARE JUST ESSENCE HERE.
WHICH MEANS?
WHICH MEANS RUN!

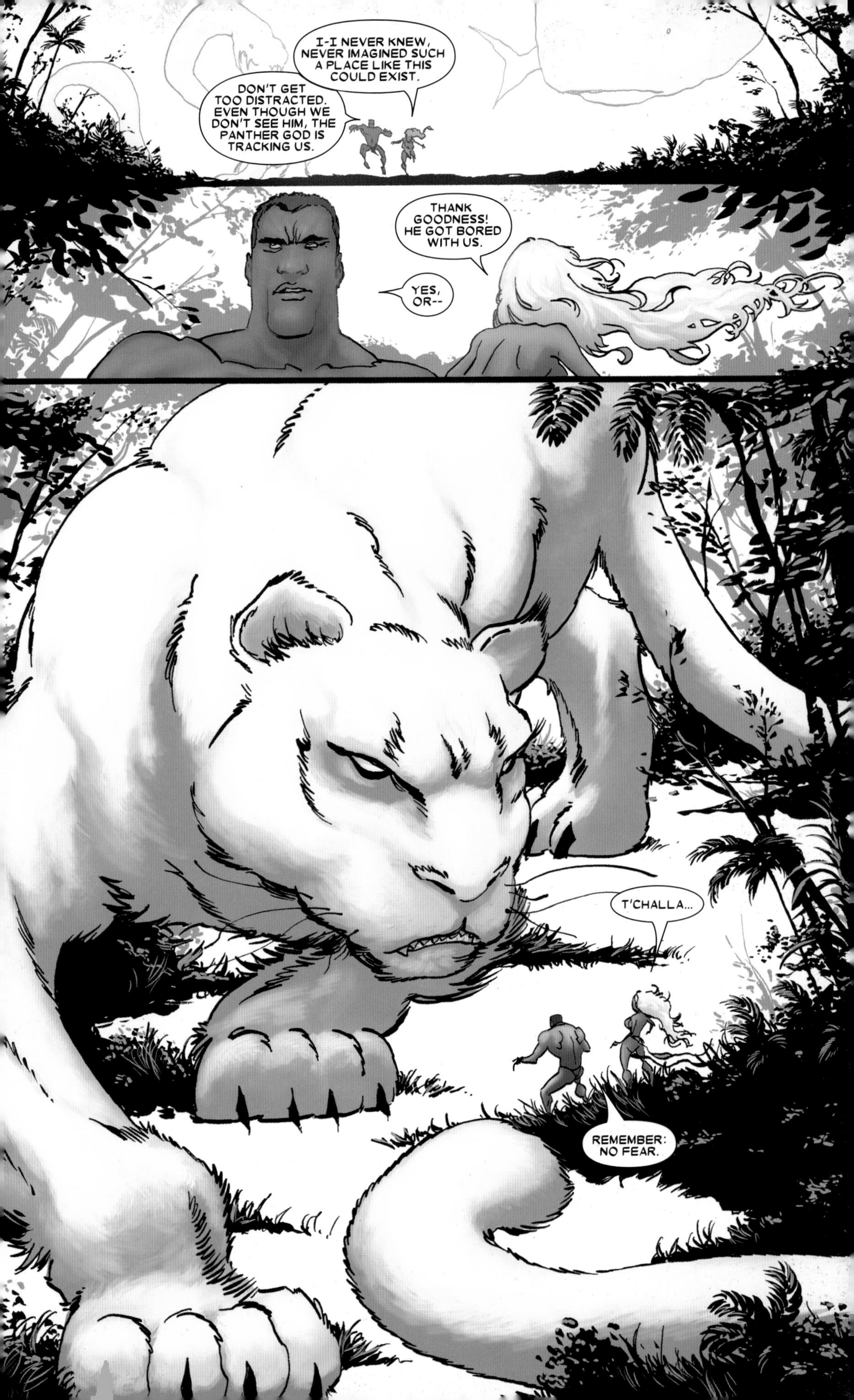
I-I NEVER KNEW, NEVER IMAGINED SUCH A PLACE LIKE THIS COULD EXIST.
DON'T GET TOO DISTRACTED. EVEN THOUGH WE DON'T SEE HIM, THE PANTHER GOD IS TRACKING US.
THANK GOODNESS! HE GOT BORED WITH US.
YES, OR--
T'CHALLA...
REMEMBER: NO FEAR.

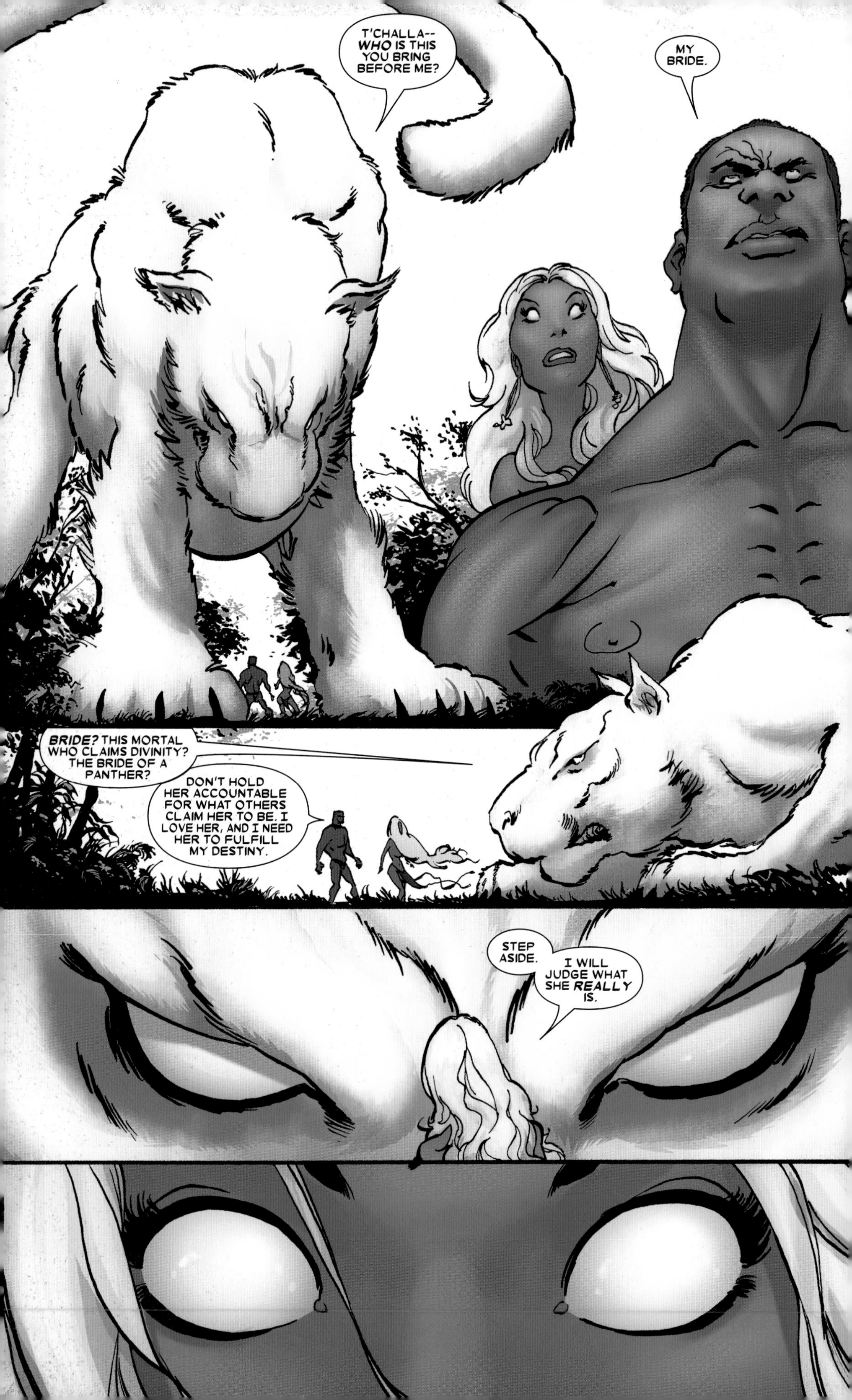
T'CHALLA-- WHO IS THIS YOU BRING BEFORE ME?
MY BRIDE.
BRIDE? THIS MORTAL WHO CLAIMS DIVINITY? THE BRIDE OF A PANTHER?
DON'T HOLD HER ACCOUNTABLE FOR WHAT OTHERS CLAIM HER TO BE. I LOVE HER, AND I NEED HER TO FULFILL MY DESTINY.
STEP ASIDE.
I WILL JUDGE WHAT SHE REALLY IS.

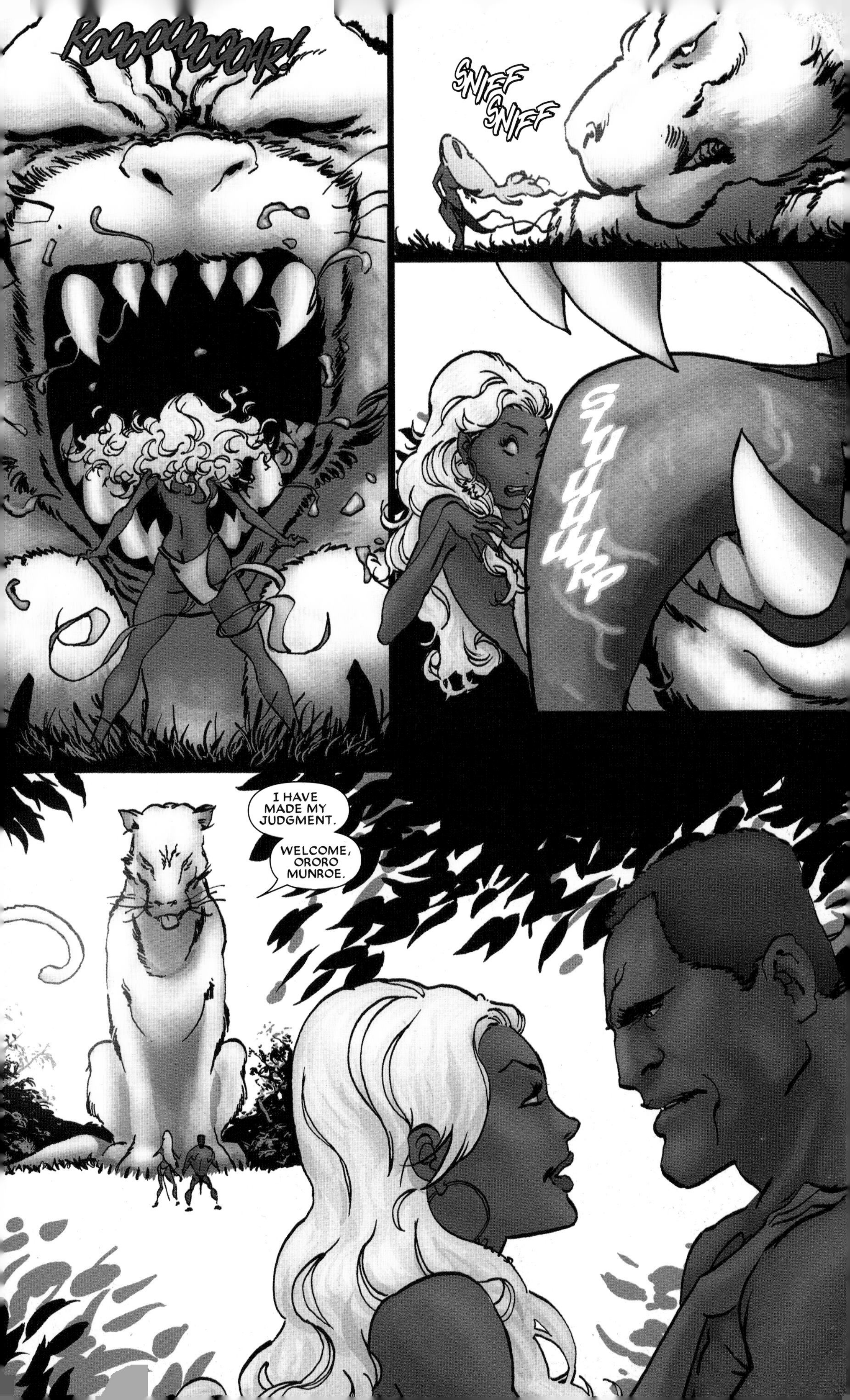

ROOOOOOOOOOAR!
SNIFF SNIFF
SLUUUUURRP
I HAVE MADE MY JUDGMENT.
WELCOME, ORORO MUNROE.

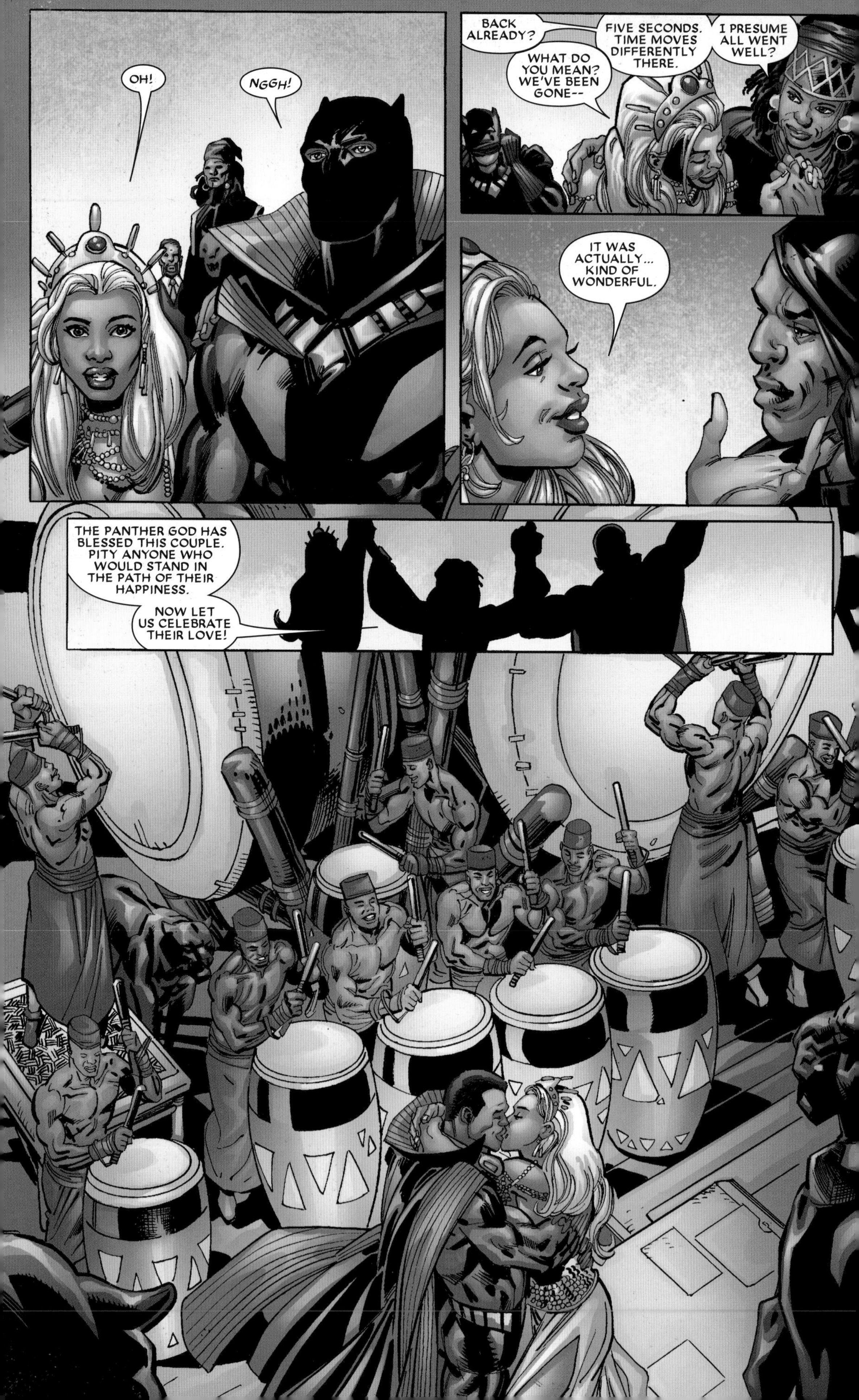
OH!
NGGH!
BACK ALREADY?
WHAT DO YOU MEAN? WE'VE BEEN GONE--
FIVE SECONDS. TIME MOVES DIFFERENTLY THERE.
I PRESUME ALL WENT WELL?
IT WAS ACTUALLY... KIND OF WONDERFUL.
THE PANTHER GOD HAS BLESSED THIS COUPLE. PITY ANYONE WHO WOULD STAND IN THE PATH OF THEIR HAPPINESS.
NOW LET US CELEBRATE THEIR LOVE!

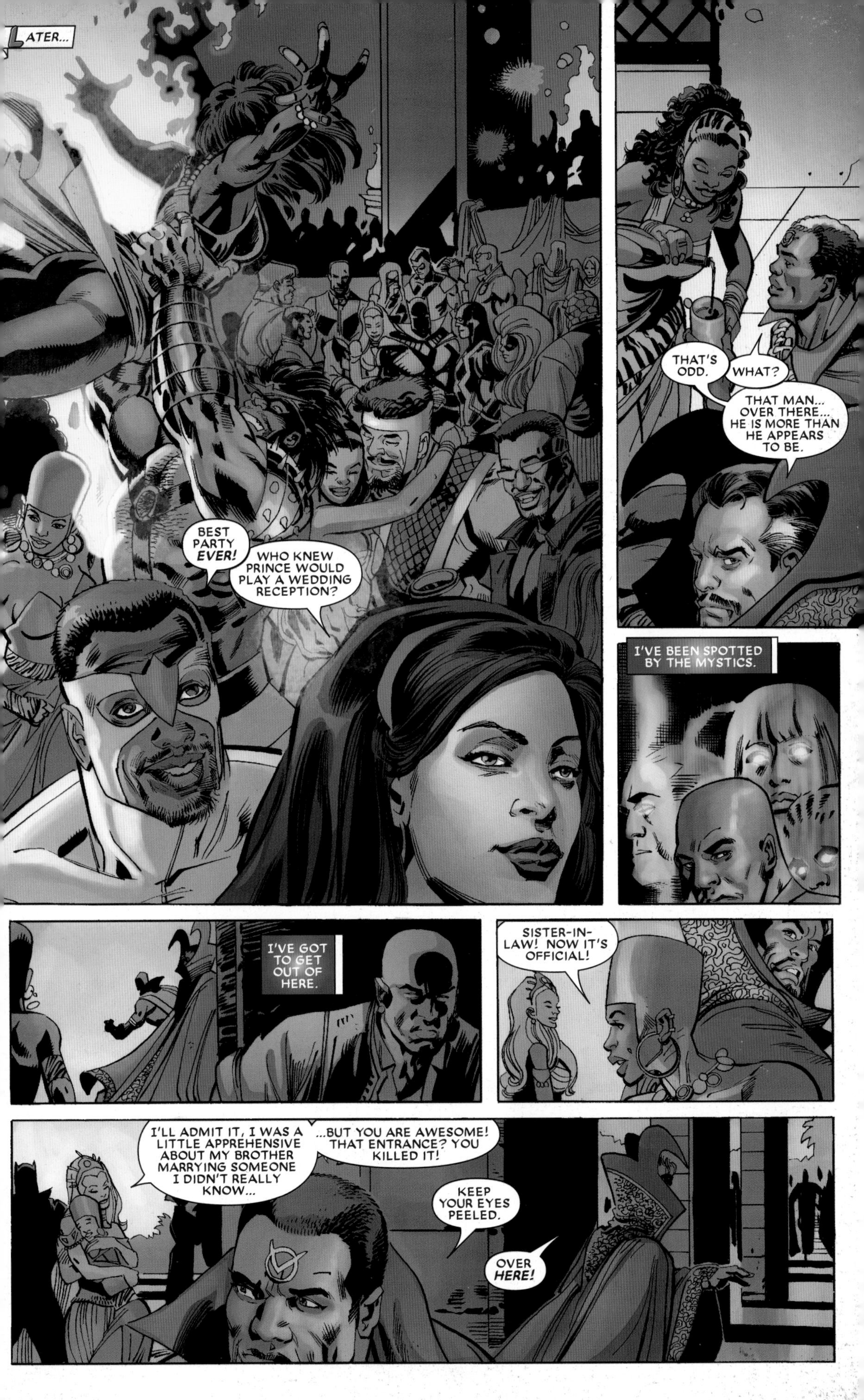
LATER...
BEST PARTY EVER!
WHO KNEW PRINCE WOULD PLAY A WEDDING RECEPTION?
THAT'S ODD.
WHAT?
THAT MAN... OVER THERE... HE IS MORE THAN HE APPEARS TO BE.
I'VE BEEN SPOTTED BY THE MYSTICS.
I'VE GOT TO GET OUT OF HERE.
SISTER-IN-LAW! NOW IT'S OFFICIAL!
I'LL ADMIT IT, I WAS A LITTLE APPREHENSIVE ABOUT MY BROTHER MARRYING SOMEONE I DIDN'T REALLY KNOW...
...BUT YOU ARE AWESOME! THAT ENTRANCE? YOU KILLED IT!
KEEP YOUR EYES PEELED.
OVER HERE!

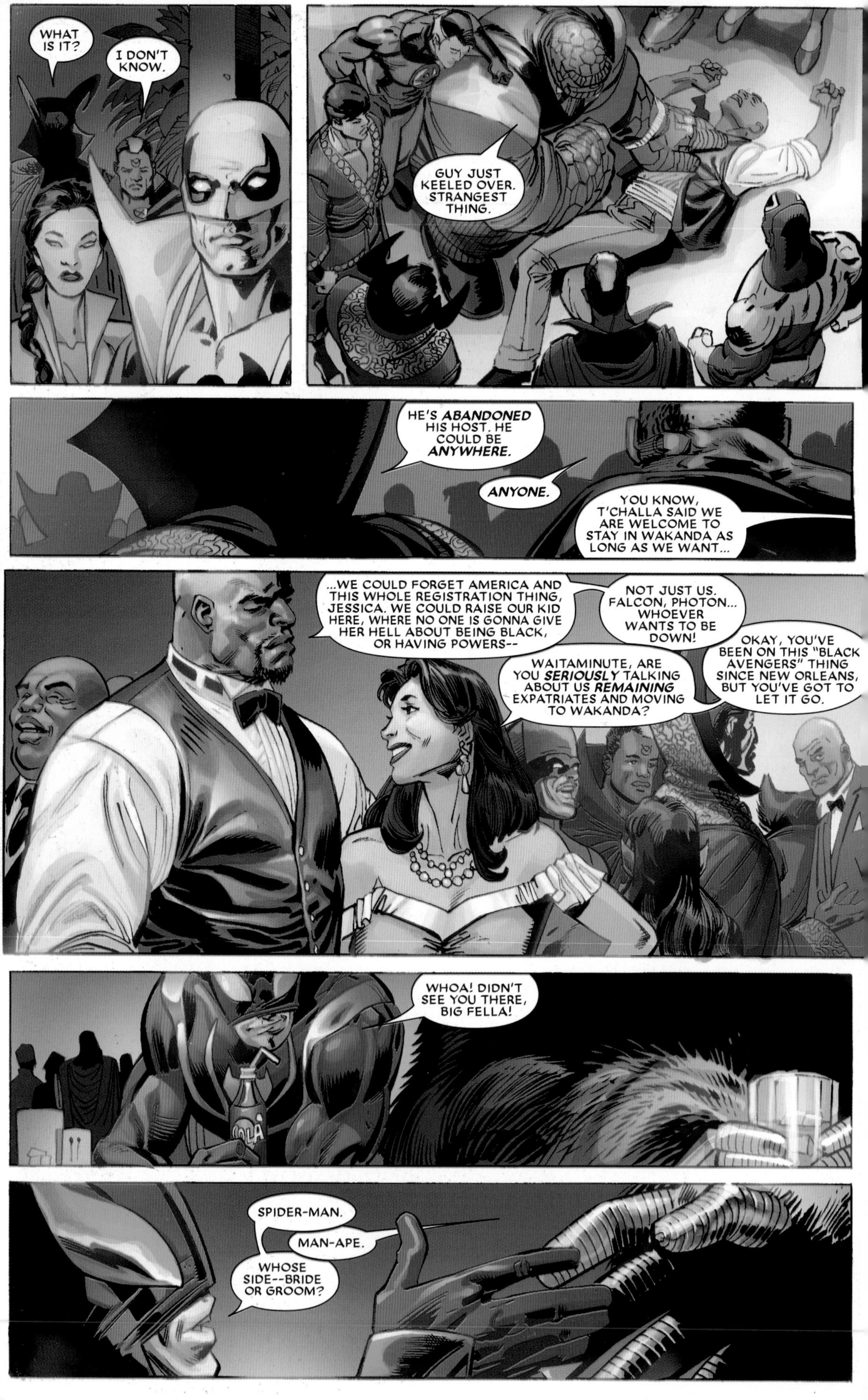

WHAT IS IT?
I DON'T KNOW.
GUY JUST KEELED OVER. STRANGEST THING.
HE'S ABANDONED HIS HOST. HE COULD BE ANYWHERE.
ANYONE.
YOU KNOW, T'CHALLA SAID WE ARE WELCOME TO STAY IN WAKANDA AS LONG AS WE WANT...
...WE COULD FORGET AMERICA AND THIS WHOLE REGISTRATION THING, JESSICA. WE COULD RAISE OUR KID HERE, WHERE NO ONE IS GONNA GIVE HER HELL ABOUT BEING BLACK, OR HAVING POWERS--
NOT JUST US. FALCON, PHOTON... WHOEVER WANTS TO BE DOWN!
WAITAMINUTE, ARE YOU SERIOUSLY TALKING ABOUT US REMAINING EXPATRIATES AND MOVING TO WAKANDA?
OKAY, YOU'VE BEEN ON THIS "BLACK AVENGERS" THING SINCE NEW ORLEANS, BUT YOU'VE GOT TO LET IT GO.
WHOA! DIDN'T SEE YOU THERE, BIG FELLA!
COLA
SPIDER-MAN.
MAN-APE.
WHOSE SIDE--BRIDE OR GROOM?

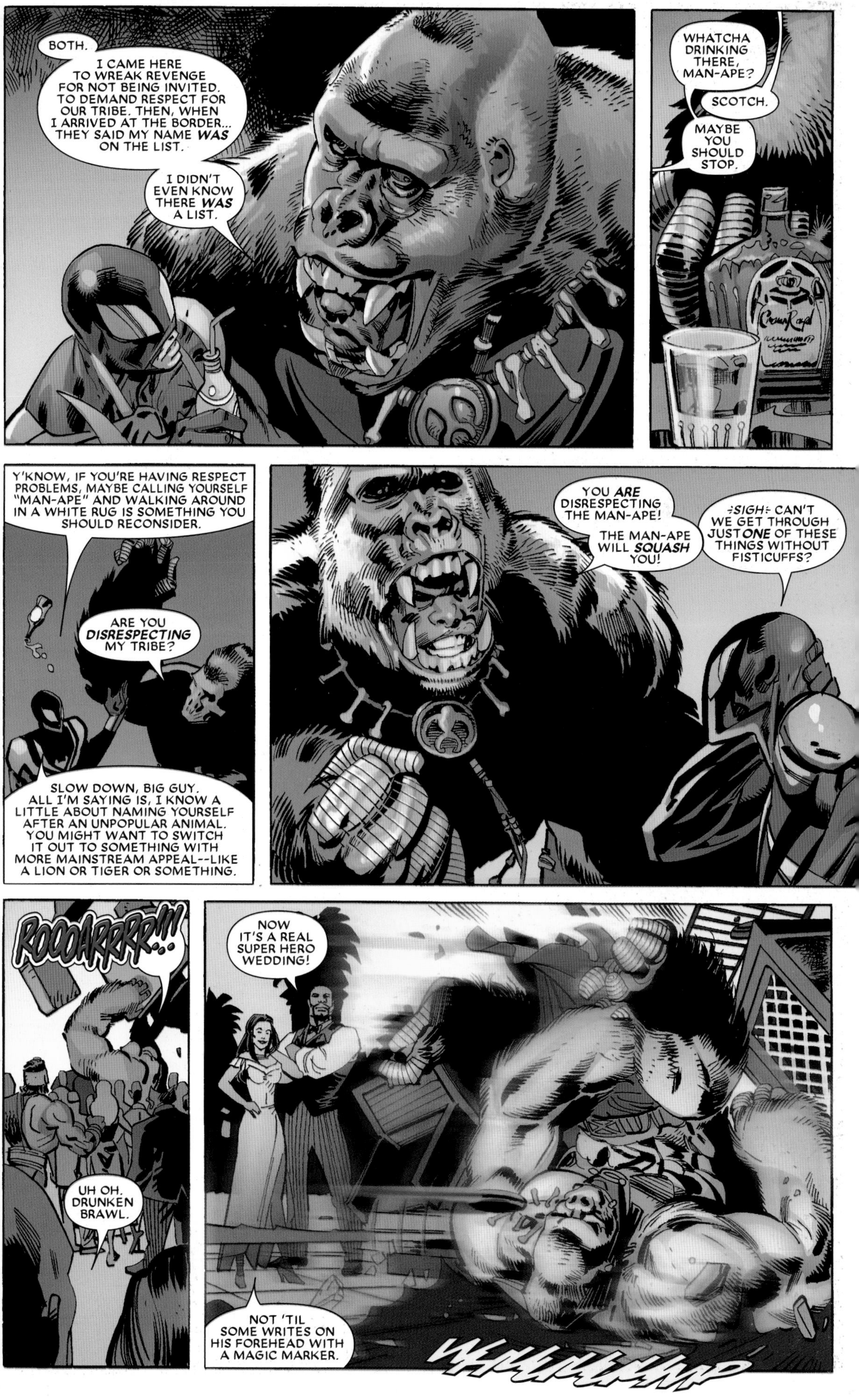
BOTH.
I CAME HERE TO WREAK REVENGE FOR NOT BEING INVITED. TO DEMAND RESPECT FOR OUR TRIBE. THEN, WHEN I ARRIVED AT THE BORDER... THEY SAID MY NAME *WAS* ON THE LIST.
I DIDN'T EVEN KNOW THERE *WAS* A LIST.
WHATCHA DRINKING THERE, MAN-APE?
SCOTCH.
MAYBE YOU SHOULD STOP.
Y'KNOW, IF YOU'RE HAVING RESPECT PROBLEMS, MAYBE CALLING YOURSELF "MAN-APE" AND WALKING AROUND IN A WHITE RUG IS SOMETHING YOU SHOULD RECONSIDER.
ARE YOU *DISRESPECTING* MY TRIBE?
SLOW DOWN, BIG GUY. ALL I'M SAYING IS, I KNOW A LITTLE ABOUT NAMING YOURSELF AFTER AN UNPOPULAR ANIMAL. YOU MIGHT WANT TO SWITCH IT OUT TO SOMETHING WITH MORE MAINSTREAM APPEAL--LIKE A LION OR TIGER OR SOMETHING.
YOU *ARE* DISRESPECTING THE MAN-APE!
THE MAN-APE WILL *SQUASH* YOU!
SIGH CAN'T WE GET THROUGH JUST *ONE* OF THESE THINGS WITHOUT FISTICUFFS?
ROOOARRRR!!!
UH OH. DRUNKEN BRAWL.
NOW IT'S A REAL SUPER HERO WEDDING!
NOT 'TIL SOME WRITES ON HIS FOREHEAD WITH A MAGIC MARKER.

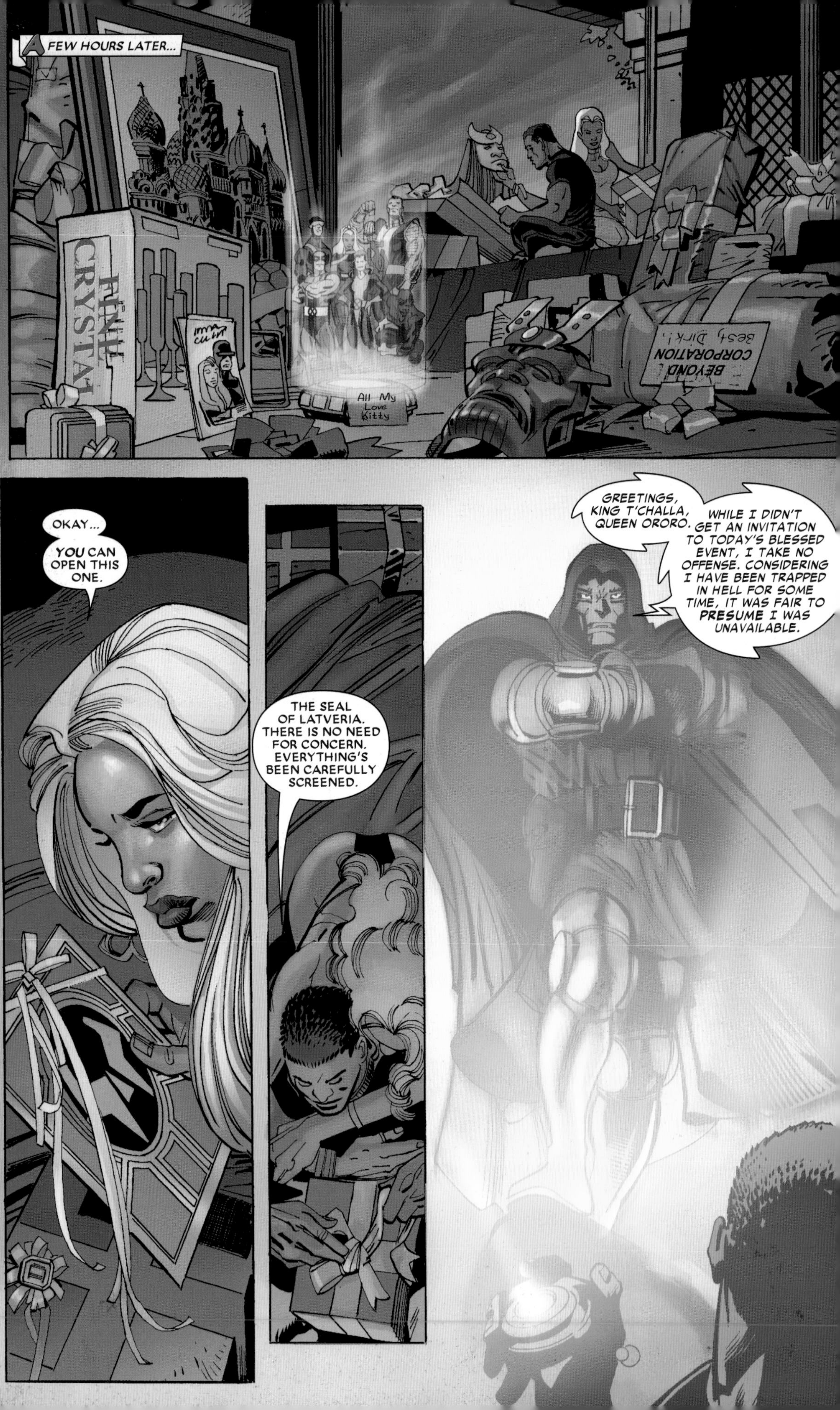
A FEW HOURS LATER...
FINE CRYSTAL
All My Love Kitty
BEYOND CORPORATION Best, Dirk!
OKAY...
YOU CAN OPEN THIS ONE.
THE SEAL OF LATVERIA. THERE IS NO NEED FOR CONCERN. EVERYTHING'S BEEN CAREFULLY SCREENED.
GREETINGS, KING T'CHALLA, QUEEN ORORO.
WHILE I DIDN'T GET AN INVITATION TO TODAY'S BLESSED EVENT, I TAKE NO OFFENSE. CONSIDERING I HAVE BEEN TRAPPED IN HELL FOR SOME TIME, IT WAS FAIR TO PRESUME I WAS UNAVAILABLE.

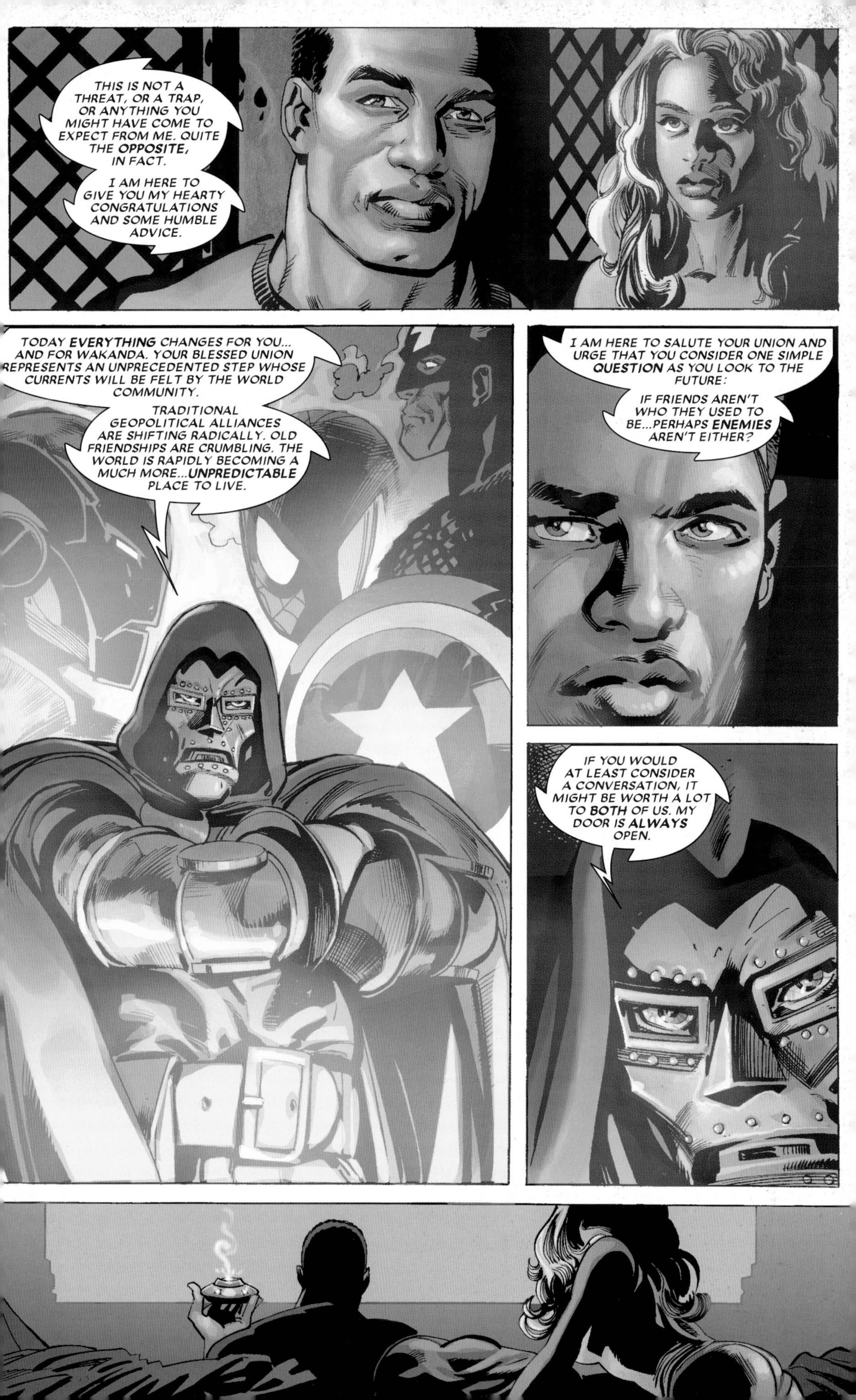
THIS IS NOT A THREAT, OR A TRAP, OR ANYTHING YOU MIGHT HAVE COME TO EXPECT FROM ME. QUITE THE OPPOSITE, IN FACT.
I AM HERE TO GIVE YOU MY HEARTY CONGRATULATIONS AND SOME HUMBLE ADVICE.
TODAY EVERYTHING CHANGES FOR YOU... AND FOR WAKANDA. YOUR BLESSED UNION REPRESENTS AN UNPRECEDENTED STEP WHOSE CURRENTS WILL BE FELT BY THE WORLD COMMUNITY.
TRADITIONAL GEOPOLITICAL ALLIANCES ARE SHIFTING RADICALLY. OLD FRIENDSHIPS ARE CRUMBLING. THE WORLD IS RAPIDLY BECOMING A MUCH MORE...UNPREDICTABLE PLACE TO LIVE.
I AM HERE TO SALUTE YOUR UNION AND URGE THAT YOU CONSIDER ONE SIMPLE QUESTION AS YOU LOOK TO THE FUTURE:
IF FRIENDS AREN'T WHO THEY USED TO BE...PERHAPS ENEMIES AREN'T EITHER?
IF YOU WOULD AT LEAST CONSIDER A CONVERSATION, IT MIGHT BE WORTH A LOT TO BOTH OF US. MY DOOR IS ALWAYS OPEN.

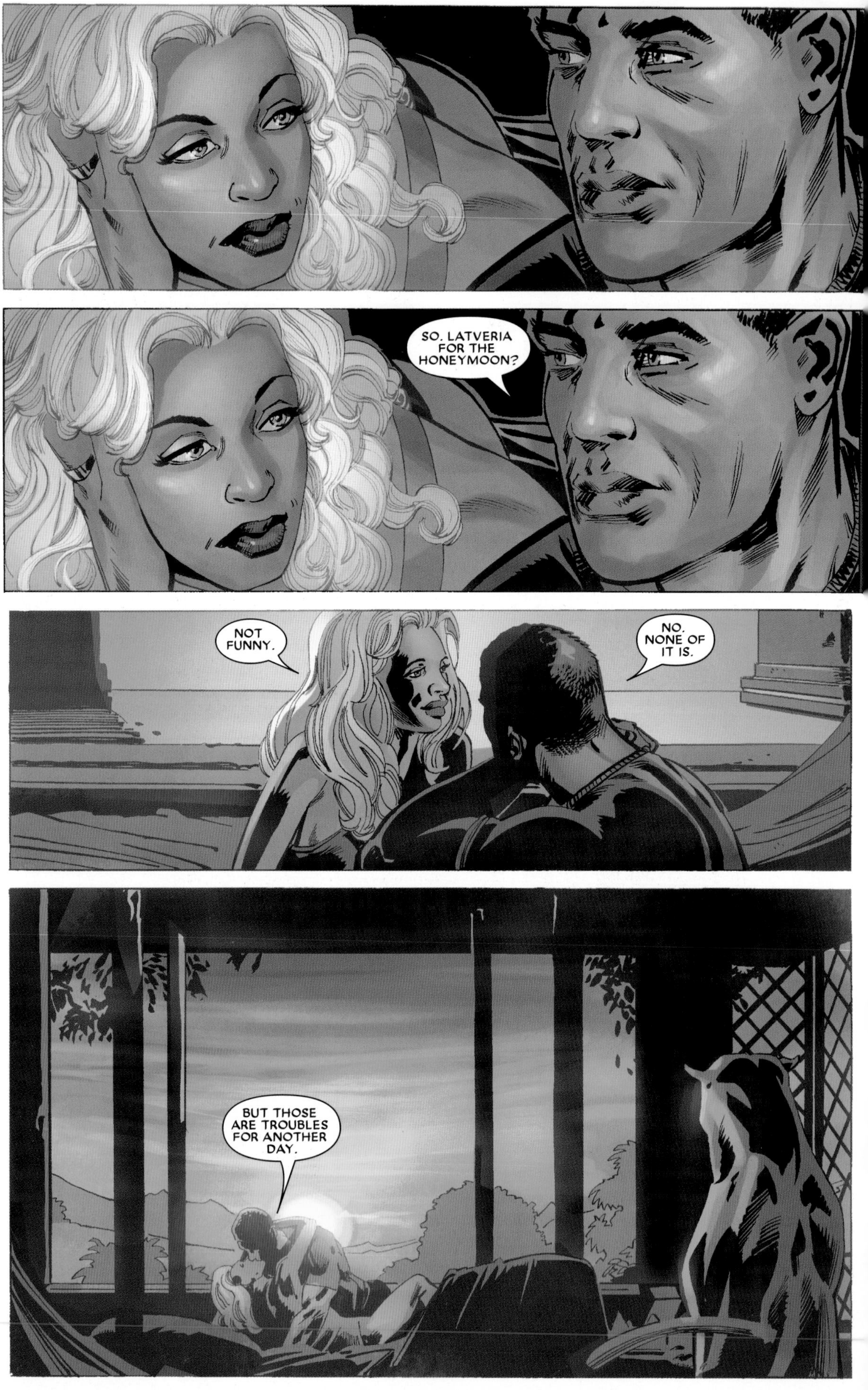
SO. LATVERIA FOR THE HONEYMOON?
NOT FUNNY.
NO. NONE OF IT IS.
BUT THOSE ARE TROUBLES FOR ANOTHER DAY.

MAP OF THE LAND OF THE WAKANDA

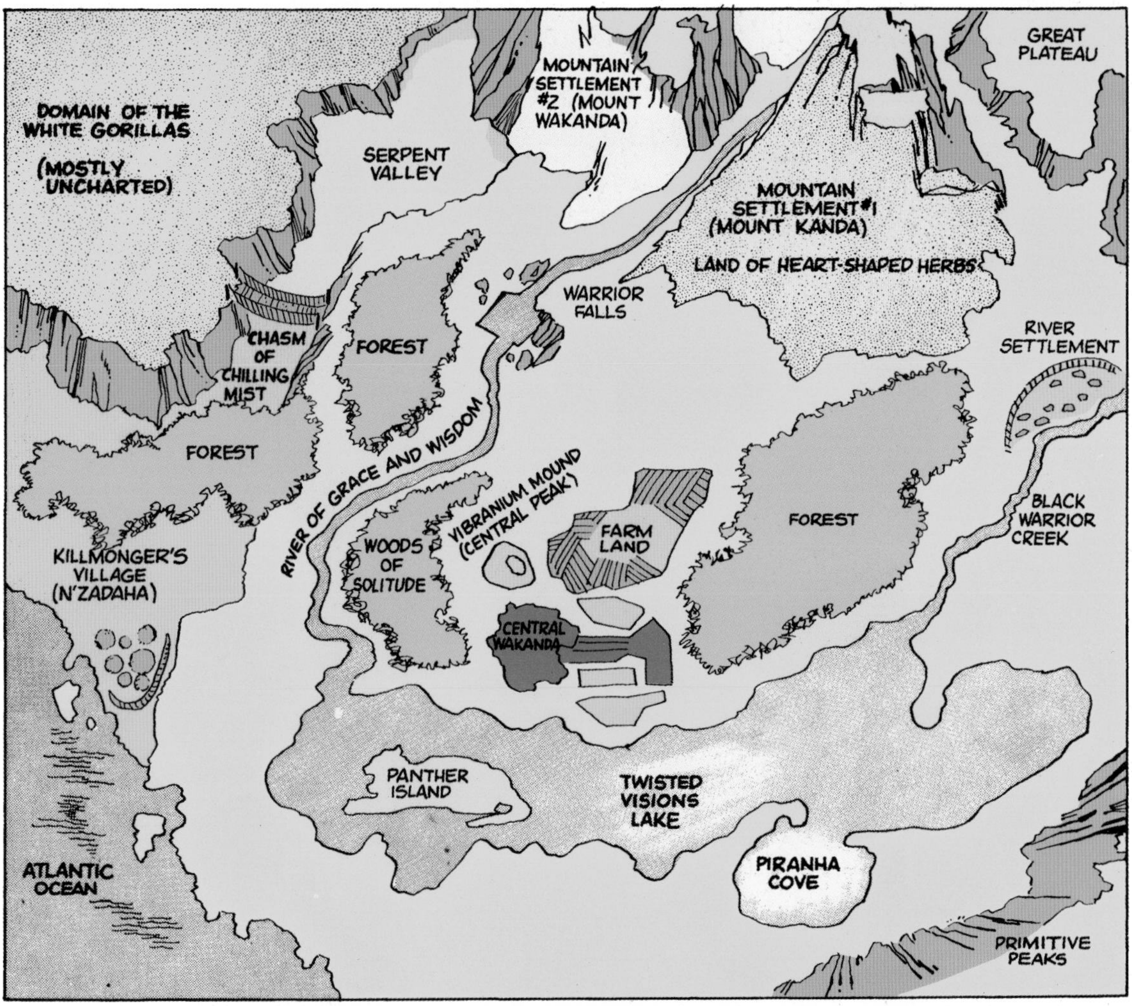

DOMAIN OF THE WHITE GORILLAS
(MOSTLY UNCHARTED)
SERPENT VALLEY
MOUNTAIN SETTLEMENT #2 (MOUNT WAKANDA)
GREAT PLATEAU
MOUNTAIN SETTLEMENT #1 (MOUNT KANDA)
LAND OF HEART-SHAPED HERBS
WARRIOR FALLS
CHASM OF CHILLING MIST
FOREST
RIVER SETTLEMENT
FOREST
RIVER OF GRACE AND WISDOM
VIBRANIUM MOUND (CENTRAL PEAK)
BLACK WARRIOR CREEK
FOREST
FARM LAND
KILLMONGER'S VILLAGE (N'ZADAHA)
WOODS OF SOLITUDE
CENTRAL WAKANDA
PANTHER ISLAND
TWISTED VISIONS LAKE
PIRANHA COVE
ATLANTIC OCEAN
PRIMITIVE PEAKS

CENTRAL WAKANDA

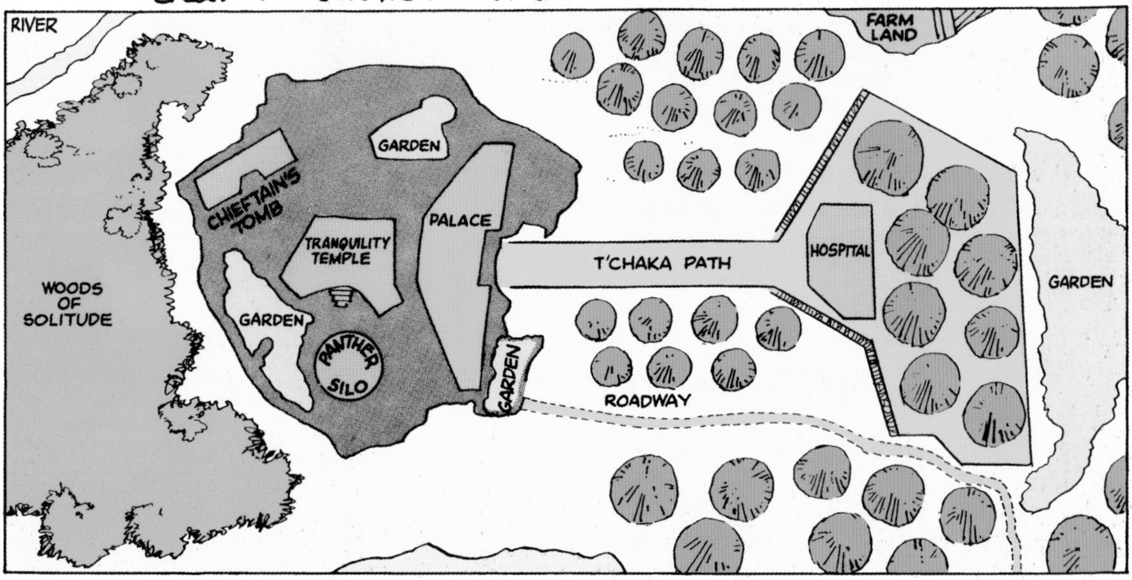

RIVER
FARM LAND
GARDEN
CHIEFTAIN'S TOMB
PALACE
TRANQUILITY TEMPLE
T'CHAKA PATH
HOSPITAL
GARDEN
WOODS OF SOLITUDE
GARDEN
PANTHER SILO
GARDEN
ROADWAY

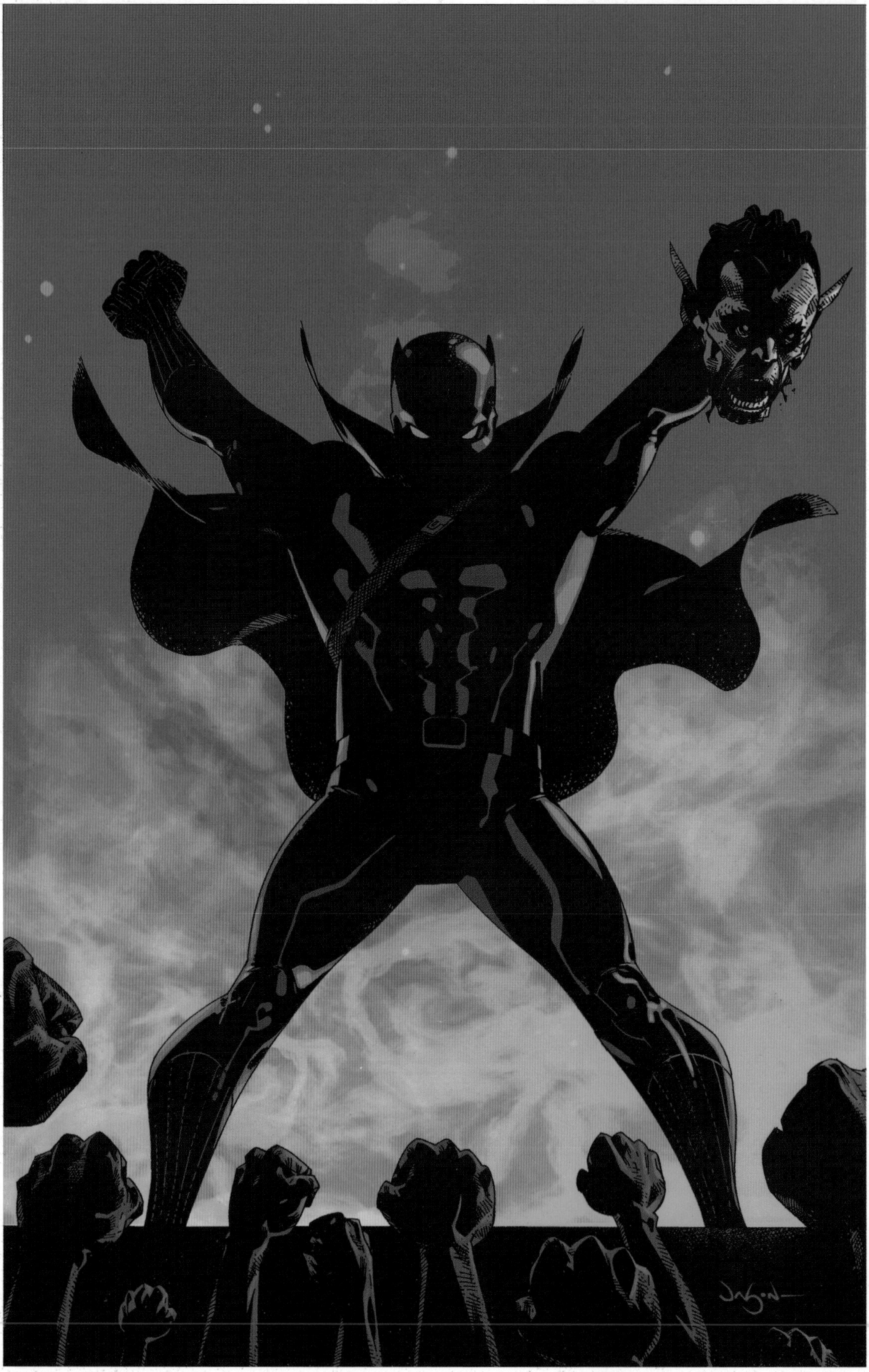

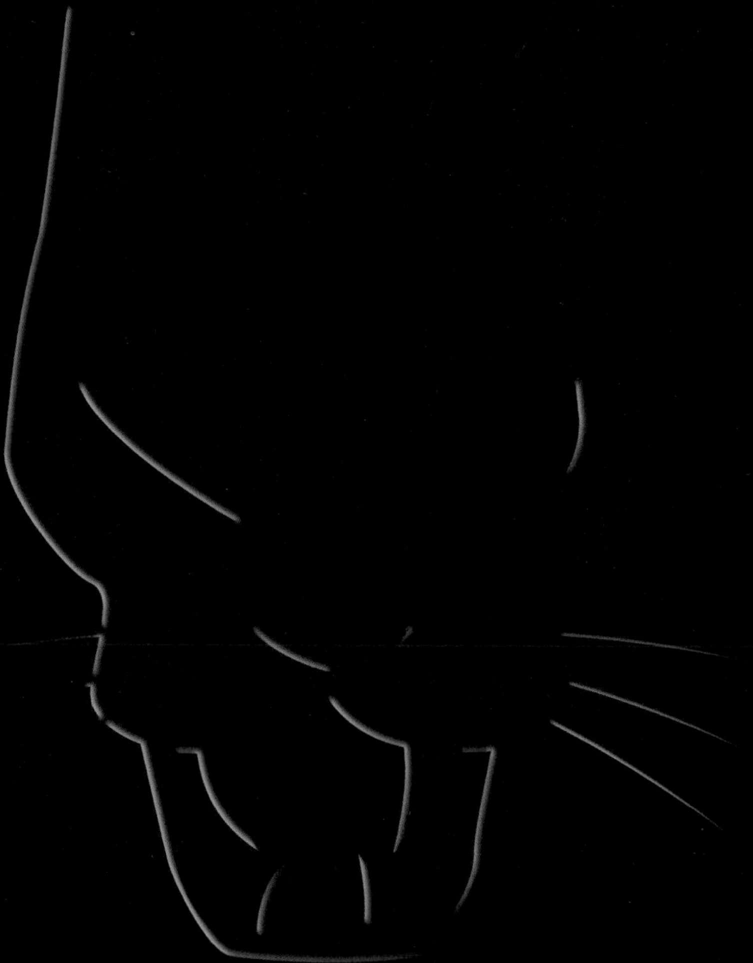

PREVIOUSLY

Unfettered by the yoke of colonization, the African warrior nation of WAKANDA flourished and became a high-tech, resource-rich, ecologically-sound paradise—one that makes the rest of the world seem primitive in comparison. Ruling over this kingdom are the BLACK PANTHER and his queen, STORM.

After a series of adventures with the Fantastic Four, the Black Panther returned home to Wakanda. However, his kingdom was not in the same state in which he left it. His longtime adversary, Erik Killmonger, had seized control of the neighboring country of Niganda and taken T'Challa's sister hostage. While the Black Panther left Wakanda to subdue his foe and rescue his sister, there was a startling discovery made by the Wakandans: T'Challa's friend and adviser Brother Voodoo was found to be an alien Skrull in disguise.

Unbeknownst to the Black Panther, shape-shifting Skrulls have infiltrated Earth. Completely undetectable, they have assumed positions of power in the government, the military, and even in the super hero community. They possess highly advanced technology, a massive armada of warships, enough soldiers to occupy the planet, and a secret weapon—Super Skrulls, who can imitate the powers of multiple heroes. And now, the invasion of Earth they've been planning for years is coming to pass...

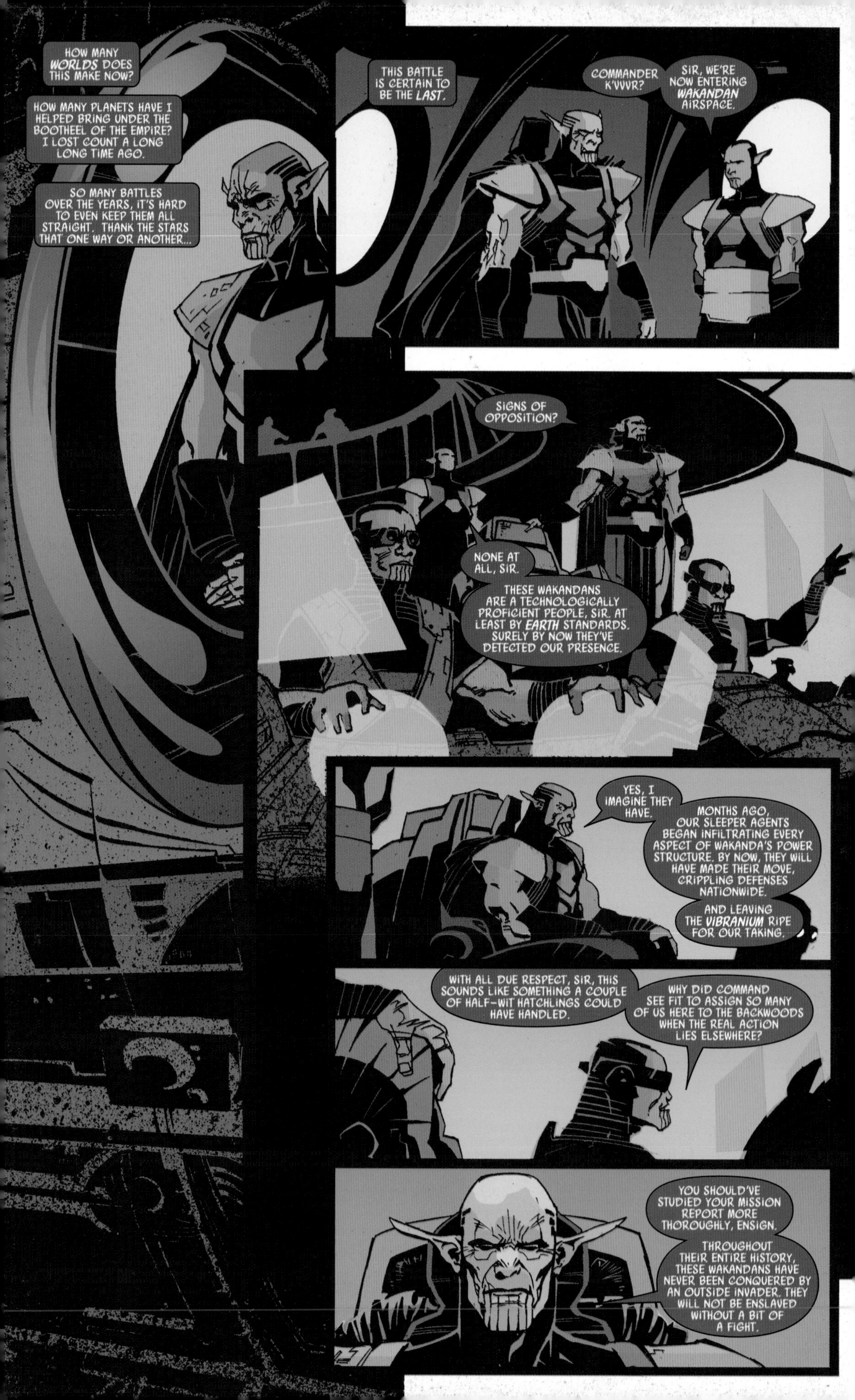

HOW MANY WORLDS DOES THIS MAKE NOW?
HOW MANY PLANETS HAVE I HELPED BRING UNDER THE BOOTHEEL OF THE EMPIRE? I LOST COUNT A LONG LONG TIME AGO.
SO MANY BATTLES OVER THE YEARS, IT'S HARD TO EVEN KEEP THEM ALL STRAIGHT. THANK THE STARS THAT ONE WAY OR ANOTHER...
THIS BATTLE IS CERTAIN TO BE THE LAST.
COMMANDER K'VVVR?
SIR, WE'RE NOW ENTERING WAKANDAN AIRSPACE.
SIGNS OF OPPOSITION?
NONE AT ALL, SIR.
THESE WAKANDANS ARE A TECHNOLOGICALLY PROFICIENT PEOPLE, SIR. AT LEAST BY EARTH STANDARDS. SURELY BY NOW THEY'VE DETECTED OUR PRESENCE.
YES, I IMAGINE THEY HAVE.
MONTHS AGO, OUR SLEEPER AGENTS BEGAN INFILTRATING EVERY ASPECT OF WAKANDA'S POWER STRUCTURE. BY NOW, THEY WILL HAVE MADE THEIR MOVE, CRIPPLING DEFENSES NATIONWIDE.
AND LEAVING THE VIBRANIUM RIPE FOR OUR TAKING.
WITH ALL DUE RESPECT, SIR, THIS SOUNDS LIKE SOMETHING A COUPLE OF HALF-WIT HATCHLINGS COULD HAVE HANDLED.
WHY DID COMMAND SEE FIT TO ASSIGN SO MANY OF US HERE TO THE BACKWOODS WHEN THE REAL ACTION LIES ELSEWHERE?
YOU SHOULD'VE STUDIED YOUR MISSION REPORT MORE THOROUGHLY, ENSIGN.
THROUGHOUT THEIR ENTIRE HISTORY, THESE WAKANDANS HAVE NEVER BEEN CONQUERED BY AN OUTSIDE INVADER. THEY WILL NOT BE ENSLAVED WITHOUT A BIT OF A FIGHT.

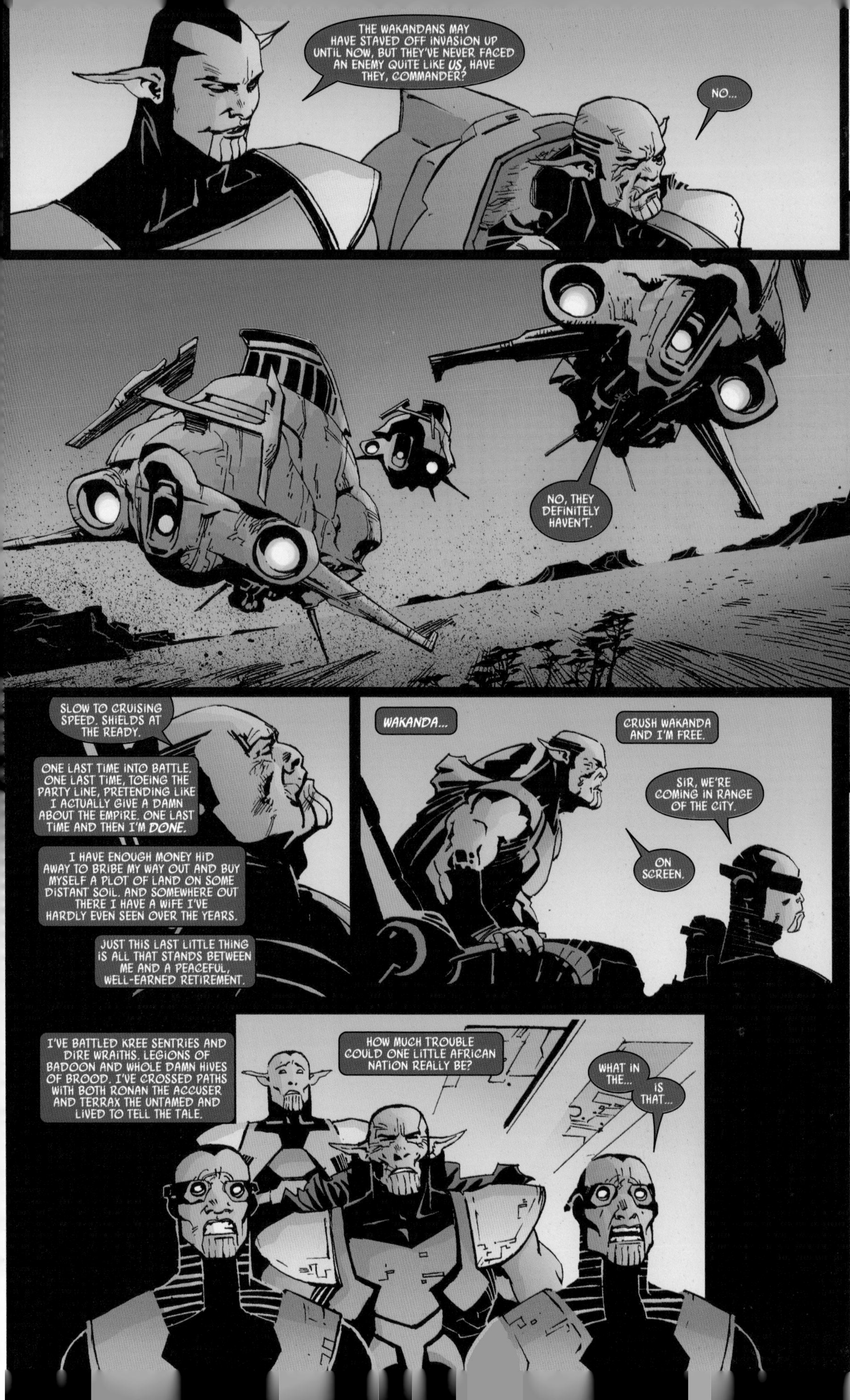
THE WAKANDANS MAY HAVE STAVED OFF INVASION UP UNTIL NOW, BUT THEY'VE NEVER FACED AN ENEMY QUITE LIKE US, HAVE THEY, COMMANDER?
NO...
NO, THEY DEFINITELY HAVEN'T.
SLOW TO CRUISING SPEED. SHIELDS AT THE READY.
ONE LAST TIME INTO BATTLE. ONE LAST TIME, TOEING THE PARTY LINE, PRETENDING LIKE I ACTUALLY GIVE A DAMN ABOUT THE EMPIRE. ONE LAST TIME AND THEN I'M DONE.
I HAVE ENOUGH MONEY HID AWAY TO BRIBE MY WAY OUT AND BUY MYSELF A PLOT OF LAND ON SOME DISTANT SOIL. AND SOMEWHERE OUT THERE I HAVE A WIFE I'VE HARDLY EVEN SEEN OVER THE YEARS.
JUST THIS LAST LITTLE THING IS ALL THAT STANDS BETWEEN ME AND A PEACEFUL, WELL-EARNED RETIREMENT.
WAKANDA...
CRUSH WAKANDA AND I'M FREE.
SIR, WE'RE COMING IN RANGE OF THE CITY.
ON SCREEN.
I'VE BATTLED KREE SENTRIES AND DIRE WRAITHS, LEGIONS OF BADOON AND WHOLE DAMN HIVES OF BROOD. I'VE CROSSED PATHS WITH BOTH RONAN THE ACCUSER AND TERRAX THE UNTAMED AND LIVED TO TELL THE TALE.
HOW MUCH TROUBLE COULD ONE LITTLE AFRICAN NATION REALLY BE?
WHAT IN THE... IS THAT...

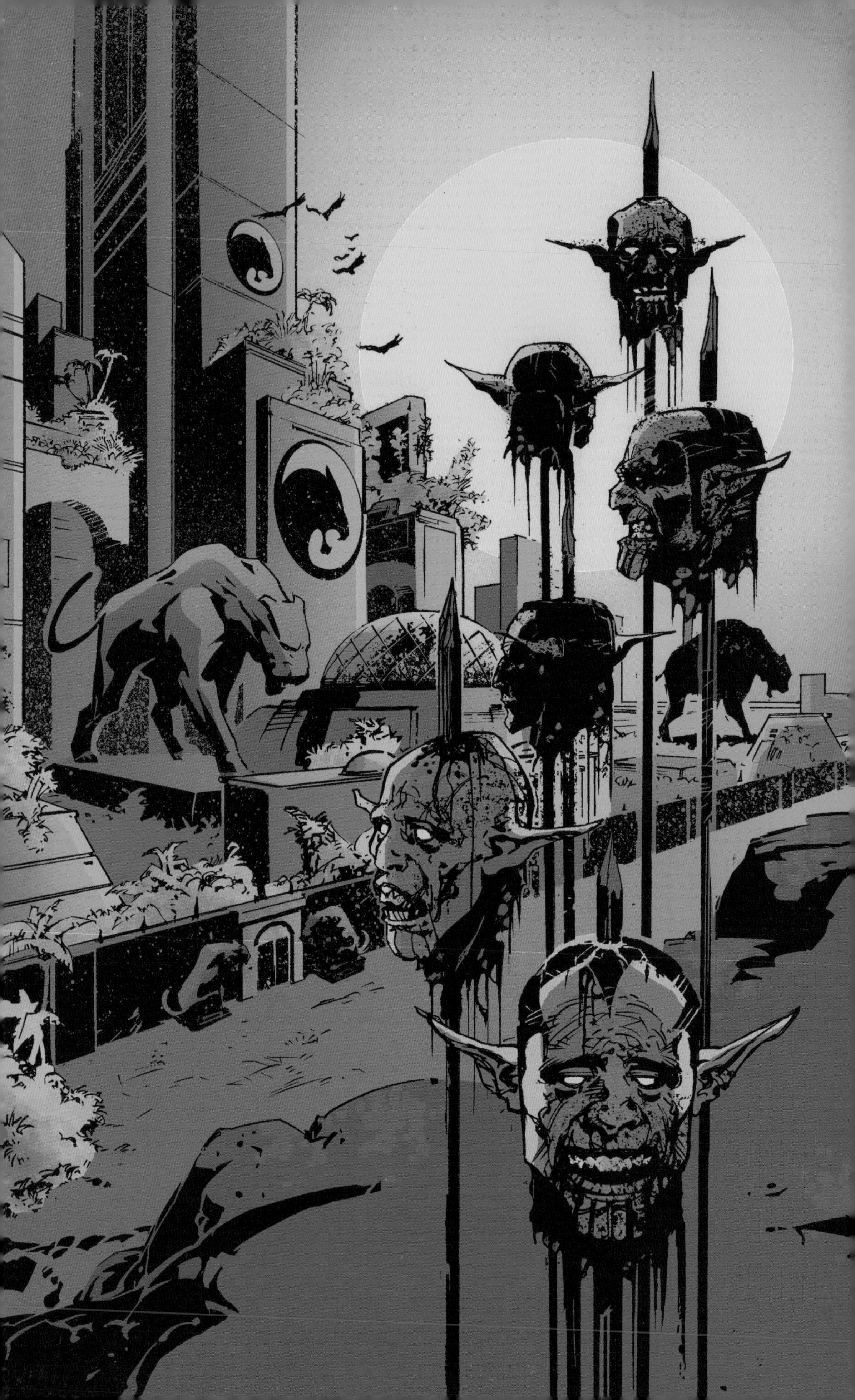

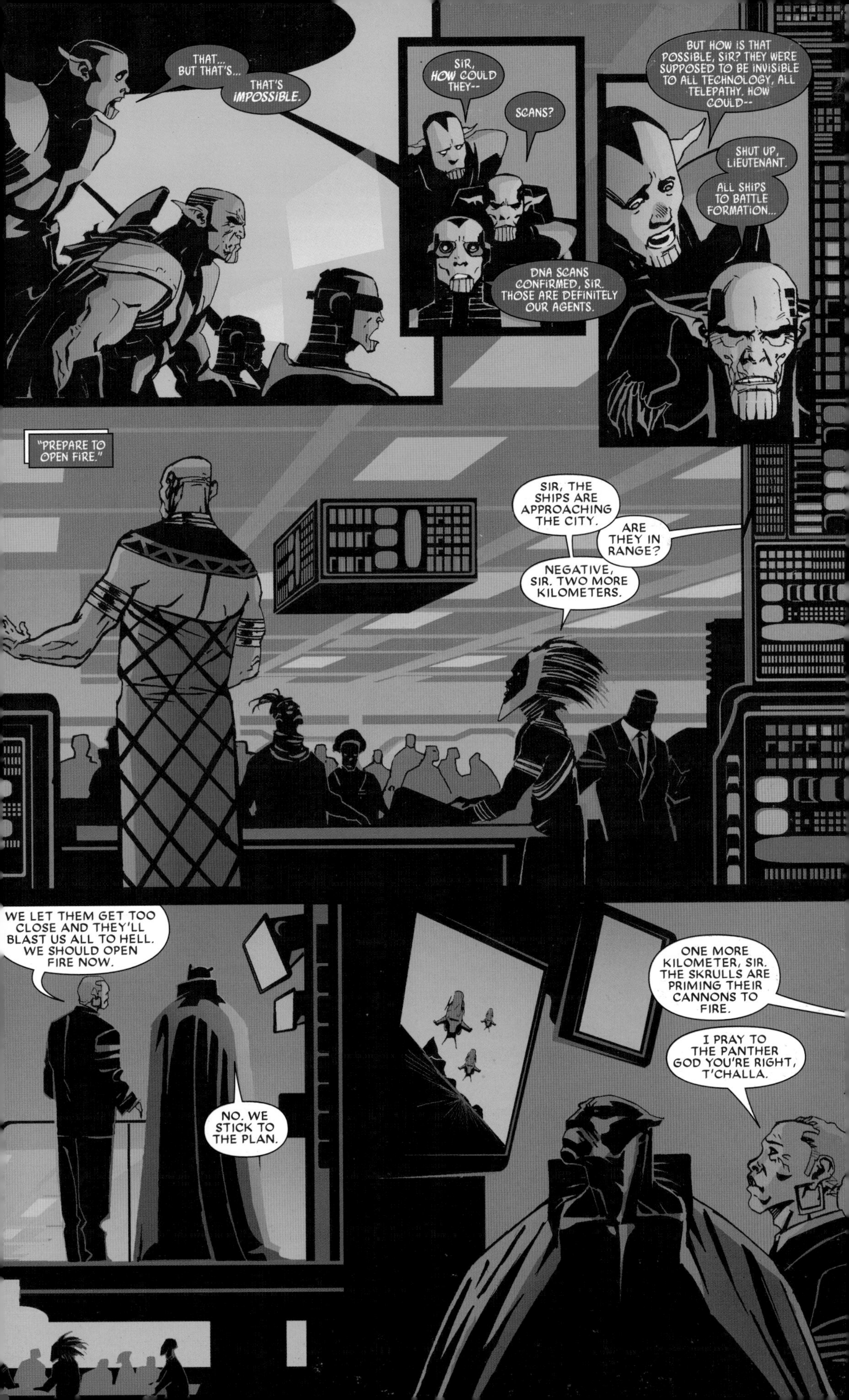
THAT... BUT THAT'S... THAT'S IMPOSSIBLE.
SIR, HOW COULD THEY--
SCANS?
DNA SCANS CONFIRMED, SIR. THOSE ARE DEFINITELY OUR AGENTS.
BUT HOW IS THAT POSSIBLE, SIR? THEY WERE SUPPOSED TO BE INVISIBLE TO ALL TECHNOLOGY, ALL TELEPATHY. HOW COULD--
SHUT UP, LIEUTENANT.
ALL SHIPS TO BATTLE FORMATION...
"PREPARE TO OPEN FIRE."
SIR, THE SHIPS ARE APPROACHING THE CITY.
ARE THEY IN RANGE?
NEGATIVE, SIR. TWO MORE KILOMETERS.
WE LET THEM GET TOO CLOSE AND THEY'LL BLAST US ALL TO HELL. WE SHOULD OPEN FIRE NOW.
NO. WE STICK TO THE PLAN.
ONE MORE KILOMETER, SIR. THE SKRULLS ARE PRIMING THEIR CANNONS TO FIRE.
I PRAY TO THE PANTHER GOD YOU'RE RIGHT, T'CHALLA.

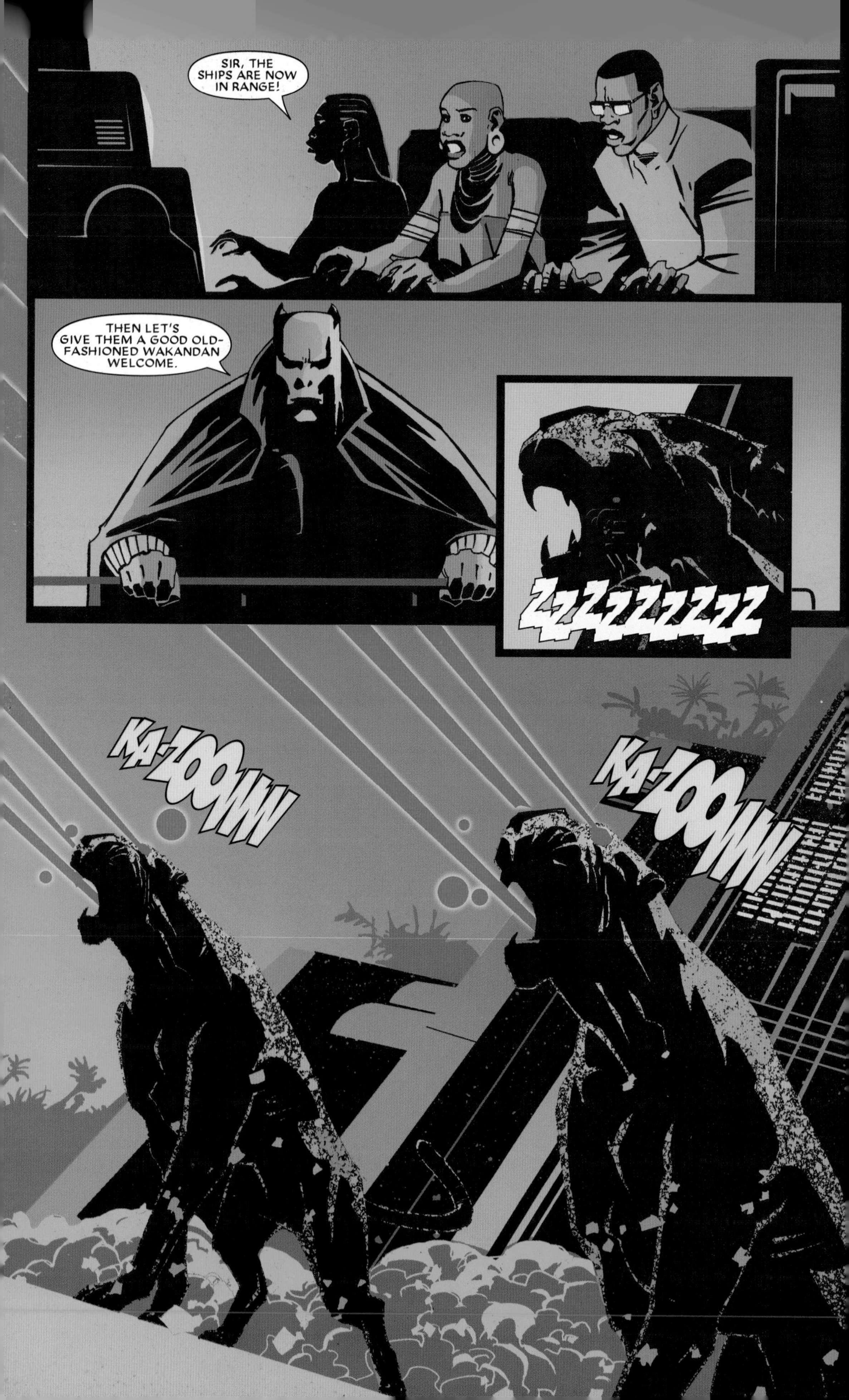
SIR, THE SHIPS ARE NOW IN RANGE!
THEN LET'S GIVE THEM A GOOD OLD-FASHIONED WAKANDAN WELCOME.
ZZZZZZZZZZ
KA-ZOOMM
KA-ZOOMM

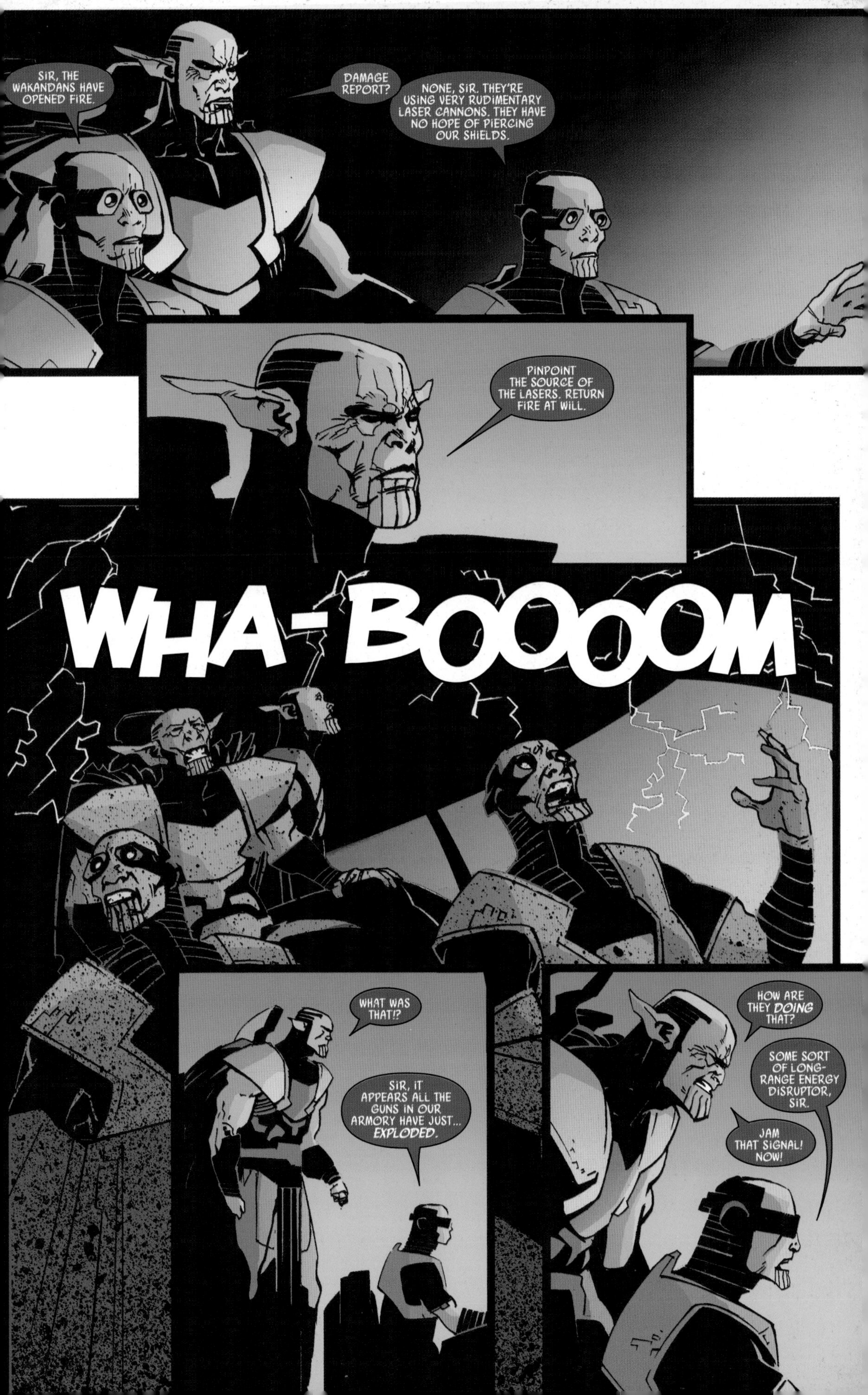
SIR, THE WAKANDANS HAVE OPENED FIRE.
DAMAGE REPORT?
NONE, SIR. THEY'RE USING VERY RUDIMENTARY LASER CANNONS. THEY HAVE NO HOPE OF PIERCING OUR SHIELDS.
PINPOINT THE SOURCE OF THE LASERS. RETURN FIRE AT WILL.
WHA-BOOOOOM
WHAT WAS THAT!?
SIR, IT APPEARS ALL THE GUNS IN OUR ARMORY HAVE JUST... *EXPLODED*.
HOW ARE THEY *DOING* THAT?
SOME SORT OF LONG-RANGE ENERGY DISRUPTOR, SIR.
JAM THAT SIGNAL! NOW!

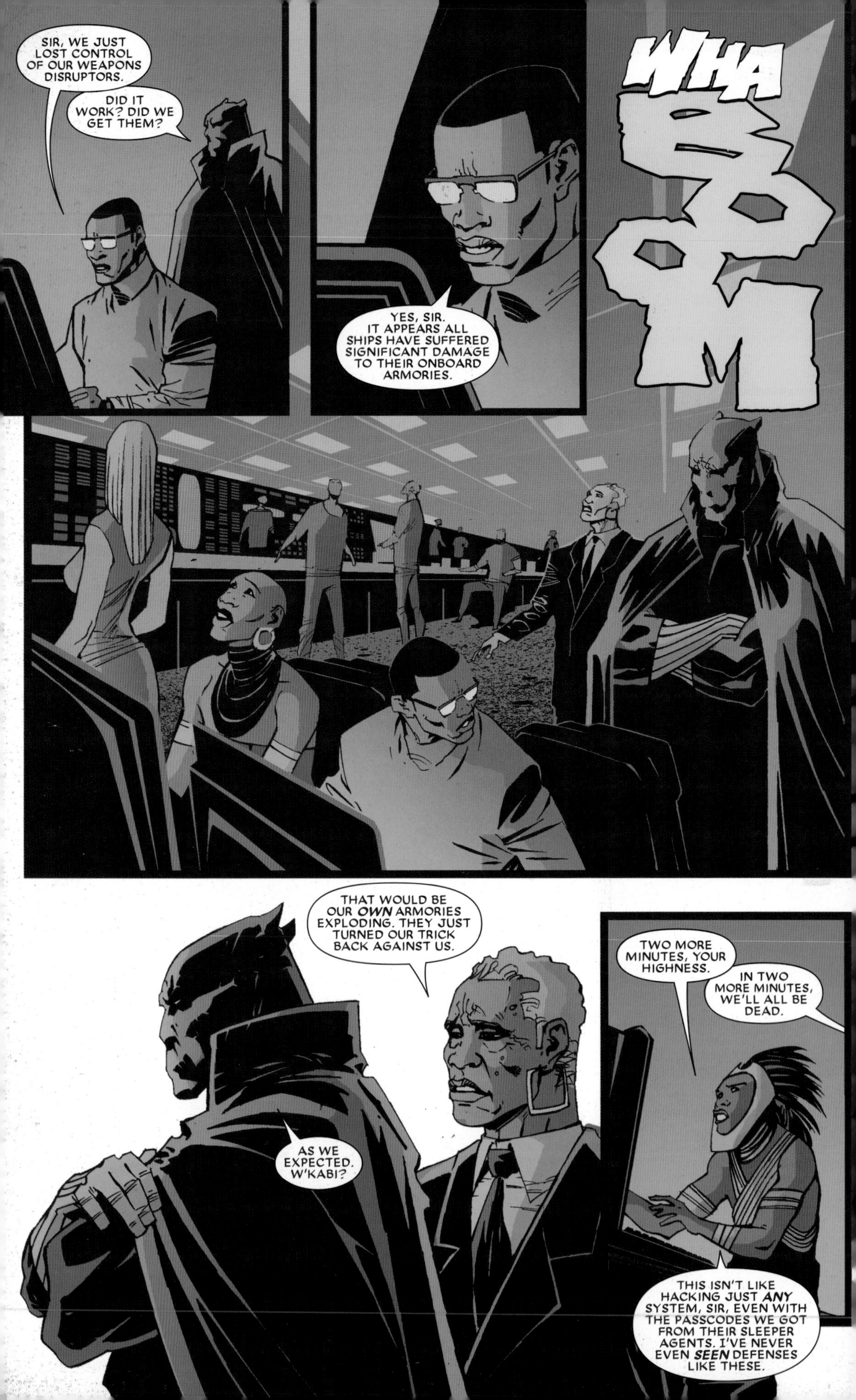

SIR, WE JUST LOST CONTROL OF OUR WEAPONS DISRUPTORS.
DID IT WORK? DID WE GET THEM?
YES, SIR. IT APPEARS ALL SHIPS HAVE SUFFERED SIGNIFICANT DAMAGE TO THEIR ONBOARD ARMORIES.
WHA BOOM
THAT WOULD BE OUR *OWN* ARMORIES EXPLODING. THEY JUST TURNED OUR TRICK BACK AGAINST US.
AS WE EXPECTED. W'KABI?
TWO MORE MINUTES, YOUR HIGHNESS.
IN TWO MORE MINUTES, WE'LL ALL BE DEAD.
THIS ISN'T LIKE HACKING JUST *ANY* SYSTEM, SIR, EVEN WITH THE PASSCODES WE GOT FROM THEIR SLEEPER AGENTS. I'VE NEVER EVEN *SEEN* DEFENSES LIKE THESE.

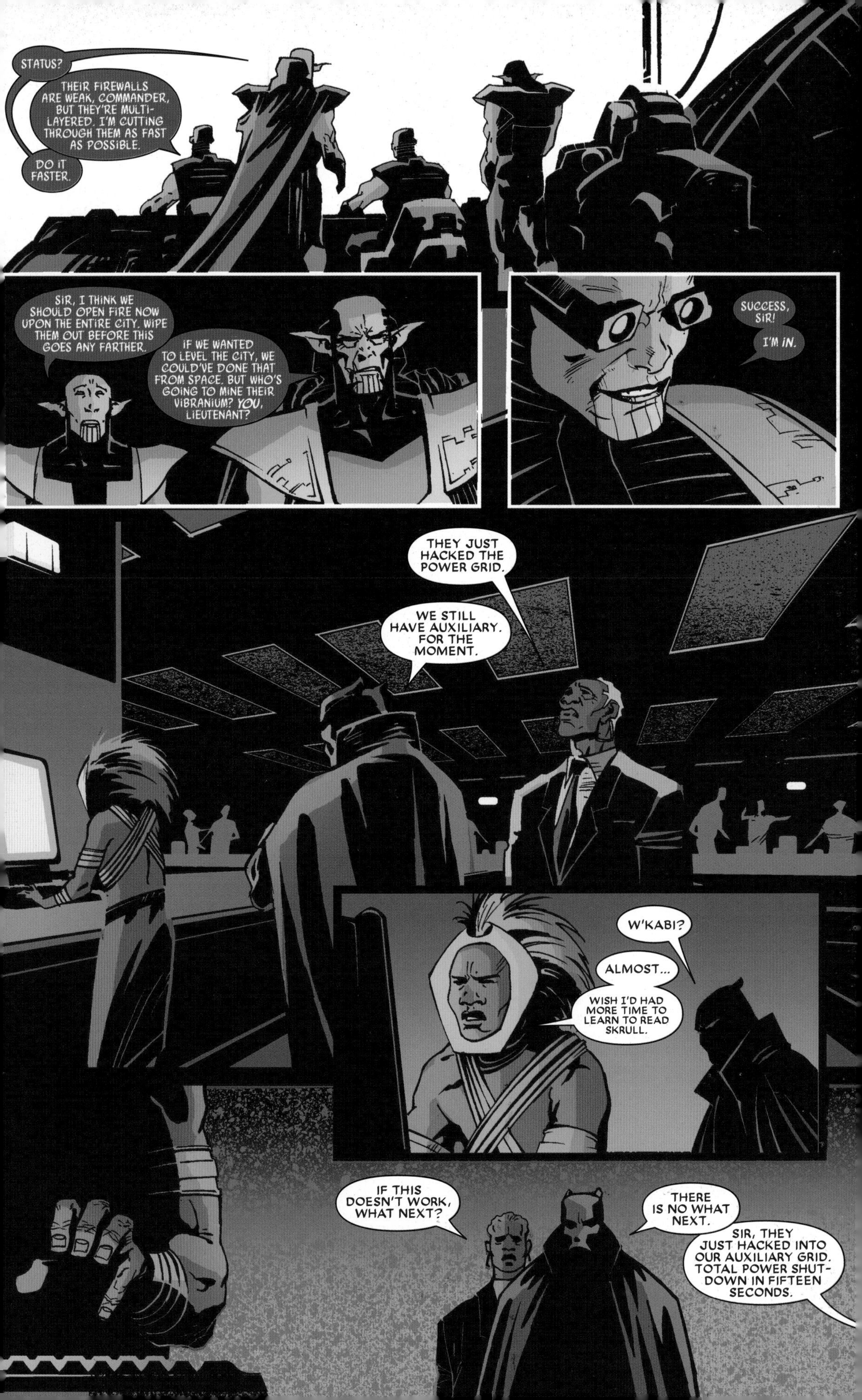
STATUS?
THEIR FIREWALLS ARE WEAK, COMMANDER, BUT THEY'RE MULTI-LAYERED. I'M CUTTING THROUGH THEM AS FAST AS POSSIBLE.
DO IT FASTER.
SIR, I THINK WE SHOULD OPEN FIRE NOW UPON THE ENTIRE CITY. WIPE THEM OUT BEFORE THIS GOES ANY FARTHER.
IF WE WANTED TO LEVEL THE CITY, WE COULD'VE DONE THAT FROM SPACE. BUT WHO'S GOING TO MINE THEIR VIBRANIUM? YOU, LIEUTENANT?
SUCCESS, SIR!
I'M IN.
THEY JUST HACKED THE POWER GRID.
WE STILL HAVE AUXILIARY. FOR THE MOMENT.
W'KABI?
ALMOST...
WISH I'D HAD MORE TIME TO LEARN TO READ SKRULL.
IF THIS DOESN'T WORK, WHAT NEXT?
THERE IS NO WHAT NEXT.
SIR, THEY JUST HACKED INTO OUR AUXILIARY GRID. TOTAL POWER SHUT-DOWN IN FIFTEEN SECONDS.

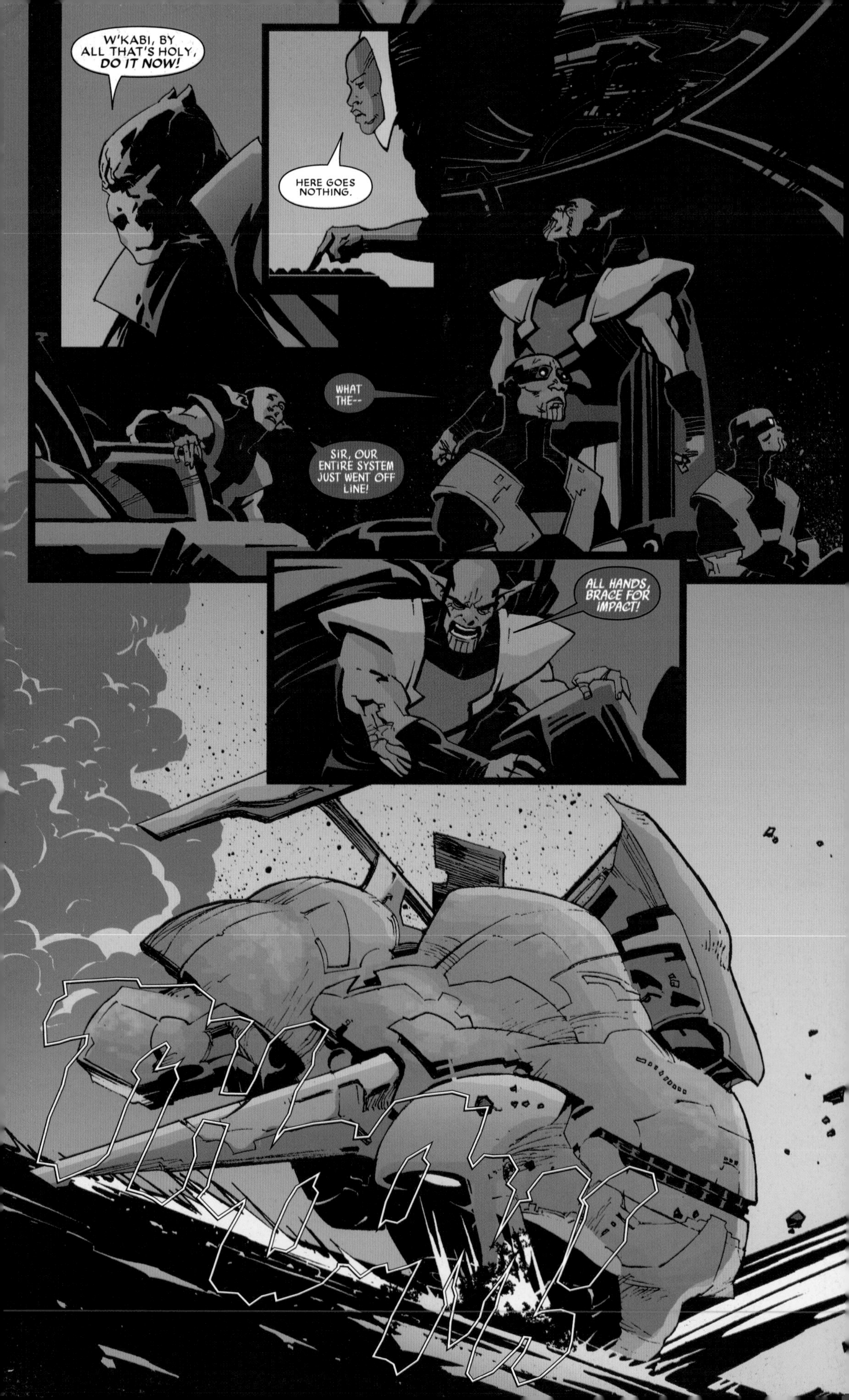
W'KABI, BY ALL THAT'S HOLY, DO IT NOW!
HERE GOES NOTHING.
WHAT THE--
SIR, OUR ENTIRE SYSTEM JUST WENT OFF LINE!
ALL HANDS, BRACE FOR IMPACT!

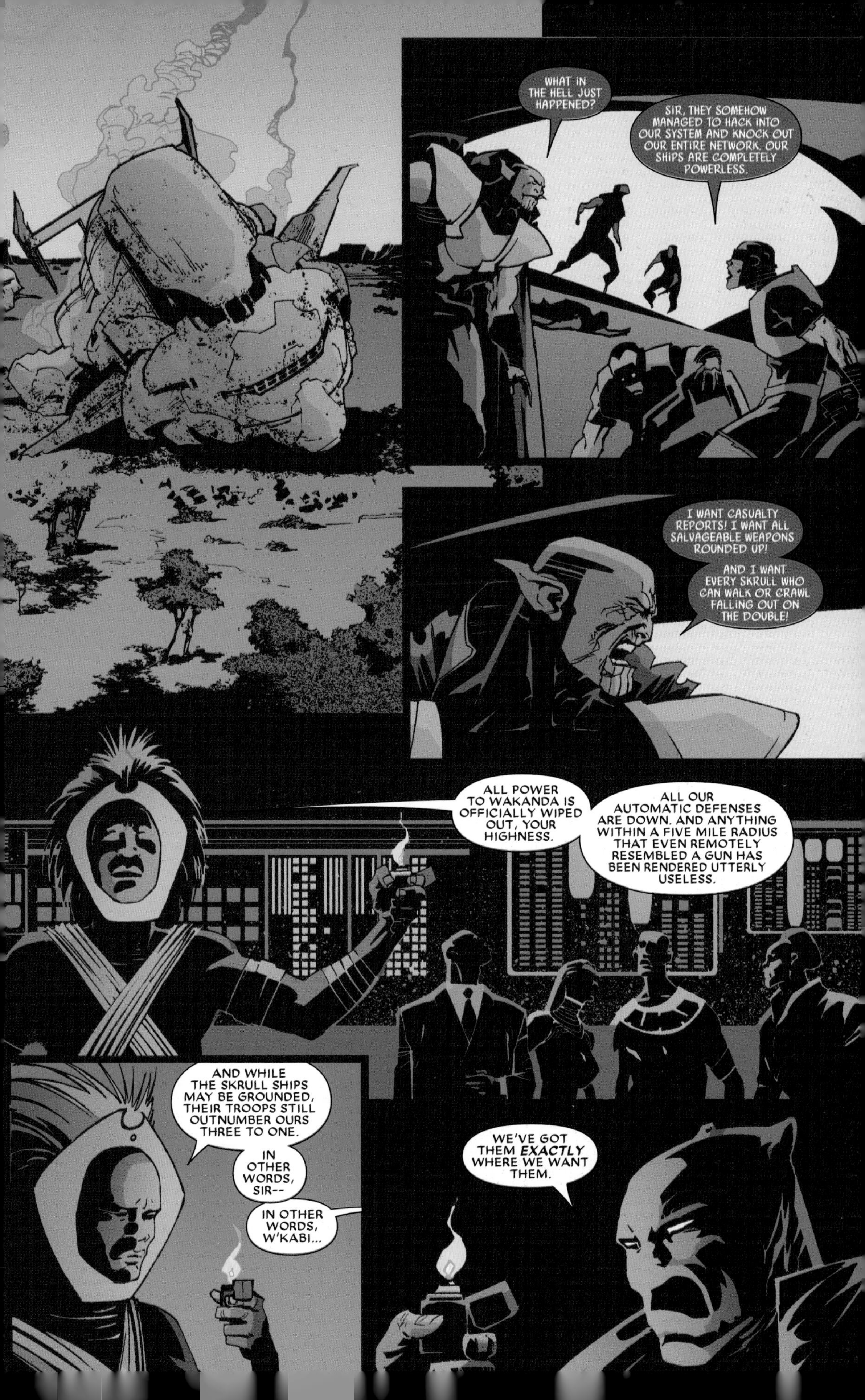
WHAT IN THE HELL JUST HAPPENED?
SIR, THEY SOMEHOW MANAGED TO HACK INTO OUR SYSTEM AND KNOCK OUT OUR ENTIRE NETWORK. OUR SHIPS ARE COMPLETELY POWERLESS.
I WANT CASUALTY REPORTS! I WANT ALL SALVAGEABLE WEAPONS ROUNDED UP!
AND I WANT EVERY SKRULL WHO CAN WALK OR CRAWL FALLING OUT ON THE DOUBLE!
ALL POWER TO WAKANDA IS OFFICIALLY WIPED OUT, YOUR HIGHNESS.
ALL OUR AUTOMATIC DEFENSES ARE DOWN. AND ANYTHING WITHIN A FIVE MILE RADIUS THAT EVEN REMOTELY RESEMBLED A GUN HAS BEEN RENDERED UTTERLY USELESS.
AND WHILE THE SKRULL SHIPS MAY BE GROUNDED, THEIR TROOPS STILL OUTNUMBER OURS THREE TO ONE.
IN OTHER WORDS, SIR--
IN OTHER WORDS, W'KABI...
WE'VE GOT THEM EXACTLY WHERE WE WANT THEM.

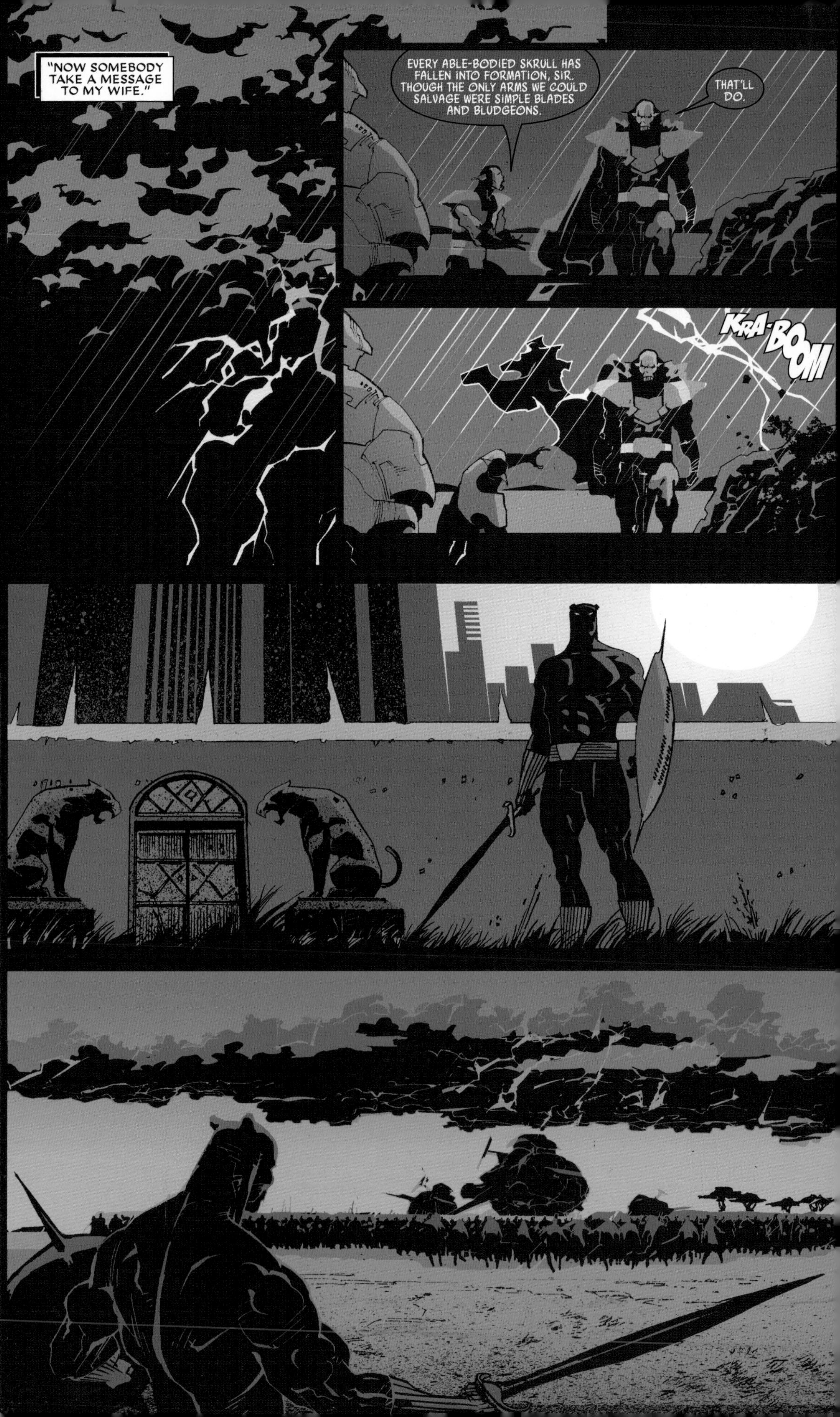
"NOW SOMEBODY TAKE A MESSAGE TO MY WIFE."
EVERY ABLE-BODIED SKRULL HAS FALLEN INTO FORMATION, SIR. THOUGH THE ONLY ARMS WE COULD SALVAGE WERE SIMPLE BLADES AND BLUDGEONS.
THAT'LL DO.
KRA-BOOM

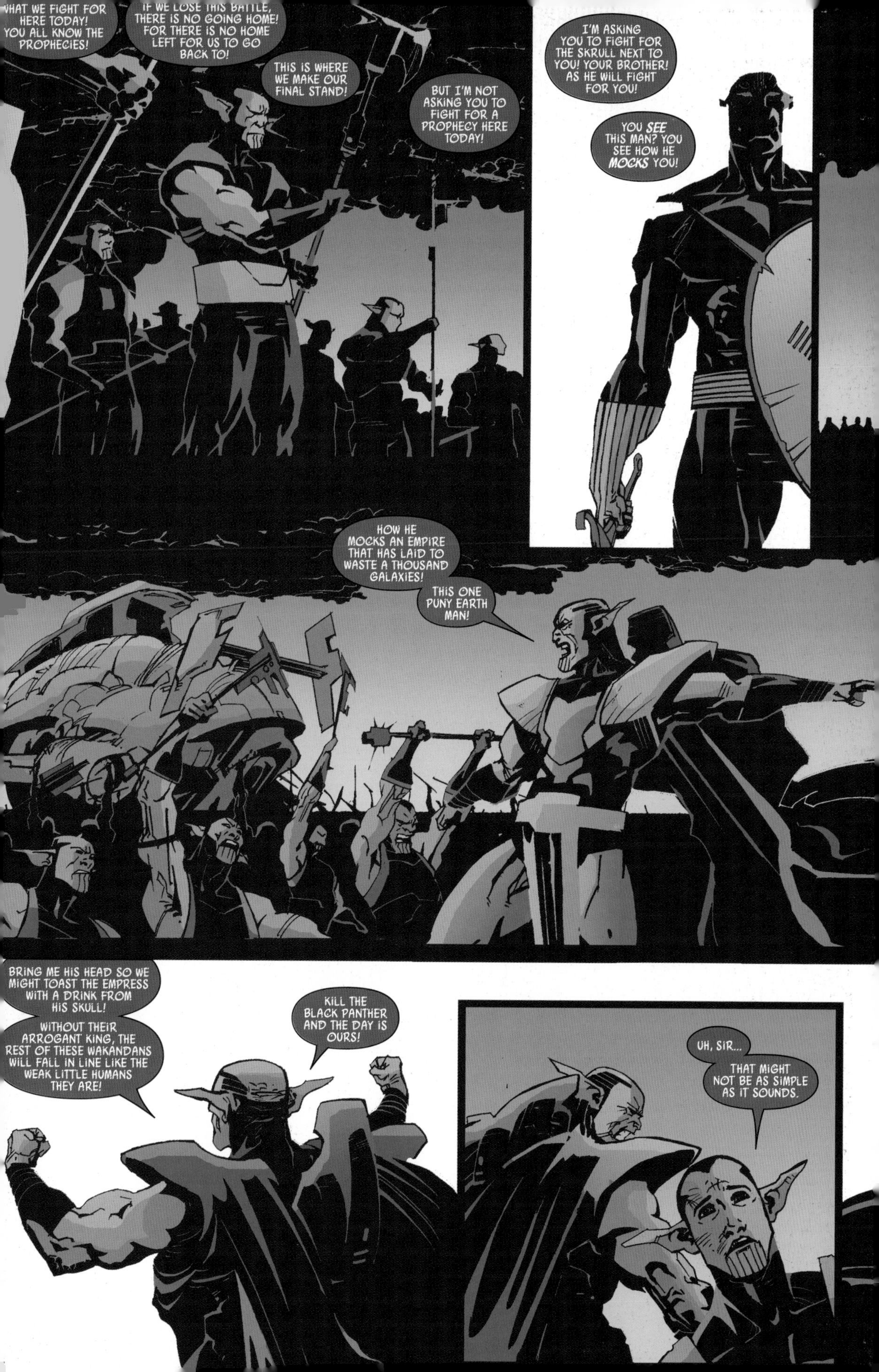
WHAT WE FIGHT FOR HERE TODAY! YOU ALL KNOW THE PROPHECIES!
IF WE LOSE THIS BATTLE, THERE IS NO GOING HOME! FOR THERE IS NO HOME LEFT FOR US TO GO BACK TO!
THIS IS WHERE WE MAKE OUR FINAL STAND!
BUT I'M NOT ASKING YOU TO FIGHT FOR A PROPHECY HERE TODAY!
I'M ASKING YOU TO FIGHT FOR THE SKRULL NEXT TO YOU! YOUR BROTHER! AS HE WILL FIGHT FOR YOU!
YOU SEE THIS MAN? YOU SEE HOW HE MOCKS YOU!
HOW HE MOCKS AN EMPIRE THAT HAS LAID TO WASTE A THOUSAND GALAXIES!
THIS ONE PUNY EARTH MAN!
BRING ME HIS HEAD SO WE MIGHT TOAST THE EMPRESS WITH A DRINK FROM HIS SKULL!
WITHOUT THEIR ARROGANT KING, THE REST OF THESE WAKANDANS WILL FALL IN LINE LIKE THE WEAK LITTLE HUMANS THEY ARE!
KILL THE BLACK PANTHER AND THE DAY IS OURS!
UH, SIR...
THAT MIGHT NOT BE AS SIMPLE AS IT SOUNDS.

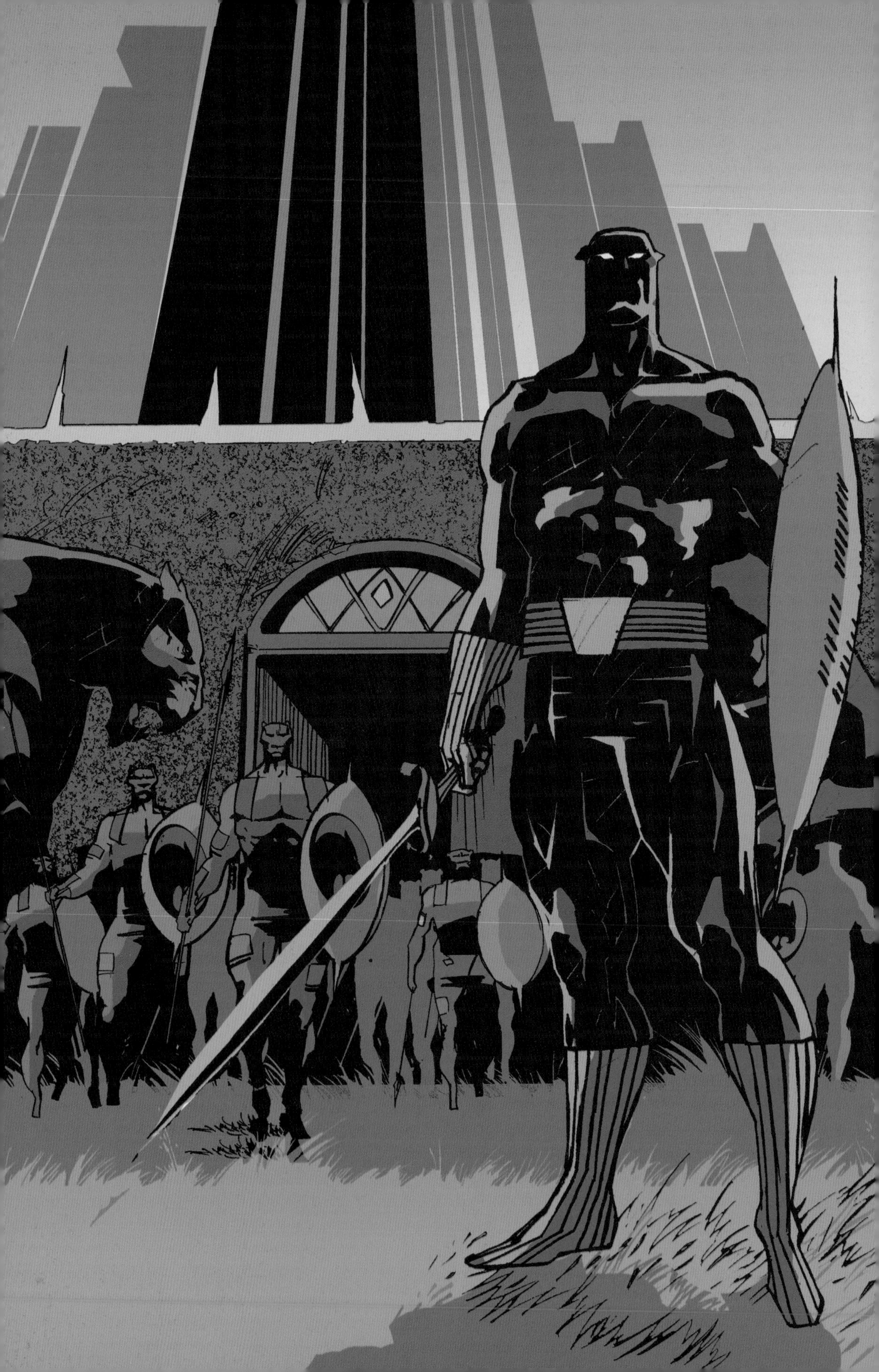

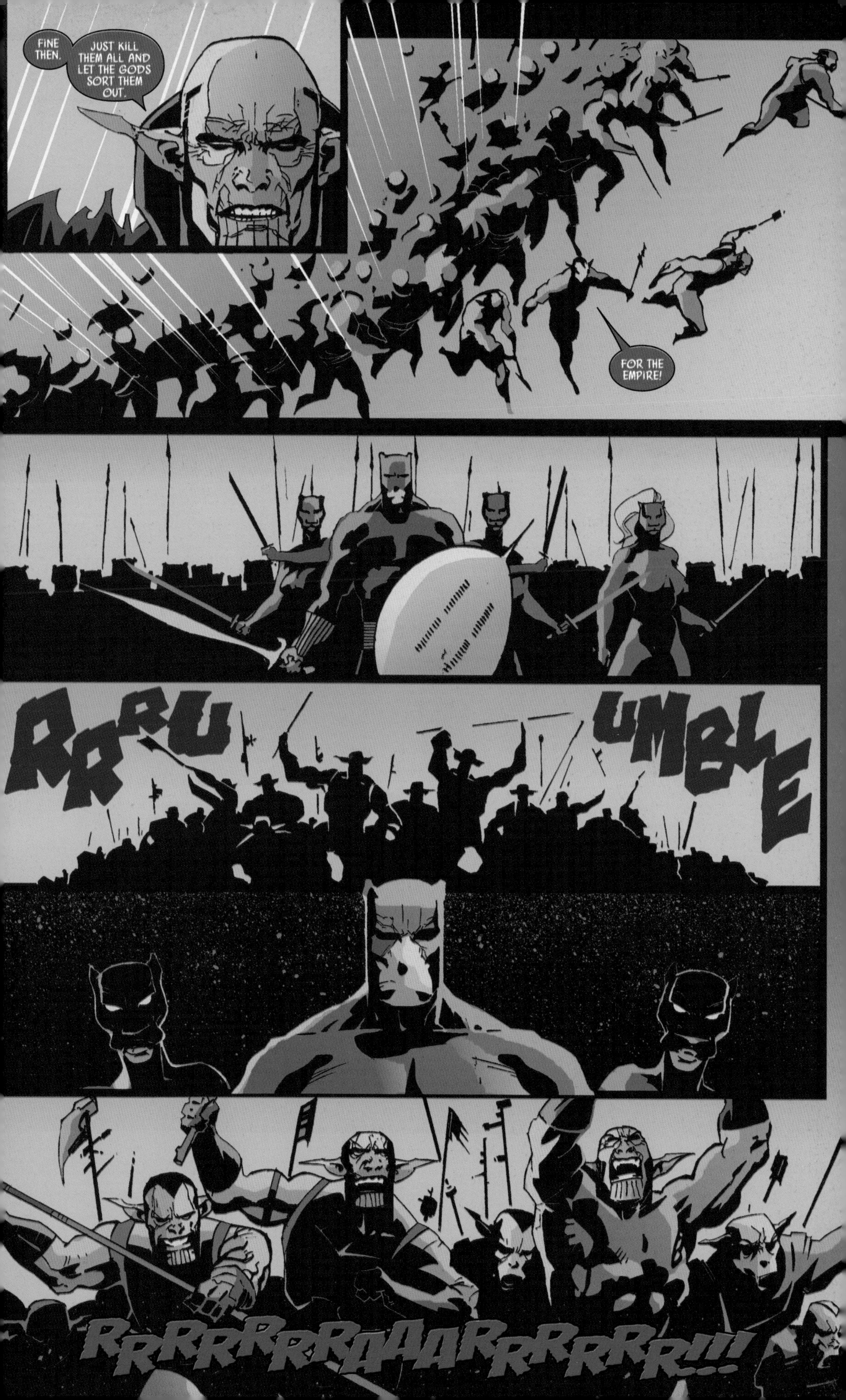
FINE THEN.
JUST KILL THEM ALL AND LET THE GODS SORT THEM OUT.
FOR THE EMPIRE!
RRRUUMBLE
RRRRRRRAAAARRRRRRR!!!

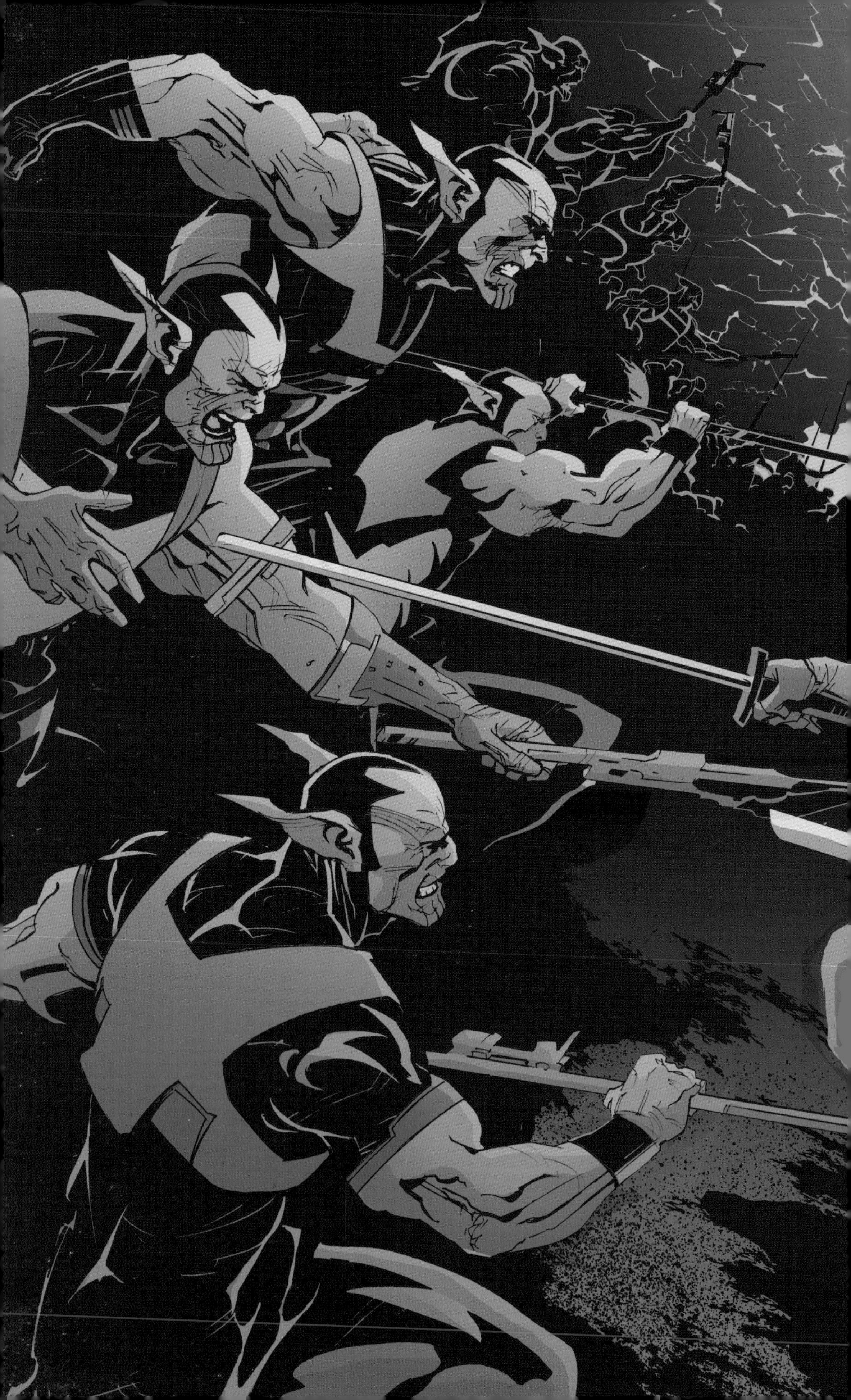

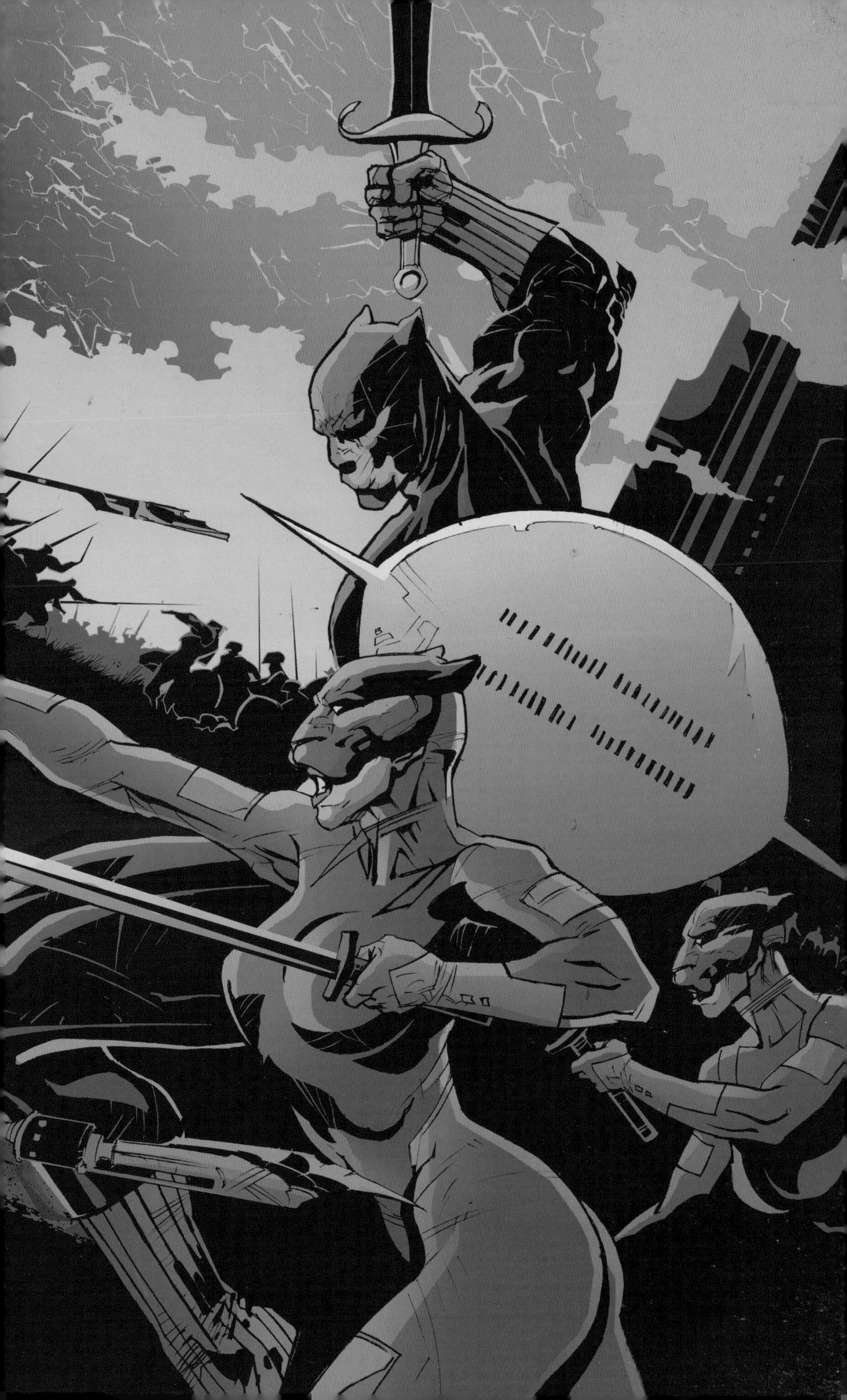

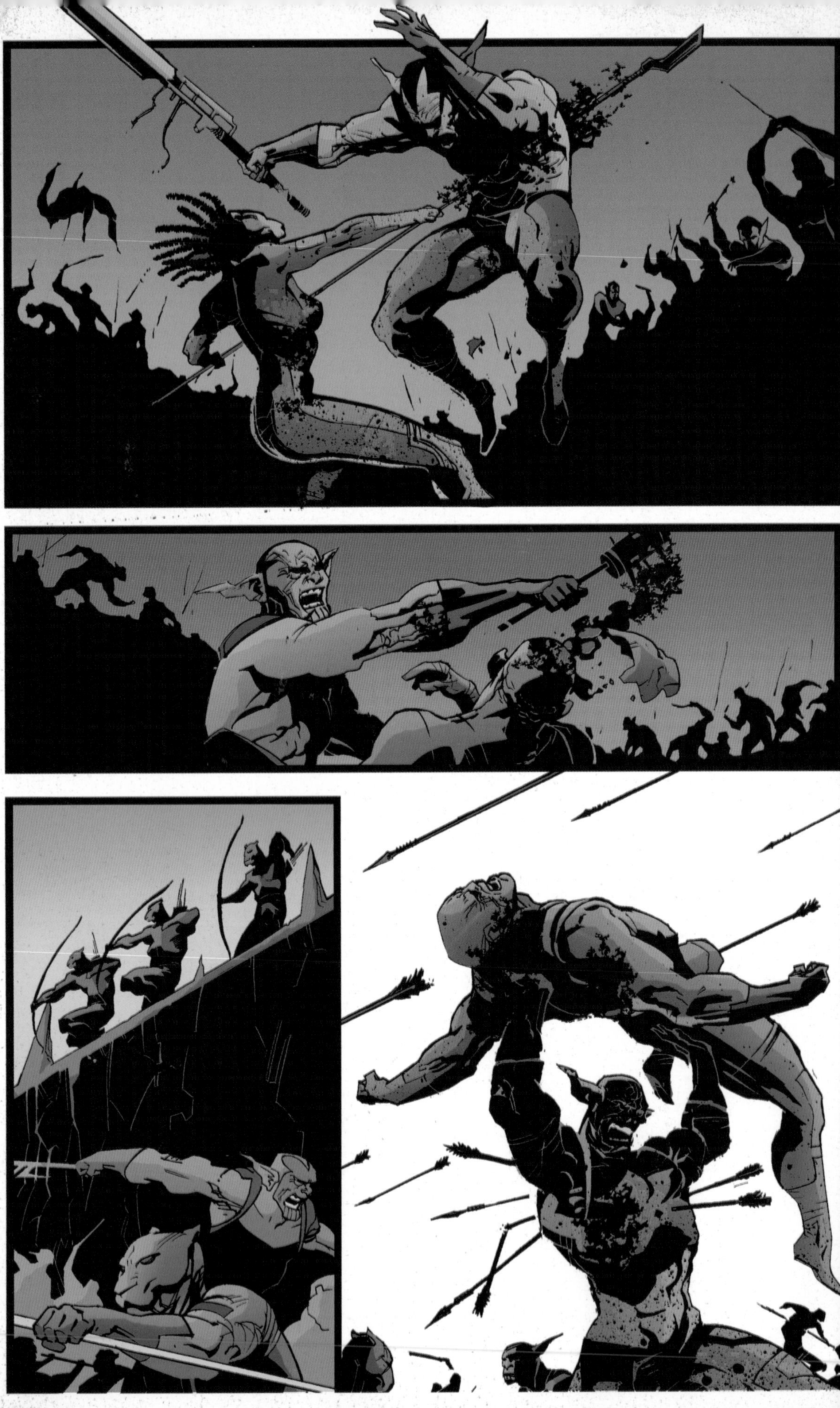

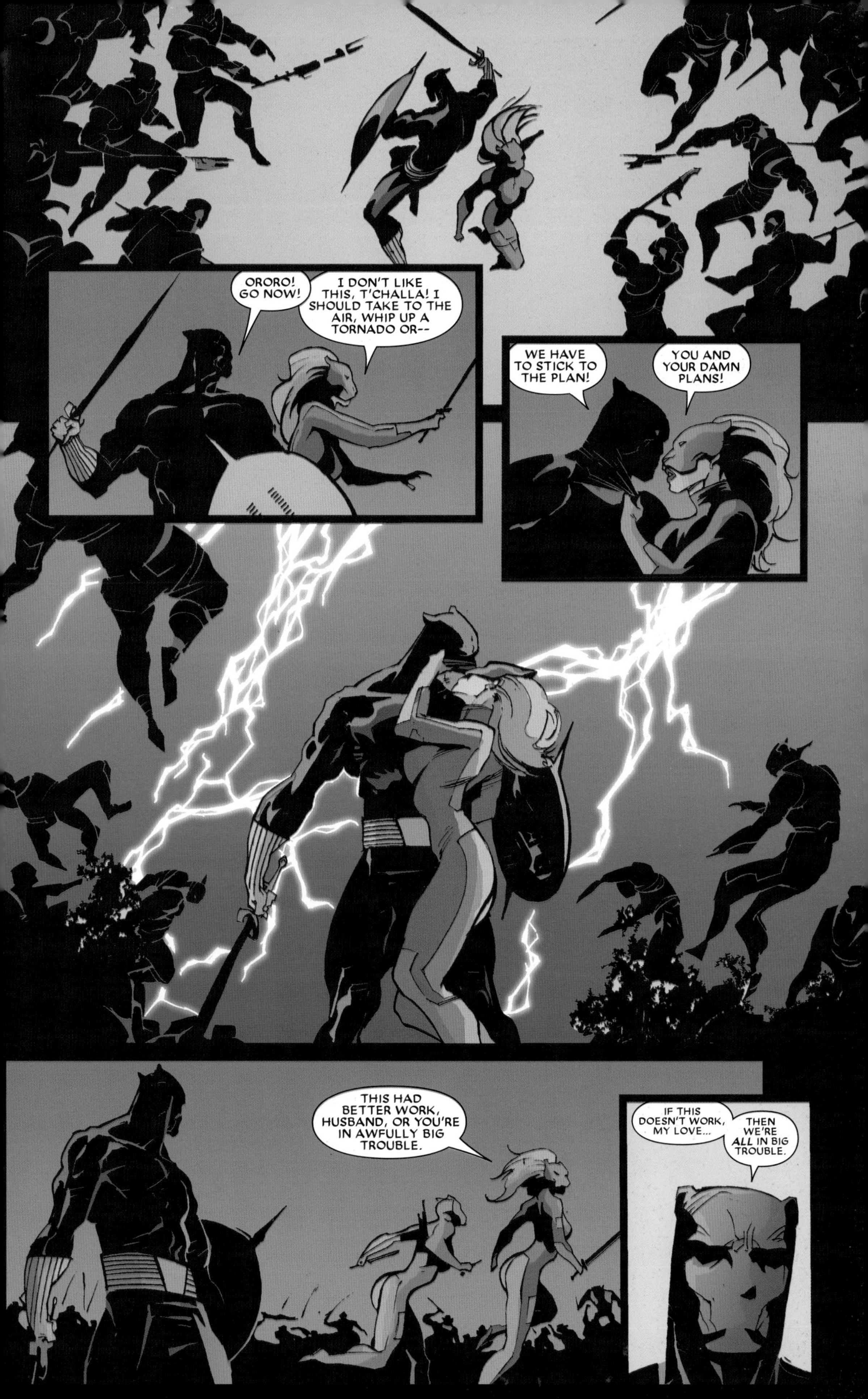
ORORO! GO NOW!
I DON'T LIKE THIS, T'CHALLA! I SHOULD TAKE TO THE AIR, WHIP UP A TORNADO OR--
WE HAVE TO STICK TO THE PLAN!
YOU AND YOUR DAMN PLANS!
THIS HAD BETTER WORK, HUSBAND, OR YOU'RE IN AWFULLY BIG TROUBLE.
IF THIS DOESN'T WORK, MY LOVE...
THEN WE'RE *ALL* IN BIG TROUBLE.

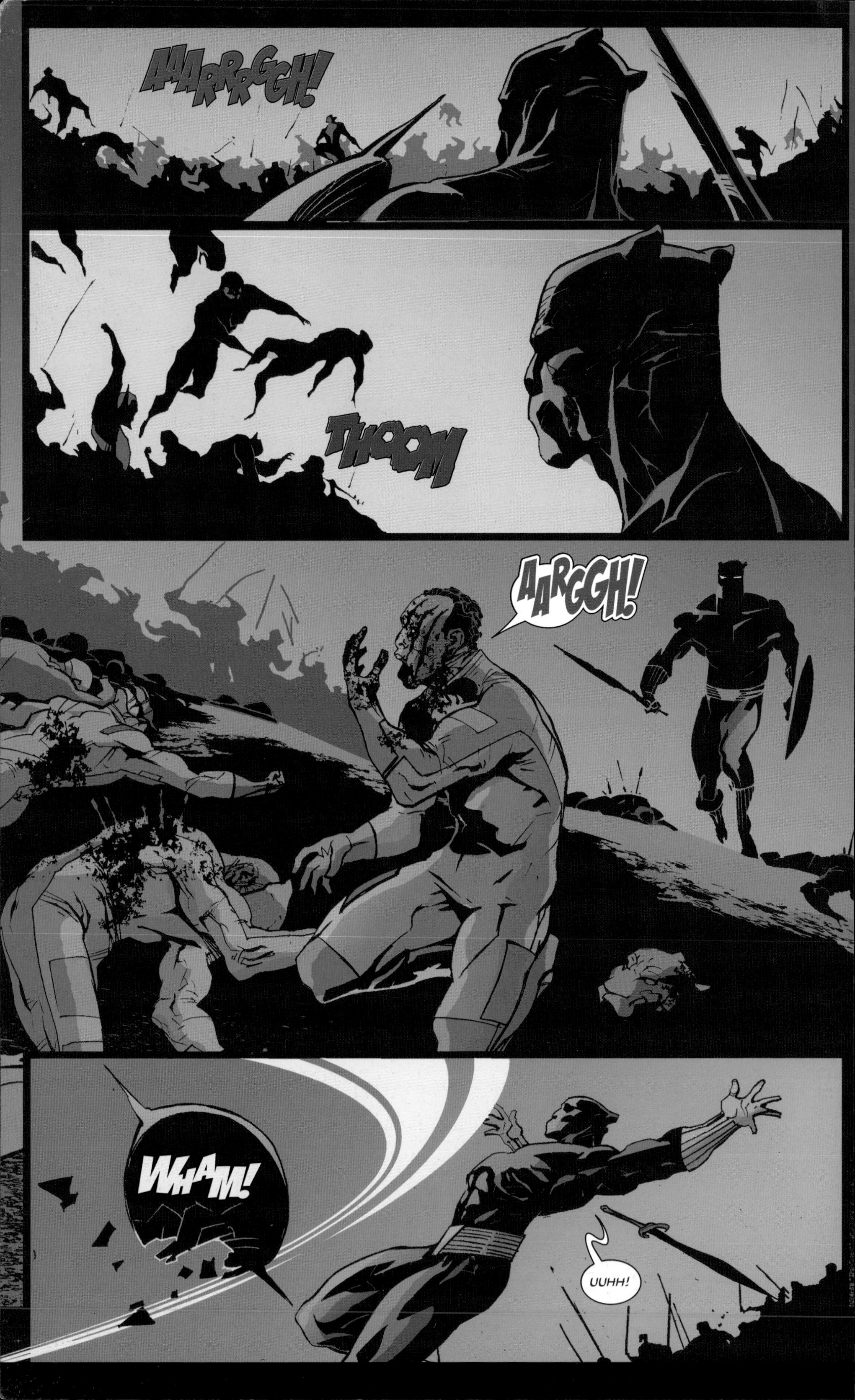
AAARRRGGH!
THOOM
AARGGH!
WHAM!
UUHH!

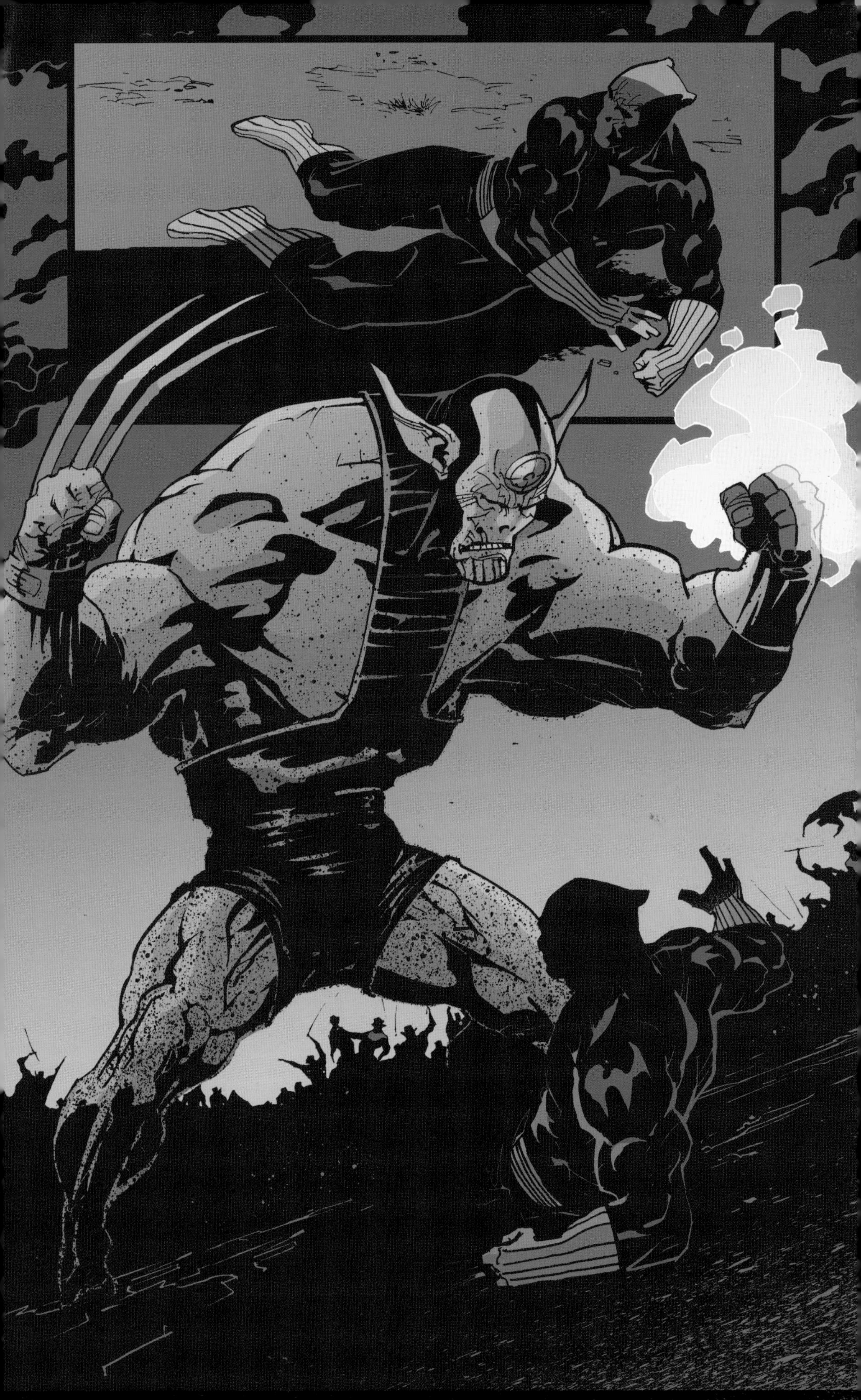

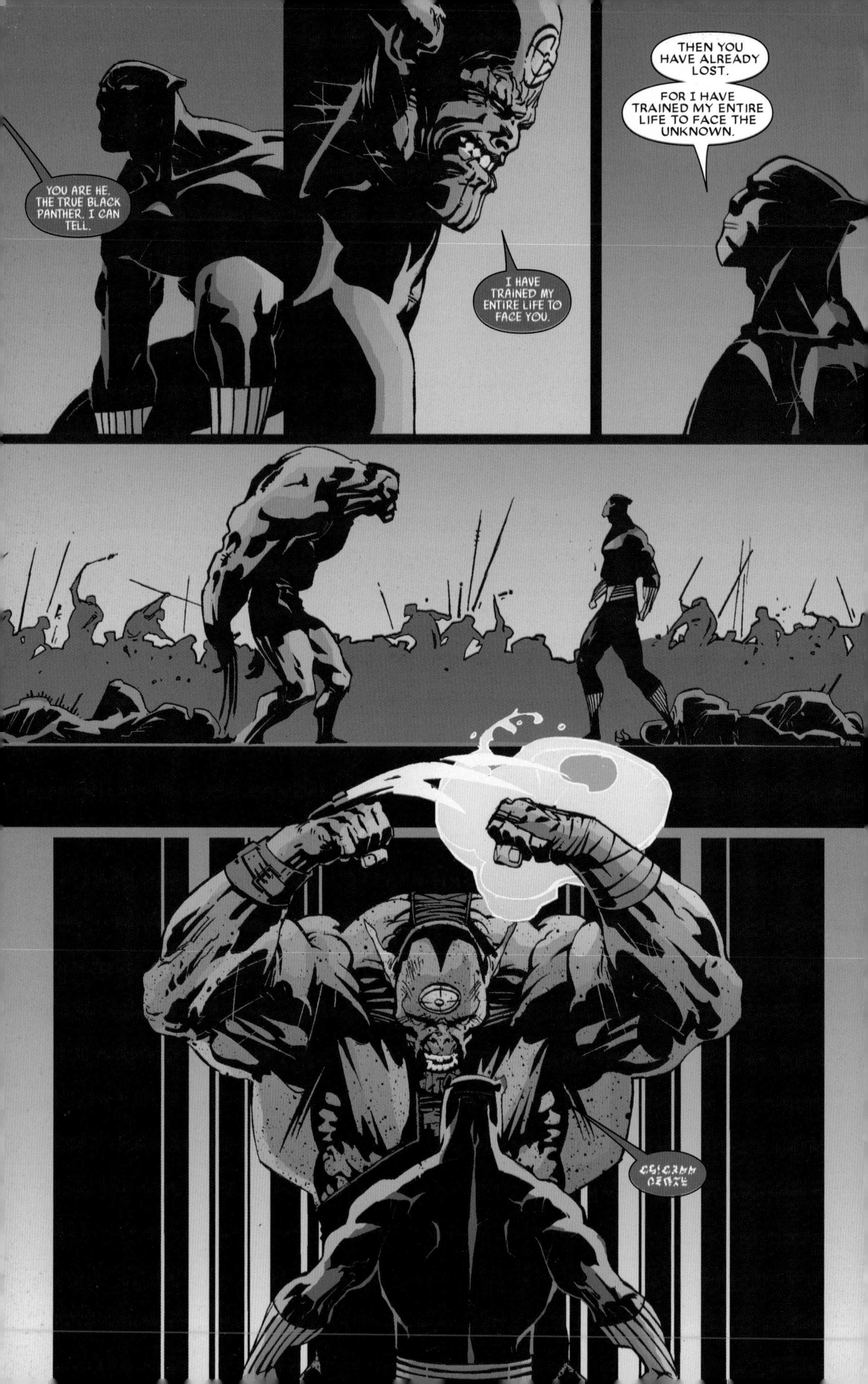
YOU ARE HE. THE TRUE BLACK PANTHER. I CAN TELL.
I HAVE TRAINED MY ENTIRE LIFE TO FACE YOU.
THEN YOU HAVE ALREADY LOST.
FOR I HAVE TRAINED MY ENTIRE LIFE TO FACE THE UNKNOWN.

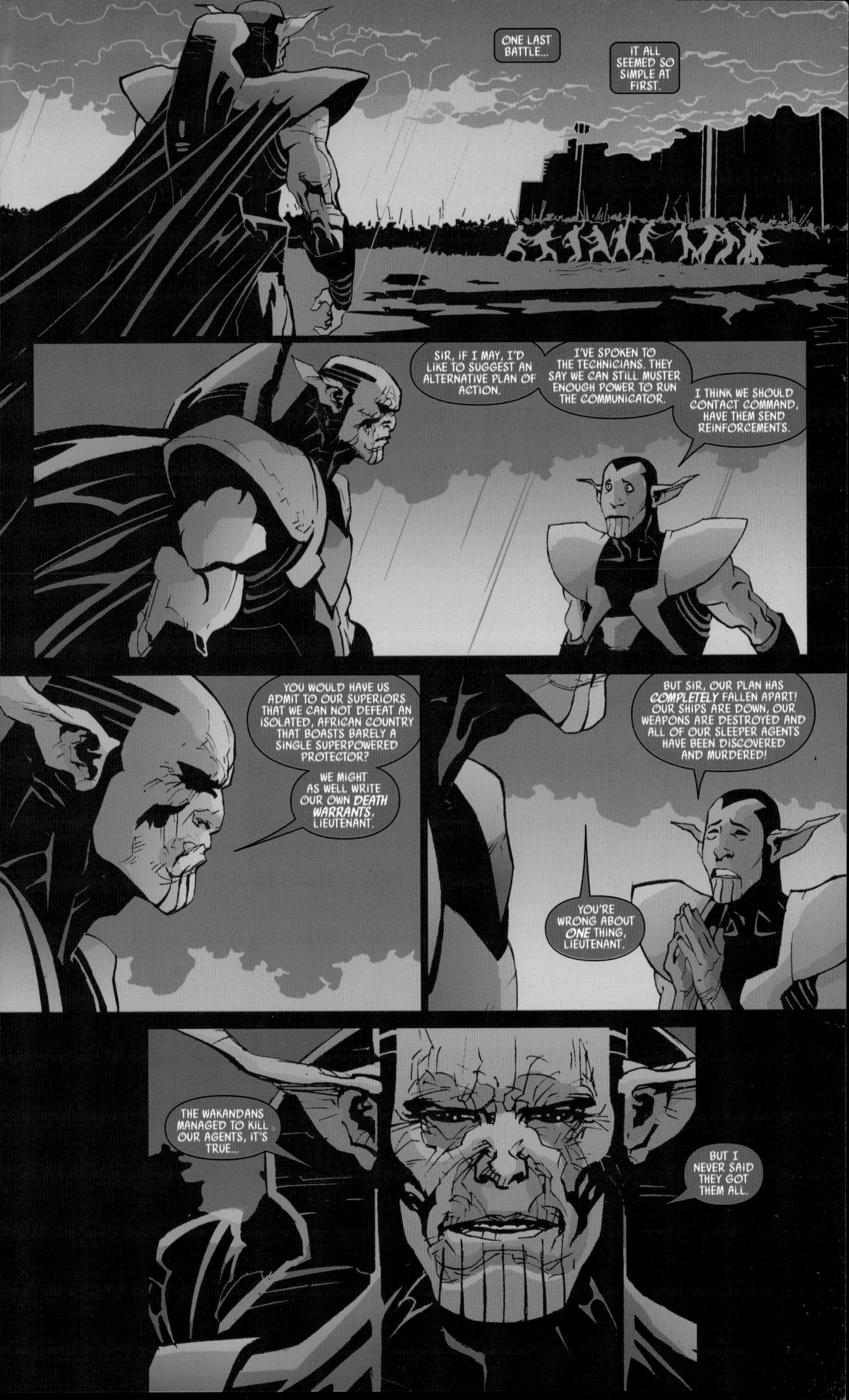
ONE LAST BATTLE...
IT ALL SEEMED SO SIMPLE AT FIRST.
SIR, IF I MAY, I'D LIKE TO SUGGEST AN ALTERNATIVE PLAN OF ACTION.
I'VE SPOKEN TO THE TECHNICIANS. THEY SAY WE CAN STILL MUSTER ENOUGH POWER TO RUN THE COMMUNICATOR.
I THINK WE SHOULD CONTACT COMMAND, HAVE THEM SEND REINFORCEMENTS.
YOU WOULD HAVE US ADMIT TO OUR SUPERIORS THAT WE CAN NOT DEFEAT AN ISOLATED, AFRICAN COUNTRY THAT BOASTS BARELY A SINGLE SUPERPOWERED PROTECTOR?
WE MIGHT AS WELL WRITE OUR OWN *DEATH WARRANTS*, LIEUTENANT.
BUT SIR, OUR PLAN HAS *COMPLETELY* FALLEN APART! OUR SHIPS ARE DOWN, OUR WEAPONS ARE DESTROYED AND ALL OF OUR SLEEPER AGENTS HAVE BEEN DISCOVERED AND MURDERED!
YOU'RE WRONG ABOUT *ONE* THING, LIEUTENANT.
THE WAKANDANS MANAGED TO KILL OUR AGENTS, IT'S TRUE...
BUT I NEVER SAID THEY GOT THEM ALL.

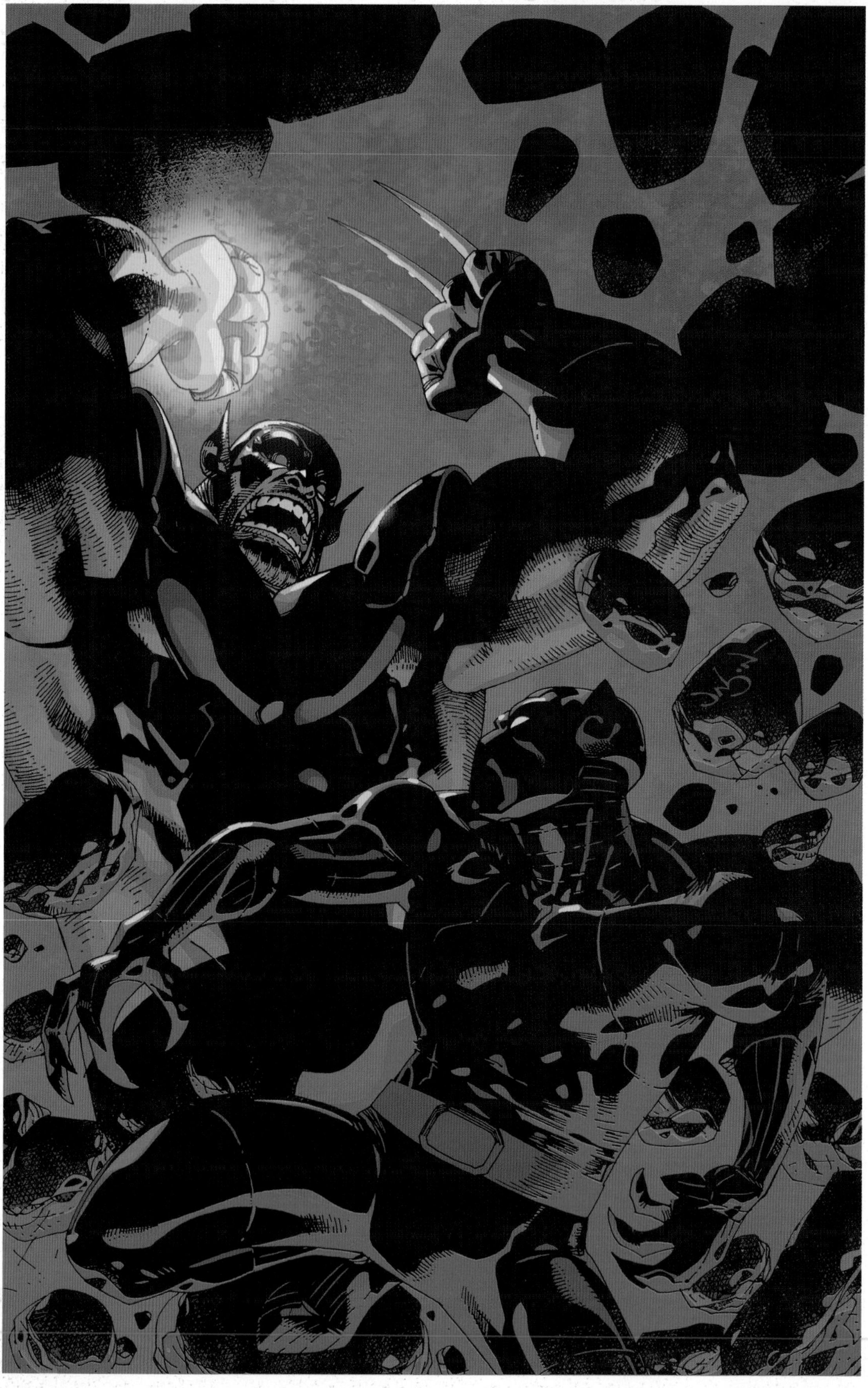

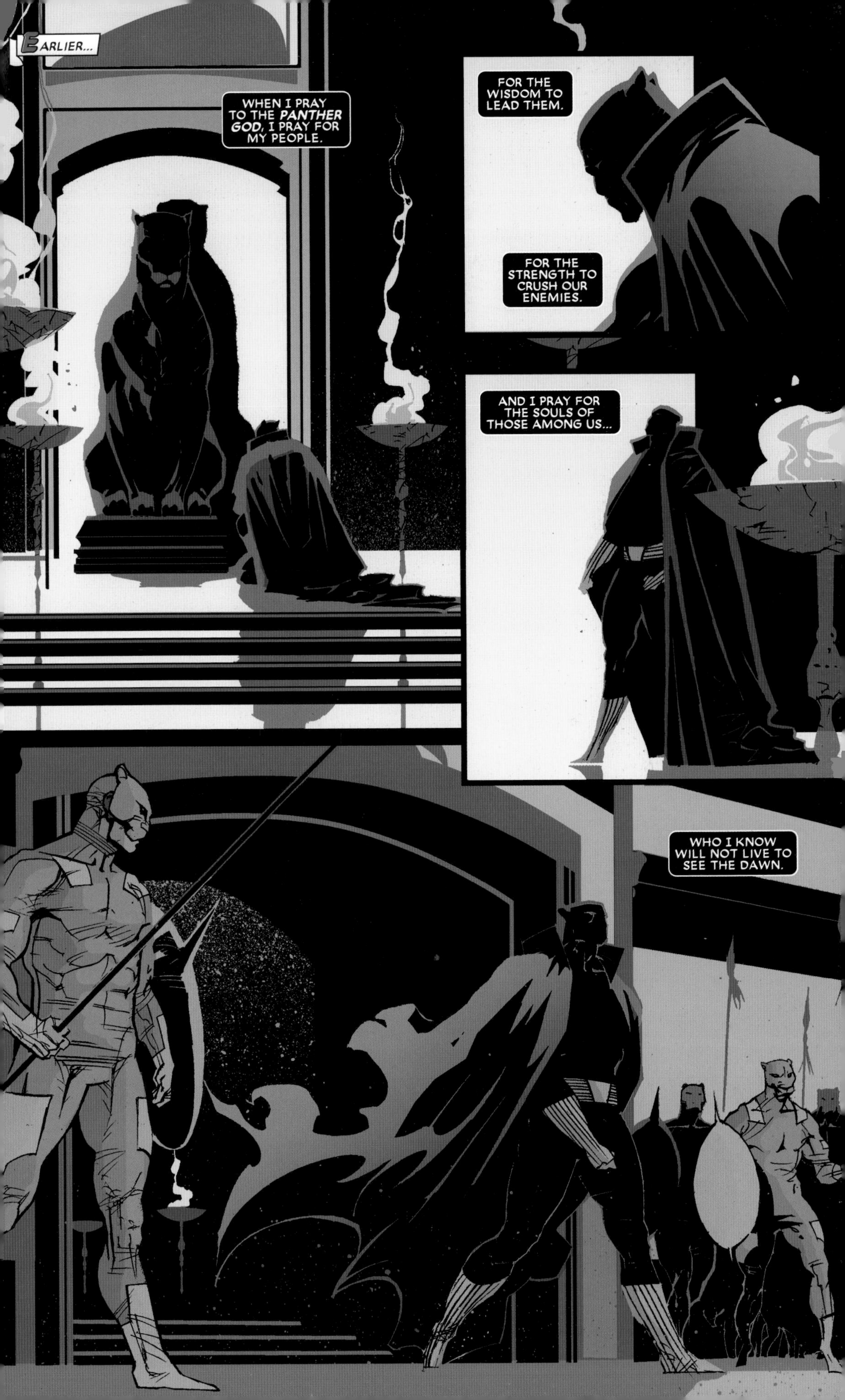
EARLIER...
WHEN I PRAY TO THE PANTHER GOD, I PRAY FOR MY PEOPLE.
FOR THE WISDOM TO LEAD THEM.
FOR THE STRENGTH TO CRUSH OUR ENEMIES.
AND I PRAY FOR THE SOULS OF THOSE AMONG US...
WHO I KNOW WILL NOT LIVE TO SEE THE DAWN.

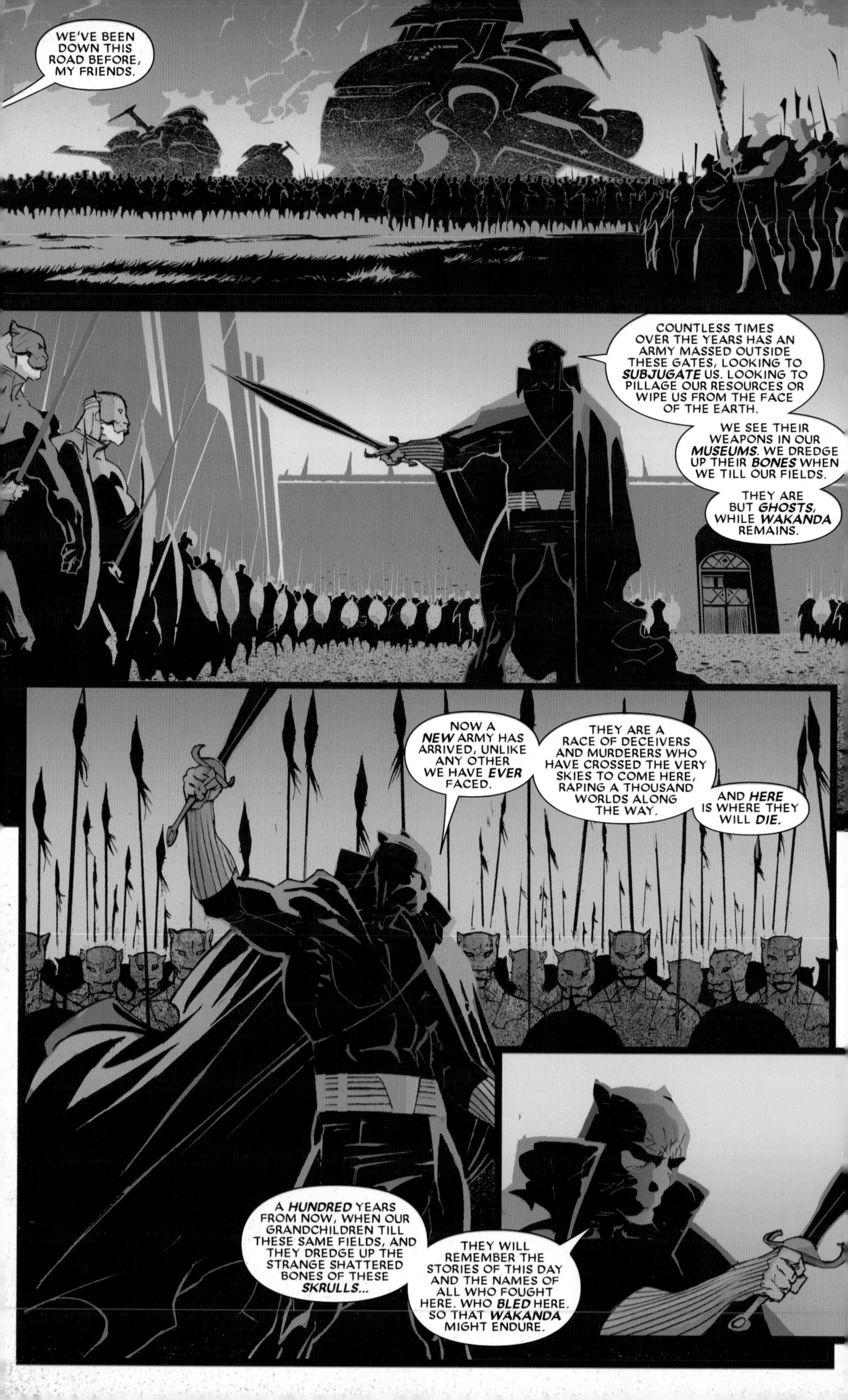
WE'VE BEEN DOWN THIS ROAD BEFORE, MY FRIENDS.
COUNTLESS TIMES OVER THE YEARS HAS AN ARMY MASSED OUTSIDE THESE GATES, LOOKING TO SUBJUGATE US. LOOKING TO PILLAGE OUR RESOURCES OR WIPE US FROM THE FACE OF THE EARTH.
WE SEE THEIR WEAPONS IN OUR MUSEUMS. WE DREDGE UP THEIR BONES WHEN WE TILL OUR FIELDS.
THEY ARE BUT GHOSTS, WHILE WAKANDA REMAINS.
NOW A NEW ARMY HAS ARRIVED, UNLIKE ANY OTHER WE HAVE EVER FACED.
THEY ARE A RACE OF DECEIVERS AND MURDERERS WHO HAVE CROSSED THE VERY SKIES TO COME HERE, RAPING A THOUSAND WORLDS ALONG THE WAY.
AND HERE IS WHERE THEY WILL DIE.
A HUNDRED YEARS FROM NOW, WHEN OUR GRANDCHILDREN TILL THESE SAME FIELDS, AND THEY DREDGE UP THE STRANGE SHATTERED BONES OF THESE SKRULLS...
THEY WILL REMEMBER THE STORIES OF THIS DAY AND THE NAMES OF ALL WHO FOUGHT HERE. WHO BLED HERE. SO THAT WAKANDA MIGHT ENDURE.

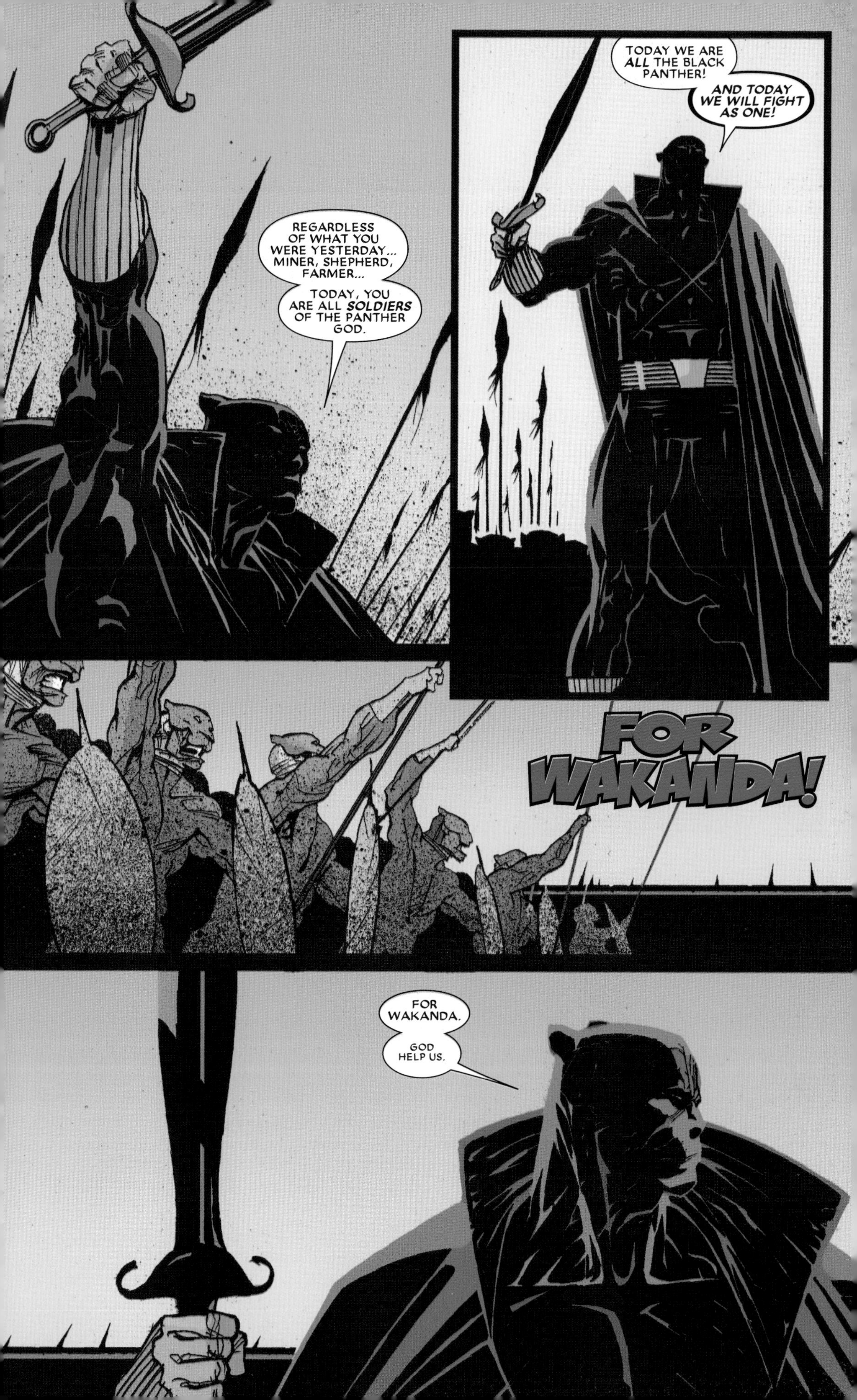
REGARDLESS OF WHAT YOU WERE YESTERDAY... MINER, SHEPHERD, FARMER...
TODAY, YOU ARE ALL **SOLDIERS** OF THE PANTHER GOD.
TODAY WE ARE ***ALL*** THE BLACK PANTHER!
AND TODAY WE WILL FIGHT AS ONE!
FOR WAKANDA!
FOR WAKANDA.
GOD HELP US.

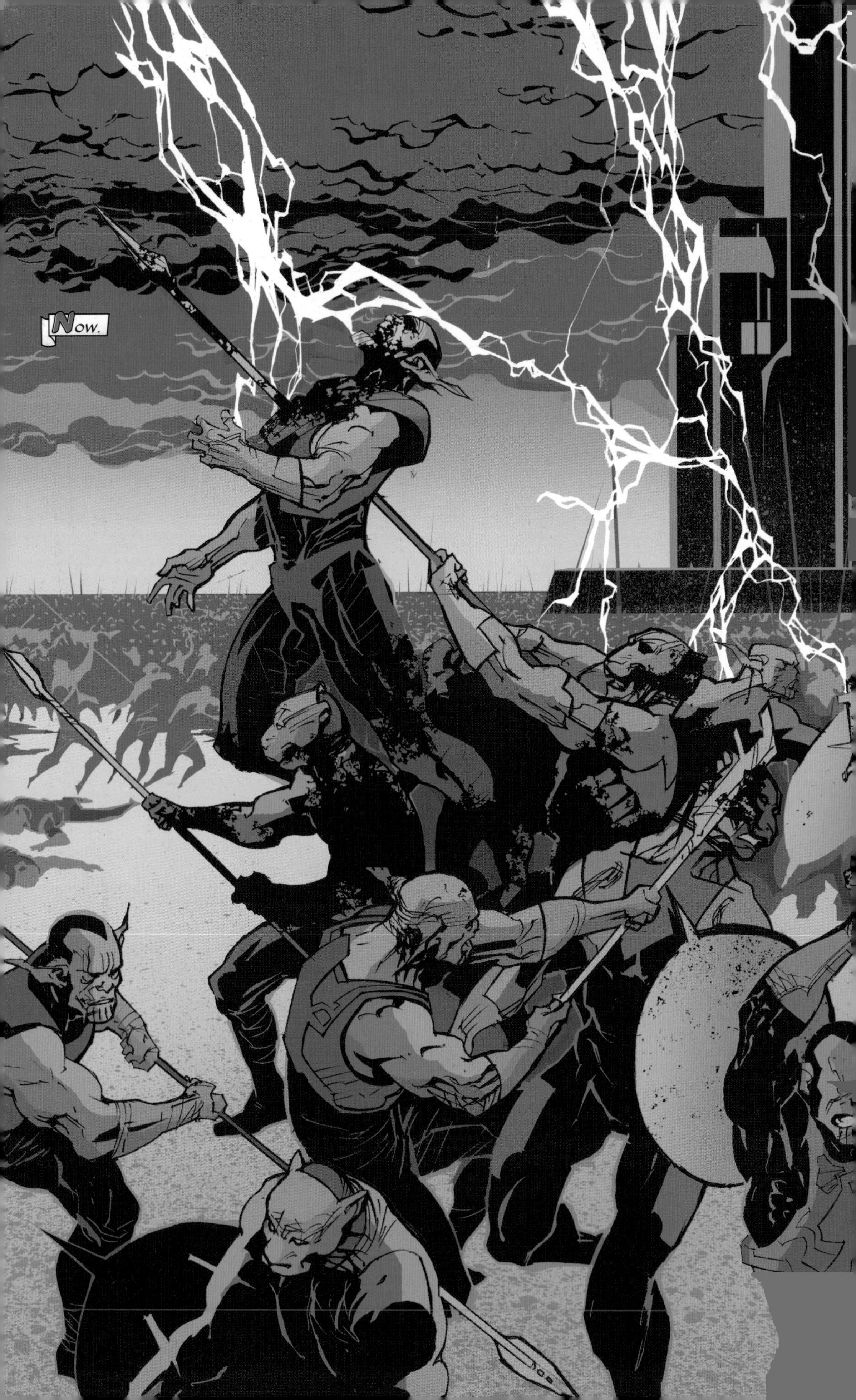
Now.

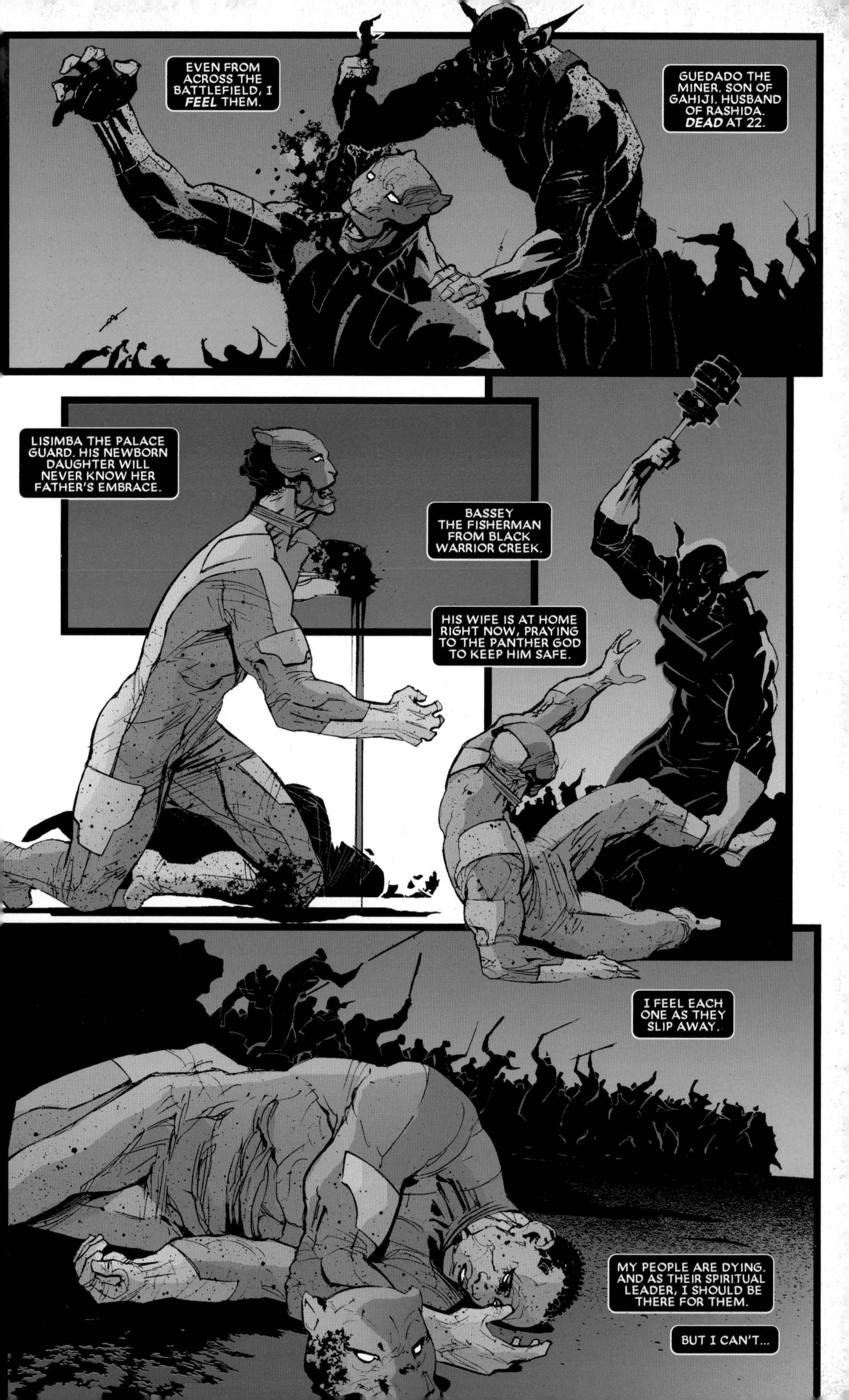
EVEN FROM ACROSS THE BATTLEFIELD, I *FEEL* THEM.
GUEDADO THE MINER. SON OF GAHIJI. HUSBAND OF RASHIDA. *DEAD* AT 22.
LISIMBA THE PALACE GUARD. HIS NEWBORN DAUGHTER WILL NEVER KNOW HER FATHER'S EMBRACE.
BASSEY THE FISHERMAN FROM BLACK WARRIOR CREEK.
HIS WIFE IS AT HOME RIGHT NOW, PRAYING TO THE PANTHER GOD TO KEEP HIM SAFE.
I FEEL EACH ONE AS THEY SLIP AWAY.
MY PEOPLE ARE DYING. AND AS THEIR SPIRITUAL LEADER, I SHOULD BE THERE FOR THEM.
BUT I CAN'T...

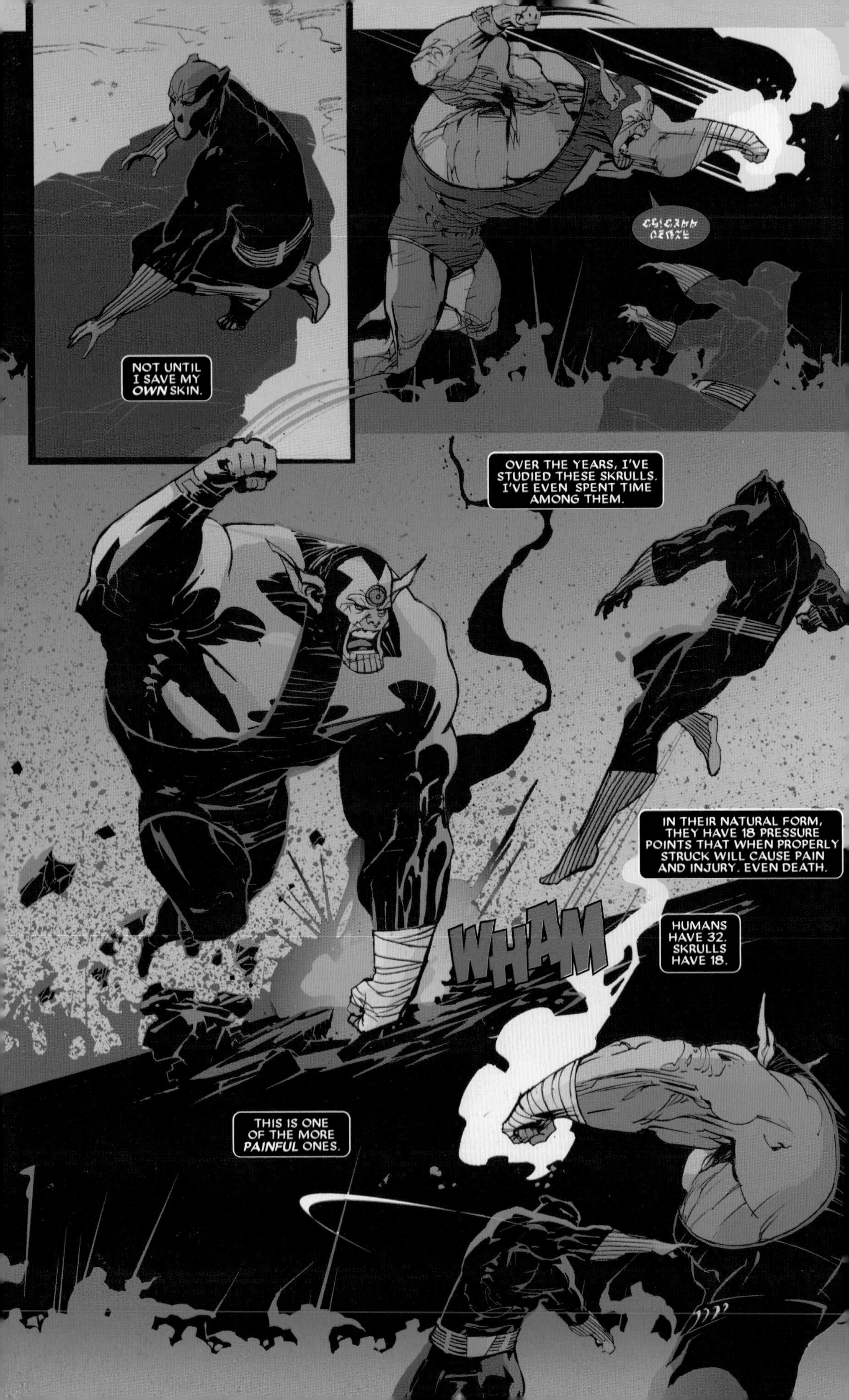
NOT UNTIL I SAVE MY *OWN* SKIN.
OVER THE YEARS, I'VE STUDIED THESE SKRULLS. I'VE EVEN SPENT TIME AMONG THEM.
IN THEIR NATURAL FORM, THEY HAVE 18 PRESSURE POINTS THAT WHEN PROPERLY STRUCK WILL CAUSE PAIN AND INJURY. EVEN DEATH.
WHAM
HUMANS HAVE 32. SKRULLS HAVE 18.
THIS IS ONE OF THE MORE *PAINFUL* ONES.

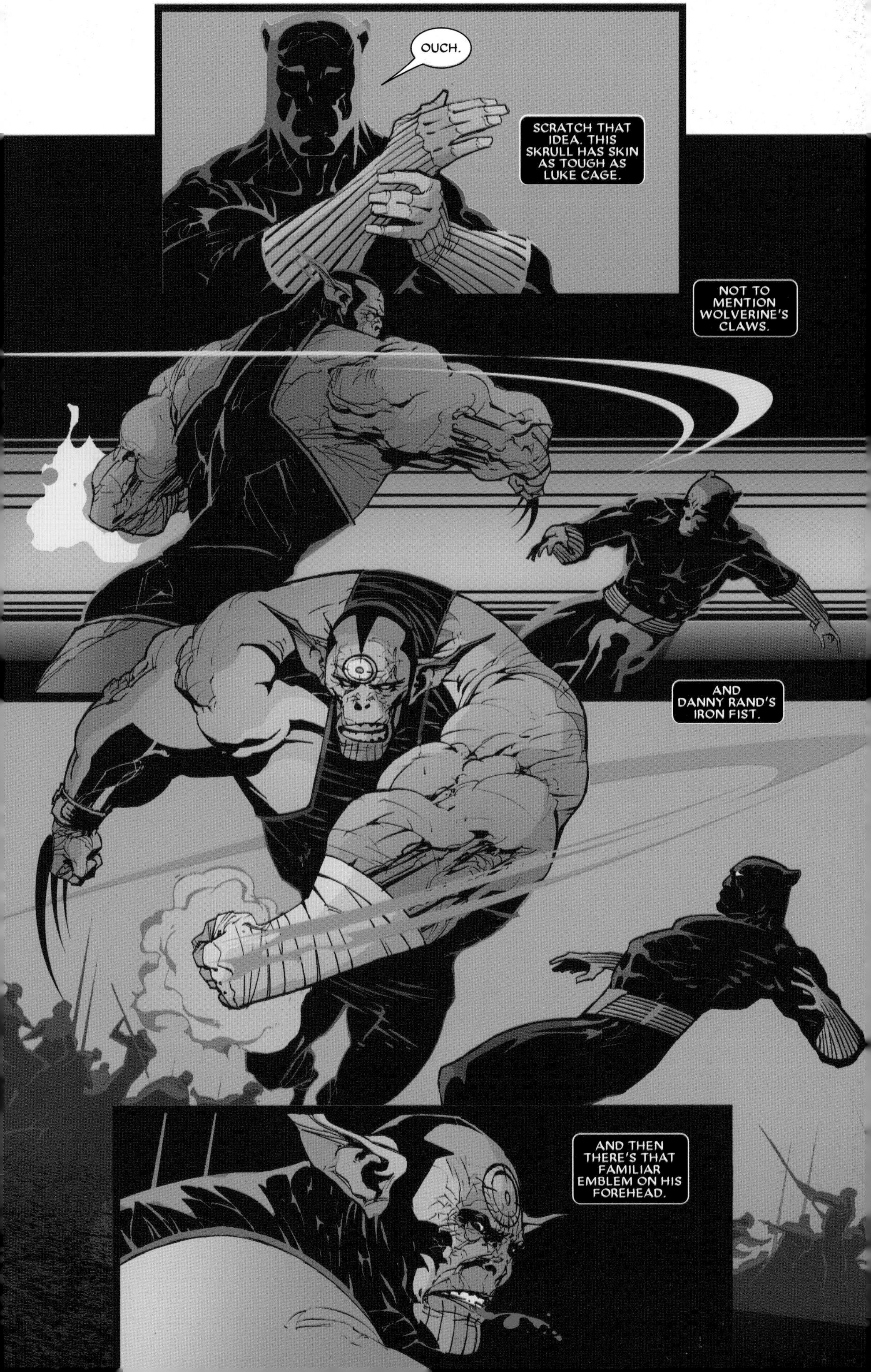
OUCH.
SCRATCH THAT IDEA. THIS SKRULL HAS SKIN AS TOUGH AS LUKE CAGE.
NOT TO MENTION WOLVERINE'S CLAWS.
AND DANNY RAND'S IRON FIST.
AND THEN THERE'S THAT FAMILIAR EMBLEM ON HIS FOREHEAD.

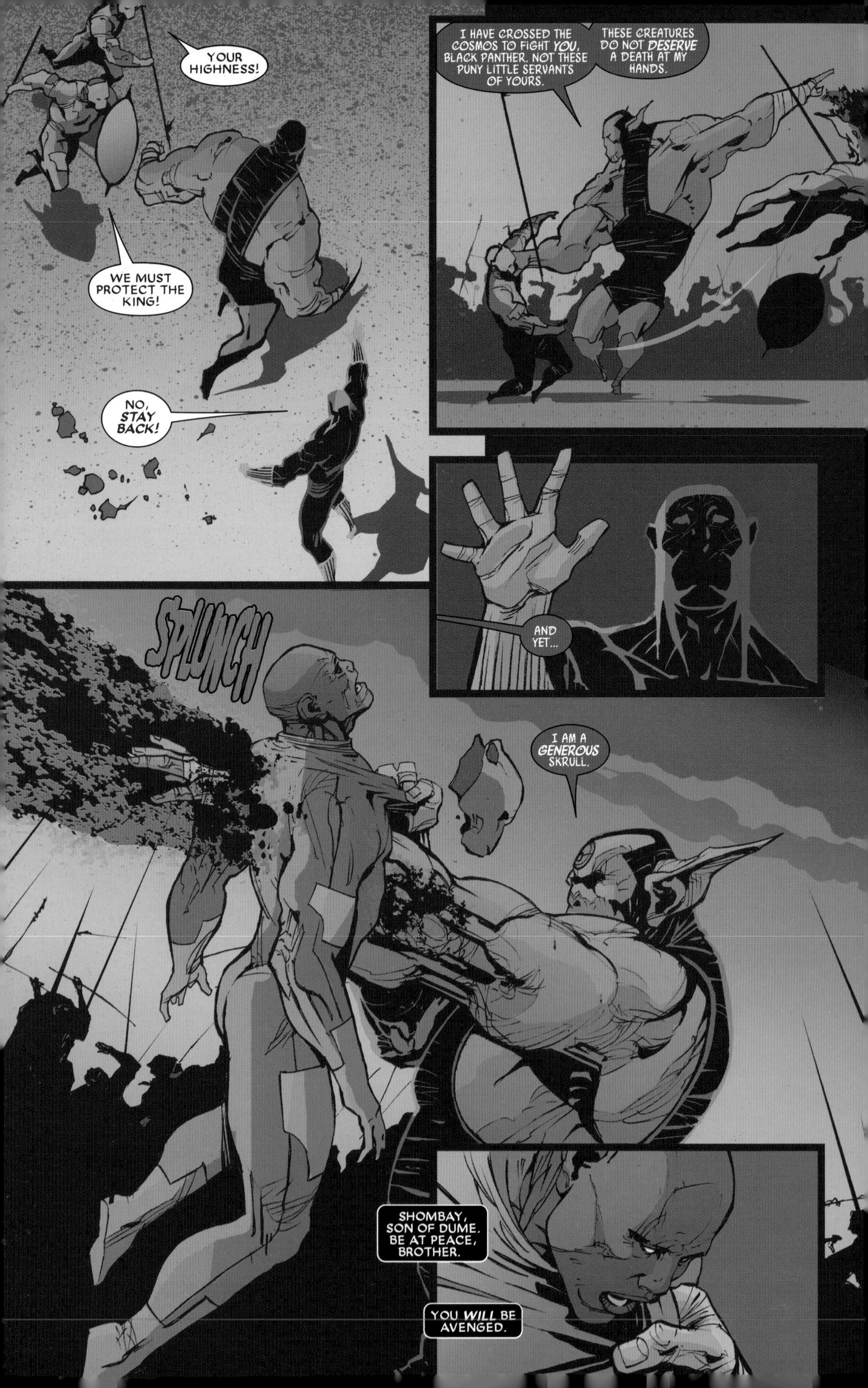
YOUR HIGHNESS!
WE MUST PROTECT THE KING!
NO, STAY BACK!
I HAVE CROSSED THE COSMOS TO FIGHT YOU, BLACK PANTHER. NOT THESE PUNY LITTLE SERVANTS OF YOURS.
THESE CREATURES DO NOT DESERVE A DEATH AT MY HANDS.
AND YET...
SPLUNCH
I AM A GENEROUS SKRULL.
SHOMBAY, SON OF DUME. BE AT PEACE, BROTHER.
YOU WILL BE AVENGED.

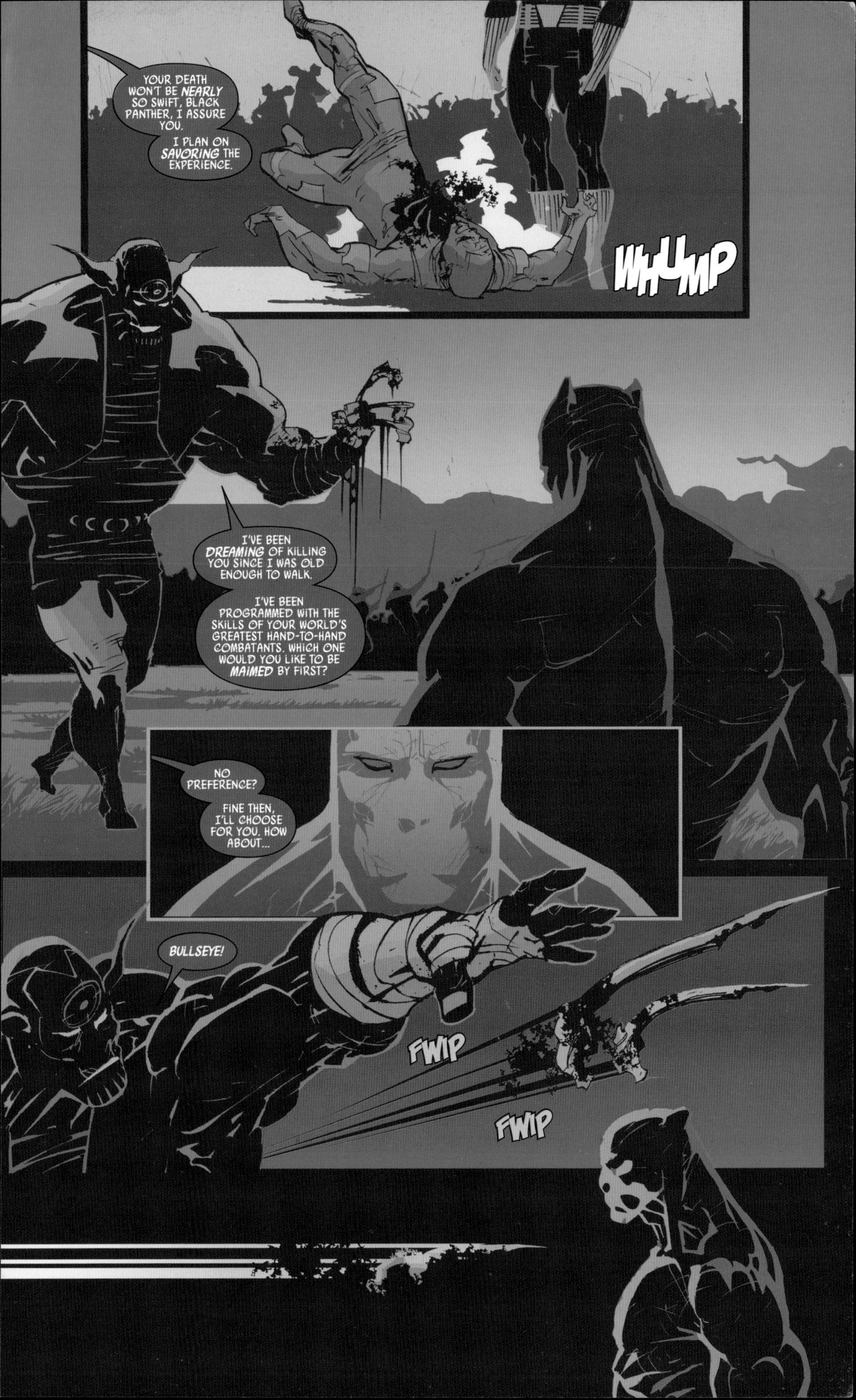
YOUR DEATH WON'T BE NEARLY SO SWIFT, BLACK PANTHER, I ASSURE YOU.
I PLAN ON SAVORING THE EXPERIENCE.
WHUMP
I'VE BEEN DREAMING OF KILLING YOU SINCE I WAS OLD ENOUGH TO WALK.
I'VE BEEN PROGRAMMED WITH THE SKILLS OF YOUR WORLD'S GREATEST HAND-TO-HAND COMBATANTS. WHICH ONE WOULD YOU LIKE TO BE MAIMED BY FIRST?
NO PREFERENCE?
FINE THEN, I'LL CHOOSE FOR YOU. HOW ABOUT...
BULLSEYE!
FWIP
FWIP

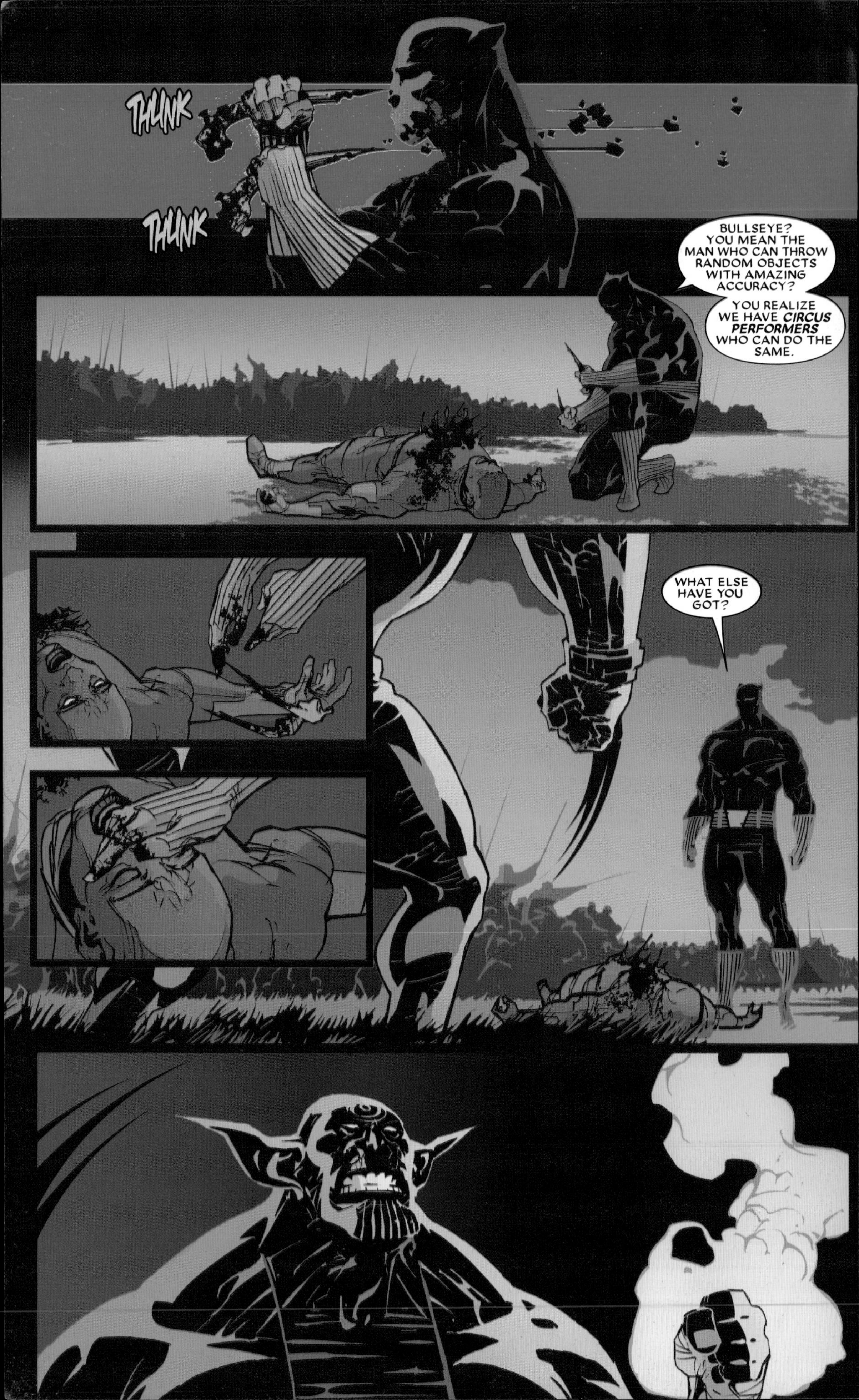
THUNK
THUNK
BULLSEYE? YOU MEAN THE MAN WHO CAN THROW RANDOM OBJECTS WITH AMAZING ACCURACY?
YOU REALIZE WE HAVE *CIRCUS PERFORMERS* WHO CAN DO THE SAME.
WHAT ELSE HAVE YOU GOT?

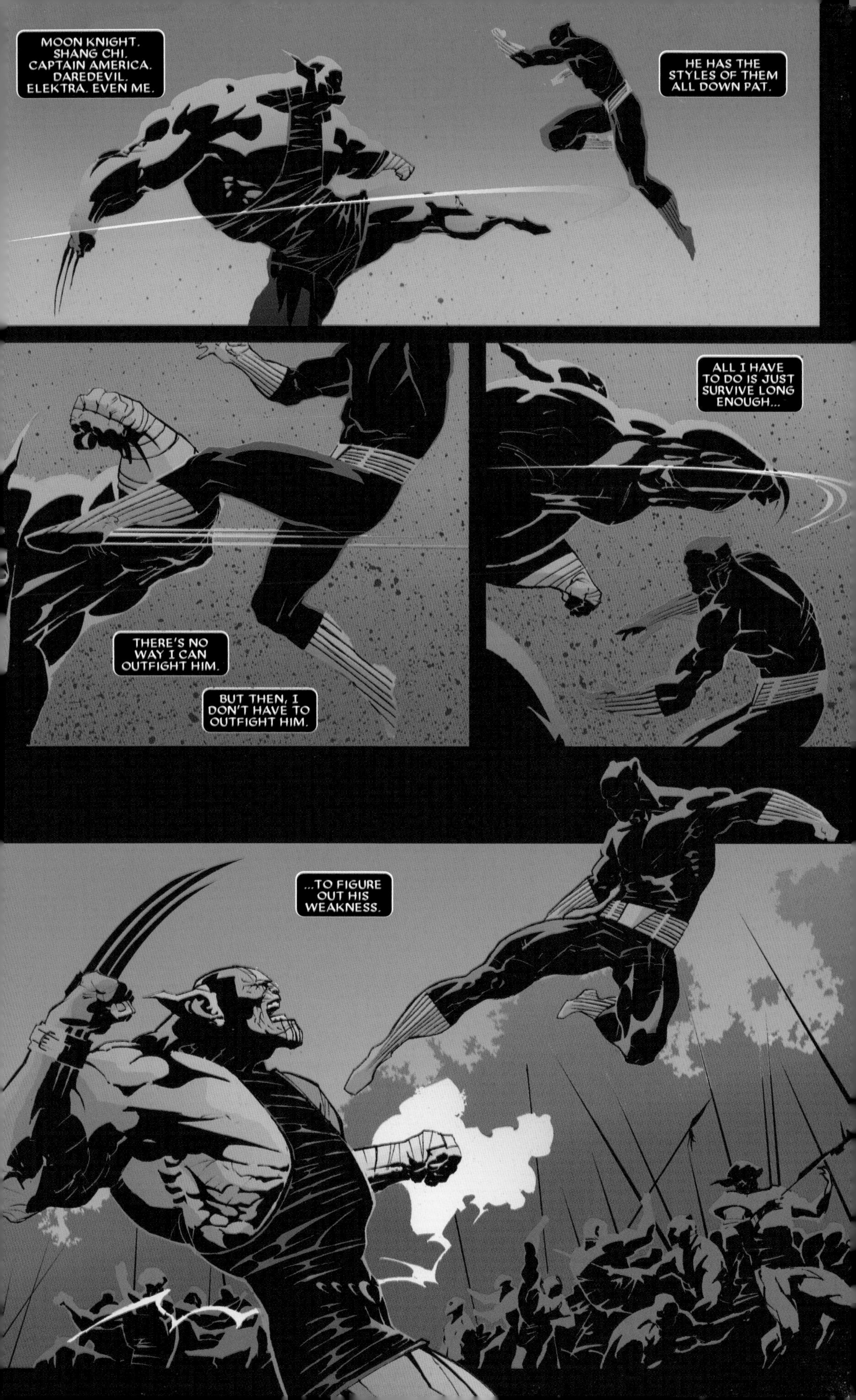
MOON KNIGHT. SHANG CHI. CAPTAIN AMERICA. DAREDEVIL. ELEKTRA. EVEN ME.
HE HAS THE STYLES OF THEM ALL DOWN PAT.
THERE'S NO WAY I CAN OUTFIGHT HIM.
BUT THEN, I DON'T HAVE TO OUTFIGHT HIM.
ALL I HAVE TO DO IS JUST SURVIVE LONG ENOUGH...
...TO FIGURE OUT HIS WEAKNESS.

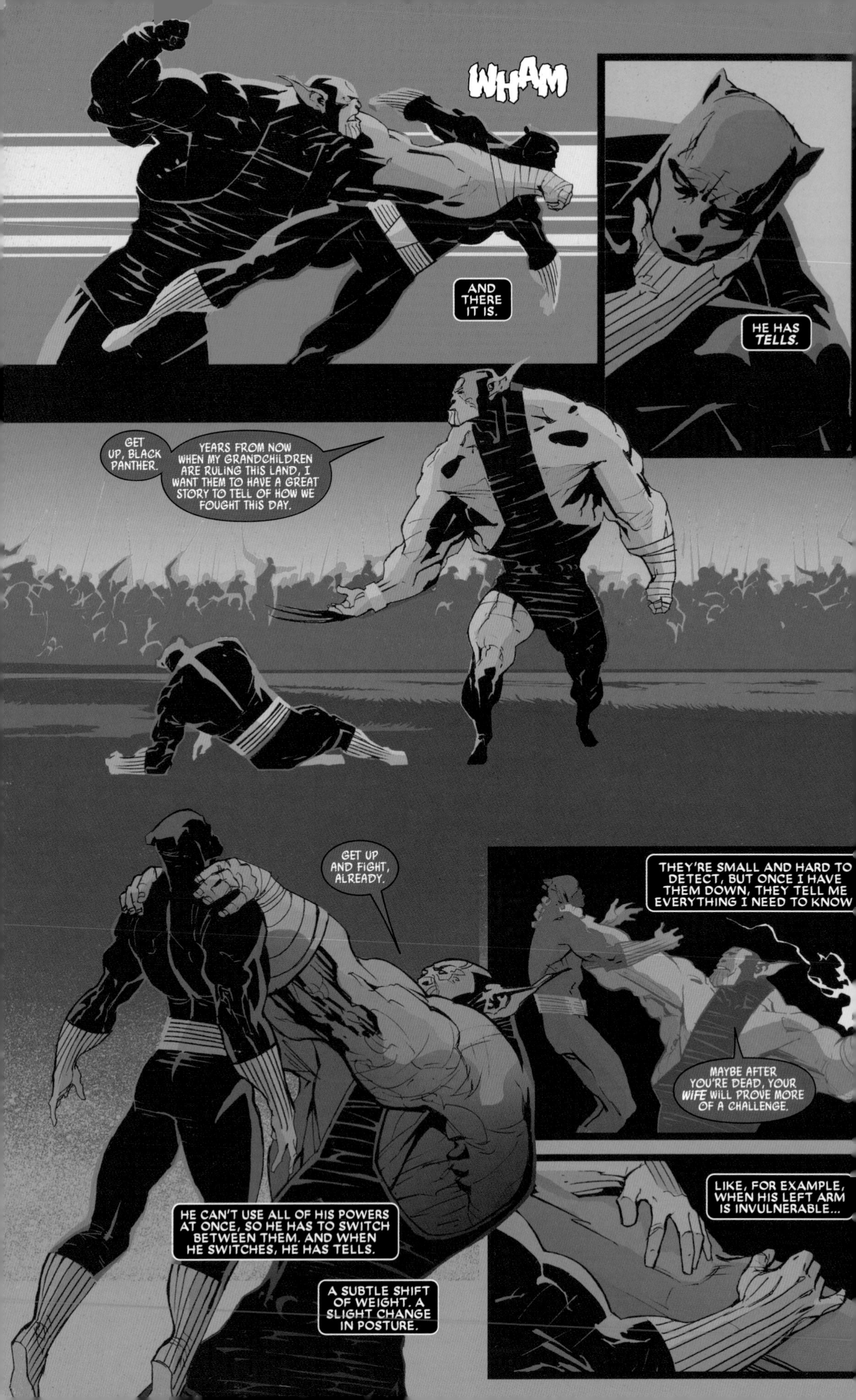
WHAM
AND THERE IT IS.
HE HAS TELLS.
GET UP, BLACK PANTHER.
YEARS FROM NOW WHEN MY GRANDCHILDREN ARE RULING THIS LAND, I WANT THEM TO HAVE A GREAT STORY TO TELL OF HOW WE FOUGHT THIS DAY.
GET UP AND FIGHT, ALREADY.
HE CAN'T USE ALL OF HIS POWERS AT ONCE, SO HE HAS TO SWITCH BETWEEN THEM. AND WHEN HE SWITCHES, HE HAS TELLS.
A SUBTLE SHIFT OF WEIGHT. A SLIGHT CHANGE IN POSTURE.
THEY'RE SMALL AND HARD TO DETECT, BUT ONCE I HAVE THEM DOWN, THEY TELL ME EVERYTHING I NEED TO KNOW
MAYBE AFTER YOU'RE DEAD, YOUR WIFE WILL PROVE MORE OF A CHALLENGE.
LIKE, FOR EXAMPLE, WHEN HIS LEFT ARM IS INVULNERABLE...

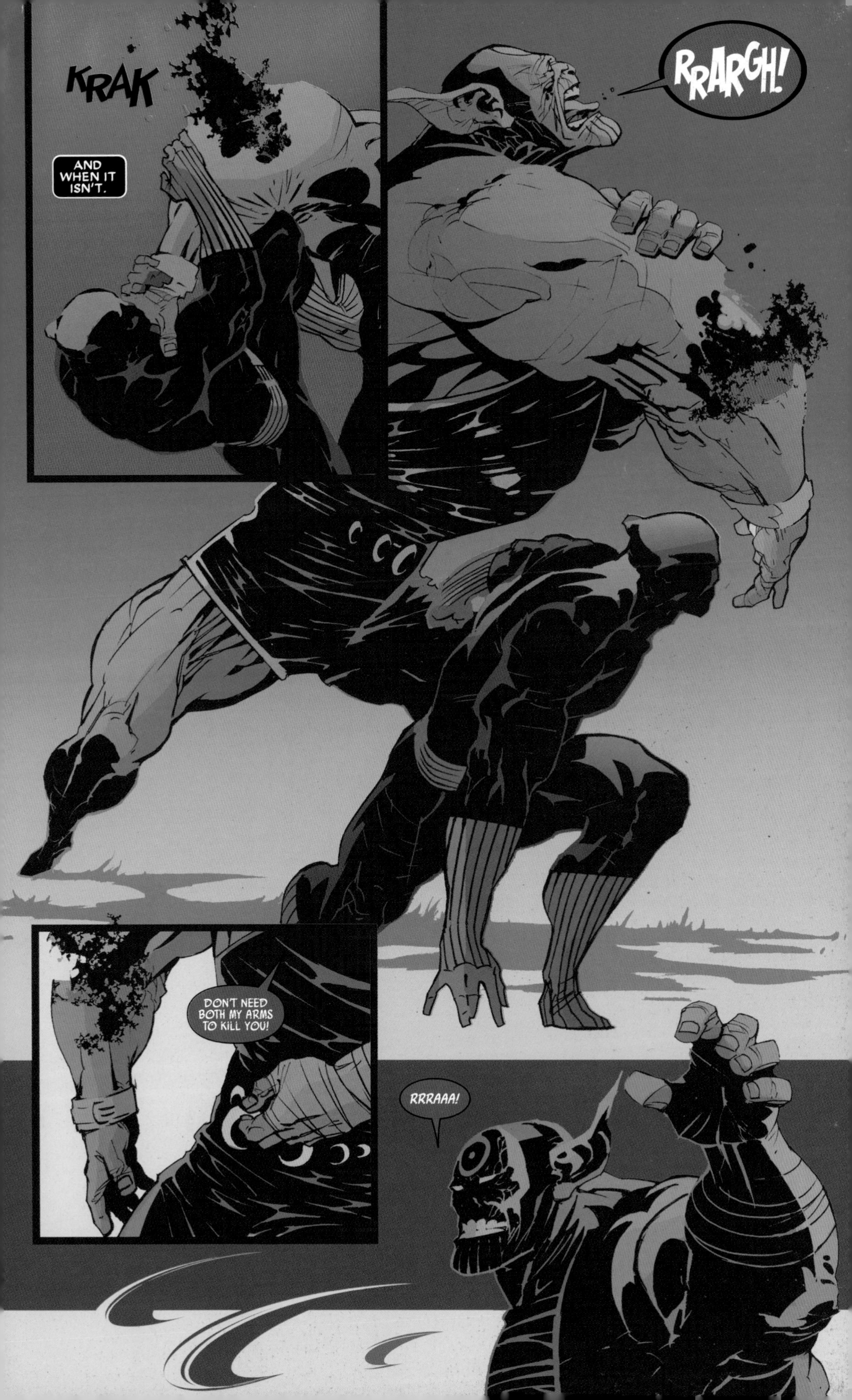
KRAK
AND WHEN IT ISN'T.
RRARGH!
DON'T NEED BOTH MY ARMS TO KILL YOU!
RRRAAA!

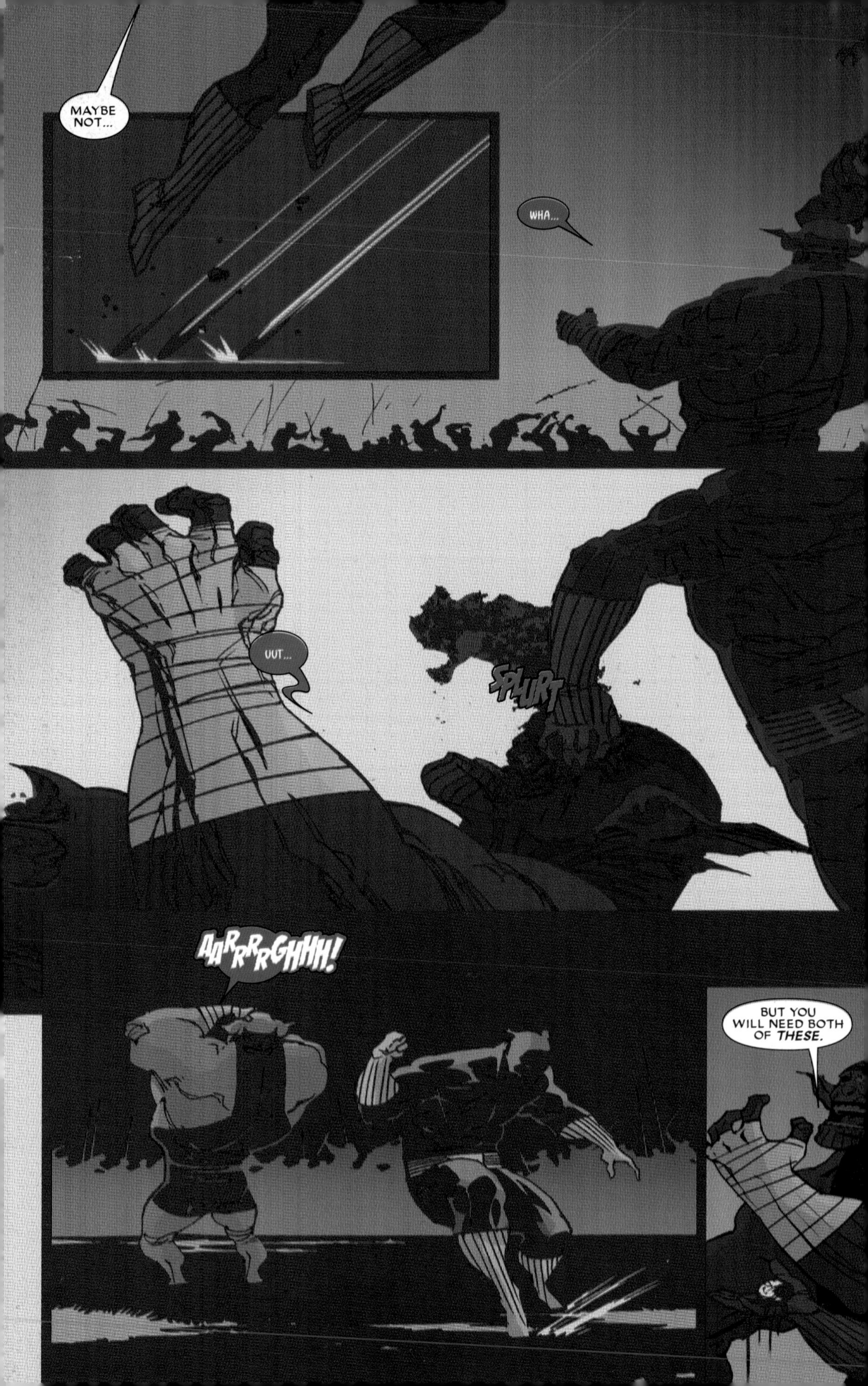
MAYBE NOT...
WHA...
UUT...
SPLURT
AARRRRGHHH!
BUT YOU WILL NEED BOTH OF *THESE.*

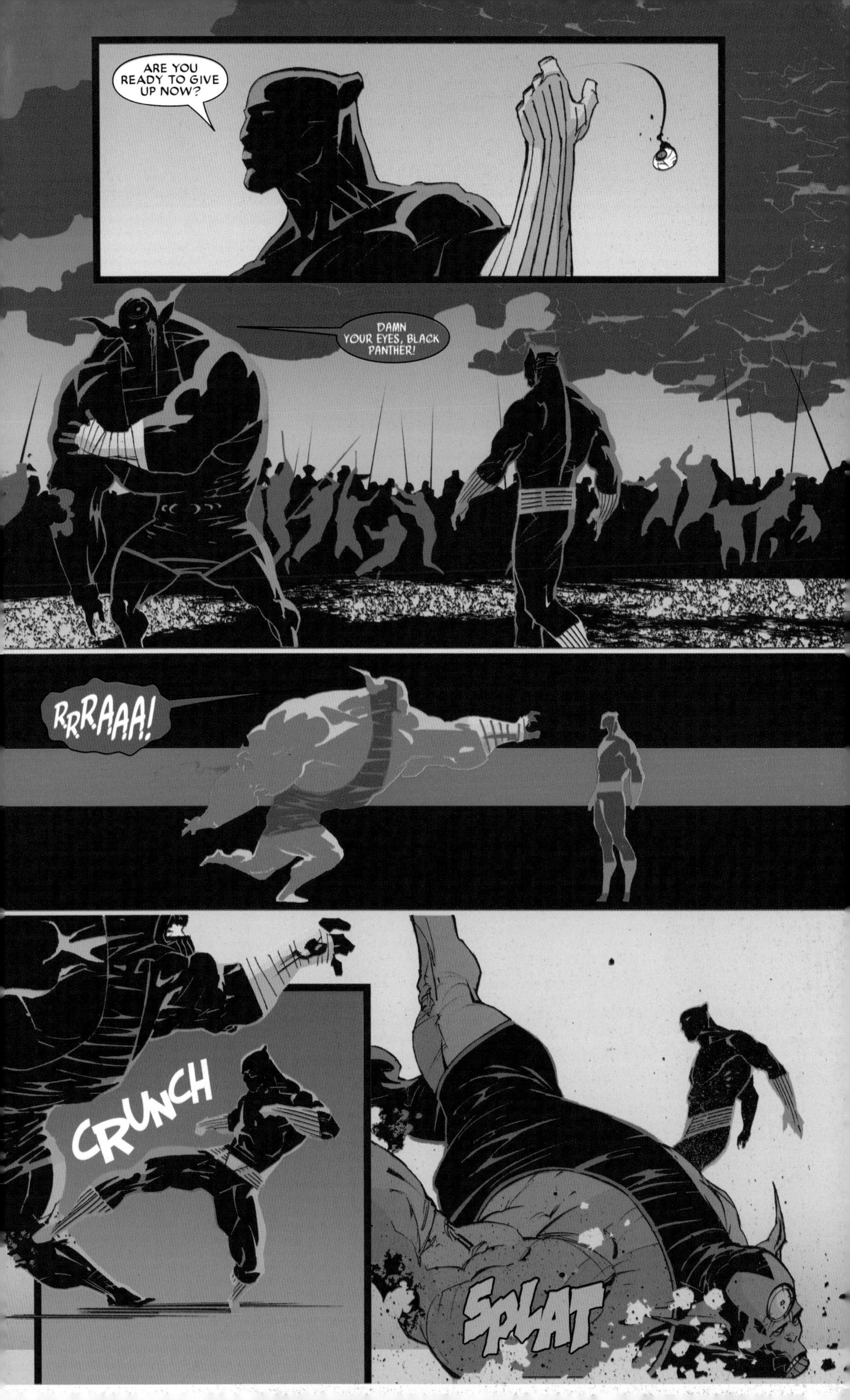
ARE YOU READY TO GIVE UP NOW?
DAMN YOUR EYES, BLACK PANTHER!
RRRAAAA!
CRUNCH
SPLAT

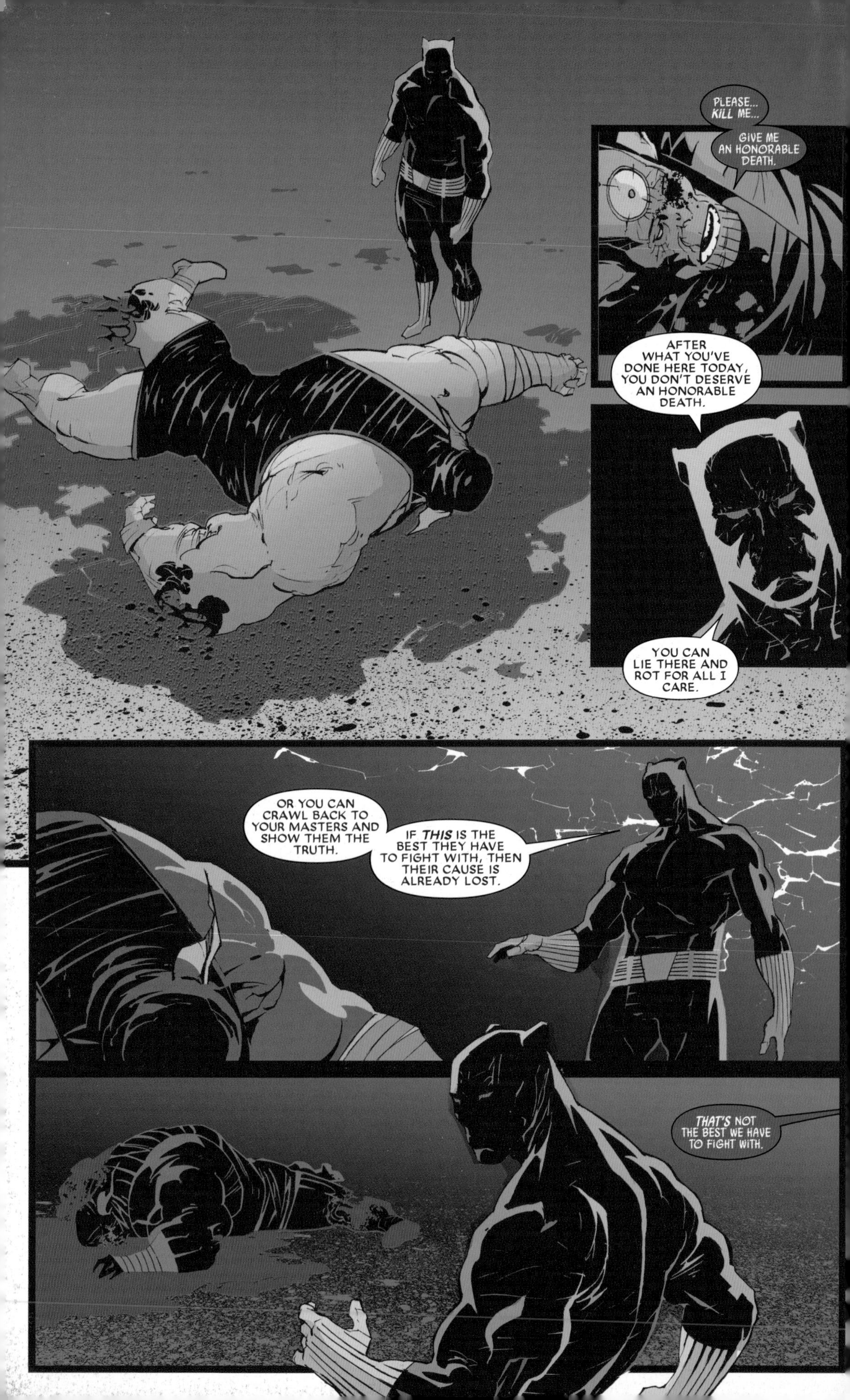

PLEASE... KILL ME...
GIVE ME AN HONORABLE DEATH.
AFTER WHAT YOU'VE DONE HERE TODAY, YOU DON'T DESERVE AN HONORABLE DEATH.
YOU CAN LIE THERE AND ROT FOR ALL I CARE.
OR YOU CAN CRAWL BACK TO YOUR MASTERS AND SHOW THEM THE TRUTH.
IF THIS IS THE BEST THEY HAVE TO FIGHT WITH, THEN THEIR CAUSE IS ALREADY LOST.
THAT'S NOT THE BEST WE HAVE TO FIGHT WITH.

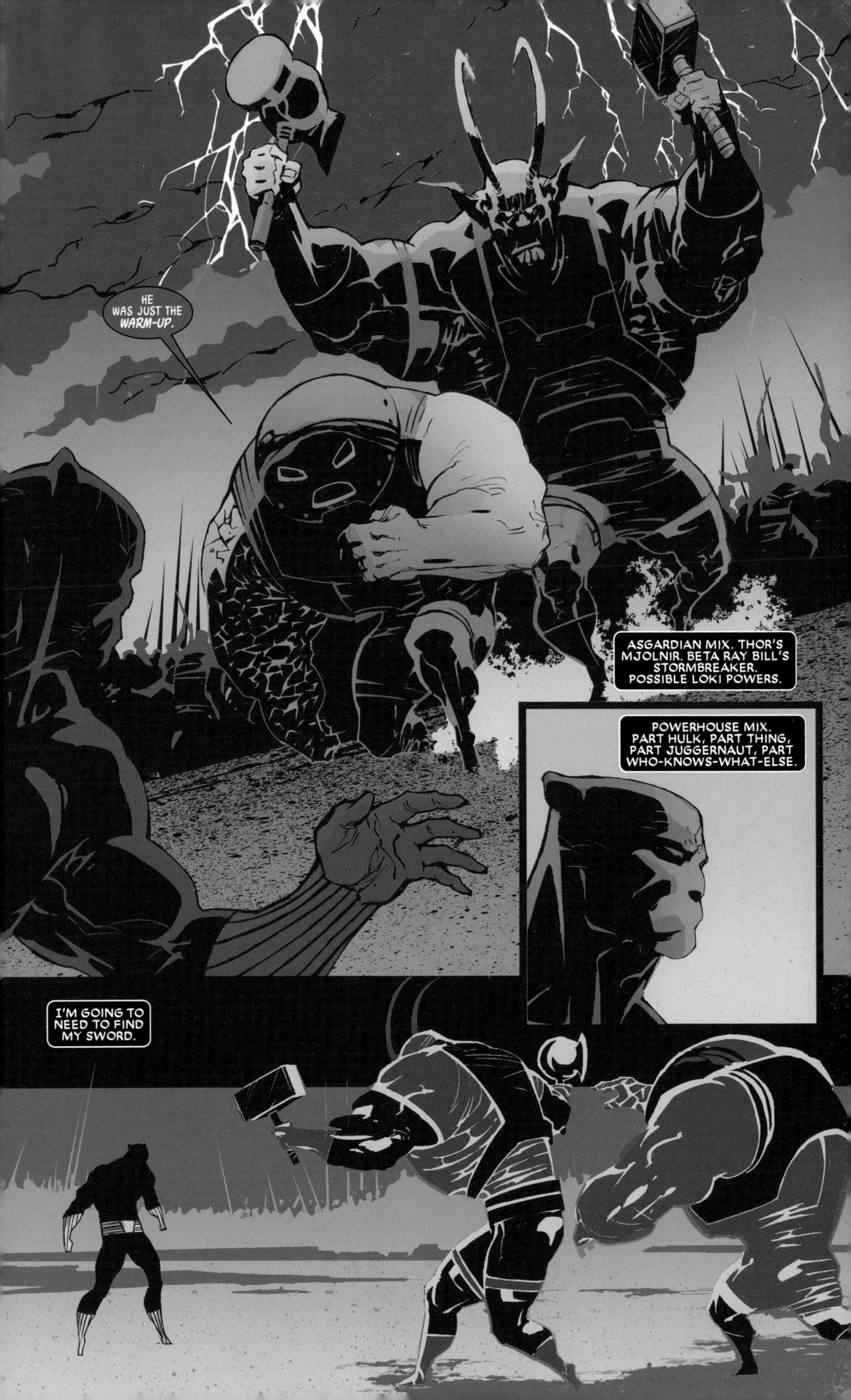

HE WAS JUST THE WARM-UP.
ASGARDIAN MIX. THOR'S MJOLNIR. BETA RAY BILL'S STORMBREAKER. POSSIBLE LOKI POWERS.
POWERHOUSE MIX. PART HULK, PART THING, PART JUGGERNAUT, PART WHO-KNOWS-WHAT-ELSE.
I'M GOING TO NEED TO FIND MY SWORD.

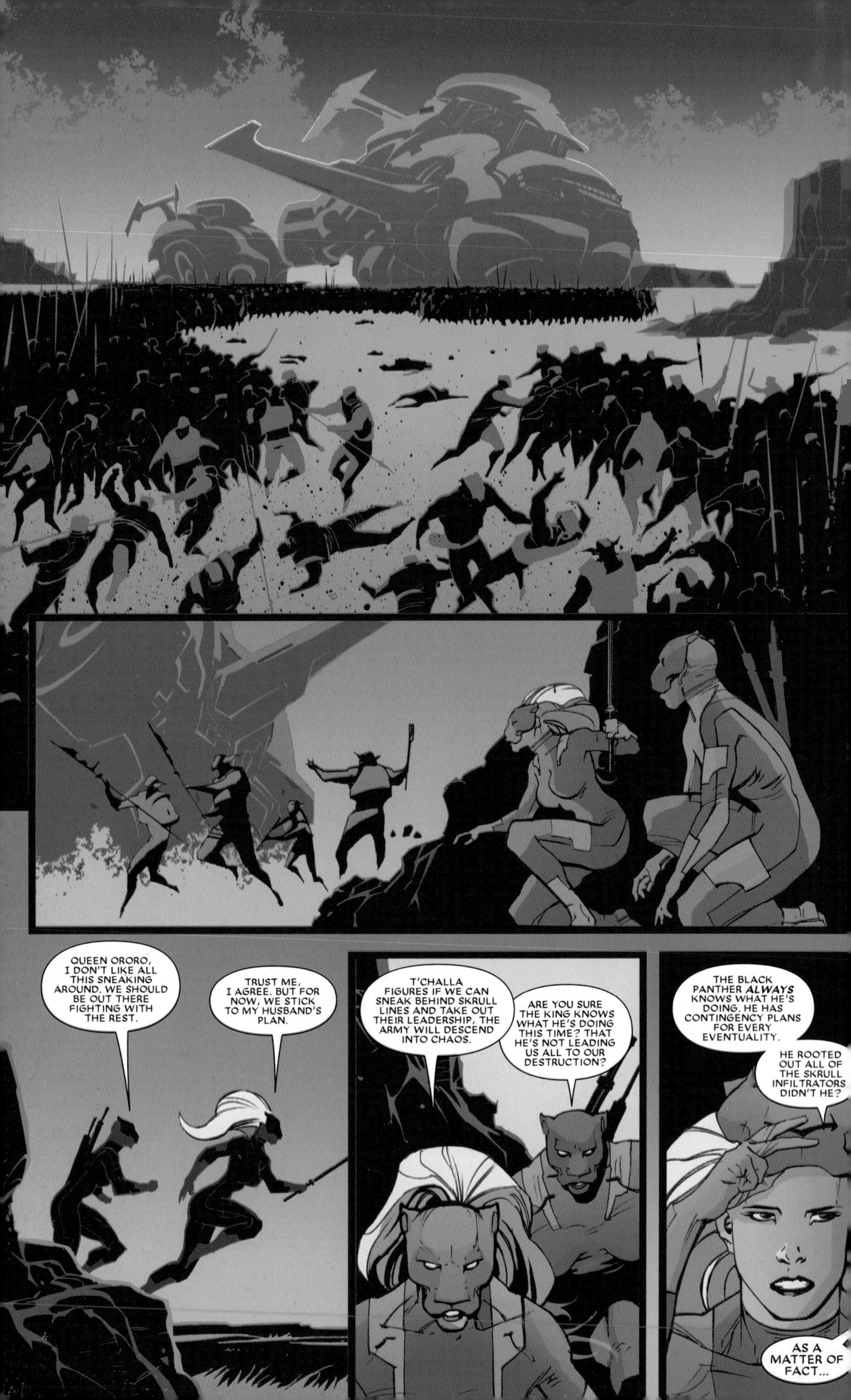
QUEEN ORORO, I DON'T LIKE ALL THIS SNEAKING AROUND. WE SHOULD BE OUT THERE FIGHTING WITH THE REST.
TRUST ME, I AGREE. BUT FOR NOW, WE STICK TO MY HUSBAND'S PLAN.
T'CHALLA FIGURES IF WE CAN SNEAK BEHIND SKRULL LINES AND TAKE OUT THEIR LEADERSHIP, THE ARMY WILL DESCEND INTO CHAOS.
ARE YOU SURE THE KING KNOWS WHAT HE'S DOING THIS TIME? THAT HE'S NOT LEADING US ALL TO OUR DESTRUCTION?
THE BLACK PANTHER *ALWAYS* KNOWS WHAT HE'S DOING. HE HAS CONTINGENCY PLANS FOR EVERY EVENTUALITY.
HE ROOTED OUT ALL OF THE SKRULL INFILTRATORS DIDN'T HE?
AS A MATTER OF FACT...

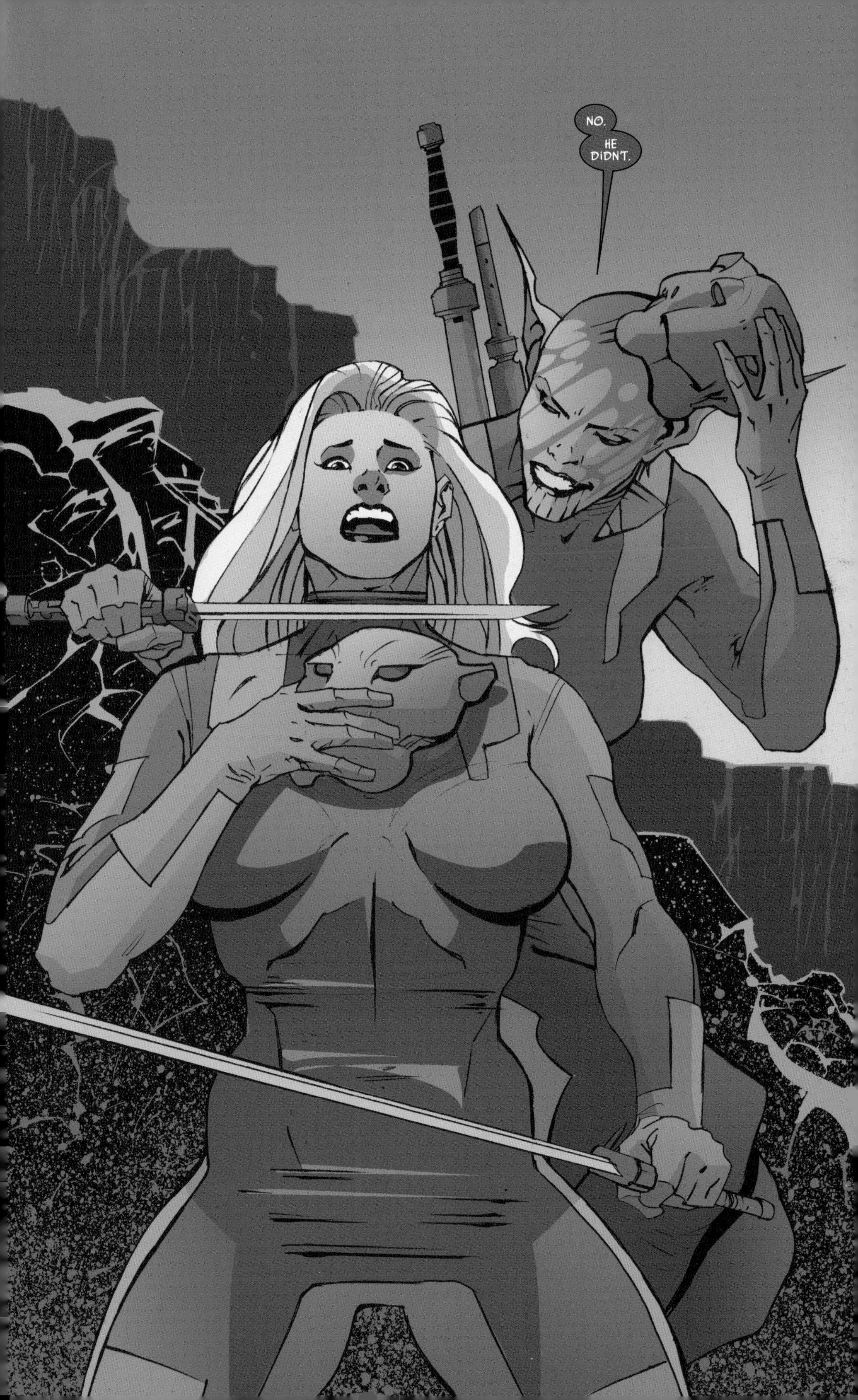
NO.
HE DIDN'T.

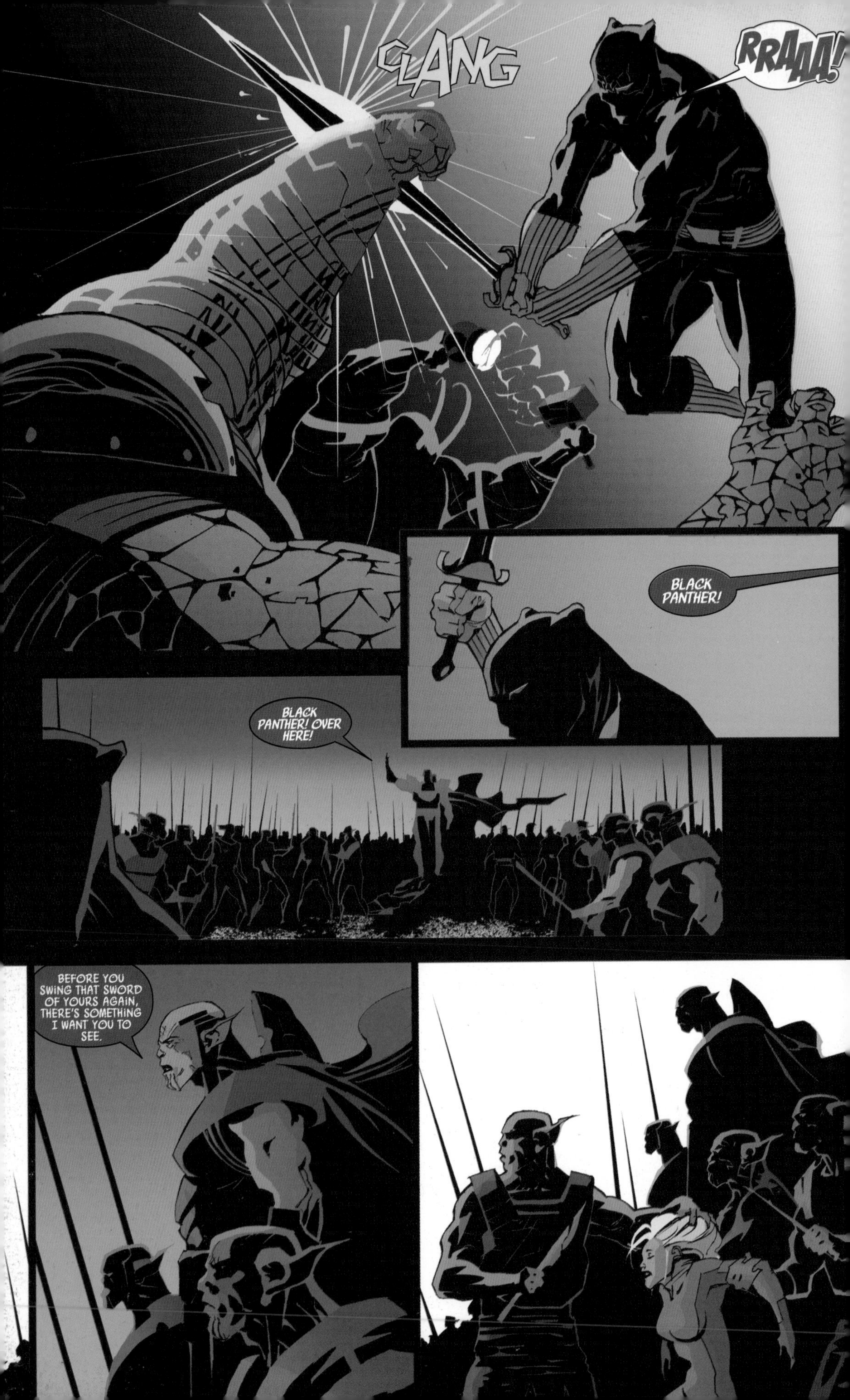
CLANG
RRAAA!
BLACK PANTHER!
BLACK PANTHER! OVER HERE!
BEFORE YOU SWING THAT SWORD OF YOURS AGAIN, THERE'S SOMETHING I WANT YOU TO SEE.

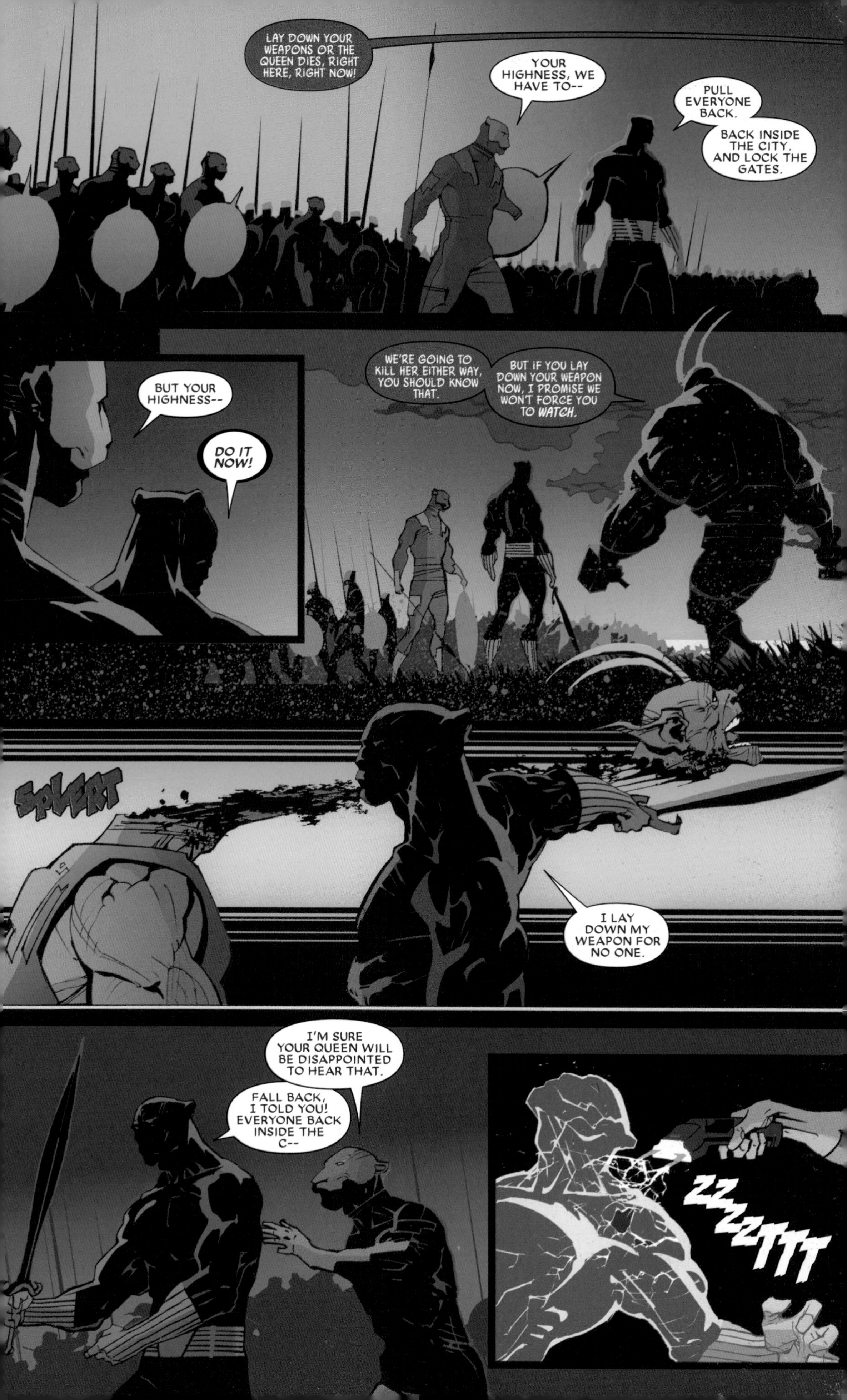
LAY DOWN YOUR WEAPONS OR THE QUEEN DIES, RIGHT HERE, RIGHT NOW!
YOUR HIGHNESS, WE HAVE TO--
PULL EVERYONE BACK.
BACK INSIDE THE CITY. AND LOCK THE GATES.
BUT YOUR HIGHNESS--
DO IT NOW!
WE'RE GOING TO KILL HER EITHER WAY, YOU SHOULD KNOW THAT.
BUT IF YOU LAY DOWN YOUR WEAPON NOW, I PROMISE WE WON'T FORCE YOU TO WATCH.
SPLERT
I LAY DOWN MY WEAPON FOR NO ONE.
I'M SURE YOUR QUEEN WILL BE DISAPPOINTED TO HEAR THAT.
FALL BACK, I TOLD YOU! EVERYONE BACK INSIDE THE C--
ZZZZTTT

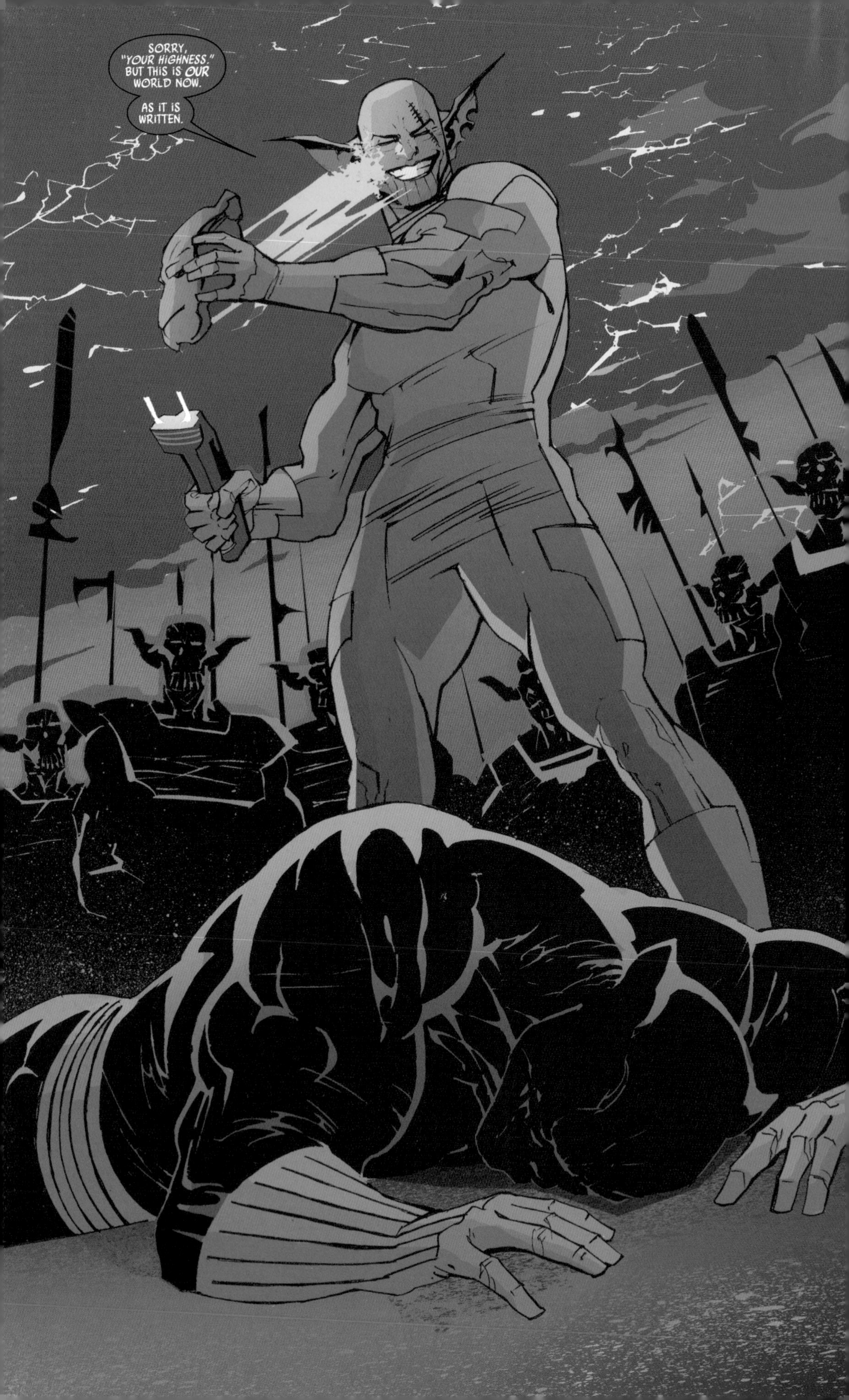
SORRY, "YOUR HIGHNESS." BUT THIS IS OUR WORLD NOW.
AS IT IS WRITTEN.

THE HIDDEN LAND OF WAKANDA!

A SPECIAL RETROSPECTIVI DETAILING WHERE IN WAKANDA "PANTHER'S RAGE" HAS TAKEN PLACE.

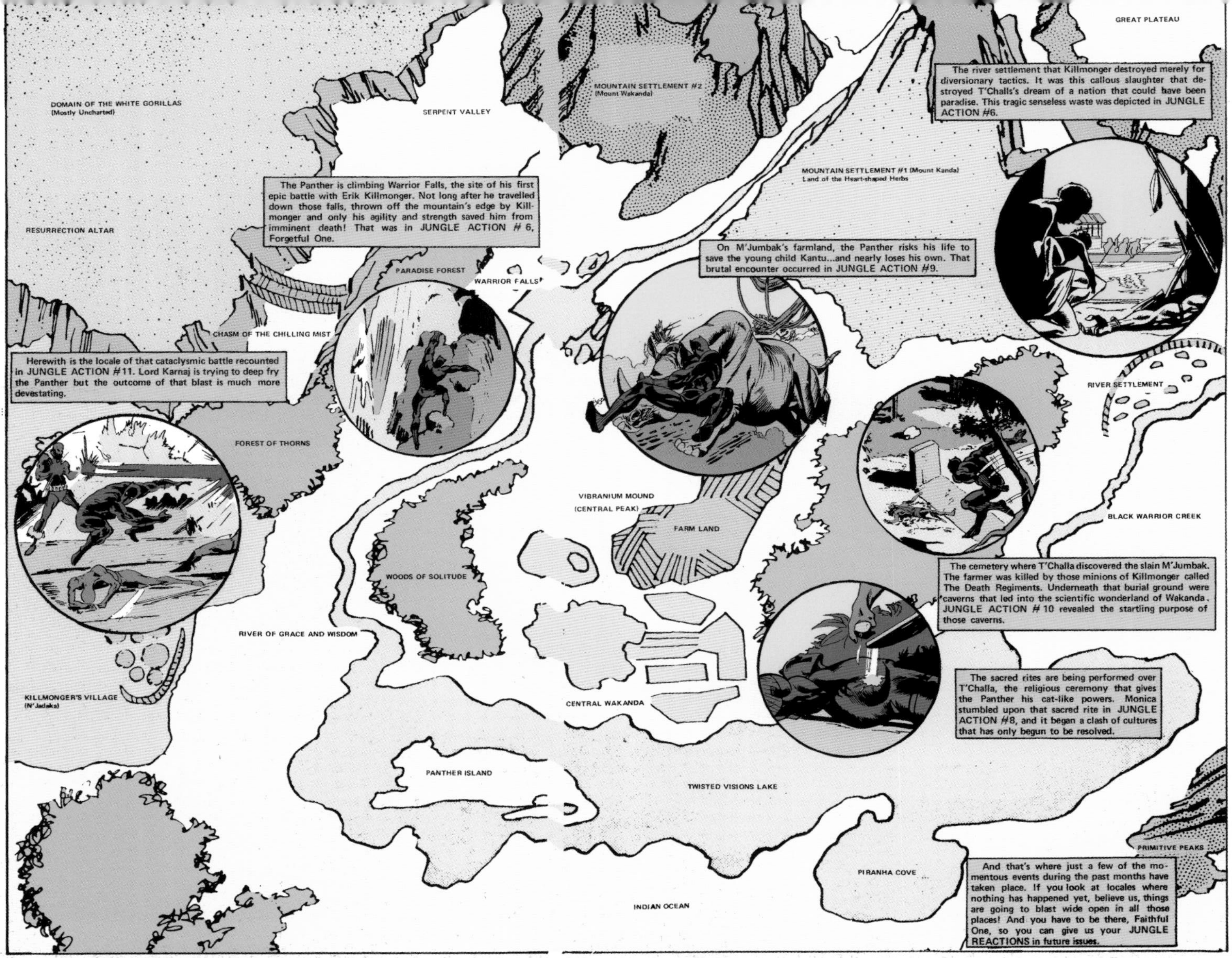

DOMAIN OF THE WHITE GORILLAS (Mostly Uncharted)
SERPENT VALLEY
MOUNTAIN SETTLEMENT #2 (Mount Wakanda)
GREAT PLATEAU
The river settlement that Killmonger destroyed merely for diversionary tactics. It was this callous slaughter that destroyed T'Challs's dream of a nation that could have been paradise. This tragic senseless waste was depicted in JUNGLE ACTION #6.
MOUNTAIN SETTLEMENT #1 (Mount Kanda) Land of the Heart-shaped Herbs
The Panther is climbing Warrior Falls, the site of his first epic battle with Erik Killmonger. Not long after he travelled down those falls, thrown off the mountain's edge by Killmonger and only his agility and strength saved him from imminent death! That was in JUNGLE ACTION # 6, Forgetful One.
RESURRECTION ALTAR
On M'Jumbak's farmland, the Panther risks his life to save the young child Kantu...and nearly loses his own. That brutal encounter occurred in JUNGLE ACTION #9.
PARADISE FOREST
WARRIOR FALLS
CHASM OF THE CHILLING MIST
Herewith is the locale of that cataclysmic battle recounted in JUNGLE ACTION #11. Lord Karnaj is trying to deep fry the Panther but the outcome of that blast is much more devestating.
RIVER SETTLEMENT
FOREST OF THORNS
VIBRANIUM MOUND (CENTRAL PEAK)
FARM LAND
BLACK WARRIOR CREEK
WOODS OF SOLITUDE
The cemetery where T'Challa discovered the slain M'Jumbak. The farmer was killed by those minions of Killmonger called The Death Regiments. Underneath that burial ground were caverns that led into the scientific wonderland of Wakanda. JUNGLE ACTION # 10 revealed the startling purpose of those caverns.
RIVER OF GRACE AND WISDOM
The sacred rites are being performed over T'Challa, the religious ceremony that gives the Panther his cat-like powers. Monica stumbled upon that sacred rite in JUNGLE ACTION #8, and it began a clash of cultures that has only begun to be resolved.
KILLMONGER'S VILLAGE (N'Jadaka)
CENTRAL WAKANDA
PANTHER ISLAND
TWISTED VISIONS LAKE
PRIMITIVE PEAKS
PIRANHA COVE
And that's where just a few of the momentous events during the past months have taken place. If you look at locales where nothing has happened yet, believe us, things are going to blast wide open in all those places! And you have to be there, Faithful One, so you can give us your JUNGLE REACTIONS in future issues.
INDIAN OCEAN

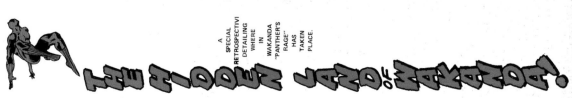

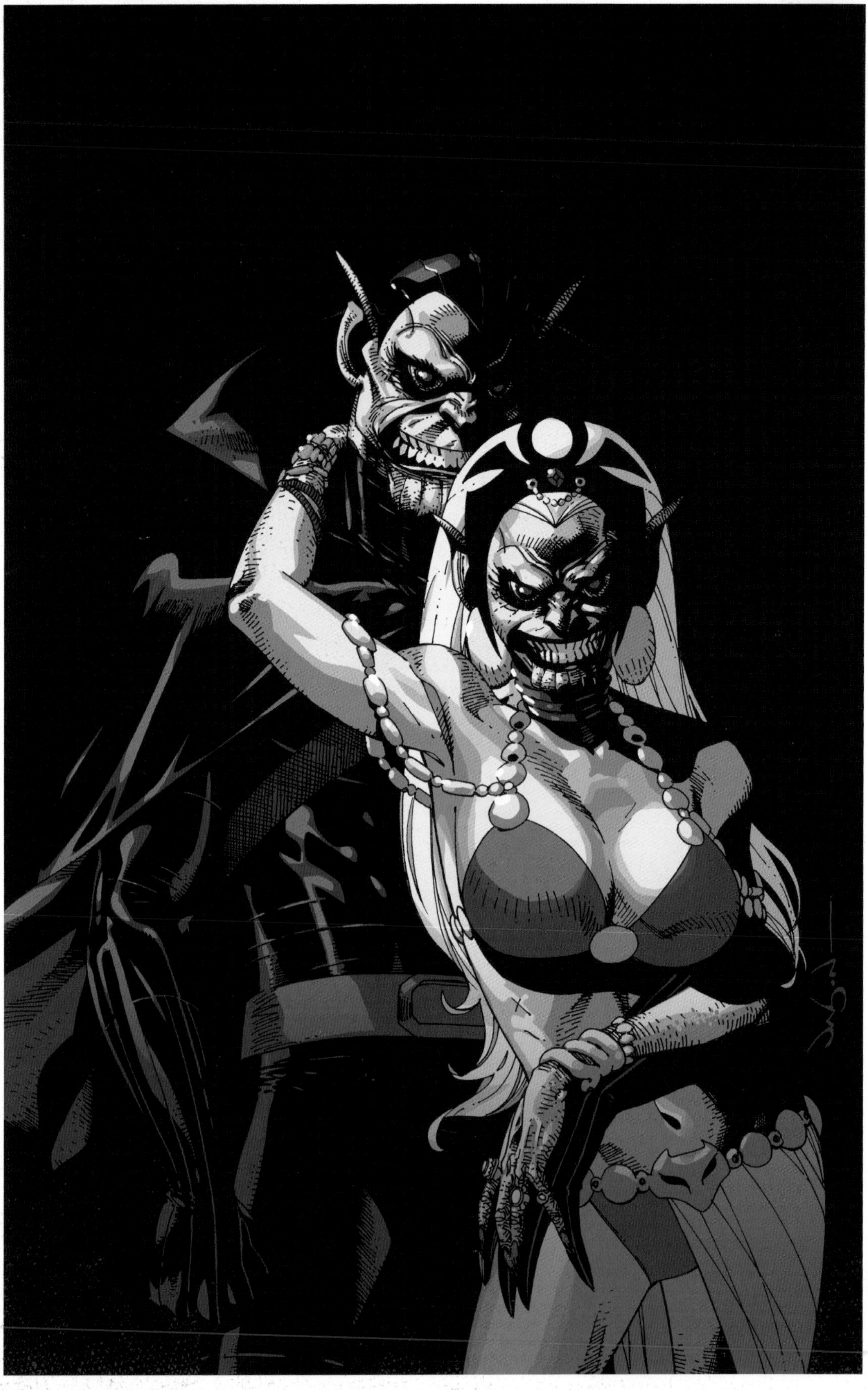

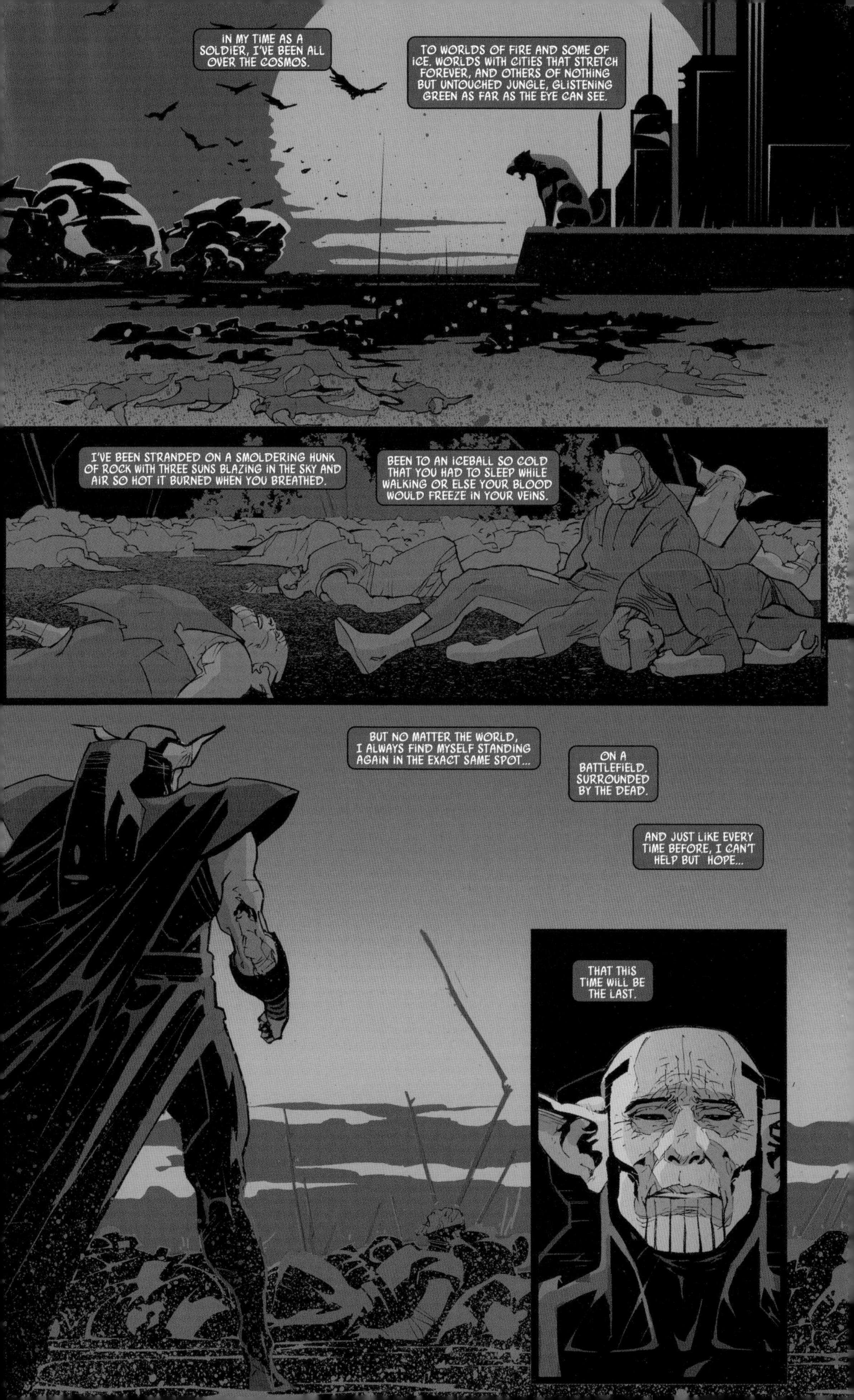
IN MY TIME AS A SOLDIER, I'VE BEEN ALL OVER THE COSMOS.
TO WORLDS OF FIRE AND SOME OF ICE. WORLDS WITH CITIES THAT STRETCH FOREVER, AND OTHERS OF NOTHING BUT UNTOUCHED JUNGLE, GLISTENING GREEN AS FAR AS THE EYE CAN SEE.
I'VE BEEN STRANDED ON A SMOLDERING HUNK OF ROCK WITH THREE SUNS BLAZING IN THE SKY AND AIR SO HOT IT BURNED WHEN YOU BREATHED.
BEEN TO AN ICEBALL SO COLD THAT YOU HAD TO SLEEP WHILE WALKING OR ELSE YOUR BLOOD WOULD FREEZE IN YOUR VEINS.
BUT NO MATTER THE WORLD, I ALWAYS FIND MYSELF STANDING AGAIN IN THE EXACT SAME SPOT...
ON A BATTLEFIELD, SURROUNDED BY THE DEAD.
AND JUST LIKE EVERY TIME BEFORE, I CAN'T HELP BUT HOPE...
THAT THIS TIME WILL BE THE LAST.

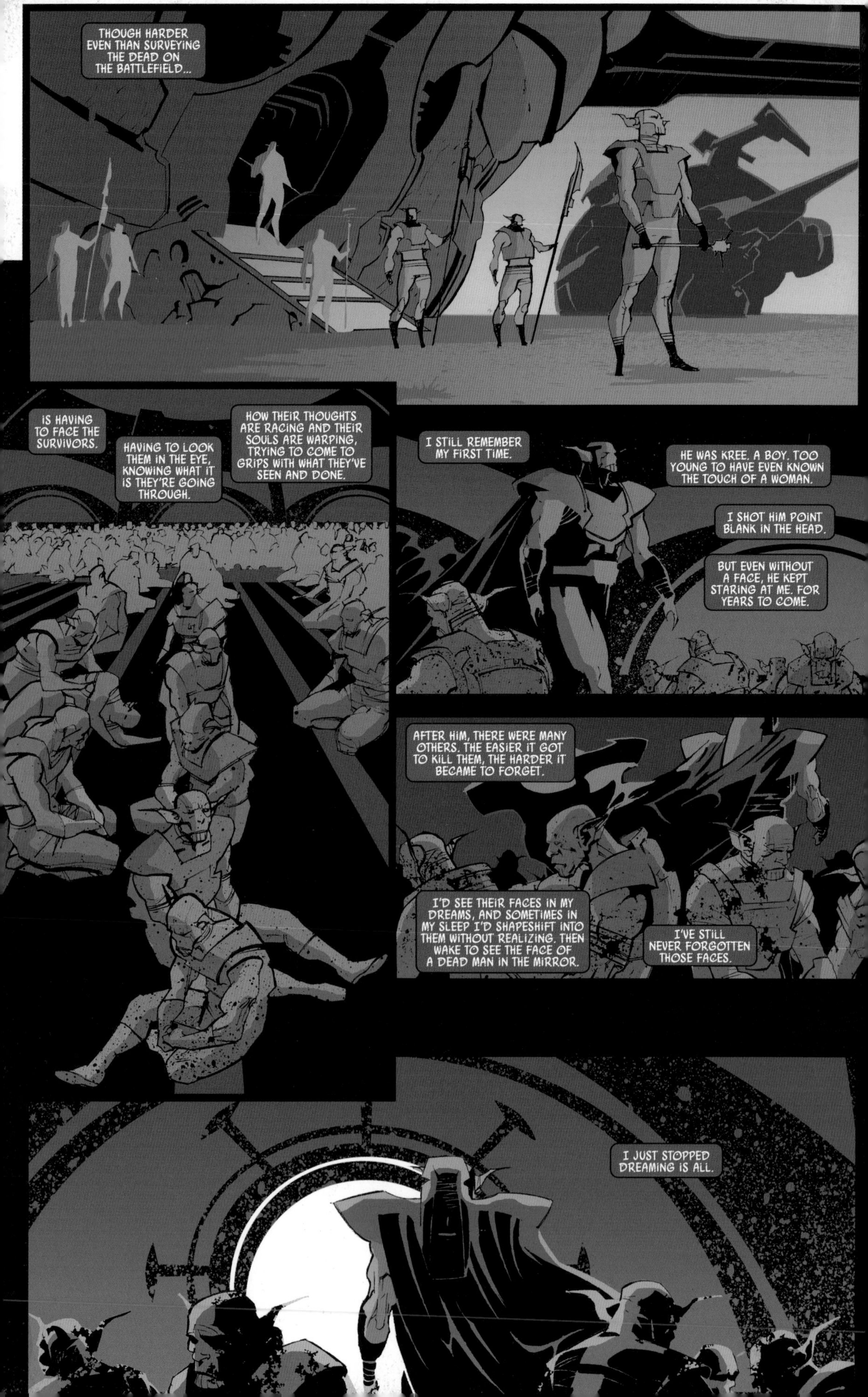
THOUGH HARDER EVEN THAN SURVEYING THE DEAD ON THE BATTLEFIELD...
IS HAVING TO FACE THE SURVIVORS.
HAVING TO LOOK THEM IN THE EYE, KNOWING WHAT IT IS THEY'RE GOING THROUGH.
HOW THEIR THOUGHTS ARE RACING AND THEIR SOULS ARE WARPING, TRYING TO COME TO GRIPS WITH WHAT THEY'VE SEEN AND DONE.
I STILL REMEMBER MY FIRST TIME.
HE WAS KREE. A BOY. TOO YOUNG TO HAVE EVEN KNOWN THE TOUCH OF A WOMAN.
I SHOT HIM POINT BLANK IN THE HEAD.
BUT EVEN WITHOUT A FACE, HE KEPT STARING AT ME. FOR YEARS TO COME.
AFTER HIM, THERE WERE MANY OTHERS. THE EASIER IT GOT TO KILL THEM, THE HARDER IT BECAME TO FORGET.
I'D SEE THEIR FACES IN MY DREAMS, AND SOMETIMES IN MY SLEEP I'D SHAPESHIFT INTO THEM WITHOUT REALIZING. THEN WAKE TO SEE THE FACE OF A DEAD MAN IN THE MIRROR.
I'VE STILL NEVER FORGOTTEN THOSE FACES.
I JUST STOPPED DREAMING IS ALL.

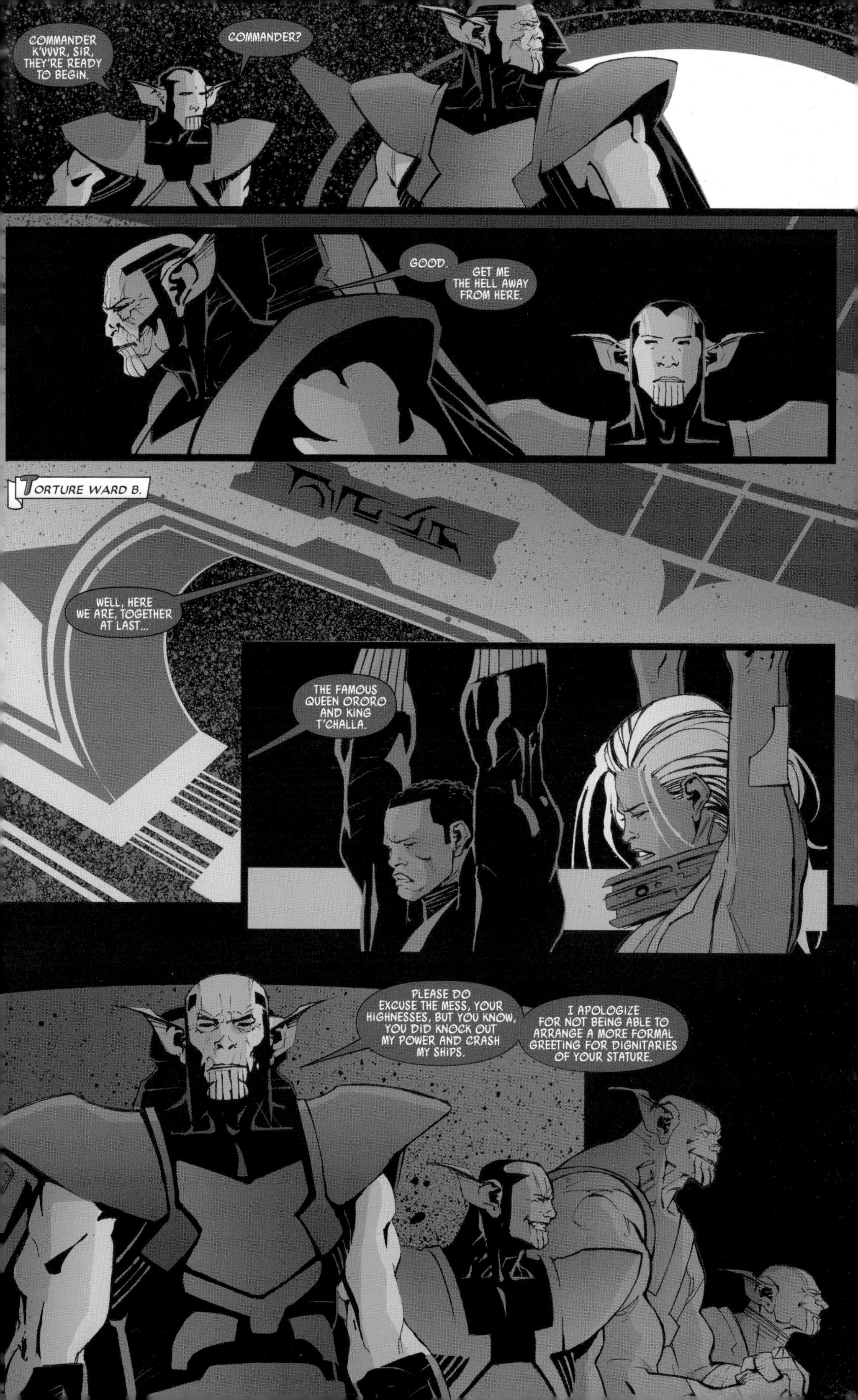
COMMANDER K'VVVR, SIR, THEY'RE READY TO BEGIN.
COMMANDER?
GOOD.
GET ME THE HELL AWAY FROM HERE.
TORTURE WARD B.
WELL, HERE WE ARE, TOGETHER AT LAST...
THE FAMOUS QUEEN ORORO AND KING T'CHALLA.
PLEASE DO EXCUSE THE MESS, YOUR HIGHNESSES, BUT YOU KNOW, YOU DID KNOCK OUT MY POWER AND CRASH MY SHIPS.
I APOLOGIZE FOR NOT BEING ABLE TO ARRANGE A MORE FORMAL GREETING FOR DIGNITARIES OF YOUR STATURE.

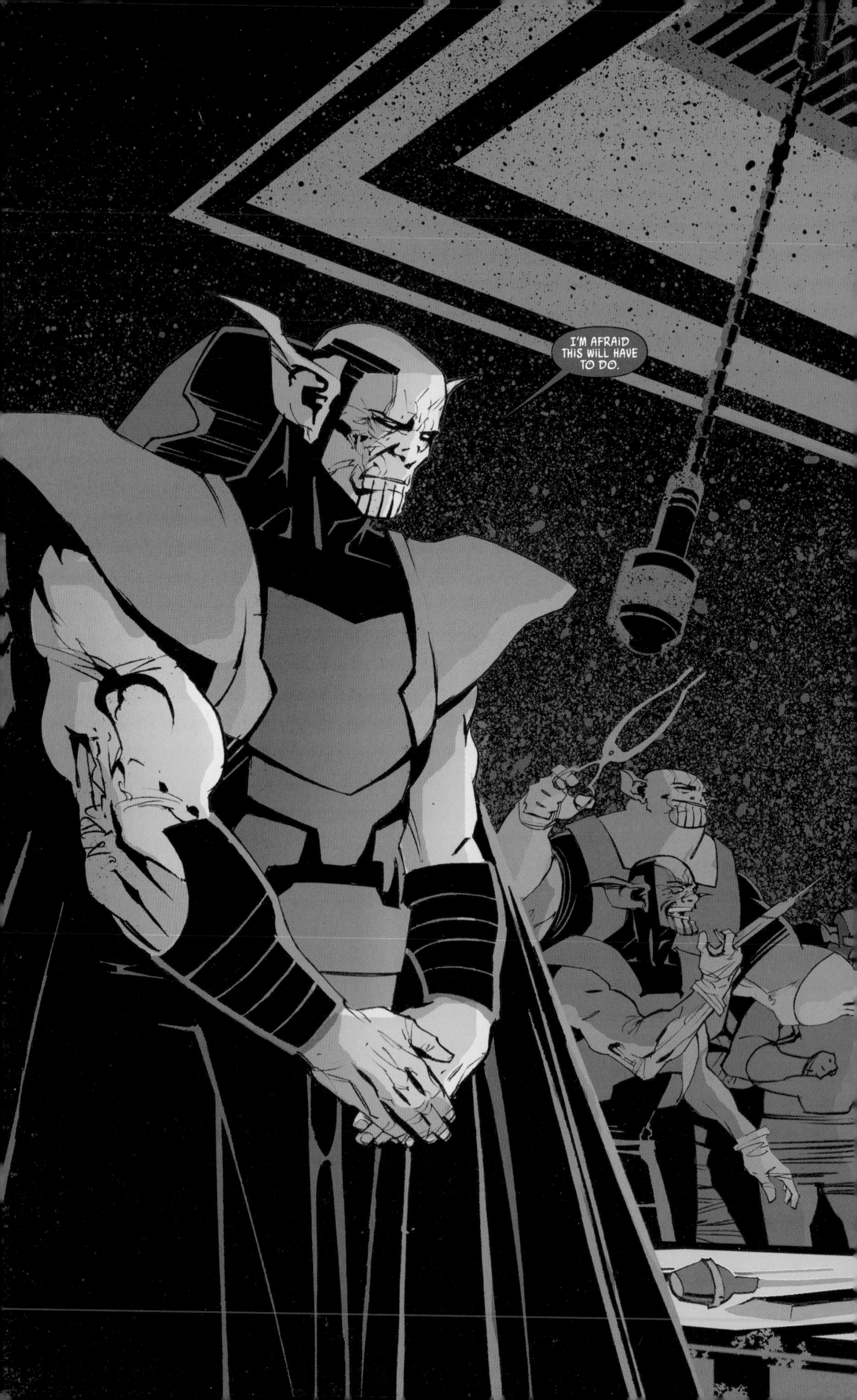
I'M AFRAID THIS WILL HAVE TO DO.

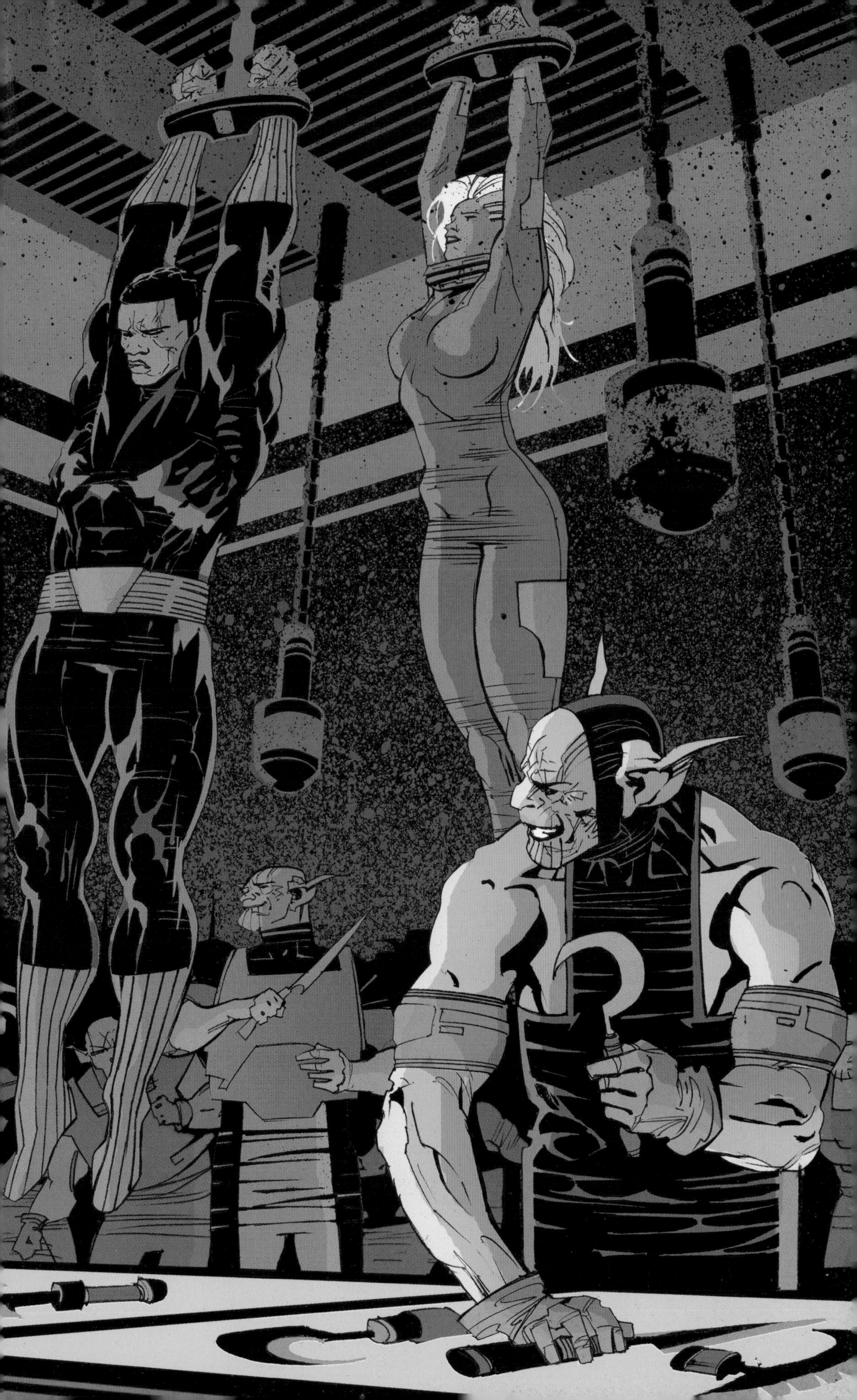

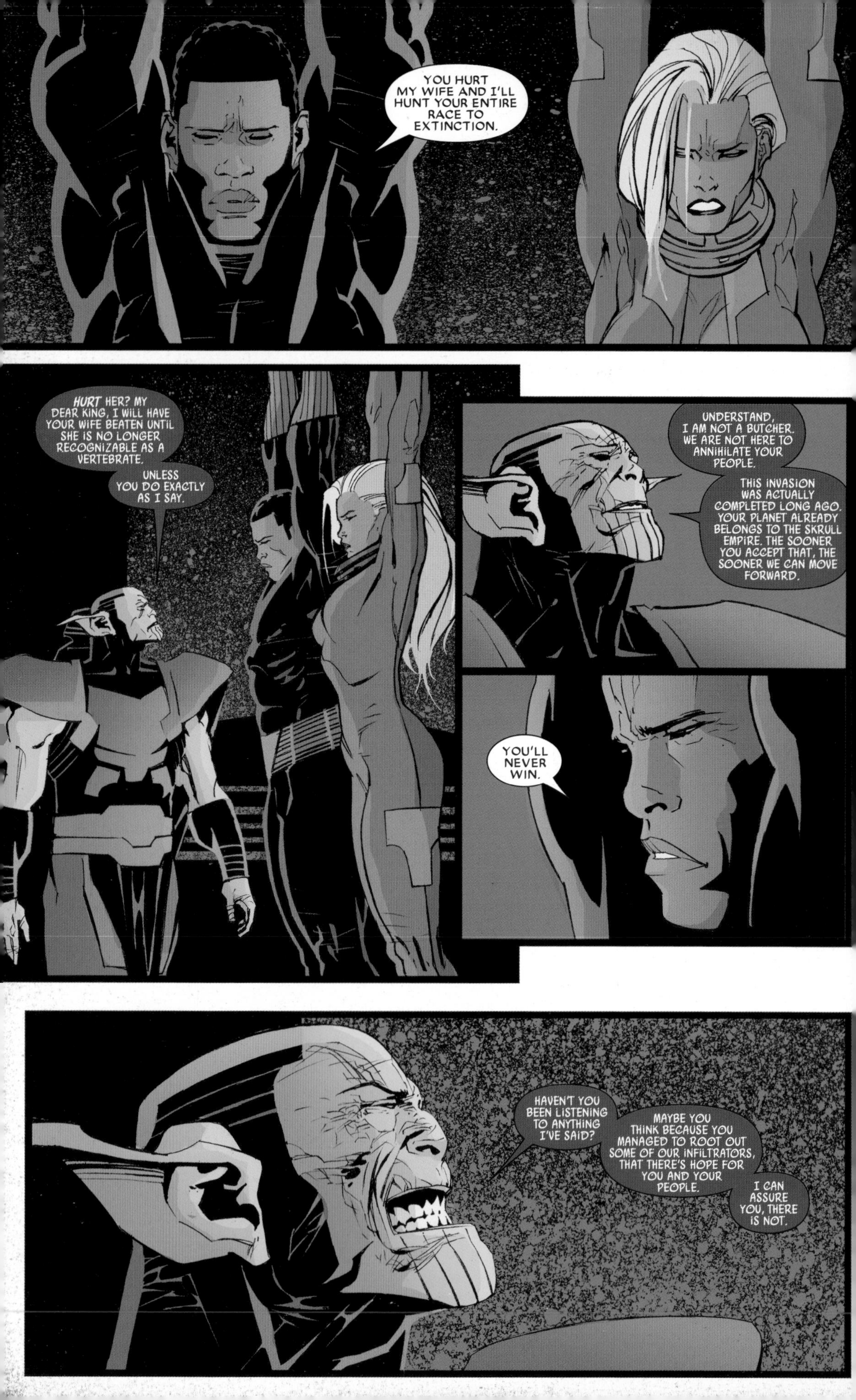
YOU HURT MY WIFE AND I'LL HUNT YOUR ENTIRE RACE TO EXTINCTION.
HURT HER? MY DEAR KING, I WILL HAVE YOUR WIFE BEATEN UNTIL SHE IS NO LONGER RECOGNIZABLE AS A VERTEBRATE.
UNLESS YOU DO EXACTLY AS I SAY.
UNDERSTAND, I AM NOT A BUTCHER. WE ARE NOT HERE TO ANNIHILATE YOUR PEOPLE.
THIS INVASION WAS ACTUALLY COMPLETED LONG AGO. YOUR PLANET ALREADY BELONGS TO THE SKRULL EMPIRE. THE SOONER YOU ACCEPT THAT, THE SOONER WE CAN MOVE FORWARD.
YOU'LL NEVER WIN.
HAVEN'T YOU BEEN LISTENING TO ANYTHING I'VE SAID?
MAYBE YOU THINK BECAUSE YOU MANAGED TO ROOT OUT SOME OF OUR INFILTRATORS, THAT THERE'S HOPE FOR YOU AND YOUR PEOPLE.
I CAN ASSURE YOU, THERE IS NOT.

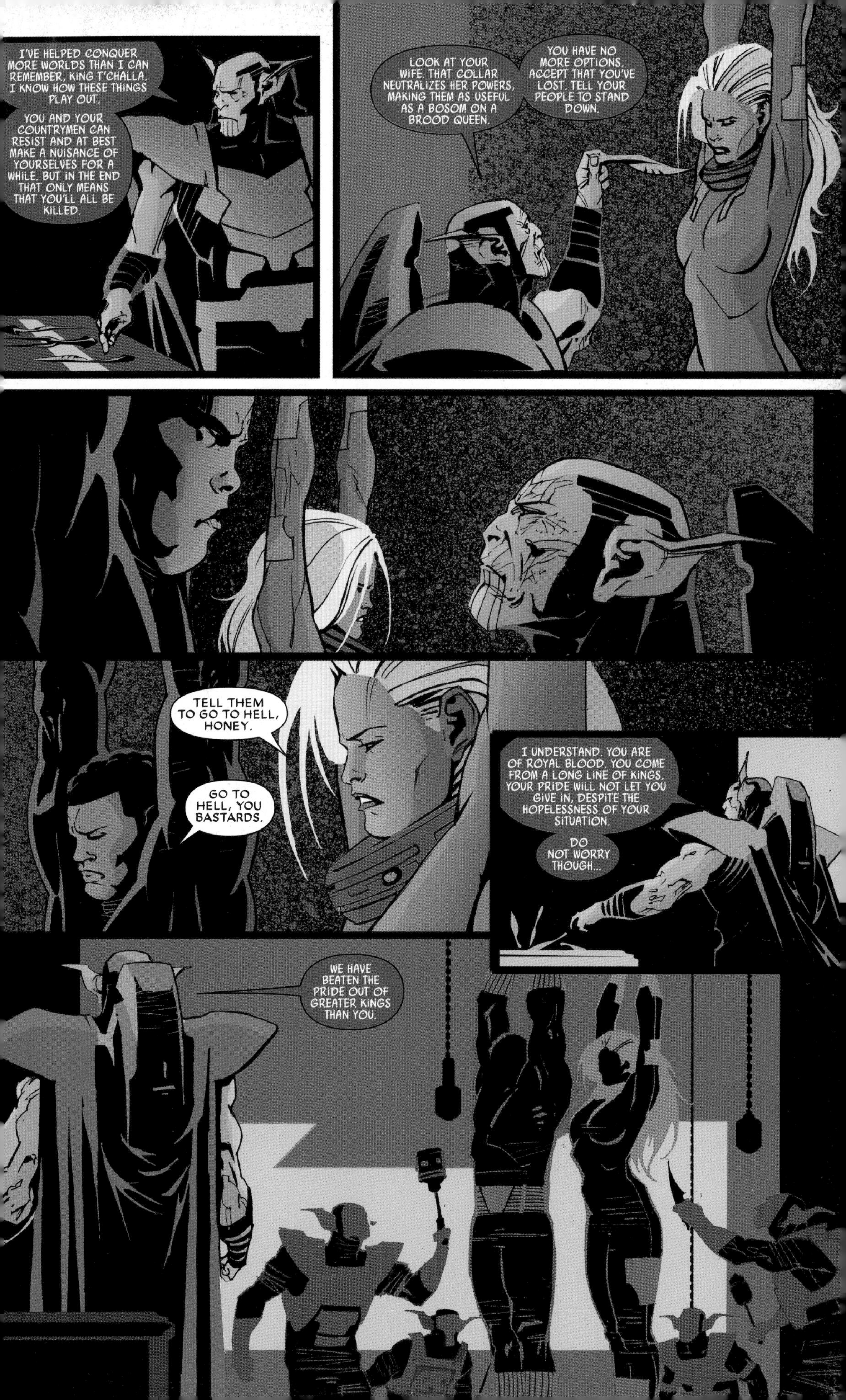
I'VE HELPED CONQUER MORE WORLDS THAN I CAN REMEMBER, KING T'CHALLA. I KNOW HOW THESE THINGS PLAY OUT.
YOU AND YOUR COUNTRYMEN CAN RESIST AND AT BEST MAKE A NUISANCE OF YOURSELVES FOR A WHILE. BUT IN THE END THAT ONLY MEANS THAT YOU'LL ALL BE KILLED.
LOOK AT YOUR WIFE. THAT COLLAR NEUTRALIZES HER POWERS, MAKING THEM AS USEFUL AS A BOSOM ON A BROOD QUEEN.
YOU HAVE NO MORE OPTIONS. ACCEPT THAT YOU'VE LOST. TELL YOUR PEOPLE TO STAND DOWN.
TELL THEM TO GO TO HELL, HONEY.
GO TO HELL, YOU BASTARDS.
I UNDERSTAND. YOU ARE OF ROYAL BLOOD. YOU COME FROM A LONG LINE OF KINGS. YOUR PRIDE WILL NOT LET YOU GIVE IN, DESPITE THE HOPELESSNESS OF YOUR SITUATION.
DO NOT WORRY THOUGH...
WE HAVE BEATEN THE PRIDE OUT OF GREATER KINGS THAN YOU.

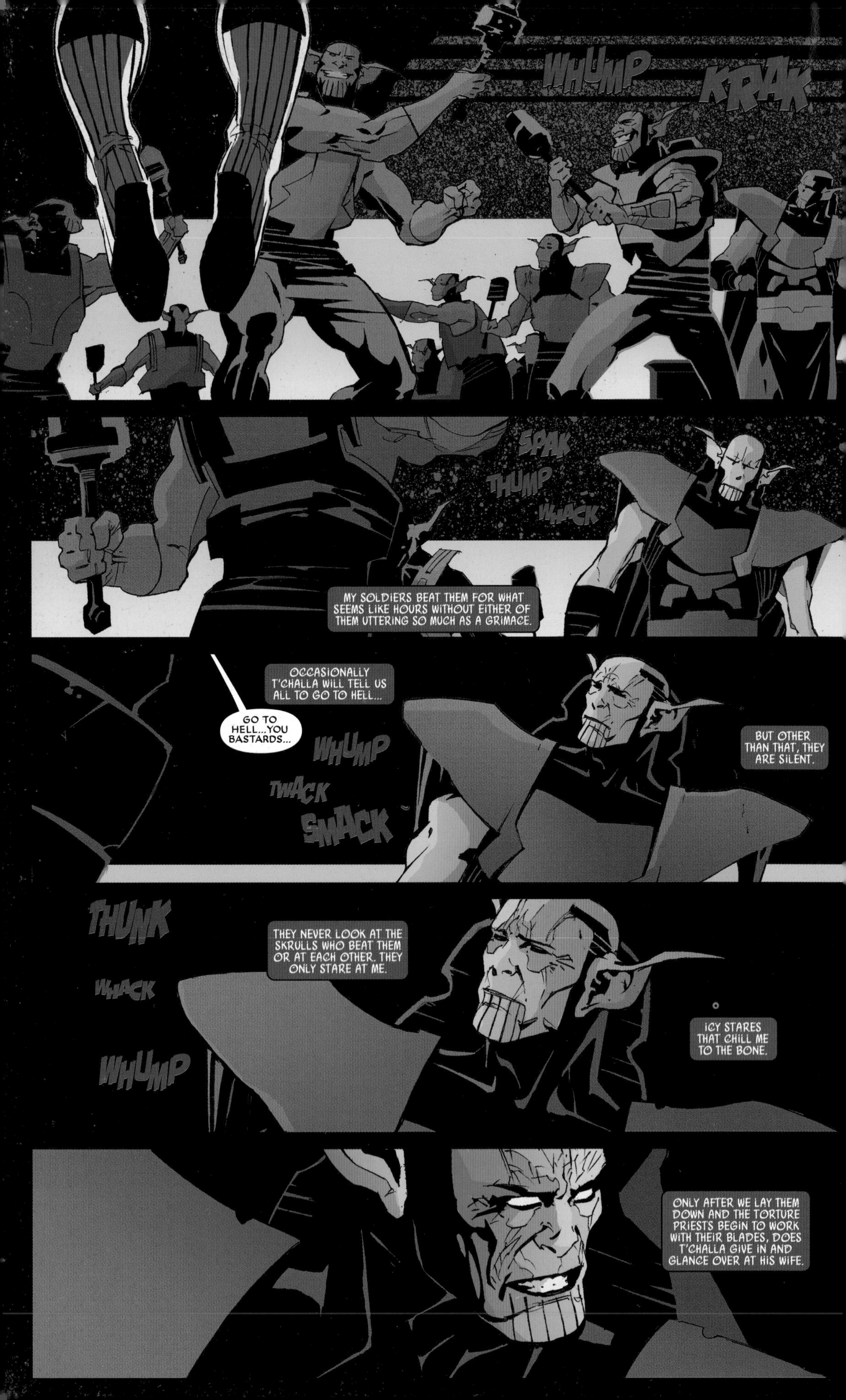
WHUMP
KRAK
SPAK
THUMP
WHACK
MY SOLDIERS BEAT THEM FOR WHAT SEEMS LIKE HOURS WITHOUT EITHER OF THEM UTTERING SO MUCH AS A GRIMACE.
OCCASIONALLY T'CHALLA WILL TELL US ALL TO GO TO HELL...
GO TO HELL...YOU BASTARDS...
WHUMP
TWACK
SMACK
BUT OTHER THAN THAT, THEY ARE SILENT.
THUNK
WHACK
WHUMP
THEY NEVER LOOK AT THE SKRULLS WHO BEAT THEM OR AT EACH OTHER. THEY ONLY STARE AT ME.
ICY STARES THAT CHILL ME TO THE BONE.
ONLY AFTER WE LAY THEM DOWN AND THE TORTURE PRIESTS BEGIN TO WORK WITH THEIR BLADES, DOES T'CHALLA GIVE IN AND GLANCE OVER AT HIS WIFE.

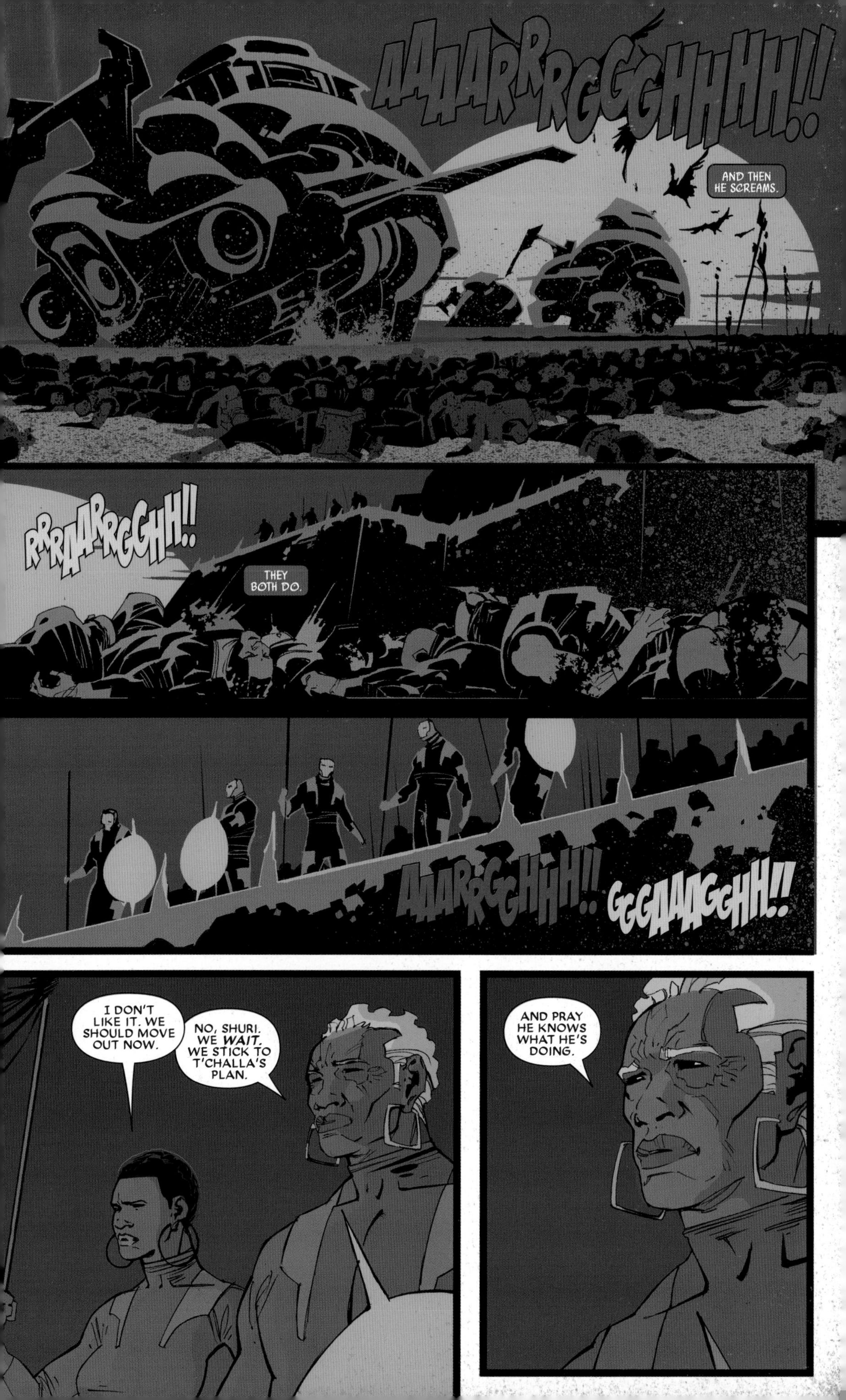
AAAARRRGGGHHHH!!
AND THEN HE SCREAMS.
RRRAARRGGHH!!
THEY BOTH DO.
AAARRGGHHHH!!
GGGAAAGGHH!!
I DON'T LIKE IT. WE SHOULD MOVE OUT NOW.
NO, SHURI. WE WAIT. WE STICK TO T'CHALLA'S PLAN.
AND PRAY HE KNOWS WHAT HE'S DOING.

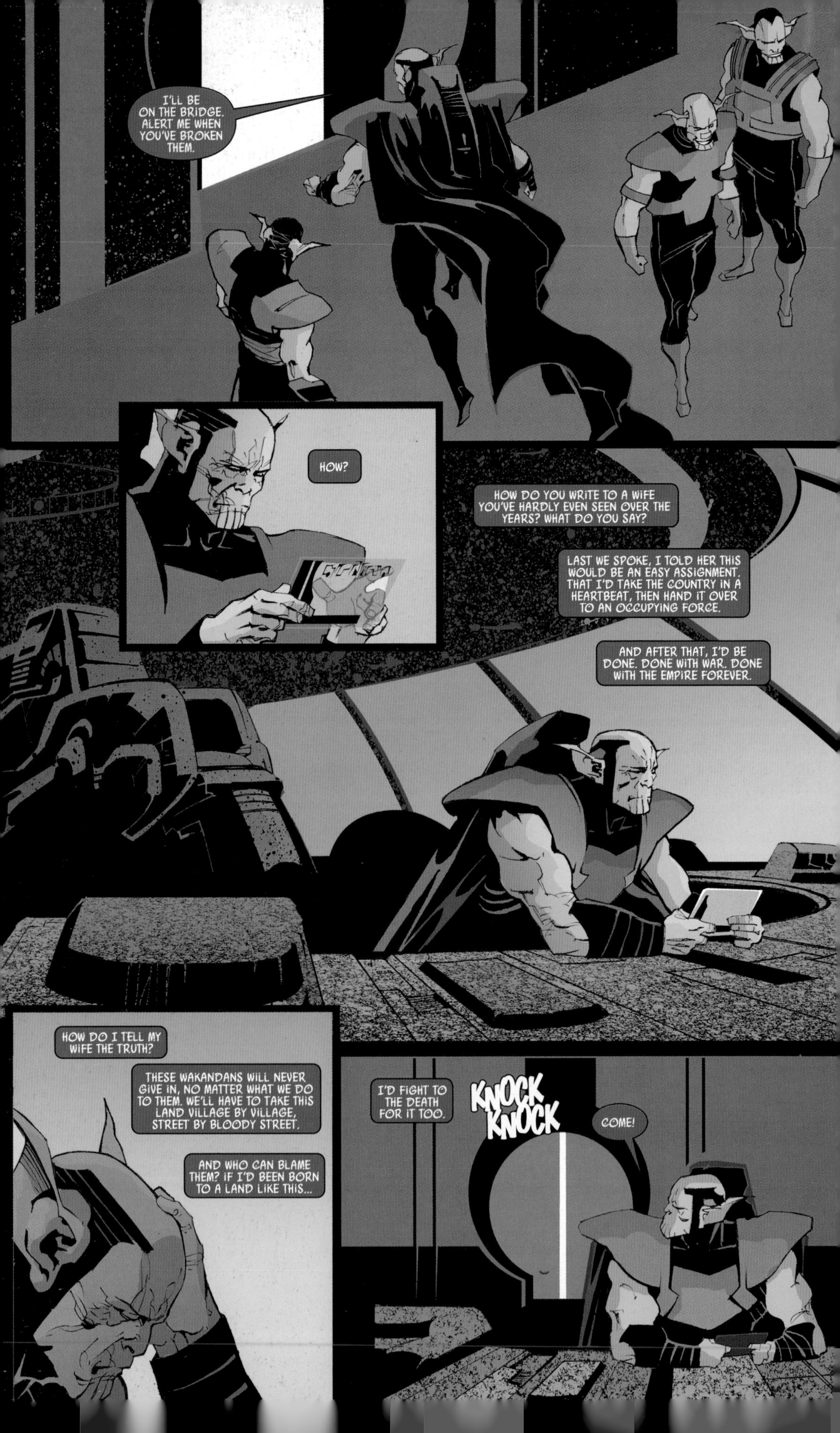
I'LL BE ON THE BRIDGE. ALERT ME WHEN YOU'VE BROKEN THEM.
HOW?
HOW DO YOU WRITE TO A WIFE YOU'VE HARDLY EVEN SEEN OVER THE YEARS? WHAT DO YOU SAY?
LAST WE SPOKE, I TOLD HER THIS WOULD BE AN EASY ASSIGNMENT. THAT I'D TAKE THE COUNTRY IN A HEARTBEAT, THEN HAND IT OVER TO AN OCCUPYING FORCE.
AND AFTER THAT, I'D BE DONE. DONE WITH WAR. DONE WITH THE EMPIRE FOREVER.
HOW DO I TELL MY WIFE THE TRUTH?
THESE WAKANDANS WILL NEVER GIVE IN, NO MATTER WHAT WE DO TO THEM. WE'LL HAVE TO TAKE THIS LAND VILLAGE BY VILLAGE, STREET BY BLOODY STREET.
AND WHO CAN BLAME THEM? IF I'D BEEN BORN TO A LAND LIKE THIS...
I'D FIGHT TO THE DEATH FOR IT TOO.
KNOCK KNOCK
COME!

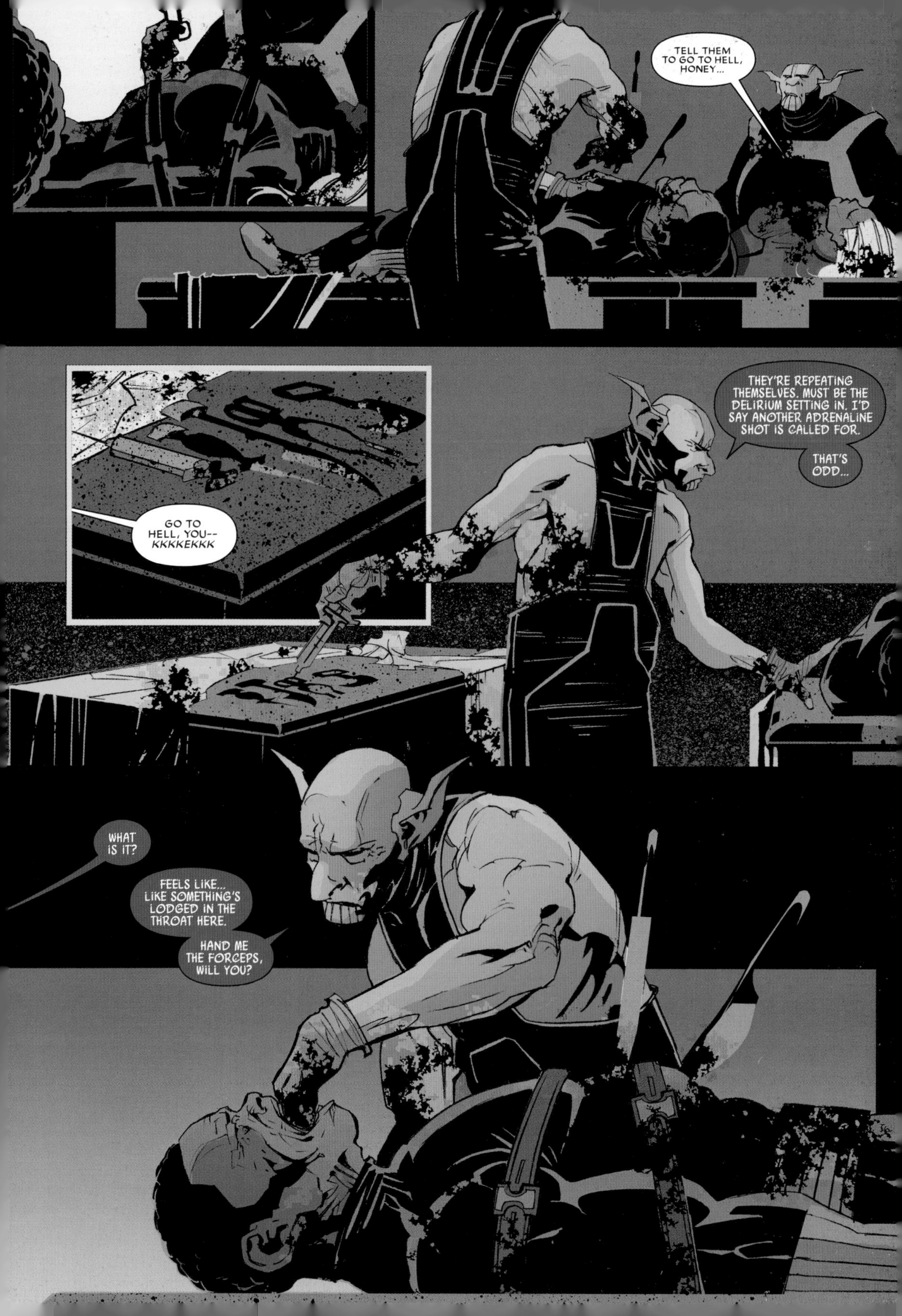
TELL THEM TO GO TO HELL, HONEY...
GO TO HELL, YOU-- KKKKEKKK
THEY'RE REPEATING THEMSELVES. MUST BE THE DELIRIUM SETTING IN. I'D SAY ANOTHER ADRENALINE SHOT IS CALLED FOR.
THAT'S ODD...
WHAT IS IT?
FEELS LIKE... LIKE SOMETHING'S LODGED IN THE THROAT HERE.
HAND ME THE FORCEPS, WILL YOU?

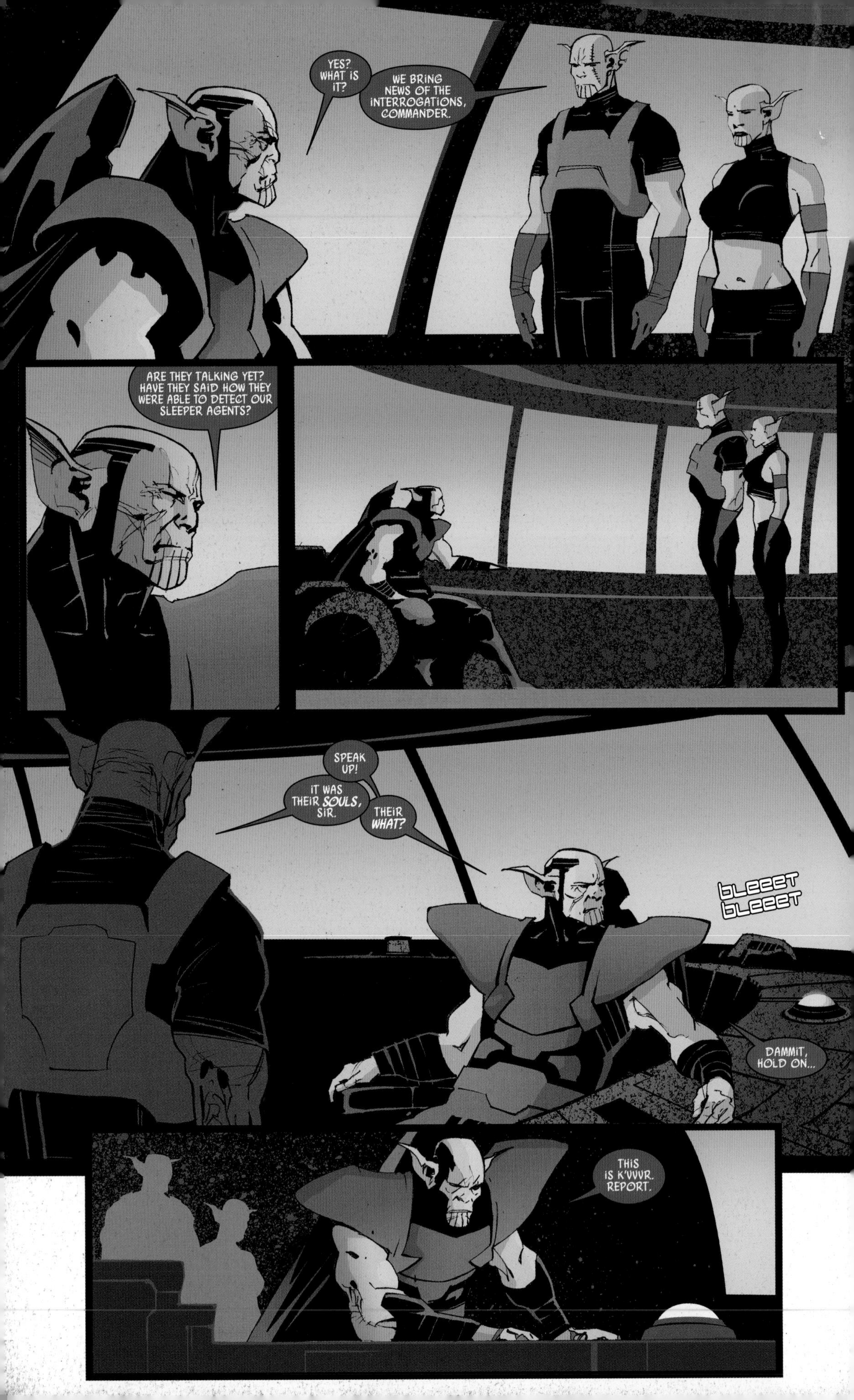
YES? WHAT IS IT?
WE BRING NEWS OF THE INTERROGATIONS, COMMANDER.
ARE THEY TALKING YET? HAVE THEY SAID HOW THEY WERE ABLE TO DETECT OUR SLEEPER AGENTS?
SPEAK UP!
IT WAS THEIR *SOULS*, SIR.
THEIR *WHAT?*
BLEEET BLEEET
DAMMIT, HOLD ON...
THIS IS K'VVVR. REPORT.

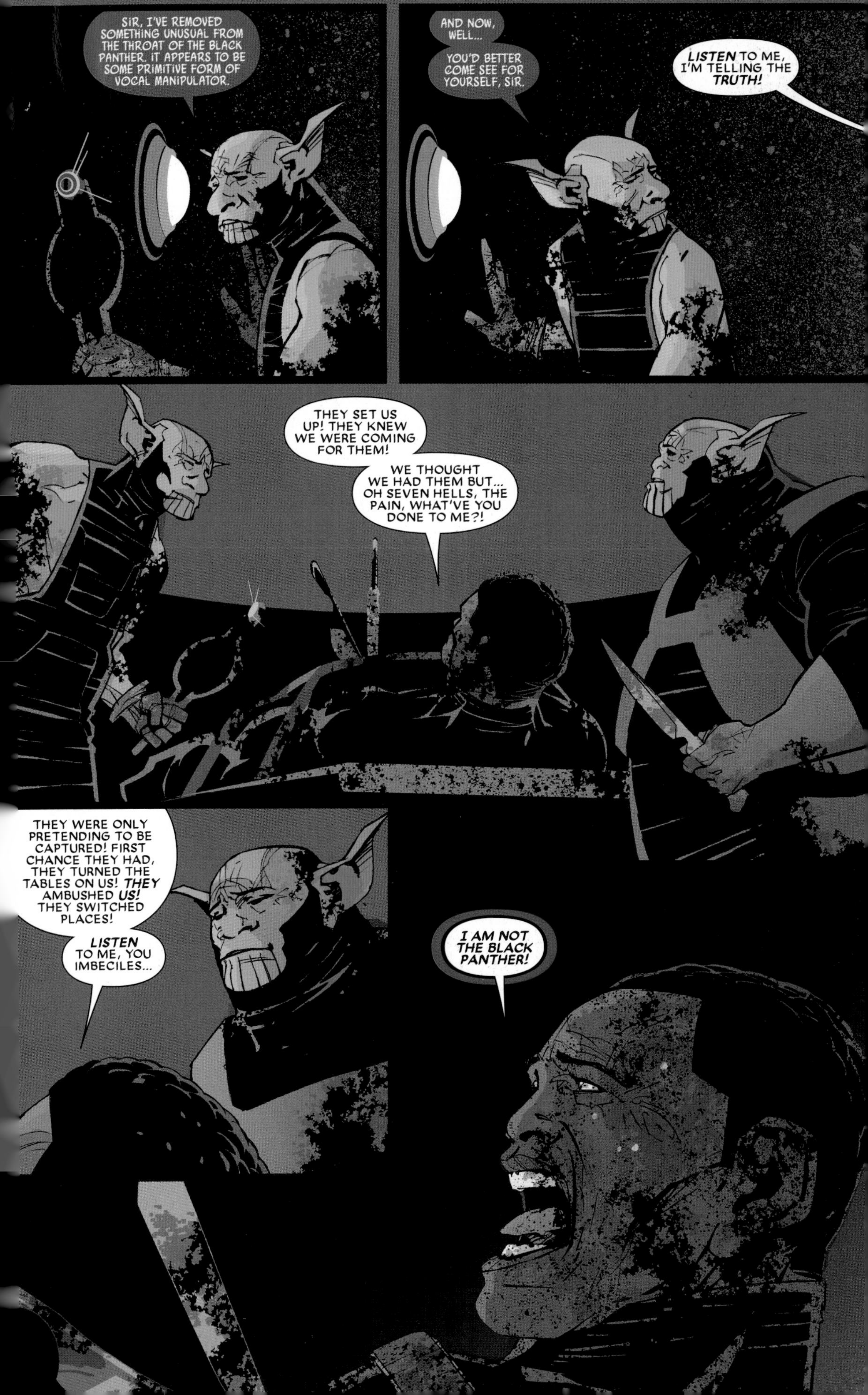

SIR, I'VE REMOVED SOMETHING UNUSUAL FROM THE THROAT OF THE BLACK PANTHER. IT APPEARS TO BE SOME PRIMITIVE FORM OF VOCAL MANIPULATOR.
AND NOW, WELL...
YOU'D BETTER COME SEE FOR YOURSELF, SIR.
LISTEN TO ME, I'M TELLING THE TRUTH!
THEY SET US UP! THEY KNEW WE WERE COMING FOR THEM!
WE THOUGHT WE HAD THEM BUT... OH SEVEN HELLS, THE PAIN, WHAT'VE YOU DONE TO ME?!
THEY WERE ONLY PRETENDING TO BE CAPTURED! FIRST CHANCE THEY HAD, THEY TURNED THE TABLES ON US! THEY AMBUSHED US! THEY SWITCHED PLACES!
LISTEN TO ME, YOU IMBECILES...
I AM NOT THE BLACK PANTHER!

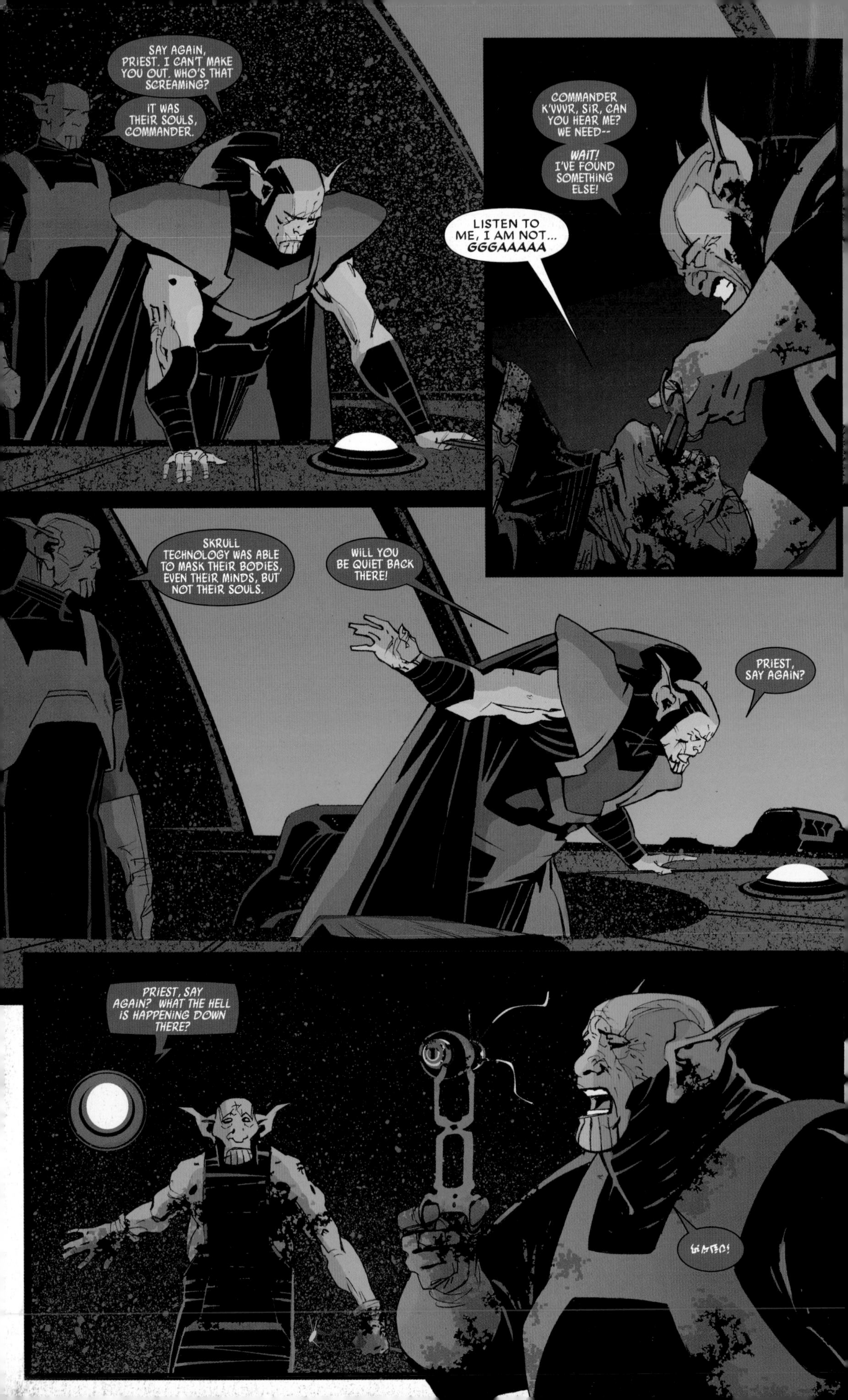
SAY AGAIN, PRIEST. I CAN'T MAKE YOU OUT. WHO'S THAT SCREAMING?
IT WAS THEIR SOULS, COMMANDER.
COMMANDER K'VVVR, SIR, CAN YOU HEAR ME? WE NEED--
WAIT! I'VE FOUND SOMETHING ELSE!
LISTEN TO ME, I AM NOT... GGGAAAAA
SKRULL TECHNOLOGY WAS ABLE TO MASK THEIR BODIES, EVEN THEIR MINDS, BUT NOT THEIR SOULS.
WILL YOU BE QUIET BACK THERE!
PRIEST, SAY AGAIN?
PRIEST, SAY AGAIN? WHAT THE HELL IS HAPPENING DOWN THERE?

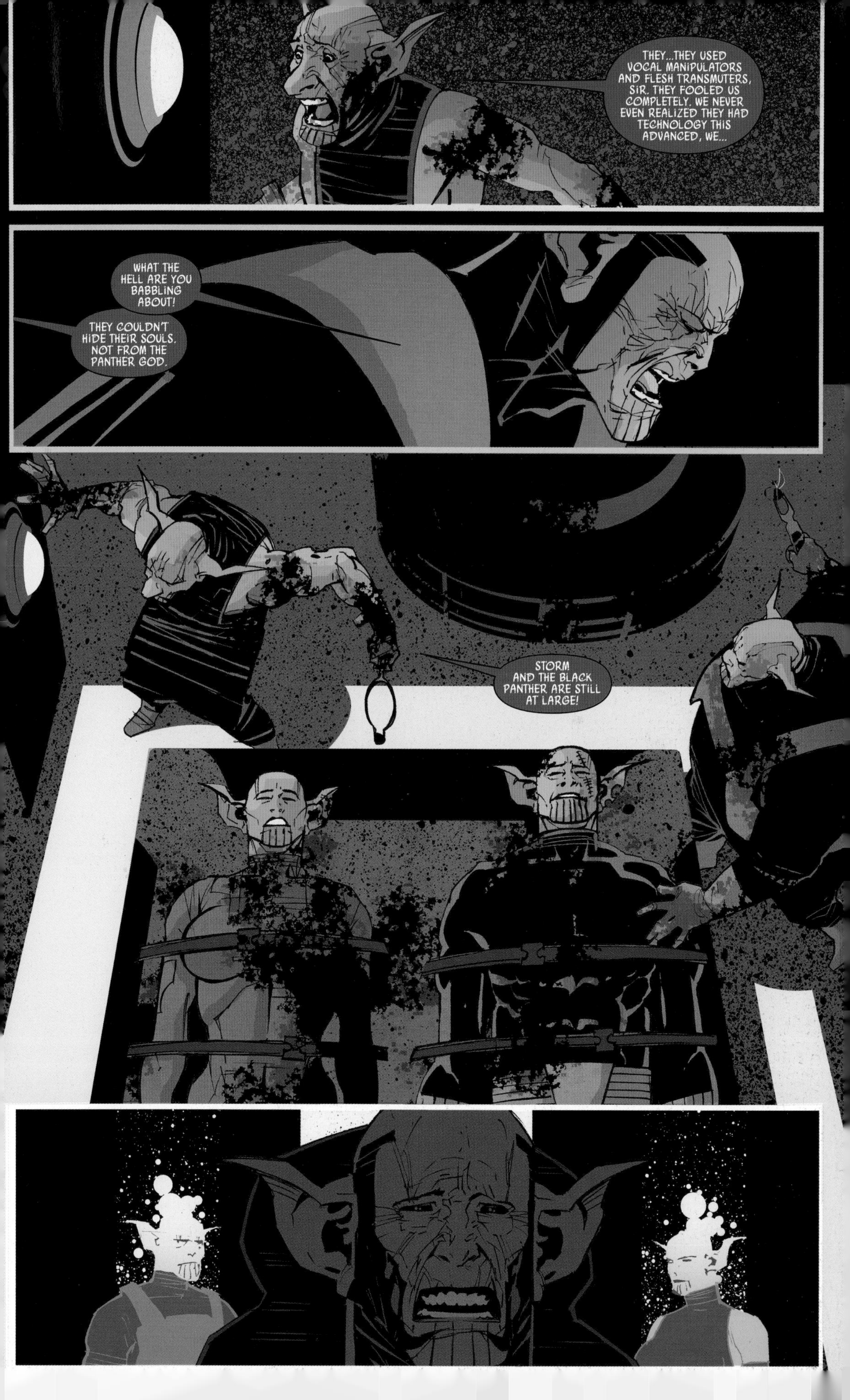
THEY...THEY USED VOCAL MANIPULATORS AND FLESH TRANSMUTERS, SIR. THEY FOOLED US COMPLETELY. WE NEVER EVEN REALIZED THEY HAD TECHNOLOGY THIS ADVANCED, WE...
WHAT THE HELL ARE YOU BABBLING ABOUT!
THEY COULDN'T HIDE THEIR SOULS. NOT FROM THE PANTHER GOD.
STORM AND THE BLACK PANTHER ARE STILL AT LARGE!

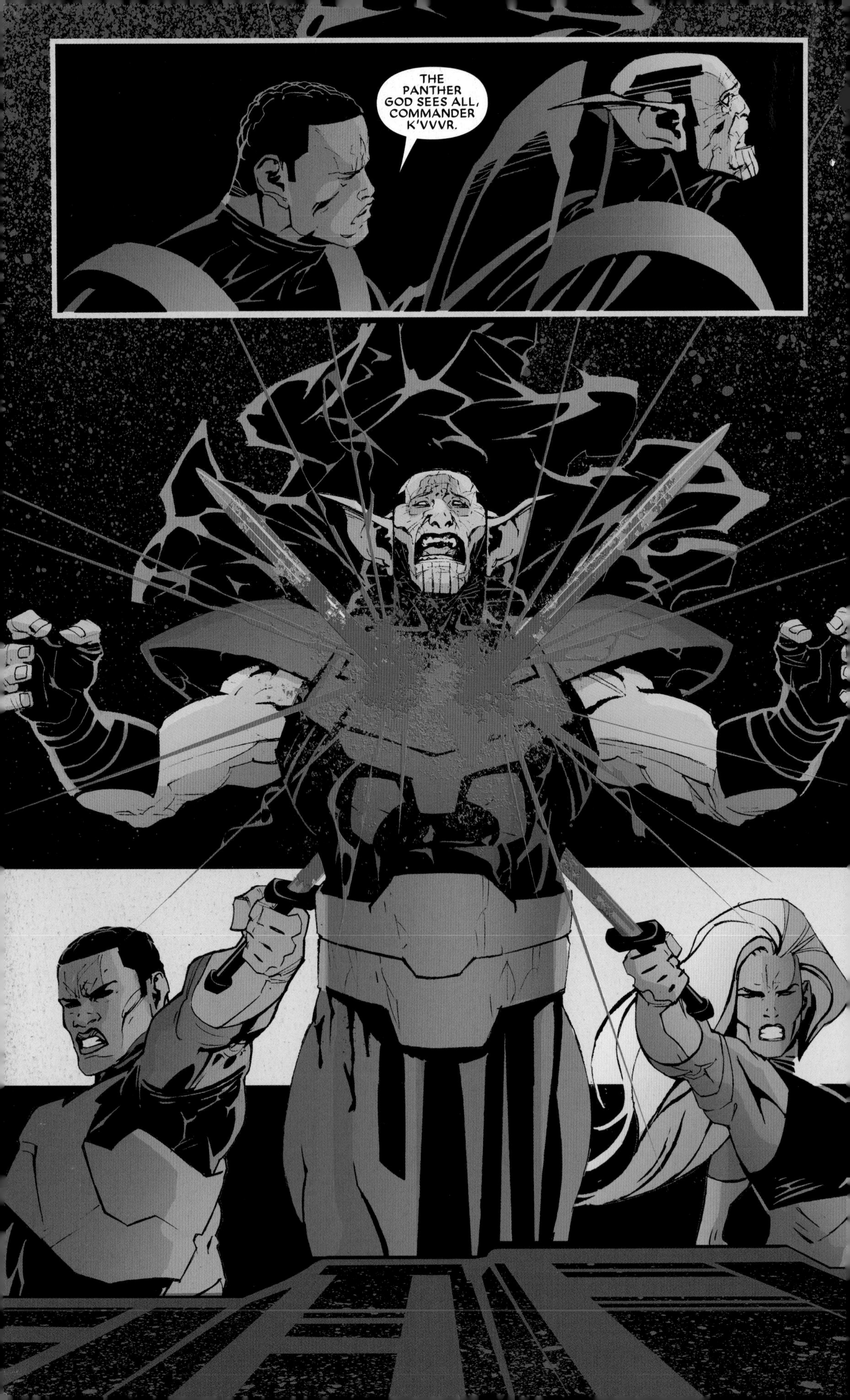
THE PANTHER GOD SEES ALL, COMMANDER K'VVVR.

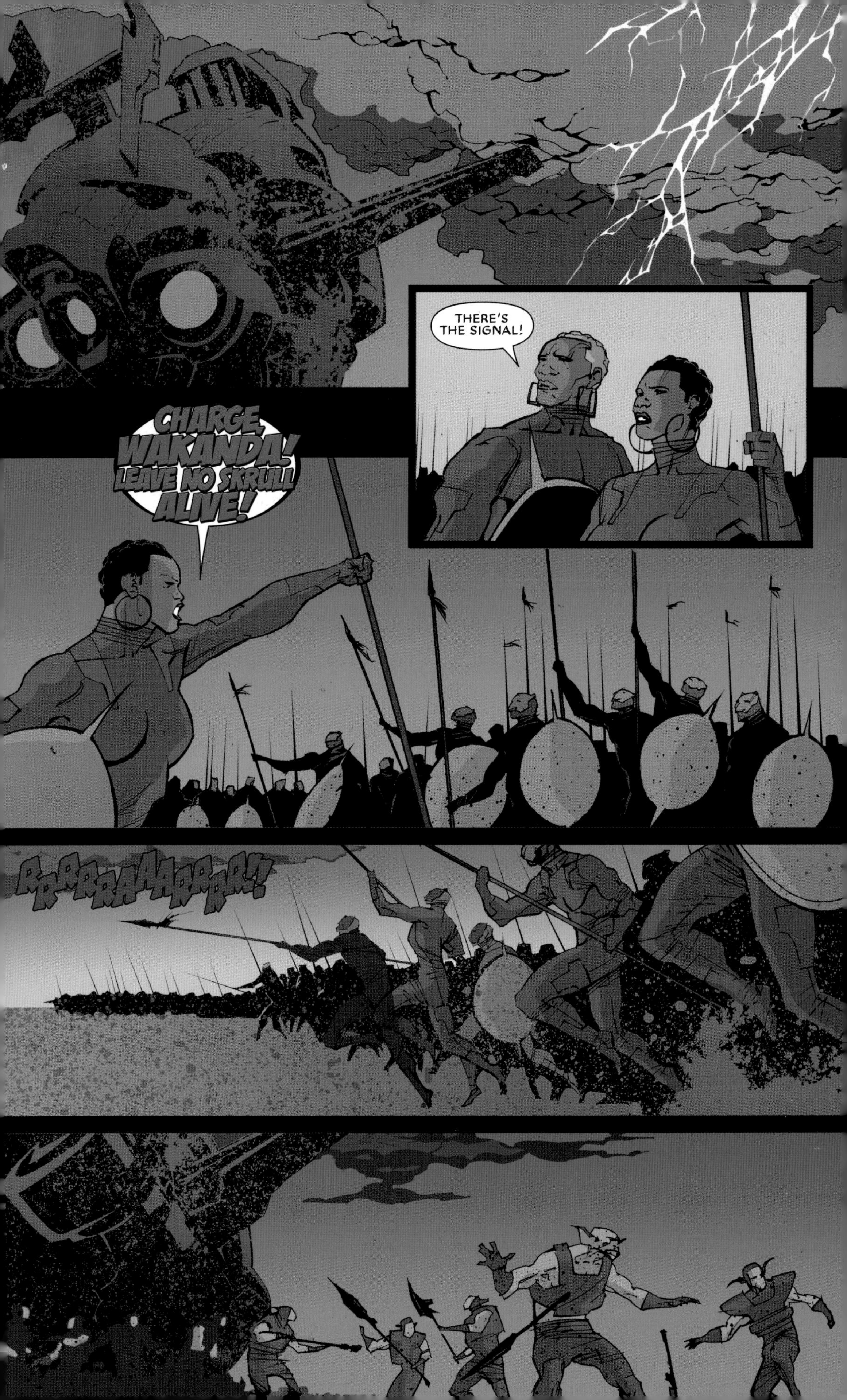
THERE'S THE SIGNAL!
CHARGE, WAKANDA! LEAVE NO SKRULL ALIVE!
RRRRRAAARRRR!!

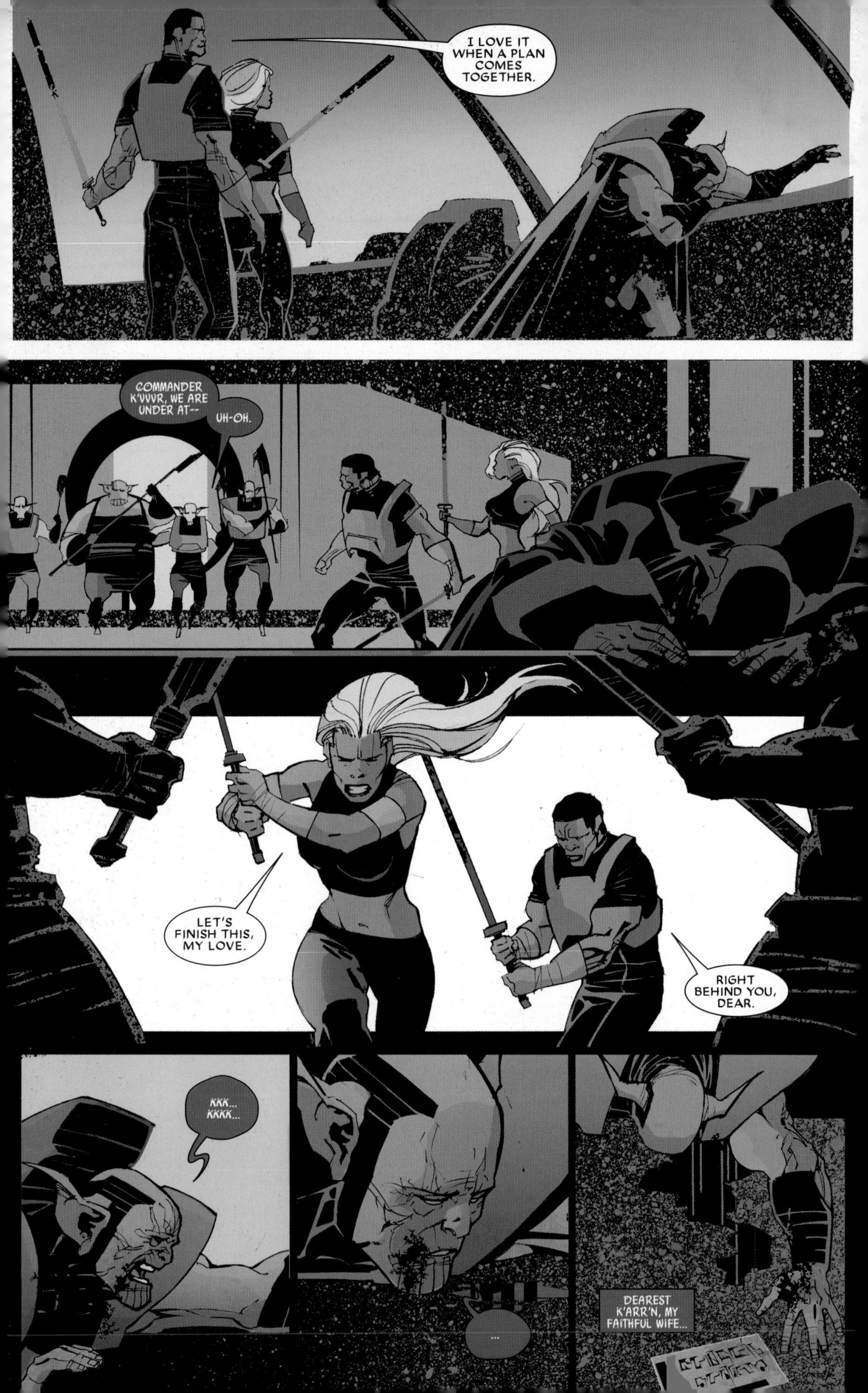

I LOVE IT WHEN A PLAN COMES TOGETHER.
COMMANDER K'VVVR, WE ARE UNDER AT--
UH-OH.
LET'S FINISH THIS, MY LOVE.
RIGHT BEHIND YOU, DEAR.
KKK... KKKK...
...
DEAREST K'ARR'N, MY FAITHFUL WIFE...

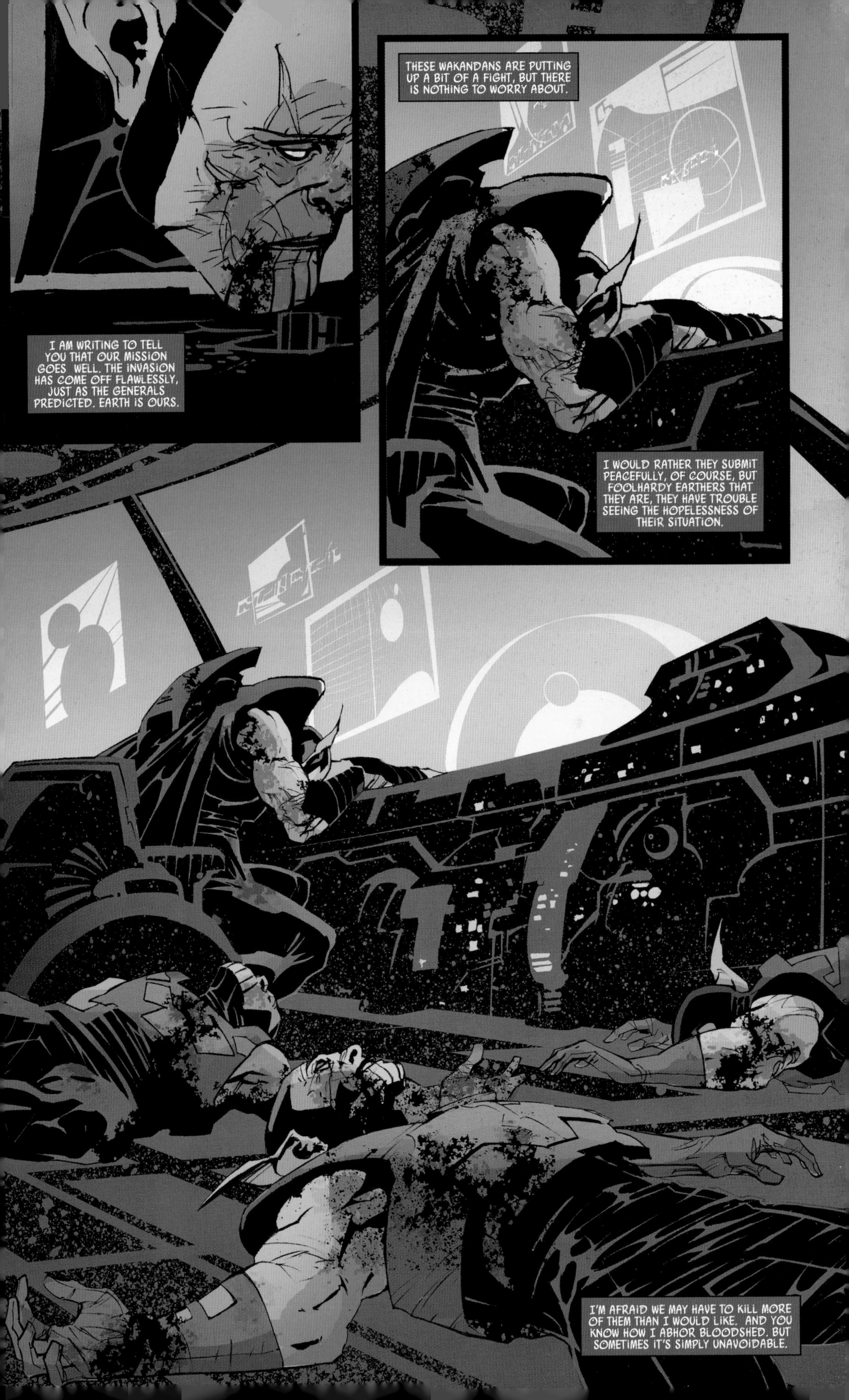
I AM WRITING TO TELL YOU THAT OUR MISSION GOES WELL. THE INVASION HAS COME OFF FLAWLESSLY, JUST AS THE GENERALS PREDICTED. EARTH IS OURS.
THESE WAKANDANS ARE PUTTING UP A BIT OF A FIGHT, BUT THERE IS NOTHING TO WORRY ABOUT.
I WOULD RATHER THEY SUBMIT PEACEFULLY, OF COURSE, BUT FOOLHARDY EARTHERS THAT THEY ARE, THEY HAVE TROUBLE SEEING THE HOPELESSNESS OF THEIR SITUATION.
I'M AFRAID WE MAY HAVE TO KILL MORE OF THEM THAN I WOULD LIKE. AND YOU KNOW HOW I ABHOR BLOODSHED. BUT SOMETIMES IT'S SIMPLY UNAVOIDABLE.

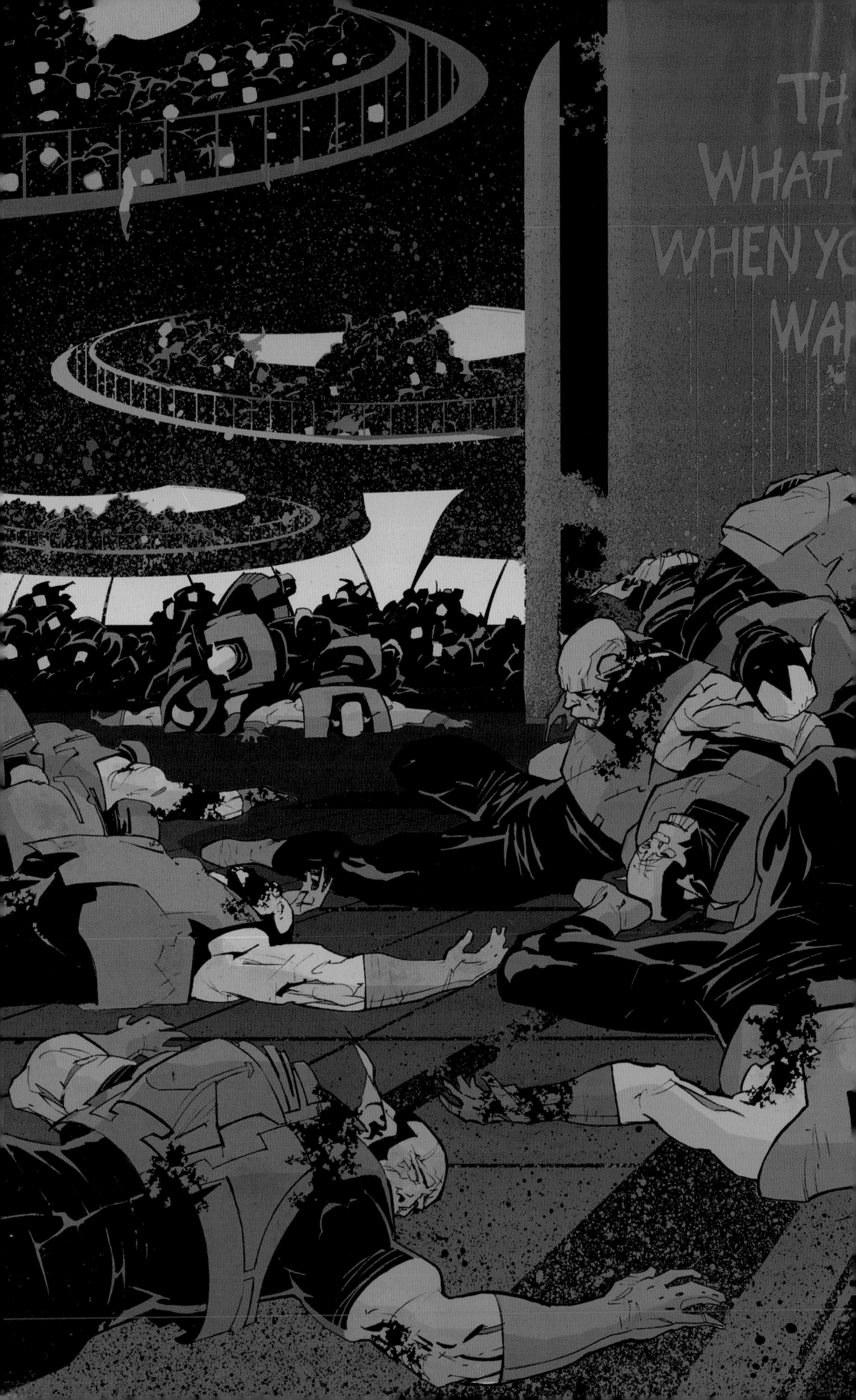
TH
WHAT
WHEN YO
WA

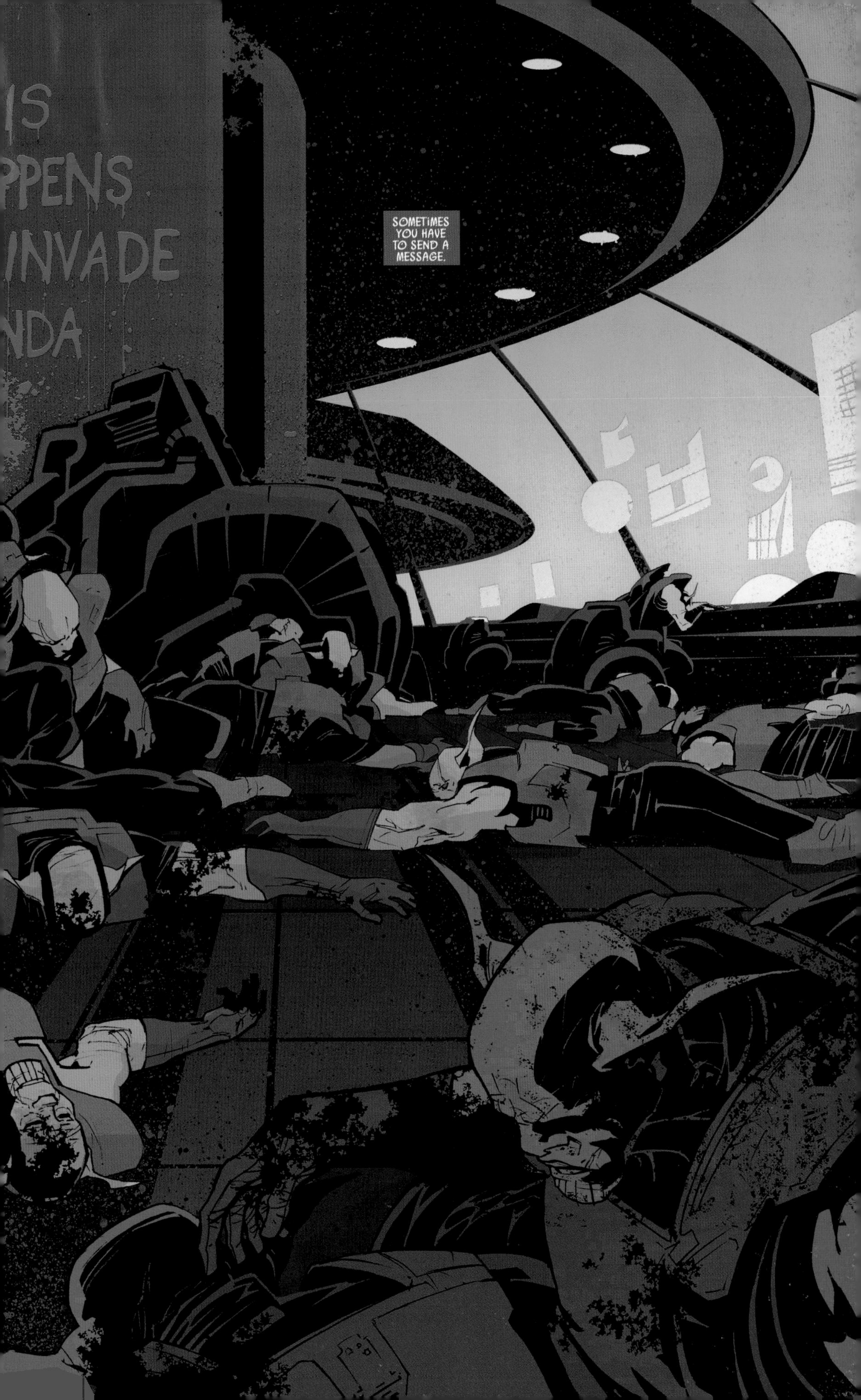
IS
PPENS
INVADE
NDA
SOMETIMES YOU HAVE TO SEND A MESSAGE.

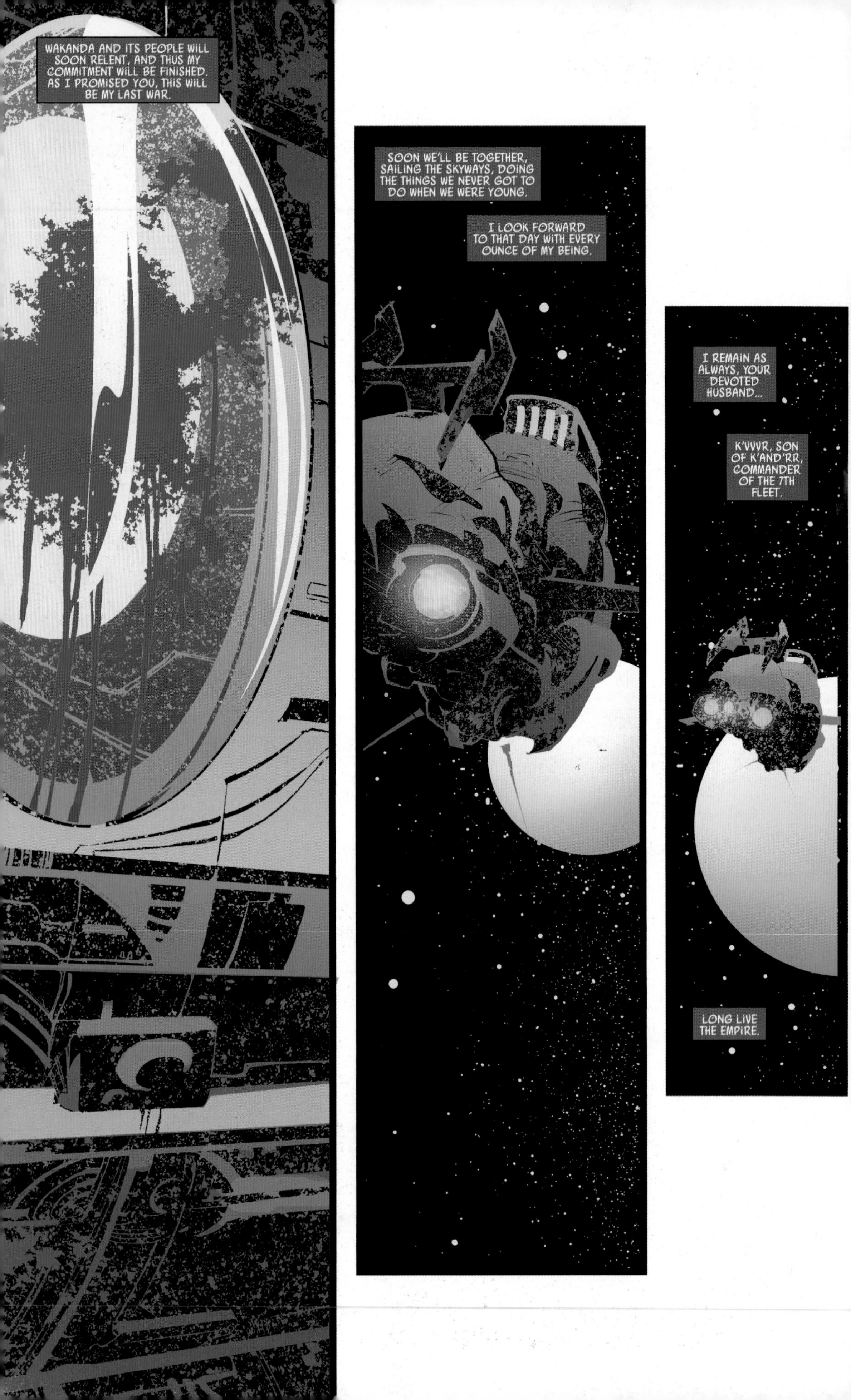
WAKANDA AND ITS PEOPLE WILL SOON RELENT, AND THUS MY COMMITMENT WILL BE FINISHED. AS I PROMISED YOU, THIS WILL BE MY LAST WAR.
SOON WE'LL BE TOGETHER, SAILING THE SKYWAYS, DOING THE THINGS WE NEVER GOT TO DO WHEN WE WERE YOUNG.
I LOOK FORWARD TO THAT DAY WITH EVERY OUNCE OF MY BEING.
I REMAIN AS ALWAYS, YOUR DEVOTED HUSBAND...
K'VVVR, SON OF K'AND'RR, COMMANDER OF THE 7TH FLEET.
LONG LIVE THE EMPIRE.

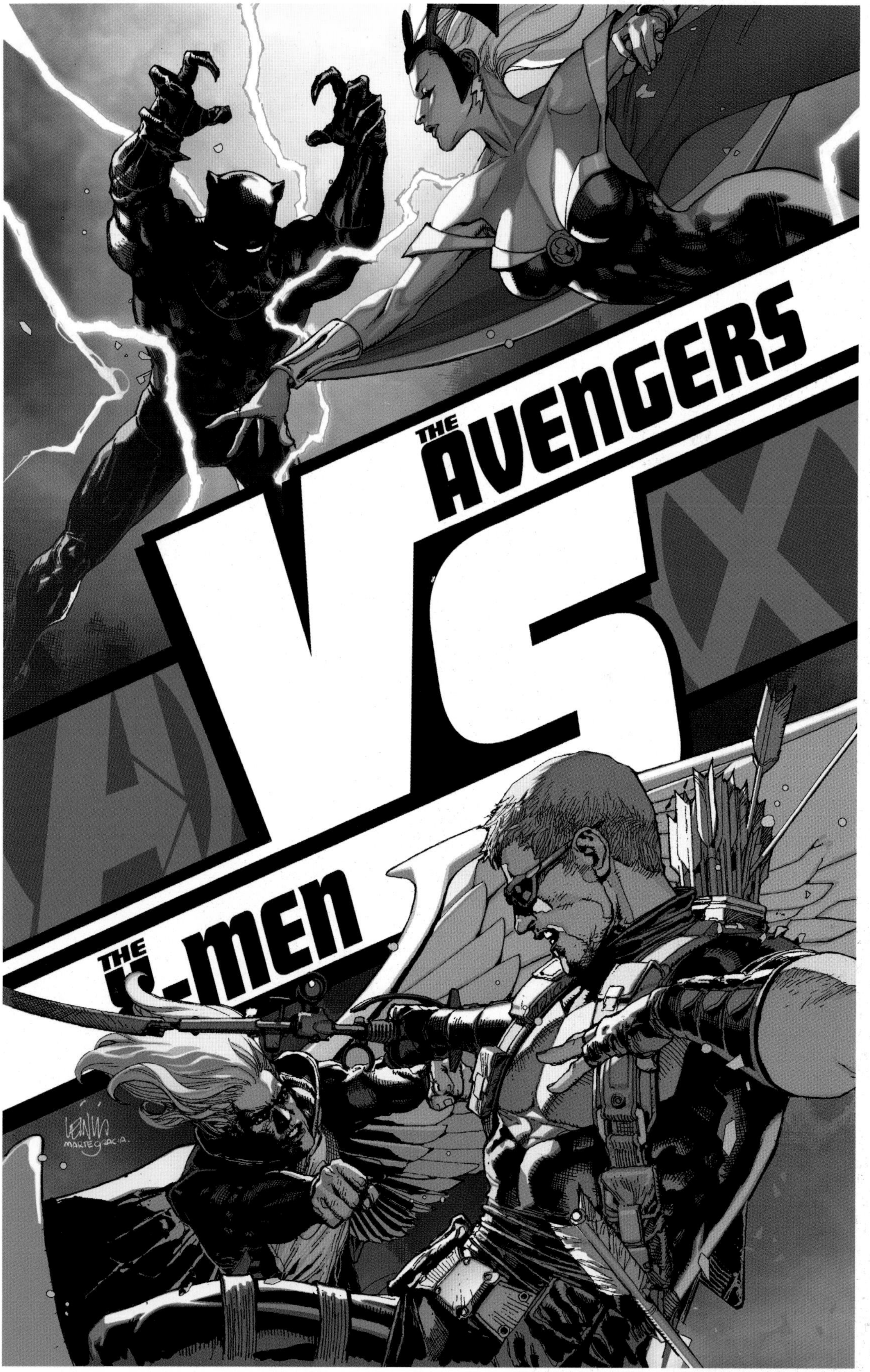
THE AVENGERS
VS
THE
-MEN

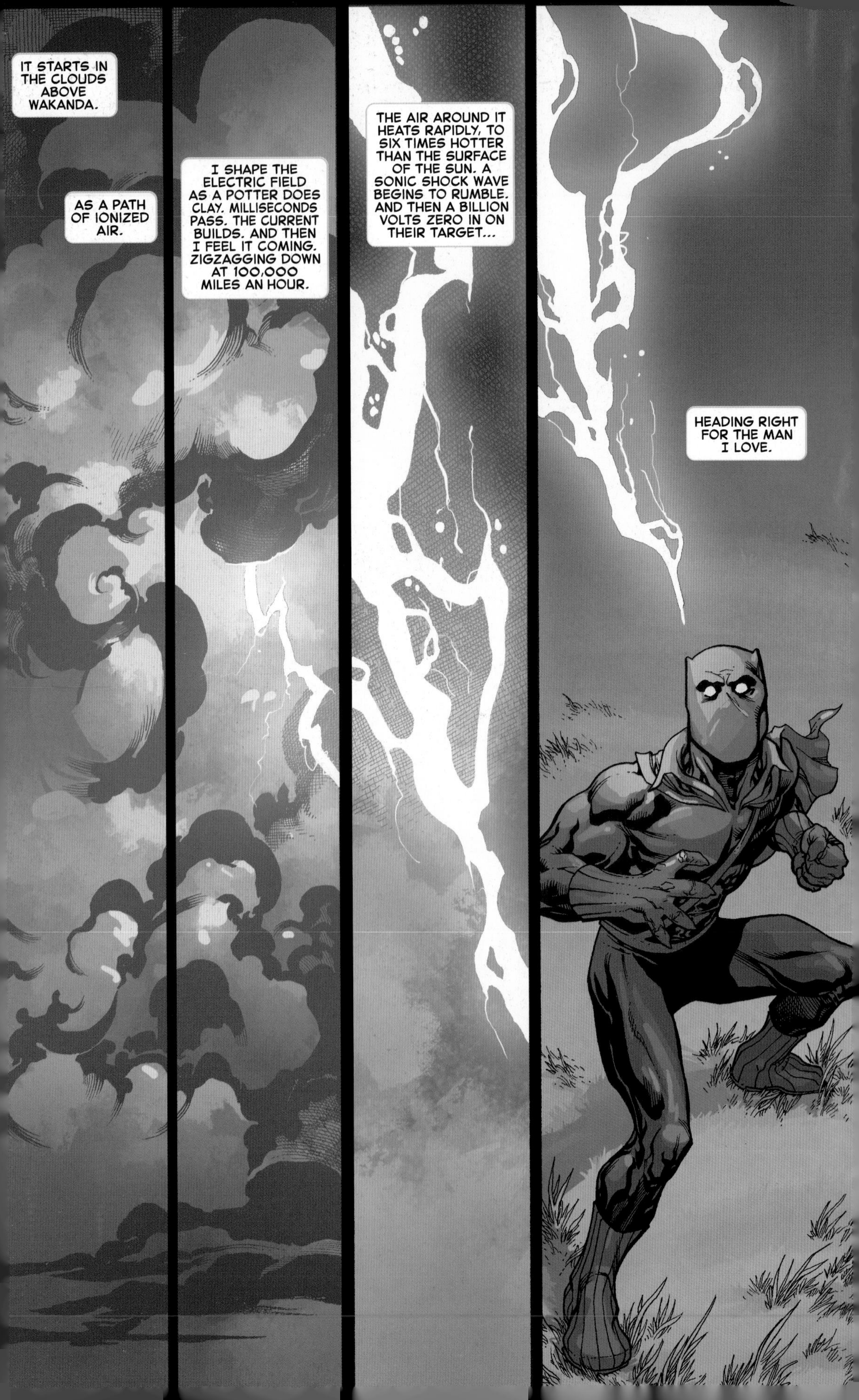
IT STARTS IN THE CLOUDS ABOVE WAKANDA.
AS A PATH OF IONIZED AIR.
I SHAPE THE ELECTRIC FIELD AS A POTTER DOES CLAY. MILLISECONDS PASS. THE CURRENT BUILDS. AND THEN I FEEL IT COMING. ZIGZAGGING DOWN AT 100,000 MILES AN HOUR.
THE AIR AROUND IT HEATS RAPIDLY, TO SIX TIMES HOTTER THAN THE SURFACE OF THE SUN. A SONIC SHOCK WAVE BEGINS TO RUMBLE. AND THEN A BILLION VOLTS ZERO IN ON THEIR TARGET...
HEADING RIGHT FOR THE MAN I LOVE.

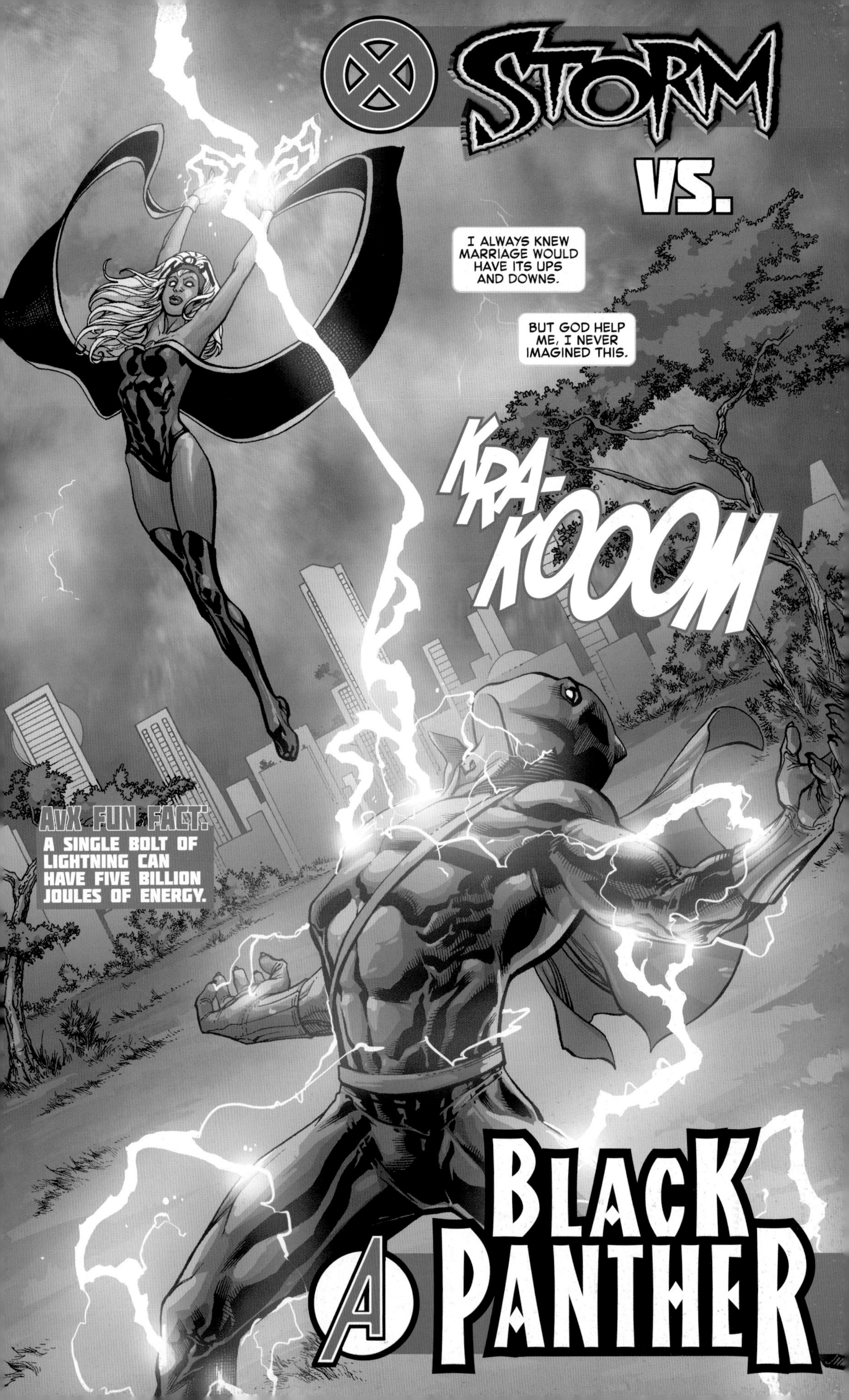
STORM
VS.
I ALWAYS KNEW MARRIAGE WOULD HAVE ITS UPS AND DOWNS.
BUT GOD HELP ME, I NEVER IMAGINED THIS.
KRA-KOOOM
AvX FUN FACT:
A SINGLE BOLT OF LIGHTNING CAN HAVE FIVE BILLION JOULES OF ENERGY.
BLACK PANTHER

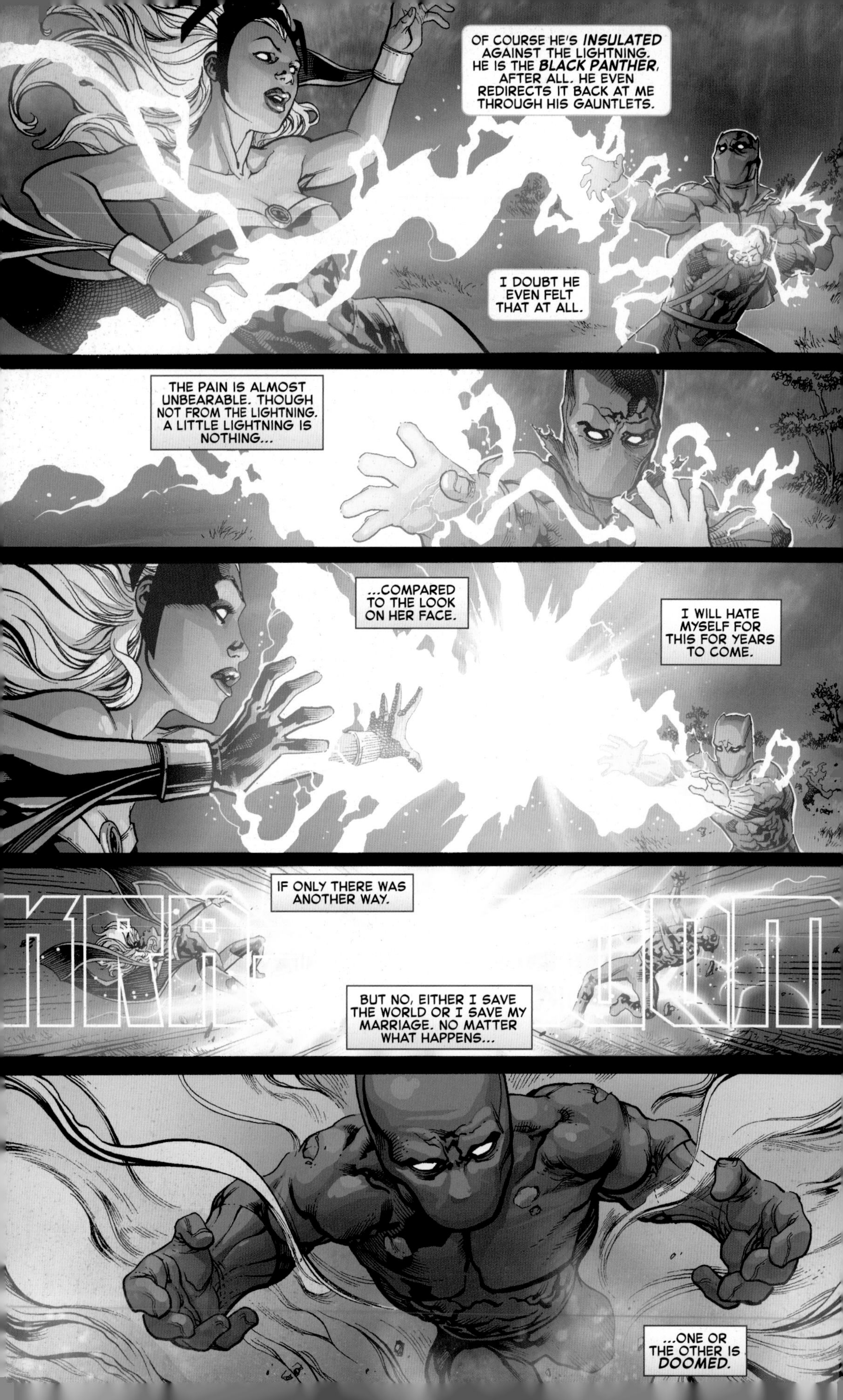
OF COURSE HE'S *INSULATED* AGAINST THE LIGHTNING. HE IS THE ***BLACK PANTHER***, AFTER ALL. HE EVEN REDIRECTS IT BACK AT ME THROUGH HIS GAUNTLETS.
I DOUBT HE EVEN FELT THAT AT ALL.
THE PAIN IS ALMOST UNBEARABLE. THOUGH NOT FROM THE LIGHTNING. A LITTLE LIGHTNING IS NOTHING...
...COMPARED TO THE LOOK ON HER FACE.
I WILL HATE MYSELF FOR THIS FOR YEARS TO COME.
IF ONLY THERE WAS ANOTHER WAY.
BUT NO, EITHER I SAVE THE WORLD OR I SAVE MY MARRIAGE. NO MATTER WHAT HAPPENS...
...ONE OR THE OTHER IS ***DOOMED.***

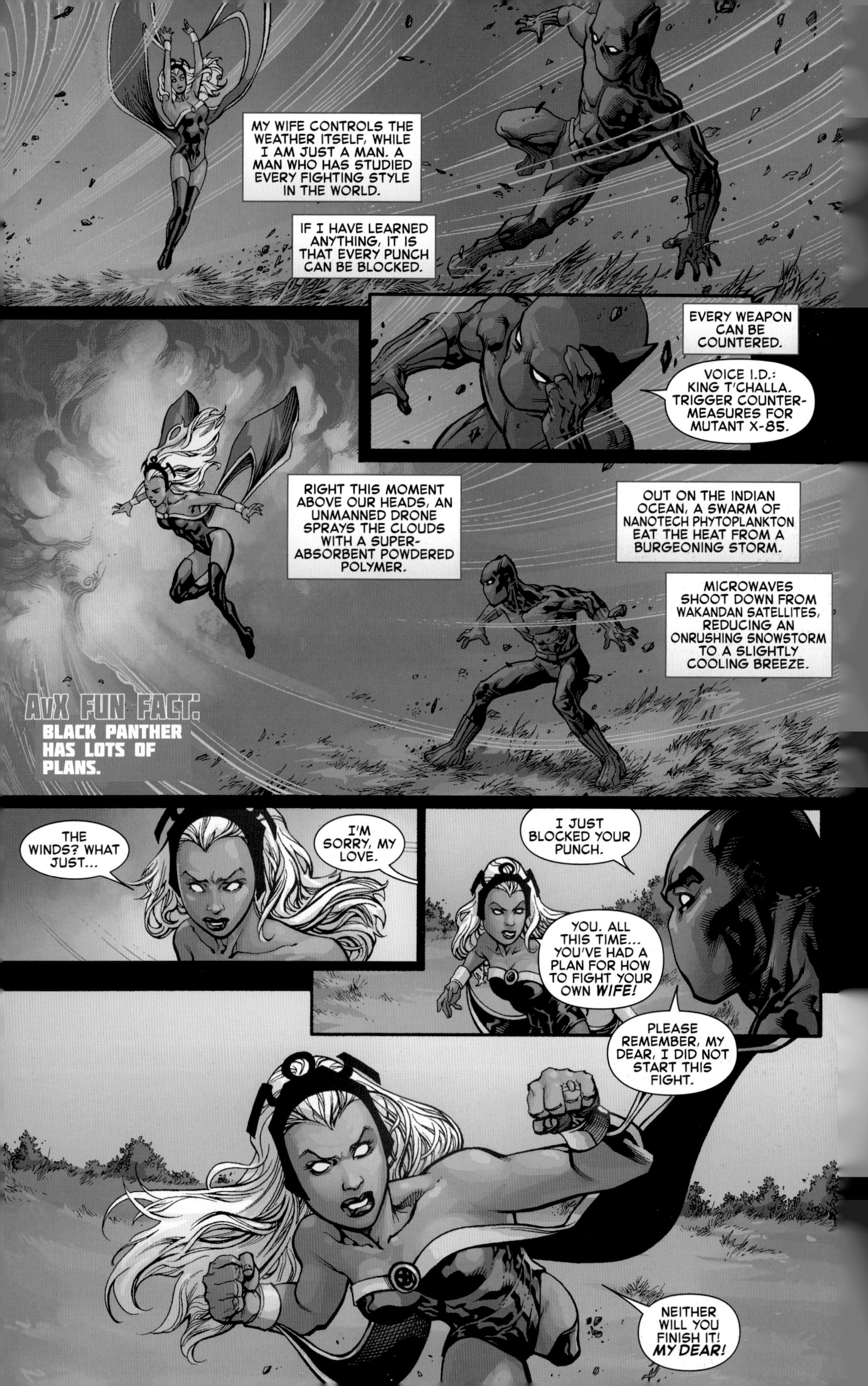
MY WIFE CONTROLS THE WEATHER ITSELF, WHILE I AM JUST A MAN. A MAN WHO HAS STUDIED EVERY FIGHTING STYLE IN THE WORLD.
IF I HAVE LEARNED ANYTHING, IT IS THAT EVERY PUNCH CAN BE BLOCKED.
EVERY WEAPON CAN BE COUNTERED.
VOICE I.D.: KING T'CHALLA. TRIGGER COUNTER-MEASURES FOR MUTANT X-85.
RIGHT THIS MOMENT ABOVE OUR HEADS, AN UNMANNED DRONE SPRAYS THE CLOUDS WITH A SUPER-ABSORBENT POWDERED POLYMER.
OUT ON THE INDIAN OCEAN, A SWARM OF NANOTECH PHYTOPLANKTON EAT THE HEAT FROM A BURGEONING STORM.
MICROWAVES SHOOT DOWN FROM WAKANDAN SATELLITES, REDUCING AN ONRUSHING SNOWSTORM TO A SLIGHTLY COOLING BREEZE.
AvX FUN FACT:
BLACK PANTHER HAS LOTS OF PLANS.
THE WINDS? WHAT JUST...
I'M SORRY, MY LOVE.
I JUST BLOCKED YOUR PUNCH.
YOU. ALL THIS TIME... YOU'VE HAD A PLAN FOR HOW TO FIGHT YOUR OWN *WIFE!*
PLEASE REMEMBER, MY DEAR, I DID NOT START THIS FIGHT.
NEITHER WILL YOU FINISH IT! *MY DEAR!*

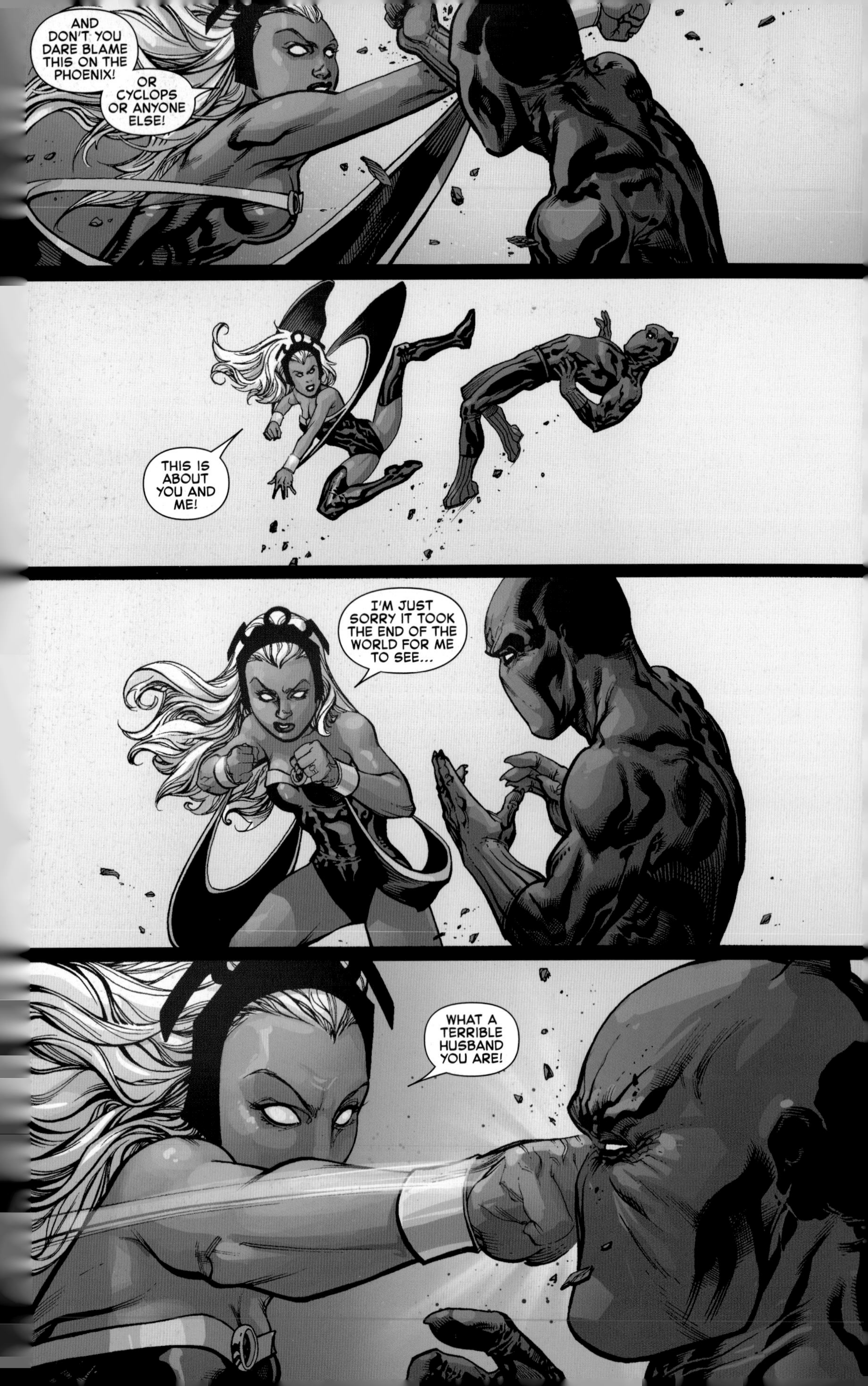
AND DON'T YOU DARE BLAME THIS ON THE PHOENIX!
OR CYCLOPS OR ANYONE ELSE!
THIS IS ABOUT YOU AND ME!
I'M JUST SORRY IT TOOK THE END OF THE WORLD FOR ME TO SEE...
WHAT A TERRIBLE HUSBAND YOU ARE!

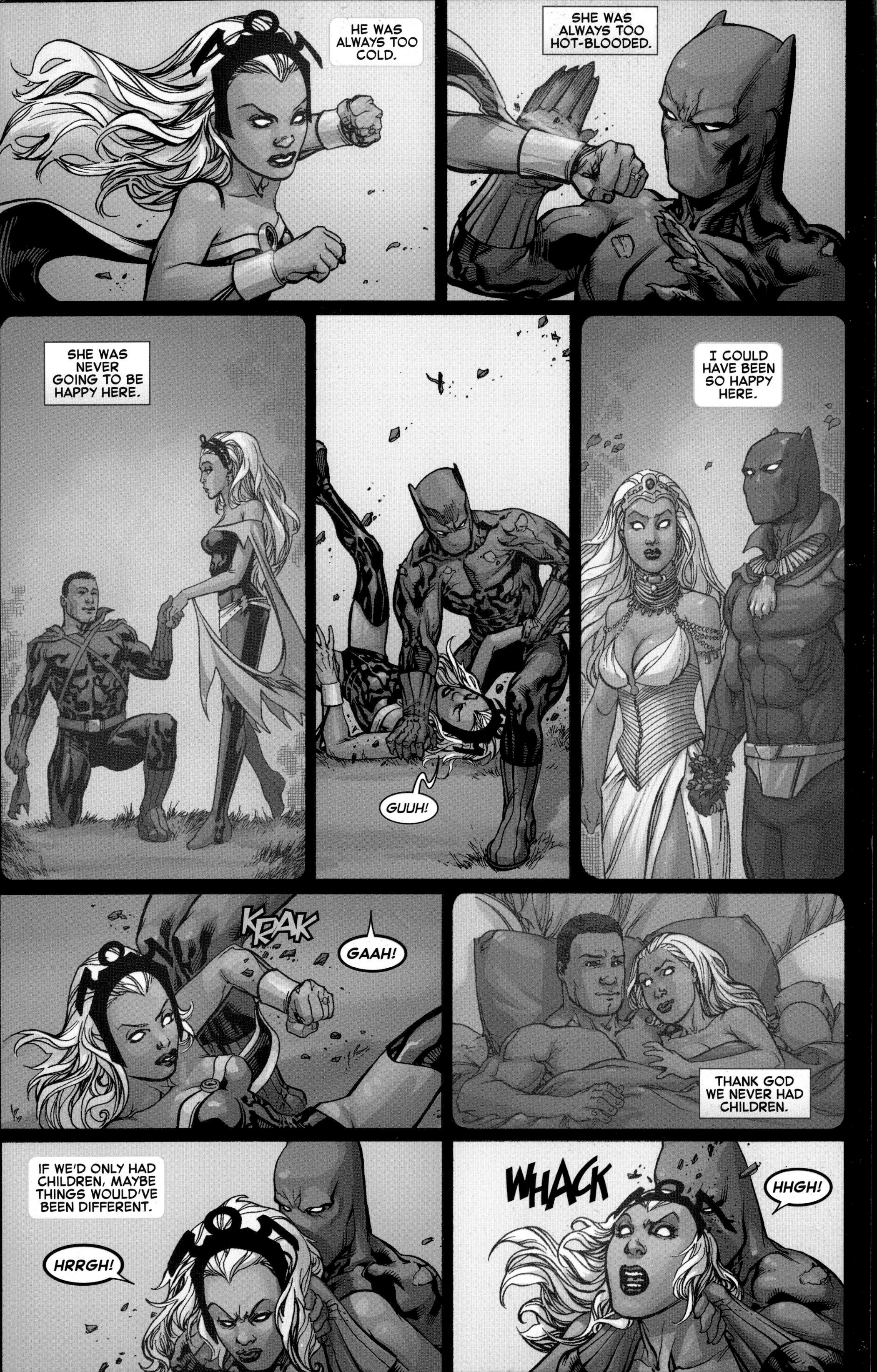

HE WAS ALWAYS TOO COLD.
SHE WAS ALWAYS TOO HOT-BLOODED.
SHE WAS NEVER GOING TO BE HAPPY HERE.
GUUH!
I COULD HAVE BEEN SO HAPPY HERE.
KRAK
GAAH!
THANK GOD WE NEVER HAD CHILDREN.
IF WE'D ONLY HAD CHILDREN, MAYBE THINGS WOULD'VE BEEN DIFFERENT.
HRRGH!
WHACK
HHGH!

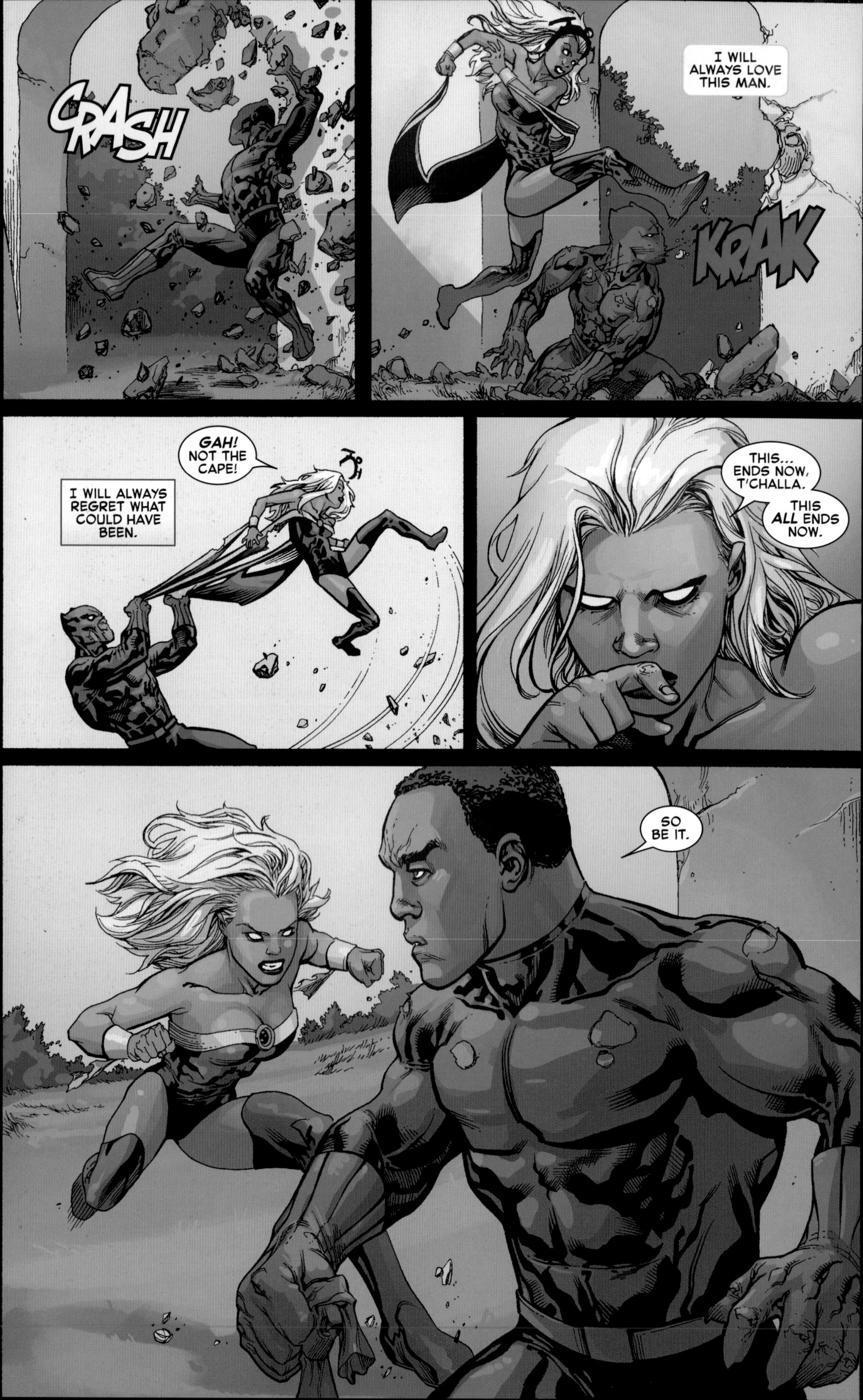
CRASH
I WILL ALWAYS LOVE THIS MAN.
KRAK
I WILL ALWAYS REGRET WHAT COULD HAVE BEEN.
GAH! NOT THE CAPE!
THIS... ENDS NOW, T'CHALLA.
THIS ALL ENDS NOW.
SO BE IT.

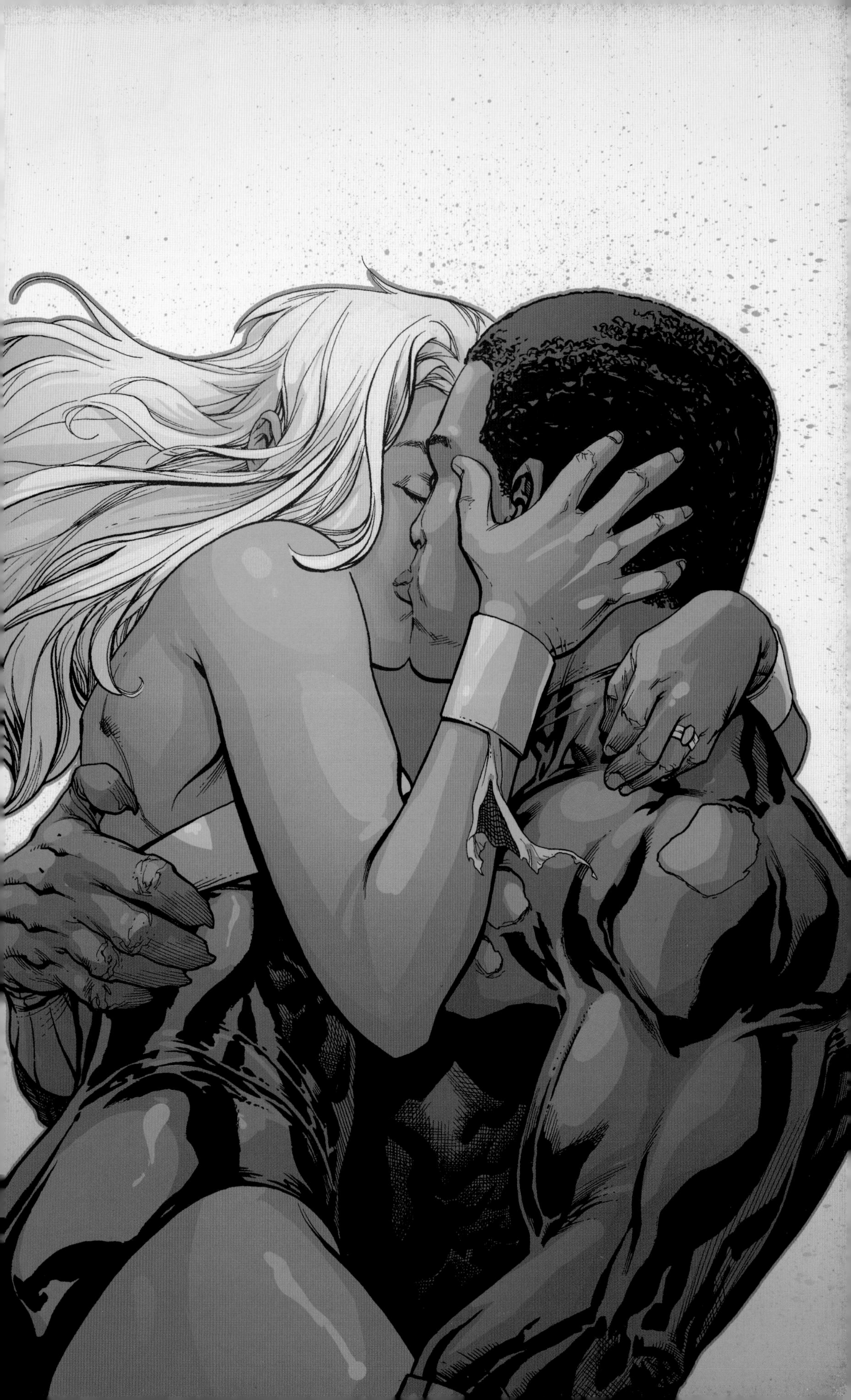

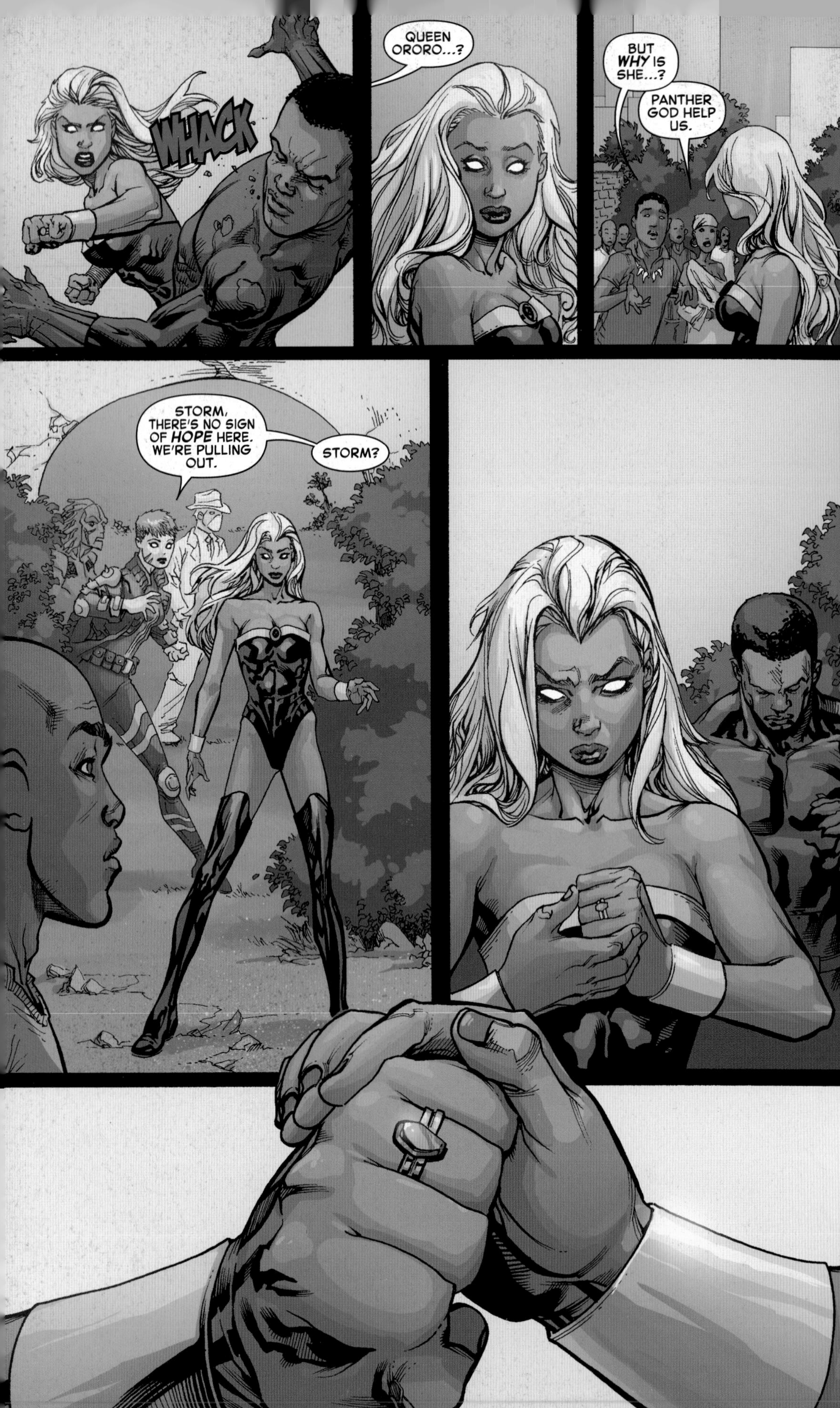
WHACK
QUEEN ORORO...?
BUT WHY IS SHE...?
PANTHER GOD HELP US.
STORM, THERE'S NO SIGN OF HOPE HERE. WE'RE PULLING OUT.
STORM?

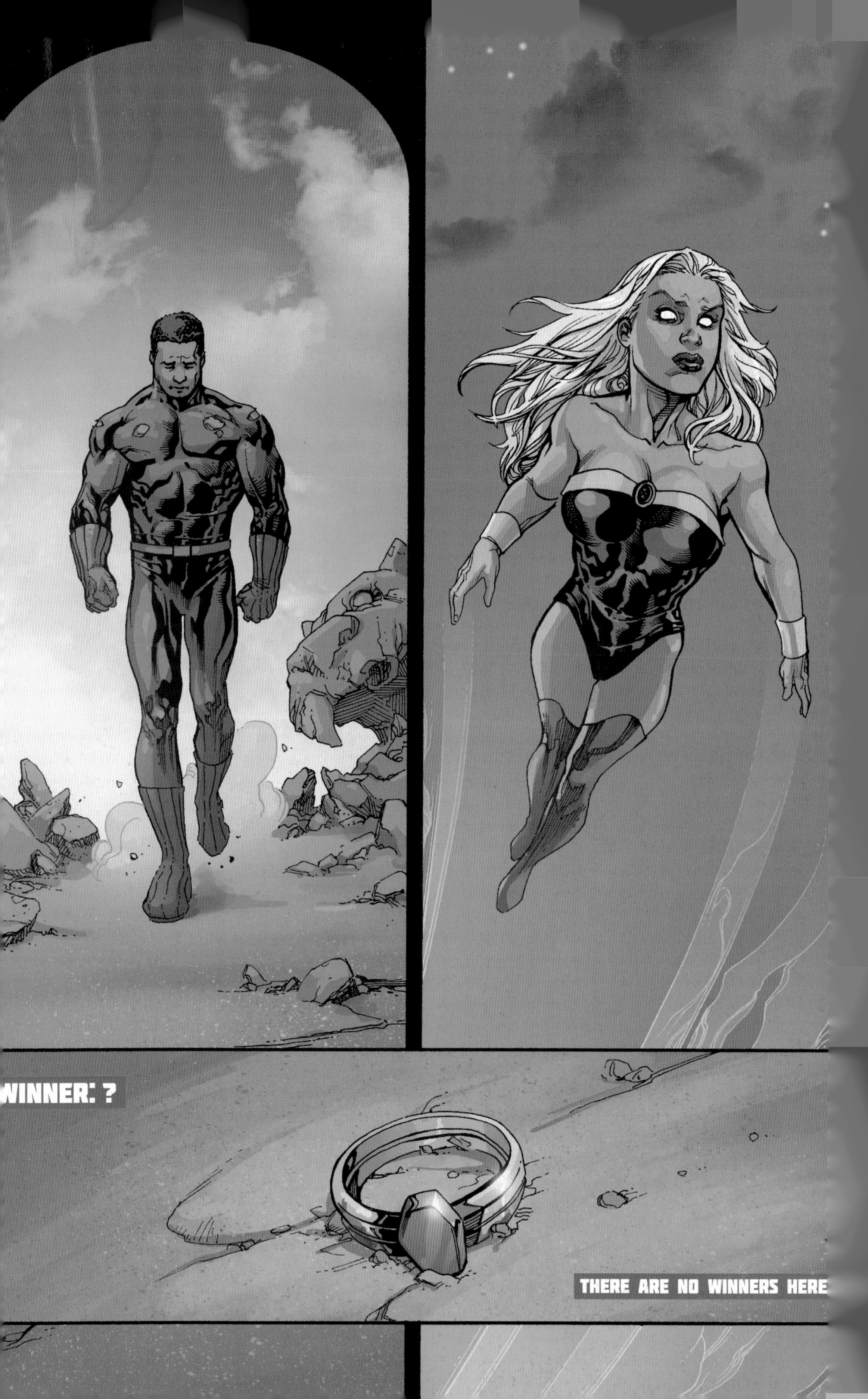
WINNER: ?
THERE ARE NO WINNERS HERE

BLACK PANTHER

Art by Shawn Martinbrough
with Chris Sprouse (inset)

HISTORY: T'Challa is heir to the centuries-old ruling dynasty of the African kingdom Wakanda, and ritual leader of its Panther Clan. His mother died in childbirth, earning him the enduring hatred of his adopted elder brother, Hunter, who also resented T'Challa for supplanting him in the royal household. Hunter would become the White Wolf, leader of the Hatut Zeraze (Dogs of War), the Wakandan secret police. Their father T'Chaka remarried, but his second wife, Ramonda, seemingly ran away with another man when T'Challa was eight. When T'Challa was a teenager, T'Chaka was murdered by Ulysses Klaw, a Dutchman seeking to plunder the rare vibranium metal unique to Wakanda, but T'Challa used Klaw's own weapon to maim him and drive him off. T'Challa studied in Europe and America, then underwent ritual trials in Wakanda – including defeating his uncle S'yan, the existing Black Panther – to win the heart-shaped herb, enhancing his abilities and linking him spiritually to the Panther God Bast. Now Wakanda's ruler as the Black Panther, he disbanded and exiled the Hatut Zeraze and continued transforming his country into a high-tech wonderland. When tribal war broke out, T'Challa restored peace by condemning the Jabari tribe, and by picking Dora Milaje ("Adored Ones") from rival tribes to serve as his personal guard and ceremonial wives-in-training.

Taught by his father to think two steps ahead of enemies and three steps ahead of friends, T'Challa saw the world's super-beings as potential threats to Wakanda. Inviting the Fantastic Four to visit him, he forced them into a series of tests, then allied with them against a returning Klaw. He also joined the American-based Avengers to spy on them from within, but soon came to regard them as true friends and staunch allies. He adopted the identity of teacher Luke Charles while in America, romancing singer Monica Lynne, later his fiancée. Dividing his time between Wakanda and America for years, he battled foes such as Jabari malcontent M'Baku the Man-Ape, rebel leader Erik Killmonger, the snake-charmer Venomm (later an ally), voodoo charlatan Baron Macabre, the Ku Klux Klan, the ghostly Soul-Strangler, the soaring Wind Eagle, mutated drug czar Solomon Prey, arms dealer Moses Magnum and the Supremacists of Azania. He also fought Kiber the Cruel during a quest for the mystic time-shifting artefacts known as King Solomon's Frogs; these produced an alternate version of T'Challa from a future ten years hence, a merry telepathic Panther with a terminal brain aneurysm. Placing his dying future self in cryogenic storage, T'Challa broke off his engagement

REAL NAME: T'Challa
ALIASES: Luke Charles, Black Leopard, Nubian Prince, the Client, Coal Tiger, has impersonated Daredevil and others on occasion
IDENTITY: Publicly known
OCCUPATION: Monarch of Wakanda, scientist; former schoolteacher
CITIZENSHIP: Wakanda
PLACE OF BIRTH: Wakanda
MARITAL STATUS: Divorced
KNOWN RELATIVES: T'Chaka (father, deceased), N'Yami (mother, deceased), Ramonda (stepmother), Bashenga (first Black Panther, ancestor, deceased), Jakarra (half-brother, deceased), Hunter (White Wolf (Hunter), adopted brother), Azzari the Wise (grandfather, deceased), Chanda (grandfather, presumably deceased), Nanali (grandmother, deceased), S'yan (uncle), Khanata, Joshua Itobo, Ishanta, M'Koni Wheeler, Zuni (cousins), Storm (ex-wife)
GROUP AFFILIATION: Illuminati, formerly Fantastic Four, Secret Avengers, Avengers, Pendragons, Queen's Vengeance, former Fantastic Force financier
EDUCATION: Ph.D in physics
FIRST APPEARANCE: Fantastic Four Vol. 1 #52 (1966)

with Monica since he feared he had no future to give her. Wakanda and Atlantis subsequently came to the brink of war during the Kiber Island incident, which revealed Wakanda to be a nuclear power. Discovering his stepmother Ramonda had not run away, but instead had been kidnapped by Anton Pretorius, he rescued her from years of captivity in South Africa. T'Challa joined the Knights of Pendragon against their enemies, the Bane, learning in the process that he housed one of the Pendragon spirits himself. He was also used as a pawn in the efforts of the munitions company Cardinal Technology to escalate the civil war in the northern nation Mohannda. T'Challa exposed Cardinal with the aid of the mercenary Black Axe and the anti-war activist Afrikaa. T'Challa's restrictions on exports of both vibranium and Wakandan technology had long annoyed foreign powers. Xcon, an alliance of rogue intelligence agents and the Russian mafia, backed a coup in Wakanda led by Reverend Achebe. Learning Achebe was empowered by the

'TWAS I WHO INVITED YOU FOR THE HUNT!

BUT, I NEGLECTED TO TELL YOU ONE THING...

IT IS YOU WHO SHALL BE HUNTED!

demon Mephisto, T'Challa sold his soul in exchange for Mephisto's, abandoning Achebe and leaving Wakanda in peace; however, T'Challa's unity with the Panther God and its link to the spirits of past Panther Clan leaders forced Mephisto to forfeit the Panther's soul. T'Challa then presented the UN with evidence of the Xcon plot and its US links, demanding sanctions against America. When Hunter and the Hatut Zeraze resurfaced during the Xcon incident, a wary T'Challa imprisoned them just prior to regaining his throne.

After T'Challa discharged Nakia from the Dora Milaje for trying to kill Monica Lynne in a fit of jealousy, Nakia was tortured by Achebe and rehabilitated by Killmonger, who shaped her into the mad warrior Malice. She was replaced in the Dora Milaje by Queen Divine Justice, an American-raised Jabari. T'Challa himself returned to the US on a diplomatic mission, leaving his Washington envoy Everett K Ross in charge as regent of Wakanda, until Killmonger tried to destroy Wakanda's economy; to thwart this, the Panther nationalised all foreign companies in Wakanda, causing a global run on the stock market, which Tony Stark (Iron Man) used to secure a controlling interest in the Wakandan Design Group. Returning home, the Panther fought Killmonger in ritual combat, but was distracted at a critical juncture by Ross and beaten nearly to death. Killmonger only relented when Ross, still regent, yielded on T'Challa's behalf, unwittingly giving the Black Panther title to Killmonger. T'Challa's life was mystically saved by his allies Brother Voodoo and Moon Knight. While T'Challa recovered, Killmonger tried to join the Avengers as the new Black Panther, and Achebe enlisted super-mercenaries such as Deadpool to attack Wakanda again. During the resultant Avengers visit to Wakanda, Ross freed Hunter, whose scheming resulted in Killmonger's seeming demise and the restoration of T'Challa's title. Wakanda next came into conflict with Deviant Lemuria during a dispute over custody of a Deviant child found in Wakanda.

As tensions mounted, warships from Wakanda, the US and Atlantis all entered the area, and Hunter made matters worse when he decided to force T'Challa to "reclaim his dignity" by reviving Klaw, who tried to spark outright war between the nations involved. In the end, Ross's negotiation skills and information supplied by Magneto and Doctor Doom resolved the conflict. While T'Challa faced attacks by Malice, Divine Justice was kidnapped by the Man-Ape, who learned she was the rightful queen of his tribe. T'Challa defeated M'Baku again, though not before he uncovered the frozen future Panther. Back in New York, the criminal Nightshade resurrected the fabled Chinese monster Chiantang the Black Dragon to use against T'Challa. Black Dragon had the Panther attacked by a mind-controlled Iron Fist, whose assault caused the brain aneurysm the future Panther had foreshadowed. Nightshade, meanwhile, managed to revive the future Panther.

At the same time, T'Challa learned that White Wolf had taken over Xcon and slain most of its leaders, who had used King Solomon's Frogs to replace the US President and Canadian Prime Minister with brainwashed future counterparts, allowing Xcon to secretly take over both countries. Hunter continued their plan and sought revenge on Tony Stark for his buy-out of Wakandan Design Group. Uncertain of how far along Hunter's plan was, T'Challa drew Stark out with a covert message, using financial finagling to seize control of Stark Enterprises and simultaneously annex a small Canadian island in Lake Superior, prompting the US and Canadian leaders to meet to discuss this crisis. The Panther and his allies, including the future Panther, then invaded the White House and foiled Xcon's plot, un-brainwashing the duplicate leaders and returning them to their own times.

Panther and his allies returned to Wakanda, where the future Panther fell into a coma. Hoping to free her tribe, Divine Justice freed the Man-Ape, but he broke his promises of non-violence by slaying the helpless future T'Challa. The original T'Challa, by now unstable and hallucinating, attacked the Jabari tribe with the intent of wiping them out; but after nearly slaying Divine Justice, he came to his senses and stopped the battle. Unable to face what he had done, the Panther handed power to his council and hid in New York. There he mentored policeman Kasper Cole (who had adopted an abandoned Panther costume), an experience which gave T'Challa the strength to face his illness, his nation and the world.

His rule was again challenged by a revived Killmonger. At the same time, T'Challa renewed his ties with the Avengers, helping them battle Scorpio, secure special United Nations status and unmask US Defence Secretary Dell Rusk as the evil Red Skull; however, the team disbanded after a series of devastating assaults by an insane Scarlet Witch.

Unbeknownst to T'Challa, the US government planned a coup in order to get access to the vibranium. They allowed Klaw to recruit a team of villains in order to support Wakandan totalitarian neighbour, Nigandia. Klaw recruited Rhino, Black Knight, Batroc the Leaper, and Radioactive Man to lead the invasion. The US government then deployed an army of Deathloks (cybernetically enhanced soldiers) to "support" T'Challa and justify an invasion, but T'Challa killed Klaw and Ororo Munroe, AKA Storm, wiped out the Deathlok army in a hurricane.

T'Challa then helped Storm reunite with her surviving family members in Africa and the US. Soon after, he proposed and the two were married in a large Wakandan ceremony attended by many superheroes. One of the couple's first tasks was to embark on a diplomatic tour, in which they visited the Inhumans, Doctor Doom, the President of the United States, and Namor of Atlantis.

During the superhero civil war, the Black Panther and Storm side with Captain America's anti-registration forces after the death of Bill Foster, AKA Giant Man. During the final battle between both sides, the Wakandan embassy in Manhattan was heavily damaged, though no Wakandans were hurt. After the confrontation, the Panther and Storm briefly filled in for vacationing Fantastic Four members Reed and Sue Richards before returning to Wakanda.

Black Panther returned to Wakanda alone, leaving Storm in New York to aid the X-Men. He once again was forced to face Erik Killmonger, and defeated him with assistance from Monica Rambeau (AKA Pulsar).

Afterward, Wakanda fended off the alien shapeshifters the Skrulls, who had infiltrated Wakandan society as part of their plan to conquer Earth.

Prince Namor attempted to recruit T'Challa for the Cabal, a secret council of supervillains. Attacked by the forces of fellow Cabal member Doctor Doom, T'Challa was left comatose. His sister Shuri was trained as the next Panther, with the mantle passing on to her officially after T'Challa awakenened from his coma and attempted to recover from his injuries.

In the aftermath, T'Challa lost all

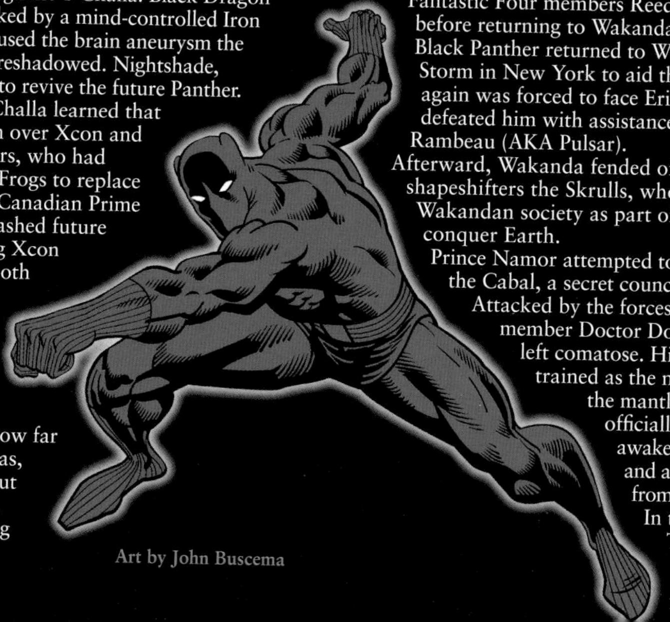

Art by John Buscema

of his enhanced attributes by being the panther totem. As a result, he worked with his sorcerer, Zawavari, to accumulate a replacement. He made a pact with another unknown panther deity and regained his attributes at an even higher level. In addition, eldritch incantations were drawn on his body, making himself highly resistant to most magic and mystic assaults. This was all done in preparation for an imminent battle with Doctor Doom, which culminated in T'Challa rendering all of the processed vibranium inert to give his people a chance to rebuild without their dependence on the element.

Next, Matt Murdock (AKA Daredevil) asked T'Challa to replace him as guardian of Hell's Kitchen, which gave T'Challa a chance to rediscover himself. With the help of Foggy Nelson, T'Challa assumed the identity of Mr. Okonkwo, an immigrant from the Congo and manager of a diner called Devil's Kitchen, so that he could blend in and learn about his neighbourhood as an ordinary man.

T'Challa soon found himself up against an ambitious new crime lord, Vlad Dinu, who styled himself "The Impaler". During an attempt by Vlad to terminate the Panther, Brian, the busboy from the Devil's Kitchen, was seriously injured by an energy blast from Vlad. The conflict between Vlad and the Panther became more personal, especially after Vlad discovered the Panther standing over his wife Angela who had been killed by a gunshot wound. The Panther obtained evidence of Vlad Dinu's crimes and turned the evidence over to the police. Vlad killed his own son Nicolae before being subdued by the Panther.

Shortly after, Daredevil returned to Hell's Kitchen, freeing T'Challa to go home to Wakanda. There, T'Challa served as a second to his sister, Shuri. In preparation for an upcoming attack on Wakanda, the panther god returned T'Challa's abilities. Empowered by the Phoenix, Namor destroyed Wakanda with a massive tidal wave. Returning to help, Storm is stunned when the Panther informed her that their marriage had been annulled.

Now, T'Challa continues to defend Wakanda from any and all threats from without and within.

HEIGHT: 6'
WEIGHT: 200 lbs
EYES: Brown
HAIR: Black

ABILITIES/ACCESSORIES: T'Challa's senses and physical attributes have been enhanced to superhuman levels by the heart-shaped herb. T'Challa is a brilliant tactician, strategist, scientist, tracker and a master of all forms of unarmed combat whose unique hybrid fighting style incorporates acrobatics and aspects of animal mimicry. Being of royal descendent of a warrior race, T'Challa is also a master of armed combat, able to use a variety of weapons but prefers unarmed combat. He is a master planner who always thinks several steps ahead and will go to extreme measures to achieve his goals and protect the kingdom of Wakanda.

T'Challa's vibranium-weave uniform absorbs the kinetic force of impacts, rendering him bulletproof. His costume's gloves can generate energy daggers and house anti-metal claws that dissolve other metals on contact. His Kimoyo Card enables global communication, picks up satellite signals, and can block most radio transmissions. His boot soles are thick vibranium alloy pads which can vibrate at various frequencies, allowing him to run up the sides of buildings, land soundlessly and without injury from a height of 50 feet, walk on water, or slice through metal. His costume is fitted with cloaking technology, allowing it to pass as normal street clothes. He also has access to the many specialised weapons and vehicles of Wakanda. The extent of technology T'Challa has access to is believed to be limitless.

POWER GRID	1	2	3	4	5	6	7
INTELLIGENCE							
STRENGTH							
SPEED							
DURABILITY							
ENERGY PROJECTION							
FIGHTING SKILLS							

POWER RATINGS

INTELLIGENCE
Ability to think and process information
1 Slow/impaired
2 Normal
3 Learned
4 Gifted
5 Genius
6 Super-Genius
7 Ominiscient

STRENGTH
Ability to lift weight
1 Weak: cannot lift own body weight
2 Normal: able to lift own body weight
3 Peak human: able to lift twice own body weight
4 Superhuman: 800lbs-25 ton range
5 Superhuman: 26-75 ton range
6 Superhuman: 76-100 ton range
7 Incalculable: in excess of 100 tons

SPEED
Ability to move over land by running or flight
1 Below normal
2 Normal
3 Superhuman: Peak range: 700 MPH
4 Speed of Sound: Mach-1
5 Supersonic: Mach-2 through orbital velocity
6 Speed of light: 186,000 miles per second
7 Warp speed: transcending light speed

DURABILITY
Ability to resist or recover from bodily injury
1 Weak
2 Normal
3 Enhanced
4 Regenerative
5 Bulletproof
6 Superhuman
7 Virtually indestructible

ENERGY PROJECTION
Ability to discharge energy
1 None
2 Ability to discharge energy on contact
3 Short range, short duration, single energy type
4 Medium range, duration, single energy type
5 Long range, long duration, single energy type
6 Able to discharge multiple forms of energy
7 Virtually unlimited command of all forms of energy

FIGHTING SKILLS
Proficiency in hand-to-hand combat
1 Poor
2 Normal
3 Some training
4 Experienced fighter
5 Master of a single form of combat
6 Master of several forms of combat
7 Master of all forms of combat